NATIONAL ATTRIBUTES AND BEHAVIOR

DIMENSIONS OF NATIONS SERIES

by R. J. Rummel

Vol. 1 – Dimensions of Nations (1972)
Vol. 2 – Field Theory Evolving (1977)
Vol. 3 – National Attributes and Behavior (1978)

National Attributes and Behavior

R. J. RUMMEL

For information address:

SAGE PUBLICATIONS, INC.
275 South Beverly Drive
Beverly Hills, California 90212

SAGE PUBLICATIONS LTD
28 Banner Street
London EC1Y 8QE, England

Printed in the United States of America

International Standard Book Number 0-8039-0392-8

Library of Congress Catalog Card No. 76-50501

FIRST PRINTING

Man is not a circle with a single center; he is an ellipse with two foci. Facts are one, ideas are the other.

Victor Hugo. *Les Misérables* VII.i.

ABOUT THE AUTHOR

R. J. RUMMEL was born in 1932, received his B.A. in 1959 and his M.A. in 1961 in political science at the University of Hawaii, and his Ph.D. in political science at Northwestern University, 1963. He has taught at Indiana University and Yale University, and is currently Professor of Political Science, University of Hawaii. Dr. Rummel has directed the Dimensionality of Nations Project from 1962 to 1975. His other publications include *Applied Factor Analysis* (1970), *Dimensions of Nations* (1972), *Peace Endangered* (1976), *Field Theory Evolving* (1977), as well as the first two volumes in the **Understanding Conflict and War** series: *The Dynamic Psychological Field* (Vol. 1), *The Conflict Helix* (Vol. 2), and *Conflict in Perspective* (Vol. 3).

ACKNOWLEDGMENTS

In 1967 I proposed to the Advanced Research Projects Agency (ARPA), Department of Defense, undertaking four primary tasks: first, to collect data on 150 national attributes and behaviors for the years 1950, 1955, 1960, 1963, and 1965; second, to determine the independent dimensions in the attributes; third, to likewise determine the dimensions in dyadic international behavior; and finally, to define the mathematical linkages between these two sets of dimensions over the years 1950-1965. This project was completed in 1973. The major data so collected and a summary of the results comprise this book. I wish to express my great debt to ARPA, and especially, to Professors Raymond Tanter and Davis Bobrow, and to Dr. George Lawrence, who worked as Deputy Directors, Human Resources Research Office, for ARPA during the years this project was under way.

Many have been associated with the project as students or assistants. All have made it an educational and research adventure, a creative gestalt. In some ways I will mention, in more I could detail, and in many of which I am unaware but can only sense, this book is a product of their intellectual efforts.

The many research assistants involved in the data collection and their subanalyses were Chung-Si Ahn, Thomas Bell, Tudor Chirila, Chang-Yoon Choi, Tal Day, John Dukesbury, Dennis Hall, Herbert Hannah, Pat Irish, Willard Keim, Kook-Chin Kim, Robert Kurtz, Richard Levy, Paul McCarthy, David McCormick, John McIlroy, Gary Murfin, Omar Nassery, Gary Oliva, George Omen, Sumie Ono, Tong-Whan Park, Yong-Ok Park, Warren Phillips, Richard Pratt, Sang-Woo Rhee, Leon Richards, Edward Schwerin, Patricia Snyder, Peter Sybinsky, Christina Uebelein, Vernon Umetsu, Richard Van Atta, Paul Williamson, and Michael Zavatsky.

Moreover, the secretarial and administrative help of Frances Shomura, Ora Mae Barber, Joyce Nakasone and Karen Pacheco kept endless paper work under control and facilitated all our efforts.

No modern quantitative project can be without computer programmers. Ours were Elsie Ahern, Judith Ann Tom, and Charles Wall, who developed numerous programs for our data screening and analysis. Mr. Wall was especially helpful in developing an integrated computer system on disk for our variety of needs.

The data collection and analyses involved numerous activities requiring careful and daily administration, which were done by Warren Phillips and his successor, Sang-Woo Rhee, as assistant directors of the project.

Over the last two years, Sang-Woo Rhee, George Omen, and Peter Sybinsky especially were involved in the data preparation and analysis for this book. Their contributions have been creative and intrinsic to the results, and they were responsible for the preparation and presentation of the appendices of data given here.

And again my wife Grace struggled to simplify and make understandable my initial drafts and associated research reports.

To all, my gratitude and thanks.

CONTENTS

Chapter 1

INTRODUCTION

1.1 THE CONTEXT

This book is a research report of the Dimensionality of Nations (DON) project. My purpose is to make available the major national data collected in the process of pursuing my research, and my major empirical results. The data are given in the appendices, and their analyses comprise the substantive chapters of the book.

The major concern of the DON project has been to develop a theoretical, empirical, and quantitative framework for understanding the nature of war and violence, and for contributing to their resolution. This has been a multidimensional effort, involving the development of an appropriate methodology, appropriate empirical concepts, a theoretical framework, and substantive-philosophical understanding. The results of some of these methodological studies are given in my *Applied Factor Analysis* (1970), which also presents the methodological models and details for technically understanding many of the analyses presented here.

The results of trying to develop appropriate empirical concepts have been published in my *The Dimensions of Nations* (1972). This work is a cross-national mapping international relations, largely focused on the year 1955. Many of the analyses presented here will improve and generalize the results of that book.

The theoretical framework is presented in *Field Theory Evolving* (Rummel, 1976), which comprises most of DON's theoretical papers. Much of the analyses presented here were done to operationalize or test field theory, and are also summarized in Chapter 15 of that book. These show that field theory has a significant ability to explain the behavior of nations.

The development of a substantive-philosophical understanding is presented partly in my *The Dynamic Psychological Field* (1975), which attempts to clarify the psychological basis and many philosophical assumptions of field theory.

Therefore, *National Attributes and Behavior* is one aspect of an ongoing effort to understand man, his international relations, and his conflicts, and should be examined within that context. However, I believe the data and results given here are of sufficient use and importance to be published on their own.

1.2 CAVEATS

As a research report, this book is meant to present the analyses and data. To provide space for all the data, I have kept my discussion of the research design and methodology to a minimum. I am quite conscious of what has been omitted. I present no general introduction to the field of research represented here and to the range of scientific work done by others to which mine relates. I do not generally explain or justify my methods and operations, except where necessary to understand the analyses. I do not compare my results with accepted propositions and other quantitative results, with the exception of those in Rummel (1972). Moreover, I do not draw out the practical and theoretical significance of these findings. Although I appreciate the need for such considerations, my interest here is purely in presenting the data and their major analyses. Therefore, I must lean on the above mentioned, related books on method, cross-national analyses, theory, psychology, and philosophy to provide some of what is omitted.

Regarding the data, these were collected specifically for the various analyses presented here. I required data for all nations on 91 attributes for each of five years, and on 182 dyads for 53 dyadic behaviors for the same years. To complete the task in a reasonable time, I had to bound my tolerance for data error by the overall research design. Because I was concerned with a series of multivariate analyses and with either delineating or linking data *patterns* rather than with actual frequencies, percentages, or data tabulations, I could accept a higher amount of error. Therefore, although my assistants tried to use the best sources, and we employed various checks to reduce clerical errors, we did not consider each datum with loving care. While appropriate for bivariate or multivariate correlational (or pattern) type analyses, including causal analysis, analyses of variance and covariance, discriminant analysis, chi-square tests, and so on, these data should be used with caution for analyses focusing on an individual datum.

Concerning the analyses, those presented here comprise the most extensive and intensive range of national multivariate analyses of which I am aware. They cover all nations in the post-World War II years; they involve the full range of national attributes, from economic, social, and cultural to demographic, political, and military; they consider the variety of international behaviors of nations, including solidary or integrative, contractual and antagonistic behaviors; they concern the many linkages between such behaviors and national attributes and the most general equations for predicting behavior; they uncover what pairs of nations are most alike in their linkages; and they point to a set of national and international social indicators.

In presenting this wealth of results, I can only summarize the most general findings. Consequently my approach has been to present as much as possible in tables and in the clearest form.

A good table is worth chapters of prose. In sum the collection of tables given here comprise an archive of empirical results on nations. Here can be found relevant empirical findings on hypotheses or theories concerning the relationships between politics, demography, development, energy, or stability; concerning the dependence of foreign policy upon national characteristics; concerning the correlates and causes of foreign conflict; and so on. I hope these results will be so exploited.

1.3 SUMMARY

Leaving all qualifications and technical considerations aside, what are the central patterns and relationships I found in the data presented here?

1.3.1 On National Societies

1. The major patterns of cross-national, cross-time variation in national attributes are along dimensions of wealth, totalitarianism, authoritarianism, power, domestic conflict, density, and Catholic culture.

2. The wealth dimension is consistently the largest pattern of national attributes, spanning the literacy, communications, nutrition, housing, GNP per capita, and bureaucratization of national societies. It is partly an economic development or modernization dimension, but includes other aspects of national societies. Wealth is the most pervasive and strongest pattern of covariance in national attributes in time and space, and at its center is the magnitude of energy consumption per capita.

3. Energy also enters into the power dimension. Energy production times population is the best indicator of a nation's power pattern. Thus, energy *consumption* per person marks a distinctive pattern of wealth; energy *production* weighted by the number of people indexes a nation's power. These two dimensions demonstrate the importance of energy.

4. The total foreign conflict of a nation is highly correlated with its power; the more the power, the more the conflict behavior of a nation.

5. National governments either vary from liberal democratic to totalitarian or to authoritarian. Totalitarianism and authoritarianism are the two major political dimensions of nations.

1.3.2 On International Behavior

6. The major independent patterns of behavior between nations comprise transactions, alignment, international organizations, relative exports, negative communications, military violence, and antiforeign behavior.

7. Conflict behavior between nations is in space and time independent of their level of transactions, comemberships in organizations, exports, and political alignments. In other words, the level of cooperation between two nations does not indicate much about their conflict behavior, and vice versa.

8. Moreover, the political alignments of nations, insofar as reflected by UN voting or bloc memberships, does not indicate much about their transactions or conflict behavior.

1.3.3 On Linkages

9. About a third of the variation in behavior between nations can be explained statistically by their various economic, political, and sociocultural distances from each other. Almost 90% of the variation in specific behaviors can be explained by such distances.

10. The behavior most *generally* dependent on distances in comemberships in international organizations. Actors are inclined to join organizations with densely populated, liberal democratic nations.

11. Nations are inclined to trade and transact less with those that are weak, small, and unstable.

12. Nations are disposed to have less conflict behavior with poor and weak nations.

13. *In general,* we can explain the conflict behavior of different actors by differences in wealth and power. However, the size of their effect and whether other differences are involved depends on the actor.

14. Six groups of actors share similar linkages between distances and behavior. The largest group involves a common linkage between power and organizational comemberships. Another large group shares a linkage between wealth and cooperation. China and the USSR, and UK and the US form separate groups. China and the USSR have a common linkage between wealth, politics and power, and cooperation with other nations. The US and UK share linkages across diverse distances, including politics and size, and their conflict with others.

15. In sum, there is a simple equation linking behavior and distances. It is

$$w_{i \to j,k} = \Sigma \alpha_{i\ell} d_{\ell,i-j},$$

where w is the behavior k of nation i to j, Σ is the summation sign, d is the distance vector (difference) between i and j on the ℓth dimension of the nation's attributes, and α is a parameter weighting the distances specifically for actor i.

Chapter 2

ATTRIBUTES AND NATIONS

2.1 DATA YEARS

The data and analyses are for the years 1950, 1955, 1960, 1963, and 1965. Why is 1950 the starting point? Enough time had passed to enable the social and political disruptions of World War II to settle and a new national order to stabilize. A new international system centered duo-politically around the Soviet Union and the United States had materialized; and 1950 marked the political-military beginning of the Cold War with the invasion of South Korea by the North, and the consequent crash rearmament of the United States.

The data series concludes with 1965, as close to the present as data availability allowed (the time collection began in 1968). Regarding the intermediary years, 1955 was a natural selection because data had already been collected and analysed for that year, as published in Rummel (1972); 1960 and 1963 were also selected to provide enough longitudinal data points to determine the effects of time on attributes and behavior.

2.2 NATIONS

Data were collected on all nations for each year in which they (1) were recognized within the family of nations as evidenced by exchange of ambassadors; (2) had a population greater than 750,000; and (3) had been independent for at least two years.

Applying these criteria, the number of nations varied by year as follows:

1950: 72
1955: 82
1960: 87
1963: 107
1965: 113

The total list of nations and their nation codes are given in Table 2.1.

2.3 ATTRIBUTES

A number of criteria directed the choice of nation attributes for which to collect data. These criteria are linked to a previous analysis, similar to that reported here (Rummel, 1972), on 236 attributes, which were selected carefully through the screening of over 500 attributes. The 236 were chosen on the basis of catholicity, statistical and arithmetical independence, sufficient data, scaling properties (its level of measurement), prior use or expert recommendation, and hypothetical and theoretical relevance to international relations (Rummel, 1972: 80-85).

The attributes analyzed here are a further reduction of that list of 236; therefore, the criteria guiding the choice of the previous attributes underlie those selected here in addition to the following.

First, attributes were selected to mark the empirically distinct patterns found among the 236 for 1955. Table 2.2 lists these patterns and those attributes selected for analysis here which index them. I should mention that the larger of these patterns have also been found in similar analyses of Cattell (1949), Cattell et al. (1952), Berry (1960), and Russett (1967), and these marker attributes, therefore, index a consistent set of empirical patterns found by different researchers for different years. Including these marker attributes here enables us to track across time the shifts in these patterns and the attributes of particular nations, such as China, the USSR, or the US as they change between 1950 and 1965.

Second, attributes were selected from the 236 according to their uniqueness. Some attributes had little relationship to others in the previous analyses. It may be, however, that these uniquely measure latent patterns that would emerge for different years or through time. Table 2.3 lists the unique attributes included here, along with a measure of their uniqueness in the 236-variable analysis.

Third, attributes were added that were not included in the previous 236-variable analysis but would help spotlight the political orientation pattern. This pattern is fuzzy: it is not clear whether it involves a communist-anticommunist or authoritarian-antiauthoritarian pattern, or a combination of both. Therefore, attributes were included to make these distinctions sharper. Table 2.4 lists these attributes.

Fourth, geographic location was defined by three attributes in the following

(text continued on p. 21)

Table 2.1. List of Nations [a]

I.D.	Political Unit	Code Abbreviation[b]	I.D.	Political Unit	Code Abbreviation	I.D.	Political Unit	Code Abbreviation
1.	Afghanistan	AFG 50	30.	Germany (Fed. Rep.)	GMW 55	56	Outer Mongolia	OUT 50
2.	Albania	ALB 50	90.	Ghana	GHA 60	57.	Pakistan	PAK 50
106.	Algeria	ALG 65	31.	Greece	GRC 50	58.	Panama	PAN 50
3.	Argentina	ARG 50	32.	Guatamala	GUA 50	59.	Paraguay	PAR 50
4.	Australia	AUL 50	91.	Guinea	GUN 63	60.	Peru	PER 50
5.	Austria	AUS 55	33.	Haiti	HAI 50	61.	Philippines	PHI 50
6.	Belgium	BEL 50	34.	Honduras	HON 50	62.	Poland	POL 50
7.	Bolivia	BOL 50	35.	Hungary	HUN 50	63.	Portugal	POR 50
8.	Brazil	BRA 50	36.	India	IND 50	64.	Rumania	RUM 50
9.	Bulgaria	BUL 50	37.	Indonesia	INS 50	114.	Rwanda	RWA 65
10.	Burma	BUR 50	38.	Iran	IRN 50	65.	Saudi Arabia	SAU 50
113.	Burundi	BRN 65	39.	Iraq	IRQ 50	100.	Senegal	SEN 63
11.	Cambodia	CAM 55	40.	Ireland	IRE 50	204.	Sierra Leone	SIE 63
83.	Cameroon	CAO 63	41.	Israel	ISR 50	101.	Somalia	SOM 63
12.	Canada	CAN 50	42.	Italy	ITA 50	66.	Spain	SPN 50
84.	Central African Rep.	CEN 63	92.	Ivory Coast	IVO 63	102.	Sudan	SUD 60
13.	Ceylon	CEY 50	163.	Jamaica	JAM 65	67.	Sweden	SWD 50
85.	Chad	CHA 63	43.	Japan	JAP 55	68.	Switzerland	SWZ 50
14.	Chile	CHL 50	44.	Jordan	JOR 50	69.	Syria	SYR 50
15.	China	CHN 50	45.	Korea (Dem. Rep.)	KON 50	109.	Tanzania	TAZ 63
16.	China (Republic of)	CHT 55	46.	Korea (Rep. of)	KOS 50	70.	Thailand	TAI 50
17.	Colombia	COL 50	80.	Laos	LAO 55	103.	Togo	TOG 63
87.	Congo (Brazzaville)	CON 63	47.	Lebanon	LEB 50	216.	Trinidad	TRI 65
86.	Congo (Leopoldville)	COP 63	48.	Liberia	LBR 50	104.	Tunisia	TUN 60
18.	Costa Rica	COS 50	49.	Libya	LYB 55	71.	Turkey	TUR 50
19.	Cuba	CUB 50	93.	Madagascar	MAD 63	72.	Union of S. Africa	UNS 50
20.	Czechoslovakia	CZE 50	94.	Malaysia	MAL 60	73.	USSR	USR 50
88.	Dahomey	DAH 63	95.	Mali	MLI 63	74.	United Kingdom	UNK 50
21.	Denmark	DEN 50	96.	Mauritania	MAT 63	75.	USA	USA 50
22.	Dominican Republic	DOM 50	50.	Mexico	MEX 50	219.	Uganda	UGA 65
23.	Ecuador	ECU 50	97.	Morocco	MOR 60	105.	Upper Volta	UPP 63
24.	Egypt (UAR)	EGP 50	51.	Nepal	NEP 50	76.	Uruguay	URA 50
25.	El Salvador	ELS 50	52.	Netherlands	NTH 50	77.	Venzuela	VEN 50
26.	Ethiopia	ETH 50	53.	New Zealand	NEW 50	81.	Vietnam (N)	VTN 55
27.	Finland	FIN 50	54.	Nicaragua	NIC 50	82.	Vietnam (S)	VTS 55
28.	France	FRN 50	98.	Niger	NIR 63	78.	Yemen	YEM 50
89.	Gabon	GAB 63	99.	Nigeria	NIG 63	79.	Yugoslavia	YUG 50
29.	Germany (D.D.R.)	GME 55	55.	Norway	NOR 50			

a. N = 113

b. The numbers next to the code abbreviation are the last two digits of the year that the nation entered the sample. Burundi, for example, became a member of the sample in 1965.

Table 2.2. Attributes Indexing Cross-National Dimensions [a]

Dimension	Attribute
Economic Development	telephones/population
	agricultural population/population
	energy consumption/population
	illiterates/population 10 years of age or older
	GNP/population
Power Bases (Size)	population x energy production
	national income
	population
	UN assessment/total UN assessment
	defense expenditure
Political Orientation	English titles translated/foreign titles translated
	bloc membership
	US aid received/USSR and US aid received
	freedom of opposition
	IFC and IBRD subscription/$(GNP)^2$ per capita
Foreign Conflict Behavior	threats
	accusations
	killed in foreign violence
	military action or not
	protests
Domestic Conflict	killed in domestic violence
	general strikes
	riots
	purges
	demonstrations
Catholic Culture	Roman Catholics/population
	air distance from US
	medicine NGO/NGO
	diplomat expelled or recalled
	divorces/marriages
Density	population/national land area
	arable land/total land area
	national area
	road length/national area
	railroad length/national area
Oriental Culture	religions
	immigrants/migrants
	average rainfall
	membership of largest religion/population
	dwellings with running water/dwellings

Table 2.2 (continued)

Dimension	Attribute
(Unlabeled) [b]	foreign college students/college students membership in neutral bloc age of country religious titles published/book titles
Seaport Dependency	emigrants/population seaborne goods/GNP law NGO/NGO unemployed/economically active population leading export/exports
Diversity	languages membership of largest language group/population ethnic groups economic aid received technical assistance received
Equality	government education expenditures/government expenditures female workers/economically active
Traders	exports/GNP foreign mail sent/foreign mail imports/trade
Sufficiency	calories consumed minus calories required/ calories required proteins/calories Russian titles translated/foreign titles translated military personnel/population balance of investments/gold stock
(Unlabeled) [b]	political parties arts and culture NGO/NGO communist party membership/population government expenditure/GNP monarchy or not

a. These dimensions are the oblique factor-dimensions of 236 attributes for 1955. See Rummel (1972, Chap. 9).

b. This particular dimension was not substantively interpretable.

Table 2.3. Unique Attributes [a]

pupils in primary school/primary school teachers
legality of government change
legitimacy of present government
largest ethnic group membership/population
assassinations
major government crises
UN payment delinquencies/assessments
balance of payments/gold stock
balance of investments

a. These are those attributes with the lowest communalities (h^2) across the dimensions of Table 2.2. See Rummel (1972: 478-479).

Table 2.4. Additional Attributes [a]

system style (0= nonmobilizational; 1 = limited mobilizational; 2 = mobilizational)
constitutional status (0 = totalitarian; 1 = authoritarian; 2 = constitutional)
electoral system (0 = noncompetitive; 1 = partly competitive; 2 = competitive)
noncommunist regime (0 = no; 1 = yes)
political leadership (0 = elitist; 1 = moderately elitist; 2 = nonelite)
horizontal power distribution (0 = negligible; 1 = limited; 2 = significant)
military participation (0 = neutral; 1 = supportive; 2 = interventive)
bureaucracy (0 = traditional; 1 = semi-modern; 2 = modern)
censorship (0 = little censorship; 1 = moderate; 2 = complete)

a. These are selected to better delineate the political orientation dimension of Table 2.2.

fashion. The geographical location of the capital or seat of the national government was determined in degrees of latitude and longitude, with North latitude and East longitude defined in the positive sense. For each nation these two polar coordinates were converted to three rectangular coordinates, called geographic x, y, and z, using the transformations

$$\text{geographic x} = R \cos\phi \cos\theta,$$

$$\text{geographic y} = R \cos\phi \sin\theta,$$

$$\text{geographic z} = R \sin\phi,$$

where ϕ is latitude, θ is longitude, and R = 3,963 miles (the earth's equatorial radius). The axis of geographic x passes through the center of the earth and intersects the Greenwich Meridian (zero degrees longitude) at the equator. Geographic y is a coordinate also passing through the earth's center and is at right angles to geographic x in the plane of the equator. Geographic z is the North-South coordinate coincident with the earth's axis of rotation. Capitals with joint positive values on all three coordinates are situated in the Northern Hemisphere, between zero degrees and 90° East longitude.

These three geographic attributes uniquely measure the location of a nation's political center and enable us to assess the relationship of geographic location to other socioeconomic, political, and cultural attributes, and international behavior.

Finally, since we are analyzing nations and their behavior over a fifteen-year span, the year of the data was included as an attribute called time. Thus, for those nations in 1950, time has the value 50; for 1955 it is 55, for 1960 it is 60, and so forth. In this way we can assess what dimensions are correlated with time.

In total, then, there are 91 attributes for which data have been collected for 1950-1965. Table 2.5 lists these attributes, along with their variable and analysis numbers, and means and standard deviations across all five years.

Appendix I gives their definitions, units, and principal sources for the data. Appendix II presents all the data for the five years, their means and standard deviations for each year, and data footnotes.

Table 2.5. Attributes and Their Codes

No.	Code	Attribute
1	TEL-PC	telephones/population
2	%A-POP	agricultural population/population
3	ENC-PC	energy consumption/population
4	ILLITE	illiterates/population 10 years of age or older
5	GNP-PC	GNP/population
6	EPXPOP	energy production x population
7	NI	national income
8	POPULA	population
9	%CT-UN	UN assessment/total UN assessment
10	DEFEXP	defense expenditure
11	E/TRSL	English titles translated/foreign titles translated
12	BLOC	bloc membership
13	US/AID	US aid received/USSR and US aid received
14	TOTALI	freedom of opposition
15	IFC/GP	IFC and IBRD subscription/$(GNP)^2$ per capita
16	THREAT	threats
17	ACCUSA	accusations
18	F-KILL	killed in foreign violence
19	MILACT	military action or not
20	PROTST	protests
21	D-KILL	killed in domestic violence
22	STRIKE	general strikes
23	RIOTS	riots
24	PURGES	purges
25	DEMONS	demonstrations
26	%CATH	Romantic Catholics/population
27	US-DIS	air distance from US
28	MED/NGO	medicine NGO/NGO
29	ER-AMB	diplomat expelled or recalled
30	DIV-MR	divorces/marriages
31	DENSITY	population/national land area
32	%ARABL	arable land/total land area
33	AREA	national area
34	RDS-KM	road length/national area
35	RRS-KM	railroad length/national area
36	RELGRP	religions
37	IM/I+E	immigrants/migrants
38	RAIN	average rainfall
39	RGRP/P	membership of largest religion/population
40	%D-WTR	dwellings with running water/dwellings
41	FST/ST	foreign college students/college students
42	NEUTRL	membership in neutral bloc
43	NATAGE	age of country

Table 2.5 (continued)

No.	Code	Attribute
44	REL-TI	religious titles published/book titles
45	EMG/POP	emigrants/population
46	SG/GNP	seaborne goods/GNP
47	LAW/NG	law NGO/NGO
48	%UNEMP	unemployed/economically active population
49	EX/EPT	leading export/exports
50	LANGRP	languages
51	LGRP/P	membership of largest language group/population
52	ETHGRP	ethnic group
53	AIDRVD	economic aid received
54	TECRVD	technical assistance received
55	%E-GVT	government education expenditures/government expenditures
56	FM/WKS	female workers/economically active population
57	EXP/GNP	exports/GNP
58	FMST/M	foreign mail sent/foreign mail
59	IP/TRD	imports/trade
60	CAL-PC	calories consumed minus calories required/calories required
61	PR/CAL	proteins/calories
62	R/TRSL	Russian titles translated/foreign titles translated
63	MIL/POP	military personnel/population
64	BOI/GO	balance of investments/gold stock
65	PARTYS	political parties
66	ART/NGO	arts and culture NGO/NGO
67	COM/POP	communist party membership/population
68	GVT/GNP	government expenditures/GNP
69	MONARC	monarchy or not
70	PUP-PT	pupils in primary school/primary school teachers
71	LAWTRA	legality of government change
72	LEGIT	legitimacy of present government
73	EGRP/P	largest ethnic group membership/population
74	ASSASS	assassinations
75	GVTCRS	major government crises
76	UNDE/A	UN payment delinquencies/assessments
77	BOP/GO	balance of payments/gold stock
78	INVBAL	balance of investments
79	STYLE	system style
80	CONSTI	constitutional status
81	ELECTO	electoral system
82	COMMUN	noncommunist regime
83	LEADER	political leadership
84	POWDIS	horizontal power distribution
85	MILPAR	military participation
86	BUREAU	bureaucracy
87	CENSOR	censorship score
88	GEOG-X	geographic x
89	GEOG-Y	geographic y
90	GEOG-Z	geographic z
91	TIME	time

Chapter 3

INTERNATIONAL BEHAVIOR

3.1 DATA YEARS AND NATION-DYADS

Since our fundamental concern is to determine the linkages between dyadic behavior and attributes, the same five years were selected for the behavior data.

Selecting nation-dyads, however, was not so simple. The total number of paired relationships among nations for any one year is more than several thousand, surely presenting a gigantic data collection task. Alternatively, a manageable sample can be provided by selecting at random a hundred or so dyads, and then collecting data on them for all five years. As a matter of fact, such a random sample had already been used for 1955 behavior data (Rummel, 1972, Chapter 16; 1969).

Here, however, I could not use a random sample for I was focusing on the directed behavior of one member of a dyad (the actor) toward the other (the object). To determine the behavior-attribute linkages of these actors, I needed a sufficient number of actors. Randomly selected dyads hardly yielded an appropriate sample, since most actors occurred only once or twice among the dyads.

Another alternative was to select a dozen actors randomly, and then take all dyadic combinations among them. This would yield enough dyads involving the same actor, but probably bias the results in terms of some dimensions. For example, with only a population of around a hundred nations to select randomly from, the dozen actors so selected might not include any developed nations, nor communist regimes, nor European nations, and so on. Yet, since my concern was to determine general linkages, the sample had to include the range of variation among nations.

To ensure such a sample, then, I did the following. A list of fourteen nations was selected carefully to represent the high, middle, and low values of nations on the major dimensions emerging from an earlier analysis of 236 attributes for 82 nations (Rummel, 1972) and 94 international relations behaviors for 82 nations (Rummel, 1972, Chapter 13). Each of the high, middle, and low positions on each dimension is represented in the list by at least two nations. To index the major cultural and regional groupings of nations, Cattell's (1950) and Russett's (1967) results were used to identify individual nations central to a cultural or regional cluster of nations.

With a representative list of fourteen nations thus choosen, I then took all dyadic combinations among them as a sample of 182 dyads. This *selected sample* ensured that the full scope of differences and similarities *among* nations would be analyzed as they related to interaction *between* nations. Table 3.1 lists the fourteen nations which formed the selected sample of dyads.

Table 3.1. Selected Nations

Brazil	Israel
Burma	Jordan
China	Netherlands
Cuba	Poland
Egypt	USSR
India	United Kingdom
Indonesia	USA

3.2 BEHAVIOR

There were two aims: one, to delimit the dimensions of dyadic behavior, 1950-1965; the other, to determine the linkages of these behavior dimensions to nation attributes. To achieve both, the same criteria should be applied in selecting both behaviors and attributes to analyze. Of special concern, however, is that data fully mirror the variety of conflict behavior possible between nations, while also spanning the variation in international relations.

These two criteria—that behaviors reflect the variety of conflict and the variety of international relations—in addition to those underlying the selection of the attributes (data availability, scaling properties, statistical independence, and so on), had already been satisfied in the selection of forty behaviors for the analysis of 1955 data previously published (Rummel, 1972, Chapter 16; 1969). Therefore, in selecting the behaviors to be analyzed, insofar as data would allow, I incorporated the forty behaviors previously analyzed, as well as additional behaviors to satisfy further the need for catholicity.

In sum, 53 behaviors were finally selected for the analysis. Organized by substantive domain, these are shown in Table 3.2 with their codes. The definitions, units, and data sources are given in Appendix III; Appendix IV lists the data, means, and standard deviations.

Table 3.2. Behaviors and Their Codes

Domain	No.	Code	Behavior A→B [a]
Communications			
	5	VISITS	official visits A→B
	6	CONFER	co-participation in international conferences A↔B
	7	BOOKS	export of books and magazines A→B
	8	R-BOOK	relative export of books and magazines A→B
	9	TRANSL	book translations A of B
	10	R-TRAN	relative book translations A of B
Conflict			
	11	WARNDF	warning or defensive acts
	12	VIOLAC	violent actions
	13	MILACT	military actions
	14	DAYSVL	duration
	15	NEGBEH	negative behavior
	16	EXPREC	expulsion or recall of diplomats and lesser officials
	17	BCTEMB	boycott or embargo
	18	AIDREB	aid to subversive groups or enemy
	19	NEGCOM	negative communications
	20	ACCUSN	accusation
	21	PROTST	protests
	22	UNOFAC	unofficial acts
	23	ATKEMB	attack on embassy
	24	NVIOLB	nonviolent behavior
Diplomacy			
	3	TREATY	treaties A↔B
	4	R-TRTY	relative treaties
	44	EMBLEG	embassy or legation A→B
	45	R-EMB	relative diplomatic representation A→B
History			
	46	WAROPP	time since opposite sides of a war A↔B
	47	WARSAM	time since on same sides of war A↔B
	48	LOSTER	A has lost, and not regained, territory to B since 1900 or not
	49	DEPEND	A once a colony, territory or part of homeland of B
	50	INDEP	independence of A and B predates 1946 or not
International Politics			
	25	WD-UN	weighted UN voting distance
	26	UWD-UN	unweighted UN voting distance
	51	COMBLC	common bloc membership
	52	COMPOS	bloc position index A↔B
	53	ALLIAN	military alliance A↔B

Table 3.2 (continued)

Domain	No.	Code	Behavior A→B
International Organizations			
	38	IGO	intergovernmental organizations (IGO) of which A and B are both members A↔B
	39	R-IGO	relative IGO A↔B
	40	NGO	nongovernmental international organizations (NGO) of which A and B are both members A↔B
	41	R-NGO	relative NGO A↔B
	42	N-IGO	IGO A↔B/common membership of A
	43	N-NGO	NGO A↔B/common membership of A
Mobility			
	27	TOURIS	tourists A→B
	28	R-TOUR	relative tourists A→B
	29	T/POPU	tourists (A→B)/A's population
	30	EMIGRA	emigrants A→B
	31	R-EMIG	relative emigrants A→B
	32	E/POPU	emigrants (A→B)/A's population
	33	STUDNT	students A→B
	34	R-STUD	relative students A→B
Trade and Aid			
	1	AID	economic aid A→B
	2	R-AID	relative economic aid A→B
	35	EXPORT	exports A→B
	36	R-EXPT	relative exports A→B
	37	E/GNP	exports (A→B)/A's GNP

a. A is the actor and B is the object.

Chapter 4

TOWARD DELINEATING DIMENSIONS AND LINKAGES

4.1 THEORETICAL CONTEXT AND RESEARCH QUESTIONS

Before analyzing the attribute and behavior data, I should provide some perspective on these efforts. Data can be analyzed in a variety of ways, and many different routes provide answers to the same question. Some theoretical context, therefore, is needed to guide the analysis and provide a framework for the research decisions made.

The theoretical orientation here is that the attributes of nations form a force field effecting the dyadic behavior of nations; that the forces in this field comprise the various socioeconomic, political, cultural, and geographic distances between nations (Rummel, 1975, 1976). Now, all nations are influenced by such a force field, which is to say that the behavior of any specific actor toward another is partly a resolution of their distance vectors, That is,

$$w_{i \to j} = \Sigma \alpha_{i\ell} d_{\ell,i-j} + u_{i \to j} \text{ ,}$$

where $w_{i \to j}$ is the behavior of actor i to object j along a specific behavioral dimension, $d_{\ell,i-j}$ is a distance vector on a specific dimension of nation attributes, $\alpha_{i\ell}$ is a weight that the specific distance has in effecting w and u_{i-j} comprises that aspect of behavior independent of distances. By theory, the amount of dyadic behavior of all nations accounted for by this force field will be substantial.

However, nations will vary in the effect that various distances have on their behavior. Because of their unique cultures, history, decision framework, and so on, the elite of each nation will perceive differently their nation's distances from others. Some nations will be affected more by ideological distance, some by power distance, some by distance in development or wealth. Accordingly, the weights, $\alpha_{i\ell}$, that the distances have in effecting behavior will vary by actor i. All nations are caught equally in a force field of distances, but the potency of these distances depends on a nation's qualities.

In sum, the transactions, conflict, diplomacy, and so forth of nations is, to a significant degree, the product of their various distances.[1] This is the theory guiding the following analyses. The aim of these analyses is then to determine

(1) whether distances do account in substantial degree for dyadic behavior, as theorized;
(2) and what distances link to what behavior.

These comprise the research questions. To answer them, however, requires engaging two instrumental questions. What are the dimensions of attributes which generate the distance-forces? What are the dimensions of dyadic behavior? And how do we determine what behavior is linked to what distances? These are the topics of the following sections.

4.2 SPACE-TIME DIMENSIONS OF ATTRIBUTES

4.2.1 The Data Matrix: Super-P Factor Analysis

What are the dimensions among the 91 attributes for the years 1950-1965? In other words, given these attributes and their different data across both nations and years, what underlying dimensions span most of this variance? This is a typical factor analysis question, but one applied to an unusual set of data.[2]

Figure 4.1 displays the matrix organization of the attribute data. The problem is to determine in the columns of data, the dimensions describing the variation across both nations and years. Factor analysis applied to variation across time alone is called P-factor analysis. For this reason, I will call the factor analysis applied to a supermatrix (a matrix composed of submatrices, where each submatrix consists of attribute data for one year for all nations, as in Figure 4.1) a *super-P factor analysis.* When this kind of analysis is applied to the data of Figure 4.1, the resulting factor-dimensions will delineate the space-time variance of the attributes.

4.2.2 The Technique: Component vs. Image Factor Analysis

There are, however, two kinds of approaches to this variance in attributes. First, we can try to determine dimensions describing as much of this variance as possible. Our aim would be simply to reproduce this variance, and the appropriate factor analysis technique is *component analysis.* Its application assumes

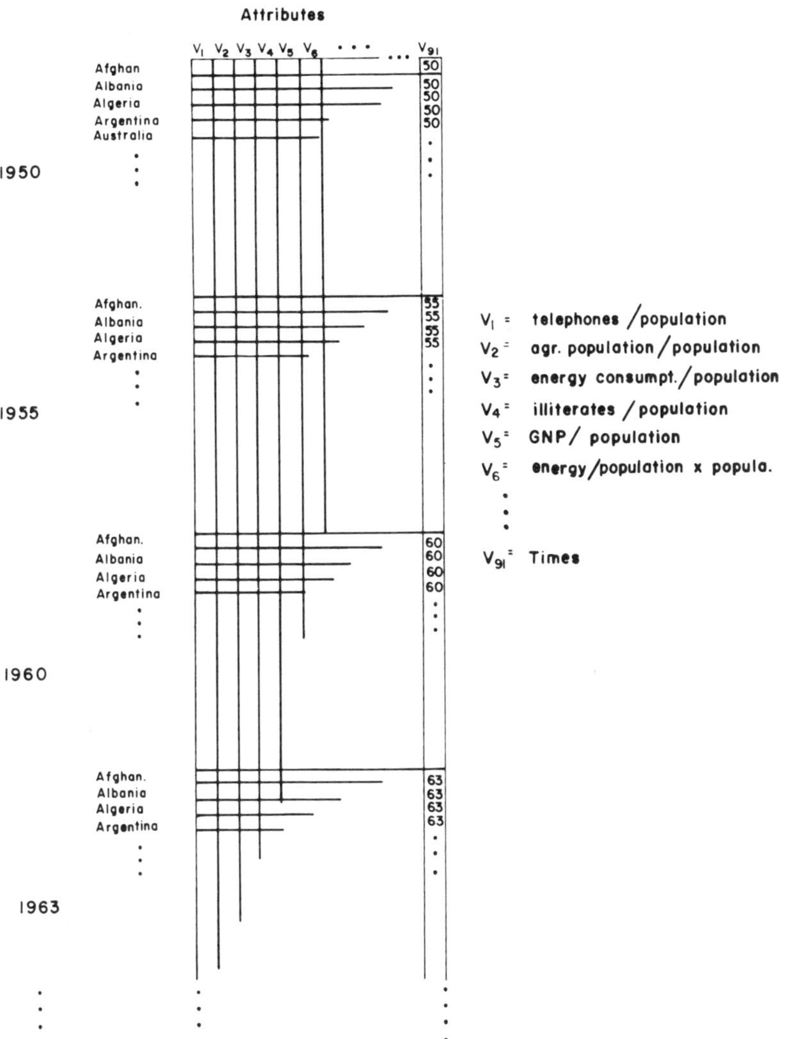
Attributes
V1 V2 V3 V4 V5 V6 . . . . . . V91
Afghan
Albania
Algeria
Argentina
Australia
1950
50
Afghan.
Albania
Algeria
Argentina
1955
55
Afghan.
Albania
Algeria
Argentina
1960
60
Afghan.
Albania
Algeria
Argentina
1963
63
V1 = telephones /population
V2 = agr. population /population
V3 = energy consumpt./population
V4 = illiterates /population
V5 = GNP/ population
V6 = energy/population x popula.
V91 = Times

Figure 4.1

that all the variance in the attributes is important and therefore we want to define the space-time dimensions that best reproduce it.

We may desire, however, to define only the common variance among the attributes. That is, we want dimensions that measure the *common* variance in attributes across space and time, leaving independent that variance due to *unique* societal, environmental, and historical influences, or individual and cultural creativity. Then, we can use *image analysis,* which is a common factor technique defining the common dimensions of attributes.[3]

Image analysis is more appropriate within the framework of field theory, since the theory assumes that the field is defined by the common variance in attributes.[4] Since the purpose here, however, is not to operationalize the theory but to present the empirical analyses that may be useful for a range of field theory irrelevant purposes, both the component and image analyses results will be presented.

4.3 SPACE-TIME DIMENSIONS OF DYADIC BEHAVIOR

4.3.1 The Dyadic Data Matrix: Super-P Factor Analysis

The data matrix for the dyadic behavior is organized the same as for attributes in Figure 4.1. It is a supermatrix, with each submatrix comprising dyadic data for a specific year. Each row of the matrix refers to a specific dyad, such as China's behavior to Cuba, Israel's to Egypt, and Poland's to the USSR: there are the same 182 dyads for each year. The columns of the matrix define the various behaviors described in the last chapter.

Super-P factor analysis also will be done on these data to delineate the major space-time dimensions of dyadic behavior.

4.3.2 The Technique: Component vs. Image Factor Analyses

The considerations that apply to the dimensions of attributes apply also to behavior. I will present the dimensions that best describe the maximum variance in the data. But also, I will present the *common* dimensions that describe the covariation between the behaviors. The first set of dimensions will be determined through component analysis; the second set, through image analysis.

4.4 MEASURING LINKAGES: CANONICAL ANALYSIS

Through the above analyses we will determine space-time dimensions of behavior and attributes. The next question is: how do these empirical dimensions of behavior link to those of attributes? Before dealing with this question, however, we must determine what in attributes we want to link to behavior.

4.4.1 Attributes, Distance Magnitudes, or Distance Vectors

What aspect of attributes is most sensible to examine systematically in explaining behavior? First, we could link the attributes of the actor nation to its behavior to the object. Or, in terms of the space-time dimensions, we could link an actor's scores on the attribute dimensions (such as wealth, power, and authoritarianism) to its dyadic scores on the behavior dimensions (such as transactions, alignment, and military violence). But this would assume (1) that an actor behaved similarly toward other nations regardless of *their* differing attributes (since the actor's scores on a dimension would not change with change in object) and (2) that all actors who share the same attributes behave similarly towards other nations. This is hardly reasonable. We do not need statistical analysis to know that the behavior of the United States, for example, does vary considerably among Cuba, China, the USSR, Argentina, the United Kingdom, and so on. And since the scores of the United States on attribute dimensions like wealth and power are constant (for a year), they cannot explain this behavioral variance.

Another approach is to link the distances between actor and object on attribute dimensions to the actor's behavior. This seems a reasonable and compelling approach, for we can well see in international relations the effects of differences in wealth and power, geographic distance, and ideological similarity.

Should such distances be magnitudes or vectors? If magnitudes, we are simply saying that the absolute differences on attribute dimensions between actor and object help explain their behavior. But wait. Is it irrelevant to an actor whether other countries have more or less wealth, energy, power, or population than it does? Will an actor behave toward two nations equally so long as both are the same absolute distance from it in power, even if one is much greater in power than the other? Of course not. Nations are quite sensitive to the *direction* that distances take, and therefore we should use a measure of distance that takes this direction into account.

Such a measure is the *distance vector*. This simply comprises the difference between actor and object on a particular attribute or dimension. It not only takes into account the direction of the difference, but also its magnitude. If another nation j is higher in power than an actor i, for example, then the distance is negative; if j is lower in power, then the distance is positive.[5]

Insofar as linkages to dyadic behavior are concerned, then, our focus is on the distance vectors in attribute space. We want to know whether the variance along the dyadic space-time behavior dimensions is explained by the variance in distances between actor and object on the attribute space-time dimensions.

4.4.2 Transforming Attribute Data

There is a psychological aspect to distances, however, which we ought to accommodate in our measurements. The larger the distance magnitudes between people, the less perception there is of unit differences. For example, those with ten and twenty million dollars are perceived by the poor person as about equally distant from himself. Yet, a person with ten million would be quite attendant to the difference between ten and twenty million. There is, thus, a diminishing salience with distance.

Similarly with nations. Incremental differences among those nations that are close in power or wealth are far more salient to the acting nation's elite than are the differences among those quite distant. A small power perceives more the differences among other small powers than it does the same unit differences between the super powers.

There are two ways of including this law of diminishing salience in the analysis. One is to do directly a logarithmic transformation of the distances. This will decrease the differences between large distances and increase those between the small. However, this is a nonlinear transformation and will mean that the distances no longer span the underlying attribute space.

A better approach log-transforms the original data in the attribute matrix. In the transformed space-time thus produced, its dimensions will then reflect these transformations, and distances between nations upon these dimensions will then span the space. Also, because they are generated by underlying log-transformed data, the distances will have diminishing magnitude with the size of the underlying raw data. In other words, transforming the raw data enables us to assume that the whole attribute space-time of nations is, *from the point of view of the actor,* increasingly compressed as we move to the attribute extremes.

In the results, I accordingly will focus on the transformed attribute data. The data for behavior has not been log-transformed, since there is no theoretical reason to apply a law of diminishing returns to behavior as well.

4.4.3 Assessing Overall Linkages Between Behavior and Attributes: The Trace Correlation

Given the above, a primary question is: How much dyadic behavior is explained by attribute distances. This is answerable by some quantity or proportion which expresses the degree to which dyadic behavior is so explained.

Consider the result of the previous analyses determining the space-time dimensions of attributes and behavior. We will have defined separately two vector spaces in terms of the empirical dimensions of each. We now want to assess the linear dependence of one space upon the other.

A technique for doing this is *canonical analysis.* This is a form of regression analysis (the regression model using one dependent variable is a special case of canonical analysis) [6] which yields a coefficient called the *trace correlation* (which is the multiple correlation coefficient in regression analysis). When squared, this coefficient measures the dependence of behavior on distances that we are after.

For a picture of this consider Figure 4.2. The attribute and dyadic behavior defined by the two sets of space-time dimensions are shown, with some overlap between the two. This overlap is that dyadic behavior completely determined

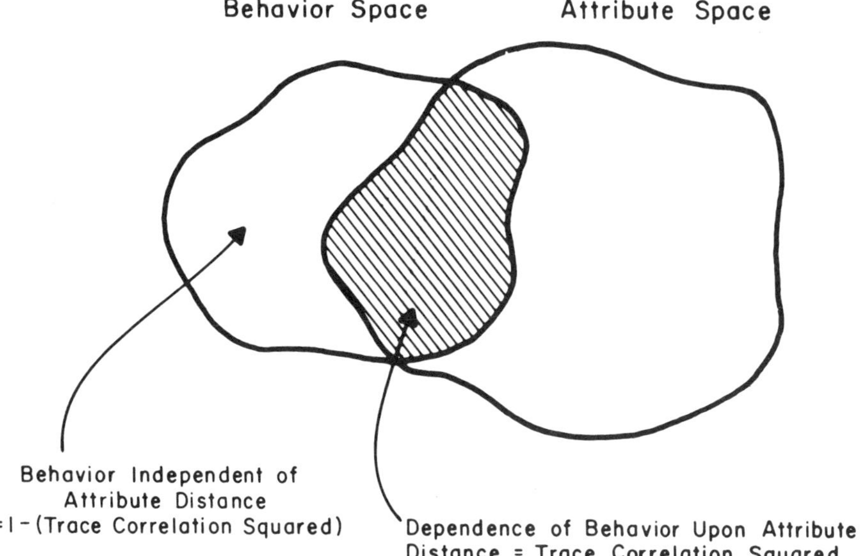

Figure 4.2

or explained by the distances. Now, the squared trace correlation will tell us what the amount of this dependence is as a proportion of the whole, and will thus explicitly answer our original question about the data linkages. The trace correlation is therefore the first aspect of these linkages we will look at.

4.4.4 Assessing Specific Linkages: The Canonical Equations

Although only a small portion of the behavior space-time may be dependent upon distances, some particular behavioral dimensions may be highly dependent. For example, although the range of dyadic behavior may have little total relationship to ideological distance, a dimension of international conflict may be wholly explained by it. We should, therefore, have some means of pulling out those specific relationships between the dimensions and distances manifesting the largest dependencies.

Our second question, then, is: What specific behavioral space-time dimensions are most related to which distances, and to what degree? Here also canonical analysis is appropriate. Besides giving us the trace correlation, it will also define those equations maximally linking behavioral dimensions to distances. These equations will be mutually independent, and along with each is defined a *canonical correlation coefficient.* When squared, this coefficient measures the proportion of the variance in the dyadic dimension dependent upon the distances.

All this will be clarified in the context of my actual interpretation of the canonical equations. The point here is to define what we want to know about the linkages and the direction their analysis will take.

4.4.5 The Distance Parameters

Let me return to the question of distances. Do distances affect actors equally, or do effects vary depending on the actor? If they affect actors equally, then each actor, such as China, the United States, and the USSR, will tend to behave equally toward another nation if the distance is the same. This hardly seems true, however. From what we know about international relations, the same distance in power, ideology, culture, or wealth does not have anything like the same behavioral effect on different actors.[7] Moreover, by the nature of distance vectors or differences, if the distance of i→j results in behavior w, then the distance j→i must result in -w. That is, if we assume distances to have equal effect, then insofar as behavior is dependent on distances, reciprocal behavior between nations is inversely related. If trade is dependent on distance in development, then the more i exports to j, the less j exports to i. This is clearly contra-experience.

As mentioned in Section 4.1, it is more reasonable to assume that each actor processes distances in terms of its own unique decision-making structure, ideology, culture, and historical experiences. Then, the same distance would have different weights for China, for the United States, for the USSR, or for Burma. Then, the behavior between nations i and j could be reciprocal, because the underlying distances i-j and j-i effecting behavior could differ in both the weights and whether they were positive or negative.

The upshot of this discussion of weights is that the canonical analysis cannot be done on all the dyads simultaneously, for this assumes that distances have equal effect on actors. To allow the weight of distances to vary for each actor, we have to carry out a separate canonical analysis of those dyads involving a particular actor. Thus, for example, all dyads involving China as an actor should be analyzed separately from all the dyads involving the United States as an actor. This will be done.

4.5 SUMMARY

I can summarize the manner in which behavior-attribute linkages will be assessed by reference to Figure 4.3. First, we begin on each side at the top of Figure 4.3 with the dyadic behavior data given in Appendix IV and the log-transformations of the attribute data given in Appendix II. Then, super-P factor analysis is separately applied to both to determine the space-time dimensions of each. The scores (factor scores) of nations or dyads on these dimension then are computed, and for the attribute dimensions, distances between nations are computed (a distance matrix for *each* dimension). Finally, as shown for each

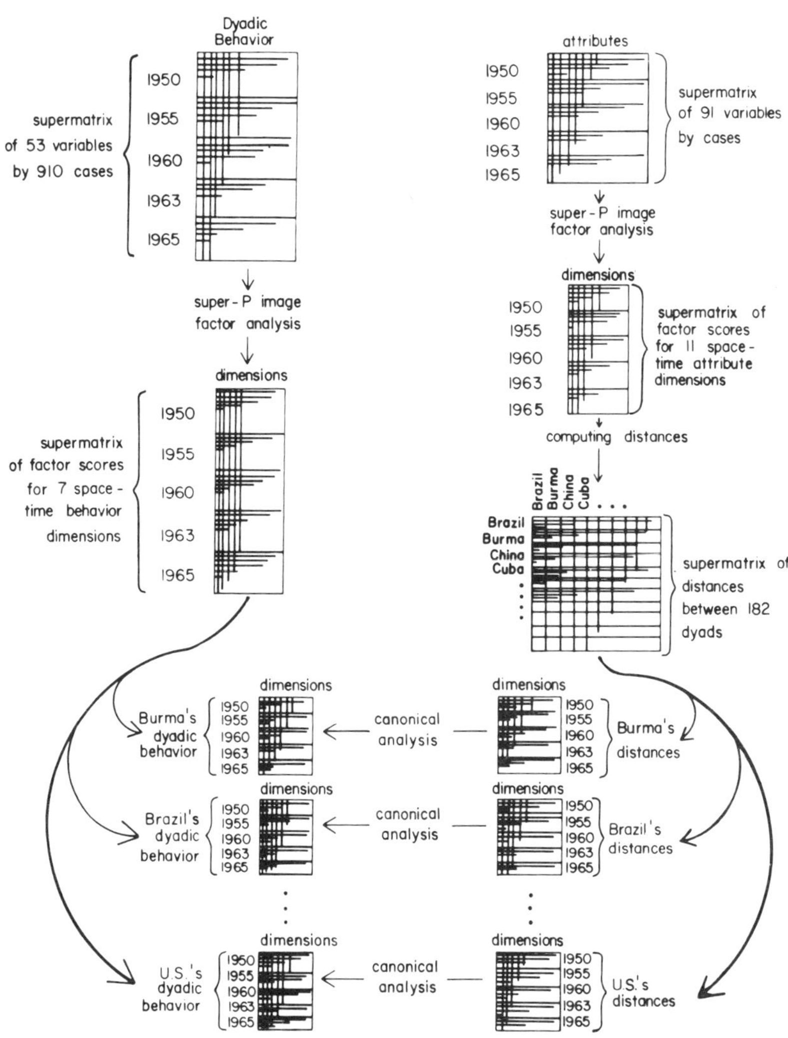
Dyadic Behavior
1950
1955
1960
1963
1965
supermatrix of 53 variables by 910 cases
super-P image factor analysis
dimensions
supermatrix of factor scores for 7 space-time behavior dimensions
attributes
supermatrix of 91 variables by cases
dimensions
supermatrix of factor scores for 11 space-time attribute dimensions
computing distances
Brazil
Burma
China
Cuba
supermatrix of distances between 182 dyads
Burma's dyadic behavior
canonical analysis
Burma's distances
Brazil's dyadic behavior
Brazil's distances
U.S.'s dyadic behavior
U.S.'s distances

Figure 4.3

sample of selected dyads involving the same actor, a canonical analysis of the actor's behavior dependency on its distances is done. There thus will be fourteen separate canonical analyses.

With this overview in mind, I can now move to determining the space-time dimensions.

NOTES

1. The evolution of this field theory and the various empirical tests applied to it, including the results presented here, are given in my *Field Theory Evolving* (1976).

2. For an overview of factor analysis as a method applied to nations, see Rummel (1967; 1972, Chapter 2). For a more detailed mathematical and methodological description, see Rummel (1970).

3. See Rummel (1970, Section 5.2).

4. This assumption is developed in Rummel (1975).

5. I compute the distance between i and j on a dimension S as $S_i - S_j$, so that the distance vector points from object to actor.

6. Unfortunately, the social sciences have yet to be widely acquainted with canonical analysis. A seminal article on it is Hotelling (1936). For a description of the mathematical model see Rummel (1976, especially Chapter 4). For extensive application to international relations paralleling that here, see the various chapters in Rummel (1976).

7. For systematic evidence of this, see the tests of Model I (which assumes distances impact equally on nations) summarized in Chapter 16 of Rummel (1976).

Chapter 5

SPACE-TIME DIMENSIONS OF NATIONS, 1950-1965

5.1 MISSING DATA AND SEPARATE ANALYSES

Given the 91 attributes for all nations described in Chapter 2 and the data of Appendix II, then what are the major dimensions accounting for the variance in this data?

One immediate methodological problem concerns missing data. Not all nations had data available for all attributes for all years. Therefore, I first subjectively estimated the most obvious data, such as zero for the number of Cuban tourists in China in 1955. These estimates are given along with the data in Appendix II. Then, we used a regression technique (Wall and Rummel, 1969) to estimate the remainder. Essentially, this involved linearly estimating a missing datum on an attribute X_k from the available data on the attributes, X_1, X_2, X_3, . . . , upon which X_k is most dependent, 1950-1965.[1]

Four different super-P factor analyses (see Section 4.2.1) were then done on the complete matrix of data and estimates. The first was a component analysis (see Section 4.2.2) of the raw data. The second was a component analysis of the log transformed data (see Section 4.4.3). Third, an image analysis (see Section 4.2.2) of the transformed data was done to define the common dimensions of nations. And finally, an oblique rotation of these image dimensions was done to define better the common patterns of interrelationships in the data.

A word on oblique rotation may be helpful. Factor analysis can be used to delineate uncorrelated (orthogonal) or correlated dimensions. Generally, because of their simplicity, uncorrelated dimensions are most desirable. However, these uncorrelated dimensions may not define the separate patterns of interrelated attributes, if these patterns are themselves correlated among nations. For example, uncorrelated dimensions may not delineate power and politics if such attributes form correlated patterns. In this case, an oblique rotation can define better these correlated patterns and measure their degree of correlation. The oblique rotation done here was applied to the attribute dimensions after determining that oblique dimensions would give a clear alternative delimitation of the empirical space-time patterns.

5.2 THE DIMENSIONS

When the results of the four analyses were considered together, twelve major dimensions common to them were found to account for an average of 52% of the variance in attributes, 1950-1965. Let us consider these dimensions in detail.

5.2.1 Wealth

The largest dimension to emerge from each of the four analyses is shown in Table 5.1. It is consistent across the analyses and measures what has been called economic development in other studies (Rummel, 1972). It represents a pattern of correlated attributes involving per capita telephones, GNP, and energy consumption, as well as proportion in agriculture, illiteracy, dwellings with water, size of the bureaucracy, calories per capita, and pupils per teacher. It is thus a general dimension delineating covariance in volume of communication, national product, energy consumed, housing quality, extent of government regulation, education and educational quality (pupils per teacher), and nutrition.

Economic development as a label for this dimension has become increasingly unsatisfactory, because it does not encompass the variety of attributes, many of which are not economic, that are highly correlated with it. These attributes imply more the notion of affluence than development. For example, the United Kingdom may be more developed economically than Canada, New Zealand, or Denmark, although these countries are more affluent. On the relevant component analysis (C) dimensions, nations with the top ten (factor) scores for 1965 are (in decreasing order) Canada, Sweden, Switzerland, New Zealand, Australia, Norway, Denmark, Belgium, the Netherlands, the United Kingdom, and Israel. This distribution would hardly be accepted as representing "economic development."

Accordingly, the dimension has been labeled wealth, by which is meant an abundance and diversity of goods and services. According to Table 5.1, abundance and diversity involve energy consumption per capita, communications, domestic product, governmental size, education, housing, and nutrition.

Table 5.1. Wealth Dimensions

Attributes		Dimensions[c,d]				Communalities[e]			
Anal. No.[a]	Code[b]	C[h]	CT[h]	IT[h]	IO	C	CT	IT	% Missing Data[f]
5	GNP-PC*	.85	.90	.91	1.10	.91	.89	.91	8.03
1	TEL-PC*	.83	.92	.93	1.11	.89	.92	.93	0.43
40	%D-WTR*	.83	.85	.84	.99	.82	.78	.76	52.49
3	ENC-PC*	.80	.88	.90	1.09	.89	.87	.88	2.60
86	BUREAU	.80	.81	.81	.96	.82	.75	.74	2.39
60	CAL-PC	.65	.75	.75	.91	.79	.67	.62	45.55
70	PUP-PT	-.52	-.51	-.52	-.61	.72	.52	.42	5.42
4	ILLITE	-.76	-.78	-.79	-.96	.89	.85	.85	0.22
2	%A-POP*	-.87	-.82	-.85	-1.01	.89	.79	.82	6.29
% total variance[g]		9.8	13.4	13.0					

* Attributes transformed to logarithms (base 10).

a. This is the analysis number. See Appendix II.

b. For the codes, see Appendix I.

c. C = the dimension from the component analysis of the raw data, and orthogonal varimax rotation of 30 factors, with a cutoff at an eigenvalue of 1.0.
   CT = the dimension from the component analysis of the log transformed data, and orthogonal varimax rotation of 12 factors, with a cutoff at an eigenvalue of 1.69.
   IT = the dimension from the image factor analysis of the log transformed data, and orthogonal varimax rotation of 12 factors, with a cutoff at an eignvalue of 1.08.
   IO = the oblique dimension from the oblique rotation (biquartimin, at 18 cycles and 1,455 iterations) of the 12 IT dimensions.

d. For the C, CT, and IT dimensions, the coefficients are the correlations (loadings) between the attribute and the dimension. For IO dimensions, the coefficients are for the primary pattern dimensions and can be interpretted as regression coefficients or, if between ± 1.00, loosely as correlations (because the correlations between the oblique dimensions are low).

e. These communalities, which are the proportion of variance in an attribute correlated with the dimensions, are across the following number of dimensions.
   C: for 30 dimensions
   CT: for 12 dimensions
   IT: for 12 dimensions

   The communalities for IO analysis are the same as for the IT, and are therefore omitted.

f. This is the percent of missing data after the subjective estimates were made that are shown in Appendix II.

Table 5.1 (continued)

g. The percent of total variance figures were not computed for the IO dimensions.

h. All signs reversed.

5.2.2 Totalitarianism

The second largest and consistent set of dimensions across the analyses involve several political attributes, as shown in Table 5.2. To enable easier interpretation, Table 5.3 shows the direction of attribute variation correlated with the dimension. Surely this is a dimension relating to the extent of totalitarian control over its citizens by a government, and mainly involving communist regimes at the totalitarian end. The dimension was not labeled communism, however, because communist regimes only exemplify this more general political dimension of totalitarianism, which, in 1965, also included nations like Burma, Cambodia, Ethiopia, Ghana, Portugal, Spain, and Yemen.

Table 5.2. Totalitarianism

Attributes		Dimensions[c,d]				Communalities[e]			% Missing Data[f]
Anal. No.[a]	Code[b]	C	CT	IT	IO	C	CT	IT	
82	COMMUN[h]	.93	.90	.92	1.03	.93	.90	.89	0.22
62	R/TRSL	.86	.83	.86	1.00	.82	.78	.79	54.23
12	BLOC	.80	.76	.76	.83	.90	.80	.79	0.0
13	US/AID*	.69	.68	.70	.79	.73	.60	.56	14.32
87	CENSOR[h]	.61	.70	.63	.49	.77	.74	.71	1.74
14	TOTALI[h]	.56	.68	.63	.49	.82	.75	.72	0.43
81	ELECTO[h]	-.57	-.68	-.61	-.44	.82	.78	.77	1.95
80	CONSTI	-.75	-.83	-.79	-.70	.86	.82	.81	0.43
79	STYLE	-.79	-.78	-.77	-.82	.78	.73	.69	0.22
67	COM/POP*[h]	-.82	-.56	-.59	-.75	.80	.77	.74	1.95
% total variance[g]		9.1	10.1	9.6					

*, a-h. See notes to Table 5.1

h. Scaling on attribute reversed from that shown in Appendix II to accord with the dimension's label. With the reversal of scaling the signs for the attribute were also reversed.

Because of the scaling on the attributes, the positive direction on the dimensions is toward nontotalitarianism. See Table 5.3.

Table 5.3. Scaling of Attributes on Totalitarianism Dimension

	Attribute	Sign on Dim.[a]	Totalitarianism: totalitarian	Totalitarianism: nontotalitarian
82	COMMUN	+	communist regime	noncommunist regime
62	R/TRSL[b]	+	high Russian translation to total translation	low Russian translation to total translation
80	CONSTI[b]	-	totalitarian	constitutional
79	STYLE	-	mobilizational	nonmobilizational
12	BLOC	+	communist bloc	Western bloc
13	US/AID	+	low US aid to total aid	high US aid to total aid
67	COM/POP[b]	-	high communist party membership to population	low communist party membership to population
87	CENSOR	+	complete or fairly complete censorship	relatively no censorship
14	TOTALI	+	no freedom of group opposition	freedom of group opposition
81	ELECTO[b]	-	noncompetitive electoral system	competitive

a. From Table 5.2.

b. Scaling reversed from Appendix I. Note that because of the scaling on the attributes, the positive direction of the dimension is toward nontotalitarianism.

This dimension is nearly identical to that found in previous cross-sectional analyses of nations (Rummel, 1972). What is most interesting, however, is that it is now one of two political dimensions. The second will be described next.

5.2.3 Authoritarianism

In previous analyses, the totalitarian dimension appeared ambiguous. Consequently, more political variables were included here in the hope of clarifying its nature. As a result, in the component analysis of raw data (C) and the oblique rotation (IO), a second political dimension emerges as shown in Tables 5.4 and 5.5. The latter gives the direction of attribute variation.

Note the differences between Tables 5.5 and 5.3. The attribute (STYLE), which measures the degree to which the population is mobilized toward a government-defined goal, is missing on the authoritarian dimension. Moreover, correlated with authoritarianism is the degree of military intervention (MILPAR) and the elitism of the leadership (LEADER). What we have here is a dimension reflecting the existence of nontotalitarian dictatorial regimes, mainly those involving a charismatic leader or military junta who rule by decree and permit

Table 5.4. Authoritarianism

Attributes		Dimensions[c,d]				Communalities[e]			% Missing Data[f]
Anal.No.[a]	Code[b]	C[h]	CT	IT	IO	C	CT	IT	
37	IM/I+E	.61	---	---	.67	.65	---	---	62.04
14	TOTALI	.56	---	---	.98	.82	---	---	0.43
84	POWDIS	.42	---	---	1.02	.84	---	---	0.87
81	ELECTO[i]	-.45	---	---	-1.04	.82	---	---	1.95
65	PARTYS[i]	-.49	---	---	-.72	.71	---	---	1.95
80	CONSTI[i]	---	---	---	-1.01	---	---	---	0.43
87	CENSOR	---	---	---	.95	---	---	---	1.74
83	LEADER	---	---	---	.91	---	---	---	1.52
85	MILPAR[i]	---	---	---	.70	---	---	---	
% total variance[g]		2.56							

*, a-h. See notes to Table 5.1.

i. See note h to Table 5.2. The positive direction of the dimension is in the direction of nonauthoritarianism.

Table 5.5. Scaling of Attributes on Authoritarianism Dimension

Attribute		Sign on Dim.[a]	Authoritarianism: Authoritarian	Authoritarianism: Nonauthoritarian
37	IM/I+E	+	low proportion of immigrants to migrants	high proportion of immigrants to migrants
14	TOTALI	+	no freedom of group opposition	freedom of group opposition
65	PARTYS	-	few political parties	many political parti
81	ELECTO	-	noncompetitive electoral system	competitive
84	POWDIS	+	little horizontal power distribution	horizontal power distribution
80	CONSTI	+	totalitarian	constitutional
87	CENSOR	+	complete or fairly complete censorship	relatively no censorship
83	LEADER	+	elitist	nonelitist
85	MILPAR	+	military are interventive	military are neutral

a. From Table 5.5

b. Scaling reversed from Appendix I. Note that because of the scaling on the attributes, the positive direction of the dimension is towards nonauthoritarianism.

little political freedom. Outside politics, however, people are largely free to pursue their own interests.

How do these two dimensions fit comparative typologies of political regimes or governments? Recently, Finer (1970) has developed a typology according to which he classifies political regimes in terms of (1) how much the mass is involved in governing, (2) how much obedience of the mass is out of fear or commitment, and (3) the degree to which political arrangements follow the current values of the mass. In terms of answers to these three questions, according to Finer, regimes can be located in a political space defined by two dimensions. One is that of political participation (rule by persuasion and bargaining) versus political exclusion (rule by coercion). The other dimension is group autonomy of politics versus group dependency. Figure 5.1 shows these two dimensions with the appropriate location of some specific regimes, as Finer categorizes them. Overlaying his typology in bold line are the two dimensions emerging from our analysis. They fit his space in terms of the distribution of nations on them, but are oblique dimensions radiating from the liberal democracies, which are both nonauthoritarian and nontotalitarian.

In sum, totalitarianism and authoritarianism give a more refined view of political attributes than has emerged from previous quantitative analyses, but a view that can be seen best in the *common* oblique dimensions of nations. Note that authoritarianism does not appear in the CT and IT analysis; for the C analysis it appears with no more than moderate correlations for some of the attributes, not including leadership (LEADER) and military participation (MILPAR). Thus, the definition of authoritarianism as a dimension depends on a specific approach to the data.

5.2.4 Power

As shown in Table 5.6, a power space-time dimension emerges from the attribute data, and is consistent across the four analyses. Highly correlated with it are energy production times population, defense expenditures, national income, and population. Each has been suggested by one scholar or another as measures of power. That they all should be highly intercorrelated with this dimension buttresses our interpretation of its nature.

Aside from the power measures, protests, accusations, and threats also are correlated with the dimension. In former cross-national analyses, these conflict attributes formed a separate foreign conflict dimension. Here, they merge with power, and indicate that the more powerful a nation over the period 1950-1965, the more foreign conflict behavior it engaged in. That is, great powers are most conflictful. Why do these results differ from the analyses of 1955 attribute data (Rummel, 1972, Section 9.3) and other cross-national analyses (Rummel, 1972, Chapter 14)?

One explanation is that we are now dealing with conflict variance in time and space, rather than for a single year. Another is that 1955 may have been an odd

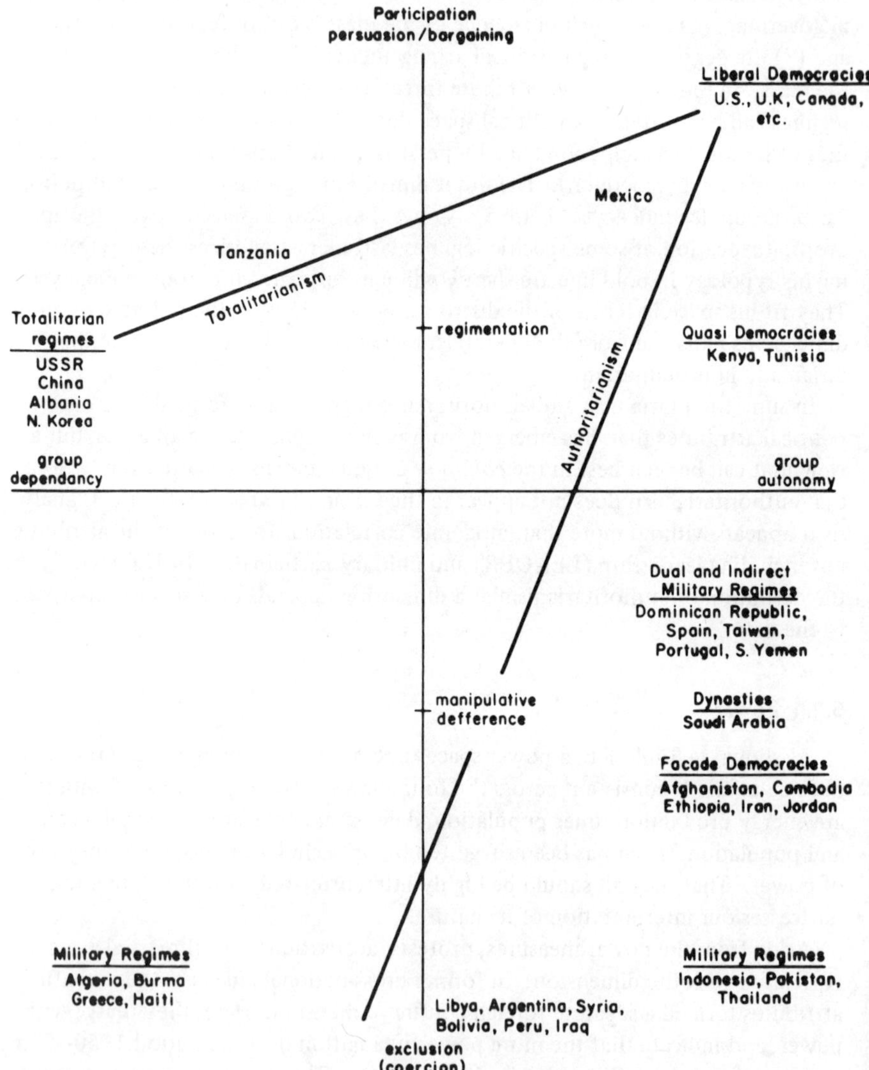
Participation
persuasion/bargaining
Liberal Democracies
U.S., U.K, Canada, etc.
Mexico
Tanzania
Totalitarianism
Totalitarian regimes
USSR
China
Albania
N. Korea
regimentation
Quasi Democracies
Kenya, Tunisia
Authoritarianism
group dependancy
group autonomy
Dual and Indirect Military Regimes
Dominican Republic, Spain, Taiwan, Portugal, S. Yemen
manipulative defference
Dynasties
Saudi Arabia
Facade Democracies
Afghanistan, Cambodia
Ethiopia, Iran, Jordan
Military Regimes
Algeria, Burma
Greece, Haiti
Military Regimes
Indonesia, Pakistan, Thailand
Libya, Argentina, Syria, Bolivia, Peru, Iraq
exclusion
(coercion)

Figure 5.1

Table 5.6. Power

Attributes		Dimensions[c,d]				Communalities[e]			% Missing
Anal. No.[a]	Code[b]	C	CT	IT	IO	C	CT	IT	Data[f]
10	DEFEXP*	.94	.61	.45	.46	.93	.89	.90	17.57
7	NI*	.92	.58	.41	.40	.94	.89	.91	14.75
9	%CT-UN*	.89	.45	---	---	.90	.66	---	5.21
78	INVBAL*	.89	---	.42	.45	.84	---	.22	29.07
6	EPXPOP*	.82	.83	.70	.73	.93	.78	.75	4.56
20	PROTST*	.76	.73	.68	.73	.72	.62	.58	2.17
17	ACCUSA*	.61	.64	.60	.66	.80	.66	.59	1.08
8	POPULA*	.43	.66	.49	.50	.91	.86	.88	0.0
16	THREAT*	.42	.58	.56	.60	.78	.38	.34	1.08
% total variance[g]		7.7	6.3	4.7					

*, a-g. See Table 5.1.

year, unrepresentative of the relationship between power and foreign conflict. One way to gain perspective on this is to consider the results of doing a separate component analyses on 91 attributes for each of the five years. When this is done, and the power factor arrayed as in Table 5.7, 1955 appears indeed an odd year: of the five years, foreign conflict and power are most independent for 1955. We can conclude, therefore, that given the by-year results and those in Table 5.6 for the super-P analysis, that foreign conflict and power are interrelated.

5.2.5 Size

In previous analyses, power and size were one dimension. And so they are here in the CT analyses. But in the C, IT, and IO analysis, as shown in Table 5.8, size is separable from power. Population in the C analysis and population, national income, and area in the IT and IO analyses are also highly correlated with a dimension of sheer size.

Size is surely an aspect of power and is correlated with it (.47 between the oblique dimensions). The population and area of a nation influence both its adversaries and friends. But aside from size, power is also a productive capacity. An ability to generate and transform resources and redistribute them to the needs of Power. Thus, the dimension we are calling power involves primarily energy *production* and to a lesser extent defense *expenditures.*

5.2.6 Catholic Culture

Another dimension shown in Table 5.9 is Catholic culture. It involves the proportion of Catholics in the population, as well as the geographic location of

Table 5.7. By-Year Results for the Power Dimension

	Power Dimensions[a]				
Attributes	1950	1955	1960	1963	1965
78 INVBAL	.59	.94	.92	.94	.92
25 DEMONS	.73			.92	
9 %CT-UN	.87	.93	.93	.95	.90
6 EPXPOP	.90	.84	.78	.73	.88
16 THREAT	.94		.61	.86	
7 NI	.94	.95	.95	.95	.90
17 ACCUSA		.54	.85		.69
10 DEFEXP		.97	.96	.97	.94
33 AREA			.65		.68
29 ER-AMB			.76		
20 PROTST			.85	.84	.82
8 POPULA					.53
% Total Variance	6.8	7.3	9.5	9.2	8.0

a. The dimension for a year is from the varimax, rotated results of a component analysis of the raw data on the 91 attributes of Appendix I for that year. Only correlations above or equal to an absolute .50 are shown.

Table 5.8. Size

Attributes		Dimensions[c,d]				Communalities[e]			% Missing
Anal. No.[a]	Code[b]	C[h]	CT	IT	IO	C	CT	IT	Data[f]
8	POPULA*	.79	---	.73	.89	.91	---	.88	0.0
53	AIDRIVD*	.61	---	---	---	.72	---	---	30.15
6	EPXPOP*	.46	---	.44	.69	.93	---	.75	4.56
7	NI*	---	---	.61	.74	---	---	.91	14.75
10	DEFEXP*	---	---	.57	.70	---	---	.90	17.57
33	AREA*	---	---	.51	.74	---	---	.83	0.0
% total variance[g]		2.6		3.4					

*, a-h. See notes to Table 5.1.

the nation (largely focused in Central and South America), the distance from the US, and the ratio of divorces to marriages. This is a dimension that is gradually breaking up as more non-Catholic nations enter the international system. Table 5.10 shows this. The Catholic culture dimension is weak in 1963, and in 1965 it all but disappears. The likelihood is that, with the increased number of independent nations since 1965, the Catholic culture dimension will have disappeared as a major pattern of attributes.

Table 5.9. Catholic Culture Dimensions

Attributes		Dimensions[c,d]				Communalities[e]			% Missing
Anal. No.[a]	Code[b]	C[h]	CT[h]	IT	IO	C	CT	IT	Data[f]
26	%CATH	.84	.67	.76	.83	.85	.76	.72	0.87
42	NEUTRL	.49	---	.55	.60	.80	---	.62	1.30
69	MONARC	-.52	---	---	---	.76	---	---	0.0
30	DIV-MR	-.68	-.48	-.54	-.57	.76	.52	.48	38.83
27	US-DIS*	-.69	---	-.42	-.44	.85	---	.58	0.0
89	GEOG-Y	-.78	-.69	-.77	-.83	.89	.85	.81	0.0
% total variance[g]		4.5	3.5	4.1					

*, a-h. See notes to Table 5.1

Table 5.10. By-Year Results for the Catholic Culture

Attributes	1950	1955	1960	1963	1965
28 MED-NGO	-.36	.55	-.53		.80
42 NEUTRL	-.53		-.58		.62
69 MONARC	.55				
30 DIV-MR	.70		.66		
27 US-DIS	.76	-.81	.71	.61	
89 GEOG-Y	.82	-.85	.80	.74	
26 %CATH	-.89	.86	-.87	-.75	(.47)
66 ART-NGO			-.53		
48 %UNEMP			-.70		
36 RELGRP				.59	
15 IFC/GP					-.52
41 FST/ST					-.72
% Total Variance	5.6	5.1	5.9	5.0	4.6

a. See note to Table 5.7.

5.2.7 Domestic Conflict

Table 5.11 presents the super-P results delineating a domestic conflict dimension. Except for the component analysis of raw data, the various domestic conflict attributes form a consistent interrelated pattern among nation attributes.

5.2.8 Remaining Dimensions

Little need be said here about the remaining space-time dimensions. They are shown in Table 5.12. Since time emerges as a separate dimension, it is independent

Table 5.11. Domestic Conflict Dimensions

Attributes		Dimensions[c,d]				Communalities[e]			% Missing
Anal. No.[a]	Code[b]	C	CT[h]	IT	IO	C	CT	IT	Data[f]
22	STRIKE	.81	.57	.43	.44	.75	.44	.28	0.65
23	RIOTS*	.64	.66	.55	.59	.75	.58	.44	0.65
21	D-KILL*	---	.59	.52	.55	---	.46	.36	2.17
24	PURGES	---	.59	.46	.49	---	.40	.25	0.65
75	GVTCRS	---	.58	.45	.48	---	.39	.25	0.87
25	DEMONS*	---	.51	.42	.45	---	.46	.33	0.65
% total variance[g]		1.82	3.6	2.8					

*, a-h. See notes to Table 5.1

Table 5.12. Remaining Dimensions

Density

Attributes		Dimensions[c,d]				Communalities[e]			% Missing
Anal. No.[a]	Code[b]	C[h]	CT[h]	IT[h]	IO	C	CT	IT	Data[f]
31	DENSITY	.78	.82	.79	.80	.85	.77	.75	0.88
32	%ARABL	.78	.75	.70	.73	.77	.70	.63	10.63
35	RRS-KM*	.75	.65	.65	.68	.85	.87	.85	7.81
34	RDS-KM*	.60	.60	.60	.63	.72	.83	.81	17.35
58	FMST/M*	.58	---	---	---	.75	---	---	51.84
33	AREA*	---	-.58	-.60	-.64	---	.85	.83	0.0
% total variance[g]		3.9	4.0	3.6					

Diversity

Attributes		Dimensions[c,d]				Communalities[e]			% Missing
Anal. No.[a]	Code[b]	C	CT	IT	IO	C	CT	IT	Data[f]
50	LANGRP	.83	.81	.74	.79	.84	.75	.67	5.86
52	ETHGRP	.54	.62	.63	.67	.70	.59	.51	9.11
43	NATAGE	.43	.46	.52	.54	.77	.56	.52	0.65
73	EGRP/P	-.50	-.61	-.64	-.67	.75	.57	.52	0.0
51	LGRP/P	-.87	-.77	-.69	-.73	.84	.65	.56	25.60
% total variance[g]		3.3	3.9	3.7					

Table 5.12. (continued)

Geographic

Attributes		Dimensions [c,d]				Communalities [e]			% Missing
Anal. No. [a]	Code [b]	C [h]	CT	IT	IO	C	CT	IT	Data [f]
41	FST/ST	.77	.67	---	---	.74	.53	---	34.27
88	GEOG-X	.51	.59	.68	.77	.71	.71	.62	0.0
42	NEUTRL	-.54	-.52	---	---	.80	.65	---	1.30
38	RAIN	---	---	-.53	-.63	---	---	.50	1.30
% total variance [g]		2.3	3.5	2.2					

Import Dependency

Attributes		Dimensions [c,d]				Communalities [e]			% Missing
Anal. No. [a]	Code [b]	C	CT	IT [h]	IO	C	CT	IT	Data [f]
59	IP/TRD*	.76	.76	.60	.63	.79	.65	.44	9.54
53	AIDRVD*	---	.44	.49	.54	---	.52	.39	30.20
57	EXP/GNP*	---	-.67	-.49	-.52	---	.66	.45	26.25
% total variance [g]		2.1	2.5	2.00					

Time

Attributes		Dimensions [c,d]				Communalities [e]			% Missing
Anal. No. [a]	Code [b]	C [h]	CT [h]	IT [h]	IO	C	CT	IT	Data [f]
55	%E-GVT*	.86	.52	.41	.47	.80	.34	.23	24.95
91	TIME	.53	.79	.68	.73	.81	.70	.55	0.0
% total variance [g]		1.8	2.8	2.1					

*, a-h. See notes to Table 5.1.

of the major dimensions previously discussed. There are no major patterns among attributes through the years 1950-1965 which so linearly increase or decrease with time as to overcome their cross-national variance. If the data covered a 50- to 100-year period, the linear changes in many attributes, such as national income and population, would introduce enough covariance to be correlated with time. But the fifteen-year period covered here, as indicated by the time dimension, is not sufficient to do this.

5.3 AND DIMENSIONS FOR 236 ATTRIBUTES

How well do the above space-time dimensions for 1950-1965 fit the dimensions for 236 attributes found for 1955 (Rummel, 1972, Chapter 9)? The comparison could be tricky, because we have four separate analyses that could be compared. My question is fairly simple, however. Since the dimensions we interpreted are those we will subsequently focus on, how well do these compare? Table 5.13 provides an answer.

Wealth was the largest dimension in both the 1955 and 1950-1965 analyses. It has simply been given a new label.

Political orientation in the 1955 analysis has split into the two correlated dimensions of totalitarianism and authoritarianism.

Size, or what was alternatively called power bases, is also split into size and power. And the formerly independent dimension of foreign conflict has now combined with power, 1950-1965. This combination also has held through separate year-by-year analyses, with the exception of the 1955 analysis of the 91 attributes.

Table 5.13. Comparison Dimensions for 236 Attributes

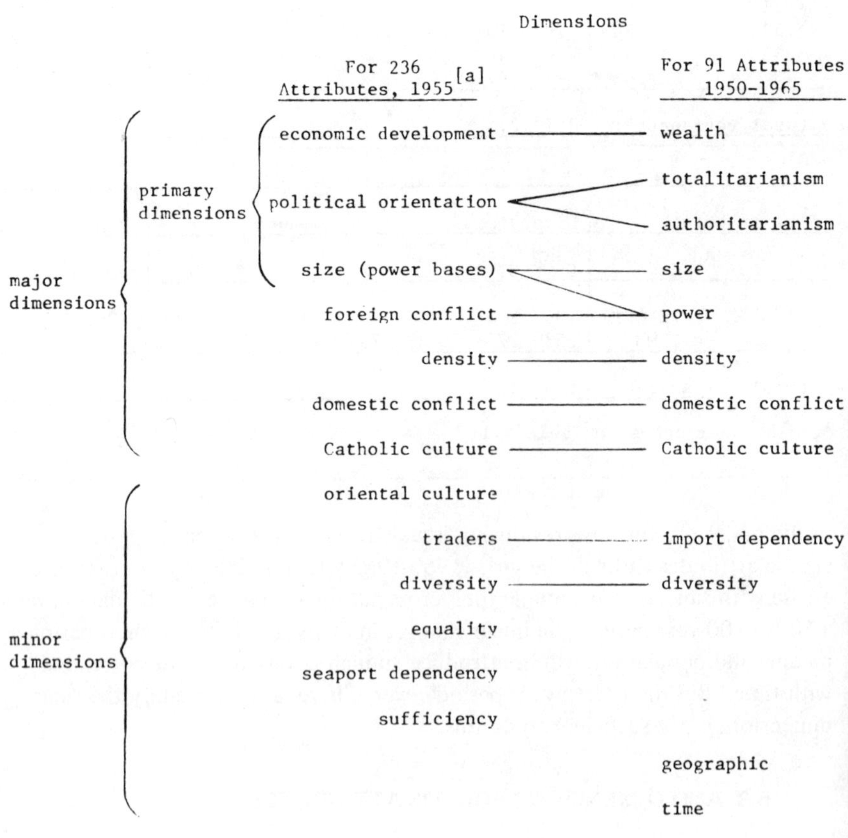

		Dimensions	
		For 236 Attributes, 1955[a]	For 91 Attributes 1950-1965
major dimensions	primary dimensions	economic development	wealth
		political orientation	totalitarianism
			authoritarianism
		size (power bases)	size
		foreign conflict	power
		density	density
		domestic conflict	domestic conflict
		Catholic culture	Catholic culture
minor dimensions		oriental culture	
		traders	import dependency
		diversity	diversity
		equality	
		seaport dependency	
		sufficiency	
			geographic
			time

a. From Rummel (1972, Table 9.3).

Thus, the three primary dimensions, which were the largest in the 236-attribute analysis and accounted for 40% of the variance in all these attributes, also exist over the period 1950-1965 and account for an average of 35% of the variance. However, the three primary 1955 dimensions turn into five dimensions for 1950-1965.

Turning to the remaining major dimensions shown in Table 5.13, foreign conflict is lost as an independent dimension: it merges with power. Density, domestic conflict, and Catholic culture are identical in both analyses. Among all the major dimensions for 1955, foreign conflict is the only one to disappear.

Finally, the minor dimensions, which are those involving only a few attributes and accounting for small amounts of variance, are predictably unstable. Of the six minor dimensions for 1955, only traders and diversity are found in the 1950-1965 data. However, the geographic and time dimensions of the 1950-1965 data should not be expected to be related to the 1955 dimensions, since both are defined by attributes not included in that analysis.

The twelve dimensions shown in the right of Table 5.13 now comprise our space-time dimensions of attributes. These are the dimensions I will link to behavior, after I next define the space-time dimensions of behavior space.

NOTE

1. The factor analyses to be reported in this chapter should be exactly reproducible from the data given in Appendix II, if missing data are estimated using the method ($\hat{Y}$-estimation) reported in Wall and Rummel (1969).

Chapter 6

SPACE-TIME DIMENSIONS OF BEHAVIOR

6.1 MISSING DATA AND SEPARATE ANALYSES

The missing data for the dyadic behavior variables, 1950-1965, were treated in the same way as the attributes. First, common sense estimates were inserted. They are shown along with the data in Appendix IV. Then, the remaining missing data were estimated using our regression estimation technique.[1]

Two super-P factor analyses were done on the behavior data: one, a component analysis of raw data (C); and the other, an image analysis of the raw data (I) to determine the *common* behavioral dimensions. There was no need to log-transform the behavioral raw data, since by theory the law of diminishing salience operated on distances and not on behavior; the actual behavior of nations is assumed to reflect transformed distances.

In addition to the image orthogonal rotation (IO), two oblique rotations were done. The first was the biquartimin rotation (IB), which was used for the attribute super-P analysis of Chapter 5 and in Rummel (1972). Upon study, however, this rotation did not yield good simple structure (Rummel, 1970, Section 16.2.2). The dimensions appeared more correlated than allowed for by the biquartimin rotation. Accordingly, a quartimin (Rummel, 1970, Section 17.3.2) rotation was done, delineating simpler and more interpretable dimensions. It is this quartimin solution that will be focused on here. For the comparison, however, the component and the orthogonal, biquartimin, and quartimin dimensions will be presented together.

6.2 THE DIMENSIONS

6.2.1 Transactions

The largest common space-time dimension (IQ) of dyadic behavior is transactions, as shown in Table 6.1. This is a broad cluster of intercorrelated dyadic activities involving communications (books and conferences), trade (exports), population mobility (tourists), comembership in international organizations, and in the case of the quartimin dimension, relative embassies. Broadly, it comprises a cooperative, contractual type of behavior. Conflict is not correlated with this dimension, meaning that these transactions are independent of the existence of an actor's conflict behavior.[2]

6.2.2 International Organizations

The largest dimension in the component analysis and the second largest in the image analysis delineates international organizations, as shown in Table 6.2. Comembership in governmental (IGO) and nongovernmental (NGO) international organizations, whether considered relative to the actor's total memberships (R-IGO and R-NGO) or to the size of the organizations (N-IGO and N-NGO), comprise a highly intercorrelated pattern.

6.2.3 Negative Communications

Negative communications has consistently appeared as an independent pattern of dyadic behavior, whether conflict data is analyzed in the context of other forms of behavior (Rummel, 1972, Chapter 16; 1969), analyzed alone for all dyads having conflict (Rummel, 1968), or analyzed through (super-P) component time series (Phillips, 1969). Here, we can see from Table 6.3 that negative communications is a strong pattern involving not only the total number of negative communications of the actor to an object, but also accusations and protests. Moreover, this pattern involves the total negative behavior (severance of diplomatic relations, withdrawal of aid, cancellation of visits, expulsion of diplomats, and so forth) of actor to object, as well. Negative behavior had been found to be an independent pattern in previous analyses, but here from the perspective of 1950-1965, it merges with negative communication.

6.2.4 Alignment

Table 6.4 shows a fourth pattern, comprising common bloc membership (COMBLC) and bloc distance (COMPOS) on the one hand, and UN voting distances (WD-UN; D-UN) on the other. That is, allies tend to vote together in the United Nations.

(text continued on p. 61)

Table 6.1. Transactions Dimensions

Behavior Variables		Dimensions[c,d]					Communalities[e]		% Missing Data[f]
			IO[h]						
Anal. No.[a]	Code[b]	C	1	7	IB	IQ	C	IO	
7	BOOKS	(.91)	.45	(.68)	(.81)	(.91)	.88	.69	11.43
40	NGO	.42	.35	(.54)	(.68)	(.85)	.85	.77	0
38	IGO	.33	.23	.47	(.59)	(.81)	.86	.76	0
6	CONFER	(.82)	.35	(.60)	(.71)	(.77)	.76	.51	0
8	R-BOOKS	(.71)	.11	(.66)	(.72)	(.72)	(.82)	.46	15.38
45	R-EMB	-.04	.10	-.28	-.19	(-.68)	.86	.32	0
35	EXPORT	(.73)	(.62)	(.54)	(.73)	(.67)	.88	.79	1.43
27	TOURIS	.47	(.52)	.32	.47	(.53)	.76	.48	19.34
53	ALLIAN	.42	(.50)	.33	.49	.42	.67	.57	0
30	EMIGRA	.43	.06	(.53)	(.60)	.40	.75	.35	13.5
28	R-TOUR	.24	.47	.17	.29	.37	.54	.26	18.5
3	TREATY	.35	.47	.33	(.50)	.24	.73	.52	0
1	AID	.06	.49	-.02	.09	.18	.79	.25	4.62
2	R-AID	.07	.46	-.06	.04	-.01	.74	.24	4.95
% total variance[g]		7.47	5.86	6.57					

a. This is the variable number. See Appendix III.

b. For the variable codes, see Appendix III.

c. C = the dimension from the component analysis of the raw data, and orthogonal varimax rotation of twenty factors, with a cutoff at an eigenvalue of .82.
IO = the dimension from the image (common) factor analysis of the raw data, and orthogonal varimax rotation of nine factors, with a cutoff at an eigenvalue of 1.10.
IB = the dimension from a biquartimin oblique rotation of the nine image factors (30 cycles and 13,189 iterations).
IQ = the dimension from a quatrimax oblique rotation of the nine image factors (30 cycles and 13,500 iterations).
Loadings $\geq |.50|$ are shown in parentheses.

d. For the C and IO dimensions, the coefficients are the correlations between the behavioral variables and dimension. For the IB and IQ dimensions, the coefficients are for the primary pattern dimensions and can be interpreted as regression coefficients.

e. These communalities, which are the proportion of variance in a behavioral variable correlated with the dimensions, are across the following number of dimensions.
C: for 20 dimensions
I: for 9 dimensions.

f. This is the percent of missing data after the subjective estimates were made that are shown in Appendix IV.

g. Variance figures are given only for the orthogonal factors.

h. There are two orthogonal dimensions (number 1 and 7) that were similar to the component and image oblique transaction dimensions. Accordingly, both are included here.

Table 6.2. International Organizations Dimensions

Behavior Variables		Dimensions[c,d]				Communalities[e]		% Missing data[f]
Anal. No.[a]	Code[b]	C	IO	IB	IQ	C	IO	
39	R-IGO	(.86)	(.81)	(.85)	(1.14)	.84	.75	.55
41	R-NGO	(.89)	(.83)	(.87)	(1.13)	.88	.78	0
42	N-IGO	(.80)	(.79)	(.82)	(1.09)	.79	.72	.88
43	N-NGO	(.85)	(.82)	(.85)	(1.05)	.87	.80	0
38	IGO	(.54)	(.62)	(.63)	(.68)	.86	.76	0
40	NGO	.43	(.51)	(.52)	.48	.85	.77	0
% total variance[g]		7.32	7.45					

a-g. See notes to Table 6.1.

Table 6.3. Negative Communications Dimensions

Behavior Variables		Dimensions[c,d]				Communalities[e]		% Missing data[f]
Anal. No.[a]	Code[b]	C	IO	IB	IQ	C	IO	
20	ACCUSN	(.90)	(.92)	(1.07)	(1.20)	.87	.88	0
19	NEGCOM	(.92)	(.93)	(1.09)	(1.20)	.91	.90	0
15	NEGBEH	(.81)	(.79)	(.95)	(.87)	.83	.71	0
21	PROTST	(.71)	(.57)	(.70)	(.63)	.68	.39	0
16	EXPREC	.46	.49	(.56)	(.62)	.72	.28	0
12	VIOLAC	.47	.45	(.58)	.38	.72	.37	0
11	WARNDF	.40	.41	(.56)	.28	.61	.37	0
% total variance[g]		7.1	7.50					

a-g. See notes to Table 6.1.

Table 6.4. Alignment Dimensions

Behavior		Dimensions[c,d]				Communalities[e]		% Missing data[f]
Anal. No.[a]	Code[b]	C	IO	IB	IQ	C	IO	
25	WD-UN	(.92)	(.80)	(.83)	(.90)	.89	.70	22.31
51	COMBLC	(-.74)	(-.82)	(-.86)	(-.87)	.88	.80	0
26	UWD-UN	(.88)	(.74)	(.75)	(.85)	.86	.63	22.20
52	COMPOS	(.70)	(.80)	(.84)	(.85)	.86	.78	0
% total variance[g]		5.75	5.93					

a-g. See notes to Table 6.1.

Table 6.5. Remaining Dimensions

Behavior Variables		Dimensions[c,d]				Communalities[e]		% Missing data[f]
Anal. No.[a]	Code[b]	C	IO	IB	IQ	C	IO	
Relative Exports Dimensions								
37	E/GNP	(.81)	(.81)	(.85)	(1.23)	.86	.72	3.52
36	R-EXPT	(.61)	(.71)	(.75)	(1.00)	.83	.74	4.18
29	T/POPU	(.87)	(.60)	(.62)	(.93)	.82	.38	18.24
% total variance[g]		4.37	4.29					
Antiforeign Behavior Dimensions								
22	UNOFAC	(.79)	(.65)	(.74)	(.97)	.81	.47	0
24	NVIOLB	(.85)	(.60)	(.71)	(.84)	.79	.45	0
17	BCTEMB	(.79)	(.58)	(.68)	(.83)	.77	.42	0
% total variance[g]		4.12	2.87					

Table 6.5. (continued)

Behavior Variables		Dimensions[c,d]				Communalities[e]		
Anal. No.[a]	Code[b]	C	IO	IB	IQ	C	IO	% Missing data[f]
		Military Violence Dimensions						
14	DAYSVL	(.96)	(.89)	(.96)	(1.31)	.95	.81	0
13	MILACT	(.95)	(.89)	(.97)	(1.30)	.95	.82	0
11	WARNDF	.42	.43	(.52)	(.51)	.61	.37	0
12	VIOLAC	.29	.39	.49	.43	.72	.37	0
% total variance[g]		4.08	4.07					
		Aid Dimensions						
35	EXPORT	.29	*	(.69)	*	.88	.79	1.43
27	TOURIS	.38		(.56)		.76	.48	19.34
53	ALLIAN	.20		(.55)		.67	.57	0
3	TREATY	.25		(.54)		.73	.52	0
7	BOOKS	.08		(.52)		.88	.69	11.43
1	AID	(.87)		(.51)		.79	.25	4.62
28	R-TOUR	.39		(.50)		.54	.26	18.5
2	R-AID	(.84)		.48		.74	.24	4.95
% total variance[g]		3.9						
		Unnamed Dimensions						
33	STUDNT	(.83)	(.57)	(.63)	(.90)	.85	.44	11.1
34	R-STUD	(.89)	(.50)	(.54)	(.77)	.84	.29	11.1
3	TREATY	.25	.39	.45	(.65)	.73	.52	0
4	R-TREATY	.15	.49	(.56)	(.64)	.74	.33	0
5	VISITS	.10	.32	.33	(.60)	.57	.16	0
36	R-EXPT	.12	.40	(.52)	.28	.83	.74	4.18
38	IGO	-.03	-.17	-.03	(-.62)	.86	.76	0
% total variance[g]		3.4	3.87					

* No aid-related dimensions emerged.
a-g. See notes to Table 6.1.

6.2.5 Remaining Dimensions

Table 6.5 shows the remaining behavior dimensions. Both antiforeign behavior and military violence dimensions emerge, as they have in other analyses of behavior (see Section 6.2.3). There is a relative export dimension, manifesting an actor's exports to another nation relative to the size of its GNP, and an aid dimension.

Aid, as a pattern, is unique to the component analysis. In the image analysis it appears only in the biquartimin rotation, and even then not too clearly. Nonetheless, the pattern is included here because of its importance to international relations.

Finally, there is a dimension that consistently involves students across the various analyses and in the quartimin rotation broadens to include international organizations, treaties, and visits. It is tempting to call this a student dimension, but the quartimin dimension indicates that it is a pattern relating more to behavior than to student movements. It seems to be a residual transaction dimension, with a correlation of .73 with the transaction dimension. This is unusually high in oblique rotation and suggests that transactions occur along a major dimension, but that a minor and somewhat independent cluster exists involving students, international organizations, treaties and visits.

6.3 AND 1955 BEHAVIOR DIMENSIONS

Data on 40 dyadic behaviors for 1955 have been analyzed previously and published (Rummel, 1972, Chapter 16; 1969). This involved the same selected sample used here, as well as a randomly selected sample of 164 dyads; the results of independently analyzing the two samples correlated .84 (intraclass). We, therefore, can focus on the 1955 selected sample results in comparison to what we have found across dyads and years.

Table 6.6 links the dimensions of the 1955 analysis with those delineated here. Some of the dimensions are similar between analyses, although in most cases the labels have been revised for clarity and better communication. The differences that appear are partly a consequence of the different behaviors analyzed, or my leaving uninterpreted the very small dimensions in the 1950-1965 analyses. More specifically, the 1955 self-determination voting dimension could not emerge for 1950-1965, because no specific UN voting dimensions were included in the analysis here. The 1955 dimension however had the 1955 UN voting distance correlated with it, and therefore, as shown in Table 6.6, merged with alignment, which includes UN voting distance.

Foreign students was a small 1955 dimension including student movements and mail. But mail data were not available across the years and could not be included in this study, and therefore foreign students was found to be a unique behavior in the component results. In the image orthogonal and biquartimin results, however, the student dimension comprises a weak pattern and generalizes

Table 6.6. Comparison To Dimension Previously Published

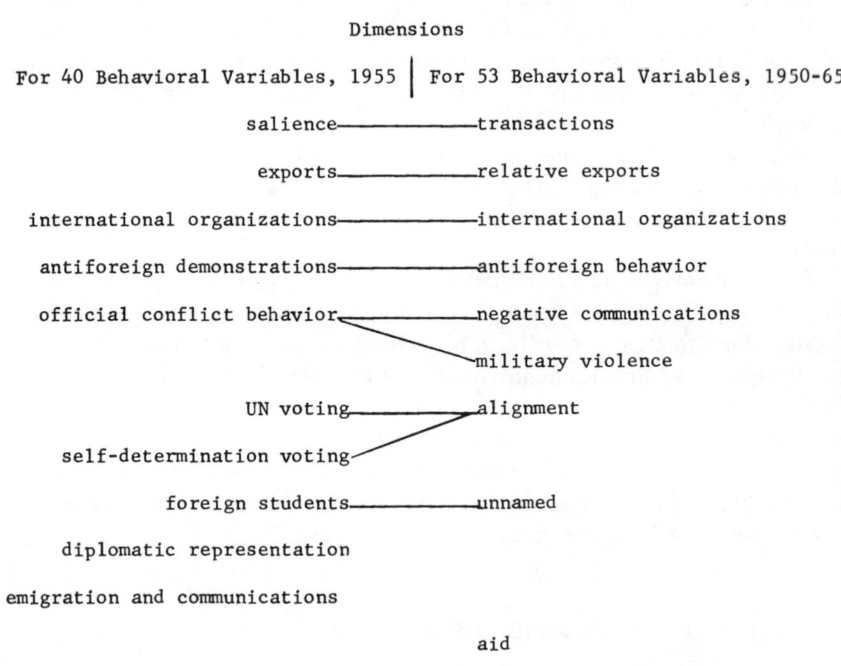

Dimensions	
For 40 Behavioral Variables, 1955	For 53 Behavioral Variables, 1950-65
salience	transactions
exports	relative exports
international organizations	international organizations
antiforeign demonstrations	antiforeign behavior
official conflict behavior	negative communications
	military violence
UN voting	alignment
self-determination voting	
foreign students	unnamed
diplomatic representation	
emigration and communications	
	aid

to other kinds of transactions in the quartimin rotation. It was therefore left unnamed.

Mail was also central to the emigration and communications dimension, and without mail to correlate with, emigrants came out as a unique behavior.

Diplomatic representation involved embassies and legations i→j in 1955, both in total number and relatively. Such a pattern also emerged for 1950-1965, but since it was a small dimension and only involved total and relative embassies and legations, it was excluded from my discussion of the 1950-1965 results.

Finally, consider the conflict results. What was a combination of negative communications and military violence, and labeled official conflict behavior for 1955, separates into negative communication and military violence. Why should this be so? Was 1955 an odd year?

Table 6.7 shows what conflict dimensions emerge when the dyadic behavior variables are analyzed separately for each year. The super-P 1950-1965 dimensions are also shown for easy comparison. From the table we can see that the conflict patterns vary by year, existing in one year and disappearing in another. The most consistent dimension is the negative communications one found by the super-P analysis. It also exists for 1950, 1955, and 1960, but loses NEGBEH in 1963 and PROTST in 1965. The upshot of this by-year instability in conflict behavior is that we cannot expect a dimension of conflict delineated for one year also to be a space-*time* dimension.

As for being an odd year, 1955 did have a conflict dimension comprising both negative communications and violence (VIOLAC), as shown in Table 6.7. And in no other year have violent actions, negative communications, and negative behavior correlated with the same dimension. Therefore, 1955 was different in this sense, and the previously published 1955 results were a consequence of this uniqueness.

6.4 INTERCORRELATIONS AMONG DIMENSIONS

How correlated are the transactions, alignment, negative communications, and other dimensions? If one were to focus on the orthogonal dimensions, the answer would be simple. By definition, all dimensions would have zero correlations. However, the oblique dimensions (IB, IQ) are correlated, and such correlations are of substantial interest.

Table 6.8 presents the intercorrelations for the quartimin rotation. The correlations for the biquartimin rotation are much lower but in the same directions. As can be seen, the transactions dimension is highly correlated with international organization, relative exports, and the unnamed dimension. The latter appears from the loadings in Table 6.5 and the high (.73) correlation to be a transaction type of dimension distinct from, but closely related to, the one we are calling transactions. These interrelations can be seen better through a higher-order factor analysis of the correlations in Table 6.8.

6.5 HIGHER-ORDER DIMENSIONS

Table 6.9 shows the higher-order dimensions resulting from an analysis of the intercorrelations among the (first-order) oblique dimensions partly shown in Table 6.8. The three higher-order dimensions show that there are three independent clusters of oblique first-order dimensions; that is, *the original space of 53 behavioral variables for 182 nation-dyads for 1950-1965 is at the most general level divisible into three independent behavioral dimensions.*

These three higher-order dimensions thus define the most general empirical concepts, the most general lines of empirical covariation in international behavior reflected in our data. The first of these shown in Table 6.9 is a *general transaction dimension.* It involves the relative exports, unnamed (which comprised a cluster of treaties, relative treaties, students, relative students, and IGOs), international organizations, and transaction dimensions. And no conflict dimensions! The highest loading a first-order conflict dimension has on this higher-order generalized transaction dimension is .125 (not shown).

Table 6.7. Comparison of Conflict Dimensions to By-Year Results

Dimensions/Behaviors	Super-P [d]		By-Year Dimensions[e]																
			1950				1955[f]		1960[g]			1963					1965[g]		
Negative Communications[a]	C	IO	D_2	D_7	D_9	D_{13}	D_2	D_3	D_2	D_3	D_{10}	D_4	D_5	D_{11}	D_{13}	D_{14}	D_2	D_3	D_9
19. NEGCOM	.92	.93	.97				.90		.93				.87				.90		
20. ACCUSN	.90	.92	.97				.88		.92				.87				.88		
15. NEGBEH	.81	.79	.93				.84		.81						.81		.60		-.64
21. PROTST	.71	.57	.81				.78		.71		-.50		.51		.68				
Antiforeign Behavior[b]																			
24. NVIOLE	.85	.60	.70				.63		.57					.68					.88
22. UNOFAC	.79	.65		.86							.80	.88							.86
17. BCTEMB	.79	.58						.72						.62	.56				.88
Military Violence[b]																			
13. MILACT	.95	.89	.63					.94		.95						.77		.96	
14. DAYSVL	.96	.89				.83		.96		.93		.92						.95	
Unique Behavior[c]																			
16. EXPREC					.71				.81						.74		.82		
12. VIOLAC						.66	.70			.80						.89		.90	
11. WARNDF			.65					.81		.64						.82		.75	
18. AIDREB					.78						.84						.94		
23. ATKEMB				.94								.95							

a. From Table 6.3.
b. From Table 6.5
c. These are behaviors with low communalities, and with low correlations with the above conflict dimensions.
d. For the definitions of C and IO, see Table 6.1.

Table 6.7. (continued)

e. A component factor analysis of the behavior data was done separately for each year. Fifteen dimensions were orthogonally rotated (varimax), at an eigenvalue of 1.0 for each year (in the case of 1950, fourteen factors were rotated). Only the conflict dimensions are given here, and only a loading of greater or equal to an absolute .50. The subscripts on D stand for the factor number in the analysis of that year.

f. ATKEMB (D_7), AIDREB (D_{12}), and UNOFAC (D_{13}) each loaded highly on a single factor.

g. ATKEMB (D_{11}) loads highly on a single factor.

Table 6.8. Intercorrelations Among Behavior Dimension[a]

		Transactions 1	International Organizations 2	Negative Communications 3	Alignment 4	Relative Exports 5	Antiforeign Behavior 6	Military Violence 7
1	Transactions							
2	International Organizations	(.55)						
3	Negative Communications	.30	.01					
4	Alignment	.05	.13	.27				
5	Relative Exports	(.58)	(.68)	.06	-.08			
6	Antiforeign Behavior	-.18	.03	.25	.32	.08		
7	Military Violence	-.14	-.18	.12	.07	-.05	.47	
8	Unnamed	(.73)	(.69)	.18	.03	(.70)	-.09	-.25

a. From the quartimin oblique results. Correlations ≥|.50| shown in parentheses.

The higher-order generalized transaction dimension comprises all the non-conflict-oriented activities (assuming alignment is conflict oriented), such as trade, treaties, organizational memberships, migrants, student movements, tourists, and the like. This dimension surely represents the integration or transaction pattern of international relations and the line of nonconflict-oriented, cooperative activity of nations.

The second dimension in Table 6.9 is military conflict, comprising the anti-foreign behavior and military violence first-order dimensions. The third higher-order dimension involves negative communications and alignment (bloc membership and UN voting distance). Clearly, we have two general conflict patterns here, one defining violence and the other, independent conflict-oriented diplomatic behavior.

What is most interesting about these higher-order results is that they divide conflict and transactions along independent dimensions. This means that we cannot predict the transactions of one nation with another from their conflict, nor *can we predict their conflict from the transactions of one with another.* The last point is worth pondering, for there are many theories of international relations which assume that the way to peace lies along an increasing density of transactions, or that integrative type behavior decreases the probability of conflict. Moreover, there is the current assumption of US-Soviet detente: that cooperative bonds will provide a structure of peace. These results, showing generalized transactions and conflict behavior to be independent, render that assumption questionable for the period 1950-1965.

Table 6.9. Higher Order Dimensions

First-Order Dimensions	Dimensions[a]			
	1	2	3	h^2
Relative Exports	.89			.83
Unnamed	.89			.84
International Organizations	.85			.73
Transactions	.79			.73
Military Violence		.84		.72
Antiforeign Behavior		.83		.77
Negative Communication			.79	.65
Alignment			.77	.61
% total variance	37.1	19.0	17.4	73.4

a. These are the orthogonally rotated (eigenvalue≥ 1.00) dimensions from component analysis of the oblique correlation matrix partly given in Table 6.8. Only loadings ≥|.30| are shown.

NOTES

1. Subsequent to the factor analyses to be reported here, data were corrected on students and relative students for China to the USSR, 1950, and Cuba to the US, 1960; and on aid and relative aid for the USSR to all others and the US to all others for 1955. The impact of these changes on the reported results is negligible. The corrected data are given in Appendix IV.

2. I will deal with correlations between the various dimensions in the final section. Anticipating that discussion, I should note that the oblique transaction dimension also has little correlation with the conflict dimensions.

Chapter 7

INTERNATIONAL SOCIAL INDICATORS

Considerable data are given in Appendices II and IV, and a variety of their analyses have been presented in previous chapters. Given all these data and analyses, what are appropriate *indicators* for the range of variation in the data and their interrelationships? The purpose of this chapter is to suggest such a list.

This list will not only be useful in itself, but will also provide indicators for assessing the linkages between international dyadic behavior and national attribute distances. Such a use of the indicators will be reported in subsequent chapters.

7.1 CRITERIA

There are a number of criteria for selecting indicators of the kind we seek.

(1) *Data must be readily available in a simple form.* Clearly, if an indicator is to be used, data must be easily available, and, moreover, in a comprehensible form. Thus, for example, factor scores, Guttman scales, or additive scales would be undesirable unless they already are used and understood widely (as is GNP, an additive scale).

(2) *Data on an indicator should be comparable.* For some potential indicators, the definitions under which data are aggregated vary from nation to nation. GNP and national income, for example, are variables for which the data do not mean the same between, say, Poland and France, and for which exchange rate

conversion to common currency adds additional elements of noncomparability. Given the instability of exchange rates, any variable dependent on their conversion could not make a desirable indicator.

(3) *Each indicator should be measured on at least an interval scale.* Then each nation or nation-dyad usually will have a distinct value on the indicator, and the associated data can be used in a variety of statistical and mathematical analyses and models. If the choice must be between ordinally scaled indicators, then the one having more discrete values is preferred.

(4) *Each indicator should index a distinct dimension of variation among nations.* A dimension of nations is a pattern of intercorrelated characteristics or behaviors and a basic indicator should be central to the pattern. Why this should be so may not be immediately evident. Consider "the organization of political power" (POWDIS), which is a political attribute correlated with both the wealth and totalitarianism dimensions (see Chapter 5). How are we to interpret the correlation of political power with other attributes, such as trade, threats, alliances, or domestic unrest? This correlation may be due to variance associated with national wealth, with totalitarianism, or with both. However, if an attribute indexing only one dimension of nations is used, then the variance involved in its correlations would not be ambiguous. Moreover, because the attribute indexes a pattern of intercorrelated attributes (or behaviors), the correlations or findings that hold for one–the indicator–hold also for the others involved in the pattern. This enables comparison of results for attributes (or behaviors) within the same pattern, and facilitates relating the indicators to a variety of policy interests.

(5) *The set of indicators should encompass the major variance among nations.* If each indicator indexes a dimension, then the major dimensions reflecting most of the variation among nations should be indexed by the set of indicators. Such a set enables an analyst to cover the major differences and similarities among nations, which would be useful, for example, in linking domestic characteristics and capabilities to foreign conflict, trade, balance of payments, aid, and diplomatic interaction. Moreover, the set would serve as a collection with known correlates and from which specific measures could be selected for secondary analyses, additional data collections, and monitoring.

These are five scientific criteria; they satisfy a need for a scientifically based set of social indicators. Our concern, however, is not only scientific but also practical. We want indicators that enable us to foresee social problems, to assess priorities, and to facilitate taking steps to help alleviate these problems. Thus, some additional criteria are required.

(6) *The indicators should be socially manipulable.* Clearly, if we are not only to foresee problems and assess priorities, but to try to deal with them and to avoid those problems we forsee, we must be able to change the situation: we must be able to alter by policy the central variables. Thus, if we have a choice, say, between national area and energy production as indicators, the latter can be significantly and consciously altered by national policy, while the former usually is unalterable except by recourse to violence or subversion.

(7) *The indicator should be well known and directly meaningful to the policy-making and debating community.* Cute variables with nice statistical properties or faddish appeal may satisfy scientific criteria and make professional peers happy, but they may be unknown to the public and useless to the policy maker. An indicator must have a face validity to it and be the subject of much interest in its own right. Thus, other criteria being equal, GNP is preferable to the GINI number (area under the Lorentz curve) of income equality, population is preferable to coastline length/square root of area, and energy production is preferable to a primacy measure of large cities.

These seven criteria constitute the framework for determining a useful set of social indicators of cross-national variation and dyadic behavior and their linkages.

7.2 INDICATORS OF NATIONAL SOCIETIES

Relevant to the above criteria, a first list of social indicators has been suggested (Rummel, 1972, Chapter 11) on the basis of the analysis of 236 attributes for 1955 data (Section 5.3). The data and analysis here, although involving fewer attributes, in effect, cover a greater range of variance and are both cross-national and cross-time 1950-1965.[1] Table 7.1 presents this first list on the left and on the right the suggested indicators of national societies derived from the results of Chapter 5. The table is organized so that the two sets of indicators can be compared. I will discuss Table 7.1 indicator by indicator.

7.2.1 Energy Consumption per Capita

This was selected in the 1955 analysis as an indicator of economic development and has also been selected here as an indicator of the renamed wealth space-time dimension. It well fits the criteria for an indicator. Data are cross-nationally comparable. It is highly correlated with the associated dimension, and is thus a good index to the cluster of communication, technological, economic, educational and international attributes clustered around the associated dimension. It is easily understood and of momentous contemporary policy importance. And it is manipulable, as demonstrated by the Arab oil boycott of 1973-74.

7.2.2 A Totalitarianism Scale

The 1955 analysis delineated a political orientation dimension for which the appropriate indicator was deemed to be bloc membership, an attribute also highly correlated with the totalitarianism dimension found here for the 1950-1965 data. The problem with bloc membership, however, is its lack of discrimination (it measures only Western, neutral, and Eastern bloc membership) and its obsoleteness. The attribute does not fit well the variety of political orientations in the world today and the passing of the bipolar, Cold War period of international

Table 7.1. National Social Indicators

236-Attribute Analysis, 1955[a]		91-Attribute Analysis 1950-1965	
Dimension	Indicator	Indicator	Dimension[b]
1. economic development	energy consumption per capita	energy consumption per capita	wealth
2. political orientation	bloc membership	(system style) + (communist regime) (freedom of political opposition) + (constitutional status) + (electoral system) + (censorship)	totalitarianism authoritarianism
3. foreign conflict behavior	threats	energy production x population	power
4. size (power bases)	population	population	size
5. Catholic culture	Roman Catholics/ population	Roman Catholics/ population	Catholic culture
6. domestic conflict behavior	domestic killed	number of riots	domestic confli
7. density	population/area	population/area	density
8. density	language groups	(language groups) + (ethnic groups)	diversity
9.		imports/trade	import dependenc
10.		year	time

a. The dimensions and indicators are from Rummel (1972: 269, Table 11.1).

b. These are the dimensions described in Chapter 5.

relations. Accordingly, a more discriminating indicator was sought, one that would measure the continuum that is totalitarianism while discriminating it from authoritarianism.

No one attribute highly correlated with the totalitarianism dimension satisfies these requirements. Consequently, I formed a *totalitarianism scale* by adding together the appropriate attributes in the totalitarianism cluster. The scale is then the sum of:

(1) system style (STYLE)
    0 = nonmobilized population
    1 = some mobilization
    2 = highly mobilized

(2) communist regime (COMMUN)
    0 = noncommunist
    2 = communist

The scale of (2) in Appendix I has been reversed so that both STYLE and COMMUN would be measured in the direction of high totalitarianism.

7.2.3 An Authoritarianism Scale

As shown in Table 7.1, the political orientation dimension in the 1955 data was found to consist of two dimensions for 1950-1965. The second, or authoritarian, dimension suffers from the same problem as the totalitarian one. We lack a good continuous single, political indicator of the dimension. Accordingly, here also I summed together attributes to form an *authoritarianism scale.* This comprises the sum of:

(1) freedom of political opposition (TOTAL)
- 0 = unrestricted
- 1 = some restriction
- 2 = opposition not permitted

(2) constitutional status (CONSTI)
- 0 = constitutional
- 1 = authoritarian
- 2 = totalitarian

(3) electoral system (ELECTO)
- 0 = competitive
- 1 = partly competitive
- 2 = noncompetitive

(4) censorship (CENSOR)
- 0 = no censorship
- 1 = some censorship
- 2 = complete or fairly complete censorship

The scales for each of these attributes have been reversed from those given in Appendix I to accord with the direction of high authoritarianism.

7.2.4 Energy Production x Population

In the 1955, 236-attribute analysis, there emerged a size dimension with which energy production x population was highly correlated. Nonetheless, population (or national income) as the simpler and more understandable attribute was selected as the proper indicator. However, events that have since then shown the importance of energy *production* and the completion of the 91-attribute analysis point to a split between size and power. Especially, both current events and our most recent analyses show that the most appropriate indicator, even though complex, is energy production x population. The number of people a country has, weighted by the amount of energy it can produce per person—energy production times population—is highly correlated with a variety of measures of a nation's power (see Section 5.2.4). Contemporary events surely show the influence and power that energy production gives a nation.

7.2.5 Population

The number of people a country has is a central indicator of its size, and its choice as an indicator clearly satisfies our criteria.

7.2.6 Roman Catholics/Population

Catholic culture emerged both in the 1955 analysis and the analyses presented here, although a yearly analysis of the 1950-1965 attribute data would show this dimension to be increasingly weak in time. I still suggest that the proportion of Roman Catholics in the population is the obvious indicator.

7.2.7 Riots

As shown in Table 7.1, in the 1955 analysis the variable domestic killed was selected as the best indicator of domestic conflict. However, in the results reported here, violent domestic deaths had a low correlation with the domestic conflict dimension in the component analysis (Table 5.11) and a moderate loading in the others. Riots, however, was consistently correlated with the dimension across all analyses, and therefore was selected as indicator.

7.2.8 Population/Area

Density has been extracted in both the 1955, and 1950-1965 analyses. The same indicator, population over area, is surely the appropriate choice here.

7.2.9 A Diversity Scale

In the 1955 analysis a diversity dimension was delineated, and the number of language groups in a nation was selected as the appropriate indicator. Unfortunately, this indicator does not provide enough discrimination between nations. Accordingly, I decided to add the number of ethnic groups to the number of language groups to form a scale of diversity. This scale will correlate better with the dimension and enable the heterogeneity of nations like the US, Canada, India, and the USSR, to be measured in contrast with more homogeneous nations like S. Korea, W. Germany, and Sweden.

7.2.10 Imports/Trade and Year

The remaining two indicators have no corresponding dimension in the 1955 analysis and are for the minor space-time dimensions. The first is the imports-to-trade ratio, which measures the import dependency of a nation. The second is time, which simply indicates the year of the data.

7.2.11 Geographic X

A geographic dimension was extracted, but I propose no indicator for it, although a nation's longitude would suffice, since the attribute most highly correlated with the dimension (geographic X) is this measure of longitude. My reason for omitting it as an indicator is based on an interest in distances between nations. In the linkage analysis, therefore, I will simply measure the geographic distance between nation's "home territory," instead of using the geographic x dimension.

7.3 INDEPENDENCE BETWEEN ATTRIBUTE INDICATORS

I have presented above a list of indicators on which data is presented in Appendix II and which map the cross-national, cross-time variance in national societies. Those interested in using these indicators can determine from Chapter 5 and from the data the degree to which these indicators satisfy one or another criteria.

I can present here, however, one kind of information on the indicator's independence. If, as I say, these indicators measure independent clusters of coveriation in national societies, then they should be statistically independent of each other. Are they?

In answer to this, I took the data on the indicators, estimated missing data, and computed the matrix of coefficients of determination (squared correlation coefficients) between them. The results are presented in Table 7.2. The coefficient (x 100) measures the percent of variance in common between the indicators. From the table, we can see that most indicators have near zero covariance.

The most highly correlated indicators are those for the dimensions that we know from Chapter 5 are oblique to each other. The authoritarian and totalitarian scales share 40% of their variance, showing that the selected indicator formed scales that would discriminate between these political types. And the power and size indicators—energy production x population and population—share 67% of their variance.

The squared multiple correlations down the principal diagonal show to what degree each indicator's variance is measured jointly by all the other indicators. In general, each indicator is independent of the others, with the possible exception of energy production x population and population.

In general, however, taking into account all the coefficients in Table 7.2, we can see that the indicators selected to index national societies comparatively and through time are independent. Moreover, they span national variation, are measureable and have available data, are well known, and index important dimensions of nations.

Table 7.2. Coefficients of Determination Between Indicators of National Societies

	Coefficients[a]										
	1	2	3	4	5	6	7	8	9	10	11
1. energy consumption per capita	.53										
2. totalitarian scale	.01	.51									
3. authoritarian scale	(-).08	.40	.55								
4. energy production x population	.15	.02	.00	.80							
5. population	.01	.04	.00	.67	.78						
6. diversity scale	(-).03	.00	.02	.00	.02	.17					
7. population/area	.06	.00	(-).02	.00	.01	(-).04	.20				
8. riots	.00	.00	(-).01	.10	.17	.00	.02	.21			
9. imports/trade	(-).02	.00	.01	(-).02	.00	.00	.02	.00	.10		
10. Catholics/population	.00	(-).02	(-).06	(-).02	(-).02	(-).08	.00	.00	(-).03	.16	
11. time	.00	.00	.00	.00	.00	.02	.00	.01	.01	(-).01	.05

a. The coefficients in the principal diagonal are the squared multiple correlation coefficients of an indicator regressed on all the rest. In the off-diagonals are the squared product moment correlation coefficients. The negative in parenthesis means that the correlation was negative. Sample size is 461.

7.4 INDICATORS OF INTERNATIONAL BEHAVIOR

Let us now turn to the international behavior indicators. Table 7.3 shows those indicators previously suggested and the revised list based on the analyses here. I will consider the indicators in the order shown in the table's right column.

7.4.1 Exports A→B

A major space-time dimension for 1950-1965 is transactions. In the behavior variables correlated with it, the dimension is similar to the salience dimension for 1955, as shown by the high correlation of tourists, the indicator for 1955, with transactions (Table 6.1). Exports, however, is a better choice of indicator. Much more data are available on exports than tourists, the data are more consistently defined from nation to nation and thus are more comparative, and exports is a well-known and researched international behavior.

7.4.2 Weighted UN Voting Distance

This suggested indicator is the same as that chosen for 1955. It is a complex indicator, which is not well known or easily understood, and its choice therefore appears to violate some of our criteria. But consider the behaviors correlated with the alignment dimension. We really have a choice only between common bloc membership or the UN voting measures.

Common bloc membership is simply a three-valued scale indicating whether two nations have common, different, or opposing bloc memberships. Clearly, this scale does not well discriminate, and is increasingly difficult to apply to the contemporary post-Cold War period.

The voting measures do discriminate and do reflect the fluid politics of a multialignment system. However, the fact that I used a distance measure calculated across voting dimensions would seem to make the indicator only unusable to those able and willing to do a prior component analysis. For this reason, I selected the *weighted* UN voting distance. The weighted distance[2] is the sum of the distances on each UN voting dimension, weighted by the proportion of voting variance the dimension describes. Let d_{A-B} stand for the UN voting distance between two nations. Then

$$d_{A-B} = \sqrt{\sum_{\ell=1}^{p} (S_{A\ell} - S_{B\ell})^2 V_\ell}$$

where $S_{A\ell}$ and $S_{B\ell}$ are the factor scores of nations A and B on the ℓth voting dimension, and V_ℓ is the proportion of voting variance the ℓth dimension

Table 7.3. International Social Indicators

	40 Behaviors Analysis, 1955[a]		53 Behaviors Analysis, 1950-1965[b]	
	Dimension	Indicator	Indicator	Dimension
1.	Salience	tourists A→B	exports A→B	transactions
2.	UN voting	weighted UN voting distance A↔B	weighted UN voting distance	alignment
3.	international organizations	IGO A↔B/A's IGO memberships	IGO A↔B/A's common memberships	international organizations
4.	exports	exports A→B/A's GNP	exports A→B/A's GNP	relative exports
5.	official conflict behavior	military violence factor score A→B	military acts A→B	military violence
6.	antiforeign demonstrations	antiforeign behavior factor score A→B	unofficial actions A→B	antiforeign behavior
7.	emigration and communication	emigrants A→B/A's population		
8.	foreign students	students A→B/A's students to all nations		
9.	diplomatic representation	embassy or legation A→B/A's total embassies or legations		
10.	self-determination voting	UN voting distance on "Self Determination" issue pattern A↔B		
			negative communications A→B	negative communications
			aid A→B	aid

a. The dimensions and indicators are from Rummel (1969).
b. These are the dimensions described in Chapter 6.

describes. Were d_{A-B} computed across all the voting dimensions in the data (including the smallest ones), it would be equivalent to

$$d_{AB} = \alpha + \beta d^*_{AB},$$

$$d^*_{AB} = \sqrt{\sum_{k=1}^{m} (X_{Ak} - X_{Bk})^2},$$

where α and β are parameters and X_{Ak} and X_{Bk} are the votes of A and B on roll call X_k.

Therefore, because we are interested in the indicator comparatively—in measuring a dyad's relative voting alignment—we can use d^*_{AB} in place of d_{AB}. *Thus, the indicator can be measured by simply computing the distance across actual UN votes.* Since this is only a matter of taking the difference in votes (where, say a no = 0, abstain = 1, and yes = 2) between two countries, squaring, summing across all roll calls, and taking the square root of the result, the indicator can be generated with relative ease, and without undertaking computer analyses.

7.4.3 IGO A⟷B/A's Common Memberships

This indicator is similar to that chosen for 1955, except for the denominator. For 1955, comemberships A⟷B was divided by the number of nation A's memberships. The ratio then measured the importance of the comemberships A⟷B. Clearly, these comemberships would vary in importance depending upon nation A's general involvement in international organizations. However, a simple count of nation A's organizational memberships does not take into account organizational size. Nation A may have joined mainly the large international organizations, in which case its comembership with nation B would be less significant than if A had joined mainly very small organizations. Consequently, I chose the indicator that norms comemberships A⟷B by the total memberships of all organizations of which A is a member.

7.4.4 Exports A→B/A's GNP

This is the same indicator selected for the 1955 data.

7.4.5 Military Acts A→B

For 1955, the military violence factor score was selected as a measure of official conflict behavior. Unfortunately, factor scores are neither easily understandable nor reproducible. To overcome this problem, in part, I included no such factor score variables in the 53 behaviors analyzed for 1950-1965. Therefore, we can select as a conflict indicator an easily countable behavior such as the number of military acts A→B, which is highly correlated with the military violence dimension and comprises a count of the number of continuous military actions (exceeding 24 hours) short of war, discrete military actions (less than 24 hours), and clashes.

7.4.6 Negative Communications A→B

This indicator comprises the number of negative oral or written communications A→B, and would include warnings, threats, protests, denunciations, ultimatums, accusations, and verbal attacks.

7.4.7 Unofficial Actions A→B

For 1955, antiforeign behavior factor scores were proposed as an indicator of antiforeign demonstrations. For the 1950-1965 data, we can use an actual count of unofficial actions A→B as an indicator of such a dimension. These comprise any unofficial antiforeign actions of nation A's citizens against the persons, property, or symbols of B. This would include attacks on an embassy, flag, or diplomatic vehicles, or any antiforeign demonstrations, boycotts, or strikes.

7.4.8 Aid A→B

The final indicator is aid A→B, which had no counterpart in the analysis of 40 behavior variables for 1955.

7.4.9 Remaining Indicators for 1955

Table 7.3 shows that there are still four indicators previously suggested that have no counterpart here. What of these?

Regarding the emigrants and communication dimension for 1955, this came out in the 1950-1965 analysis as a dimension in the component analysis involving only the emigration behaviors (EMIGRA, R-EMIG, E/POPU); in the image analyses, no such dimension emerged. Therefore, for 1950-1965, the emigration indicator would be representing only unique emigration variance. However, if an indicator of emigration would be useful in a particular analysis, then the one suggested from the 1955 analysis would do.

Regarding the 1955 foreign students dimension, for 1950-1965 this comprised, in the component analysis, a dimension only involving students (STUDNT and R-STUD). In the image analysis rotations, the dimension lost its specificity to students and was difficult to interpret (and thus was left unnamed); therefore, no student indicator was selected.

The observations made for emigrants and students also apply to diplomatic representation, which emerged in the component analysis as a dimension involving only representation (EMBLEG and R-EMB), and which did not emerge in the image analysis.

Finally, the self-determination voting dimension has no counterpart in the 1950-1965 data, because no individual UN voting dimensions were included in the analysis. The 1955 indicator may be useful only for that year, since its variance may be captured by the other indicators, especially the weighted UN voting distance.

7.5 INDEPENDENCE BETWEEN BEHAVIORAL INDICATORS

For the indicators of national societies, we determined the degree of independence between the indicators by computing their coefficients of determination. Table 7.4 shows these coefficients for the behavior indicators. As can be seen, generally the indicators are statistically independent. Even the squared multiple correlations in the diagonal are low, with the highest being for exports. Only about 5% of the variation in exports overlaps with all the other indicators. I will thus conclude that this set of indicators measures independent sources of international behavior variance.

Table 7.4. Coefficients of Determination Between Indicators of International Behavior

	Coefficients[a]						
	1	2	3	4	5	6	7
1. exports A→B	.25						
2. weighted UN voting distance	(-).01	.05					
3. IGO A↔B/A's common memberships	.07	(-).01	.10				
4. exports A→B/A's GNP	.09	(-).02	.05	.14			
5. military acts A→B	.00	.00	.00	.00	.04		
6. negative communications A→B	.00	.01	.00	.00	.07	.11	
7. unofficial actions A→B	.00	.00	.00	.09	.00	.03	.07
8. aid A→B	.00	.00	.00	.00	.00	.00	.13

a. See note to Table 7.2.

7.6 LINKAGES BETWEEN INDICATORS

With the list of national and international indicators, we can now ask how they are linked.

These indicators are the best representations of the space-time dimensions delineated in Chapters 5 and 6. By best I mean they satisfy the criteria of Section 7.1, which include the indicator being among, if not the most, highly correlated with a dimension.

7.7 AND THE CRITERIA

Finally, let us return to the criteria I specified in Section 7.1. How well do the suggested indicators fit these seven criteria? Referring to individual indicators, these criteria concern data availability and comparability, level of measurement, indexing dimensions, manipulability, meaningfulness, and the ability of the indicators to span cross-national, cross-time variance.

Table 7.5 shows how each indicator and the set of indicators fit the various criteria. In general, the suggested indicators form a set spanning the cross-national, cross-time dimensions of nations. Moreover, comparable data are available on most of the indicators, levels of measurement are appropriate, and each indicator is meaningful and manipulable. Furthermore, each *uniquely* indexes a space-time dimension of national societies or international behavior.

NOTES

1. See Section 2.3 for the criteria involved in selecting the attributes.
2. See Rummel (1970, Section 22.1) for a discussion of distances in a multidimensional space.

Table 7.5. Indicators and Criteria[a]

	Criteria[b]						
	data			dimensionality		praxis	
	availability	comparability	interval scale	index a dimension	span social variation	meaningfulndss	manipulable
National Social Indicators							
1. energy consumption per capita	E	E	Yes	Yes		E	F
2. totalitarianism scale	E	F[f]	No	Yes		F[i]	F
3. authoritarianism scale	E	F	No	Yes		F[i]	F
4. energy production x population	E	E	Yes	Yes		F	F
5. population	E	E	Yes	Yes		E	P
6. Roman Catholic population	E	E	Yes	Yes		E	P
7. riots	P[c]	F	Yes	Yes		E	E
8. population/area	E	E	Yes	Yes		E	P
9. diversity scale	F[d]	F[g]	Yes	Yes		F[i]	P
10. imports/trade	E	E	Yes	Yes		E	E
11. year	E	E	Yes	Yes		E	No
International Social Indicators							
1. exports	E	E	Yes	Yes		E	E
2. weighted UN voting distance	E	E	No	Yes		P[j]	E
3. IGO comemberships/A's common memberships	E	E	Yes	Yes		F	E
4. exports/A's GNP	E	E	Yes	Yes		E	E
5. negative communications	P[c]	F	Yes	Yes		E	E
6. unofficial actions	P[c]	F	Yes	Yes		E	E
7. aid	F[e]	F[h]	Yes	Yes		E	E
the indicator set					Yes		

a. For the criteria, see Section 7.1.

b. E = excellent fit; F = fair; P = poor.

c. Cross-national data on this indicator are mainly available from the public press; however, their quality is poor.

d. Data on the number of language and ethnic groups are not available for all nations, and the quality of such data varies considerably by nation.

e. The availability and validity of aid data are controlled by many governments.

f. There is an inevitable ambiguity associated with defining political attributes, such as freedom of group opposition, and difficulty in fitting such definitions to many nations.

Table 7.5. (continued)

g. There is lack of uniformity in the cross-national definitions of domestic ethnic and language groups.

h. Aid figures vary in their inclusion of long- and short-term gifts, grants, loans, as well as in what they classify under these categories.

i. While the underlying dimension is meaningful, the indicators are newly formed scales; therefore they are not known as scales by the policy and academic community. Nonetheless, the scale ingredients are so well known and their summation to form the scale is simple, so that the scale should have at least a fair meaningfulness.

j. A distance measure is not well known and not simple.

Chapter 8

LINKAGE ANALYSIS

The purpose of the above analyses was to provide two kinds of information as shown in Figure 4.3. The first has to do with the space-time attribute dimensions of nations and their indicators, along which the distances between nations could be measured. The second concerns the dyadic behavior dimensions and their indicators. With a definition of these behavioral indicators and the attribute distances, we can now determine whether this behavior is linked quantitatively to these various distances. In this chapter, I will report the major results of this linkage analysis.

8.1 THE DEPENDENCE OF DYADIC BEHAVIOR ON DISTANCES

Figure 4.3 shows that fourteen different sets of linkages between behavior and distances must be determined: one for each set of dyads involving the same actor. Each is a super-P analysis, in that it will be across the five years. Figure 8.1, which illustrates the analysis for the United States as actor, should clarify what is being linked in these analyses.

The linkages discussed will be in terms of the indicators. I could use instead the scores of nations or dyads on each dimension (the factor scores), but indicators provide more understandable and usable results and provide better continuity with other research. Indicators, such as energy consumption per capita or population are meaningful in their own right and usually are well understood with considerable research surrounding them; factor scores are abstract and intrinsic to the specific analysis.

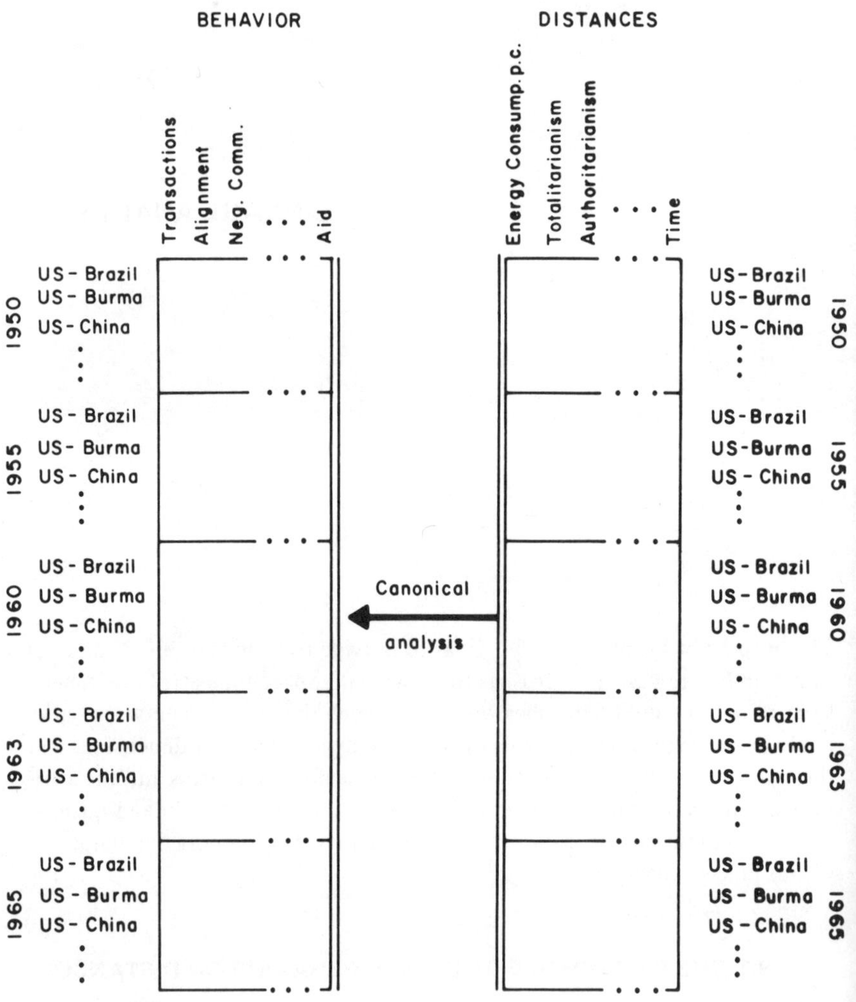

Figure 8.1

The indicators developed in the last chapter will not all be used in raw form, however. The basic idea is that the distances between nations on the attribute indicators will be significantly linked to their dyadic behavior. But the salience of some distances probably decreases with magnitude (Section 4.4.3), and some provision for this should be made. Accordingly, the data on five indicators[1] were transformed to logarithms (base 10) prior to the linkage analysis, as shown in Table 8.1.

I will present the linkage results in terms of the dimension names, for this then provides a more general conceptual understanding of the linkages. It should

Table 8.1. Linkage Analysis: Indicators and Dimensions

Attribute Dimension	Indicator
Wealth	log 10 (energy consumption per capita)
Totalitarianism	totalitarian scale
Authoritarianism	authoritarianism scale
Power	log 10 (energy production x population)
Size	log 10 population
Diversity	diversity scale
Density	population/area
Domestic Conflict	log 10 riots
Import Dependency	log 10 (imports/trade)
Catholic Culture	Catholics/population
	geographic distance[a]
Behavioral Dimensions	**Indicator**
Transactions	exports A→B
Alignment	weighted UN voting distance
International Organizations	IGO A↔B/A's common membership
Relative Exports	exports A→B/A's GNP
Military Violence	military acts A→B
Antiforeign Behavior	unofficial actions A→B
Negative Communications	negative communications A→B
Aid	aid A→B

a. See Section 7.2.11.

be recognized in each case, however, that the underlying measurement of the dimensions is in terms of the indicators shown in Table 8.1.

Turning now to the canonical super-P analyses, Table 8.2 presents the findings for each actor. At the right of the table are shown the results of random number analyses, which enable the magnitudes of the empirical traces to be evaluated. On the average, the indicators explain about one-third of *all* the variation in the dyadic behavior for each actor. For each actor there are at least two independent kinds of distance-behavior linkages explaining on the average 86% (.93 squared x 100) and 69% (.83 squared x 100) of the variation in specific behavioral indicators (to be detailed below).

These results are considerably better than random, as can be seen in Table 8.2. Note especially that none of the first random canonical correlations are significant and that on the average they account for 38% of "behavior" compared to

Table 8.2. Dependence of Dyadic Behavior on Distances

Actor	Real Data						Random Numbers[c]	
	Correlation[a]	Significant Canonical Correlations[b]					Trace Correlation[a]	First Ca[nonical] Correlat[ion]
Brazil[e,f]	.60 (.36)	.94	.85				.41 (.17)	.64
Burma[e,f,g]	.63 (.40)	.89	.76				.40 (.16)	.56
China[e]	.59 (.35)	.94	.83	.72			.40 (.16)	.6[illegible]
Cuba[e]	.56 (.31)	.95	.79				.39 (.15)	.5[illegible]
Egypt[e,g]	.65 (.42)	.89	.85	.64	.57		.41 (.17)	.6[illegible]
India[e]	.60 (.36)	.92	.84	.75			.44 (.19)	.66
Indonesia[e]	.57 (.32)	.91	.79				.39 (.15)	.64
Israel[e]	.60 (.36)	.95	.81	.74			.33 (.11)	.49
Jordan[e]	.61 (.37)	.90	.81	.73			.41 (.17)	.6[illegible]
Netherlands[g]	.61 (.37)	.96	.74	.68			.44 (.19)	.70
Poland[f,g]	.63 (.40)	.93	.86				.40 (.16)	.60
USSR	.59 (.35)	.93	.92				.41 (.17)	.6[illegible]
UK	.67 (.45)	.93	.89	.84	.74	.58	.42 (.18)	.7[illegible]
US	.62 (.38)	.95	.82	.79			.39 (.15)	.56
Average	.61 (.37)	.93	.83				.40 (.16)	.6[illegible]

a. The figures in parentheses are the proportion of variance (trace correlation squared) in the act[or] behavior on the eight behavioral indicators accounted for by the eleven indicator distances.

b. These are significant at a Z-score ≥ 2.00, which is a one-tailed p ≤ .0227. For the methodologi[cal] details on the canonical equations, correlations, and determination of significance, see Rummel (197[illegible] Chapter 4, Section 2).

c. Seven columns of computer generated random numbers (nonnormal) were regressed onto eleven distances between dyads on the attribute indicators. Where one, two, or three behavioral indicators for an actor had to be omitted due to zero variance, the corresponding number of random number columns was also omitted.

c. The highest Z-score for these first canonical correlations is 1.8; the average Z-score is .172.

e. The aid indicator could not be used for this actor due to zero variance.

f. The military violence indicator could not be used for this actor due to zero variance.

g. The antiforeign behavior indicator could not be used for this actor due to zero variance.

86% for the real data. Thus, the variance explained by the canonical analysis is empirically meaningful, and not due to random covariance or a small number of degrees of freedom in the canonical fit.[2]

What do these results mean? They show that the *socioeconomic, political and cultural distances do explain a considerable amount of dyadic behavior.* Of course, not all dyadic behavior is explained, but at least a third is dependent upon attribute distances.[3] And this is a theoretically and practically meaningful chunk of behavior to so explain, when it is considered that we are dealing with such diverse actors as Cuba, China, the USSR, Brazil, and Burma; with such different objects of their behavior as the United States, Poland, Israel, the Netherlands, and Indonesia; with such a range of behavior as exports, treaties, UN voting, military violence, tourists, and joining international organizations; and with such different years as those between 1950 and 1965. Then to account consistently for a third of the space-time variation in behavior by distances for all these actors is indeed to establish that *international behavior is linked to the similarities and differences between nations.*

8.2 SPECIFIC LINKAGE EQUATIONS

Canonical analyses measure the dependence of behavior on distances. They also provide equations showing which specific behavior is linked to what particular distances and to what degree. For example, a particular canonical analysis may show that three independent equations linking behavior and distances account for the significant overall dependence of behavior on distances. My concern in this section is to present the more interesting of these equations for the indicators.

Table 8.2 listed the significant canonical correlations for the canonical analyses of the indicators representing the dimensions. Each equation linking specific behavioral dimensions (indicators) and distances has a canonical correlation, which measures how good the particular linkage is. By squaring the canonical correlation and multiplying by 100, we can tell what percent of the variance in the specific behavior linked to distances is explained by the equation. For example, for the canonical analysis of Brazilian behavior, 1950-1965, one equation was found that linked specific behavioral dimensions and distances with a correlation of .94 (the first canonical correlation for Brazil in Table 8.2). In other words, 88% (.94 squared x 100) of the variation in some Brazilian dyadic behavior can be explained by the variation in Brazil's attribute distances from other nations. Clearly, judging from the size of the canonical correlations in Table 8.2, there are a number of near perfect linkages in the overall dyadic data. For comparison, the highest canonical correlation is shown in Table 8.2 for each of the random number analyses. In no case do the random number results approach that for the actual behavior; nor do they have a z-score above the significance threshold of 2.00 in any case.

Let us now focus on significant equations. There are clearly too many to detail here, but we can deal with the most interesting. Table 8.3 presents the canonical equations for distances on wealth, totalitarianism, power, and size. The table is organized by primary distance and by actor. The coefficients in the table are from the canonical structure matrices (not given here), which are similar to orthogonal factor loading matrices in that the coefficients are correlations.

How are the correlations in Table 8.3 to be interpreted? Recall that we input distances (actor nation minus object nation) on each of the attribute indicators listed in Table 8.1. Now, these are distance vectors (differences) and not distance magnitudes, which complicates the interpretation. But fortunately, we have an easy approximation. If we correlate one variable x with another variable y, where $y = c_i - z_j$, and c_i is a constant, then the correlation r_{xy} between x and y will equal the inverse of that between x and z. That is, $r_{xy} = -r_{xz}$. Now, let $c_i - z_j$ stand for the distance of the object nation j from the actor nation i, where c_i is the actor nation's magnitude on some attribute indicator, say, population; z_j is the object nation's magnitude on the same indicator and z ranges across a variety of nations j. Then, if the correlation of some behavior, say, alignment, is .74 with the distance of j from i, the correlation of j's population with the alignment between i and j will be -.74. *That is, by reversing the signs on the distances, we, in effect, have the correlation between the object nation's attributes and the actor's behavior.*

This is only an approximation because the actor's values are not constant across the five years; and for some attributes like riots, where an actor's values can sharply alter in time, the interpretation must be applied with caution. Nonetheless, it gives a very helpful basis for understanding the correlations (coefficients) shown in Table 8.3. If the actor's attributes can shift rapidly in time, we can handle this by interpreting the object's magnitudes as relative to the actor. For example, if the correlation between distance in riots and alignment is positive, we can say that the less riots of the object nation *relative to the actor,* the more the actor aligns with the object.

To make sure Table 8.3 is clear, and to illustrate the above interpretations, consider the equation involving wealth for the USSR (row seven). Writing this equation out,

-.84 (negative communications) + .53 (alignment) - .64 (I.O.)
- .60 (military violence)
≑ .71 (wealth) - .52 (totalitarianism) - .64 (authoritarianism) + .56 (power)

with a canonical correlation of .92 (center column), and where ≑ signifies approximate equality.[4]

Now, the coefficients on the right of the approximation are the correlations of the specified distances with the equation; those on the left are the correlations of dyadic behavioral indicators with the equation. Because the distances are

(text continued on p. 94)

Table 8.3. Canonical Equations [a]

Primary Attribute Distance [b]	Actors [c]	Behavior									Attribute Distances										
		Transactions	Negative Communications	Alignment [d]	International Organizations	Relative Exports	Antiforeign Behavior	Military Violence	Aid	Canonical Correlation	Wealth	Totalitarianism	Authoritarianism	Power	Size	Diversity	Density	Domestic Conflict	Import Dependency	Catholic Culture	Geographic
Wealth	Brazil	-.87	-.51		-.89	-.85				.94	.65		-.59								.68
	Burma			.55	-.60					.89	.68										-.74
	Egypt	-.78		.58		-.73				.85	.76			.67							
	India	-.89		.56	-.70	-.89				.92	.75		-.60								
	Indonesia	-.88			-.51	-.84				.91	.75		-.58								
	Israel	-.77			-.66	-.88				.95	.74	-.52	-.66								
	USSR		-.84	.53	-.64			-.60		.92	.71	-.52	-.64	.56							
Totalitarianism	China	-.85				-.71				.83		.70	.55			.59					
	Israel			.82						.74		.50									
	Jordan			.53	.54					.73		.61									
	Netherlands			.51						.74		.56	.52								.56
	Poland	-.90		-.73		-.95				.93		.67	.54			.63					
	USSR	-.90		-.67		-.77			-.50	.93		.71									

Table 8.3. (continued)

Primary Distance [b]	Actors [c]	Behavior								⇐	Attribute Distances										
		Transactions	Negative Communications	Alignment [d]	International Organizations	Relative Exports	Antiforeign Behavior	Military Violence	Aid	Canonical Correlation	Wealth	Totalitarianism	Authoritarianism	Power	Size	Diversity	Density	Domestic Conflict	Import Dependency	Catholic Culture	Geographic
Authoritarianism	Cuba				.93					.79			.61								-.80
	Egypt				.88					.89	-.58		.69								
	Netherlands	.86			.93	.93				.96	-.56	.54	.65				-.66				
	Poland				.98					.86	-.71	.55	.72				-.50				
	UK	.78			.91	.86				.93	-.61	.55	.70								
	US	.83		.62	.92	.88				.95		.62	.75				-.64				
Power	Brazil	(-.49)			(.43)	(-.47)				.85				.73							
	China		-.86	.65						.94	.54		-.54	.72							
	Cuba	-.72	-.56			-.68		-.50		.95				.85							
	India		-.79		.57					.84				.76	.58					-.55	.51
	Indonesia				.69					.79				.66							
	Israel				.74					.81		.55		.70							
	UK	(-.46)				(-.45)	(.43)			.89				.76							
	US								-.64	.79				.69	.60	.62				-.50	
Size	Burma	-.89			-.59	-.86				.78		-.51			.53						
	Jordan				.83					.90		.57	.60		.64						

Table 8.3. (continued)

a. The values in the table are the product-moment correlations of the column variable with the particular canonical equation. Each row represents a significant canonical equation for the indicated actor. Only those canonical equations are shown which are highly correlated with wealth, totalitarianism, authoritarianism, power, or size. Only correlations greater than or equal to an absolute .50 are shown, with some exceptions given in parentheses. The indicators shown in Table 8.1 were used in the canonical analyses.

b. Those equations are grouped together which are highly correlated with the indicated distance.

c. An actor may appear more than once, since each actor has a number of independent (orthogonal) equations. For the number of significant canonical equations for each actor, see the canonical coefficients listed by actor in Table 8.2.

d. Scaling reversed. The higher the magnitude, the closer in UN voting distance.

differences and not magnitudes, it is not easy to interpret the relationships involved. But by remembering that the correlation between distance and some behavior is the inverse of that between the object nation's attribute and the behavior, we can interpret the above equation as follows. From the perspective of the Soviet Union, it tends to align more with, to direct less negative communication and military violence toward, and to join fewer IO's with nations the more totalitarian, authoritarian, poorer, and weaker they are for the years 1950-1965. Thus, for the Soviet Union there is a partial explanation of her alignments, conflict behavior and IO comemberships accounting for 85% of this variance, which is in terms of the wealth, power, and the domestic politics of the object nation.

Consider a second example from Table 8.3, taken for China (row eight) on the totalitarianism primary distance. The equation for China is

$$-.85 \text{ (transactions)} - .71 \text{ (relative exports)} \doteq .70 \text{ (totalitarianism)} + .55 \text{ (authoritarianism)} + .59 \text{ (diversity)},$$

with a correlation of .83 and a fit of 69%.

In words and remembering our way of interpreting this, the less totalitarian, authoritarian, and diverse the object nation, the fewer China's transactions and relative exports with her for the years 1950-1965.

The equations presented in Table 8.3 present a wealth of detail, and are fascinating reading for those interested in the empirical nature of international relations. Many hypotheses and theories about such relations can be checked against the results shown. But our purpose here is to present a summary overview of the results, and enough detail in Table 8.3, to enable others to weigh against these findings their special theories and hypotheses.

A summary of Table 8.3 can take two directions. First, I could present the most general equations holding for the most actors. And second, I could present the major independent groupings of actors in terms of the similarities of their canonical equations. I will do both in the next two chapters.

NOTES

1. By virtue of the importance of the indicators in the subsequent analyses, the data given on the indicators in the appendices were reprocessed. Specialized studies were consulted for better data, some missing data were located, and estimates were recomputed after an analysis of the distributions for each nation (dyad) on each indicator for the five years. Thus, the results of analyzing the indicators shown here and in the next chapter differ slightly from what would be found by analyzing the data given on the original variables in the appendix and estimating missing data using the ($\hat{Y}$-estimations) technique described in Wall and Rummel (1969). These differences are not substantial, however.

2. The sample size is 65, and the total number of variables included is, at the most, 19 (8 behavioral indicators and 11 distances). Nineteen is sufficiently close to 65 to raise a degrees-of-freedom question. The random number analyses help to show that the effect of the degrees of freedom on the canonical results is minor. The same point is made by the significance levels for the canonical variates, which will be discussed in the next section.

3. The emphasis here is on the indicators. If factor scores for the image results are used (and similarly log transformed) the distances account for 43% of the variance. This better fit is understandable, since factor scores smooth the extremes on the variables and better measure the dimensions involved.

4. This is approximate because the coefficients below an absolute .50 are not included for other distances and behaviors, and the error (residuals) are ignored.

Chapter 9

THE MOST GENERAL LINKAGES

With the wealth of equations linking behavior and attribute distances that we now have, I should be able to make some general statements about these linkages, 1950-1965. This I can do as systematically as in the previous analyses.

Consider how a complete matrix of canonical equations would look for all significant equations and actors, as shown in Figure 9.1. Each cell of the matrix would contain the correlation coefficient of the column attribute distance or behavior with the row-equation for a particular actor. Let us now fill in this matrix with all correlations (not just those above an absolute .50) and with all the equations with the significant canonical correlations shown in Table 8.2. There are then thirty-nine equations across all fourteen actors.

When we ask for the most general equations in the results, in effect, we mean to ask about what distances and behaviors most often cluster together in the matrix of Figure 9.1. This question is about the pattern of covariation in the table, and can be answered using factor analysis. Thus, a way of determining systematically the most general equations for the canonical results is to factor analyze the matrix of canonical coefficients (the canonical structure matrix).

The results of doing so are shown in Table 9.1.[1] Each of the five columns gives a general equation linking distances and behavior latent in all the significant equations ($p \leq .05$, two-tailed) found for the fourteen actors. Thus, for the first column we find

$$.86\ (\text{IO}) \doteq -.40\ (\text{wealth}) + .93\ (\text{totalitarianism}) + .96\ (\text{authoritarianism}) + .48\ (\text{diversity}) - .84\ (\text{density}) - .44\ (\text{Catholic culture}),$$

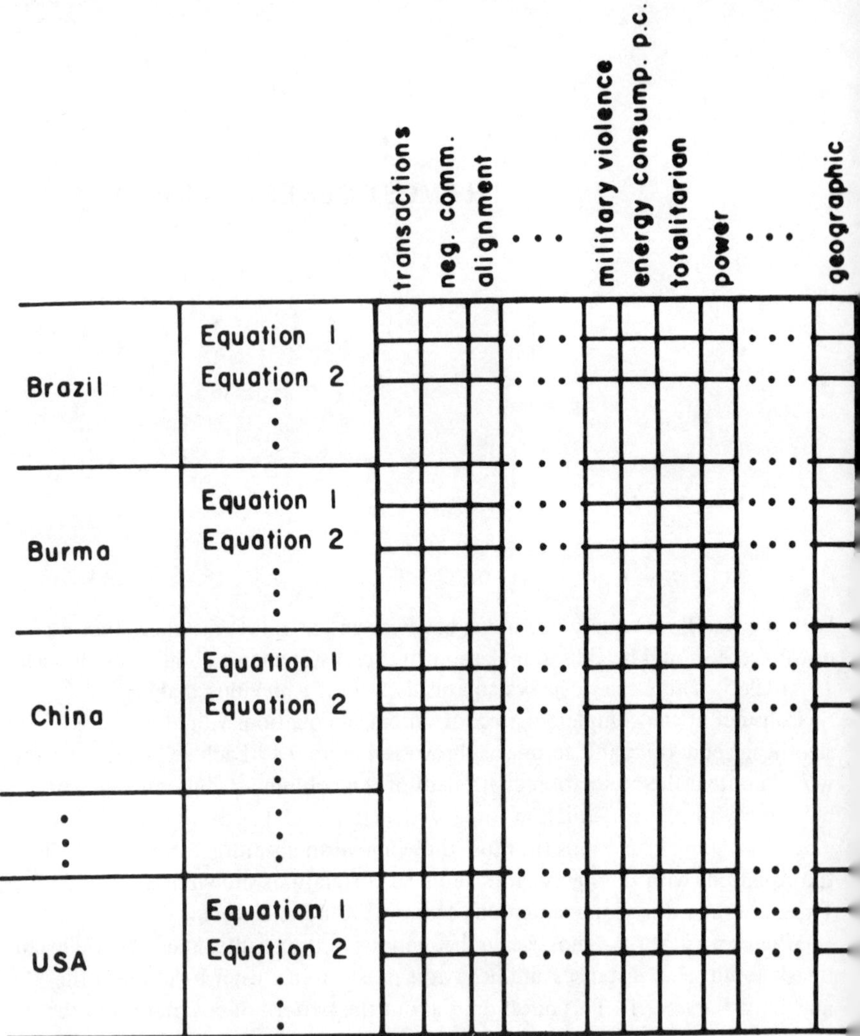

Figure 9.1

and this equation accounts for 22.5% of the variance in all the coefficients among the thirty-nine equations.

Remembering again how we can interpret these distances, we can say that in general, *the wealthier, denser, more Catholic, less totalitarian, less authoritarian, and diverse the object nation relative to the actor, the more an actor tends to join IO's with it.* To turn this around, comemberships in international organizations tend to be a function of wealthy, densely populated, homogeneous Catholic and democratic societies. This is the most general equation to be found in all the cononical linkage equations.

The second most general equation is in column four: it accounts for 15% of

Table 9.1. Cross Actor Common Linkages Between Attribute Distances and Behavior[a]

Variables	1	2	3	4	5	h^2
Wealth	-.40		.50		.54	.78
Totalitarianism	.93					.88
Authoritarianism	.96					.95
Power			.44	.77		.91
Size				.80		.85
Diversity	.48					.53
Density	-.84					.74
Domestic Conflict				.64	-.42	.62
Import Dependency				-.54		.47
Catholic Culture	-.44				.64	.73
Geographic		-.50				.43
Transactions		.76		-.58		.94
Negative Communications			-.83			.72
Alignment[b]		.72				.65
International Organizations	.86					.90
Relative Exports		.76		-.56		.93
Antiforeign Behavior			-.49			.36
Military Violence			-.61			.41
Aid					.57	.35
% total variance	22.5	11.5	11.1	15.0	9.0	

a. These are the orthogonally rotated dimensions of an image factor analysis of the matrix partly given in Table 8.3. The matrix factored comprised all the complete significant equations, where the matrix cells were the correlations between variables and equations. Where an equation lacked a score (for example, since many developing nations do not give aid, aid had to be omitted from the analysis for these nations), a correlation of .00 was inserted.

b. Scale reversed. Higher magnitudes mean closer UN voting distance.

the variance. There is no need to present the equation here. We can simply interpret it as showing that *the weaker, smaller, less stable, and more dependent on imports the object nation relative to the actor, then the less the actor's transactions and relative exports with it.* [2]

The third most general equation accounting for 11.5% of the variance is shown in column 2. This is purely a geographic distance linkage. *The closer the actor is to the object nation, the more transactions, alignment, and relative exports the actor directs toward it.*

The next general equation (column 3) ties wealth and power to conflict. *The poorer and weaker the object nation relative to the actor, the less negative communications, antiforeign behavior, and military violence the actor directs toward it.*

Finally, the last general equation concerns aid. *The poorer, more unstable, and non-Catholic the object nation relative to the actor, the more aid the actor directs toward it.*

In summary and considering only the larger coefficients of the distances in Table 9.1, we find general equations separately linking dyadic conflict and cooperation. For conflict, we find a conflict-wealth-power linkage, where dyadic conflict is purely related to the wealth-power distances.

For cooperation, we find four different general linkages. The most general is an *IO-politics-density linkage,* where comemberships in international organizations is largely a function of democratic political characteristics and relative density. Second, we have a *transactions-alignment-exports-geographic distance linkage,* whereby closer nations have more cooperative interaction. Third, there is a general *transaction-export-power-size linkage,* relating dyadic transactions and relative exports mainly to power and size. Fourth, there is a *wealth-power-conflict linkage,* such that actors direct less conflict towards poorer and weaker nations. Finally, the weakest is an *aid-wealth-stability-Catholic linkage.*

These five general linkages underlie the thirty-nine significant equations for the fourteen actors, 1950-1965. These show that the data contain patterned relationships between attribute distance and important international behaviors. Wealth, power, and politics indeed relate to transactions, conflict, trade, and alignment. Clues to some of these relationships are suggested in Tables 8.3 and 9.1.

Finally, there is one more aspect of Table 9.1 to note: the communalities (h^2). The larger the communalities, the more a distance contributes to the general equations or the more a behavior is explained by the equations. Thus, we find that the distance contributing most to accounting for behavior in these general equations is authoritarianism (.95), next is power (.91), and totalitarianism (.88) is third. By far the dyadic behavior best explained in general is transactions (.94), followed by relative exports (.93), and international organizations (.90). The worst attribute distances (in finding general-across-actors linkages) and behavior are geographic distance and aid. Considering dyadic international behavior as a whole, then, the most productive distances to focus on are political orientation and power. Indeed, these are the elements students of international relations have traditionally focused upon in order to explain international behavior. And those behaviors most tied to these distances are transactions, exports, and international organization comemberships.

NOTES

1. I am indebted to Peter Sybinsky for originating all the analyses reported in this chapter and the text.

2. The relationship between import dependency and dyadic relative exports is not tautological. Nations may have relatively low imports to their total trade (thus being trade independent), while another nation is sending to it high exports relative to that nation's GNP. Indeed, if there is any tautological relationship, it should be the opposite of that shown.

Chapter 10

COMMON ACTORS AND THEIR LINKAGES

The previous chapter has shown what general equations exist among the thirty-nine dyadic linkages for the fourteen nations. This chapter will focus on the similarity between actors in the linkages they manifest. Are China and the USSR similar; what about the USSR and the United States? Is there a similarity in linkages between developed and underdeveloped, nontotalitarian and totalitarian, or powerful and weak actors? The way to determine this is to Q-factor analyze the same complete matrix of canonical coefficients exemplified in Figure 9.1, and used to generate Table 9.1. We factor by rows (the actors and equations) rather than by columns (the distances and behaviors), and the resulting dimensions (when rotated) define the clusters of actors with similar equations.

These results are shown in the upper half of Table 10.1, where the coefficients are the correlations between the actors and each of the common groups (columns). The bottom half of the table presents the general equation (factor scores) manifesting the similarity of actors within each group.

There are seven groups of actors, the first being by far the largest. It includes all fourteen actors except the Netherlands, the Soviet Union, and the United States. Regarding the equation for this group, the signs of the factor scores can be interpreted in the same way as the correlations of Table 9.1. We, therefore, can read the general equation for those actors in this group as: the less the object's power, and the greater his diversity and Catholic culture relative to these actors, the more the actors join international organizations with, and the less their transactions with and relative exports to the object. This is a group of actors which focus their cooperation on international organizations to the

Table 10.1. Groups of Actors Showing Common Linkages Between Distances and Behavior

	Groups[a]						
	1	2	3	4	5	6	7
Actor							
Brazil	.93	.93					
Burma	.69	.76					
China	.69				.92		
Cuba	.71	.75					
Egypt	.73		.74	.91			
India	.79	.84					
Indonesia	.92	.83					
Israel	.88	.93	.92				
Jordan	.75		.60	.84			
Netherlands		.97	.74				
Poland	.63	.77					
USSR					.84		
UK	.75	.97				.90	.70
US		.89				.82	.87
Associated Equation[b]							
wealth		-1.79			1.41		
totalitarianism			1.60		-1.13		1.17
authoritarianism		1.05			-1.35		1.01
power	2.02				1.70		
size						-1.21	
diversity	-1.36					-2.37	1.94
density		-1.32				-1.08	
domestic conflict							-1.51
import dependency			1.51	-1.64			-1.41
Catholic culture	-1.52			1.06			1.08
geographic			1.26	-1.93			
transactions	-1.44	1.73			1.34		
negative communications				1.78	-1.72		-2.00
alignment[c]			2.82	1.82	1.62		
international organizations	1.75	1.80					-1.01
relative exports	-1.40	1.77			1.23		
antiforeign behavior							
military violence				1.66		2.35	
aid							

a. These groups result from a Q-factor analysis of the complete matrix employed to determine the common linkages shown in Table 9.1. Component analysis was used, and the groups shown in the table are the orthogonally rotated components. Only loadings greater than or equal to an absolute .60 are shown.

Note that each actor may appear with high loadings in more than one group, since each nation had more than one canonical equation (more than one row of matrix). If an actor has more than one high loading on the same factor, only the highest is shown.

b. This part of the table gives the factor scores of each indicator on the actor group shown above. Only factor scores greater than or equal to an absolute 1.00 are shown.

In the original computer output some actors had negative loadings on the group factor. This only indicated that their equations had all the signs reversed from those for the positive loading actors. These negative loadings were therefore all made positive, which in no way affects our interpretation of the results.

c. Scale reversed. Higher factor scores mean closer distance in UN voting.

exclusion of exports and transactions *if* the object nation is weak, diverse, and Catholic relative to them. Power here is the main distance. This can be called an *organizational-power linkage group.*

The second group also includes most nations, but now China, Egypt, Jordan, and the USSR are omitted. This group cooperates with other nations mainly dependent on their wealth. Specifically, the wealthier the object nation relative to them, the less authoritarian, and the denser it is, the greater their transactions and relative exports to it and the more they cojoin international organizations with it. This can be called a *cooperation-wealth linkage group.*

The third group involves Egypt, Israel, Jordan, and the Netherlands. To them the relative totalitarianism of the object nation is crucial in their alignments. That is, the less totalitarian and import-dependent the object nation and the further away, the more they are inclined to align with it. This is an *alignment-politics linkage group.*

The remaining groups involve two actors. The first includes China and the USSR, showing that they both transact and align more with, export more to, and send lesser negative communications to relatively poor, weak, totalitarian, and authoritarian nations. *They form a cooperation-wealth-politics-power linkage group.* Another group comprises Egypt and Jordan, who align and have conflict more with object nations the more relatively import-dependent, non-Catholic, and closer geographically they are. Egypt and Jordan constitute a *cooperation-conflict-geographic distance linkage group.* Finally, the two groups involving only the United Kingdom and the United States show that they have two different linkage equations in common. One shows that they have more military violence with the larger, relatively more diverse and denser object nations; the other shows that they direct less negative communications to and join less international organizations with object nations the less totalitarian, authoritarian, diverse, and Catholic they are and the more unstable and import dependent. The United Kingdom and the United States form *violence-conflict-diversity linkage groups.*

In summary, we find that certain actors are similarly affected by distances. The same distances are linked to the same dyadic behaviors in the same ways. There are seven such groups of actors, some showing common linkages between organization memberships and relative power; between cooperation and relative wealth; between alignment and relative politics; between cooperation and relative wealth, politics, and power; between cooperation and conflict and geographic distance; and between violence and conflict and relative diversity.

REFERENCES

Berry, Brian J. L. "An Inductive Approach to the Regionalization of Economic Development." In *Essays on Geography and Economic Development,* edited by Norton Ginsburg. Chicago: University of Chicago Press, 1960.

Cattell, Raymond B. "The Dimensions of Culture Patterns By Factorization of National Characters," Journal of Abnormal and Social Psychology 44 (October 1949): 443-469.

_______. "The Principal Culture Patterns Discoverable in the Syntal Dimensions of Existing Nations," Journal of Social Psychology 32 (November 1950): 215-253.

_______, H. Bruel, and H. P. Hartman. "An Attempt at More Refined Definitions of the Cultural Dimensions of Syntality in Modern Nations," American Sociological Review 17 (August 1952): 408-421.

Finer, S. F. *Comparative Government.* New York: Basic Books, 1970.

Hotelling, H. "Relations Between Two Sets of Variates," Biometrika, 28 (1936): 321-377.

Phillips, Warren R. "Dynamic Patterns of International Conflict." Ph.D. dissertation and Research Report No. 33. Honolulu: Dimensionality of Nations Project, University of Hawaii, 1969. Mimeographed.

Rummel, R. J. "Understanding Factor Analysis," Journal of Conflict Resolution, 11 (December 1967): 444-480.

_______. "International Pattern and Nation Profile Delineation." In *Computers and the Policy-Making Community,* edited by Davis B. Bobrow and Judah L. Schwartz. Englewood Cliffs, N.J.: Prentice-Hall, 1968.

_______. "Indicators of Cross-National and International Patterns," American Political Science Review 62 (March 1969): 127-147.

_______. *Applied Factor Analysis.* Evanston, Ill.: Northwestern University Press, 1970.

_______. *The Dimensions of Nations.* Beverly Hills, Calif.: Sage Publications, 1972.

_______. *The Dynamic Psychological Field.* Volume 1 in understanding conflict and war. New York: Halsted Press (a Sage Publications book), 1975.

_______. *Field Theory Evolving.* Beverly Hills, Calif.: Sage Publications, 1976,

Russett, Bruce M. *International Regions and the International System: A Study in Political Ecology.* Chicago: Rand McNally, 1967.

Wall, Charles, and R. J. Rummel. "Estimating Missing Data." Research Report No. 20. Honolulu: Dimensionality of Nations Project, University of Hawaii, 1969. Mimeographed.

APPENDICES

Appendix I

ATTRIBUTE VARIABLES: DEFINITIONS, UNITS, AND PRINCIPAL SOURCES

The following pages provide the necessary information for understanding the attribute variable data presented in Appendix II.

The *Set Numbers* (20-34) were used to facilitate the administrative organization of the DON project's data collection. Initially there were seven variables per data set, but due to unavailability or unreliability of data, some variables were omitted prior to analysis. In addition, with the exception of Set 20 (the first set), all variables are footnoted by set number. The footnotes are included at the end of each data set listing in Appendix II, along with a table of mean and standard deviation information.

The *Variable Numbers* (1-90) are consistent throughout all of the analyses presented in this book. In Appendix II, the variable numbers appear at the top of each column of data, and are also included in the mean and standard deviation tables.

The rest of the information contained in this appendix includes: the names of the attribute variables; the abbreviation codes used to identify the variables in subsequent analyses; the definitions of the attributes; the units for which the raw data are given in the tables; and the primary source(s) for each variable.

SET 20 (VARIABLES 1-7)

1 Telephones per capita (TEL-PC)

Data on "the number of public and private telephones in use, which can be connected to a central exchange" are in units representing the number of telephones for every ten thousand people in the nation (i.e., the datum times 10^{-4} is the number of telephones per person for each nation). *Statistical Yearbook,* UN.

2 Percentage of Population Engaged in Agricultural Production (%A-POP)

Agricultural population is defined as "all persons who depend upon agriculture for a livelihood, that is to say, persons actively engaged in agriculture and their nonworking dependents." *Yearbook of Food and Agricultural Statistics:* "Production."

3 Energy Consumption per capita (ENC-PC)

Energy includes solid and liquid fuels, natural and imported gas, hydro and imported electricity, and nuclear. Data are expressed in kilograms of coal equivalent energy per capita. *Statistical Yearbook,* UN; and *World Energy Supplies,* UN.

4 Percentage of Illiterates in Population, 10 Years of Age or Older (ILLITE)

Literacy is defined as "the ability to read and write." For some countries, however, literacy includes those who can read *or* write. *Demographic Yearbook,* UN.

5 Gross National Product per capita (GNP-PC)

Gross national product is defined as the "total value of goods and services produced in a country in a year's time." Data are given in US dollars. *The Role of Foreign Aid in the Development of Other Countries;* Norton Ginsburg (ed.), *Atlas of Economic Development.*

6 Energy Production Times Population (EPXPOP)

Energy production includes the primary sources of energy—coal and lignite, crude petroleum, natural gas, hydro-electricity, and nuclear. This measure has been suggested as a measure of the military strength of a nation in Quincy Wright's *The Study of International Relations* (1955: 599). Each datum is the product of (energy production standardized plus 20) times (population standardized plus 20) times 10^{-1}. *Statistical Yearbook,* UN.

7 National Income (NI)

National income is defined as "the sum of the incomes accruing within a year to the factors of production supplied by the normal residents of a country, before deduction of direct taxation, and equals the sum of compensation of employees, income from unincorporated enterprises, rent, interest and dividends accruing to households, savings of corporations, direct taxes on corporations and general government income." National incomes were converted to US dollars using exchange rate data. Because many countries give data on several kinds of exchange rates, if available, only the *free rate* (a rate that rises or falls to some extent in response to private purchases and sales) was used. If such data were not available, the following rates, in decreasing order of desirability, were used: selling or import rates, buying or export rates or the official rate. Data are in units of one hundred million US dollars. *Statistical Yearbook,* UN.

SET 21 (VARIABLES 8-14)

8 Population (POPULA)

Both the actual data and the estimates are, insofar as possible, "modified present-in-area counts. This means that they include data for jungle tribes, aborigines, nomadic peoples, displaced persons, and refugees, as well as national armed forces and diplomatic personnel stationed outside the territory, and that they exclude alien armed forces, alien diplomatic personnel, and enemy prisoners of war stationed inside the country." Data are in units of 10,000 persons. *Demographic Yearbook,* UN.

9 Percent of Contribution to UN's Total Assessment (%CT–UN)

The assessment of each nation divided by the total UN assessment for all member nations. A datum times 10^{-2} constitutes a percentage.[1] *Statesman's Yearbook.*

10 Defense Expenditure (DEFEXP)

Includes the total current and capital outlays found under the defense classification in the national account tables of the primary source. Because data are given in domestic currencies, exchange rates were used to convert them to US dollars. The same procedures used in calculating national incomes (variable 7) were followed. Data are in units of one million US dollars. *Statistical Yearbook,* UN; *SIPRI Yearbook of World Armaments and Disarmament; World Military Expenditures,* US/ACDA.

11 Percentage of English Titles Translated (E/TRSL)

The number of English book titles (for all nonperiodical publications) translated, divided by all foreign titles translated in each nation for each year. A datum times 10^{-1} constitutes a percentage. *Statistical Yearbook,* UN.

12 Bloc Membership (BLOC)

A rating scale, where 0 = Eastern bloc, 1 = neutral bloc, 2 = Western bloc. Eastern and Western bloc memberships are determined by the military treaties or alliances with the Soviet Union or the United States, respectively. The neutral bloc, a residual category, consists of those nations with no military treaties or alliances with either bloc leader. *Statesman's Yearbook;* and T. N. Dupuy, *The Almanac of World Military Power.*

13 Ratio of US Aid Received, to Soviet and US Aid Received (US/AID)

The total US aid received by a nation for any given year is divided by the total Soviet and US aid a nation received for the same year. To avoid undefined cases when the denominator is zero, one million is added to both the US and the Soviet aid. A datum times 10^{-4} constitutes a ratio.[2] *New York Times* (March 22, 1959); *The Foreign Assistance Program* Annual Report to the US Congress.

14 Freedom of Political Opposition (TOTALI)

A rating scale, where 0 = political opposition not permitted (groups are not allowed to organize for political action), 1 = restricted political opposition allowed (groups are permitted to organize in politics, but their oppositional role is limited and they may not campaign for control of the government), 2 = political opposition mostly unrestricted (groups can organize for political action and they may campaign for control of the government). *Statesman's Yearbook; The Worldmark Encyclopedia of the Nations;* and *The Political Handbook and Atlas of the World.*

SET 22 (VARIABLES 15-21)

15 IFC and IBRD Subscriptions per GNP^2 per capita (IFC/GNP)

The numerator represents the subscriptions of member nations to the International Finance Corporation and the International Bank of Reconstruction and Development. The denominator, GNP^2 per capita, is intended to measure the economic resources of a nation, its need for economic aid or its ability to give aid to other nations. Gross domestic product (excludes incomes received from abroad) data are used in place of GNP for some nations. These economic resources are believed to be best indexed by an exponential rather than a linear function of GNP. Data are in units of ten million. *International Finance Corporation Annual Report; International Bank of Reconstruction and Development* Annual Report; *Demographic Yearbook,* UN; *Statistical Yearbook,* UN.

16 Threats (THREAT)

A frequency count of the number of publicly reported threats made by a nation in one year toward any other nation in the international system. A threat is any official diplomatic communication or governmental statement asserting that if a particular country does or does not do a particular thing it will incur negative sanctions. *New York Times; The New International Yearbook; Keesing's Contemporary Archives; Facts on File; Britannica Book of the Year.*

17 Accusations (ACCUSA)

A frequency count of the number of publicly reported accusations made by a nation in one year toward any other nation in the international system. An accusation is any official diplomatic or governmental statement involving charges and allegations of a derogatory nature against another country. Same sources as variable 16.

18 Number of Citizens Killed in Foreign Violence (F-KILL)

The total number of deaths resulting directly from any violent interchange between a nation and all other nations during each year for which data was collected. Same sources as variable 16.

19 Presence or Absence of Military Action (MILACT)

A dichotomous scale with 0 = no military action and 1 = military action. Military action is defined as any military clash involving gunfire between countries, but excludes any actions classified as war. War is defined as any military clash in which more than .02% of a nation's population are militarily involved. Same sources as variable 16.

20 Protests (PROTST)

A frequency count of the number of publicly reported protests made by each nation, in one year, toward other nations in the international system. A protest is any official diplomatic communication or governmental statement that complains about or objects to the policies of another country. Same sources as variable 16.

21 Number of Citizens Killed in Domestic Violence (D-KILL)

The total number of deaths that are a direct consequence of any domestic intergroup violence in the nature of strikes, riots, coups, banditry, etc. This excludes murders, executions, and suicides. Where only casualty figures were given, the number killed was assumed to be 20% of that figure. Where more than one figure for a particular incident, or a series of incidents, was given, the median value was taken. Same sources as variable 16.

SET 23 (VARIABLES 22-28)

22 General Strikes (STRIKE)

A frequency count of the number of publicly reported general strikes that take place within each nation for each year. A general strike is one in which 1000 or more industrial or service workers and more than one employer are involved. It is aimed at national government policies or authority. General strikes *do not* include those whose nature is to force government or private industry to grant wage or working concessions. Same sources as variable 16.

23 Riots (RIOTS)

A frequency count of the number of publicly reported riots that take place within each nation for each year. A riot is any violent demonstration or clash of more than 100 citizens involving the use of physical force. Same sources as variable 16.

24 Purges (PURGES)

A frequency count of the number of publicly reported purges that take place within each nation for each year. A purge is any systematic jailing or execution of elite within the regime or the opposition. If elimination of the opposition continues over a period of time without a relaxation of more than three months, then it is considered as one purge. Same sources as variable 16.

25 Demonstrations (DEMONS)

A frequency count of the number of publicly reported demonstrations that take place within each nation for each year. A demonstration is any peaceful, public gathering of at least 100 people for the primary purpose of displaying or voicing their opposition to government policies or authority, including those demonstrations of a strictly antiforeign nature. These are discrete events limited on one day and to a particular group of people. Same sources as variable 16.

26 Percentage of Roman Catholics in Population (%CATH)

A percentage calculation based on the recorded number of Roman Catholics in each nation's population. Where the percentage turned out to be less than one percent, a zero percentage was recorded for that particular country.

Population figures were taken from variable 8. A datum times 10^{-1} constitutes a percentage. *Catholic Encyclopedia,* Supplement II; *Demographic Yearbook,* UN; *National Catholic Almanac; Worldmark Encyclopedia of the Nations.*

27 Air Distance from the US (US-DIS)

The shortest distance between national borders as directly measured from a 24-inch globe. A datum times 10^{-3} gives a distance in inches; one inch is equal to 330 miles.

28 Percentage of Membership in Medical NGO's (MED/NGO)

The number of medical international nongovernmental organizations to which each nation is a member, divided by its total NGO membership. A datum times 10^{-2} constitutes a percentage. *Yearbook of International Organizations.*

SET 24 (VARIABLES 29-35)

29 Diplomats Expelled or Recalled (ER-AMB)

The number of publicly reported expulsions or recalls of its diplomatic personnel each nation has had for each year. Diplomatic personnel refers to ambassadors or lesser officials serving as official representatives of a nation at foreign embassies or other diplomatic legations. Same sources as variable 16.

30 Ratio of Divorces to Marriages (DIV-MR)

The number of divorces per 10,000 marriages for each nation for each year. "A divorce is a final legal dissolution of a marriage . . . by a judicial decree which confers on the parties the right of civil and/or religious remarriage." *Demographic Yearbook,* UN.

31 Density (DENSITY)

The number of people per square kilometer of national land area. National land area refers to "the total area of the specific geographical units, including inland water as well as such uninhabited or uninhabitable stretches of land as may lie within their mainland boundaries." *Demographic Yearbook,* UN.

32 Percentage of Arable Land Area (%ARABL)

Arable land refers to "land planted to crops . . . land temporarily fallow, temporary meadows for mowing or pasture, garden land, and area under fruit trees, vines, fruitbearing shrubs, and rubber plantations." For total land area, see variable 33. A datum times 10^{-1} constitutes a percentage. *Yearbook of Food and Agricultural Statistics:* "Production," FAO; *Demographic Yearbook,* UN.

33 National Land Area (AREA)

Refers to "the total area of the specific geographical units, including inland water as well as such uninhabited or uninhabitable stretches of land as may lie within their mainland boundaries." Data are presented in thousands of square kilometers. Same sources as variable 32.

34 Roads to National Land Area (RDS-KM)

The total length in kilometers of all a nation's usable roads, divided by the total national land area; see variable 33. Data are expressed in units of thousands of kilometers per square kilometer. Norton Ginsburg (ed.) *Atlas of Economic Development;* S. H. Steinberg (ed.) *The Statesman's Yearbook;* Moody's *Governments and Municipalities.*

35 Railroads to National Land Area (RRS-KM)

The total length in kilometers of all railroads usable in each nation, divided by the total national land area; see variable 33. Railroads include all double track without discriminating the width of gauge. Data are expressed in units of ten thousand kilometers per square kilometer. Same sources as variable 34.

SET 25 (VARIABLES 36-42)

36 Religious Groups (RELGRP)

The number of religions in each nation with membership exceeding one percent of the total population. Christianity is divided into Protestant and Catholic, but otherwise divisions are between the major religions (Islam, Hindu, Buddhist, etc.) reported by each country. *Demographic Yearbook,* UN.

37 Ratio of Immigrants to Migrants (IM/I+E)

Immigrants to a country are newly arrived aliens intending to remain for a period exceeding one year. Migrants include immigrants and emigrants. Emigrants are nationals leaving their country with the intention of staying abroad for a period exceeding one year. A datum times 10^{-2} constitutes a percentage. *Demographic Yearbook,* UN; *Encyclopaedia Britannica World Atlas; The Worldmark Encyclopedia of the Nations;* Yale Political Data Program.

38 Average Yearly Rainfall (RAIN)

The mean of monthly recorded rainfall for each year, which in turn is averaged across all reporting stations within each nation. Data are given in millimeters. *World Weather Records;* Rand McNally *World Atlas.*

39 Percentage Population of the Largest Religious Group (RGRP/P)

For the definition of religious groups, see variable 36. Population data were taken from the same census as that for the religions. Data are given as percentages. *Demographic Yearbook,* UN; *The Worldmark Encyclopedia of the Nations.*

40 Percentage of Dwellings with Running Water (%D-WTR)

A dwelling is "a room or suite of rooms . . . in a permanent building . . . which . . . is intended for private habitation and is not . . . used wholly for other purposes. It should have a separate access to a street or to a common space within the building." Running water refers to water piped in from the outside. A datum times 10^{-1} constitutes a percentage. *Statistical Yearbook,* UN.

41 Percentage of Foreign College Students (FST/ST)

The total number of foreign college students divided by all college students for the same year. A datum times 10^{-1} constitutes a percentage. *Basic Facts and Figures,* UNESCO.

42 Neutral Bloc Membership (NEUTRL)

A dichotomous scale, where 0 = neutral bloc member, 1 = nonneutral bloc member. Neutral bloc nations have no military treaties or alliances with either the United States or the Soviet Union. T. N. Dupuy, *The Almanac of World Military Power; Statesman's Yearbook; Treaties and Alliances of the World.*

SET 26 (VARIABLES 43-48)

43 Nation Age (NATAGE)

A rating based on the date at which a nation became a politically recognizable unit, according to the following scale:

0 = B.C.
1 = 1 - 1499 A.D.
2 = 1500 - 1799 A.D.
3 = 1800 - 1899 A.D.
4 = 1900 - 1945 A.D.
5 = 1946 - 1965 A.D.

A political unit is defined as having an internationally recognized border and some form of central administration. Thus, independence is a sufficient, but not a necessary condition for a political unit. For example, Pakistan became a politically recognizable unit as of her independence in 1948, but India, although gaining independence at the same time, has been a politically recognizable unit for centuries. *An Encyclopedia of World History; Statesman's Yearbook; The Worldmark Encyclopedia of the Nations.*

44 Percentage of Religious Titles Published (REL/TI)

The number of religious book titles published in each nation for each year, divided by the total number of book titles published for the same year. Book titles "cover all nonperiodical publications, including pamphlets, first editions of originals and new translations, re-editions and the more important government reports." A datum times 10^{-2} constitutes a percentage. *Statistical Yearbook,* UN.

45 Emigrants to Population (EMG/POP)

Nationals leaving their country with the intention of staying abroad for a period exceeding one year. A datum times 10^{-3} constitutes a percentage. *Demographic Yearbook,* UN; *Encyclopaedia Britannica World Atlas; The Worldmark Encyclopedia of the Nations;* Bouscaren, *International Migrations Since 1945* (New York: Praeger, 1963).

46 Seaborne Goods to GNP (SG/GNP)

Seaborne goods are the "weight of goods (including packing) in external trade loaded onto and unloaded from seagoing vessels of all flags at the ports of the country in question." For GNP data, see variable 5. A datum times 10^{-5} constitutes the ratio. Norton Ginsburg (ed.) *Atlas of Economic Development; Statistical Yearbook,* UN.

47 Percentage of Membership in Legal NGOs (LAW/NG)

The total number of legal international nongovernmental organizations which a nation belongs to, divided by the total number of NGOs of which that nation is a member. A datum times 10^{-2} constitutes a percentage. *Yearbook of International Organizations.*

48 Percentage of Unemployed (%UNEMP)

The number of unemployed, divided by the total economically active population. A datum times 10^{-2} constitutes a percentage. *Statistical Yearbook,* UN; *The Worldmark Encyclopedia of the Nations; Yearbook of Labor Statistics.*

SET 27 (VARIABLES 49-55)

49 Leading Export to Total Exports (EX/EPT)

The largest SITC (Standard International Trade Classification) category export, or the largest commodity export not identified by SITC label, divided by total exports. A datum times 10^{-2} constitutes a percentage. *Yearbook of International Trade Statistics; Worldmark Encyclopedia of the Nations.*

50 Language Groups (LANGRP)

The total number of language groups in each nation with a membership exceeding at least one percent of the total population. *Demographic Yearbook,* UN; *The Worldmark Encyclopedia of the Nations.*

51 Percentage Population of the Largest Language Group (LGRP/P)

The membership of the largest language group in a nation divided by the nation's total population. A datum times 10^{-1} constitutes a percentage. Same sources as variable 50.

52 Ethnic Groups (ETHGRP)

The total number of ethnic or racial groups in each nation, with a membership exceeding one percent of the total population. Data are taken as reported by nations, according to what they consider their major ethnic and/or racial divisions. Same sources as variable 50.

53 Economic Aid Received (AIDRVD)

Data include the amount committed in grants or long-term loans, "in cash and in kind, including with the latter category the provision of services as well as commodities." Long-term loans are, "those for which there is a schedule of repayments extending beyond a period of five years from the date the loan becomes effective. Grants and loans specifically linked to the defense of the recipient country, such as a transfer of military equipment, direct military expenditures and financial contributions for the support of military forces are excluded." Data are given in units of one hundred thousand US dollars. *Geographical Distribution of Financial Flows to Less Developed Countries,* OECD.

54 Technical Assistance Received (TECRVD)

Technical assistance includes all domestic technical assistance and relief projects. Data are given in units of thousands of US dollars. *United Nations Assistance Committee Report of the Technical Assistance Board.*

55 Percentage of Government Expenditures on Education (%E-GVT)

The total amount of governmental education expenditures, divided by the total amount of governmental expenditures for the same year. A datum times 10^{-2} constitutes a percentage. *Statistical Yearbook,* UN.

SET 28 (VARIABLES 56-58)

56 Percentage of Female Workers (FM/WKS)

The number of female workers in a nation, divided by the total number of economically active workers. Economically active workers "consist of all persons who are, or who seek to be, engaged in producing goods and services; whether employed or unemployed at the time of the census inquiry." A datum times 10^{-2} constitutes a percentage. *Demographic Yearbook,* UN; *The Worldmark Encyclopedia of the Nations; Yearbook of Labor Statistics.*

57 Exports to GNP (EXP/GNP)

The total amount of exports (f.o.b.) divided by the gross national product. For GNP data, see variable 5, A datum times 10^{-2} constitutes a percentage. Norton Ginsburg (ed.) *Atlas of Economic Development; Statistical Yearbook,* UN.

58 Percentage of Foreign Mail Sent (FMST/FM)

The amount of foreign mail *sent* out of a nation divided by the total foreign mail *sent* and *received* in the same year. Mail includes "letters (air mail, ordinary mail and registered), postcards, printed matter, business papers, small merchandise samples, small packets, and phonopost packets. It includes all mail carried without charge, but excludes ordinary packages with a declared value." *Statistical Yearbook,* UN.

SET 29 (VARIABLES 59-64)

59 Imports to Total Trade (IP/TRD)

Total trade includes imports (c.i.f.) and exports (f.o.b.). Data for most countries exclude goods imported into the customs area and re-exported without being cleared for domestic consumption. Goods passing through a country only for the purposes of transport are excluded from all figures. A datum times 10^{-2} constitutes a percentage. *Statistical Yearbook,* UN.

60 Caloric Sufficiency per capita (CAL-PC)

The amount of calories consumed per capita minus the amount of calories required is divided by the amount of calories required. Calorie requirements are calculated by the UN on the basis of climate, work load, and average body build. A datum times 10^{-2} constitutes a percentage. *Report on the World Social Situation,* UN.

61 Protein to Calorie Consumption (PR/CAL)

Grams of proteins, per capita, divided by calories, per capita. The caloric data are for foodstuffs, excluding alcoholic beverages. A datum times 10^{-2} constitutes a percentage. *Statistical Yearbook,* UN; Norton Ginsburg (ed.) *Atlas of Economic Development; Encyclopaedia Britannica World Atlas.*

62 Percentage of Russian Titles Translated (R/TRSL)

The number of Russian book titles translated divided by the total number of foreign book titles translated. Book titles, "cover all nonperiodical publications, including pamphlets, first editions of originals and new translations, re-editions and the more important government reports." A datum times 10^{-2} constitutes a percentage. *Statistical Yearbook,* UN.

63 Percentage of Military Personnel (MIL/POP)

Military personnel divided by population. Personnel data exclude civilians employed by the armed forces. A datum times 10^{-2} constitutes a percentage. *Statesman's Yearbook; The Worldmark Encyclopedia of the Nations.*

64 Balance of Investments to Gold Stock (BOI/GO)

The balance of investments is the average annual income from investments in other nations, minus payments on foreign domestic investments. Information on gold stocks were averaged for "liquid holdings" over a three-year period around the data year. Nations which had zero gold stock during this period were given one million in the denominator to avoid an indeterminate ratio. *International Financial Statistics.*

SET 30 (VARIABLES 65-70)

65 Number of Political Parties (PARTYS)

The total number of political parties within each nation having a membership of more than one percent of the total population. *Political Handbook and Atlas of the World.*

66 Percentage of Membership in Artistic and Cultural NGOs (ART/NGO)

The number of all artistic and cultural international nongovernmental organizations to which each nation is a member, divided by the total number of all NGOs for the same nation for the same year. A datum times 10^{-2} constitutes a percentage. *Yearbook of International Organizations.*

67 Percentage of Communist Party Membership (COM/POP)

The reported communist party membership for each nation, divided by the total population of the same nation (see variable 8). A datum times 10^{-3} constitutes a percentage. US State Department, *World Strength of the Communist Party Organizations; Demographic Yearbook,* UN.

68 Government Expenditures to GNP (GVT/GNP)

Government expenditures refer to the budgeted current and capital outlays of the national government. Redemption of debt is excluded, as are certain capital transfers. Grants to foreign governments are included. For gross national product data see variable 5. A datum times 10^{-2} constitutes a percentage. Norton Ginsburg (ed.) *Atlas of Economic Development; Statistical Yearbook,* UN.

69 Monarchy (MONARC)

A country is considered a monarchy if heredity is the primary means of succession to the chief of state and/or the chief executive position. No distinction is made between constitutional and absolute monarchies. Rating scale: 0 = nonmonarchy; 1 = monarchy. *Statesman's Yearbook; The Worldmark Encyclopedia of the Nations.*

70 Primary School Pupils to Primary School Teachers (PUP/PT)

The total number of pupils in primary school divided by the total number of primary school teachers. A datum times 10^{-2} constitutes a ratio. *Basic Facts and Figures,* UNESCO; Arthur S. Banks, *Cross-Polity Time-Series Data; Report on the World Social Situation,* UN.

SET 31 (VARIABLES 71-77)

71 Legality of Governmental Change (LAWTRA)

This dichotomous rating scale is based on the legality of the change between the previous and the present government, where 0 = present government came into being through nonlegal means (e.g., illegal elections, revolutions), or if there has been only one government since independence, it came into being illegally; 1 = present government came into being through legal means. Government refers to the executive head of government. Legality refers to the constitutional provisions for transferring power, or, in the absence of a constitution, the traditional practice of a country (e.g., hereditary transference of power). *The Worldmark Encyclopedia of the Nations; Statesman's Yearbook; Political Handbook and Atlas of the World; Britannica Book of the Year.*

72 Legitimacy of Present Government (LEGIT)

Government refers to the executive head of government. A dichotomous rating scale, where 0 = present government came into being through means other than revolution; 1 = present government came into being through revolution. Revolution refers to any illegal or forced change in the top governmental elite, any attempt at such a change, or any successful or unsuccessful armed rebellion whose aim is independence from the central government. Same sources as variable 71.

73 Percentage population of the Largest Ethnic Group (EGRP/P)

The population of the largest ethnic or racial group in a nation, divided by the total population. A datum times 10^{-1} constitutes a percentage. *Demographic Yearbook,* UN; *The Worldmark Encyclopedia of the Nations.*

74 Assassinations (ASSASS)

The number of publicly reported, politically motivated murders or attempted murders of high government officials or politicians. Among high government officials are included the governors of states or provinces, the mayors of large cities, members of the cabinet, and the members of the national legislature. Among politicians are included members of the inner core of the ruling party or group, and leaders of the opposition. Same sources as variable 16.

75 Major Government Crises (GVTCRS)

The number of publicly recorded rapidly developing situations (excluding revolution) which threaten to bring the immediate downfall of the present government. A vote of no confidence by a parliamentary majority or the forced resignation or impeachment of top officials are also considered major government crises. A new major government crisis is not counted unless at least three months of stability have intervened since the previous crisis. Same sources as variable 16.

76 Delinquent UN Payments to Total Assessments (UNDE/A)

A percentage calculation based upon the total outstanding delinquencies for each member-nation, divided by that member-nation's total UN assessment for the same year. *Information Annex II; Statesman's Yearbook.*

77 Balance of Payments to Gold Stock (BOP/GO)

Balance of payments refers to the short-term balance of payments, averaged over a three-year period around the data year, divided by "liquid holdings" over the same three-year period. Nations that had zero gold stock during these periods were given one million in the denominator to avoid an indeterminate ratio. As a result, the ratios are biased slightly in the direction of being too high for countries with no gold stock. Data are given in ratios times ten. *International Financial Statistics.*

SET 32 (VARIABLES 78-84)

78 Investment Balance (INVBAL)

The average annual income from investments in other nations minus payments on foreign domestic investments. Data are in units of millions of US dollars. *Balance of Payments Yearbook,* IMF.

79 System Style (STYLE)

A rating scale of the degree to which a nation's population is internally mobilized toward some specific national goals or programs, where 0 = no mobilization, 1 = limited mobilization, 2 = highly mobilized. Banks and Textor, *A Cross-Polity Survey.*

80 Constitutional Status (CONSTI)

A rating scale of the types of national constitutions, with 0 = totalitarian, 1 = authoritarian, and 2 = constitutional. Same source as variable 79.

81 Electoral System (ELECTO)

A rating scale of the degree to which a nation's political parties are allowed to compete in the general election process, where 0 = no competition allowed, 1 = some competition allowed, and 2 = system is openly competitive. Same source as variable 79.

82 Communist Regime (COMMUN)

A dichotomous measure of whether or not a nation's government is classified as communistic, where 0 = yes, and 1 = no. Same data source as variable 79.

83 Political Leadership Style (LEADER)

A rating scale of the degree to which the political leadership of a nation is elitist, with 0 = elitist government, 1 = moderately elitist and 2 = non-elite. Same data source as variable 79.

84 Horizontal Power Distribution (POWDIS)

A rating scale of the degree to which a nation distributes its power within the governmental structure, where 0 = none, or negligible power distribution, 1 = limited power distribution and 2 = significant power distribution. Same source as variable 79.

SET 33 (VARIABLES 85-87)

85 Military Participation (MILPAR)

A rating scale of the degree to which a nation's military organizations participate in the governmental processes of that country, where 0 = military plays a neutral role, 1 = military is supportive of the governmental party in power and 2 = military actively intervenes in the nation's governmental practices. *The Almanac of World Military Power;* Banks and Textor, *A Cross-Polity Survey.*

86 Bureaucracy Style (BUREAU)

A rating scale of the degree to which a nation's bureaucracy is traditional or modern, where 0 = traditional or post colonial, 1 = semi-modern, 2 = modern. Banks and Textor, *A Cross-Polity Survey.*

87 Censorship Score (CENSOR)

A rating scale indicating the degree to which a nation's press is controlled by the national government, where 0 = complete or fairly complete censorship of news, 1 = some censorship of the news, 2 = no censorship, other than the usual laws about libel and the controlling of news of a national security nature. Journalism Quarterly 37 (1960); *New York Times Index; The Worldmark Encyclopedia of the Nations.*

SET 34 (VARIABLES 88-90)

88 Geographic-X (GEOG-X)

See variable 90.

89 Geographic-Y (GEOG-Y)

See variable 90.

90 Geographic-Z (GEOG-Z)

These variables are an index of the geographical location of the capital, or the place containing the administrative seat of the central government, of each nation. The location is represented on the surface of a sphere by utilizing a three-dimensional space. North latitude and East longitude are given the positive sign. The following equations give the formulas used for calculating the three geographic indexes:

$$\text{GEOG-X} = R \cos \phi \cos \theta$$
$$\text{GEOG-Y} = R \cos \phi \sin \theta$$
$$\text{GEOG-Z} = R \sin \phi$$

where ϕ is latitude, θ is longitude, and R = 3,963 miles (the equatorial radius of the Earth). Rand McNally, *The International Atlas.*

NOTES

1. In preparation for computer analysis all data were punched without decimal points; therefore, in Appendices II and IV the decimal point is always immediately to the right of any data entry. For this reason many of the percentage variables carry the unit transformation "times 10^{-2}," or some other negative exponential.

For example, the US's percent contribution to the UN for 1950 is 3979. The unit transformation for variable 9 is "times 10^{-2}," so the actual percentage should be read as: 39.79%.

2. Thus, the unit 5000 (i.e., 1/2) represents nations who received no US or Soviet aid. Figures greater than 5000 indicate a nation's reliance on US aid, and figures less than 5000 indicate nations more dependent on Soviet aid.

Appendix II

ATTRIBUTE DATA, 1950-1965: FOOTNOTES, MEANS, AND STANDARD DEVIATIONS FOR YEARLY AND SUPER-P ANALYSES

1. QUALIFICATIONS

The user of these data is warned that *these data were collected for a particular type of analysis.* In all cases, our tolerance for data error and source reliability was a function of the role these data would play in defining the dimensions of national attributes and behavior, and their linkages, as given in this book.

These dimensions would be relatively insensitive to gross data error, as long as the *patterns* of correlation between variables remained stable.[1] Moreover, minor systematic errors and frequent random errors would have little effect on the dimensions being sought, as long as such errors were not outliers in the data.[2]

The upshot is that *the potential user of these data must gauge whether the confidence he can place in them is adequate to his use.* Although the data are suited to our task, we do not feel they are sufficiently accurate overall for interpretation or use as individual data or for the blanket application of percentages, frequency counts, or other calculations highly sensitive to individual values.[3] They are, we feel, sufficiently accurate for the application of covariance and correlational techniques, including cross-tabulation and cross-plotting. We place the greatest confidence in these data, however, when used in multivariate analyses, such as multiple regression, canonical analysis, discriminant analysis, multidimensional scaling, and factor analysis.

2. DATA COLLECTION AND CHECKING

Some words about our collection and checking of these data may be helpful. Because in sum we were involved in collecting and screening some 300,000 data, only about 45,000 of which are displayed here, and because data publication was not our primary goal, we could not focus on individual data or attributes. We constantly had to assess the time and resources to be invested in searching for the best data and in assuring the accuracy of our recording, against the resources needed to complete our collection and analyses. Accordingly, data were collected and recorded on the following basis.

2.1 Sources

We could not do a thorough comparative analysis of sources for each variable. We selected what we felt to be the best source among those most readily available, which usually turned out to be UN statistical data sources, without investigating whether better specialized studies on the particular data (such as population) were available. Only when data were not easily available were specialized studies sought, and then we often had to fill in data from a variety of such sources. In some instances, we had to accept data from where we could find them, even though known to be approximations.

We usually gave preference to sources listing data for all countries. This not only eased our task but also we felt there would be common definitions and standards underlying the data on a variable.

2.2 Recording

Over the decade that data have been collected for DON, numerous assistants were involved. Most were graduate or undergraduate students, with various tolerances and dependability for such tasks. To help avoid the consequent errors, data were either double collected by different assistants and compared or double-checked against the source. All hand calculations (for example, of density or percentage of the population in agriculture) were done twice, by different assistants.

2.3 Error

One has to collect such data as presented here and prepare them for analyses to appreciate the points at which mistakes can be made. To eliminate as many clerical errors as possible, data were double punched (verified) on computer cards, and then all extremes of greater than two times the standard deviation of a variable were rechecked. Finally, if there was still doubt, sources were compared.

In addition, the results of factor analyzing the data were not accepted automatically. If unreasonable or contra-intuitive results were obtained (as sometimes happened), the data were systematically rechecked and errors eliminated.

2.4 Missing Data

Where data were missing but a particular value was obviously appropriate based on our general knowledge, such an estimate was used (and recorded as an estimate in a footnote). For example, zero was estimated as the figure on US aid to mainland China. Of course, all estimates were not so obvious, and the user will have to judge for himself whether he wishes to accept them in specific cases. As a rough guide, we felt that our estimates could be off by as much as a half a standard deviation on a variable without seriously influencing our results.[4]

3. DATA AVAILABILITY

The data listed herein have been deposited on computer tape with the University of Michigan International Relations Archive (The Inter-University Consortium for Political Research/Center for Political Studies/International Relations Archive/Ann Arbor, Michigan 48106) and are available from them. Please do not request data tapes from the DON project, because we are not organized for such general dissemination purposes.

4. DATA

The following tables present the data in a time-series format.

As an example of using these data, the first line of data on the first page gives those data on the first seven variables for Afghanistan in 1950; the second line gives the data on the same variables for 1955. Variable numbers are included at the top of each page. At the end of each data set the *mean* and *standard deviation* for each variable for each year and for the super-P with and without missing data regression estimates ($\hat{Y}$) are also printed.

It is important to remember that different attributes have different unit measures. These units are discussed in Appendix 1, and are also included in the tables of means and standard deviations.

With the exception of data set 20, all data are footnoted by data set. Footnotes are given after the data. For all data sets the letter "A" indicates the item of data is an estimate; either as reported in the primary or secondary source, the result of extrapolation of data available from other time points, or as a result of common sense or practical knowledge by the data collector or project director.

Some data sets contain blank columns. These represent variables that were excluded from the final analysis as a result of insufficient or unreliable data.

FORMAT OF DATA

Set	Variables						
20	*1* TEL-PC	*2* %A-POP	*3* ENC-PC	*4* ILLITE	*5* GNP-PC	*6* EPXPOP	*7* NI
21	*8* POPULA	*9* %CT-UN	*10* DEFEXP	*11* E/TRSL	*12* BLOC	*13* US/AID	*14* TOTALI
22	*15* IFC/GNP	*16* THREAT	*17* ACCUS	*18* F-KILL	*19* MILACT	*20* PROTST	*21* D-KILL
23	*22* STRIKE	*23* RIOTS	*24* PURGES	*25* DEMONS	*26* %CATH	*27* US-DIS	*28* MED/NGC
24	*29* ER-AMB	*30* DIV-MR	*31* DNSITY	*32* %ARABL	*33* AREA	*34* RDS-DM	*35* RRS-KM
25	*36* RELGRP	*37* IM/I+E	*38* RAIN	*39* RGRP/P	*40* %D-WTR	*41* FST/ST	*42* NEUTRL
26	*43* NATAGE	*44* REL/TI		*45* EMB/POP	*46* SG/GNP	*47* LAW/NG	*48* %UNEMP
27	*49* EX/EPT	*50* LANGRP	*51* LGRP/P	*52* ETHGRP	*53* AIDRVD	*54* TECRVD	*55* %E-GVT
28			*56* FM/WKS		*57* EP/GNP		*58* FMST/F
29	*59* IP/TRD		*60* CAL-PC	*61* PR/CAL	*62* R/TRSL	*63* MIL/PP	*64* BOT/GO
30	*65* PARTYS	*66* ART/NGO	*67* COM/POP	*68* GVT-PC	*69* MONARC		*70* PUP-PT
31	*71* LAWTRA	*72* LEGIT	*73* EGRP/P	*74* ASSASS	*75* GVTCRS	*76* UNDE/C	*77* BOP/GO
32	*78* INVBAL	*79* STYLE	*80* CONSTI	*81* ELECTO	*82* COMMUN	*83* LEADER	*84* POWDIS
33	*85* MILPAR	*86* BUREAU				*87* CENSOR	
34	*88* GEOG-X	*89* GEOG-Y	*90* GEOG-Z				

		1	2	3	4	5	6	7	
1	20	4A	75A	8	97A	50A	3912	5A	1950
1	20	5	75A	5	97F	58	3905	6A	1955
1	20	6A	75D	15	95H	52	3903	6C	1960
1	20	6A	85N	20	97L	80	3918	11A	1963
1	20	6C	87	27	93A	83	3918	10	1965
2	20	8A	70A	160A	54B		3883A		1950
2	20	10	70A	160	28F		3879		1955
2	20	34	69D	305	28A	175G	3875	2A	1960
2	20	60	60A	323	29		3886		1963
2	20	71	59	321	24	380	3887		1965
106	20	117	58	319	88A	221	3950	21	1965
3	20	464	20	762	13	331	3936	51	1950
3	20	590	20	983	13	377	3932	35	1955
3	20	627	19	1088	9G	459	3934	76	1960
3	20	657	20AD	1137	6	614	3960	76	1963
3	20	664	20A	1330	9A	851	3962		1965
4	20	1414	12	3138	2	952	3932	69	1950
4	20	1725	12	3546	2F	1185	3928	97	1955
4	20	2100B	11G	3918	1C	1543B	3928	129	1960
4	20	2337	11G	4196	2L	1679	3945	155	1963
4	20	2468	10	4565	1AJ	1993	3952	184	1965
5	20	727	22	1861	2F	531	3907	31	1955
5	20	994	23	2155	2C	878	3897	48	1960
5	20	1208	20	2541	2L	1041	3910	59	1963
5	20	1390	14A	2631	1AJ	1281	3912	70	1965
6	20	795	10	3623	3	775	3944	55	1950
6	20	990	10	4228	3	1049	3938	74	1955
6	20	1243	7G	3958	1C	1259	3918	92	1960
6	20	1468	10B	4647	4L	1360	3928	114	1963
6	20	1647	6	4894	1AJ	1776	3926	136	1965
7	20	26A	66A	132A	69	66	3889A		1950
7	20	36	66B	145	69	62	3885		1955
7	20	70A	65D	152	69H	110C	3879	3	1960
7	20	53A	67B	161	68L	154	3890	4C	1963
7	20	58C	60	185	68	140	3893	5	1965
8	20	104	61A	218	51	258	3897A	115	1950
8	20	138	61F	289	51	191	4023		1955
8	20	146	52G	337	39G	183C	4043	100	1960
8	20	157C	52G	366	53L	196	4079	180D	1963
8	20	163C	56	364	39	238	4087	156	1965
9	20	81A	55A	304A	24B		3903A	1A	1950
9	20	81	55	793	35E	285	3903	8	1955
9	20	308C	64G	1298	13	591A	3899	37A	1960
9	20	279	75B	1960	10	637	3913	49C	1963
9	20	340	57	2573	10K	817	3916	57B	1965
10	20	3A	80A	22A	30B	43	3930	6	1950
10	20	4	80B	34	58E	51	3924	9	1955
10	20	6A	70	53	40H	67	3922	12	1960
10	20	9	80B	48	43L	72	3938	12	1963
10	20	8	62	49	40	71	3940	15	1965
113	20	6C	95	99	91	45	3901	1	1965
11	20	6	70	20	83F		3887	3	1955
11	20	6	70D	35	64G	106	3883	5A	1960
11	20	7C	81G	47	83L	127	3895	6C	1963
11	20	8C	77A	49	69	135	3897	7	1965
83	20	8C	80A	60	93L	92	3893		1963
83	20	8AC	84	77	90	128	3895	6	1965
12	20	2124A	20	6703	3	1196	3926	128	1950
12	20	2642	16	5280	5E	1656	3980	207	1955

		1	2	3	4	5	6	7	
12	20	3033	11	5663	2I	2035	4000	275	1960
12	20	3513	10A	6556	3L	2076	4058	302	1963
12	20	3796	9A	7597	1AJ	2454	4075	359	1965
84	20	15	75A	28	98M	90	3884		1963
84	20	22	84	73	93A	89	3887	1	1965
13	20	23		80	36	119	3901	8	1950
13	20	32		87	36	126	3897	11	1955
13	20	37	49G	110	30H	140	3893	12	1960
13	20	39A	53G	114	38L	142	3906	13	1963
13	20	39AC	50	108	25A	118	3909	15	1965
85	20	6	75A	16	95M	40	3889		1963
85	20	9	95	30	95	73	3891	2	1965
14	20	232	38A	757	20B	258	3900	14B	1950
14	20	221	38E	788	27E	177	3897	40	1955
14	20	251	28	839	16G	605	3893	37	1960
14	20	286C	28B	1109	13	483	3909	27	1963
14	20	302	28	1045	16	643	3911	36	1965
15	20	5	85		52A				1950
15	20	5	85	159A	46A	58	5331	335	1955
15	20	5	69A	540B	39A	74F	6065B		1960
15	20	5A	78I	392	35A	62A	5975B	420A	1963
15	20	5	69	461A	32A	107	6054B		1965
16	20	47	50B	384	56A	90A	3903	8	1955
16	20	92	50G	513	40C	148	3899	12	1960
16	20	114C	46B	573	42	169	3915	17	1963
16	20	134	47A	651	22	227	3918	23	1965
17	20	90	53	266A	38B	355	3922A	35	1950
17	20	129	53	416	44E	332	3918	23	1955
17	20	191	46	516	38H	235	3922	30	1960
17	20	220C	46	533	48L	292	3939	39	1963
17	20	246AC	50	527	38	202	3944	44	1965
87	20	86	68	139	80C	150	3883		1963
87	20	95C	65	119	80	143	3885	1	1965
86	20	20A	80	80	85	80	3917	10D	1963
86	20	13AC	70	83	63A	81	3920	10A	1965
18	20	125	55A	250	21	125	3883A	1	1950
18	20	122	55B	210	21	315	3879	3	1955
18	20	137	49G	215	18G	389C	3873	4	1960
18	20	149	51J	251	19A	317	3884	4	1963
18	20	148C	48A	336	16	390	3887	5	1965
19	20	226	44A	485	22B	373	3895	18	1950
19	20	232	44F	645	24E	359	3891	19	1955
19	20	296	42G	847	24H	383	3887		1960
19	20	309	42G	906	23L		3898	42C	1963
19	20	290	34	984	20	419	3901	39B	1965
20	20	312A	25	3023	3	113	3946		1950
20	20	557	25	3885	5E	543	3970		1955
20	20	744	18	4755	2I	1394A	3978	149A	1960
20	20	932	18	5631	3L	1714A	4001	240C	1963
20	20	1054	16A	5643	1AJ	1589	3998	242B	1965
88	20	13C	75A	26	95M	138	3886		1963
88	20	17	84	42	95	70	3889	2	1965
21	20	1677	24	2088	2	742	3893	27	1950
21	20	2014	24	2496	2F	924	3887	34	1955
21	20	2341	18G	2829	0C	1299	3881	48	1960
21	20	2667	25H	3714	2L	1620	3893	59	1963
21	20	2866	14	4097	1AJ	2101	3895	80	1965
22	20	28	46	94	57	189		4A	1950
22	20	43	46	158	57	198	3883	5	1955

		1	2	3	4	5	6	7	
22	20	66	50G	158	57H	234	3879	5	1960
22	20	83C	70B	177	58L	269	3889	7	1963
22	20	86C	59	166	36	254	3891	8	0965
23	20	28	51A	125	44	125	3889	3	1950
23	20	34	51F	135	44	190	3885	5	1955
23	20	67	56G	186	33G	181	3881	7	1960
23	20	92C	70B	176	19	199	3893	7	1963
23	20	83C	57	214	32	218	3895	10	1965
24	20	57A		152	75	127	3940	23	1950
24	20	66		243	75	134	3934	26	1955
24	20	90A	57	290	75H	141	3934	32	1960
24	20	94	62J	298	70	135A	3956	33D	1963
24	20	112AC	56A	306	70	160	3962	47	1965
25	20	38A	64A	108A	58	161	3885	3	1950
25	20	46	64F	105	58	228	3881	4	1955
25	20	66	60G	128	51G	229C	3877	4	1960
25	20	77A	62H	152	31	261	3887	6	1963
25	20	68C	57	134	52	270	3889	7	1965
26	20	1	87A	0	97		3922		1950
26	20	3	87B	6	97F	45	3924	6	1955
26	20	6	90	8	96H	45	3918	7A	1960
26	20	8	90	9	98L	47	3933	9A	1963
26	20	11	89A	13	95	52	3936	12	1965
27	20	814	34	1191	3	422	3895	17	1950
27	20	1089	34	1184	2E	943	3887	33	1955
27	20	1370	32	1650	0C	1113	3881	39	1960
27	20	1606	22B	2070	2L	1195	3893	47	1963
27	20	1813	28A	2711	1AJ	1757	3893	64	1965
28	20	562	25	1991	3	706	4088		1950
28	20	720	25	2166	3	1044	4062	371	1955
28	20	954	18	2419	4I	1322	4056	463	1960
28	20	1115	18	2833	4L	1601	4072	608	1963
28	20	1255	16A	2972	1AJ	1918	4076	745	1965
89	20	65	74	194	59	200	3883		1963
89	20	87	85A	217	88A	283	3887	2	1965
29	20	643	21	4143	2F	295	4000	51A	1955
29	20	802	18D	4660	2C	1239A	3990	168A	1960
29	20	942	21	5324	2A		4012	349C	1963
29	20	1039	20A	5821	1AJ	1610	4006	374E	1965
30	20	794	15	3373	2F	759	4222	319	1955
30	20	1126	13G	3673	2C	1337	4212	551	1960
30	20	1371	8	4128	2A	1652	4241	720	1963
30	20	1549	8A	4404	1AJ	1974	4225	864	1965
90	20	35	58G	99	75H	233		12A	1960
90	20	42	70J	104	78L	226	3898	13A	1963
90	20	44	60	103	78A	285	3901	18	1965
31	20	103	52	214	24	201	3903A	5	1950
31	20	153	52	341	24	251	3895	18	1955
31	20	208	54G	443	18	421	3909	27	1960
31	20	420	47B	551	14	507	3903	33	1963
31	20	594	54	784	18	690	3905	48	1965
32	20	14A	62	143	70	251	3889	4	1950
32	20	34	62	132	70	184	3885	5	1955
32	20	47	65G	170	70H	262C	3879	9	1960
32	20	48A	75B	171	73L	183	3891	7	1963
32	20	63AC	64	203	70	296	3893	12	1965
91	20	12A	91K	102	85A		3889		1963
91	20	17C	85	114	90	73	3891	2	1965
33	20	13	90A	32A	89				1950
33	20	13	90D	36	89	91	3885	1	1955

		1	2	3	4	5	6	7	
33	20	10	83G	38	90H	71	3881	3A	1960
33	20	9C	83G	30	88L	80	3891	3	1963
33	20	9AC	80	46	90	74	3893	3	1965
34	20	22A	76A	146	66	146	3885	2	1950
34	20	45	76F	127	66	120	3881	3	1955
34	20	31	67G	160	53	199C	3875	3	1960
34	20	42C	67G	165	30	206	3886	4	1963
34	20	41C	65	184	55	235	3889	4	1965
35	20	125A		977A	5B	430	3918A	40	1950
35	20	186		1901	5E	386	3922	21	1955
35	20	243	36	2080	3	848A	3916	66A	1960
35	20	501	36	2584	2	696A	3929	100AC	1963
35	20	558	29A	2818	2	1054	3930	145B	1965
36	20	5	70	101	82	56	4926	200	1950
36	20	6	70	111	82	70	4883	209	1955
36	20	10	73G	140	72G	81	4928	296	1960
36	20	15	72B	168	72A	86	5082	321	1963
36	20	18	70	172	76	99A	5133	432	1965
37	20	6A	58A	54	83	205	4101		1950
37	20	9	58C	116	92	129	4097	70	1955
37	20	13	68G	134	57G	69	4121	58A	1960
37	20	15C	80H	111	57A	80	4161	45	1963
37	20	16	67	114	57	81	4172	82	1965
38	20	15	80A	240A	90		3992		1950
38	20	32	80D	159	88F	115	3948		1955
38	20	53A	60	344	83	206C	3998	39	1960
38	20	72A	60	353	80A	216	4048	36	1963
38	20	84C	58A	379	77K	240	4080	54	1965
39	20	35	75	176A	69B		3906	6	1950
39	20	61	75D	265	88F	163	3948	8	1955
39	20	81	48G	531	86G	211C	3958	12	1960
39	20	77A	55B	641	80A	228	3987	14C	1963
39	20	79AC	48	501	80	233	3995	18	1965
40	20	276	49	1111	3	269	3889	11A	1950
40	20	380	49	1291	2F	514	3883	12	1955
40	20	565	35G	1844	1I	654C	3879	15	1960
40	20	680C	35	2232	2L	784	3891	19	1963
40	20	753	32A	2257	1AJ	972	3891	22	1965
41	20	230	18	794	6	1111			1950
41	20	378	18	1127	7		3881	10	1955
41	20	559	13	1243	16G	1213	3875	19	1960
41	20	782	13G	1485	10	1111	3887	20	1963
41	20	1008	12	2227	10	1327	3887	28	1965
42	20	269	44	637	13B	378	4030	138	1950
42	20	455	44	722	23E	441	4006	173	1955
42	20	778	28G	1135	8G	684	4004	253	1960
42	20	999	27G	1564	8A	830	4025	352	1963
42	20	1160	30	1784	7	1121	4026	475	1965
92	20	33A	90H	82	92A	196	3890	5	1963
92	20	44C	81	156	80	251	3893	7	1965
163	20	274C	50A	894	15	497	3891	7	1965
43	20	351	31	740	3F	239	4159	182	1955
43	20	593	30D	1166	2	458	4159	323	1960
43	20	879	25	1531	3L	617	4188	489	1963
43	20	1429	24A	1783	2	852	4185	706	1965
44	20	31		79	83				1950
44	20	70		111	83F	70	3881	1	1955
44	20	141A	35G	191	68G	153	3875	3	1960
44	20	137A	35G	260		199	3885	4A	1963
44	20	136AC	34	314	63A	242	3887	4	1965

		1	2	3	4	5	6	7	
45	20	4A			35				1950
45	20	20A			30E		3899		1955
45	20	44A	44D		27	177E	3907		1960
45	20	64A	44L	392	16A		3919		1963
45	20	97A	50A	450A	23	207	3911		1965
46	20	4	50		33				1950
46	20	20	50	138	30E	84	3930	17	1955
46	20	44	62G	261	15H	66	3934	13	1960
46	20	64C	57	390	16	114	3955	25	1963
46	20	97C	55A	448	15	102	3960	29	1965
80	20	8		7	81				1955
80	20	7		22	85H	60	3875	1C	1960
80	20	4C	95I	39	83L	87	3887	2A	1963
80	20	4C	81	38	85	66	3889	1	1965
47	20	111A	70A	317	52	238	3883	3	1950
47	20	230	70C	464	53F	273	3881	4	1955
47	20	317	50D	520	50H	399	3875	6A	1960
47	20	417A	60B	611	53L	383	3886	4D	1963
47	20	436AC	55	622	14	465	3889	10	1965
48	20	0		0	93		3885		1950
48	20			24	93F	160	3879		1955
48	20		81G	81	92I	175	3873	1	1960
48	20	29A	81G	170	90	170	3883	2C	1963
48	20	28AC	79	280	90	190	3885	2	1965
49	20	63		181	93F	90	3879	1	1955
49	20	70A	72	281	81	162	3875	2A	1960
49	20	80C	80J	286	93L	359	3918	3A	1963
49	20	93C	40	309	68A	641	3969	11	1965
93	20	30	80D	37	66L	90	3895		1963
93	20	30	85	48	65	92	3897	6	1965
94	20	109	81G	241	49	279		15	1960
94	20	206	72	479	23	295	3902	17C	1963
94	20	140C	55A	340	57	307	3905	23	1965
95	20	9		18	95M	53	3891		1963
95	20	11	91A	22	95	51	3893	3	1965
96	20	10C		32	95A	135	3883		1963
96	20	13A	78	95	97A	124	3885	1	1965
50	20	111A		599	43B	183	3976	44	1950
50	20	119		635	54E	183	3976	60	1955
50	20	149	54G	915	33	353C	3992	111	1960
50	20	165	54B	939	20	402	4021	139	1963
50	20	193	52	963	29	455A	4030	176	1965
97	20	111	56G	139	86G	157C		16	1960
97	20	111	69J	143	50	173	3912	18	1963
97	20	107	55	158	88A	191	3914	23	1965
51	20	0A	95A	0A	95B				1950
51	20	0	95D	1A	97F	47	3897		1955
51	20	0	94G	4	95	52	3893	5A	1960
51	20	2A	95K	5	97L	59	3904	6A	1963
51	20	3C	92	10	93A	73	3907	7A	1965
52	20	773	14	1958	3	495	3928	39	1950
52	20	1039	14	2377	2F	707	3920	64	1955
52	20	1405	10	2691	1C	987	3914	93	1960
52	20	1690	10	3199	2L	1159	3927	118	1963
52	20	1914	8A	3442	1AJ	1546	3930	157	1965
53	20	1927	19	2448A	3	1042	3889	17	1950
53	20	2502	19	1882	2F	1264	3883	23	1955
53	20	3143	14G	2029	1I	1532	3879	31	1960
53	20	3551	16H	2052	2L	1720	3891	35	1963
53	20	3897	13	2546	1AJ	1977	3893	45	1965

		1	2	3	4	5	6	7	
54	20	29	70A	95A	62B	95	3883		1950
54	20	30	70F	153	63E	241	3879		1955
54	20	57	60G	189	50G	243	3875	3A	1960
54	20	91A	60G	243	31	301	3885	4	1963
54	20	72C	58	241	50	345	3887	5	1965
98	20	6A	97G	12	60	40	3888		1963
98	20	6	87	0	99	71	3891	3	1965
99	20	11C	70A	32	88L	93	4019	33A	1963
99	20	12C	80	45	68	84	4039	39	1965
55	20	1378	19	4360	3	610	3904	18	1950
55	20	1715	19	2333	2F	962	3889	27	1955
55	20	2022	19	2740	0C	1263	3883	35	1960
55	20	2283	19	3151	2L	1516	3896	43	1963
55	20	2441	17A	3548	1AJ	1909	3899	54	1965
56	20	0A	75A		83				1950
56	20	78	75D		43F		3879		1955
56	20	78			28C	332E	3873		1960
56	20	117C	71N	392	22A		3884		1963
56	20	127C	58		30K	455	3885		1965
57	20	3		37A	81B	73	4089	55	1950
57	20	5		41	86E	55	4078	41	1955
57	20	9	75G	68	81G	68	4084	63A	1960
57	20	11	75G	79	80A	81	4120	71	1963
57	20	13	81A	89	80	107	4130	97	1965
58	20	138	49	250	28	250		2	1950
58	20	216	49	379	28	325	3879	3	1955
58	20	270	46G	493	27G	386B	3873	4	1960
58	20	333C	48	910	17	488	3884	4	1963
58	20	376	43A	1040	22	504	3887	5	1965
59	20	35	56	0	32	84A		2A	1950
59	20	36	56	58	32	128	3881	2	1955
59	20	62	55G	87	26G	156	3875	2	1960
59	20	68C	50H	102	20	193	3886	2	1963
59	20	69	50	148	32	215	3887	4	1965
60	20	56	66A	190	53	119	3907	8	1950
60	20	68	66B	275	58E	138	3903	11	1955
60	20	107	50G	494	39G	204	3899	19A	1960
60	20	115C	58H	562	39A	262	3913	20	1963
60	20	118C	50	549	39	361	3916	25	1965
61	20	10	69	101A	38	166	3934	30	1950
61	20	23	69	116	38	185	3934	35	1955
61	20	46	61G	143	25	158	3934	38	1960
61	20	49C	60A	190	25A	134	3953	37A	1963
61	20	51C	58A	204	28	161	3960	70	1965
62	20	92A	47	2090	6B		4064		1950
62	20	131	47	2622	5A	468	4072	44	1955
62	20	297	38	3097	4	716A	4066	167A	1960
62	20	355	45H	3431	3	644A	4096	115AC	1963
62	20	411	36A	3508	3	911	4100	133AB	1965
63	20	180	42	259	42	165	3907	14A	1950
63	20	293	42	297	42	205	3897	16	1955
63	20	447	42	379	38G	284	3891	21	1960
63	20	537	42	459	27	322	3904	24	1963
63	20	598	39A	500	36	402	3905	33	1965
64	20	85		454A	23B		3940A		1950
64	20	94		1038	23D	312	3952		1955
64	20	225C	67D	1404	1C	493A	3950	71A	1960
64	20	200A	73	1801	8		3973		1963
64	20	249	60	1981	4	809	3976		1965
114	20	3AC	95	0	93A	39	3911	1	1965

		1	2	3	4	5	6	7	
65	20	10	85A	117A	97		3946		1950
65	20	15	85D	184	97F	199	3972	4	1955
65	20	44A	75D	233	90H	167	3979	9C	1960
65	20	41A	85D	279	97L	175	4020	9A	1963
65	20	41AC	46	370	90A	225	4045	18	1965
100	20	72	80A	110	51	200	3889	5A	1963
100	20	72	75	143	93A	195	3891	6	1965
204	20	26A	75G	89	93L	100	3886		1963
204	20	25C	89	84	90	143	3887	3	1965
101	20	9A	90A	21	94A	42	3887		1963
101	20	16C	89	40	95	60	3889	1	1965
66	20	239	48	579	18B	182	3978	35	1950
66	20	371	48	609	24E	255	3966	70	1955
66	20	587	41G	823	13	338	3960	88	1960
66	20	730	38G	988	10	487	3975	107	1963
66	20	877	38	1045	9	690	3976	186	1965
102	20	20	86G	51	85C	95		10	1960
102	20	26C	86J	57	60	110	3911	11	1963
102	20	27C	77A	81	93A	102	3914	13	1965
67	20	2393	24	3196	3	781	3916	52	1950
67	20	3057	24	2743	2F	1170	3899	80	1955
67	20	3525	14G	3491	0C	1649	3893	111	1960
67	20	4018	14G	3975	2L	1977	3905	138	1963
67	20	4382	13	4463	1AJ	2497	3907	171E	1965
68	20	1902	16	1123A	3	977	3900	39	1950
68	20	2440	16	1427	2F	1226	3891	56	1955
68	20	3095	11	1938	1C	1608	3885	73	1960
68	20	3463	11	2548	2L	1924	3898	90	1963
68	20	3797	10A	2672	1AJ	2340	3901	115	1965
69	20	37		124A	72			9A	1950
69	20	90		192	73F	104	3885	5	1955
69	20	109	47G	261	71G	154	3881	6A	1960
69	20	136C	56	289	66A	167	3893	8	1963
69	20	149	56A	344	65	215	3895	8	1965
109	20	19C	75J	46	93L	66	3904	6	1963
109	20	20C	86	51	93A	64	3891	7	1965
70	20	3A	66	22	46	66		12	1950
70	20	5	66	51	46	103	3924	20	1955
70	20	17	82G	62	29	101	3928	23	1960
70	20	19C	82B	84	28A	106	3950	27	1963
70	20	25	78	127	32	125	3956	33	1965
103	20	19	91	34	93L	73	3885		1963
103	20	43	79	61	93A	95	3887	1	1965
216	20	402C	21	3711	20	619	3889	6	1965
104	20	94A	68	166	75H	181B		7	1960
104	20	104	68G	200	74A	185	3891	8C	1963
104	20	115	64	229	70A	215	3893	8	1965
71	20	31	72	258	68B	177	3946	32	1950
71	20	60	72	225	65	270	3940	65	1955
71	20	110	75	246	62G	203	3940	49	1960
71	20	96	65	299	58A	238	3959	58	1963
71	20	113	75	350	56	260	3964	76	1965
72	20	373	22	2110	71	276	3952	53	1950
72	20	438	22	2511	58F	372	3952	44	1955
72	20	588	30	2338	65C	448	3950	63	1960

		1	2	3	4	5	6	7	
72	20	628	44	2464	63A	545	3971	71	1963
72	20	670	29A	3050	58A	600	3978	93	1965
73	20	102	35A	1500A	16	273		135	1950
73	20	145	35A	2205	19E	749	5005	445	1955
73	20	186	35G	2832	2G	1097D	5225	1700A	1960
73	20	289A	35G	3233	1	898	5485	1876	1963
73	20	293A	32	3597	1	1379	5578	2150B	1965
74	20	1073	6A	4415	3	735	4344	302	1950
74	20	1334	6E	4969	2F	998	4305	430	1955
74	20	1563	4G	4907	1I	1372	4228	583	1960
74	20	1723	6M	5093	2L	1552	4250	723	1963
74	20	1951	4	5132	1AJ	1822	4229	805	1965
75	20	2846	13A	7543	3B	1908	6121	2410	1950
75	20	3390	13	7745	3E	2334	6113	3302	1955
75	20	4115	8	8047	2G	2830	6043	4170	1960
75	20	4458	8	8508	2	3048	6299	4750	1963
75	20	4813	6A	9203	1AJ	3520	6335	5684	1965
219	20	25C	91	40	78A	113	3897	6	1965
105	20	4A	91H	9	95M	40	3892		1963
105	20	4	86	21	93A	53	3895	2	1965
76	20	380	19	633	19		3887A		1950
76	20	437	19	657	15	573	3883	10	1955
76	20	557	15	851	10G	480	3877	11	1960
76	20	638	15	829	7	478	3887	11C	1963
76	20	680C	17A	882	9	393	3889	16	1965
77	20	134	40	782	51	681	4040	26	1950
77	20	181	40	2125	51	762	4094	37	1955
77	20	271	31	2623	34G	961B	4127	58	1960
77	20	296	31	2752	17	728	4168	67C	1963
77	20	328	29A	2520	20	869	4173	64	1965
81	20	10A	75A		36		3881		1955
81	20	11A	75A		36G	66A	3907		1960
81	20	14A	75A	39	20		3924	47	1963
81	20	14A	77		35	100	3928		1965
82	20	10	80A	37	50A		3911		1955
82	20	11	80D	52	10C	85	3903	10	1960
82	20	14C	90	61	10C	114	3918	13	1963
82	20	14	85	143	55A	118	3920	17	1965
78	20	0A		0A	97				1950
78	20	0		0	97F		3887		1955
78	20	0		6	75H	90	3883	2A	1960
78	20	2C	75A	7	98L	90	3893	6	1963
78	20	16C	92	20	90	98	3895		1965
79	20	53A	73	415	25		3932	20A	1950
79	20	91	73	587	25	296	3930	47	1955
79	20	141	50	875	21	231	3928	34A	1960
79	20	169	50	1025	15	303	3947	56	1963
79	20	213	47A	1194	15	451	3950	60B	1965

		8	9	10	11	12	13	14	
1	21	1200	5			1	8649	0	1950
1	21	1200	8			1	2143	0	1955
1	21	1380A	6			1	4947	0	1960
1	21	1538	5	13S		1	4200	0E	1963
1	21	1505A	5	23		1	5789K	1	1965
2	21	120	0			0	5000	0	1950
2	21	138				0	2941	0	1955
2	21	161	4		85	0	675	0	1960

		8	9	10	11	12	13	14	
2	21	176	4	56R	55	0		0E	1963
2	21	187	4	70	678	0	5000	0	1965
106	21	1192A	10	100	0I	1	9418	1	1965
3	21	1720	185	163AC	492	2	9635	1	1950
3	21	1912	132	231	549	2	9844	1	1955
3	21	2067	111	285	453	2	N	2	1960
3	21	2169	101	296	465	2		2Z	1963
3	21	2255A	92	412	514	2	3962	2	1965
4	21	819	197	130C	J	2	5652	2A	1950
4	21	920	180	470	J	2	5000	2	1955
4	21	1031	179	419	J	2	7142	2	1960
4	21	1092	166	913	J	2	5000A	2Z	1963
4	21	1139	158	838	J	2	5000	2	1965
5	21	697		8	542	1	8947	2	1955
5	21	705	43	73	420	1	6667	2	1960
5	21	717	45	101	455	1	5000A	2Z	1963
5	21	726	53	118	527	1	5000	2	1965
6	21	864	135	167C		2	9947	2A	1950
6	21	887	138	376H	424	2	5000	2	1955
6	21	915	130	363	541	2	6667	2	1960
6	21	929	120	462	479	2	5000A	2Z	1963
6	21	946	115	501	462	2	5000	2	1965
7	21	302	8	6E		2	8529	2	1950
7	21	324	5	2		2	9703	2	1955
7	21	345A	4	5A		2	9367	2	1960
7	21	360	4	8S		2		2Z	1963
7	21	433A	4	15	750I	2	9310	1	1965
8	21	5265	185	342AC	452	2	9667	2	1950
8	21	5846	132	268		2	9828	2	1955
8	21	6988A	102	293	489	2	N	2	1960
8	21	7752	103	314A	490	2		2Z	1963
8	21	8077A	95	449	559	2	9963	2	1965
9	21	724	0	40E	21	0	5000	0A	1950
9	21	750			30	0	629	0	1955
9	21	787	16		33	0	269	0	1960
9	21	808	20	254AC	58	0	100	0Z	1963
9	21	820	17	250	64	0	76L	0	1965
10	21	1849	15	25C	172	1	7826	2	1950
10	21	1966	13	77		1	5238	2	1955
10	21	2233A	8	86	933	1	N	1	1960
10	21	2374	7	102	714	1	9000	1Z	1963
10	21	2473A	6	110	673	1	8305	0	1965
113	21	321A	4	0		1	6875	2	1965
11	21	410				1	9750	2	1955
11	21	544A	4			1	N	0	1960
11	21	589	4	45S	0	1		0P	1963
11	21	614A	4	53		1	1000K	1	1965
83	21	501	4	17S		1		2	1963
83	21	523A	4	15		1	8734	2	1965
12	21	1371	320	350C	J	2	8214	2A	1950
12	21	1570	363	2008H	J	2	5000	2	1955
12	21	1791	311	1536	J	2	5000	2	1960
12	21	1892	312	1457	J	2	5000A	2	1963
12	21	1960	317	1535	J	2	5000	2	1965
84	21	130	4	2S		1		0P	1963
84	21	137A	4	3		1	6296	0	1965
13	21	754	0	1C		1	5000	2	1950
13	21	872		6	692	2	5238	2	1955

8	9	10	11	12	13	14	
13 21 990A	10	15	557	1	N	2	1960
13 21 1059	9	15S	777	1	2600	2E	1963
13 21 1116A	8	13	652	1	8275	2	1965
85 21 321	4	2S		1		1P	1963
85 21 331A	4	3		1	7619	0	1965
14 21 581	45	41C	706	2	9448	2	1950
14 21 676	30	126		2	8780	2	1955
14 21 769	27	104	391	2	N	2	1960
14 21 822	26		273	2		2Z	1963
14 21 871	27	119	364	2	9924	2	1965
15 2146350	0	876		0	33	0A	1950
15 2160819A	0	2500		0	70	0	1955
15 2165000A	0	2420		0	26	0	1960
15 2168000	0	5500AS		0	600	0	1963
15 2170000A	0	6000		0	1694L	0	1965
16 21 891	562			2	9930	1	1955
16 21 1061A	501		794	2	9918	0	1960
16 21 1170	457	218S	754	2	9800A	0E	1963
16 21 1244	426	218	817	2	9839	0	1965
17 21 1126	37	41C		2	8000	2	1950
17 21 1266A	41	63		2	8462	0	1955
17 21 1542A	31	57		2	9273	2	1960
17 21 1694	26		400	2		2E	1963
17 21 1802A	23	61	500I	2	9734	2	1965
87 21 81	4	5S	0	1	1300M	1P	1963
87 21 84A	4	5		1	5000	0	1965
86 21 1501	7	12S		1		2P	1963
86 21 1563A	5	31	0I	2	9626	1	1965
18 21 80	4	1C		2	6552	2	1950
18 21 95	4	2		2	8630	2	1955
18 21 117	4	2		2	9193	2	1960
18 21 134	4	2S		2		2E	1963
18 21 149	4	2		2	9425	2	1965
19 21 536	29	40D		2	8039	2	1950
19 21 613A	30			2	6000	1	1955
19 21 683	25			0	N	0	1960
19 21 724	22	200S		0	200	0	1963
19 21 763	2	213		0	546L	0	1965
20 21 1234	90	192AC	107	0	5000	0	1950
20 21 1309	94	1008F	41	0	1887	0	1955
20 21 1365	87		60	0	2590	0	1960
20 21 1395	117	1420A	74	0	800	0	1963
20 21 1416	111	1410	103	0	1515L	0	1965
88 21 223	4	4S		1		0Z	1963
88 21 237A	4	4		2	6428	0	1965
21 21 431	79	47D		2	9887	2A	1950
21 21 444	74	150H	545	2	5000	2	1955
21 21 458	60	142	506	2	5000	2	1960
21 21 468	58	218	519	2	5000A	2	1963
21 21 476	62	286	483	2	5000	2	1965
22 21 212	5	18D		2	5238	1	1950
22 21 253A	5			2	5652	1	1955
22 21 303	5	43		2	5454	2	1960
22 21 338	5	34		2	9700A	2P	1963
22 21 362A	4	35		2	9887	1	1965
23 21 320	5	4E		2	7959	2	1950
23 21 369	4	18		2	8413	2	1955
23 21 432Q	6	19		2	9065	2	1960

		8	9	10	11	12	13	14	
23	21	481	6	17		2		2Z	1963
23	21	515A	5	24	I	2	9674	2	1965
24	21	2043	79	98C		1	5833	2A	1950
24	21	2306A	40	216		1	9854	1	1955
24	21	2583A	32	C	747	1	8511	0	1960
24	21	2797	25	237A	827	1	5000	0Z	1963
24	21	2939A	23	392	735I	1	9933	0	1965
25	21	186	5	4AC		2	5652	2	1950
25	21	219A	6	7		2	6429	2	1955
25	21	245	5	6		2	6551	1	1960
25	21	272	4	8	0	2		1E	1963
25	21	293A	4	9		2	9516	1	1965
26	21	1500	8			1	5652	0	1950
26	21	2000	12			1	8361	0	1955
26	21	2060A	6			1	N	0	1960
26	21	2180	5	22S		1		0P	1963
26	21	2270A	4	30		2	9547	0	1965
27	21	403	0			1	7778	2	1950
27	21	424		70	467	1	5000	2	1955
27	21	443	36	100	543	1	7727	2	1960
27	21	454	37	119	544	1	5000A	2E	1963
27	21	461	43	139	586	0	5000	2	1965
28	21	4280	600	1770AC	492	2	9989	2A	1950
28	21	4328	590	2977H	551	2	7917	2	1955
28	21	4568	640	3361	543	2	8000	2	1960
28	21	4785	594	3767	553	2	5000A	2	1963
28	21	4876	609	5125	527	2	5121	2	1965
89	21	46	4	2S		1		1P	1963
89	21	46A	4	3		1	7143	1	1965
29	21	1680	0			0	5000	0	1955
29	21	1616	0			0	1097	0	1960
29	21	1609	0	1245R		0	700	0	1963
29	21	1596		740		0	490L	0	1965
30	21	5017	0	1920		2	9537	2	1955
30	21	5322	0	2256		2	8076	2	1960
30	21	5543	0	4360		2	5000A	2	1963
30	21	5684	741	4979	509	2	5000	2	1965
90	21	678A	7			1	N	0	1960
90	21	734	9	31	0	1	3300	0P	1963
90	21	774A	8	42	0I	1	7872	0	1965
31	21	796	17	347C	254	2	9962	2	1950
31	21	797A	21	138H	404	2	9835	2	1955
31	21	833A	23	162	453	2	9913	2	1960
31	21	848	23	185	345	2		2Z	1963
31	21	855	25	210	439	2	2857	2	1965
32	21	279	5	5C		2	7222	2	1950
32	21	326	7	7		2	9180	1	1955
32	21	381A	8	10		2	9090	2	1960
32	21	418	5	9		2		2Z	1963
32	21	444	4	14	286I	2	9328	1	1965
91	21	336	4	5S		1	6200	0Z	1963
91	21	351A	4	11		2	9574	0	1965
33	21	311	4	3C		2	8361	2	1950
33	21	331A	4	4		2	9310	2	1955
33	21	416	4			2	9285	0	1960
33	21	423	4	7A		2		0E	1963
33	21	440A	4	9	0I	2	7560	0	1965
34	21	137	4	3C		2	5652	1	1950
34	21	166A	4	3		2	7436	1	1955

		8	9	10	11	12	13	14	
34	21	194	4	4		2	8333	2	1960
34	21	214	4	8		2		2Z	1963
34	21	218A	4	6		2	8387	2	1965
35	21	931	0		47	0	5000	0	1950
35	21	984			120	0	1538	0	1955
35	21	998	42		143	0	629	0	1960
35	21	1009	56	524A	83	0	500	0E	1963
35	21	1015	56	320	100	0	591L	0	1965
36	21	35800	325	345C	714	1	9844	2A	1950
36	21	39383A	330	524	342	1	4875	2	1955
36	21	42903A	246	560	349	1	9746	2	1960
36	21	46049	203	990	390	1	8300	2P	1963
36	21	48665A	185	2077	469	1	9958	2	1965
37	21	7550	0	252D		1	9818	1	1950
37	21	8170A	56	266	336	1	8936	1	1955
37	21	9351A	47		676	1	9185	1	1960
37	21	10004	45	1200S	471	1	7800	1E	1963
37	21	10488A		870	811	1	2000	1	1965
38	21	1877	45	77AC		2	9029	0	1950
38	21	1833A	25	90		1	9923	0	1955
38	21	2018A	21A	211A	583	2	N	1	1960
38	21	2218	20	226A	458	2		1P	1963
38	21	2481A	20	296	458	2	1375	1	1965
39	21	510	17	20AC		1	5238	0	1950
39	21	615A	11	53		2	7959		1955
39	21	662A	9	104		1	2352	1	1960
39	21	776	9	138		1	600	1P	1963
39	21	818A	8	197	500	0	8550	1	1965
40	21	297	0	14C	J	1	9743	2A	1950
40	21	292		26	J	1	5000	2	1955
40	21	283	16	25	J	1	5000	2	1960
40	21	284	14	30	J	1	5000A	2	1963
40	21	288	16	33	J	1	5000	2	1965
41	21	126	12	67C		1	9826	2A	1950
41	21	175	17	39		1	9818	2	1955
41	21	211	14	171	389	1	9822	2	1960
41	21	238	15	182A	398	1	9800A	2E	1963
41	21	256	17	413	473	2	9832	2	1965
42	21	4628	0	600C	414	2	9976	2A	1950
42	21	4806		974	473	2	9905	2	1955
42	21	4964	225	978	446	2	9827	2	1960
42	21	5064	224	1283	434	2	5000A	2	1963
42	21	5158	254	1939	435	2	8765	2	1965
92	21	366	4	11S		1		0P	1963
92	21	384A	4	13		1	8461	0	1965
163	21	179	5	5		2	8888	2	1965
43	21	8900		457	481	2	9840	2	1955
43	21	9321	219	449	573	2	9588	2	1960
43	21	9590	227	599	628	2	5000A	2	1963
43	21	9795	277	781	576	2	9850	2	1965
44	21	127	0			1	6970	1	1950
44	21	144		32		2	9083	2	1955
44	21	170A	4		765	1	9811	2	1960
44	21	183	4	51A		1	9800	2P	1963
44	21	191A	4	60		1	9772	0	1965
45	21	898A	0			0	5000	0	1950
45	21	942	0			0	2632	0	1955
45	21	1060A	0			0	3448	0	1960
45	21	1150	0	180AS		0	600	0	1963
45	21	1210A	0	350		0	657L	0	1965

		8	9	10	11	12	13	14	
46	21	2051	0			2	9921	1	1950
46	21	2153	0	151		2	9968	1	1955
46	21	2470A	0	227	531	2	9953	2	1960
46	21	2687	0	158	626	2	9900A	1P	1963
46	21	2838	13	113	552	2	9946	1	1965
80	21	155				1	5000	2	1955
80	21	181A	4			1	9773	1	1960
80	21	251	4	17S	0	1		1Z	1963
80	21	263A	4	27	0	1	9801	1	1965
47	21	126	6	5AC	600	1	6000	2	1950
47	21	147	5	11		1	8969	2	1955
47	21	208A	5			1	8850	2	1960
47	21	228	5	25	0	1		2P	1963
47	21	241A	5	30	0	2	6296	2	1965
48	21	170A	4			1	8077	2	1950
48	21	125	4			1	9471	2	1955
48	21	99A	4			1	8850	0	1960
48	21	103	4	2S		1		0P	1963
48	21	107A	4	3		2	9769	0	1965
49	21	111A				2	9355	2	1955
49	21	135A	4			1	9704	0	1960
49	21	150	4	17S		1		0P	1963
49	21	162A	4	28		2	6666	0	1965
93	21	594	4	9S		1		2P	1963
93	21	626Q	4	11		1	8507	2	1965
94	21	691	17	29		1	6000	2	1960
94	21	890	13	50		1		2P	1963
94	21	942A	15	117	1000	1	8412	2	1965
95	21	439	4	9S		1	5300	0P	1963
95	21	453A	4	10		2	7368	0	1965
96	21	102	4	2S		1		1P	1963
96	21	105A	4	2		1	5121	1	1965
50	21	2572	63	41AC	520	2	9786	2A	1950
50	21	3002A	80	57	617	2	8592	2	1955
50	21	3499	71	89	634	2	9794	1	1960
50	21	3987	74	101	424	2		1P	1963
50	21	4269A	81	134	793	2	9910	2	1965
97	21	1163A				1	N	1	1960
97	21	1266	14	113S	0	1	9600	1E	1963
97	21	1332A	11	103		1	9731	2	1965
51	21	700	0			1	5238	1	1950
51	21	856A				1	7826	1	1955
51	21	918A	4			1	N	0	1960
51	21	973	4	5S		1		0Z	1963
51	21	1010A	4	5		1	9305	0	1965
52	21	1011	140	221C	524	2	9965	2A	1950
52	21	1075	125	511H	514	2		2	1955
52	21	1148	101	456	561	2	5000	2	1960
52	21	1197	101	641	553	2	5000A	2	1963
52	21	1229	111	750	497	2	5000	2	1965
53	21	192	50	22C	J	1	5000	2A	1950
53	21	214	48	77	J	2		2	1955
53	21	237	42	75	J	2	5000	2	1960
53	21	254	41	74	J	2	5000A	2Z	1963
53	21	263	38	113	J	2		2	1965
54	21	105	4			2	6296	1	1950
54	21	125A	4			2	8214	2	1955

		8	9	10	11	12	13	14	
54	21	141	4			2	9259	1	1960
54	21	154	4	8S		2		1E	1963
54	21	166A	4	8		2	9607	2	1965
98	21	314	4	5S		1		0Z	1963
98	21	351A	4	6		2	7222	0	1965
99	21	5530	21	48S		1		2	1963
99	21	5800A	17	66	0I	1	9725	2	1965
55	21	328	50	47C		2	9890	2A	1950
55	21	343	50	152H	604	2	5000	2	1955
55	21	358	49	141	760	2	5000	2	1960
55	21	367	45	193	755	2	5000A	2	1963
55	21	372	44	266	747	2	5000	2	1965
56	21	89	0			0	5000	0A	1950
56	21	83A				0	2128	0	1955
56	21	94A				0	662	0	1960
56	21	103	4	25S		0	300	0E	1963
56	21	110A	4	15		0	261L	0	1965
57	21	7504	70	228C		1		1	1950
57	21	8438A	67	200		2	9911	2	1955
57	21	9270	40		333	2	9965	1	1960
57	21	9868	42	189	753	2	9700	1E	1963
57	21	10288A	37	588	673	2	8725	1	1965
58	21	80	5			2	7222	2	1950
58	21	92A	5			2	7959	2	1955
58	21	106	4			2	7435	2	1960
58	21	117	4	0		2		2Z	1963
58	21	125A	4	1		2	9610	2	1965
59	21	141	4	10E		2	6429	0	1950
59	21	157A	4	5		2	9145	0	1955
59	21	175A	4			2	8360	1	1960
59	21	191	4	12S		2		1P	1963
59	21	203A	4	7		2	9145	1	1965
60	21	841	20	23AC	429	2	8780	2	1950
60	21	940A	18	34		2	9911	2	1955
60	21	1013A	11	50		2	9487	1	1960
60	21	1096	10	73A	125	2		1Z	1963
60	21	1165A	9	115	263	2	9734	1	1965
61	21	1987	29	35C	J	2	9941	2A	1950
61	21	2376A	45	78	J	2	9695	2	1955
61	21	2741A	43	68	J	2	9606	2	1960
61	21	3024	40	70	J	2	A	2	1963
61	21	3235A	35	76	J	2	9734	2	1965
62	21	2498	95	938E		0	98	0A	1950
62	21	2729	173	877	72	0		1	1955
62	21	2970	137		223	0	2500	0	1960
62	21	3069	128	5175	250	0	300	0Z	1963
62	21	3150	145	1390	243	0	2023L	1	1965
63	21	849	0	43C	600	2	9429	0A	1950
63	21	877A		85	348	2	5000	0	1955
63	21	883	20	83	245	2	8148	0	1960
63	21	904	16	150	253	2	5000A	0Z	1963
63	21	920	15	232	263	2	8888	0	1965
64	21	1609	0	95E	10	0	5000	0A	1950
64	21	1733A			30	0	505	0	1955
64	21	1840A	34		48	0	355	0	1960
64	21	1881	32	685R	43	0	300	0E	1963
64	21	1903	35	540	58	0	352L	0	1965
114	21	311A	4	1A		1	5833	2	1965

		8	9	10	11	12	13	14	
65	21	600	8			1	6970	0A	1950
65	21	604A	7			1	5652	0	1955
65	21	604AC	6			1	5000	0	1960
65	21	660	7	113S		1		0P	1963
65	21	675A	7	131		1	6428	0	1965
100	21	333	5	11S		1	2900M	1Z	1963
100	21	349A	4	15		2	7142	1	1965
204	21	230	4	2S		1		2E	1963
204	21	237A	4	3		1	1944K	2	1965
101	21	233	4	4S		1	7000	1P	1963
101	21	250A	4	5		1	8969	2	1965
66	21	2798	0	79D	496	1	9342	0A	1950
66	21	2898A		99	450	2	9915	0	1955
66	21	3030A	93	192	421	1	9922	0	1960
66	21	3108	86	369	391	1	5000A	0Z	1963
66	21	3160A	73	577	366I	2	9857	0	1965
102	21	1177A	6			1	N	0	1960
102	21	1283	7	25		1	6800	0E	1963
102	21	1354A	6	33	0	1	8936	2	1965
67	21	704	198	195C	622	1	9658	2A	1950
67	21	726	159	527	608	1		2	1955
67	21	748	139	562	616	1	5000	2	1960
67	21	760	130	710	680	1	5000A	2A	1963
67	21	773	126	843	673	1	5000	2	1965
68	21	471	0	117C	455	1	5000	2A	1950
68	21	498	0	185	383	1		2	1955
68	21	536	0	215	674	1	5000	2	1960
68	21	577	0	305	529	1	5000A	2	1963
68	21	595	88	356	562	1	5000	2	1965
69	21	322	12	16D		1	5238	2	1950
69	21	386A	8	28		1	5000	2	1955
69	21	457				1	8089	1	1960
69	21	500	5	100AS		1	3100	1E	1963
69	21	523A	5	95	441	1	6774	1	1965
109	21	979	4	1	364	1	2400M	1Z	1963
109	21	1167A	4	6	1000I	1	8823	0	1965
70	21	1831	27	13C	714	2	9038	1	1950
70	21	2030A	18	46		2	9802		1955
70	21	2539A	16	65		2	9642	0	1960
70	21	2884	16	77		2	9500A	0E	1963
70	21	3074A	14	84		2	9771	0	1965
103	21	157	4	1A		1		0E	1963
103	21	164A	4	3		1	6969	2	1965
216	21	97	4	5		2	7959	2	1965
104	21	440A	5			1	N	1	1960
104	21	431	5	7S		1	9500	1	1963
104	21	436A	5	14		1	9819	1	1965
71	21	2093	91	185C	356	2	9915	2	1950
71	21	2407	65	228		2	9910	2	1955
71	21	2775	59	127	258	2	9630	2	1960
71	21	2989	40	284	329	2	9900	2E	1963
71	21	3115A	35	425	379	2	5034	2	1965
72	21	1232	112	31C	682	1	9074	2A	1950
72	21	1399A	78	67		2	5000	2	1955
72	21	1594A	56	112		1	7826	1	1960
72	21	1704	53	179	461	1	5000A	1	1963
72	21	1787A		320	91I	1	5000	1	1965

ATTRIBUTE DATA, 1950-1965

		8	9	10	11	12	13	14	
73	21	19300	740B	20717C	235	0	5000	0A	1950
73	21	20020	1758B	11888	54	0	5000	0	1955
73	21	21440	1362		193	0	5000	0	1960
73	21	22476	1497	15444	130	0	5000	0	1963
73	21	23056	1492	46000	122	0	5000	0	1965
74	21	5062	1137	2075C	J	2	9988	2A	1950
74	21	5122	885	5031	J	2	9730	2	1955
74	21	5251	775	4514	J	2	5000	2	1960
74	21	5380	758		J	2	5000A	2	1963
74	21	5444	721	5855	J	2	9960	2	1965
75	21	15112	3979	12303C	J	2	5000	2	1950
75	21	16593	3333	44428	J	2	5000	2	1955
75	21	18068	3251	47690	J	2	5000	2	1960
75	21	18942	3202	53429	J	2	5000	2	1963
75	21	19459	3191	51884	J	2	5000	2	1965
219	21	755A	4	9		1	7674	2	1965
105	21	467	4	8S		1		0P	1963
105	21	486A	4	3		1	6153	0	1965
76	21	237	18	17E		2	6552	1	1950
76	21	262A	18			2	5833	2	1955
76	21	254A	12			2	9435	2	1960
76	21	265	11	17S	192	2		2Z	1963
76	21	272A	10	18	187	2	5000	2	1965
77	21	499	27	56C		2	7826	2	1950
77	21	578	44	111		2	5455	2	1955
77	21	745A	50	167	500	2	9456	2	1960
77	21	814	52	135	200	2		2Z	1963
77	21	872A	50	174	333	2	9765	2	1965
81	21	1430	0			0	98	1	1955
81	21	1592	0			1	1908	0	1960
81	21	1780	0	300S		1	400	0	1963
81	21	1900A	0	425		0	290L	0	1965
82	21	1200	0		356	2	5000	1	1955
82	21	1410A	0		600	1	9945	0	1960
82	21	1532	0	267S	400	1	9900A	0	1963
82	21	1612A	8	258	773	2	9963	0	1965
78	21	450	4			1	5000	0	1950
78	21	450	4			1	5000	0	1955
78	21	500AC	4			1	6734	0	1960
78	21	500	4	10S		1	8600	0P	1963
78	21	500A	4	11		1	8529	0	1965
79	21	1615	33	560D	78	1	9871	0A	1950
79	21	1759	44	328	215	1	6134	0	1955
79	21	1840	35		181	1	9871	0	1960
79	21	1906	38	403S	23	1	2000	0	1963
79	21	1951	36	396	191	1	9246L	0	1965

		15	16	17	18	19	20	21	
1	22	0	0	1	0	0	0	0	1950
1	22	244	0	0	0	0	2	0	1955
1	22		0	0	600A	1	0	0	1960
1	22	1010	0	0	0	0	0	0	1963
1	22	2904	0	0	0	0	0	0	1965
2	22	0	0	10	0	1	1	0	1950
2	22	0	0	1	0	0	0	0	1955
2	22		0	1	0	0	0	1	1960
2	22		0	2	0	1	0	0	1963
2	22		0	3	0	0	0	0	1965
106	22		0	2	0	0	0	0	1965

		15	16	17	18	19	20	21	
3	22	0B	0	0	0	0	1	0	1950
3	22	55	0	0	1	1	0	4279	1955
3	22	860	0	1	0	0	0	1	1960
3	22	273	0	0	0	0	0	36	1963
3	22	230	0	0	0	1	1	1	1965
4	22	269	0	1	261J	1	1	0	1950
4	22	187	0	0	0	1	0	0	1955
4	22	220	0	1	0	0	0	0	1960
4	22	56	0	1	1	1	0	0	1963
4	22	118	0	0	17A	1	0	0	1965
5	22	308	0	2					1955
5	22	185	0	0	0	0	2	0	1960
5	22	59	0	1	0	0	0	0	1963
5	22	84	0	0	0	0	0	0	1965
6	22	433	0	1	0	0	0	8	1950
6	22	279	0	0	0	0	0	0	1955
6	22	312	0	3	50	1	1	8	1960
6	22		0	1	0	0	0	0	1963
6	22	152	0	0	0	0	0	10	1965
7	22	5303	0	4	0	0	0	21	1950
7	22	7083	0	0	0	0	0	0	1955
7	22	1770	0	0	0	0	0	16	1960
7	22	1060	0	0	0	0	1	8	1963
7	22	2536	0	0	0	0	0	115	1965
8	22	299	0	0	0	0	1	6	1950
8	22	2730	0	0	0	0	0	0	1955
8	22		0	0	0	0	1	0	1960
8	22	336	1	0	0	0	0	9	1963
8	22	816	0	0	0	0	0	0	1965
9	22	0	0	13	1	1	4	0	1950
9	22	0	0	1	0	10	0	0	1955
9	22		0	0	0	0	0	0	1960
9	22		0	2	0	0	0	0	1963
9	22		0	3	0	0	0	0	1965
10	22	0	0	1	0	0	0	266	1950
10	22	3549	0	0	28A	1	0	122	1955
10	22	4017	0	1	0	0	0	17	1960
10	22	2020	0	0	0	0	0	1200	1963
10	22	3216	0	0	0	0	0	53	1965
113	22		0	0	0	0	0	0	1965
11	22	0	0	0	0	0	0	0	1955
11	22		0	0	16A	1	0	0	1960
11	22		0	3	3	1	0	0	1963
11	22		4	7	23A	1	1	15	1965
83	22	1010	0	0	0	0	0	0	1963
83	22		0	0	0	0	0	0	1965
12	22	166	0	0	294J	1	1	0	1950
12	22	91	0	5	0	0	0	0	1955
12	22	88	0	0	0	0	0	0	1960
12	22	45	0	2	0	0	0	3	1963
12	22	64	0	2	0	0	1	0	1965
84	22		0	0	0	0	0	0	1963
84	22		0	0	0	0	0	0	1965
13	22	0	0	0	0	0	1	0	1950
13	22	1302	0	0	0	0	0	0	1955
13	22	758	0	0	0	0	0	0	1960
13	22	1515	0	0	0	0	0	0	1963
13	22	3882	0	0	0	0	0	0	1965

		15	16	17	18	19	20	21	
85	22		0	0	0	0	0	0	1963
85	22		0	1	0	0	0	1	1965
14	22	904B	0	0	0	0	0	0	1950
14	22	1986	0	0	0	0	0	0	1955
14	22	250	0	0	0	0	0	3	1960
14	22		0	0	0	0	0	5	1963
14	22	260	1	2	1	1	1	0	1965
15	22	0	0	49	99999AJ	1	13	0	1950
15	22	0	1	78	2D	1	0	0	1955
15	22	0	0	42	0	1	2	0	1960
15	22		0	42	10	1	7	200	1963
15	22		2	71	42A	1	19	0	1965
16	22	2091	1	17	4	1	0	0	1955
16	22	26087	0	4	14	1	0	0	1960
16	22	7565	0	0	147	1	1	0	1963
16	22		0	1	100A	1	0	0	1965
17	22	247B	0	0	0	0	0	53	1950
17	22	303	0	0	0	0	0	0	1955
17	22	828	0	0	0	0	0	8	1960
17	22	392	0	0	0	0	0	2090	1963
17	22	1277	0	0	0	0	0	57	1965
87	22		0	0	0	0	0	0	1963
87	22		0	4	0	0	0	0	1965
86	22	604	0	2	0	0	0	5230	1963
86	22		0	4	0	1	0	9208	1965
18	22	1600B	0	1	0	0	1	0	1950
18	22	253	0	6	0	1	0	20	1955
18	22		0	0	0	0	0	0	1960
18	22	100	0	0	0	0	0	0	1963
18	22	484	0	0	0	0	0	0	1965
19	22	469B	0	0	0	0	1	0	1950
19	22	535	0	0	0	0	0	2	1955
19	22		0	42	0	1	4	82	1960
19	22		0	21	0	1	4	500	1963
19	22		0	19	0	0	0	0	1965
20	22	7862	0	13	0	1	5	0	1950
20	22	0	1	7	0	1	2	0	1955
20	22		0	3	0	0	2	0	1960
20	22		0	0	0	0	0	0	1963
20	22		0	2	0	0	1	0	1965
88	22		0	0			0	0	1963
88	22		0	0	0	0	0	0	1965
21	22	286	0	1	0	0	0	0	1950
21	22	217	0	0	0	0	0	0	1955
21	22	225	0	0	0	0	0	0	1960
21	22	65	0	0	0	0	0	0	1963
21	22	83	0	0	0	0	0	0	1965
22	22	265B	0	0	0	0	1	0	1950
22	22	263	0	0	0	0	0	0	1955
22	22	472	0	6	0	0	0	8	1960
22	22	133	3	4	0	0	0	30	1963
22	22	588	0	0	3000AD	1	0	3028	1965
23	22	640B	0	1	0	0	1	0	1950
23	22	311	0	1	0	0	0	0	1955
23	22	917	0	1	0	0	0	7	1960
23	22	325	0	0	0	0	0	8	1963
23	22	701	0	0	0	0	0	3	1965
24	22	1610	0	4	10	1	2	0	1950
24	22	1543	1	34	225AD	1	2	0	1955

		15	16	17	18	19	20	21	
24	22		0	8	1	1	1	0	1960
24	22	727	0	7	928A	1	1	0	1963
24	22		5	7	928A	1	0	0	1965
25	22	206	0	1	0	0	1	0	1950
25	22	105	0	0	1	1	0	0	1955
25	22		0	0	0	0	0	0	1960
25	22	150	0	0	0	0	0	1	1963
25	22	506	0	0	0	0	0	0	1965
26	22	C	0	1	0	0	1	0	1950
26	22	900	0	0	0	0	0	0	1955
26	22	2508	0	1	0	0	0	0	1960
26	22		0	3	0	0	1	100	1963
26	22	1661	0	0	0	0	0	0	1965
27	22	530B	0	0	0	0	0	0	1950
27	22	122	0	0	0	0	0	0	1955
27	22	139	0	0	0	0	0	0	1960
27	22		0	0	0	0	0	0	1963
27	22	54	0	0	0	0	0	0	1965
28	22	247	0	4	1001A	1	1	5	1950
28	22	134	0	13	300A	1	3	0	1955
28	22	132	0	4	2795A	1	4	40	1960
28	22	36	1	0	0	0	10	0	1963
28	22	59	0	4	0	0	8	0	1965
89	22	500	0	0			0	0	1963
89	22		0	0	0	0	0	0	1965
29	22	0	0	10	0	0	0	0	1955
29	22		0	6	0	0	0	0	1960
29	22		0	2	0	1	5	0	1963
29	22		0	9	0	0	1	3	1965
30	22	138	0	3	0	0	0	0	1955
30	22	111	0	13	0	0	0	0	1960
30	22	34	0	0	0	0	0	0	1963
30	22	48	1	4	0	0	2	0	1965
90	22		1	4	0	0	0		1960
90	22	590	0	3	0	0	0	19	1963
90	22	745	0	4	0	0	0	0	1965
31	22	5531B	0	3	1000A	1	0	0	1950
31	22	50	0	8	0	0	2	0	1955
31	22	340	0	1	0	1	1	24	1960
31	22	97	0	0	0	0	1	0	1963
31	22	124	0	2	0	1	0	47	1965
32	22	114B	0	2	0	0	1	0	1950
32	22	218	0	0	1	1	0	10	1955
32	22	309	0	3	0	0	0	0	1960
32	22	100	0	0	0	0	0	2	1963
32	22	206	0	0	0	0	0	10	1965
91	22		0	0	0	0	0	0	1963
91	22		0	1	0	0	0	0	1965
33	22	0B	0	1	0	0	1	0	1950
33	22	889	0	0	0	0	0	0	1955
33	22		0	0	0	0	0	1	1960
33	22		0	6	0	0	0	200	1963
33	22	6617	0	0	0	0	1	0	1965
34	22	343	0	0	0	0	1	0	1950
34	22	500	0	1	0	0	0	0	1955
34	22	751	0	0	0	0	1	0	1960
34	22	300	0	0	0	0	0	8	1963
34	22	672	0	0	0	0	0	1	1965

		15'	16	17	18	19	20	21	
35	22	0	0	6	0	0	4	0	1950
35	22	0	0	1	0	0	0	0	1955
35	22		0	2	0	0	1	0	1960
35	22		0	1	0	0	0	0	1963
35	22		0	0	0	0	0	0	1965
36	22	3540	0	5	25A	1	2	90	1950
36	22	2535	0	11	12D	1D	2	399	1955
36	22		0	12	0	0	3	41	1960
36	22	1092	1	9	0	0	11	514	1963
36	22	1682	1	33	4572A	1	9	62	1965
37	22	0A	0	1	0	0	1	20	1950
37	22	984	0	4	0	0	0	4176	1955
37	22		0	5	0	0	0	14	1960
37	22		1	2	65A	1	0	57	1963
37	22		2	11	83A	1	1	99999AJ	1965
38	22	C	0	1	0	0	0	0	1950
38	22	1683	0	1	0	0	0	0	1955
38	22	1063	0	1	0	0	0	12	1960
38	22	454	0	0	11A	1	0	584	1963
38	22	634	0	0	3	1	1	3	1965
39	22	C	0	0	0	0	0	0	1950
39	22	448	0	4	0	0	0	0	1955
39	22	502	1	2	0	0	0	17	1960
39	22	190	0	5	0	0	0	1655	1963
39	22	335	0	2	0	1	1	0	1965
40	22	0			0	0		0	1950
40	22	0	0	1	0	0	4	0	1955
40	22	499	0	0	0	0	0	0	1960
40	22	159	0	0	0	0	0	0	1963
40	22	222	0	1	0	0	0	0	1965
41	22	0	0	11	15A	1	2	0	1950
41	22	12	2	66	437AD	1	0	0	1955
41	22	107	1	9	13A	1	0	0	1960
41	22	60	0	4	8A	1	0	0	1963
41	22	148	0	4	21A	1	2	0	1965
42	22	272	0	3	0	0	2	15	1950
42	22	233	0	3	1	1	0	0	1955
42	22	78	0	1	0	0	2	8	1960
42	22	37	0	0	0	0	0	9	1963
42	22	107	0	0	0	0	0	0	1965
92	22	505	0	0	0	0	0	0	1963
92	22	839	0	3	0	0	0	0	1965
163	22	608	0	1	0	0	0	0	1965
43	22	592	0	3	0	0	0	0	1955
43	22	342	0	4	0	0	2	60	1960
43	22	70	0	0	0	0	0	0	1963
43	22	92	0	0	0	0	0	0	1965
44	22	0	0	7	9A	1	0	0	1950
44	22	5143	0	6	4A	1	0	0	1955
44	22		0	10	0	0	0	0	1960
44	22	300	0	2	26A	1	0	44	1963
44	22	1368	0	3	7A	1	1	0	1965
45	22	0	0	4	99999AJ	1	2	0	1950
45	22	0	0	3	0	1	0	0	1955
45	22	0A	0	0	14	1	0	0	1960
45	22		0	3	7A	1	0	0	1963
45	22		0	5	2	1	0	0	1965
46	22	0	0	1	47000AJ	1	3	293	1950
46	22	83	1	18	0	1	0	0	1955
46	22		0	2	4	1	0	115	1960

		15	16	17	18	19	20	21	
46	22	210	0	0	2	1	0	0	1963
46	22	849	0	1	29A	1	0	1	1965
80	22		0	3	0	1		0	1955
80	22		0	1	0	1	0	2	1960
80	22		0	3	0	0	0	1120	1963
80	22		0	3	9AH	1	0	0	1965
47	22	630B	0	0	0	0	0	0	1950
47	22	500	0	1	0	1	0	0	1955
47	22		0	0	0	1	0	2	1960
47	22	113	0	2	3	1	1	0	1963
47	22	175	0	0	0	0	1	0	1965
48	22	0			0	0		0	1950
48	22	0	0	0	0	0	0	0	1955
48	22		0	1	0	0	0	0	1960
48	22		0	0	0	0	0	0	1963
48	22	4032	0	3	0	0	0	0	1965
49	22	0	0	0	0	0			1955
49	22		0	0	0	0	0	0	1960
49	22	337	0	0	0	0	0	0	1963
49	22	304	0	0	0	0	0	0	1965
93	22	1010	0	0	0	0	0	0	1963
93	22		0	0	0	0	0	0	1965
94	22	931	0	1	0	0	0	0	1960
94	22	360	0	3	7A	1	0	10	1963
94	22	1504	0	6	20A	1	0	0	1965
95	22		0	0	0	0	0	0	1963
95	22		0	2	0	0	0	0	1965
96	22		0	0	0	0	0	0	1963
96	22		0	0	0	0	0	0	1965
50	22	757	0	0	0	0	1	0	1950
50	22	779	0	0	0	0	0	28	1955
50	22	400	0	0	0	0	0	13	1960
50	22	148	0	0	0	0	0	3	1963
50	22	197	0	0	0	0	0	20	1965
97	22	2414	1	7	0	0	0	0	1960
97	22	883	0	3	12	1	1	0	1963
97	22	1445	0	0	0	0	0	25	1965
51	22	0	0	0	0	0	0	0	1950
51	22	0	0	0	0	0	0	0	1955
51	22		0	3	0	0	2	0	1960
51	22		0	1	0	0	0	50	1963
51	22		0	0	0	0	0	0	1965
52	22	1113	0	0	1000A	1	0	0	1950
52	22	618	0	3	0	0	0	0	1955
52	22	495	0	0	0	0	0	0	1960
52	22	156	0	0	0	0	0	0	1963
52	22	188	0	0	0	0	0	0	1965
53	22	0	0	0	22	1	0	0	1950
53	22	0	0	1	0	0	0	0	1955
53	22	0	0	0	0	0	0	9	1960
53	22		0	0	0	0	1	0	1963
53	22	163	0	0	0	1	0	0	1965
54	22	840B	0	1	0	0	1	0	1950
54	22	167	1	7	0	1	1	0	1955
54	22	7	0	2	0	0	1	2	1960
54	22	300	0	0	0	0	0	2	1963
54	22	312	0	0	0	0	0	0	1965

		15	16	17	18	19	20	21	
98	22		0	0	0	0	0	0	1963
98	22		0	0	0	0	0	0	1965
99	22	1120	0	0	0	0	0	0	1963
99	22	1652	0	0	0	0	0	80	1965
55	22	410	0	0	0	0	0	0	1950
55	22	190	0	0	0	0	0	0	1955
55	22	234	0	2	0	0	0	0	1960
55	22	22	0	0	0	0	0	0	1963
55	22	99	0	0	0	0	1	0	1965
56	22	0	0	2	0	0	0	0	1950
56	22	0	0	0	0	0	0	0	1955
56	22		0	0	0	0	0	0	1960
56	22		0	0	0	0	0	0	1963
56	22		0	1	0	0	0	0	1965
57	22	2481	0	5	25A	1	0	0	1950
57	22	4813	0	19	2D	1	4	0	1955
57	22		0	4	0	1	4	0	1960
57	22	1122	1	2	0	1	1	133	1963
57	22	1701	2	23	3451A	1	8	0	1965
58	22	40B				0		0	1950
58	22	23	0	0	0	0	0	0	1955
58	22	13	0	0	0	0	0	200	1960
58	22	7	0	0	0	0	1	0	1963
58	22	289	0	0	0	0	0	1	1965
59	22	124				0		0	1950
59	22	669	0	0	0	0	0	10	1955
59	22	1504	0	0	0	0	0	0	1960
59	22	300	0	0	0	0	0	2	1963
59	22	643	0	2	0	0	0	0	1965
60	22	1471B	0	1	0	0	1	250	1950
60	22	1175	0	1	0	0	0	0	1955
60	22	838	0	0	0	0	0	2	1960
60	22	295	0	2	0	0	0	10	1963
60	22	231	0	3	0	0	0	183	1965
61	22	274B	0	3	50A	1	0	243	1950
61	22	222	0	2	0	1	0	0	1955
61	22	738	0	0	0	0	0	0	1960
61	22	252	0	1	0	0	0	0	1963
61	22	1200	0	1	0	0	0	55	1965
62	22	0	0	5	0	0	3	0	1950
62	22	0	0	5	0	0	3	0	1955
62	22		0	3	0	0	0	0	1960
62	22		0	1	0	0	0	0	1963
62	22		0	9	0	0	1	0	1965
63	22	0	0	0	0	0	0	0	1950
63	22	0	5	5	0	0	2	0	1955
63	22	0	0	0	0	0	0	0	1960
63	22		0	3	148A	1	1	0	1963
63	22		0	2	33	1	1	0	1965
64	22	0	0	4	0	0	0	0	1950
64	22	0	0	0	0	0	1	0	1955
64	22		0	1	0	0	0	0	1960
64	22		0	0	0	0	0	0	1963
64	22		0	2	0	0	0	0	1965
114	22		0	0	0	0	0	0	1965
65	22	0	0	0	0	0	1	0	1950
65	22	0	0	12	0	1	2	0	1955
65	22		0	0	0	0	0	0	1960
65	22	925	1	2	59A	1	0	0	1963
65	22	2145	0	0	0	1	0	0	1965

		15	16	17	18	19	20	21	
100	22	1680	0	0	0	0	0	0	1963
100	22	2540	0	1	0	0	0	0	1965
204	22		0	0	0	0	0	0	1963
204	22	3250	0	3	0	0	0	0	1965
101	22		0	3	0	1	1	4	1963
101	22	18850	0	0	0	0	0	0	1965
66	22	0A	0	0	0	0	1	0	1950
66	22	0	0	5	0	0	0	0	1955
66	22	581	0	2	0	0	0	4	1960
66	22		0	0	0	0	0	0	1963
66	22	134	0	0	0	0	1	0	1965
102	22		0	0	0	0	1	0	1960
102	22	1010	0	0	0	0	0	0	1963
102	22	4239	0	1	0	0	0	155	1965
67	22	0	0	0	0	0	0	0	1950
67	22	121	0	0	0	0	1	0	1955
67	22	99	0	0	0	0	0	0	1960
67	22	27	0	1	0	0	1	0	1963
67	22	42	0	0	0	0	0	0	1965
68	22	0	0	0	0	0	0	0	1950
68	22	0	0	0	0	0	0	0	1955
68	22	0	0	0	0	0	1	0	1960
68	22		0	0	0	0	0	0	1963
68	22		0	0	0	0	0	0	1965
69	22	C	0	3	0	1	0	3	1950
69	22	159	0	11	140A	1	0	0	1955
69	22		0	3	3A	1	0	0	1960
69	22	475	0	6	4	1	0	82	1963
69	22		0	8	10A	1	2	24	1965
109	22		0	0			0	0	1963
109	22		1	1	0	0	0	0	1965
70	22	1590B	0	0	1000A	1	0	0	1950
70	22	698	0	4	2	1	0	0	1955
70	22	2313	0	1	0	1	0	0	1960
70	22	1010	0	3	0	0	0	0	1963
70	22	1245	0	1	17A	1	0	0	1965
103	22		0	0	0	0	0	1	1963
103	22	12360	0	0	0	0	0	0	1965
216	22		0	0	0	0	0	0	1965
104	22	2143	0	3	6A	0	0	0	1960
104	22	755	0	2	0	0	0	0	1963
104	22	1510	0	6	0	0	0	0	1965
71	22	658	0	1	5500A	1	0	0	1950
71	22	296	0	4	0	1	2	0	1955
71	22	422	0	0	0	1	1	16	1960
71	22	290	0	0	0	1	0	28	1963
71	22	548	0	4	3	1	1	0	1965
72	22	1066	0	1	0	1	0	0	1950
72	22	625	0	4	0	0	1	0	1955
72	22	628	0	0	0	0	2	122	1960
72	22	266	0	2	0	0	0	44	1963
72	22	313	0	2	0	0	1	0	1965
73	22	0	0	102	0	1	17	0	1950
73	22	0	1	144	0	1	6	0	1955
73	22		4	89	0	1	13	0	1960
73	22		2	30	1	1	17	212	1963
73	22		2	56	0	0	8	0	1965

ATTRIBUTE DATA, 1950-1965

		15	16	17	18	19	20	21	
74	22	476	0	11	686J	1	1	0	1950
74	22	308	0	24	27A	1	15	0	1955
74	22	264	0	1	0	0	2	0	1960
74	22	95	2	8	6A	1	8	0	1963
74	22	145	0	5	43A	1	12	0	1965
75	22	58	2	73	33629J	1	12	0	1950
75	22	42	0	62	0	1	7	0	1955
75	22	44	1	64	3	1	10	2	1960
75	22	17	5	6	72	1	24	3	1963
75	22	26	1	35	1395G	1	31	0	1965
219	22	3509	1	4	1	1	1	0	1965
105	22		0	0	0	0	0	0	1963
105	22		0	1	0	0	0	0	1965
76	22	C	0	0	0	0	0	0	1950
76	22	12	0	0	0	0	0	0	1955
76	22	178	0	0	0	0	0	0	1960
76	22		0	0	0	0	0	0	1963
76	22		0	1	0	0	0	0	1965
77	22	45B	0	0	0	0	1	1	1950
77	22	38	0	0	0	0	0	0	1955
77	22	156	0	5	0	0	0	3	1960
77	22		0	1	0	0	0	145	1963
77	22	213	0	0	0	0	2	20	1965
81	22		0	7	1	1			1955
81	22		0	8	0	1	1	0	1960
81	22		0	3	0	1	0	0	1963
81	22		0	30	8915AG	1	19	0	1965
82	22		0	6	0	1			1955
82	22		0	1	4816A	1	1	78	1960
82	22	755	0	2	5665A	1	1	36010	1963
82	22		1	8	11243H	1	1	19	1965
78	22	0			0	0		0	1950
78	22	0	0	2	25A	1	0	0	1955
78	22		0	0	0	0	0		1960
78	22		0	0	3	1	0	1003	1963
78	22		0	1	10007	1	0	200	1965
79	22	C	0	30	0	1	5	0	1950
79	22	26	0	10	0	1	1	0	1955
79	22	816	0	2	0	0	1		1960
79	22	150	0	1	0	1	0	0	1963
79	22		0	3	0	0	0	0	1965

		22	23	24	25	26	27	28	
1	23	0	0	0	0	0	18250	1667	1950
1	23	0	0	0	0	0	18250	909	1955
1	23	0	0	0	0	0B	13500C	0	1960
1	23	0	0	0	0	0B	13500C	0	1963
1	23	0	1	0	0		13500C	0	1965
2	23	0	0	0	0	100	12125	952	1950
2	23	0	0	0	0	100E	12125	741	1955
2	23	0	0	0	0	61	12125	0	1960
2	23	0	0	0	0	54A	12125	294	1963
2	23	0	0	0	0	62	12125	732	1965
106	23	0	0	1	2	42	10125	738	1965
3	23	0	0	0	0	950	10250	1341	1950
3	23	6	17	3	6	936	10250	1642	1955
3	23	0	0	0	0	894	10250	1458	1960
3	23	1	3	1	0	885	10250	1530	1963
3	23	1	6	0	3	880	10250	1568	1965

	22	23	24	25	26	27	28	
4 23	0	1	0	0	223	20875	1143	1950
4 23	0	0	0	0	229	20875	1180	1955
4 23	0	0	0	0	190	11750D	1016	1960
4 23	0	0	0	0	208	11750D	1111	1963
4 23	0	0	0	0	229	11750D	1145	1965
5 23	0	0	0	0	895	10375	916	1955
5 23	0	0	0	0	894	10375	806	1960
5 23	0	0	0	0	890	10375	940	1963
5 23	0	0	0	0	846	10375	949	1965
6 23	4	3	0	1	995	9250	906	1950
6 23	0	2	0	1	960A	9250	899	1955
6 23	3	4	0	2	958	9250	810	1960
6 23	0	1	0	1	950	9250	778	1963
6 23	0	2	0	0	950	9250	809	1965
7 23	1	1	1	0	940	7750	667	1950
7 23	0	0	0	0	946	7750	1182	1955
7 23	0	0	0	0	949	7750	880	1960
7 23	0	1	1	0	941	7750	1042	1963
7 23	1	4	3	0	937	7750	1394	1965
8 23	0	1	0	0	932	5375	1296	1950
8 23	0	0	1	0	934	5375	1484	1955
8 23	0	0	0	0	935	5375	1256	1960
8 23	2	1	0	2	932	5375	1389	1963
8 23	0	0	1	5	930	5375	1491	1965
9 23	0	0	1	0	6	12500	1011	1950
9 23	0	0	0	0	1	12500	889	1955
9 23	0	0	0	0	6	12500	476	1960
9 23	0	0	1	0	7A	12500	1099	1963
9 23	0	0	1	0	7	12500	1403	1965
10 23	0	0	0	0	9	19500	227	1950
10 23	0	0	0	0	12	19500	676	1955
10 23	0	0	0	0	9	12375C	430	1960
10 23	0	1	0	0	9	12375C	636	1963
10 23	0	0	0	1	9	12375C	727	1965
113 23	0	0	1	0	520	20125	0	1965
11 23	0	0	0	0	4	21500	769	1955
11 23	0	0	0	0	11	13375C	833	1960
11 23	0	0	0	0	9	13375C	556	1963
11 23	0	0	0	0	9	13375C	323	1965
83 23	0	0	0	0	200	15500	0	1963
83 23	0	0	0	0	219	15500	220	1965
12 23	0	1	0	0	391	0	982	1950
12 23	0	0	0	0	447	0	1197	1955
12 23	0	0	0	0	440	0	1084	1960
12 23	0	0	0	1	433	0	1177	1963
12 23	0	1	0	0	460	0	1209	1965
84 23	0	0	0	0	123	16500	0	1963
84 23	0	0	0	0	140	16500	270	1965
13 23	0	0	0	0	67	24000	658	1950
13 23	0	0	0	0	71	24000	410	1955
13 23	0	0	0	0	75	17250C	479	1960
13 23	0	0	0	0	67	17250C	609	1963
13 23	0	1	0	0	68	17250C	746	1965
85 23	0	0	0	0	29	14125	0	1963
85 23	0	0	1	0	32	14125	0	1965
14 23	3	0	0	0	900	9125	1488	1950
14 23	0	0	0	1	896	9125	1627	1955
14 23	0	1	0	0	890	9125	1154	1960

	22	23	24	25	26	27	28	
14 23	1	1	0	0	895	9125	1374	1963
14 23	0	1	0	2	884	9125	1311	1965
15 23	0	0	0	0	7	13000	1391	1950
15 23	0	0	1	0	5	13000	1000	1955
15 23	0	0	0	0	4	5375	667	1960
15 23	0	24	0	0	4A	5375C	2500	1963
15 23	0	0	0	0	4	5375C	1024	1965
16 23	0	0	0	0	15	18000	948	1955
16 23	0	1	0	0		9625C	619	1960
16 23	0	0	0	0	18	9625C	1192	1963
16 23	0	0	0	0	22	9625C	1899	1965
17 23	0	0	0	0	995	3125	1111	1950
17 23	0	0	0	0	995	3125	1361	1955
17 23	0	0	0	0	975	3125C	1233	1960
17 23	0	0	0	0	973	3125	1303	1963
17 23	0	5	0	0	967	3125	1480	1965
87 23	0	0	0	0	352	17000	135	1963
87 23	0	1	1	0	350	17000	291	1965
86 23	0	0	0	0	331	17500	392	1963
86 23	0	0	0	1	366	17500	385	1965
18 23	0	0	0	0	940	3000	943	1950
18 23	0	0	0	0		3000	1609	1955
18 23	0	0	0	0	955	3000	891	1960
18 23	0	0	0	0	957	3000	985	1963
18 23	0	0	0	0	759	3000	1438	1965
19 23	0	0	0	0	808	375	1901	1950
19 23	0	4	0	7	909	375	2000	1955
19 23	0	1	0	1	843	375	1485	1960
19 23	0	0	0	0	840	375	1681	1963
19 23	0	0	1	0	806	375	1913	1965
20 23	0	0	1	0	750	10375	1029	1950
20 23	0	0	0	0	750	10375	1171	1955
20 23	0	0	0	0	606	10375	1147	1960
20 23	0	0	0	0	631A	10375	1433	1963
20 23	0	0	0	0	640	10375	1520	1965
88 23	0	0	0	0	138	13875	0	1963
88 23	0	0	0	1	132	13875	204	1965
21 23	0	0	0	0	6	9375	1056	1950
21 23	0	0	0	0	6	9375	1055	1955
21 23	0	0	0	0	6	9375	922	1960
21 23	0	0	0	0	6	9375	1034	1963
21 23	0	0	0	0	6	9375	1012	1965
22 23	0	0	0	0	991	1875	1163	1950
22 23	0	0	0	0	982	1875	1625	1955
22 23	0	0	0	0	955	1875	789	1960
22 23	0	0	0	0	956	1875	843	1963
22 23	0	0	1	0	952	1875	1058	1965
23 23	0	0	0	0	940	5000	921	1950
23 23	0	0	1	1	942	5000	1351	1955
23 23	0	0	0	0	942	5000	0	1960
23 23	0	3	0	0	940	5000	1410	1963
23 23	2	2	2	1	940	5000	1703	1965
24 23	0	0	0	0	5	14375	1176	1950
24 23	0	0	1	1	9	14375	1387	1955
24 23	0	0	0	0	7	14375	893	1960
24 23	0	0	0	0	6	14375	978	1963
24 23	0	1	1	0	6	14375	1076	1965
25 23	0	0	0	0	980	2750	714	1950
25 23	0	0	0	0	980	2750	1711	1955

	22	23	24	25	26	27	28	
25 23	0	1	0	0	978	2750	1486	1960
25 23	0	0	0	0	979	2750	1667	1963
25 23	0	0	0	0	977	2750	2033	1965
26 23	0	0	0	0	3	18125	714	1950
26 23	0	0	0	0	0	18125	500	1955
26 23	0	0	0	0	6	18125	0	1960
26 23	0	0	0	0	6	18125	0	1963
26 23	0	0	0	0	6	18125	526	1965
27 23	0	0	0	0	0	9500	1088	1950
27 23	0	0	0	0	0	9500	1235	1955
27 23	0	0	0	0	0	7875C	896	1960
27 23	0	0	0	4	1	7875C	1045	1963
27 23	0	0	0	0	1	7875C	1108	1965
28 23	1	4	0	0	977	8500	954	1950
28 23	0	0	0	2	965	8500	962	1955
28 23	2	2	1	0	828	8500	860	1960
28 23	2	2	0	0	827	8500	782	1963
28 23	0	0	0	0	826	8500	852	1965
89 23	0	0	0	0	436	16625	0	1963
89 23	0	0	0	0	464	16625	263	1965
29 23	0	0	0	0	110	9875	0	1955
29 23	0	0	0	0	110	9875	729	1960
29 23	0	0	0	0	110	9875	979	1963
29 23	0	0	0	0	110	9875	1223	1965
30 23	0	0	0	0	453	9500	875	1955
30 23	0	0	0	0	480	9500	850	1960
30 23	0	0	0	0	476	9500	782	1963
30 23	0	0	0	0	476	9500	853	1965
90 23	0	0	2	0	105	13250	0	1960
90 23	0	0	0	0	87	13250	303	1963
90 23	0	0	1	0	100	13250	606	1965
31 23	1	0	0	0	4	12625	1240	1950
31 23	0	0	0	0	4	12625	1333	1955
31 23	0	1	0	0	8	12625	937	1960
31 23	0	1	0	0	6	12625	1203	1963
31 23	1	3	1	10	6	12625	1276	1965
32 23	0	0	0	0	968	2125	1014	1950
32 23	0	0	2	1	969	2125	1140	1955
32 23	0	0	0	1	922	2125	826	1960
32 23	0	0	0	0	926	2125	1056	1963
32 23	0	1	1	0	920	2125	1375	1965
91 23	0	0	0	0	9	11500	385	1963
91 23	0	0	0	0	9	11500	1000	1965
33 23	0	0	0	0	0	1625	1163	1950
33 23	0	0	0	0	990	1625	1341	1955
33 23	0	0	0	0	690	1625	900	1960
33 23	0	0	1	0	791	1625	962	1963
33 23	0	0	1	0	787	1625	1351	1965
34 23	0	0	0	0	978	2000	968	1950
34 23	0	0	0	0	978	2000	1905	1955
34 23	0	0	0	0	980	2000	1333	1960
34 23	0	0	0	0	973	2000	1264	1963
34 23	0	1	0	0	962	2000	1505	1965
35 23	0	0	0	0	680	11125	1139	1950
35 23	0	0	1	0	680	11125	1273	1955
35 23	0	0	0	0	556	11125	1055	1960
35 23	0	0	1	0	592A	11125	1319	1963
35 23	0	0	0	0	594	11125	1341	1965

		22	23	24	25	26	27	28	
36	23	2	5	0	0	3	19500	980	1950
36	23	1	2	1	6	11	19500	972	1955
36	23	1	10	2	0	14	12125C	1070	1960
36	23	0	4	1	5	15	12125C	1176	1963
36	23	0	6	0	10	15	12125C	1272	1965
37	23	0	0	1	0	5	24500	615	1950
37	23	0	0	0	1	11	24500	545	1955
37	23	0	0	0	1	13	10875D	909	1960
37	23	0	0	0	2	14	10875D	944	1963
37	23	0	1	1	4	16	10875D	955	1965
38	23	0	0	1	1	1	15375	678	1950
38	23	0	0	1	0	0	15375	690	1955
38	23	0	1	1	1	1	14000C	1364	1960
38	23	0	2	0	1	1	14000C	1497	1963
38	23	0	0	0	0	1	14000C	1509	1965
39	23	0	0	0	0	35	15500	540	1950
39	23	0	0	0	0	35	15500	1273	1955
39	23	0	0	0	1	33	14250C	933	1960
39	23	0	1	1	0	27	14250C	1023	1963
39	23	0	0	1	0	33	14250C	1124	1965
40	23	0	0	0	0	933	7500	1188	1950
40	23	0	0	0	0	943	7500	1009	1955
40	23	0	0	0	0	940	7500	840	1960
40	23	0	0	0	0	942	7500	853	1963
40	23	0	0	0	0	943	7500	926	1965
41	23	0	0	0	0	28	15375	1404	1950
41	23	0	0	0	0	5	15375	1377	1955
41	23	0	0	0	0	18	15375	1270	1960
41	23	0	0	0	1	19	15375	1376	1963
41	23	0	0	0	0	18	15375	1308	1965
42	23	5	4	0	1	985	10250	1023	1950
42	23	0	2	0	2	990	10250	1009	1955
42	23	3	7	0	0	995	10250	835	1960
42	23	0	6	0	0	995	10250	807	1963
42	23	0	0	0	0	994	10250	818	1965
92	23	0	0	1	0	80	12875	244	1963
92	23	0	0	0	0	91	12875	137	1965
163	23	0	0	0	0	76	1375	610	1965
43	23	0	0	0	0	0	12250	1004	1955
43	23	2	7	0	13	3	3875C	983	1960
43	23	0	1	0	0	3	3875C	1183	1963
43	23	0	0	0	1	3	3875C	1195	1965
44	23	0	0	0	0	20	15000	769	1950
44	23	0	0	0	0	18	15000	370	1955
44	23	0	0	0	0	29	15500	667	1960
44	23	0	0	0	2	27	15500	741	1963
44	23	0	0	0	0	26	15500	1364	1965
45	23	0	0	0	0	8	14000	303	1950
45	23	0	0	0	0	0	14000	0	1955
45	23	0	0	0	0	4	6125C	0	1960
45	23	0	0	0	0	5A	6125C	370	1963
45	23	0	0	0	0	4	6125C	286	1965
46	23	0	0	1	0	9	14875	303	1950
46	23	0	0	0	1	8	14875	600	1955
46	23	0	7	0	2	13	6875C	874	1960
46	23	0	0	0	7	21	6875C	884	1963
46	23	0	16	2	15	24	6875C	857	1965
80	23					0	20250	0	1955
80	23	0	0	0	0	12	12500C	0	1960

	22	23	24	25	26	27	28	
80 23	0	0	0	0	13	12500	0	1963
80 23	0	0	0	0	13	12500C	0	1965
47 23	0	0	0	0	476	15250	1000	1950
47 23	0	0	0	0	493	15250	1024	1955
47 23	0	0	0	0	581	15250	1220	1960
47 23	0	0	0	0	409	15250	1156	1963
47 23	0	0	0	0	312	15250	1185	1965
48 23	0	1	0	0	6	12625	0	1950
48 23	0	0	0	0	8	12625	1875	1955
48 23	0	0	0	0	7	12625	1176	1960
48 23	0	0	0	0	9	12625	612	1963
48 23	0	0	0	0	10	12625	806	1965
49 23	0	0	0	0	29	12375	0	1955
49 23	0	0	0	0	39	12375	0	1960
49 23	0	0	0	0	31	12375	645	1963
49 23	1	0	0	0	25	12375	652	1965
93 23	0	0	0	0	185	24125	0	1963
93 23	0	0	0	0	195	24125	248	1965
94 23	0	0	0	0	22	15250C	594	1960
94 23	0	0	0	0	25	15250	643	1963
94 23	0	1	1	1	25	15250C	936	1965
95 23	0	0	1	0	7	10500	714	1963
95 23	0	0	0	0	8	10500	500	1965
96 23	0	0	0	0	3	8750	0	1963
96 23	0	0	0	0	3	9750	0	1965
50 23	0	0	0	1	985	0	1132	1950
50 23	0	2	0	0	982	0	1479	1955
50 23	0	0	0	0	945	0	1398	1960
50 23	0	0	0	0	943	0	1467	1963
50 23	0	1	0	0	941	0	1481	1965
97 23	1	0	0	0	44	9500	1132	1960
97 23	0	0	0	0	33	9500	909	1963
97 23	1	3	0	0	33	9500	877	1965
51 23	0	0	0	0	1	20125	0	1950
51 23	0	0	0	1	0A	20125	0	1955
51 23	0	0	1	0	0	13375C	0	1960
51 23	0	0	0	0	0	13375C	714	1963
51 23	0	0	0	0	0	13375C	370	1965
52 23	0	0	0	0	385	9250	913	1950
52 23	0	0	0	0	385	9250	944	1955
52 23	0	0	0	0	396	9250	795	1960
52 23	0	0	0	0	404	9250	736	1963
52 23	0	0	0	0	385	9250	775	1965
53 23	0	0	0	0	136	19125	1131	1950
53 23	0	0	0	0	136	19125	991	1955
53 23	0	0	0	0	126	12750D	766	1960
53 23		0	0	0	141	12750D	921	1963
53 23	0	0	0	0	144	12750D	972	1965
54 23	0	0	0	0	962	2125	1190	1950
54 23	0	0	0	0	959	2125	1364	1955
54 23	0	0	0	0	944	2125	845	1960
54 23	0	1	0	0	939	2125	1111	1963
54 23	0	0	0	0	941	2125	1413	1965
98 23	0	0	0	0	4	13125	0	1963
98 23	0	0	0	0	4	13125	455	1965
99 23	0	0	0	0	50	14000	507	1963
99 23	0	6	1	0	56	14000	659	1965

	22	23	24	25	26	27	28	
55 23	0	0	0	0	0	8625	954	1950
55 23	0	0	0	0	1	8625	961	1955
55 23	0	0	0	0	2	7625C	918	1960
55 23	0	0	0	0	2	7625	1013	1963
55 23	0	0	0	0	2	7625C	1009	1965
56 23	0	0	0	0	1	14250	0	1950
56 23	0	0	0	0	0	14250	0	1955
56 23	0	0	0	0	0A	7000C	0	1960
56 23	0	0	0	0	0	7000C	0	1963
56 23	0	0	0	0	0A	7000C	0	1965
57 23	0	0	0	0	4	19125	750	1950
57 23	0	0	1	1	0	19125	588	1955
57 23	0	0	0	0	3	13250C	640	1960
57 23	0	7	0	1	3	13250C	696	1963
57 23	0	0	0	0	3	13250C	898	1965
58 23	0	0	1	0	620	3250	755	1950
58 23	0	0	0	0	930	3250	1429	1955
58 23	1	0	0	0	758	3250	1316	1960
58 23	0	1	0	0	719	3250	1463	1963
58 23	1	0	0	1	730	3250	1742	1965
59 23	0	0	0	0	940	10000	1276	1950
59 23	0	0	1	0	961	10000	1538	1955
59 23	0	0	0	0	949	10000	1261	1960
59 23	0	0	1	0	926	10000	1405	1963
59 23	0	0	0	0	915	10000	1549	1965
60 23	1	0	0	0	985	5250	1250	1950
60 23	0	1	0	0	985	5250	1551	1955
60 23	0	0	0	0	954	5250	1532	1960
60 23	2	2	1	6	962	5250	1601	1963
60 23	0	0	0	0	950	5250	1645	1965
61 23	0	0	0	0	706	18875	1359	1950
61 23	0	0	1	0	829	18875	1232	1955
61 23	0	0	0	0	824	10750C	1128	1960
61 23	0	0	0	0	755	10750C	1356	1963
61 23	0	0	0	2	861	10750C	1445	1965
62 23	0	0	0	0	700	10250	1173	1950
62 23	0	0	0	0	980	10250	1208	1955
62 23	0	1	0	0	930	10250	973	1960
62 23	0	0	0	0	968	10250	1170	1963
62 23	0	0	0	0	917	10250	1186	1965
63 23	0	0	0	0	962	8625	1629	1950
63 23	0	0	0	0	968	8625	1678	1955
63 23	0	0	0	0	905	8625	1111	1960
63 23	0	0	0	0	915	8625	1311	1963
63 23	0	1	1	1	915	8625	1452	1965
64 23	0	0	2	0	174	11375	1101	1950
64 23	0	0	1	0	168	11375	1081	1955
64 23	0	0	0	0	171A	11375	1056	1960
64 23	0	0	0	0	102	11375	1389	1963
64 23	0	0	0	0	111	11375	1472	1965
114 23	0	0	0	0	263	20000	417	1965
65 23	0	0	0	0	0	16000	1428	1950
65 23	0	0	0	0	0	16000	3000	1955
65 23	0	0	0	0	0	16000	0	1960
65 23	0	0	0	0	1	16000	1875	1963
65 23	0	0	0	0	1	16000	1290	1965
100 23	0	0	0	0	52	10375	448	1963
100 23	0	0	0	0	48	10375	505	1965
204 23	0	0	0	0	10	12000	0	1963
204 23	0	0	0	0	14	12000	290	1965

		22	23	24	25	26	27	28	
101	23	0	1	0	0	1	19750	0	1963
101	23	0	0	0	0	1	19750	0	1965
66	23	0	0	0	0	1000	8375	1484	1950
66	23	0	0	0	2	734	8375	1689	1955
66	23	0	0	0	0	747	8375	1042	1960
66	23	0	0	0	0	997	8375	1254	1963
66	23	0	1	0	2	747	8375	1265	1965
102	23	0	0	0	0	22	15750	345	1960
102	23	0	0	0	0	30	15750	270	1963
102	23	0	0	1	3	35	15750	482	1965
67	23	0	0	0	0	9	9250	1074	1950
67	23	0	0	0	0	4A	9250	1109	1955
67	23	0	0	0	0	4	8000C	980	1960
67	23	0	0	0	0	5	8000	1081	1963
67	23	0	0	0	0	4	8000C	1120	1965
68	23	0	0	0	0	424	10000	1016	1950
68	23	0	0	0	0	422	10000	947	1955
68	23	0	0	0	0	416	10000	814	1960
68	23	0	0	0	0	397	10000	949	1963
68	23	0	0	0	0	404	10000	984	1965
69	23	1	0	0	0	31	15000	769	1950
69	23	0	0	1	1	33	15000	1111	1955
69	23	0	0	0	0	48	15000	1321	1960
69	23	0	8	2	2	31	15000	1026	1963
69	23	0	0	1	0	31	15000	1064	1965
109	23	0	0	0	0	170	19875	339	1963
109	23	0	0	0	0	180	19875	761	1965
70	23	0	0	0	0	2	20875	1111	1950
70	23	0	0	0	0	0	20875	1169	1955
70	23	0	0	0	0	5	12875C	855	1960
70	23	0	0	0	0	4	12875C	1224	1963
70	23	0	0	0	0	5	12875C	1437	1965
103	23	0	0	0	0	141	13750	0	1963
103	23	0	0	0	0	166	13750	227	1965
216	23	0	0	0	0	354	4875	169	1965
104	23	0	0	0	0	41	11500	901	1960
104	23	0	0	1	0	13	11500	774	1963
104	23	0	0	0	0	9	11500	828	1965
71	23	0	0	0	0	1	13125	1543	1950
71	23	0	0	0	0	1	13125	1613	1955
71	23	0	4	2	7	0	13125	1166	1960
71	23	0	1	0	2	1	13125	1358	1963
71	23	0	1	0	0	1	13125	1444	1965
72	23	1	2	0	0	50	19875	1045	1950
72	23	0	0	0	4	48	19875	969	1955
72	23	2	6	0	0	55	19875	1061	1960
72	23	0	1	0	1	58	19875	1260	1963
72	23	0	0	0	0	58A	19875	1300	1965
73	23	0	0	0	0		6000	1228	1950
73	23	0	0	1	0	53	6000	1325	1955
73	23	0	0	0	0	48	125C	503	1960
73	23	0	0	0	0	44	125C	879	1963
73	23	0	0	2	0	44	125C	1055	1965
74	23	0	0	0	0	61	7625	885	1950
74	23	0	0	0	0	87	7625	952	1955
74	23	0	0	0	1	86	7625	925	1960
74	23	0	3	0	6	80	7625	1008	1963
74	23	0	1	0	0	118	7625	1020	1965

	22	23	24	25	26	27	28	
75 23	0	1	0	2	183	0	1020	1950
75 23	0	1	0	1	220	0	1237	1955
75 23	0	2	0	5	222	0	1093	1960
75 23	0	8	0	67	232	0	1250	1963
75 23	0	0	0	1	234	0	1258	1965
219 23	0	0	0	0	320	19125	795	1965
105 23	0	0	0	0	32	12875	0	1963
105 23	0	0	0	0	35	12875	0	1965
76 23	0	0	0	0	800A	12375	1264	1950
76 23	0	0	0	0	800A	12375	1674	1955
76 23	1	0	0	0	807	12375	1022	1960
76 23	0	0	0	0	853	12375	1307	1963
76 23	1	0	0	0	666	12375	1388	1965
77 23	0	0	0	0	912	3250	1616	1950
77 23	0	0	0	0	948	3250	1867	1955
77 23	1	2	0	1	930	3250	1488	1960
77 23	0	1	3	1	927	3250	1745	1963
77 23	0	1	1	0	925	3250	1743	1965
81 23					37	20000	0	1955
81 23	0	0	0	0	37	11875C	1429	1960
81 23	0	0	0	0	26	11875C	625	1963
81 23	0	0	0	0	31	11875C	556	1965
82 23					156	21000	1395	1955
82 23	0	0	0	0	77	12875C	990	1960
82 23	0	3	0	6	94	12875C	873	1963
82 23	1	6	1	12	94	12875C	839	1965
78 23	0	0	0	0	0	19125	0	1950
78 23	0	0	0	0	0	19125	0	1955
78 23	0	0	1	0	0A	19125	0	1960
78 23	0	0	0	0	0	19125	0	1963
78 23	0	0	0	0	0A	19125	0	1965
79 23	0	0	0	0	368	11000	1410	1950
79 23	0	0	0	0	318	11000	1464	1955
79 23	0	0	0	0	309	11000	959	1960
79 23	0	0	0	0	319	11000	1220	1963
79 23	0	0	0	0	326	11000	1311	1965

	29	30	31	32	33	34	35	
1 24	1		19A	100A	647A	1	0	1950
1 24	0		18	139	647	1	0	1955
1 24	0		21	140	647	1	0	1960
1 24	0		23		647	1	0	1963
1 24	0		23	121L	647	1	0	1965
2 24	0		41D	121	29	76		1950
2 24	0		48	122	29	76	3	1955
2 24	0	770	56	170	29	93	3	1960
2 24	1	795	61	172	29	107	6	1963
2 24	0	741D	65	172	29	107	6	1965
106 24	0	774D	5	29L	2382		2	1965
3 24	1	0BD	6	107	2777	93	16	1950
3 24	0	0BC	7	108	2777	144	17	1955
3 24	2	0B	7	70	2777	205	17	1960
3 24	0	0B	8	70L	2777	205	25	1963
3 24	0	0BD	8	105L	2777	205	25	1965
4 24	0	974	1	15	7687	65	6	1950
4 24	0	660	1	30	7687		6	1955
4 24	0	930	1	40	7687		6	1960
4 24	1	925	1	43	7687	69	3	196
4 24	0	908	1	48L	7687	73	3	1965

		29	30	31	32	33	34	35	
5	24		1340	83	211	84		71	1955
5	24	0	1360	84	210	84	370	70	1960
5	24	0	1396	86	202	84	373	70	1963
5	24	0	1485	87	206	84	373	79	1965
6	24	0	708	279	332	31	352	161	1950
6	24	0	600	291	322	31	355	158	1955
6	24	2	770	300	310	31	368	148	1960
6	24	0	830A	304	290	31	371	145	1963
6	24	0	836	310	303	31	371	142	1965
7	24	0		3	30A	1099	9	2	1950
7	24	0		3	28	1099	9	2	1955
7	24	0		3	30	1099	11	3	1960
7	24	0		3		1099	15	3	1963
7	24	0		3		1099	15	3	1965
8	24	0	0BD	6	22	8512	30	4	1950
8	24	0	0B	7	22	8512	54	4	1955
8	24	3	0B	8	30	8512	56	4	1960
8	24	0	0B	9		8512	64	4	1963
8	24	0	0B	10		8512	64	5	1965
9	24	2	763	65D	387	111	283	32	1950
9	24	0	640	68	386	111		39	1955
9	24	0	1010	71	420	111		50	1960
9	24	0	1247	73	405	111	258	52	1963
9	24	0	1316	74	411	111	263	52	1965
10	24	0		27	129	678	25	4	1950
10	24	0		29	127	678	25	4	1955
10	24	0		30	130	678	23	4	1960
10	24	0		35	218	678	23	3	1963
10	24	0		36	234	678	23	3	1965
113	24	0		115	371	28	0	0	1965
11	24	0		25	114	181	19	2	1955
11	24	0		29	140	181	21	2	1960
11	24	0		33	160	181	29	2	1963
11	24	0		34	162	181	29	2	1965
83	24	0		11		475	19	1	1963
83	24	0		11		475	19	1	1965
12	24	0	429	1	37	9976		6	1950
12	24	0	340	2	41	9976		6	1955
12	24	0	540	2	40	9976	43	6	1960
12	24	0	587	2	42	9976	44	6	1963
12	24	1	614	2	44L	9976	45	6	1965
84	24	0		2	96	623		8	1963
84	24	0		2	95L	623		8	1965
13	24	0	333	114	215	66		21	1950
13	24	0	580	131	231	66		21	1955
13	24	0	320	151	230	66		21	1960
13	24	0	324A	162	227	66	165	21	1963
13	24	1	193D	171	285	66	170	21	1965
85	24	0		2	62L	1284			1963
85	24	0		3	55L	1284			1965
14	24	0	0BD	8	80	757	63	11	1950
14	24	0	0B	9	74	757		11	1955
14	24	0	0B	10	70	757	75	11	1960
14	24	1	0B	11		757	75	11	1963
14	24	0	0B	11	60	757	75	11	1965
15	24	1		48	94	9561A	13	2	1950
15	24	0		60	110A	9561	19	3	1955
15	24	0		68D	110	9561	19	3	1960
15	24	0		72		9561	19	3	1963
15	24	0		73		9561	21	3	1965

		29	30	31	32	33	34	35	
16	24	0		248	243	36	436	103	1955
16	24	0	600	295	240	36	450	103	1960
16	24	0	525	325	250L	36	458	103	1963
16	24	0	524	346	247	36	461	128	1965
17	24	0	0BD	10	19	1138	16	3	1950
17	24	0	0B	11	43	1138	23	3	1955
17	24	0	0B	12	40	1138	29	3	1960
17	24	0	0B	13	45	1138	36	3	1963
17	24	0	0B	16		1138	36	3	1965
87	24	0		2	18	342		1	1963
87	24	0		2	18	342		1	1965
86	24	2		6	209	2345	62	2	1963
86	24	0		7		2345	62	2	1965
18	24	0	254	16	149	51	12	16	1950
18	24	1	380	19	120A	51	12	16	1955
18	24	0	220	23	120A	51	24	16	1960
18	24	1	159	27	118L	51	65	16	1963
18	24	0	209	28	122	51	65	16	1965
19	24	0		47	171	115	29	82	1950
19	24	0		51	171	115	29	82	1955
19	24	4		59	170	115	116	157	1960
19	24	0	1331	63		115	116	157	1963
19	24	0	1328	67		115	116	157	1965
20	24	10	977	96	431	128	553	103	1950
20	24	0	840	102	423	128	553	103	1955
20	24	0	1420	107	450	128	553	103	1960
20	24	2	1538	109	422	128	569	103	1963
20	24	0	1667	111	421	128	569	103	1965
88	24	0		20	133	113	52	5	1963
88	24	0		21	137L	113	52	5	1965
21	24	0	1771	100	628	43	1319	112	1950
21	24	0	1360	103	634	43	1347	107	1955
21	24	0	1940	106	650	43	1369	100	1960
21	24	0	1674	109	651	43	1407	93	1963
21	24	1	1568	110	630	43	1426	91	1965
22	24	0		42	136	49	57	27	1950
22	24	0	1000	49	139	49	84	20	1955
22	24	1	820	61	140	49	98		1960
22	24	0	1136	68		49	129	29	1963
22	24	0	945	74		49	129	29	1965
23	24	0	320D	12	109	284	28	4	1950
23	24	0	340	14		284	28	4	1955
23	24	0		16	110	284	39	5	1960
23	24	0		17	107L	284	33	5	1963
23	24	0	428	18	102L	284	59	5	1965
24	24	0	2217	20	25	1000	14	8	1950
24	24	0		23	26	1000	18	7	1955
24	24	2	2300	26	30	1000	20	6	1960
24	24	0	2156	28	25	1000	30	7	1963
24	24	4	2212	30	27	1000		7	1965
25	24	0	317	100A	127	21	86	29	1950
25	24	0	500	110	272	21	152	33	1955
25	24	1	440	117D	320	21	381	33	1960
25	24	0	525	127	238	21	405	38	1963
25	24	0	650	137	310L	21	405	38	1965
26	24	0		14	104	1222		1	1950
26	24	0		17	104	1222		1	1955
26	24	0		17		1222	5	1	1960
26	24	0		18	97	1222	5	1	1963
26	24	0		18	103	1222	5	1	1965

		29	30	31	32	33	34	35	
27	24	0	1070	12	74	337	174	14	1950
27	24	0	920	13	77	337	192	15	1955
27	24	0	1210	13	80	337	199	16	1960
27	24	0	1251	13	80	337	198	16	1963
27	24	0	1265	14	82	337	204	16	1965
28	24	1	1069	78	385	547	1307	76	1950
28	24	0	580	79	387	547		73	1955
28	24	0	940	83	380	547		72	1960
28	24	0	892	87	388	547	1433	71	1963
28	24	2	1007	89	376L	547	1433	69	1965
89	24	0		2	4	268			1963
89	24	0		2	5L	268			1965
29	24	0	1900	156	487	108			1955
29	24	0	1410	150	470	108	426	150	1960
29	24	0	1662	149	463	108	421	149	1963
29	24	0	2053	148	463	108	423	147	1965
30	24	0	1280	204	353	248	521	149	1955
30	24	0	880	215	350	248	545	147	1960
30	24	0	1002	224	339	248	613	144	1963
30	24	0	1124	229	333	248	625	143	1965
90	24	1		28	220	239		4	1960
90	24	0		31		239	36	3	1963
90	24	0		32	106L	239	38	3	1965
31	24	0		60	262	132	167	20	1950
31	24	0		60	265	132	358	20	1955
31	24	0	430	64	280	132	358	20	1960
31	24	0	397	64	296	132	358	20	1963
31	24	0	435	65	292L	132		20	1965
32	24	0	243	26	132	109	50	11	1950
32	24	0	360	30	135	109	73	11	1955
32	24	0	350	35	130	109		11	1960
32	24	0	438	38		109		11	1963
32	24	0	272	41	138L	109		11	1965
91	24	0		14		246	43	3	1963
91	24	0		14		246	43	3	1965
33	24	0		111	164	28	57	11	1950
33	24	0		119	132	28	107	11	1955
33	24	0		126	130	28	107	11	1960
33	24	3		160		28	107	14	1963
33	24	0		158		28	107	14	1965
34	24	0	283	9	36	112	20	12	1950
34	24	0	260	15	89	112	22	12	1955
34	24	0	290	17	90	112		12	1960
34	24	0	446	18	71	112	26	11	1963
34	24	0	487	20	73L	112	26	11	1965
35	24	4	1059	100D	622	93	276	123	1950
35	24	0	1100	105	623	93	310	96	1955
35	24	0	1910	107	610	93	310	96	1960
35	24	1	2174	108	602	93	314	95	1963
35	24	1	2271	109	608	93	314	95	1965
36	24	0		113	435	3045	124	18	1950
36	24	1		116	482	3045	127	18	1955
36	24	1		136	490	3045	220	18	1960
36	24	1		151	532L	3045	247		1963
36	24	1		159	533L	3045	260		1965
37	24	0	1241	51	74	1492		5	1950
37	24	0		55	119	1492	43	4	1955
37	24	0		62	120	1492	54	4	1960
37	24	0		67		1492	54	4	1963
37	24	0		70	85L	1492	54	4	1965

		29	30	31	32	33	34	35	
38	24	0	2085	12	103	1648			1950
38	24			13	103	1648D	13	2	1955
38	24	0	1720	12	100	1648	13	2	1960
38	24	0	1777	13	103	1648	18	2	1963
38	24	1	1676	14		1648	21	2	1965
39	24	0	1211	12	54	435	6	4	1950
39	24	1		12	123	435	11	5	1955
39	24	0	830	16	170	435	11	5	1960
39	24	2	1024	15	258	435	11	5	1963
39	24	0	1294D	18	172L	435	11	5	1965
40	24		0B	42	187	70	1127	64	1950
40	24	0	0B	41	176	70	1151	59	1955
40	24	0	0B	40	200	70	1176	40	1960
40	24	0	0B	40	186	70	1191	21	1963
40	24	0	0B	41	180	70	1203	21	1965
41	24	0	1281	60A	167A	21A	105	19	1950
41	24	0	1520	85	173	21	114	29	1955
41	24	0	1180	102	200	21	143	33	1960
41	24	0	1300	115	191	21	181	33	1963
41	24	0	1133	124	191L	21	190	33	1965
42	24	0	0B	154	552	301	576	72	1950
42	24	0	0B	159	524	301	582	73	1955
42	24	0	0B	164	530	301	603	71	1960
42	24	1	0B	168	512	301	640	70	1963
42	24	0	0B	171	508	301	664	68	1965
92	24	0		11		322	87	2	1963
92	24	0		12	64	322	101	2	1965
163	24	0	850	163	218L	11	1391	36	1965
43	24	0	880	241	136	370	380	75	1955
43	24	0	800	252	160	370	396	75	1960
43	24	1	747	259	165L	370	401	76	1963
43	24	0	805	265	155L	370	401	75	1965
44	24	0	2000	14	53	97	7		1950
44	24	0		15	92	97	15		1955
44	24	0	1540	17D	100	97	22		1960
44	24	0	1281	20	122	97	26		1963
44	24	0	1374	22	118	97	26		1965
45	24	0		71	198	127		50	1950
45	24	0			193	121D		41	1955
45	24	0		67	150	121		41	1960
45	24	0		89		121		41	1963
45	24	0		100		121			1965
46	24	0		218	199	94	296	29	1950
46	24	0		230	206	98D	285	30	1955
46	24	0		250	210	98		30	1960
46	24	0		273	214	98	404	30	1963
46	24	0	411	288	236L	98	404	32	1965
80	24					237	12	0	1955
80	24	0		8	40	237	12	0	1960
80	24	0		8	42AL	237	12	0	1963
80	24	0		8	34	237	24	0	1965
47	24	0	658	140	311	10	50	80	1950
47	24	1		137	278	10	50	80	1955
47	24	0	670	158	280	10	50	80	1960
47	24	0	703	212	300	10	50		1963
47	24	0	654	231	300	10	50		1965
48	24			15A	163	111	9	0	1950
48	24	0		11	171	111	9	1	1955
48	24	0		12	170	111	14	1	1960
48	24	0		9	369L	111	17	3	1963
48	24	0		10	346	111	17	3	1965

		29	30	31	32	33	34	35	
49	24			1	17	1760	2	0	1955
49	24	0		1	20	1760	2	0	1960
49	24	0	2561	1	14	1760		0	1963
49	24	0	2434	1		1760		0	1965
93	24	0		10	45	587	64	2	1963
93	24	0		11	49	587	68	2	1965
94	24	0		53	190	333	33	5	1960
94	24	0		32	168	333	38	5	1963
94	24	0		28	101	333	43	5	1965
95	24	0		4		1202	11		1963
95	24	0		4		1202	11		1965
96	24	0		1	3L	1031			1963
96	24	0		1	3	1031			1965
50	24	1	447	13	51	1973		12	1950
50	24	0	420	15	101	1973		12	1955
50	24	0	630	18	120	1973	24	12	1960
50	24	1	747	19	121L	1973	27	12	1963
50	24	0	848	22		1973	30	12	1965
97	24	1		26	190	445		4	1960
97	24	2		28	178	445	51	4	1963
97	24	2		30	178L	445	53	4	1965
51	24	0		50	222	141	3	1	1950
51	24	0		60	276	141	4	1	1955
51	24	0		67D	280	141	6	1	1960
51	24	0		69	277	141	6	1	1963
51	24	0		72	130	141	6	1	1965
52	24	1	777	316	331	34	764	94	1950
52	24	0	900	331	255	34	803	94	1955
52	24	0	670	342	320	34		94	1960
52	24	0	613	356	294	34		94	1963
52	24	0	572	366	285	34	1306	94	1965
53	24	0	947	7	37	269	424	21	1950
53	24	0	540	8	19	269	429	20	1955
53	24	0	1050	9	20	269	430	20	1960
53	24	0	960	9	26	269		19	1963
53	24	0	834	10	30	269		19	1965
54	24	0	386	7	46	130		3	1950
54	24	0	360	8	58	130		4	1955
54	24	0	200	10	120	130	47	3	1960
54	24	0	426	11	129	130	47	3	1963
54	24	0	468	13	67	130	47	3	1965
98	24	0		2	118	1267			1963
98	24	0		3	91L	1267			1965
99	24	0		60	236	924	78	3	1963
99	24	0		62	236L	924	87	3	1965
55	24	0	853	10	25	324	138	14	1950
55	24	0	640	11	26	324	144	14	1955
55	24	0	830	11	30	324	160	14	1960
55	24	0	1012	11	28	324	165	14	1963
55	24	0	1020	11	26	324	203	13	1965
56	24	0		1AD	A	1565A			1950
56	24	0		1		1565		1	1955
56	24	0		1	20	1565	5	1	1960
56	24	0		1		1565	5	1	1963
56	24	0		1	22	1565		1	1965
57	24	0		79	219	947		11	1950
57	24	0		87	258	947	102	12	1955
57	24	0		98	310	947	120	12	1960

		29	30	31	32	33	34	35	
57	24	3		104	272L	947	120	12	1963
57	24	1		109	298L	947	120	12	1965
58	24		923D	11	60A	76	22	3	1950
58	24	0		12	61	76	30	3	1955
58	24	0	1000	14	70	76	37	3	1960
58	24	0	1190	16	79	76	82	3	1963
58	24	0	1234	16	74L	76	66	3	1965
59	24		0BD	4	10A	407		3	1950
59	24	0	0B	4	13	407		3	1955
59	24	0	0B	4	20	407	6	3	1960
59	24	0	0B	5	20	407	10	3	1963
59	24	0	0B	5	23L	407	11	3	1965
60	24	0		7	13	1285	19	3	1950
60	24	0		8	14	1285	31	2	1955
60	24	0	340	8	10	1285	31	2	1960
60	24	0	272	9	14	1285	32	2	1963
60	24	0	255	9	21L	1285	32	3	1965
61	24	0	0BD	67	274	300	88	5	1950
61	24	0		74	215	300	97	4	1955
61	24	0		93	230	300	165	4	1960
61	24	0	0B	101	373	300	181	4	1963
61	24	0	0B	108	278L	300	187	3	1965
62	24	5	412	80	539	313	311	92	1950
62	24	0	440	88	520	313	315	86	1955
62	24	2	610	95	520	313	334	86	1960
62	24	1	889	98	511	313	339	86	1963
62	24	1	1176	101	501	313	365	86	1965
63	24	0	147	92	367	92	293	39	1950
63	24	0	140	95	449	92	318	39	1955
63	24	0	100	97	430	92	300	39	1960
63	24	0	93	98	446	92	312	39	1963
63	24	0	93	100	475L	92	320	39	1965
64	24	4	1260	68D	392	238	292	31	1950
64	24	0		74	424	238		51	1955
64	24	1	2020	77	460	238	292	46	1960
64	24	0	2066	79	441	238		46	1963
64	24	0	2248	80	440	238		46	1965
114	24	0		118	385L	26			1965
65	24	0		4AE	0E	2150E	1		1950
65	24	0		4	1	2150	1		1955
65	24	0		4	0	2150	1		1960
65	24	0		3	1	2150	1		1963
65	24	1		3	2	2150	1		1965
100	24	0		17	281	196		9	1963
100	24	0	125D	18	292	196		9	1965
204	24	0	1000	31	514	72	97	8	1963
204	24	0	1333	32	508L	72	97	8	1965
101	24	0		4	16	638		0	1963
101	24	0		4		638		0	1965
66	24	0	0B	56	381	505	218	35	1950
66	24	0	0B	58	397	505	239	36	1955
66	24	0	0B	60	410	505	258	36	1960
66	24	0	0B	62	412	505	264	36	1963
66	24	0	0B	63	408	505	265	37	1965
102	24	0		5	30	2506	1	2	1960
102	24	0		5		2506	1	2	1963
102	24	0		5		2506	1	2	1965
67	24	1	1478	16	84	450	201	37	1950
67	24	0	980	16	84	450	202	36	1955

		29	30	31	32	33	34	35	
67	24	0	1800	17	80	450	212	34	1960
67	24	1	1589	17	73	450	214	31	1963
67	24	0	1593	17	71	450	216	30	1965
68	24	0	1143	115	120	41	397	127	1950
68	24	0	840	121	109	41	412	127	1955
68	24	2	1190	130	110	41	427	124	1960
68	24	0	1073	140	98	41	427	124	1963
68	24	0	1104D	144	98L	41	432	124	1965
69	24	0	968	17	189	185		9	1950
69	24	0		23	254	185	21	10	1955
69	24	0	930	25	320	185	24	10	1960
69	24	0	1053	28	481	185	23	5	1963
69	24	2	925	29	331L	185	23	5	1965
109	24	0		10	126	940			1963
109	24	2		11	125	940			1965
70	24	0	292	36	92	514	15	6	1950
70	24	0	160	39	152	514	15	6	1955
70	24	0		51	150	514	20	7	1960
70	24	0	626A	56	197L	514	22	7	1963
70	24	0	456D	60	222L	514	22	7	1965
103	24	0		28	386	56	77	7	1963
103	24	0		29	386	56	82	7	1965
216	24	0	50	190	280L	5	800	20	1965
104	24	2		33	350	164	95	12	1960
104	24	0		36	344L	164	95	12	1963
104	24	4	1906D	27	264L	164	96	12	1965
71	24	0	1587	27	199	781	28	10	1950
71	24	0	400	31	317	781	32	10	1955
71	24	1	1640	35	330	781	59	10	1960
71	24	1	1522A	39	334	781	76	10	1963
71	24	0	1565	40	335	781	75	10	1965
72	24	0	644	10	56	1221		18	1950
72	24	0	1240	11	72	1221	123	18	1955
72	24	0	1160	13	80	1221	147	18	1960
72	24	0	1155A	14	99	1221	151	18	1963
72	24	0	1225	15		1221	152	17	1965
73	24	2		9AD	101	22402		5	1950
73	24	1		9	99	22402	9	5	1955
73	24	3		10	100	22402	11	6	1960
73	24	1		10	103L	22402	15	6	1963
73	24	3	179D	10	108L	22402	17	6	1965
74	24	3	800	208	305	244	1205	128	1950
74	24	0	560	210	291	244	1240	125	1955
74	24	0	580	215	300A	244	1261	122	1960
74	24	1	841	221	303	244	1310	105	1963
74	24	4	880D	224	307	244	1325	90	1965
75	24	6	2310	19	235	9363	511	40	1950
75	24	0	2080	21	241	9363	580	38	1955
75	24	7	2580	19	200	9363	594	40	1960
75	24	3	2588	20	198	9363	615	40	1963
75	24	3	2689D	21	192L	9363	623	36	1965
219	24	0		32	161L	236	103	80	1965
105	24	0		17	179	274	61		1963
105	24	0		18		274	61		1965
76	24	0	717	13AD	83	187	222	16	1950
76	24	0		14	120	187	221	17	1955
76	24	0	1000	15	120	187	221	17	1960
76	24	0	708	14	123	187	222	17	1963
76	24	0	681	15	105	187	222	17	1965

		29	30	31	32	33	34	35	
77	24	0	283	6	22	912	7	1	1950
77	24	0	360	6	32	912	18	1	1955
77	24	1	510	8D	30A	912	27	1	1960
77	24	1	487	9	27	912	31	1	1963
77	24	0	463	10	30A	912	31	1	1965
81	24					159	85	4	1955
81	24	0		103	80	159		5	1960
81	24	0		112	82	159	85	5	1963
81	24	0		120	127	159	85	6	1965
82	24					171	76	8	1955
82	24	0		83	170	171	94	8	1960
82	24	0		90	181L	171	111	8	1963
82	24	1		94	172	171	117		1965
78	24			23		195		0	1950
78	24	0		23		195		0	1955
78	24	0		26		195		0	1960
78	24	0		26		195		0	1963
78	24	0		26		195		0	1965
79	24	4	961	63	304	256	189	45	1950
79	24	0	800	69	321	256	202	46	1955
79	24	0	1310	72D	260	256	207	46	1960
79	24	0	1351	75	324	256	228	46	1963
79	24	0	1243	76	325	256	224	46	1965

		36	37	38	39	40	41	42	
1	25	1A		342C	100A			0	1950
1	25	1A		342C	100A			0	1955
1	25	1		342A	100H	50A		0	1960
1	25	1B	0B	342A	100A	50A	4	0	1963
1	25	1		342A	99		2	0	1965
2	25	3	1000AB	1201C	72		0	1	1950
2	25	3B		1201C	72		16	1	1955
2	25	3		1434	73	50A	6	1	1960
2	25	3	0B	1434	72	50A	2	1	1963
2	25	3		1434	65		7	1	1965
106	25				84	674	231	0	1965
3	25	3	844	637	94	467		1	1950
3	25	3	642	637	94		60	1	1955
3	25	3H		630	93H			1	1960
3	25	3		630	94		43	1	1963
3	25	3		630	88	603	54	1	1965
4	25	2	897	778	65	768	11	1	1950
4	25	2	787	778	65	630	45	1	1955
4	25	2G	749	778A	67H		56	1	1960
4	25	2	682	778A	65		56	1	1963
4	25	2	706	778A	67		53	1	1965
5	25	2	880	1350	90	342	320	0	1955
5	25	2G	190	1009	90	636	269	0	1960
5	25	2	483	1009	90	636	204	0	1963
5	25	2	462	1009	90	636	191	0	1965
6	25	1A	388	733C	95A	561	51	1	1950
6	25	1A	609	733C	95A	484	53	1	1955
6	25	1	568	768	95A	484	52	1	1960
6	25	2B	776B	768	95	484	61	1	1963
6	25	2		768	95	484	84	1	1965
7	25	2	465	542	96			1	1950
7	25	2B	470	542	96			1	1955
7	25	2		1135	95			1	1960
7	25	2		1135	96		26	1	1963
7	25	2		1135	94		6	1	1965

		36	37	38	39	40	41	42	
8	25	2		1709	94	156		1	1950
8	25	2		1709A	94	156		1	1955
8	25	2G		1586	90			1	1960
8	25	2		1586	94			1	1963
8	25	2		1586	93			1	1965
9	25	2		634A	85		9	1	1950
9	25	2		634A	85		13	1	1955
9	25	2G	100	634	80		13	1	1960
9	25	2	56	634	85		12	1	1963
9	25	2		634	80	282	11	1	1965
10	25	5		3103	83			0	1950
10	25	5		3103	83		24	0	1955
10	25	4H		3397	85	50A		0	1960
10	25	5		3397	83	50A		0	1963
10	25	5	134	3397	85		1	0	1965
113	25				52		395	0	1965
11	25	3B		1610A	83		219	0	1955
11	25	3		1610	83A		91	0	1960
11	25	3		1610	83		77	0	1963
11	25	3		1610	90		20	0	1965
83	25	4B		2286			29	0	1963
83	25	4		2286	48		89	0	1965
12	25	4		728	51	740	47	1	1950
12	25	4		728	51	869		1	1955
12	25	4		679	48		64	1	1960
12	25	4	725	679	51		63	1	1963
12	25	4		679	46	952	35	1	1965
84	25	4B	0B	508				0	1963
84	25	4		508	60			0	1965
13	25	4		1878	64			0	1950
13	25	4	991	1878	64			1	1955
13	25	4	970	1669	64		2	0	1960
13	25	4	993	1669	64		1	0	1963
13	25	4		1669	64	103	1	0	1965
85	25	4B	0B	254				0	1963
85	25	4		254	52			0	1965
14	25	2		1305	90	545	67	1	1950
14	25	2		1305	90	545	17	1	1955
14	25	2G		1351	95		18	1	1960
14	25	2		1351	90		16	1	1963
14	25	2		1351	88		6	1	1965
15	25	3		1556	26			1	1950
15	25	3B		1556	26			1	1955
15	25	3H		1557A	26A	100A		1	1960
15	25	3		1557A	26	100A		1	1963
15	25	3		1557A	20			1	1965
16	25	4A	558	1887A			3	1	1955
16	25	4		1887		100A	3	1	1960
16	25	3B		1887		100A	7	1	1963
16	25	3		1887	93A		6	1	1965
17	25	1	233AB	1763A	94	256		1	1950
17	25	1B	353	1763A	94	256	22	1	1955
17	25	1A	253	1763	96	256	22	1	1960
17	25	1	326	1763	94	256	19	1	1963
17	25	1	213	1763	97	256A	19	1	1965
87	25	4B	0B	1270			214	0	1963
87	25	4		1270	50		377	0	1965

		36	37	38	39	40	41	42	
86	25	4B		1270			202	0	1963
86	25	4		1270	46			1	1965
18	25	1A		1880	96A			1	1950
18	25	1A	495	1880	96A	985	72	1	1955
18	25	1A		1979	96A	590	34	1	1960
18	25	1B		1979	96	590	36	1	1963
18	25	1	517	1979	76	590	35	1	1965
19	25	2A		2528AC	84A			1	1950
19	25	2A		2528AC	84A	389	17	1	1955
19	25	2		2528	84A	389		1	1960
19	25	1B		2528	84	389	15	1	1963
19	25	1	353	2528	81	389	14	1	1965
20	25	3A		489C	75	356	36	1	1950
20	25	3A	467	489C	75		26	1	1955
20	25	3H	316	602	75	491		1	1960
20	25	2B	393	602	75	491	22	1	1963
20	25	2	293	602	64	491	23	1	1965
88	25	4B		1016				0	1963
88	25	4		1016	68		2	1	1965
21	25	1	468	560	97			1	1950
21	25	1B	412	560	97	635	23	1	1955
21	25	1A	530	673	97	929	15	1	1960
21	25	1	506	673	97	929	15	1	1963
21	25	1		673	96	967	15	1	1965
22	25	2		1407C	98	52	36	1	1950
22	25	2	488	1407C	98	52	29	1	1955
22	25	2G	982	1429	98A	59	6	1	1960
22	25	2	996	1429	98	59	6	1	1963
22	25	2		1429	97	81		1	1965
23	25	2		1260	99		33	1	1950
23	25	2B		1260	99		39	1	1955
23	25	1		1131	94	252	31	1	1960
23	25	2		1131	99	252	30	1	1963
23	25	2		1131	94		31	1	1965
24	25	2		83	92			0	1950
24	25	2		83	92		51	0	1955
24	25	2H		83A	91H	100A	63	0	1960
24	25	2		83A	92	100A	71	0	1963
24	25	2		83A	93		95	0	1965
25	25	1A		1893	98A			1	1950
25	25	1A	497	1893	98A	398		1	1955
25	25	1A		1859	98A	100A		1	1960
25	25	1B	0B	1859	98	100A		1	1963
25	25	1		1859	98		18	1	1965
26	25	2		1259C	46			0	1950
26	25	2D		1259C	46A			0	1955
26	25	2H		1259A	46A	50A	107	0	1960
26	25	2	0B	1259A	46	50	102	0	1963
26	25	2		1259A	90		50	1	1965
27	25	2	0AB	614	95	252	2	1	1950
27	25	2	0	614	95		6	0	1955
27	25	2G	344	568	92	471	5	0	1960
27	25	2	629	568	95	471	3	0	1963
27	25	2		568	93	471	3	1	1965
28	25	2	597	734	97A		100	1	1950
28	25	2B		734	97A	584	95	1	1955
28	25	2H	703	755	97H	685	133	1	1960
28	25	2	353	755	83	685	100	1	1963
28	25	2	647	755	83	915	64A	1	1965

		36	37	38	39	40	41	42	
89	25	3B	0B	2032	51B			0	1963
89	25	3		2032	48			0	1965
29	25	2		631	82		12	1	1955
29	25	2G		594	82	657		1	1960
29	25	2		594	82	657		1	1963
29	25	2		594	80	657		1	1965
30	25	2	275	631	51		83	1	1955
30	25	2G	648	839	52H	967	74	1	1960
30	25	2	589	839	51	967	72	1	1963
30	25	2		839	51	982	70	1	1965
90	25	3H	470	1397A			85	0	1960
90	25	3B	0B	1397A			65	1	1963
90	25	3		1397A	62		43	0	1965
31	25	2		838C	98			1	1950
31	25	2		838C	98	121		1	1955
31	25	3H		687	96	392	27	1	1960
31	25	2		687	98	392	37	1	1963
31	25	2		687	97	287	32	1	1965
32	25	2		1317C	97			1	1950
32	25	2	492	1317C	97			1	1955
32	25	2G		1345	96	100A	26	1	1960
32	25	2		1345	97	100A	26	1	1963
32	25	2		1345	92	113	32	1	1965
91	25	2B		2032	45B			0	1963
91	25	2		2032	61			1	1965
33	25	2A		1398C	92A			1	1950
33	25	2A		1398C	92A	419			1955
33	25	2		1333	92	419A		1	1960
33	25	1B	0A	1333	79	419A	0A	1	1963
33	25	1		1333	80	419		1	1965
34	25	2	1000AB	1753A	98	60A		1	1950
34	25	2		1753A	98			1	1955
34	25	2G		1753	97	121		1	1960
34	25	2	0	1753	98	121		1	1963
34	25	2		1753	96	121	69	1	1965
35	25	4		640C	68	170		1	1950
35	25	4B		640C	68	239		1	1955
35	25	4		596	68	259	10	1	1960
35	25	4		596	68	259	9	1	1963
35	25	4		596	59	259	14	1	1965
36	25	4		1666	85			0	1950
36	25	4	508	1666	85		5	0	1955
36	25	4G		1643	85	100A	3	0	1960
36	25	4		1643	85	100A	4	0	1963
36	25	4		1643	83		4	0	1965
37	25	5		1941C	89			0	1950
37	25	5B		1941C	89		17	0	1955
37	25	5		1941A	90	50A	8	0	1960
37	25	5		1941A	89	50A	8	0	1963
37	25	5		1941A	85			0	1965
38	25	1		196	85			1	1950
38	25	1B		196	85		1	0	1955
38	25	1		227	95H			1	1960
38	25	1		227	85		3	1	1963
38	25	1		227	98	131	4	1	1965
39	25	3		145	94			0	1950
39	25	3	399	145	94	210	37	1	1955
39	25	3G		203	94H	210A	37	0	1960
39	25	3	0B	203	94	210	37	0	1963
39	25	3		203	96		35	1	1965

		36	37	38	39	40	41	42	
40	25	2		1377	94			0	1950
40	25	2		1377	94	293	186	0	1955
40	25	2G	400	1010	94	510	200A	0	1960
40	25	2	443	1010	94	510	213	0	1963
40	25	2		1010	94	510	154	0	1965
41	25	5	850	439A	91			0	1950
41	25	5B	903	439A	91			0	1955
41	25	4H	766	439	90A	895	77	0	1960
41	25	5	959	439	91	895	77	0	1963
41	25	5	939	439	89	895	25	1	1965
42	25	1	163	1016	98	427	7	1	1950
42	25	1B	161	1016	98	359	14	1	1955
42	25	1	667	755	99		13	1	1960
42	25	1	254	755	98		14	1	1963
42	25	1		755	99	623	15	1	1965
92	25	4B		2032			430	0	1963
92	25	4		2032	65		518	0	1965
163	25				74	209	355	1	1965
43	25	2B		1831	89	815	6	1	1955
43	25	2	403	1846	89A		6	1	1960
43	25	2	491	1846	89		6	1	1963
43	25	2	499	1846	89A	949	7	1	1965
44	25	2A		415A	92	91	0	0	1950
44	25	2A		415A	92	91	0	1	1955
44	25	2H		415	92H	213	1	0	1960
44	25	2B		415	92	213	13	0	1963
44	25	2	508	415	94		5	0	1965
45	25	3		734				1	1950
45	25	3B		734				1	1955
45	25	3A		734A				1	1960
45	25	3		734A				1	1963
45	25	3		734A				1	1965
46	25	4		1244	17		0	1	1950
46	25	4B		1244	17		0	1	1955
46	25	4		1291	17A	121	1	1	1960
46	25	4		1291	17	121	1	1	1963
46	25	4		1291	17A	121	1	1	1965
80	25	1A		1829					1955
80	25	1A		1429		50A		0	1960
80	25	1B		1429		50	0A	0	1963
80	25	1		1429				0	1965
47	25	2A		674C	54A			0	1950
47	25	2A		674C	54A		348	0	1955
47	25	2H		674	54H		408	0	1960
47	25	2B		674	54A		360	0	1963
47	25	2	500	674	50		532	1	1965
48	25	2	1000B	3429A	99A			0	1950
48	25	2B		3429A	99		16	0	1955
48	25	3A		3429A	99A			0	1960
48	25	3B	0B	3429A	98A			0	1963
48	25	3		3429A	70		86A	1	1965
49	25	2F		254A	95		36	1	1955
49	25	3H		254	93H			0	1960
49	25	2	0B	254	95			0	1963
49	25	2	547	254	95A		58	1	1965
93	25	3B		1270			28	0	1963
93	25	3	468	1270			213	0	1965
94	25	2A		2540A				0	1960
94	25	2B		2540A			7	0	1963
94	25	2		2540A	50		8	0	1965

	36	37	38	39	40	41	42	
95 25	2B		762	90B			0	1963
95 25	2		762	62			1	1965
96 25	1B	0B	254	99B			0	1963
96 25	1		254	99			0	1965
50 25	2		725	98	434		1	1950
50 25	2	313	725	98	171	15	1	1955
50 25	2G	933	905	98A	235	11	1	1960
50 25	2	388	905	98	235	11	1	1963
50 25	2	380	905	94	235		1	1965
97 25	2		508A	91G	527	268	0	1960
97 25	2D	49	508A		527	180	0	1963
97 25	2		508A	95A		99	0	1965
51 25	2		1328A				0	1950
51 25	2B		1328A				0	1955
51 25	2		1328		50A		0	1960
51 25	2		1328		50A	0A	0	1963
51 25	2		1328				0	1965
52 25	2	582	757	42	802		1	1950
52 25	2	476	757	42	896	42	1	1955
52 25	2G	404	767	43	900A	31	1	1960
52 25	2	574	767	42	900A	24	1	1963
52 25	2	601	767	41	900A		1	1965
53 25	2	701	1285	74			0	1950
53 25	2	689	1285	74		27	1	1955
53 25	2G	591	1284A	74A	877	24	1	1960
53 25	2	697	1284A	74	877	33	1	1963
53 25	2	655	1284A	74A	903	21	1	1965
54 25	2		2358C	96			1	1950
54 25	2		2358C	96		32	1	1955
54 25	2G		2358	96A	125	32	1	1960
54 25	2		2358	96	125	21	1	1963
54 25	2		2358	94	125	19	1	1965
98 25	2G		381	69B			0	1963
98 25	2		381	99			1	1965
99 25	4B	956	1778	23B		25	0	1963
99 25	4		1778	42		22	0	1965
55 25	1		1091	99		12	1	1950
55 25	1		1091	99		19	1	1955
55 25	1G	420	894	96	928	22	1	1960
55 25	1	513	894	99	928	17	1	1963
55 25	1A		894	96	928	14	1	1965
56 25	1		254A				1	1950
56 25	1B		254A				1	1955
56 25	1		254A		50A		1	1960
56 25	1	0B	254A		50A	0A	1	1963
56 25	1		254A				1	1965
57 25	2		771A	86			0	1950
57 25	2		771A	86		1	1	1955
57 25	2G		771A	88	100A	3	1	1960
57 25	2		771	86	100A	6	1	1963
57 25	2		771	88		2	1	1965
58 25	2		2490C	93	444A		1	1950
58 25	2B		2490C	93		28	1	1955
58 25	2		2580	93H		33	1	1960
58 25	2		2580	93		30	1	1963
58 25	2	3	2580	73		27	1	1965
59 25	2A		1429	98A	1		1	1950
59 25	2A		1429	98A		18	1	1955
59 25	2		1443	98	100A		1	1960

		36	37	38	39	40	41	42	
59	25	1B		1443	93	100A	21	1	1963
59	25	1		1443	92	107A	21	1	1965
60	25	1		692	95			1	1950
60	25	1B		692	95			1	1955
60	25	1A	254	692	95	247		1	1960
60	25	1	234	692	95	247		1	1963
60	25	1		692	95	250A		1	1965
61	25	3		2116C	83			1	1950
61	25	3	239	2116C	83			1	1955
61	25	3G		2116A	83			1	1960
61	25	3	873	2116A	83	100		1	1963
61	25	3	947	2116A	86		19	1	1965
62	25	4		678	72		1	1	1950
62	25	4B	786	678	72	299A	7	1	1955
62	25	4A	30	577	72A	299	6	1	1960
62	25	4	16	577	72	299	4	1	1963
62	25	4	5	577	92	391	5	1	1965
63	25	1		651	97	145A	13	1	1950
63	25	1		651	97	145	5	1	1955
63	25	1	54	853	97	289	5	1	1960
63	25	1	52	853	97	289	4	1	1963
63	25	1	17	853	92	289	5	1	1965
64	25	3	0B	587	80			1	1950
64	25	3B		587	80		11	1	1955
64	25	3H		553	75		10	1	1960
64	25	3		553	80		5	1	1963
64	25	3		553	90	123	3	1	1965
114	25				26		110	0	1965
65	25	1		79A	100			0	1950
65	25	1B		79A	100			0	1955
65	25	1		79	99A	50A		0	1960
65	25	1		79	100	50A	80	0	1963
65	25	1		79	99		227	0	1965
100	25	3G		1016	90	877	581	0	1963
100	25	3		1016	90	877	628	1	1965
204	25	1B		2032			575	0	1963
204	25	1	511	2032			202	0	1965
101	25	1B	0B	254				0	1963
101	25	1		254	99			0	1965
66	25	1	140	608C	100	342		0	1950
66	25	1	216	608C	100	342	35	0	1955
66	25	1	410	566	100	342	33	1	1960
66	25	1	107	566	100	342	53	1	1963
66	25	1	181	566	100	450	58	1	1965
102	25	2A		457A	66			0	1960
102	25	2D		457A	65A		5	0	1963
102	25	2		457A	65	788	38	0	1965
67	25	2	685	580	94			0	1950
67	25	2B	703	580	94	670		0	1955
67	25	1H	633	555	94	902		0	1960
67	25	2	637	555	94	902		0	1963
67	25	2	756	555	94	943	19	0	1965
68	25	2		1351	56	900A	253	0	1950
68	25	2	736A	1351	56	988	304	0	1955
68	25	2G	433	1351	53	961	327	0	1960
68	25	2	462	1351	56	961	300	0	1963
68	25	2	431	1351	58	961	263	0	1965

		36	37	38	39	40	41	42	
69	25	2		321	86A		124	0	1950
69	25	2B		321	86A		172	0	1955
69	25	3H		321	86H	419A	192A	0	1960
69	25	2		321	86A	419A	272	0	1963
69	25	2		321	82		234	0	1965
109	25	4B	527	1270	52B			0	1963
109	25	4	395	1270	55		336	0	1965
70	25	2		1652	94			1	1950
70	25	2		1652	94		0	1	1955
70	25	2H	13	1652	95H	50A	1	1	1960
70	25	3G	1000B	1652	94	50A	2	1	1963
70	25	3	19	1652	93		1	1	1965
103	25	4B		1270	75B			0	1963
103	25	4		1270	70		520	0	1965
216	25		346		36	323	234	1	1965
104	25	2		254A	90G		232	0	1960
104	25	3D		254A	91A		177	0	1963
104	25	3	476	254A	92		84	0	1965
71	25	1		590C	98		14	1	1950
71	25	1		590C	98	336	34		1955
71	25	1	117	605	99		39	1	1960
71	25	1	49	605	98		33	1	1963
71	25	1	998	605	99		37	1	1965
72	25	3	467	445	49			0	1950
72	25	3	561	445	49		69	1	1955
72	25	3A	436	445A	58G			0	1960
72	25	3	841	445A	59		58	0	1963
72	25	3	802	445A	59A		50	0	1965
73	25	2A	1000AB	376	50A		4	1	1950
73	25	2A		376	50A		5	1	1955
73	25	2A		480	50A			1	1960
73	25	2B		480	50A			1	1963
73	25	2		480	50		4	1	1965
74	25	3	345	702	55A	945	81	1	1950
74	25	3B	384	702	55A	945	112	1	1955
74	25	3	476	815	55A	987	96	1	1960
74	25	3	305	815	55A	987	114	1	1963
74	25	3	444	815	55	987	71	1	1965
75	25	3	879	811	34	839	13	1	1950
75	25	3B	918	811	34	895	14	1	1955
75	25	4		812	35	929	15	1	1960
75	25	3		812	34	929	17	1	1963
75	25	3	238	812	35A	929	15	1	1965
219	25		431		30			0	1965
105	25	3B		914				0	1963
105	25	3		914	26			0	1965
76	25	1A		965C	85A			1	1950
76	25	1A		965C	85A			1	1955
76	25	1		1146	85A		65	1	1960
76	25	1B		1146	85		65	1	1963
76	25	1		1146	67		22	1	1965
77	25	1A		1057C	92A	302		1	1950
77	25	1A	568	1057C	92A	302		1	1955
77	25	1	579	956	92A		26	1	1960
77	25	1B	467	956	93		26	1	1963
77	25	1		956	93			1	1965
81	25	3A		1727					1955
81	25	3A		1778A				0	1960

		36	37	38	39	40	41	42	
81	25	3B		1778A				0	1963
81	25	3		1778A				1	1965
82	25	5A		1579					1955
82	25	5		1579	65A		6	1	1960
82	25	3B		1579	65A		5	1	1963
82	25	3		1579	65		1	1	1965
78	25	2		381A	99A			0	1950
78	25	2B		381A	99				1955
78	25	2A		381A	99A	50A		0	1960
78	25	2		381A	99A	50A	0A	0	1963
78	25	2		381A	99			0	1965
79	25	3		916C	41		5	0	1950
79	25	3	511	916C	41	288	6	0	1955
79	25	3	374	916	50H		4	0	1960
79	25	3		916	41		7	0	1963
79	25	3		916	41	424	10	0	1965

		43	44	45	46	47	48	
1	26	2		0AB		0		1950
1	26	2		0	0	0		1955
1	26	2				588		1960
1	26	2	1333	0B		667		1963
1	26	2	741			0		1965
2	26	1		0AB		476		1950
2	26	1	40	0		370	0E	1955
2	26	1	70			370		1960
2	26	1	70	0B		294		1963
2	26	1	80			244		1965
106	26	5	0		943	328		1965
3	26	3	355	147	314	690		1950
3	26	3	190	154	266	597		1955
3	26	3	220		206	599		1960
3	26	3	381		125J	482		1963
3	26	3	401		137	459	530	1965
4	26	3	717	255	209	163		1950
4	26	3	610	386	189	186	10E	1955
4	26	3	550	500	184	339	38	1960
4	26	3	436	617	214	408	79	1963
4	26	3	346	700	221	368	130	1965
5	26	1	530	53	0	267	570	1955
5	26	1	500	100		357	350	1960
5	26	1	513	32		394	209	1963
5	26	1	549	61		414	270	1965
6	26	1	800	510	351	396		1950
6	26	1	710	369	383	357	840	1955
6	26	1	670	400	363	339	540	1960
6	26	1	726	226B	369	288	293	1963
6	26	1	758	434	389	284	240	1965
7	26	3		358		933		1950
7	26	3		336	0	727		1955
7	26	3				880		1960
7	26	3				556		1963
7	26	3				485		1965
8	26	3			94	648		1950
8	26	3	1370		380	522		1955
8	26	3	890		206	578		1960
8	26	3	1075		209J	505		1963
8	26	3			189	517		1965
9	26	1	84			674		1950
9	26	1	50	11	56	444		1955

		43	44	45	46	47	48	
9	26	1	10	0	48	272		1960
9	26	1	50	2	106D	262		1963
9	26	1	50	0	124	271		1965
10	26	1			184	227		1950
10	26	1	1070		262	405		1955
10	26	1			230	0		1960
10	26	1			191J	182		1963
10	26	1	2050		178	182		1965
113	26	5	2941		140	0		1965
11	26	1	1300			769		1955
11	26	1	1820		145	417		1960
11	26	1	1658		100J	278		1963
11	26	1	986		164	323		1965
83	26	5	556		262	328		1963
83	26	5	1000		174	330		1965
12	26	3	804	15	321	307	349	1950
12	26	3	640		263	329	440	1955
12	26	3	630		223	389	700	1960
12	26	3	602	187	265	392	548	1963
12	26	3	804		256	359	390	1965
84	26	5		0B		0		1963
84	26	5	0			270		1965
13	26	1	1274		297	395		1950
13	26	1	1420	2	305	410	280AI	1955
13	26	1	1520	0	342	359		1960
13	26	1	1280	1	321J	457	511	1963
13	26	1	1390	13	328	448		1965
85	26	5		0B		0	0	1963
85	26	5				313		1965
14	26	3			457	595	1364	1950
14	26	3	360		537	476		1955
14	26	3	450		221	769	740	1960
14	26	3	476		322J	556	166	1963
14	26	3	220		287	574	540	1965
15	26	0				522		1950
15	26	0				0	0E	1955
15	26	0				0		1960
15	26	0				313		1963
15	26	0				551		1965
16	26	5	180	0	195	603		1955
16	26	5	670		300	619		1960
16	26	5	185		335J	530		1963
16	26	5	220		309	506	340	1965
17	26	3		308	144	598		1950
17	26	3	180	159	144	592	0E	1955
17	26	3		100	184	730		1960
17	26	3		128	144J	728		1963
17	26	3	578	83	237	658		1965
87	26	5		0B	1437J	135	500	1963
87	26	5			1840	291		1965
86	26	5			103J	196		1963
86	26	5			85	231		1965
18	26	3		3010	540	943		1950
18	26			3650	237	345		1955
18	26	3			166	1089		1960
18	26	3	0		195K	682		1963
18	26	3			199	654		1965

		43	44	45	46	47	48	
19	26	3			569	563		1950
19	26	3	210		436A	500	1220E	1955
19	26	3	50			568		1960
19	26	3	79			420		1963
19	26	3	14			391		1965
20	26	4		0B		245	0E	1950
20	26	4	50	17		341		1955
20	26	4	60	0		358		1960
20	26	4	43	20		344		1963
20	26	4	40	40		320		1965
88	26	5			296	435		1963
88	26	5			195	816		1965
21	26	1	509	591	455	344	266	1950
21	26	1	450	603	457	395	970F	1955
21	26	1	330	500	361	362	430	1960
21	26	1	313	555	326	359	154	1963
21	26	1	285	618	281	337	240	1965
22	26	3	261	1558	250	1163		1950
22	26	3		1602	337	625		1955
22	26	3		0	500	789		1960
22	26	3	282	9	347J	602		1963
22	26	3		17	377	577		1965
23	26	3		175	155	1053		1950
23	26	3			170	721		1955
23	26	3			171	0		1960
23	26	3			171J	641		1963
23	26	3			194	714		1965
24	26	0		0AB	319	535		1950
24	26	0	1460		253	546	540H	1955
24	26	0	1030		323	312	371	1960
24	26	0	707	0B	471J	543	152	1963
24	26	0	796		364	556	190	1965
25	26	3		3985	100	714		1950
25	26	3		3969	95	263		1955
25	26	3	480		100	135		1960
25	26	3	267	0B	160K	648		1963
25	26	3	0		176	732		1965
26	26					1428		1950
26	26	0				500		1955
26	26	0	1460		51	645		1960
26	26	0		0B	77K	727		1963
26	26	0			72	658		1965
27	26	3	454	348	589	238	17	1950
27	26	3	710	41	357	272		1955
27	26	3	630	0	392	339	150	1960
27	26	3	739	14	372	394	163	1963
27	26	3	748	15	297	427	140	1965
28	26	1	830	15	168	336		1950
28	26	1	740		162	316	40G	1955
28	26	1	790	100	122	339		1960
28	26	1	753	442	130	293	49	1963
28	26	1	517	487	138	281		1965
89	26	5		0B	1741	417	0	1963
89	26	5	0		1669	526		1965
29	26	1	340		68	0	0B	1955
29	26	1	460		22	312	1E	1960
29	26	1	694		22D	210		1963
29	26	1	744		35	216		1965
30	26	1	640	97	133	297	510	1955
30	26	1	720	700	105	340	120	1960

		43	44	45	46	47	48	
30	26	1	699	723	95	286	65	1963
30	26	1	638	999	90	281	60	1965
90	26	5			251	337	40	1960
90	26	5	1227	1B	248J	455	56	1963
90	26	5	3067		236	364		1965
31	26	0	290			578		1950
31	26	0	280	420	250	508	2330G	1955
31	26	0	850	600	195	551	239	1960
31	26	0	843	1180	227	601	191	1963
31	26	0	872	1371	1968	565		1965
32	26	3			97	580	0E	1950
32	26	3	100	2320	128	526		1955
32	26	3	340		92	826	0E	1960
32	26	3	222		88K	634	25	1963
32	26	3	418		116	688		1965
91	26	5	0		795	385	2	1963
91	26	5	0		784	333		1965
33	26	2				1163		1950
33	26	2	320		150	732		1955
33	26	2			342	800		1960
33	26	2	2051		204	769	8	1963
33	26	2	3200		242	811		1965
34	26	3		0AB		968		1950
34	26	3	620	0	342	317		1955
34	26	3			217	667		1960
34	26	3	370	0B	218K	920		1963
34	26	3			239	968		1965
35	26	1	729			443		1950
35	26	1	40		0	364		1955
35	26	1	70			367		1960
35	26	1	73			366		1963
35	26	1	82			457		1965
36	26	0			82	367	31	1950
36	26	0	1370	42	77	408		1955
36	26	0	960		71	392	80	1960
36	26	0	621		68J	385	138	1963
36	26	0	619		77	345		1965
37	26	5	914		73	154	0E	1950
37	26	5	990		147	273	0B	1955
37	26	5	770		297	325	27	1960
37	26	5	1580		258J	278	33	1963
37	26	5			260	281		1965
38	26	1				1017		1950
38	26	1	700		736	805		1955
38	26	1	1050		1159	714		1960
38	26	1			1384J	588		1963
38	26	1	975		1540	613		1965
39	26	1				811		1950
39	26	1	1430	4151	879	727	0AE	1955
39	26	1	910		91	667	8	1960
39	26	1	1853	0B	81J	568	4	1963
39	26	1	1732		1027	787		1965
40	26	0	2270	118		250	238	1950
40	26	0	1550	1406		367	680	1955
40	26	0	2170	100	747A	344	570	1960
40	26	0	3102	47		307	450	1963
40	26	0	3564			370	560	1965
41	26	5	299	2383	117	526		1950
41	26	5	1630	224	407	486	400B	1955

		43	44	45	46	47	48	
41	26	5	1560	300	125	540	80	1960
41	26	5		112	139J	482	48	1963
41	26	5	1182	74	127	443		1965
42	26	0	642	306	149	397	781	1950
42	26	0	490	303	219	407	980	1955
42	26	0	650	800	209	342	420	1960
42	26	0	587	84	249	307	251	1963
42	26	0	707	97	244	313	360	1965
92	26	5			441J	732	2	1963
92	26	5			402	411		1965
163	26	5	500		1393	244		1965
43	26	1	170		209	430	160	1955
43	26	1	200	200	231	468	110E	1960
43	26	1	194	221	266	533	86	1963
43	26	1	194	294	262	478	80	1965
44	26	0				0		1950
44	26	0			1A	741	0B	1955
44	26	0			263	889		1960
44	26	0	0		182J	556		1963
44	26	0	0		200	606		1965
45	26	1				303		1950
45	26	1				0		1955
45	26	1				0		1960
45	26	1				0		1963
45	26	1				0		1965
46	26	1				303		1950
46	26	1	260		97	200		1955
46	26	1	530		183	388	411E	1960
46	26	1	787	5	168J	476	842	1963
46	26	1	924		233	514	740	1965
80	26	1		0		0		1955
80	26	1				1333		1960
80	26	1	192			526		1963
80	26	1	0			1200		1965
47	26	0	505		350	750		1950
47	26	0	1010		472	709	1500G	1955
47	26	0	1010		2793	427		1960
47	26	0	1372		4333J	503		1963
47	26	0	1046		3478	569		1965
48	26	3		0B		1111		1950
48	26	3	0		1021	625		1955
48	26	3			2023	1176		1960
48	26	3		0B	2414	1020		1963
48	26	3	0		7246	806		1965
49	26	5	0		389	0		1955
49	26	5			416	417		1960
49	26	5		1B	4626J	323		1963
49	26	5			5793	217		1965
93	26	5	2561		153J	353		1963
93	26	5	1824		151	331		1965
94	26	5			450	99	116	1960
94	26	5	813		2243J	143	401	1963
94	26	5	1136		858	292		1965
95	26	5				0		1963
95	26	5				250		1965
96	26	5		0B		0	274	1963
96	26	5			449	2667		1965

	43	44	45	46	47	48	
50 26	3		26	133	425		1950
50 26	3	160	24	125	387	90B	1955
50 26	3	420		43	652		1960
50 26	3	177	130	55J	533		1963
50 26	3	76	134	55	510		1965
97 26	1	250		724	0	68	1960
97 26	1		363	648J	374	63	1963
97 26	1		146	571	351		1965
51 26	2				0		1950
51 26	2			0	0	0E	1955
51 26	2				0		1960
51 26	2				357		1963
51 26	2				0		1965
52 26	2	696	502	778	330		1950
52 26	2	580	533	1053	329	130	1955
52 26	2	410	400	932	342	120	1960
52 26	2	431	270	936	303	76	1963
52 26	2	505	352	776	310	70	1965
53 26	3	1077	406	250	178	1	1950
53 26	3	520	442	250	135	0E	1955
53 26	3	470	600	198	268	12	1960
53 26	3	377	587	183	164	10	1963
53 26	3	383	707	192	282		1965
54 26	3			260	476		1950
54 26	3			162	303		1955
54 26	3			892	1127		1960
54 26	3			97K	617		1963
54 26	3			169	435		1965
98 26	5				0	3	1963
98 26	5				455		1965
99 26	5	1641	5	236J	362	11	1963
99 26	5		5	399	440		1965
55 26	1	608	71	931D	381	65	1950
55 26	1	400	76	716	348	120	1955
55 26	1	490	0	638	318	170	1960
55 26	1	349	310	609	348	126	1963
55 26	1	460	376	577	382	120	1965
56 26	1				0		1950
56 26	1		0	0	0		1955
56 26	1				909		1960
56 26	1		0B		0		1963
56 26	1				313		1965
57 26	5			81	250	43	1950
57 26	5			94	368	300B	1955
57 26	5	2070		126	443	56	1960
57 26	5	1453		113J	348	56	1963
57 26	5	1732		100	327		1965
58 26	4				755		1950
58 26	4				440	1210B	1955
58 26	4				965		1960
58 26	4				813		1963
58 26	4			685	710	760	1965
59 26	3				638		1950
59 26	3			0	440		1955
59 26	3				901		1960
59 26	3				744		1963
59 26	3				845		1965
60 26	3			240	588		1950
60 26	3	180		380	535	0E	1955
60 26	3	410		468	723		1960

	43	44	45	46	47	48	
60 26	3	349	12	400J	569		1963
60 26	3	453		320	581		1965
61 26	5	741		66	388		1950
61 26	5	370	11	208	362	1400B	1955
61 26	5	1500		253	359	676	1960
61 26	5	218	0	256K	424	694	1963
61 26	5	266	0	360	418	710	1965
62 26	1	207	9		510		1950
62 26	1	80	9	124	338	0B	1955
62 26	1	130	100	101	395		1960
62 26	1	172	65	119D	407		1963
62 26	1	149	102	92	387		1965
63 26	1	406	258	1354	498		1950
63 26	1	560	340	328	493		1955
63 26	1	180	400	254	542		1960
63 26	1	514	437	247	378		1963
63 26	1	0	968	227	353		1965
64 26	3		0B		550		1950
64 26	3	120		0	631	0B	1955
64 26	3	50		24	389		1960
64 26	3	86			278		1963
64 26	3	46		35	260		1965
114 26	5		74		0		1965
65 26	2				0		1950
65 26	2	2900			0		1955
65 26	2				3333		1960
65 26	2	1464	0B		625		1963
65 26	2			3843	968		1965
100 26	5	0		475J	299		1963
100 26	5			525	303		1965
204 26	5	395			357	47	1963
204 26	5	2500		935	290		1965
101 26	5		0B	466	0		1963
101 26	5	0		383	526		1965
66 26	1	413	212		352	154	1950
66 26	1	700	233	192	322	110AI	1955
66 26	1	1070	100	253	541	98	1960
66 26	1	1016	601	230	444	84	1963
66 26	1	697	53	196	441		1965
102 26	5	430		149	345		1960
102 26	5	0		194J	541		1963
102 26	5			169	361		1965
67 26	1	686	183	550	382	71	1950
67 26	1	580	175	428	388	250	1955
67 26	1	540	200	344	342	140	1960
67 26	1	491	202	312	360	62	1963
67 26	1	412	207	300	373	120	1965
68 26	1	853	57		339	4	1950
68 26	1	750	42	0	336	50	1955
68 26	1	1000	200		360	4	1960
68 26	1	811	155		366	3	1963
68 26	1	762	171		372		1965
69 26	0				769		1950
69 26	0			4347	741	0E	1955
69 26	0			3624	943		1960
69 26	0			3351J	641	1051	1963
69 26	0	284		2515	638	740	1965

		43	44	45	46	47	48	
109	26	5	1867	32	228K	0		1963
109	26	5		27	223	109		1965
70	26	1				556		1950
70	26	1	1490		158	909		1955
70	26	1	1490	600	181	427		1960
70	26	1	1102	1B	201J	408		1963
70	26	1			266	402		1965
103	26	5			157	357	3	1963
103	26	5			632	682		1965
216	26	5			5180	169	1400	1965
104	26	5			657	180		1960
104	26	5			699J	258		1963
104	26	5	600		811	237		1965
71	26	1	316			741		1950
71	26	1	320		83	599	240AI	1955
71	26	1	630	0	98	671	47	1960
71	26	1	487	2	102	578	17	1963
71	26	1	434	3	110	583		1965
72	26	4	1251	119	264	249	104	1950
72	26	4		89	227	271		1955
72	26	4		100	202	364	46	1960
72	26	4	644	42	207	268	173	1963
72	26	4		51	203	292		1965
73	26	1		0AB		351		1950
73	26	1	20	0		241	0B	1955
73	26	1	50		2	279		1960
73	26	1	50	0B	40D	293		1963
73	26	1	40		29	273		1965
74	26	1	569	270	258	391	168	1950
74	26	1	540	227	284	338	120	1955
74	26	1	550	200	224	359	170	1960
74	26	1	565	199	213	351	249	1963
74	26	1	510	522	196	369	150	1965
75	26	2	660	18	50	454	558	1950
75	26	2	670	15	63	442	440	1955
75	26	2	740		60	473	560	1960
75	26	2	692		60	426	596	1963
75	26	2	363		59	428	450	1965
219	26	5		30		227		1965
105	26	5				0	1	1963
105	26	5				370		1965
76	26	3		0A		575		1950
76	26	3	310			544	0AI	1955
76	26	3	110			620		1960
76	26	3	0			621		1963
76	26	3	0			662		1965
77	26	3			2235	909		1950
77	26	3	110	1701	2654	783		1955
77	26	3	150		2308	702		1960
77	26	3	108	48	2919J	638		1963
77	26	3		30	2519	642		1965
81	26	1				0		1955
81	26	1				0		1960
81	26	1				0		1963
81	26	1				0		1965
82	26	1	650			465		1955
82	26	1	1020			396		1960

		43	44	45	46	47	48	
82	26	1	849		192J	556		1963
82	26	1	1237	24	292	516		1965
78	26					0		1950
78	26	0				0		1955
78	26	0				0		1960
78	26	0				0		1963
78	26	0			2690	0		1965
79	26	4	23			641	57E	1950
79	26	4	50	293	85	502	270	1955
79	26	4	100	100	156	465	191	1960
79	26	4	77		172	431	276	1963
79	26	4	174	46	117	398	610	1965

		49	50	51	52	53	54	55	
1	27		4	574	5	212FG			1950
1	27	3370B	4B	574	5B	307	473		1955
1	27		4	574	5	151	792		1960
1	27	2113	4	574	5	310R	806		1963
1	27	2316	4	574	5	929	20500	1110	1965
2	27		2	962	2				1950
2	27		2B	962	2B		0	960	1955
2	27	5722	2	962	2		8		1960
2	27		2	962	2		51	2075B	1963
2	27		2	962	2				1965
106	27		2		2	4042	44200	1700	1965
3	27	1609	1	806	1	965FG		878	1950
3	27	3700	1B	806	1B	-325	15	1600L	1955
3	27	1466	1	806	1	397	450	870	1960
3	27	1809	1	806	1	820Q	296	1222	1963
3	27	2496	1	806	1	-294	700	2340	1965
4	27	5106	1	990	1	1013G			1950
4	27	4230	1B	990	1		0	720	1955
4	27	4052	1	990	1	0A	0A	1326	1960
4	27	3503	1	990	1	0P		1466	1963
4	27	2952	1	990	1		40H	1120	1965
5	27	2650	1	981	1B		50	1240	1955
5	27	2191	1	981	1	0A	0A	894	1960
5	27	883	1	981	1			858	1963
5	27	739	1	981	1		40H		1965
6	27	1415	2	417	2	2575F	200	742I	1950
6	27	2780	2	401	2B		0	1410	1955
6	27	2521	2	401	2	0A	0A	1852	1960
6	27	735	2	401	2			2160A	1963
6	27	926	2	401	2		40H	1880	1965
7	27	9205B	4	367	2	165FG		1443	1950
7	27	7050	4	305	2	715	342	2800	1955
7	27	5992	4	305	2	133	452	2189	1960
7	27	7073	4	305	2	530Q	563	2438A	1963
7	27	6173	4	305	2	340	700		1965
8	27	6721	2	975	3	1053F		1055	1950
8	27	5760	2	866	3	3158	429	610	1955
8	27	5617	2	866	3	246	485	785A	1960
8	27	5320	2	866	3	2020Q	448	871	1963
8	27	4429	2	866	3	2206	26500	750	1965
9	27	3291	3	900	4			725	1950
9	27	8210	3B	900	4B		0	870	1955
9	27	1236	3	900	4				1960
9	27	1182	3	900	4			740	1963
9	27	880	3	900	4	1283			1965

	49	50	51	52	53	54	55	
10 27	8767	3	848	3	104G		690I	1950
10 27	8250	3	848	3	231	707	760	1955
10 27	6629	3	848	3	84	840		1960
10 27	6333	3	848	3	330R	557	928	1963
10 27	6176	3	848	3	149	600	1470	1965
113 27		2		3	49	500	2300	1965
11 27		4B	780	5B		181		1955
11 27	4002	4	780	5	262	286		1960
11 27	5261	4	780	5	220R	529	1900B	1963
11 27	4923	4	780	5	112	900	2200	1965
83 27	3221	4B				653		1963
83 27	2727	4		5	403	700	1150	1965
12 27	1623	5	591	11	117G			1950
12 27	1930	5	528	11	0A	0A	1070	1955
12 27	1512	5	528	11	0A	0A		1960
12 27	1164	5	528	11	0P			1963
12 27	1072	5	528	11		40H	2260	1965
84 27	4836	8A		10B		207	995B	1963
84 27	5397	8		11	158	200	1270	1965
13 27	5033	2	614	5	2G		1573	1950
13 27	6460	2	434	5	313	496	1330	1955
13 27	6174	2	434	5	148	439		1960
13 27	6687	2	434	5	160R	418	1473B	1963
13 27	6313	2	434	5	576	800	1290	1965
85 27	7695	8A				161	1032B	1963
85 27	7746	8			183	400	1930	1965
14 27	5069	1	999	3	442F		1503	1950
14 27	6210	1B	999	3B	20	407	1950	1955
14 27	3816	1	999	3	244	695	1318	1960
14 27	6502	1	999	3	1470Q	567	1319	1963
14 27	3285	1	999	3	1204	1000		1965
15 27	2976	4	687	2				1950
15 27	2130	4B	687	2B		0	1000K	1955
15 27		4	687	2				1960
15 27		4	687	2			1286B	1963
15 27		4	687	2	39			1965
16 27	5850D	3B	786	4B	3834	249		1955
16 27	4076	3	786	4	1046	182		1960
16 27	3084	3	786	4	740Q	160	2335D	1963
16 27	2527	3	786	4	675	400	1350	1965
17 27	7768	1	912	3	74F		538	1950
17 27	7400	1B	912	3B	325	342	660	1955
17 27	7152	1	912	3	4	515	1069	1960
17 27	6784	1	912	3	1070Q	430	1303	1963
17 27	6381	1	912	3	616	600	1300	1965
87 27	4631	8A		4		170	1506B	1963
87 27	4266	8		4	159	300	1680	1965
86 27	4281	6B		3B	870Q	389	2883D	1963
86 27	5186	6		4	1493	39000	1600	1965
18 27	9000C	2	975	2	4FG		1496	1950
18 27	4490	2	820	2	176	115	2420	1955
18 27	5118	2	820	2	47	87	2649	1960
18 27	4777	2	820	2	110R	82	2533	1963
18 27	4170	2	820	2	252	200		1965
19 27	8583	1	951	3			2181	1950
19 27	7880	1B	951	3	144	14	2000	1955
19 27	6801	1	951	3	4	147		1960
19 27	8674	1	951	3		138	950B	1963
19 27	8779	1	951	3	170	300	1110	1965

		49	50	51	52	53	54	55	
20	27	1126	2	720	4			960	1950
20	27		2	720	4B		0	1030	1955
20	27	1973	2	720	4				1960
20	27		2	720	4				1963
20	27		2	720	5	46		800	1965
88	27	6354	5B		7B		177	1496	1963
88	27	2925	5		8	180	400	2270	1965
21	27	1948	1	984	1	1230F	500	1087	1950
21	27	2400	1B	984	1B		0	1150	1955
21	27	1367	4	984	1	0A	0A	1334	1960
21	27	1111	4	984	1			1543B	1963
21	27	1009	3	984A	1		40H	2280	1965
22	27	5057	2	977	3	3G		440	1950
22	27	6170	2	829	3	16	53		1955
22	27	4761	2	829	3	2	31	812	1960
22	27	5823	2	829	3	180R	94	955	1963
22	27	4641	2	829	3	785	200		1965
23	27	3462	2	593A	3	78FG		1974D	1950
23	27	4100	2	593	3B	235	298	1460	1955
23	27	6374	2	593	3	162	408	1110	1960
23	27	5921	2	593	3	160R	495	1577	1963
23	27	5382	2	593	3	212	800	1860	1965
24	27	8671				2FG		1159	1950
24	27	7860				712	791		1955
24	27	7069	3		2	1057	712	1485	1960
24	27	5304	3B		2B	2090Q	1265	1399	1963
24	27	5610	3		2	3891	1100	1910	1965
25	27	8962	1	999	3	128F		1124	1950
25	27	8760	1B	999	3B	139	159	1420	1955
25	27	6565	1	999	3	20	112	1824	1960
25	27	4878	1	999	3		182	2228A	1963
25	27	5063	1	999	3	176	200	2190	1965
26	27	5091		400		99G			1950
26	27	3700		400		178	294	1100	1955
26	27	5645	8	400	8	180	501		1960
26	27	5053	8A	400	8B	240R	645	1100B	1963
26	27	6648	8	400	8	317	1000	910	1965
27	27	3087	2	911	1	247GF	1300	899	1950
27	27	4920	2	866	1B		39	1690	1955
27	27	2393	2	866	1	0A	0A	1579	1960
27	27	2941	2	866	1			1863	1963
27	27	2833	2	866	1		40	2250	1965
28	27	532	1	921	3	9520EF		615	1950
28	27	2680	1B	921	3B		0	890	1955
28	27	1302	1	921	3	0A	0A		1960
28	27	837	1	921	3			1184	1963
28	27	730	1	921	3		40	2150	1965
89	27	3996	3B		8B		161	771B	1963
89	27	3322	3		8	161	300	2040A	1965
29	27	3000B	1	999	1B		0		1955
29	27	4143	1	999	1				1960
29	27		1	999	1			550B	1963
29	27		1	999	1	194			1965
30	27		1	946	1B		0	960	1955
30	27	1964	1	946	1	0A	0A	825	1960
30	27	1307	1	946	1			822	1963
30	27	1351	1	946	1			1030	1965
90	27	6532	11		19	48	294	1455	1960
90	27	7353	11B		19	270Q	518	1716	1963
90	27	6567	11		19	803	800		1965

	49	50	51	52	53	54	55	
31 27	4204	2	978	4	1933FG			1950
31 27		2	936	4B		112	670	1955
31 27	3589	2	936	4		250		1960
31 27	4071	2	936	4	400Q	152	1065	1963
31 27	3445	2	936	4	1332	300		1965
32 27	8276	2	596	2	17FG		1489	1950
32 27	5500	2	457	2	527	191	1070	1955
32 27	6583	2	457	2	175	213		1960
32 27	5073	2	457	2	110R	231		1963
32 27	4920	2	457	2	127	300	1550	1965
91 27	5981	4B		14A		228		1963
91 27		4		14	240	500	1940	1965
33 27	5242	2	838	2	6FG		1122	1950
33 27	3340	2B	838	2B	401	310	1340	1955
33 27	5556	2	838	2	106	204	1056	1960
33 27	4500A	2	838	2		146	1111A	1963
33 27		2	838	2	61	300	1710	1965
34 27	3947		667	4	1FG		938	1950
34 27	3350		667A	4	71	126	1260	1955
34 27	4567	2	667A	4	75	200	1826	1960
34 27	4037	2B	667A	4		184	2000	1963
34 27	4218	2	667A	4	127	200		1965
35 27	1550	2	957	2				1950
35 27	1550	2B	957	2B		0	960	1955
35 27	1231	2	957	2		9		1960
35 27	440	2	957	2		18	2751B	1963
35 27		2	957	2	149		1010	1965
36 27	2050	11	421		567EF		1525D	1950
36 27	3000	11	381		3089	945	900	1955
36 27	1954	11	381		4478	2150	1383	1960
36 27	1561	11	381		9780Q	1545	1445	1963
36 27	1433	11	381		13110	25700		1965
37 27	4205				1398FG		827D	1950
37 27	2500				392	779	570	1955
37 27	1598	2			175	965	499	1960
37 27	3542	2B			1160Q	969	117A	1963
37 27	3256	2			649	1400		1965
38 27	2766						899	1950
38 27	7730				2980	992		1955
38 27	5232				316	960		1960
38 27	6137				270Q	1118	1500B	1963
38 27	6809	4			3370	1400	660	1965
39 27	5333	3	799	4	68FG		1000	1950
39 27	4500	3B	799	4B	99	444	1120	1955
39 27	9654	3	799	4	18	453	1351	1960
39 27	9394	3	799	4	50R	403	1867	1963
39 27	8868	3	799	4	83	600	2250	1965
40 27	3143	1	999	1	453EG	40H	851D	1950
40 27	3500	1B	999	1B		0	998	1955
40 27	2716	1	999	1	0A	0A	1162	1960
40 27	2512	1	999	1				1963
40 27	2342	2	999A	1		40H	1490	1965
41 27	4615	12	500	2	2216G		327D	1950
41 27	7180	12	204	2B	1709	346	1000	1955
41 27	2881	12	204	2	255	308	829	1960
41 27	3317	12	204	2	1320Q	193	885	1963
41 27	3581	3	204A	2	1527	400	1390	1965
42 27	1032	1	999	1	4123EG	700	847	1950
42 27	4200	1B	999	1B		2	1450	1955
42 27	1324	1	999	1			1345	1960
42 27	770	1	999	1			1873	1963
42 27	693	1	999	1		40H	2270	1965

		49	50	51	52	53	54	55	
92	27	4339	5B		8B		355	1730B	1963
92	27	3837	5		8	388	400	2040	1965
163	27	2377	1		2	99	300	1160	1965
43	27	1290C	1B	999	1B		86	1820	1955
43	27	2286	1	999	1	0A	140	1075	1960
43	27	668	1	999	1	0P	100	1494B	1963
43	27	587	1	999	1		200	2270	1965
44	27	1767			3	52F		81D	1950
44	27	2100C			3B	545	334		1955
44	27	3749	3		3	704	368	714	1960
44	27	2634	3B		3	830Q	336	769A	1963
44	27	2452	3		3	689	500	1070	1965
45	27		1	999	1				1950
45	27		1B	999	1B		0		1955
45	27		1	999	1				1960
45	27	4370A	1	999	1				1963
45	27		1	999	1	132			1965
46	27	4897	1	999	1	981FG			1950
46	27	3010	1B	999	1B	10467	33	1910	1955
46	27	2423	1	999	1	2552	141	1461	1960
46	27	994	1	999	1	2650Q	110	1358A	1963
46	27	1036	1	999	1	2205	400	1720	1965
80	27	3680J			2		74	1240	1955
80	27		5		3	334	279		1960
80	27	4000A	5B		3B	390R	350		1963
80	27		5		3	682	35800	790	1965
47	27	1154			7	19G		941	1950
47	27				7B	205	163	1040	1955
47	27	1241	3		7	134	233	1181	1960
47	27	1934	3B		7		170	1302	1963
47	27	793	3		7	113	300	1550	1965
48	27	8333D	5	200		2FG		833D	1950
48	27	8990	5B	200		90	165	780B	1955
48	27	4728	5	200		87	207		1960
48	27	5935	5	200		340Q	211	667	1963
48	27	7330	4		4	364	400	1390	1965
49	27	2460B	2B		3	7	602		1955
49	27	3414	2		3	426	629		1960
49	27	9872	2		3	260Q	485		1963
49	27	9940	2		3	59	700	1480	1965
93	27	2895	2B		14B		477		1963
93	27	3152	2		14	508	600	1600	1965
94	27	1728	4	451	6	136	313	1560	1960
94	27	4513	4	451	6B	210R	525	1597A	1963
94	27	1121	5		6	344	1100		1965
95	27	3929	8A		9B		212	1200B	1963
95	27	2860	8		9	216	800	1570	1965
96	27	2543	4B		5B		74		1963
96	27	418	4		5	93	400	1600	1965
50	27	1924	2	883	4	701F		907	1950
50	27	1800B	2	642	4B	7	309	1310	1955
50	27	2274	2	642	4	170	412	1283	1960
50	27	1988	2	642	4	860Q	367	2244A	1963
50	27	1893	2	642	4	654	900		1965
97	27	2419	7		2	617	329		1960
97	27	2645	7B		2	1170Q	445	2030B	1963
97	27	2596	7		3	1437	25700	1760	1965

		49	50	51	52	53	54	55	
51	27		3		2	2G		377D	1950
51	27		3B		2B	159	119	830B	1955
51	27		3		2	87	208		1960
51	27		3		2	130R	282	824B	1963
51	27		3		2	178	600	790	1965
52	27	512	1	999	2	4835EF	200	789	1950
52	27		1B	999	2		0	1530	1955
52	27	933	1	999	2	0A	0A	2155	1960
52	27	778	1	999	2			2474	1963
52	27	667	1	999	2		40H	2530	1965
53	27	4144	2	935	2			809D	1950
53	27	2500	2B	935	2B		0	920	1955
53	27	3419	2	935	2	0A	0A	960	1960
53	27	3731	2	935	2	0P		1089	1963
53	27	2910	2	935	2		90S	1050	1965
54	27	3765	3	660A	5	56FA			1950
54	27	3800	3	660	5B	125	129	1190	1955
54	27	3467	3	660	5	80	152		1960
54	27	3991	3	660	5		172	1463B	1963
54	27	4639	2	660	5	110	300	1810	1965
98	27	6338	5B		7		293	996B	1963
98	27	5893	4	750	2	192	400	1200	1965
99	27	3351	3B		8	160Q	1121	870	1963
99	27	2628	3		8	1086	26900		1965
55	27	1163	1	997	1	954E	300	568	1950
55	27	2840	1	953	1B		0	1270	1955
55	27	1755	1	953	1	0A	0A	928	1960
56	27	955	1	953	1			1155	1963
55	27	820	1	953	1			1480	1965
56	27				3				1950
56	27	8000B			3B		0		1955
56	27		1		3				1960
56	27		1A		3		25		1963
56	27		1		3	363			1965
57	27	5204	6	544		307EG		410D	1950
57	27	6200	6	488		3877	929	489M	1955
57	27	4304	6	488		2070	972	418	1960
57	27	3713	6	488		5010Q	734	395B	1963
57	27	3368	6	488		5731	23400	329	1965
58	27	5455	2	919	6	2FG		1951	1950
58	27	6100	2	739	6B	104	106	2180	1955
58	27	6979	2	739	6	127	91	2065	1960
58	27	4243	2	739	6	140R	153	1963	1963
58	27	5083	2	918	6	331	200	2710	1965
59	27	2156	2	542	2	51FG			1950
59	27	2240B	2	307	2B	121	299	1260	1955
59	27	2646	2	307	2	60	341		1960
59	27	2618	2	307	2		297	1593B	1963
59	27	3274	2	307	2	96	500	1550	1965
60	27	3516	3	650	6	34FG		1249	1950
60	27	3400	3B	650	6B	904	67	1290	1955
60	27	1766	3	650	6	-118	398	1599	1960
60	27	1955	3	650	6	220Q	462	1897A	1963
60	27	2330	3	650	5	705	700		1965
61	27	4273	8	248	1	1380FG		2652	1950
61	27		8	200	1	700	357	2800	1955
61	27	2568	8	200	1	301	474	2808	1960
61	27	2323	8	200	1	300Q	339	2592	1963
61	27	2135	10	370	1	1092	900		1965

		49	50	51	52	53	54	55	
62	27		2	875	1			903D	1950
62	27		2	767	1B		0	1080	1955
62	27	1619	2	767	1		83		1960
62	27	1614	2	767	1		209	916	1963
62	27	1166	2	767	1	191	300		1965
63	27	1170	1	997	1	315EG	40	861	1950
63	27	3300	1B	997	1B		0	950	1955
63	27	1856	1	997	1			1117	1960
63	27	981	1	997	1		23	848	1963
63	27	865	1	997	1		90S	860	1965
64	27		3	857A	3			1254D	1950
64	27	4200	3	785	3B		0	790	1955
64	27		3	785	3				1960
64	27		3	785	3		26		1963
64	27		3	785	3	264			1965
114	27		2		2	84	400	2360	1965
65	27		1	999	0	53G			1950
65	27	9900B	1B	999	1B	29	103		1955
65	27		1	999	1	119	157		1960
65	27	7673	1	999	1		209	920B	1963
65	27	8381	1	999	1	2	400	1300	1965
100	27	3530	4B		11AB		340	1273B	1963
100	27	4144	4		7	475	500	1470	1965
204	27	6354	4B			90R	216	1300B	1963
204	27	6423	4			468	400	1440	1965
101	27	4602	4B		3	240R	644		1963
101	27	3303	4		3	287	1300	690	1965
66	27	1916				528G		725D	1950
66	27						15	850	1955
66	27	2122	3				23	696	1960
66	27	1831	3B			400R	34	702	1963
66	27	1941	3			490	90S	1200	1965
102	27	5466	6	514	23	377	474	1014	1960
102	27	5952	6	514	23A	250R	480		1963
102	27	4673	6	514	23	402	800	1580	1965
67	27	1953	1	918	1	516E	100	950	1950
67	27		1	918	1B		0	1290	1955
67	27	1392	1	918	1	0A	0A	1147	1960
67	27	1179	1	918	1			1239	1963
67	27	1089	1	918	1			2110	1965
68	27	1867	4	722	4			260	1950
68	27	2610	4	683	4B		0	373	1955
68	27	1561	4	683	4	0A	0A	436	1960
68	27	1443	4	683	4			389	1963
68	27	1414	3	693	4			410	1965
69	27	2740B				5G		1806	1950
69	27	5070				32	402		1955
69	27	5239	1		5		514	1450	1960
69	27	4848	1B		5B	130R	479	1485A	1963
69	27	4441	1		5	583	600	1960	1965
109	27	3641	12	397	24	360R	524	1563	1963
109	27	2317	12	397	24	383	800		1965
70	27	5332			2	428G		574	1950
70	27	5300			2	55	536	1740	1955
70	27	3743	2	905	2	538	695	1920	1960
70	27	3670	2	905	2	460Q	680	1825	1963
70	27	1016	2	905	2	468	18400	1730	1965
103	27	2606	4B		19		308	1634A	1963
103	27	2525	4		15	134	600		1965

		49	50	51	52	53	54	55	
216	27		4		5	193	300	1030	1965
104	27	1485	2		3		286		1960
104	27	1934	2B		3B	950Q	264	2143B	1963
104	27	440	2		3	920	17500	2390	1965
71	27	2642	3	871	3	1199EG		1193	1950
71	27	3730	3	759	3B		568	1420	1955
71	27	2041	3	759	3		500	1237	1960
71	27	2130	3	759	3	2200Q	551	1557A	1963
71	27	2165	3	759	3	3852	100	1900	1965
72	27	2707	11	206	4			450D	1950
72	27	1620	11	168	4		0	290	1955
72	27	1871	11	168	4			504	1960
72	27	1400	11	168	4	0P		406A	1963
72	27	1383	11	168	4				1965
73	27		11A	594A	10	0A	0A	1415I	1950
73	27	2210C	11A	594A	10	0A	0A	1340	1955
73	27	1022	11	594	10	0A	0A	1409	1960
73	27		11	594	10A	0PQ	0A	1575	1963
73	27		11	594	10A	0A	0A		1965
74	27	1009	1	851	1	9573E	2000	614D	1950
74	27	1700	1	851	1B	0A	0A	1320	1955
74	27	1904	1	851	1	0A	0A	1152	1960
74	27	1218	1	851	1			1211	1963
74	27	1198	1	851	1			1340	1965
75	27	1078	1	908	2	0A	0A	695	1950
75	27	1970	1B	908	2	0A	0A	555	1955
75	27	1581	1	908	2	0A	0A	753	1960
75	27	630	1	908	2	0P	0A	892A	1963
75	27	732	1	908	2	0A	0A	1192	1965
219	27		5			366	400	1030	1965
105	27	5552	1B		9		235	1266B	1963
105	27	6244	1		9	175	200	1650	1965
76	27	6047	1	999	2	331FG			1950
76	27	3490	1B	999	2B	186	144	2480N	1955
76	27	2588	1	999	2	61	206		1960
76	27	3026	1	999	2		215	1904B	1963
76	27	3224	1	999	2	-14	200		1965
77	27	7138	1	999	3	52FG		661	1950
77	27	9500	1	999	3B	-48	176	650	1955
77	27	6737	1	999	3	66	381	1027	1960
77	27	6579	1	999	3	610Q	330	1201	1963
77	27	6511	1	999	4	324	500	1800	1965
81	27						0		1955
81	27		3		8				1960
81	27	4000A	3A		8			1380B	1963
81	27		3		8	324		520	1965
82	27				3		104		1955
82	27	5610	3		4	1871	250		1960
82	27	4367	3B		4B	2270Q	239	559M	1963
82	27	7329	3		4	3156	26500		1965
78	27		1		3	0G			1950
78	27		1B	999	3B	2	47		1955
78	27		1	999	3	47	79		1960
78	27		1	999	3		118		1963
78	27		1	999	3	124	300	540	1965
79	27	2354	7	732	9	427F		793A	1950
79	27	2950B	7	705	9		792	1120	1955
79	27	1338	7	705	9		657		1960
79	27	866	7	705	9	1780Q	400		1963
79	27	1018	7	705	9	1181	100	1450	1965

		56	57	58	
1	28				1950
1	28				1955
1	28				1960
1	28				1963
1	28				1965
2	28	4189A			1950
2	28	4160			1955
2	28	3973			1960
2	28	3973			1963
2	28	3630			1965
106	28	180	2422	48	1965
3	28	1984	926	29	1950
3	28	1990	1290	15	1955
3	28	2250A	1136	42	1960
3	28	2250A	1475	32	1963
3	28	1640	778	37	1965
4	28	2250	1754	34A	1950
4	28	2240	1600	34	1955
4	28	2506	1239	35	1960
4	28	2506	1423	38	1963
4	28	2500	1285	40	1965
5	28	3880	1890	45	1955
5	28	4036	1517	49	1960
5	28	4036	1731	50	1963
5	28	3600	1720	51	1965
6	28	2356	2458	49	1950
6	28	2360	2980	61	1955
6	28	2151	3277	62	1960
6	28	2951A	3415	52	1963
6	28	2570	3806	50	1965
7	28	4265	5650		1950
7	28	4270	4940		1955
7	28		1349		1960
7	28		1269		1963
7	28	4220	1815		1965
8	28	1466B	992	44	1950
8	28	1460		45	1955
8	28	1788A			1960
8	28	1788A	528		1963
8	28	1150	828	72	1965
9	28	4426		38	1950
9	28	4420	1060A		1955
9	28				1960
9	28				1963
9	28	4570	1755		1965
10	28	2710	1786		1950
10	28	2720	2270		1955
10	28		1517	3	1960
10	28		1978	29	1963
10	28	5120	1278	28	1965
113	28		4452		1965
11	28				1955
11	28	4258			1960
11	28	4258			1963
11	28	3670	1265		1965
83	28	3977A		46	1963
83	28	3810	2074		1965
12	28	2141	1754		1950
12	28	2210	1700		1955

	56	57	58	
12 28	2734	1524		1960
12 28	2734	1624		1963
12 28	1970	1685		1965
84 28	5208A			1963
84 28		2131		1965
13 28	2416	3812	47	1950
13 28	2180	3700	41	1955
13 28		2770	39A	1960
13 28		2563	39	1963
13 28	1410	3100	41	1965
85 28				1963
85 28		1125		1965
14 28	2511	103		1950
14 28	2500	3970	72A	1955
14 28	2218	1054		1960
14 28	2218	1585	52	1963
14 28	1420	1228		1965
15 28				1950
15 28		70		1955
15 28				1960
15 28				1963
15 28	1300			1965
16 28	1930	770	33	1955
16 28		1045	40	1960
16 28	2101A	1844	40	1963
16 28		1587		1965
17 28		985		1950
17 28	1870	1390	4A	1955
17 28		1285	17	1960
17 28		987		1963
17 28	1160	1482	17A	1965
87 28				1963
87 28		3916		1965
86 28				1963
86 28	4960	2639		1965
18 28	1481B	292		1950
18 28	1540	2700		1955
18 28	1500A			1960
18 28	1500	1939		1963
18 28	960	1927		1965
19 28	1320	3210		1950
19 28	1300	2700		1955
19 28				1960
19 28				1963
19 28	900	2143		1965
20 28	3546	5910		1950
20 28	3520	1400A		1955
20 28	4401A			1960
20 28	4401A			1963
20 28	4290	1195		1965
88 28	5045A			1963
88 28	5250	848		1965
21 28	3350	2116	49A	1950
21 28	3370	2580	46	1955
21 28	3110	2509	43	1960
21 28	3110	2239	46	1963
21 28	3180	2320	47	1965
22 28	1566B	2100		1950
22 28	1580	2300		1955

	56	57	58	
22 28	2813	2535		1960
22 28	2813	2260		1963
22 28		1372		1965
23 28	2823B	1162		1950
23 28	2830	1260		1955
23 28	1667	1839		1960
23 28	1667	1844		1963
23 28	1050	1601		1965
24 28	1352B	1944	39	1950
24 28	620	1280	40	1955
24 28	785		41	1960
24 28	785	1374	44	1963
24 28	480	1285	44	1965
25 28	1692B	1700		1950
25 28	1660	2140	41A	1955
25 28	1728		20	1960
25 28	1728	2265	43	1963
25 28	1130	2392	44	1965
26 28			40	1950
26 28		720	41	1955
26 28		834		1960
26 28				1963
26 28		990		1965
27 28	4091B	1888	36	1950
27 28	4070	1970	29	1955
27 28	3941	2006	36	1960
27 28	3941	1868	35	1963
27 28	3480	1761	37	1965
28 28	3500A	1117		1950
28 28	3420	1090	61	1955
28 28	3343	1136		1960
28 28	3343	1011		1963
28 28	2820	1074		1965
89 28	4545A			1963
89 28	4350	7384		1965
29 28	3980	3500A	64A	1955
29 28			69	1960
29 28	4495		68	1963
29 28	3980	1194	73	1965
30 28	3600	1610	51	1955
30 28	3638	1604	57	1960
30 28	3638	1552	60	1963
30 28	3030	1621	63	1965
90 28	3860		31	1960
90 28	3860	1845	44	1963
90 28	3140	1318	42	1965
31 28	1796	2	17	1950
31 28	1800	910	31A	1955
31 28	3269	578		1960
31 28	3269	757	34	1963
31 28	2780	555		1965
32 28	1237	971		1950
32 28	1280	1650		1955
32 28	1240A	1190		1960
32 28	1240A	2040		1963
32 28	790	1420		1965
91 28				1963
91 28		2101		1965
33 28	4914			1950
33 28	4900	1200		1955

		56	57	58	
33	28				1960
33	28				1963
33	28	5380	1131		1965
34	28	4462B	1050		1950
34	28	4410	2340		1955
34	28		1658		1960
34	28	1228	1907		1963
34	28	770	2466		1965
35	28	2892	416		1950
35	28	2900	1600		1955
35	28	3633A			1960
35	28	3633			1963
35	28	3550	1411		1965
36	28	2915B	630		1950
36	28	2920	470		1955
36	28	3153		45	1960
36	28	3153	449	49	1963
36	28	2790	349	42	1965
37	28		463	26A	1950
37	28		920	36	1955
37	28	2767		33	1960
37	28	2767	867	41	1963
37	28	2320	836	38	1965
38	28			32	1950
38	28			25A	1955
38	28				1960
38	28				1963
38	28	830	2191		1965
39	28	752		52	1950
39	28	760	5190	51	1955
39	28		4671		1960
39	28		5579		1963
39	28	230	4620		1965
40	28	2520	2433	51	1950
40	28	2550	2060	45	1955
40	28	2703	2314	41	1960
40	28	2703	2387	43	1963
40	28	2010	2214	43	1965
41	28	2500	260	59	1950
41	28	2560	1000	42	1955
41	28	2667	824	46	1960
41	28	2667	1408	44	1963
41	28	2030	1195	47	1965
42	28	2508	851		1950
42	28	2510	880	52	1955
42	28	2678	1075	49	1960
42	28	2678A	1121	51	1963
42	28	1950	1269	48	1965
92	28	4703A	3710		1963
92	28	4730	2876		1965
163	28	3030	2474	44	1965
43	28	3850	940	46	1955
43	28	3940	949	45	1960
43	28	3990A	877	45	1963
43	28	3850	999	47	1965
44	28			39	1950
44	28		800	53	1955
44	28	513			1960
44	28	513		47	1963
44	28	260	606	67A	1965

	56	57	58	
45 28				1950
45 28				1955
45 28				1960
45 28				1963
45 28				1965
46 28	3555			1950
46 28	4000	100	37A	1955
46 28			45A	1960
46 28	3255A	309		1963
46 28	2340	603	42	1965
80 28				1955
80 28				1960
80 28				1963
80 28		57		1965
47 28		1110	43	1950
47 28		830	40	1955
47 28			32	1960
47 28		803	37	1963
47 28		758	41A	1965
48 28				1950
48 28		2140		1955
48 28	3659			1960
48 28	3659	5786		1963
48 28	2890	6338		1965
49 28		1290	45	1955
49 28	500		41	1960
49 28	500	9560	52	1963
49 28	270	7668	52	1965
93 28	5094A		35	1963
93 28	5070	1590	28	1965
94 28	2348	4953	42	1960
94 28	2348	3328	49	1963
94 28	2450	4346	83A	1965
95 28				1963
95 28		695		1965
96 28			39	1963
96 28	980	4461	39	1965
50 28	1365B	992	47	1950
50 28	1360	1210	48	1955
50 28	1801	618	46	1960
50 28	1801	634	46	1963
50 28	1160	576	44	1965
97 28		1934	46A	1960
97 28		1882	34	1963
97 28	590	1687	30A	1965
51 28				1950
51 28	4080			1955
51 28				1960
51 28	4072			1963
51 28	3650			1965
52 28	2448	284	54	1950
52 28	2460	3540	58	1955
52 28	2230	3555	57	1960
52 28	2230	3460	59	1963
52 28	1610	3364	65	1965
53 28	2297	2614		1950
53 28	2320	2680		1955
53 28	2444	2331		1960

	56	57	58	
53 28	2444	2066		1963
53 28	2140	1934		1965
54 28	1515	270		1950
54 28	1400	2400		1955
54 28	2128A			1960
54 28	2128	2222		1963
54 28	1230	2513		1965
98 28	1039A			1963
98 28	610	1000	34	1965
99 28		1530	39	1963
99 28	1600	1547	41	1965
55 28	2374B	1991	48	1950
55 28	2360	1920	46	1955
55 28	2270	1949	45	1960
55 28	2270	1706	44	1963
55 28	1870	2032	46	1965
56 28				1950
56 28				1955
56 28				1960
56 28				1963
56 28				1965
57 28	581	1078	40	1950
57 28	580	870	30	1955
57 28	1245		39	1960
57 28	1245	549	29	1963
57 28	880	478	37A	1965
58 28	1923B	650		1950
58 28	1980	640		1955
58 28	2059	660		1960
58 28	2059	1184		1963
58 28	1450	1253		1965
59 28	2273	1200		1950
59 28	2290	1760	48	1955
59 28	2258	989		1960
59 28	2258	1667	23	1963
59 28	1440	1307	23A	1965
60 28		1382		1950
60 28	3400	2060		1955
60 28	2779	2082		1960
60 28	2179	2278		1963
60 28	1360	1580		1965
61 28	4003	1002		1950
61 28	4010	940		1955
61 28	2553	1296		1960
61 28	2553	1679		1963
61 28	3070	1527		1965
62 28	4476		45	1950
62 28	3340	680A	44	1955
62 28	4421		57	1960
62 28	4421			1963
62 28	4010	815	56A	1965
63 28	2249B	1327	43	1950
63 28	2240	1580	58	1955
63 28	1784	1307	54	1960
63 28	1784	1472	52	1963
63 28	1310	1556	51	1965
64 28	4536A			1950
64 28	2490	720		1955
64 28				1960

		56	57	58	
64	28				1963
64	28	4810	715		1965
114	28				1965
65	28			30	1950
65	28				1955
65	28				1960
65	28				1963
65	28				1965
100	28	4091A	1914		1963
100	28	3440	1897		1965
204	28	3511			1963
204	28	3030	2617	38A	1965
101	28				1963
101	28		1800		1965
66	28	1585B	59	43	1950
66	28	1580	600	45	1955
66	28	1823	709	47	1960
66	28	1823	533	49	1963
66	28	1750	443	48	1965
102	28				1960
102	28		1846		1963
102	28	2640	1405		1965
67	28	2628B	1983	45	1950
67	28	2640	2030	41	1955
67	28	2994	2078	42	1960
67	28	2994	2052	43	1963
67	28	2980	2056	43	1965
68	28	2930B	1965	53	1950
68	28	2970	2140	56	1955
68	28	3289	2180		1960
68	28	3289	2041	55	1963
68	28	2630	2128	55	1965
69	28			43	1950
69	28	4870	3210		1955
69	28	1000			1960
69	28	1000	2124		1963
69	28	1650	1493		1965
109	28		2754		1963
109	28	720	2493		1965
70	28	4803	1417		1950
70	28	4790	1600		1955
70	28	4834	1588	24A	1960
70	28	4834	1606	33	1963
70	28	5110	1613	35	1965
103	28	4603		28	1963
103	28	3890	1730	39	1965
216	28	1790	6716		1965
104	28		1509		1960
104	28		1680		1963
104	28	300	1282		1965
71	28	4443	716	64	1950
71	28	4440	480	43	1955
71	28	4080	569	38	1960
71	28	4080	508	53	1963
71	28	3340	572	50	1965

		56	57	58	
72	28	2868	2075	45	1950
72	28	2860	1990	39	1955
72	28	2285	1734	41A	1960
72	28	2285	1495	38	1963
72	28	1660	1385	37	1965
73	28	4762			1950
73	28	4690	230		1955
73	28	5184			1960
73	28	5189			1963
73	28	4150	257		1965

		56	57	58	
74	28	3076	1700	55	1950
74	28	3080	1590	61	1955
74	28	3237	1381	57	1960
74	28	3237	1360	56	1963
74	28	3260	1334	56	1965
75	28	2748B	357	37	1950
75	28	2750	400	39	1955
75	28	2260A	399	35	1960
75	28	2260	395	23	1963
75	28	2950	396	22	1965
219	28	1200	2096		1965
105	28				1963
105	28	5620	544		1965
76	28				1950
76	28		1220		1955
76	28	2451A	1057		1960
76	28	2451	1146		1963
76	28	1930	1786		1965
77	28	1754	3403	44	1950
77	28	1780	4260	50A	1955
77	28	1867A	3440		1960
77	28	1867	3967		1963
77	28	1190	3622		1965
81	28				1955
81	28				1960
81	28				1963
81	28				1965
82	28	3750		44	1955
82	28			44	1960
82	28		535	44	1963
82	28	2800	189	44	1965
78	28				1950
78	28				1955
78	28				1960
78	28				1963
78	28		3885		1965
79	28	4444A		55	1950
79	28	3410	490	52	1955
79	28	3537	1332	49	1960
79	28	3537	1367	46	1963
79	28	3110	1240	51	1965

		59	60	61	62	63	64	
1	29					75		1950
1	29					36		1955
1	29		-1350					1960
1	29		-1772			65		1963
1	29		-1772	297		63J		1965

		59	60	61	62	63	64	
2	29					458C		1950
2	29				6280A	254		1955
2	29	6183			4314	165		1960
2	29	5966			3386	256		1963
2	29				2627	187		1965
106	29	5129		291	0R	50K		1965
3	29	4704	2196	384	164	35		1950
3	29	5580	2039	326	30	77	0	1955
3	29	5365	1020	291	254	60	-55	1960
3	29	4181	2275	290	34	53	-90	1963
3	29	4454	1451	281	94	58	-80	1965
4	29	4661	2615	373	0	56F	-115	1950
4	29	5250	2423	282		56	-400	1955
4	29	5466	2077	287		47	-180	1960
4	29	4707	2115	291	0	78	-140	1963
4	29	5320	2000	288	0	62	-127	1965
5	29	5590	1111	293	320	9	0	1955
5	29	5584	1379	293	170	31J	-3	1960
5	29	5581	1341	294	255	34	-0	1963
5	29	6744	1303	291	88	37J	-3	1965
6	29	5403	1031	321		86E	-1	1950
6	29	5050	1336	296	70	157	0	1955
6	29	5118	1679	280	186	115K	4	1960
6	29	5137	1794	296	205	117	-0	1963
6	29	5042	1718	289	48	114	1	1965
7	29	4462A				30	-13	1950
7	29	4520				37	-400	1955
7	29	5854	-2375			35J	100	1960
7	29	8522	-2250			57		1963
7	29	5339	-2250	263	0R	35J	-57	1965
8	29	4491	0	251	67		-4	1950
8	29	4780	894	246	280	18	-100	1955
8	29	5353	1574	239	428	23	-68	1960
8	29	5138	1830	236	356	19	-100	1963
8	29	4071	2170	248	262	35	-411	1965
9	29	4661A			7478	91A		1950
9	29	4590			6970	243		1955
9	29	5253			4639	172		1960
9	29	5220			5292	149		1963
9	29	5004			4296	190		1965
10	29	3952			0		-100H	1950
10	29	4430		346		32	-100	1955
10	29	5350				40A	-7	1960
10	29	4665			0	70	0	1963
10	29	5233			1495	45		1965
113	29	3564				10		1965
11	29	5430				93		1955
11	29	5758				72	-300H	1960
11	29	5459				60		1963
11	29	4952				52	-100H	1965
83	29	4779						1963
83	29	5239		254		10N		1965
12	29	5013	1402	341		32A	-49	1950
12	29	5200	1667	308		74	-100	1955
12	29	5045	1439	301		67	-61	1960
12	29	4848	1667	305	543	67A	-90	1963
12	29	4962	2045	304	581	62	-69	1965
84	29	5417						1963
84	29	5185						1965

59	60	61	62	63	64	
13 29 4275	-594	215			-1000H	1950
13 29 4290	-548	212	1150A	3	-3300H	1955
13 29 5169	-137	212	825		-900H	1960
13 29 4623	-502	219	485			1963
13 29 4312	-46	212	783	10A	-300H	1965
85 29 5577						1963
85 29 5345						1965
14 29 4662	-602	285	0	57A	-140	1950
14 29 4420	-241	310		61	-500	1955
14 29 5051	-241	328	1304	53	-144	1960
14 29 5407	1084	338	0	53A	-210	1963
14 29 4675	1084	308	0	51	-275	1965
15 29				119C		1950
15 29 3400		325A		58		1955
15 29				43		1960
15 29				36A		1963
15 29				35		1965
16 29 6200	-90	242	60A	388	0	1955
16 29 6443I	538	247	196	472K	0	1960
16 29 5216	493	249	91	463A	-10	1963
16 29 5532	762	256	87	421	-6	1965
17 29 4798	216	237		14	-52	1950
17 29 5340	-1422	221		13	-100	1955
17 29 5274	-1422	221A		12	-51	1960
17 29 5310	-517	221		19	-130	1963
17 29 4572	-259	239	0R	22	-226	1965
87 29 5961				25		1963
87 29 5804			0R	10N		1965
86 29 3780				5		1963
86 29 4886				22N	-100	1965
18 29 5679				13C		1950
18 29 5200				0	-1100	1955
18 29 5612	611				-400	1960
18 29 5662	742			9		1963
18 29 6138	742	220			-650	1965
19 29 4451				37	-11H	1950
19 29 4920		245		38	-100H	1955
19 29 5080				76		1960
19 29 6145						1963
19 29 5580				159		1965
20 29 4895			4160	109E		1950
20 29 4720			5220	172		1955
20 29 4849			2135	128		1960
20 29 4673			2283	158A		1963
20 29 4985			1639	166J		1965
88 29 7174						1963
88 29 7083						1965
21 29 5619	1564	353			-34	1950
21 29 5270	2145	279	180	92		1955
21 29 5473	2255	279	200	81	4	1960
21 29 5274	2073	280	129	214A	-10	1963
21 29 5489	2000	287	115	107	-13	1965
22 29 3308				75	-243	1950
22 29 4610				73	-200	1955
22 29 3258		236A		63	-1000	1960
22 29 4790	-45			56A		1963
22 29 4085	-45	218		53	-567	1965
23 29 3997				25	-43	1950
23 29 5170	-1853	257		54	-200	1955

		59	60	61	62	63	64	
23	29	4098	-2026	254A		39	-115	1960
23	29	4050	-2112	254		19	-90	1963
23	29	4495	-2112	247	OR	37	-227	1965
24	29	5296	129	300			-28	1950
24	29	5690	601	292	370	43	0	1955
24	29	5401	1588	294	300	46	3	1960
24	29	6370	2361	287	161	56	-10	1963
24	29	6070	2060		241	60	-12	1965
25	29	4063			0		-5	1950
25	29	4620				32	0	1955
25	29	5105	-897	281		24N	-400	1960
25	29	4967	-493	274		11		1963
25	29	5154	-493	262		21N	-42	1965
26	29	5248				13		1950
26	29	5110				10	-100	1955
26	29	5350				14J	-166	1960
26	29	5522	-769			20A	-800	1963
26	29	5639	-769	338		20J	-133	1965
27	29	5225	1703	362			-53	1950
27	29	4940	1449	310	20	91	-100	1955
27	29	5180	1268	302	287	84	-15	1960
27	29	5125	906	309	230	84A	-40	1963
27	29	5355	688	300	259	82	-49	1965
28	29	4990	1186	368	449	134	-2	1950
28	29	4910	1423	329	500	175		1955
28	29	4777	2609	333A	401	222	3	1960
28	29	5192	2490		653		0	1963
28	29	5071	2451	317	712	112	2	1965
89	29	4000						1963
89	29	3962		194				1965
29	29	4790				68		1955
29	29	5019				62		1960
29	29	4629				72		1963
29	29	4720				70		1965
30	29	4860	1660	261		38		1955
30	29	4695	1544	270		50	-6	1960
30	29	4711	1274	272		75A	-10	1963
30	29	4941	1081	275	823	72	-10	1965
90	29	5518				7J	-250	1960
90	29	5721				10	-420	1963
90	29	6046		227		10J	-450	1965
31	29	8258	415	315	188	210	-75	1950
31	29	6760	1826	322	700	172	0	1955
31	29	7757	2199	324	763	164	5	1960
31	29	7349	2075	323	1071	171A	-0	1963
31	29	7756	2075	333	854	188	-13	1965
32	29	5108					-11	1950
32	29	5140				26	0	1955
32	29	5412	-1034	265		30N	-500	1960
32	29	5204	0	269		29		1963
32	29	5505	0	263	OR	20P	-50	1965
91	29	4554						1963
91	29	4953				3N		1965
33	29	4751				13		1950
33	29	5200				15		1955
33	29	5217				12N	-400	1960
33	29	4875				13		1963
33	29	4932			OR	11N	-625Q	1965
34	29	6239	-425	269		22		1950
34	29	5370		248		22	-400	1955

		59	60	61	62	63	64	
34	29	5294	-189			21J	900	1960
34	29	5367	-236					1963
34	29	4900	236	262		18J	-9999Q	1965
35	29	5054A			7831	54		1950
35	29	4670			5100	176		1955
35	29	5276	2521		2610	107J		1960
35	29	5199	2603		2170	80		1963
35	29	5018	2975	308	1587	107J		1965
36	29	4939	-2613	203	1020	6AE	-19	1950
36	29	5250	-1667	265	1100	9	0	1955
36	29	6336	-901	257	612	10K	-36	1960
36	29	5914	-1126	258	377		-80	1963
36	29	6341	-1847	256	333	18	-89	1965
37	29	3567					-15	1950
37	29	3940			1110A	31	-400	1955
37	29	4076			541	24	-6700	1960
37	29	4229			429	37A		1963
37	29	5097		192	444	24	-269Q	1965
38	29	2142				69		1950
38	29	6670A		325	390A	71	-100	1955
38	29		-1202		179	104	-228	1960
38	29		-2103		561	81A	-280	1963
38	29	3976	-1888	266	561A	73	-272	1965
39	29	6333				220G	-4100H	1950
39	29	3440		285		98	-8100	1955
39	29	3730	-489			107	-267	1960
39	29	2900	-489			90A	-310	1963
39	29	3383	-489	290	0	91	-333	1965
40	29	6867	3359	366		44	153	1950
40	29	6490	3206	273		45	500	1955
40	29	5966	3321	261			194	1960
40	29	6098	3244	264	0		210	1963
40	29	6270	3130	262	0	50	238	1965
41	29	8879	-40	320		587E	-100H	1950
41	29	7830	1304	307		286	-5900	1955
41	29	7016	1107	298	307	303	-717	1960
41	29	6617	1186	311	2231	1050	-100	1963
41	29	6664	1265	305	1082	1050	-132	1965
42	29	5466	-122	313	685	37	-4	1950
42	29	5940	-81	290	320	56	0	1955
42	29	5643	1057	292	384	62K	-1	1960
42	29	6002	1382	294	425	97M	-0	1963
42	29	5061	1626	294	429	76	-4	1965
92	29	4250				11	-40H	1963
92	29	4600		227		10	-2700H	1965
163	29	5678		220		10N	-4300H	1965
43	29	5510	-1186	300	1140	22	-500	1955
43	29	5255	-424	309	968	25	-13	1960
43	29	5527	-85	320	811	26A	-40	1963
43	29	4915	-42	332	954	26	-58	1965
44	29	7222				110		1950
44	29	9050	-1029				0	1955
44	29	9160	-782	271		241J	100	1960
44	29	8882	288	254	0	273A	0	1963
44	29	8486	288	252		183J	200	1965
45	29					145E		1950
45	29					569		1955
45	29					362		1960
45	29					321A		1963
45	29					293		1965

		59	60	61	62	63	64	
46	29	9085A				49E		1950
46	29	9500			0A	307	500	1955
46	29	9125I			366	258	200	1960
46	29	8655			308	216A	150	1963
46	29	7257		297	492	214		1965
80	29	9310				14		1955
80	29	9231				171J		1960
80	29	9667				438		1963
80	29	9706			0R	178J		1965
47	29	7797			250	24		1950
47	29	8670				34	0	1955
47	29	8847	165	276		48J		1960
47	29	8710	823	282		47	10	1963
47	29	8501	1193	273	0	46J	14	1965
48	29	2286				29		1950
48	29	3780				32		1955
48	29	4539						1960
48	29	5691				62		1963
48	29	4375						1965
49	29	7570		261		14		1955
49	29	9839	-2137	252A		37N	5700	1960
49	29	3873	-1795			33	-30	1963
49	29	2867		266		31N	-318	1965
93	29	6077	495			0		1963
93	29	6000	495	223				1965
94	29	4904				31		1960
94	29	4842				20	-740	1963
94	29	4712			0	31	-2650	1965
95	29	7555						1963
95	29	7288		302				1965
96	29	6522						1963
96	29	2926						1965
50	29	5222			0	16	-5	1950
50	29	5430	42	269	50	16	-300	1955
50	29	6085	1059	273	112	15	-140	1960
50	29	5598	1314	277	123	16A	-190	1963
50	29	5820	1780	266	112	15	-215	1965
97	29	5286				21J	-69	1960
97	29	5351				32	-70	1963
97	29	5086		271		16J	-138	1965
51	29					64		1950
51	29					53		1955
51	29					49		1960
51	29					31		1963
51	29					20N		1965
52	29	5927	1571	314	209	199AE	17	1950
52	29	5440	1916	273	230	120	0	1955
52	29	5294	2146	264	205	115	7	1960
52	29	5460	2222	274	164	118	10	1963
52	29	5385	1111	279	239	112	12	1965
53	29	4633	3182	394	0	47C	-59	1950
53	29	5260	2879	304		53	-200	1955
53	29	4829	3220	312		42	-74	1960
53	29	4981	3144	318		46	-6800	1963
53	29	5112	3144	315		49	-4700Q	1965
54	29	4808				38A		1950
54	29	4920					-900	1955
54	29	5625				21J	-300	1960
54	29	5261				47		1963
54	29	5263		248		30J	-3250Q	1965

		59	60	61	62	63	64	
98	29	5349						1963
98	29	6032				3		1965
99	29	5225					-240	1963
99	29	5062		239	0R	2	-735	1965
55	29	6349	1439	374		104E	-16	1950
55	29	6320	1295	278	80	96	-100	1955
55	29	6240	540	276	81	95	-127	1960
55	29	6294	612	276	108	98	-190	1963
55	29	6050	647	277	50	86	-226	1965
56	29							1950
56	29							1955
56	29	5740						1960
56	29							1963
56	29					180		1965
57	29	3961	-1057	238			-11	1950
57	29	4200	-1233	235	0	19	0	1955
57	29	6246	-793	230		24	-14	1960
57	29	6807	-44	230	0		-80	1963
57	29	6639	88	227	117	20	-113	1965
58	29	8472				0		1950
58	29	7960				38	-4800H	1955
58	29	8015	175				-1000H	1960
58	29	7375	263			26		1963
58	29	7247	0	257			-2000H	1965
59	29	3171				43	-400H	1950
59	29	4520		272		47		1955
59	29	5424	862	250		57J	-200	1960
59	29	4521	862	256				1963
59	29	4519	862	271		54J	-3000Q	1965
60	29	4902			0	36	-40	1950
60	29	5280		256		40	-200	1955
60	29	4639	-422	250		43	-157	1960
60	29	5059	-717	250	0	44	-130	1963
60	29	5191	338	218	0	49	-136	1965
61	29	5186				11E	-725	1950
61	29	5640	-1776	253		21	-1200	1955
61	29	5189	-1449	239		24	-500	1960
61	29	4666	-561	230	0	16	-60	1963
61	29	5296	-654	242	0	11	-82	1965
62	29	4919A				200		1950
62	29	5030			5730	110		1955
62	29	5300	3035		2440	82		1960
62	29	5279	3035		2328	121A		1963
62	29	5122	3035	278	2291	89		1965
63	29	5961	-20	271	0	35E	2	1950
63	29	5830	-81	286	150	83	0	1955
63	29	6247	243	286	150	68	1	1960
63	29	6115	648	287	237	100M	-0	1963
63	29	6160	1215	292	145	162	-2	1965
64	29				8505	106		1950
64	29	4950			4680	100		1955
64	29	4747	2248		3365	121		1960
64	29	5172	1705		3283	118	-580H	1963
64	29	4943	1705	298	1098	104		1965
114	29			306				1965
65	29							1950
65	29	2430A				12		1955
65	29					25J	-1870	1960
65	29							1963
65	29			256		21J	-571	1965

		59	60	61	62	63	64	
100	29	5843						1963
100	29	5536				10		1965
204	29	5091						1963
204	29	5482				10	-1200H	1965
101	29							1963
101	29	6494		292		20J		1965
66	29	5008			224	143D		1950
66	29	5800	120	282	130	159	0	1955
66	29	4983	1325	274	99	141	-8	1960
66	29	7265	1245	274	99	156A	-0	1963
66	29	7565	1406	275	153	104	-4	1965
102	29	5014	-688				100H	1960
102	29	8021	-642			12		1963
102	29	5161	-1101	324	OR	12N	-700H	1965
67	29	5173	1536	339	143	101AE	5	1950
67	29	5360	679	288	110	101	0	1955
67	29	5307	679	278	299	96	17	1960
67	29	5142	536	281	225	105A	20	1963
67	29	5243	357	276	241	127	22	1965
68	29	5370	2180	365	299	45	-15	1950
68	29	5330	1617	300	210	10	0	1955
68	29	5442	2068	280	172	22P	7	1960
68	29	5741	1842	283	169		10	1963
68	29	5554	1917	278	120	20P	9	1965
69	29	4761				127C		1950
69	29	5830		319		117	0	1955
69	29	6447	84					1960
69	29	5542	335			120		1963
69	29	5579	418	301	294	103		1965
109	29	3870						1963
109	29	4484		279	OR	ON	-1400H	1965
70	29	4462			0	16AE	-3	1950
70	29	4990				22	-100	1955
70	29	5261				27K	-5	1960
70	29	5592				26A	-0	1963
70	29	5534		215	OR	41		1965
103	29	6170				27		1963
103	29	6250				10	-500H	1965
216	29	5420					-6000H	1965
104	29	6116				14J	67	1960
104	29	6498				28	-50	1963
104	29	6712		284		34J	-200	1965
71	29	5502	415	332	228	178C	-6	1950
71	29	6140	1535	319		175	0	1955
71	29	5932	2905	315	392	157	-24	1960
71	29	6531	2905	315	417	134	-30	1963
71	29	5543	2905	315	308	142	-39	1965
72	29	5492	272	284	909		-59	1950
72	29	5660	195	285		6	-100	1955
72	29	5579	973	284			-118	1960
72	29	5503	973	284	78		-30	1963
72	29	6235	973	284	0	13	-61	1965
73	29				B	147C		1950
73	29	4690			B	217		1955
73	29	5030				187		1960
73	29	4926				147A		1963
73	29	4963			B	136		1965

		59		60	61	62	63	64	
74	29	5360		1787	335	669	163	15	1950
74	29	5640		2395	262	410	179	0	1955
74	29	5531		2471	271	211	92	24	1960
74	29	5348		2395	274	832	80A	40	1963
74	29	5413		2243	273	1605	81	55	1965
75	29	4657		2046	347	578	98	7	1950
75	29	4250		2239	298	530	194	0	1955
75	29	4251		2046	294	1280	138	19	1960
75	29	4268		2124	293	1028	144	30	1963
75	29	4398		2355	293	1819	136	38	1965
219	29	3890		-1078	242		3	-1800H	1965
105	29	8043							1963
105	29	7255					2		1965
76	29	4418		989	346			-21	1950
76	29	5520		1255	324		25	0	1955
76	29	6542		2243	316A		16K	-4	1960
76	29	5175		2243	317		32	-10	1963
76	29	4399		2243	368	4375	48	-10	1965
77	29	3162		-851	272		20C	-97	1950
77	29	3410		-1702	260		30	-400	1955
77	29	3036		-213	256A		34	-130	1960
77	29	2462		170	256	0	41	-150	1963
77	29	3210		596	293	0	31	-176	1965
81	29						180A		1955
81	29						283		1960
81	29						247AM		1963
81	29						200		1965
82	29	7920				170	110A		1955
82	29	7362					110	-500H	1960
82	29	7879				0	266AM		1963
82	29	9084				0A	351		1965
78	29								1950
78	29						40		1955
78	29								1960
78	29								1963
78	29	6130					5		1965
79	29	5979				5197	124G		1950
79	29	6320		573	320	560	316	-200	1955
79	29	5934		1565	318	829	145K	-275	1960
79	29	5723		1985	313	1314	210A	-240	1963
79	29	5412		2061	294	2330	127	-316	1965
		65	66	67	68	69		70	
1	30		0	0		1		3435	1950
1	30	0	0	0	1093	1		3300	1955
1	30	0	588	0		1		3500A	1960
1	30	0H	667	0		1		5135	1963
1	30	0	1250	0	822	1		5000	1965
2	30	1	0	3667		0		5345	1950
2	30	1	370	3528		0		8600	1955
2	30	1	0	3292		0		2900	1960
2	30	1	588	3011		0		3041	1963
2	30	1	488	2834		0		2800	1965
106	30	1	246	8		0		4300	1965
3	30	2	421	233	1485	0		2289	1950
3	30	8	299	262		0		2300	1955
3	30	8I	567	363A	1610	0		2200	1960
3	30	9	461	207	1312	0		2337	1963
3	30	5	497	288	1092	0		2000	1965

		65	66	67	68	69	70	
4	30	2	408	73	1714	1	2539	1950
4	30	2	342	54	1743	0	3200	1955
4	30	6	495	56	1690	0	3300	1960
4	30	6	249	54	3568	0	2924	1963
4	30	4	511	44	3802	0	2800	1965
5	30	3	458	1004	2687	0	3600	1955
5	30	4	589	709	2615	0	2200	1960
5	30	4	546	488	2790	0	2186	1963
5	30	5	535	482	2771	0	2200	1965
6	30	4	396	347	2372	1	2427	1950
6	30	3	328	169	2051	1	2400	1955
6	30	4	496	120	2368	1	2000	1960
6	30	6	358	118	2303	1	2150	1963
6	30	5	370	137	2387	1	2500	1965
7	30	2A	400	66	2350	0	2029	1950
7	30	5	182	93		0	2600	1955
7	30	2I	480	174		0	2700	1960
7	30	6	417	166	1449E	0	3255	1963
7	30	8	424	103		0	2800	1965
8	30	5	567	114	944	0	3698	1950
8	30	9	467	171	1789	0	3100	1955
8	30	13I	729	64A		0	3300	1960
8	30	5	568	40	5405	0	3037	1963
8	30	2	517	28	2585	0	2800	1965
9	30	1	337	6906		0	2716	1950
9	30	2	333	6068	2186A	0	2500	1955
9	30	1	612	6150		0	2400	1960
9	30	2	628	6262	5697F	0	2372	1963
9	30	2	633	6712	3982	0	2300	1965
10	30	2K	227	54	1081	0	5519	1950
10	30	2	405	42	2404	0	4200	1955
10	30	1	322	9	1813	0	4200	1960
10	30	1	364	21	1873	0	4197F	1963
10	30	1	182	20	1704	0	5600	1965
113	30	1	0	0	904	1	4000	1965
11	30	3	0	25		1	3900	1955
11	30	2	417	0		1	3900	1960
11	30	2	278	0	2213F	1G	4663	1963
11	30	2	0	2	2190	1	5100	1965
83	30	2	328	0		0	4815	1963
83	30	1	330	0	1869	0	4700	1965
12	30	6	307	73	1333	1	2255	1950
12	30	4	329	48	1598	0	2700	1955
12	30	5	491	33	1525	0	2600	1960
12	30	5	478	21	1606	0	2624	1963
12	30	5	507	18	1626	0	2700	1965
84	30	1	0	0		0	6353	1963
84	30	1	270	0	2189	0	5600	1965
13	30	5P	395	66	1707	1	3559	1950
13	30	5	410	27	1875	0	3300	1955
13	30	5	240	40	2630	0	3100	1960
13	30	5	508	47	2612	0	3031	1963
13	30	10	398	23	3235	0	2800	1965
85	30	1	0	0		0	8382	1963
85	30	1	938	0		0	8300	1965
14	30	6	298	69	1511	0		1950
14	30	5	437	592		0	4000	1955
14	30	7	1014	325	1845	0	4000A	1960
14	30	7	526	304	1797	0		1963
14	30	7	492	344	2214	0	3800	1965

		65	66	67	68	69	70	
15	30		348	1251		0	3604	1950
15	30	9	1000	1759	3462B	0	3300	1955
15	30	1	667	2385A		0		1960
15	30	1	313	2647		0		1963
15	30	1	315	2643		0		1965
16	30	3	172	0	832	0	4100	1955
16	30	3	569	0	1271	0	4600	1960
16	30	3	530	0	1710E	0	4163	1963
16	30	3	506	0		0	4200	1965
17	30	2	85	44	641	0	4149	1950
17	30	4	118	40	909	0	3900	1955
17	30	2I	178	32	837	0	3800	1960
17	30	3	421	65	998	0	3626	1963
17	30	3	428	67	1448	0	3600	1965
87	30	1	541	0		0	5777	1963
87	30	1	485	0		0	6000	1965
86	30	4	686	0	1829F	0	3745	1963
86	30	1	615	0		0	3700	1965
18	30	3	0	625	833	0	2434	1950
18	30	5	230	105	1345	0	2500	1955
18	30	3I	1322	26		0	2600	1960
18	30	3	530	0	1444E	0	2609	1963
18	30	5	458	27	1349	0	2800	1965
19	30	2W	352	560	1000	0	2560	1950
19	30	4	550	490		0	3000	1955
19	30	1	611	395		0	3800	1960
19	30	1	588	387		0	3458	1963
19	30	1	652	631	4656	0	3200	1965
20	30	1	490	13590		0	3342	1950
20	30	5	390	11374		0	2600	1955
20	30	1	896	10103		0	2500	1960
20	30	1	774	11641	7	0	2482	1963
20	30	1	800	11893	3593	0	2300	1965
88	30	1	435	0		0	4136	1963
88	30	1	612	0		0	4200	1965
21	30	6	442	371	1060	1	2807	1950
21	30	4	414	383	1705	1	2900	1955
21	30	5	544	109	1618	1	3100	1960
21	30	6	503	107	1769	1	2736	1963
21	30	6	513	105	1698	1	1800	1965
22	30	1	0	94	2500	0	6359	1950
22	30	4	250	0	2428	0	6300	1955
22	30	4I	395	0	1890	0	5800	1960
22	30	4	241		2270	0	5146	1963
22	30	3	192	47	1523	0	5400	1965
23	30	6	263	156	563	0	4171	1950
23	30	8	360	136	1122	0	4200	1955
23	30	6I	0	23	1315	0	3900	1960
23	30	6	321	42	1248	0	3734	1963
23	30	7	330	49	1519	0	3700	1965
24	30	3T	535	15	2222	1	2885	1950
24	30		294	9	2092	0	3900	1955
24	30	1	491	4		0	3900	1960
24	30	0	507	4	1392	0	3866	1963
24	30	1	625	0	5896	0	3900	1965
25	30	1	0	54	1250	0	3000	1950
25	30	5	263	46	1255	0	3300	1955
25	30	5	946	41		0	3700	1960
25	30	3	463	37	982	0	3814	1963
25	30	3	325	7	1128	0	3400	1965

		65	66	67	68	69	70	
26	30	0	0	0		1		1950
26	30	0	0	0	496	1	2400	1955
26	30	0	0	0	821	1	3800	1960
26	30	0H	182	0		1	4830	1963
26	30	0	526	0	1332	1	4100	1965
27	30	6	306	744	3036	0	2725	1950
27	30	8	370	766	2504	0	2800	1955
27	30	8	518	745	2304	0	2600	1960
27	30	7	462	881	2488	0	2428	1963
27	30	7	459	1085	2383	0	2300	1965
28	30	6	371	1051		0	2385	1950
28	30	5	382	867	2175	0	2400	1955
28	30	6	520	876	2223	0	3600	1960
28	30	6	391	543	2335	0	2352	1963
28	30	6	418	574	2193	0	2500	1965
89	30	2	0	0		0	3996	1963
89	30	1	263	0		0	3900	1965
29	30	5	1111	7145		0	2500	1955
29	30	1	833	9115A		0	2400	1960
29	30	1	769	10012	7270F	0	2160	1963
29	30	1	1007	10094		0	2000	1965
30	30	6	391	120	1303	0	3500	1955
30	30	5	510	79A	2094	0	3000	1960
30	30	3	387	90	1505F	0	2764	1963
30	30	4	397	18	2284	0	2700	1965
90	30	1	337	0		0	3000A	1960
90	30	1	379	0	2286	0	3611	1963
90	30	1	485	0	1953	0	2900	1965
31	30	3	289	251	2825	1	4843	1950
31	30	3	317	251		1	4500	1955
31	30	4	523	240	1753	1	4000	1960
31	30	4	535	236	1768	1	3561	1963
31	30	5	544	234	1920	1	3600	1965
32	30	5	145	179	714	0	2347	1950
32	30	8	263	31	1310	0	2700	1955
32	30	0	642	31	958	0	3000	1960
32	30	0	423	24	793	0	3292	1963
32	30	4	375	22	1010	0	3400	1965
91	30	1	385	0		0	4887	1963
91	30	1	667	0	1922	0	4100	1965
33	30	2	465	161		0		1950
33	30	3	488	0	1157	0	4700	1955
33	30	0	900	0		0	4500A	1960
33	30	0H	865			0	4353	1963
33	30	0	811	0	861	0	4600	1965
34	30	1	0	0	750A	0	3000	1950
34	30	3	159	30	1320	0	3300	1955
34	30	2	400	21	1057	0	3200	1960
34	30	0	115	93	956	0	2921	1963
34	30	2	215	60	1047	0	2900	1965
35	30	1	316	8593A		0	3184	1950
35	30	2	364	8788	2520	0	2300	1955
35	30	1	734	4389		0	2400	1960
35	30	1	769	5159	5414F	0	2387	1963
35	30	1	793	5320	2810	0	2300	1965
36	30	5L	286	8	534	0	3439	1950
36	30	3	219	28	714	0	3500	1955
36	30	6	339	54		0	2900	1960
36	30	5	407	26	1050F	0	4849	1963
36	30	8	345	26	1559	0	3200	1965

		65	66	67	68	69	70	
37	30	14	154	40	1532	0	5922	1950
37	30	6	273	667	903	0	5200	1955
37	30	9	195	1604		0	3900	1960
37	30	6	333	1899		0	3992	1963
37	30	8	281	95		0	4200	1965
38	30	3Q	339	107		1	3797	1950
38	30	3	115	33	1379	1	2600	1955
38	30	2	325	7	1673	1	3300A	1960
38	30	0H	374	9	1508	1	3391	1963
38	30	3	377	6	3126	1	3000	1965
39	30	2R	541	235		1	2744	1950
39	30	2	364	42	2147	1	3200	1955
39	30	5	267	15	2997	0	3000	1960
39	30	0H	568	218	3369	0	2525	1963
39	30	1	449	24	2842	0	2200	1965
40	30	6	375	67	3333	0	3531	1950
40	30	6	321	3	2541	0	3800	1955
40	30	3	611	3	2430	0	3500A	1960
40	30	5	512	0	2537D	0	3503	1963
40	30	4	370	4	2868	0	3400	1965
41	30	6N	409	238	2000	0	2196	1950
41	30	12	445	200	3159	0	2400	1955
41	30	10	459	95	2814	0	2300	1960
41	30	10	482	84	2711	0	2226	1963
41	30	10	483	78	5358	0	2000	1965
42	30	9Z	480	3673	1800A	0	2737	1950
42	30	4	407	3121	2071	0	2600	1955
42	30	7	519	3608	2036	0	2200	1960
42	30	10	377	2666	1984	0	2153	1963
42	30	10	392	2617	2146	0	2200	1965
92	30	1	244	0		0	4598	1963
92	30	1	411	0	1346	0	4700	1965
163	30	2	0	0	2035	0	5600	1965
43	30	4	430	101	1369	0	3600	1955
43	30	6	516	97A	1102	0	3500	1960
43	30	6	473	118	1301	0	3058	1963
43	30	5	515	140	1105	0	2800	1965
44	30		385	157		1	4167	1950
44	30	7	0	365	4977	1	3400	1955
44	30	10	0	12		1	3400	1960
44	30	0	0	0	2888	1	3146	1963
44	30	0	0	26	2881	1	3800	1965
45	30	1	0	11136		0		1950
45	30	3	0	12362		0		1955
45	30	1	500	11321		0		1960
45	30	1	370	11304		0	4413F	1963
45	30	1	286	13223		0		1965
46	30	2	0			0	7033	1950
46	30	3	0	0	1477	0	5900	1955
46	30	2	582	0		0	5800	1960
46	30	0H	408	0	1556	0	6130	1963
46	30	2	343	0	1350	0	6200	1965
80	30	4	0	236		1	3600	1955
80	30	3	0	5		1	3200	1960
80	30	3	526	0		1G	4109	1963
80	30	3	400	0	3538	1	3700	1965
47	30	2M	0	635	1000	0		1950
47	30	6	236	546	1018	0	2700	1955
47	30	4	183	140A		0	2000	1960
47	30		201	179	2177	0	2567	1963
47	30	2	379	166	1703	0	2000	1965

	65	66	67	68	69	70	
48 30	1A	250	0		0	2667	1950
48 30	1	0	0	797	0	3200	1955
48 30	1	0	0		0	3200	1960
48 30	1	0	0		0	3229	1963
48 30	1	161	0	2629	0	3200	1965
49 30	1	0	23	2752	1	3300	1955
49 30	0	0	0		1	2900	1960
49 30	0	0	0		1	2996	1963
49 30	0	217	0	2314	1	3100	1965
93 30	7	471	0		0	7242	1963
93 30	4	331	2	2016	0	7100	1965
94 30	1	297	22	1800	0	2800	1960
94 30	1	286	22	2148	0	2712	1963
94 30	1	117	29	2674	0	2900	1965
95 30	1	1429	0		0	5493	1963
95 30	1	750	0		0	4100	1965
96 30	4	0	0		0	1989	1963
96 30	4	667	0		0	2000	1965
50 30	2	0	19	862	0	3829	1950
50 30	5	423	17	1067	0	4100	1955
50 30	5	652	214	983	0	4400	1960
50 30	2	533	130	855	0	4630	1963
50 30	3	534	12	1184	0	4700	1965
97 30	2	660	11		1	4300	1960
97 30		267	8	1342D	1	4330	1963
97 30	4	307	4		1	3900	1965
51 30		519			1		1950
51 30	5	0	21		1	2000	1955
51 30	0	0	36A		1	3300	1960
51 30	0	0	41		1	2783	1963
51 30	0	0	59		1	2900	1965
52 30	4	0	326	2487	1	3511	1950
52 30	7	358	233	2366	1	3500	1955
52 30	7	513	104	2030	1	3400	1960
52 30	7	390	100	2028	1	3238	1963
52 30	7	387	98	2346	1	3100	1965
53 30	2	447	261	1429	1	3040	1950
53 30	2	450	19	2050	0	3500	1955
53 30	2	307	17	2246	0	3000	1960
53 30	2	395	39	2121	0	2946	1963
53 30	2	376	15	1805A	0	2800	1965
54 30	2	357	475	1000	0	3111	1950
54 30	3	152	40	1020	0	3200	1955
54 30	2	845	14	1040A	0	3500	1960
54 30	3	617	0	1075	0	3628	1963
54 30	4	435	12	1157	0	3300	1965
98 30	1	909	0		0	4633	1963
98 30	1	1364	0		0	4200	1965
99 30	5	290	0		0	3075	1963
99 30	5	495	1	668	0	3300	1965
55 30	6	0	244	2143	1	2522	1950
55 30	1	389	233	1827	1	2800	1955
55 30	7	412	140	1818	1	2300	1960
55 30	7	380	109	2130	1	2207	1963
55 30	7	398	67	2186	1	2100	1965
56 30	1	327	3146		0		1950
56 30	2	1250	3610		0		1955
56 30	1	909	4574		0		1960

		65	66	67	68	69	70	
56	30	1	667	4510A		0	3081F	1963
56	30	1	313	4182		0		1965
57	30	2AX	0	7	718	1	3621	1950
57	30	8	368	2	843	0	3600	1955
57	30	0	443	4		0	3900	1960
57	30	0H	435	3	1109	0	3808	1963
57	30	2	367	3	1148	0	4000	1965
58	30	2	500	125	2000	0	3235	1950
58	30	2	330	54	1657	0	3100	1955
58	30	3	439	28	1729	0	2900	1960
58	30	3	325	0	2179	0	3152	1963
58	30	3	323	40	1506	0	3000	1965
59	30	1	0	142	714	0	3267	1950
59	30	2	330	128	806	0	2900	1955
59	30	5I	631	29	712	0	2800	1960
59	30	4	496	209	952F	0	2708	1963
59	30	4	493	246	812	0	3000	1965
60	30	3	0	119	1293	0	1017	1950
60	30	5	374	53	1852	0	3800	1955
60	30	5I	596	69	1511	0	3400	1960
60	30	4	463	73	2208	0	3582	1963
60	30	4	452	43	1697	0	4500B	1965
61	30	2	368	25	909	0	4950	1950
61	30	2	145	21	888	0	4000	1955
61	30	3	410	5	943	0	3600	1960
61	30	3	424	7	1085	0	3419	1963
61	30	2	494	5	1030	0	3100	1965
62	30	1	97	4524		0	4010	1950
62	30	4	580	5278	1573	0	4200	1955
62	30	1	821	3885		0	3300	1960
62	30	1	763	4806	5386	0	3042	1963
62	30	2	823	5476	4195	0	2800	1965
63	30	1	561	47	1244	0	3885	1950
63	30	1	428	34	1360	0	3600	1955
63	30	1	705	23	1472	0	3400	1960
63	30	1	644	22	1743	0G	3232	1963
63	30	1	643	22	1557	0	3200	1965
64	30	1	498	4475		0		1950
64	30	1	270	3437		0	2300C	1955
64	30	1	611	4533		0	2500	1960
64	30	1	648	6592		0	2416	1963
64	30	1	736	7620		0	2300	1965
114	30	1	417	0		0	6500	1965
65	30	0A	92	0		1	3375	1950
65	30	0	0	0		1	2600	1955
65	30	0	0	0		1	2300A	1960
65	30	0H	0	0		1	2027	1963
65	30	0	645	0		1	2300	1965
100	30	2	448	0		0	4671	1963
100	30	1	303	0		0	4300	1965
204	30	3	0	0	766	0	3637	1963
204	30	2	145	0	1809	0	3200	1965
101	30	3	0	0		0	2587	1963
101	30	6	526	0	1820	0	2600	1965
66	30	1	0	36	925	0	3537	1950
66	30	1	322	17	1049	1	3900	1955
66	30	1	621	17	1090	1	3500	1960
66	30	1	540	16	1148	1	3478	1963
66	30	1	529	16	1418	1	3400	1965

		65	66	67	68	69	70	
102	30	C	517	7		0	4100	1960
102	30	0	541	16	1952	0	4386	1963
102	30	4	361	59	1836	0	4900	1965
67	30	5	430	426	1979	1	2073	1950
67	30	3	333	379	2340	1	2300	1955
67	30	5	498	334	2524	1	2700A	1960
67	30	5	454	263	2462	1	1392	1963
67	30	5	438	259	2561	1	2100	1965
68	30	5	358	170	854	0	2597	1950
68	30	8	397	121	746	0	3300	1955
68	30	5	521	112	701	0	2700	1960
68	30	5	491	104	801	0	3258F	1963
68	30	8	481	67	819	0		1965
69	30	7S	438	311		0	3453	1950
69	30		494	259	1830	0	3300	1955
69	30	0	189	33		0	4600	1960
69	30	0H	128	80	1450	0	3587	1963
69	30	1	319	57	1642	0	3600	1965
109	30	1	169	0		0	5261F	1963
109	30	2	326	0	1600	0		1965
70	30	0	385	27	898	1	3589	1950
70	30	7	390	25	1145	1	3500	1955
70	30	1	427	12	1235	1	3600	1960
70	30	0H	340		1362	1	3651	1963
70	30	0	287	0	1484	1	3500	1965
103	30	3	357	0	1314D	0	10471	1963
103	30	4	227	0	1483	0	5000	1965
216	30	2	169	0		0	3500	1965
104	30	1	450	11	1671	0	6200A	1960
104	30	1	387	22	1818F	0	5704	1963
104	30	1	533	5		0	5600	1965
71	30	2AU	370	0	1553	0	4564	1950
71	30	3	369	0	1448	0	4500	1955
71	30	4	424	1	1220	0	4700	1960
71	30	5	462	3		0	4688	1963
71	30	5	417	4	1933	0	4500	1965
72	30	3	370	16	1667	1	3649	1950
72	30	5	504	11	1730	0	3300	1955
72	30	3	424	12	3243	0	3800	1960
72	30	3	429	6	1447	0		1963
72	30	3	345	0	1793	0		1965
73	30	1	547	3566	1963	0	2400	1950
73	30	1	241	3604	1328	0	1700	1955
73	30	1	503	4062		0	2500	1960
73	30	1	502	4894	5144	0	2680	1963
73	30	1	625	5205	3550	0	2600	1965
74	30	3	175	43	2932	1	2914	1950
74	30	2	369	66	2577	1	3000	1955
74	30	4	539	51	3030	1	2400A	1960
74	30	4	487	63	3321	1	2348	1963
74	30	4	531	62	3137	1	2800	1965
75	30	2	412	28	1394	0	3145	1950
75	30	2	424	J	1667	0	3200	1955
75	30	2	489	J	1843	0	3200A	1960
75	30	2	412	J	1874	0	2716	1963
75	30	2	482	J	1722	0	2800	1965
219	30	2	455	0		0	3500	1965
105	30	1	667	0		0	6638	1963
105	30	1	741	0		0	4900	1965

		65	66	67	68	69		70	
76	30	4	454	633		0		3145	1950
76	30	2	418	191	1556	0		3300	1955
76	30	2	730	157	1060	0		3500	1960
76	30	2	556	377	2889E	0		2948	1963
76	30	4	568	368	892	0		3100	1965
77	30	4Y	460	401	1667	0		3550	1950
77	30	4	181	173	1858	0		3600	1955
77	30	4	537	537	2933	0		3500	1960
77	30	6	436	369	2008	0		3459	1963
77	30	7	459	229	2088	0		3400	1965
81	30	3	0	3141		0			1955
81	30	1	1429	3141		0		4200A	1960
81	30	1	625	3371		0		6536F	1963
81	30	1	0	3684		0			1965
82	30		0	14		0		6000	1955
82	30	0	396	57A		0		5300	1960
82	30	0	397	130	2143E	0		5722	1963
82	30	2	387	192	4085	0		5800	1965
78	30	0V	0	0		1			1950
78	30	0	0	0		1		3400	1955
78	30	0	0	0		1		4700	1960
78	30	0H	0	0		0		4474	1963
78	30	0	0	0		1		4000	1965
79	30	1	0	4824		0		5690	1950
79	30	1	544	3457	2309	0		4000	1955
79	30	1	814	5348	2708	0		3300	1960
79	30	1	742	5430	1984	0		3092	1963
79	30	1	796	5279	1447	1		2900	1965

		71	72	73	74	75	76	77	
1	31	2	0	574	0	0	0		1950
1	31	2	0	574	0	0	0		1955
1	31	2	0	574	0	0	0		1960
1	31	2	0	574	0	0	0		1963
1	31	1	0	574	0	1	16		1965
2	31	1	0	962	1	0	0		1950
2	31	0	0	962	0	0	0		1955
2	31	2	0	962	0	0	3		1960
2	31	2	0	962	0	0	24		1963
2	31	2	0	962	0	0	89		1965
106	31	0	1	850A	0	1	89		1965
3	31	1	0	806	0	0	0		1950
3	31	1	0	806	3	2	92	2	1955
3	31	1	0	806	1	1	92	-5	1960
3	31	2	0	806	0	5	81	7	1963
3	31	1	0	806	3	1	71	4	1965
4	31	2	0	818	0	0	0	-42	1950
4	31	2	0	818	0	0	0	11	1955
4	31	2	0	818	0	0	0	-1	1960
4	31	2	0	818	0	0	0	-7A	1963
4	31	2	0	818	0	0	0	1	1965
5	31	1		980A	0	0	0	-4	1955
5	31	2	0	980A	0	1	50	-2	1960
5	31	2	0	980A	0	1	0	-3	1963
5	31	2	0	980A	0	0	12	1	1965
6	31	2	0	571	1	1	0	-14	1950
6	31	1	0	571	0	0	0	-0	1955
6	31	2	0	571	0	0	2	0	1960
6	31	2	0	571	0	0	22	-1	1963
6	31	2	0	571	0	0	20	-0	1965

		71	72	73	74	75	76	77	
7	31	2	0	526	0	0	0	-1	1950
7	31	0	1	526	0	0	80	52	1955
7	31	1	1	526	0	0	214	-1	1960
7	31	2	0	526	0	0	8		1963
7	31	0	1	526	2	1	85	3	1965
8	31	2	0	548	0	0	0	2	1950
8	31	2	0	548	0	1	0	-2	1955
8	31	2	0	548	0	0	0	-4	1960
8	31	2	1	548	0	2	90	5	1963
8	31	1	1	548	2	1	89	5	1965
9	31	1	0	900	0	0	0		1950
9	31	2	0	900	0	0	0		1955
9	31	2	0	900	0	0	66		1960
9	31	2	0	900	0	0	90		1963
9	31	2	0	900	0	1	60		1965
10	31	2	0	113	0	0	0	-220	1950
10	31	1	0	113	0	0	0	279	1955
10	31	1	0	113	0	0	0	-1	1960
10	31	1	1	113	0	0	51	-6	1963
10	31	1	1	113	1G	0	0	0	1965
113	31	2	0	860	3	1	89		1965
11	31	1	0	719	0	1	0		1955
11	31	2	0	719	0	0	0	-1480	1960
11	31	2	0	719	0	0	0		1963
11	31	2	0	719	0	0	24		1965
83	31	2	0	100A	0	0	0		1963
83	31	1	0	100A	0	0	26		1965
12	31	2	0	275	0	0	0	-5	1950
12	31	2	0	275	0	0	0	-0	1955
12	31	2	0	275	0	0	0	-1	1960
12	31	2	0	275	0	0	0	-4	1963
12	31	2	0	275	0	0	8		1965
84	31	2	0	500A	0	0	0		1963
84	31	1	0	500A	0	0	14		1965
13	31	1	0	397	0	0	0	-1408	1950
13	31	2	0	397	0	0	0	-404B	1955
13	31	1	0	397	0	0	0	1329B	1960
13	31	2	0	397	0	0	19	110B	1963
13	31	2	0	397	0	1	0	-18	1965
85	31	2	1	100A	0	0	0		1963
85	31	1	1	100A	0	1	89	0B	1965
14	31	2	0	680	0	0	0	3	1950
14	31	2	0	680	0	1	89	-0	1955
14	31	2	0	680	0	0	84	11	1960
14	31	2	0	680	0	0	87	6	1963
14	31	2	0	680	0	0	68	7	1965
15	31	1	1	940A	0	0	0		1950
15	31	1	1	940	0	0	0		1955
15	31	1	1	940	0	0	0		1960
15	31	2	1	940	0	0	0		1963
15	31	2	1	940	0	0	0		1965
16	31	1	0	561	0	0	99	3	1955
16	31	1	0	561	0	0	181	-3	1960
16	31	2	0	561	0	0	0	-10	1963
16	31	2	0	561	0	0	73	16	1965
17	31	2	0	636	0	1	0	-2	1950
17	31	1	1	636	0	0	0	9	1955
17	31	1	0	636	0	1	1	2	1960
17	31	1	0	636	0	0	89	8A	1963
17	31	1	0	636	1	0	89	16	1965

	71	72	73	74	75	76	77	
87 31	2	1	450	0	0	0		1963
87 31	0	1	450	5	1	89	OB	1965
86 31	0	0	600	0	0	0		1963
86 31	0	0	600	0	1	89		1965
18 31	1	0	822	0	0	0		1950
18 31	1	0	822	0	0	0	12	1955
18 31	2	0	822	0	0	25	92	1960
18 31	2	0	822	0	0	43		1963
18 31	2	0	822	0	1	89	78	1965
19 31	2	0	693	1	0	0	-1	1950
19 31	1	1	693	1	0	85	4	1955
19 31	1	1	693	1	0	84		1960
19 31	1	1	693	0	0	86		1963
19 31	0	1	693	1G	0	86		1965
20 31	1	0	622	0	0	0		1950
20 31	1	0	622	0	0	26		1955
20 31	2	0	670	0	0	16		1960
20 31	2	0	622	0	0	78		1963
20 31	2	0	670	0	0	35		1965
88 31	2	0	300	0	0	0		1963
88 31	0	1	300	0	2	89	OB	1965
21 31	2	0	984A	0	1	0	-2	1950
21 31	2	0	984	0	0	0		1955
21 31	2	0	984	0	0	0	-10	1960
21 31	2	0	984	0	0	0	-10	1963
21 31	2	0	984	0	0	12	3	1965
22 31	2	0	510	0	0	0	-9	1950
22 31	1	0	510	0	0	0	-1	1955
22 31	2	0	510	0	0	2	151	1960
22 31	2	0	510	0	0	88	-58	1963
22 31	0	1	510	0	2	87	-74	1965
23 31	2	0	341	0	0	0	-1	1950
23 31	1	0	341	0	0	6	2	1955
23 31	2	0	341E	0	0	65	2	1960
23 31	2	1	341	0	1	46	-6	1963
23 31	0	1	341	0	1	89	-7	1965
24 31	2	0	907	0	0	0	2	1950
24 31	0	1	907	0	0	0	3	1955
24 31	1	1	907	0	0	176	4	1960
24 31	0	1	907	0	0	0	5	1963
24 31	2	1	907	0	1	87	2	1965
25 31	1	0	923	0	0	0	-2	1950
25 31	0	0	923	0	0	0	1	1955
25 31	1	1	923	0	0	0	323	1960
25 31	1	0	923	0	0	0	-59	1963
25 31	1	0	923	0	0	23	6	1965
26 31	2	0	400	0	0	0		1950
26 31	2	0	400	0	0	0	-13	1955
26 31	2	0	400	0	1	152	8	1960
26 31	2	0	400	0	0	0	-23	1963
26 31	2	0	400	0	0	7	31	1965
27 31	2	0	999	0	0	0	-38	1950
27 31	2	0	999	0	0	0	-3	1955
27 31	2	0	999	0	0	0	-6	1960
27 31	2	0	999	0	0	0	-1	1963
27 31	2	0	999	0	0	19	3	1965
28 31	2	0	848	0	0	0	-1	1950
28 31	2	0	848	0	1	0	-2	1955
28 31	2	0	848	1	1	0	-6	1960
28 31	2	0	848	1	0	5	-3	1963
28 31	2	0	848	0	0	47	1	1965

		71	72	73	74	75	76	77	
89	31	2	0	240	0	0	54		1963
89	31	1	0	240	0	0	89	08	1965
29	31	1	0	999	0	0	0		1955
29	31	2	0	999	0	0	0		1960
29	31	2	0	999	0	0	0		1963
29	31	2	0	999	0	0	0		1965
30	31	1	0	999	0	0	0	-7	1955
30	31	2	0	999	0	0	0	-7	1960
30	31	2	0	999	0	1	0	-0	1963
30	31	2	0	999	0	1	0	1	1965
90	31	1	0	100A	0	0	88	2	1960
90	31	2	0	100A	2	0	34	47	1963
90	31	1	0	100A	0	0	0	1B	1965
31	31	2	0	933	0	1	0	10	1950
31	31	2	0	933	0	0	43	-9	1955
31	31	2	0	933	0	0	11	-4	1960
31	31	2	0	933	0	1	49	-2	1963
31	31	2	0	933	0	1	28	2	1965
32	31	2	0	459A	0	0	0	1	1950
32	31	1	0	459	0	0	96	-3	1955
32	31	1	0	459A	0	0	97	13	1960
32	31	0	1	459	0	0	89		1963
32	31	0	1	459	2	1	25	-10	1965
91	31	2	0	350	0	0	0		1963
91	31	2	0	350	0	0	23		1965
33	31	1	0	996	0	1	0		1950
33	31	1	0	996	0	0	0		1955
33	31	1	0	996	0	0	173	-57	1960
33	31	1	0	996	0	0	86	15	1963
33	31	1	0	996	0	0	87	258	1965
34	31	1	0	650	0	0	0		1950
34	31	2		650	0	0	0	22	1955
34	31	1	0	650	0	0	183	9	1960
34	31	0	1	650	0	0	70	-9	1963
34	31	1	1	650	0	1	89		1965
35	31	1	0	957	0	0	0		1950
35	31	1	0	957	0	0	0		1955
35	31	0	1	957	0	0	183		1960
35	31	0	0	957	0	0	90		1963
35	31	1	0	957	0	0	89		1965
36	31	1	0	200A	0	0	0	8	1950
36	31	1	0	200A	2	0	11	5	1955
36	31	2	0	200A	0	0	10	3	1960
36	31	2	0	200A	0	0	8D	1	1963
36	31	2	0	200A	1	1	16	3	1965
37	31	1	0	497	0	0	0	-4	1950
37	31	1	0	497	0	1	0	12	1955
37	31	2	0	497	1	1	0	-233	1960
37	31	1	1	497	0	0	0		1963
37	31	0	1	497	6	1	0		1965
38	31	2	0	500	0	0	0	2	1950
38	31	1	1	500	1	0	17	1	1955
38	31	1	0	500	0	1	0	3	1960
38	31	2	0	500	0	0	87	-1A	1963
38	31	2	0	500	2G	1	87	-3	1965
39	31	2	0	768	0	1	0	-60	1950
39	31	2	0	768	0	0	0	-56	1955
39	31	1	1	768	0	0	0	1	1960
39	31	0	1	768	1G	0	0	-0	1963
39	31	0	1	768	0	0	87	0	1965

		71	72	73	74	75	76	77	
40	31	1	0	999A	0	0	0	23	1950
40	31	2	0	999	0	0	0	20	1955
40	31	2	0	999	0	0	0	-11	1960
40	31	2	0	999	0	0	0	-10	1963
40	31	2	0	999	0	0	89	7	1965
41	31	1	0	906	0	1	0	116	1950
41	31	2	0	906	0	0	55	-135	1955
41	31	2	0	906E	0	1	64	-113	1960
41	31	2	0	906	0	0	37	-15	1963
41	31	2	0	906	0	0	89	-9	1965
42	31	2	0	999A	0	0	0	7	1950
42	31	2	0	999	0	0	0	-1	1955
42	31	2	0	999	0	2	19	-3	1960
42	31	2	0	999	0	0	20	1	1963
42	31	2	0	999	0	0	33	-2	1965
92	31	2	0	100A	0	0	0	0A	1963
92	31	2	0	100A	0	0	89	1B	1965
163	31	2	0	900	0	0	23	0B	1965
43	31	2	0	999	0	0	0	-48	1955
43	31	2	0	999	2	1	0	6	1960
43	31	2	0	999	0	0	0	1	1963
43	31	2	0	999	0	0	35	-2	1965
44	31	2	0	543	0	1	0		1950
44	31	2	0	543	0	1	0	-98	1955
44	31	1	0	543	11	0	0	-8	1960
44	31	2	0	543	0	0	90	155	1963
44	31	2	0	543	0	0	89	3	1965
45	31	1	0	999A	0	0	0		1950
45	31	1	0	999	0	0	0		1955
45	31	1	0	999	0	0	0		1960
45	31	2	0	999	0	0	0		1963
45	31	2	0	999	0	0	0		1965
46	31	2	0	999A	0	0	0		1950
46	31	2	0	999	0	0	0	191	1955
46	31	1	1	999	1	1	0	-87	1960
46	31	0	0A	999	0	0	0	172	1963
46	31	0	0A	999	0	1	0	-7	1965
80	31			660			0		1955
80	31	1	1	660	0	3	0	-1	1960
80	31	2	0	660	1	0	90		1963
80	31	2	0	660	0	0	89		1965
47	31	2	0	224	1	0	0		1950
47	31	2	0	224	0	0	1	-1	1955
47	31	1	0	224	0	1	88		1960
47	31	2	0	224	0	0	0		1963
47	31	2	0	224	0	0	10	1	1965
48	31	2	0	100A	0	0	0		1950
48	31	2	0	100A	1	0	0		1955
48	31	2	0	100A	0	0	0		1960
48	31	2	0	100A	0	0	90		1963
48	31	2	0	100A	0	0	72		1965
49	31	1	0	859	0	0	0	-111	1955
49	31	1	0	859E	0	1	0	-15	1960
49	31	2	0	859	0	0	0	-22	1963
49	31	2	0	859	0	0	89	1	1965
93	31	2	0	250	0	0	0		1963
93	31	2	0	250	0	0	8		1965
94	31	2	0	500	0	0	0	-460	1960
94	31	2	0	500	0	0	0	6	1963
94	31	2	0	500	0	0	18	-1590	1965

		71	72	73	74	75	76	77	
95	31	1	0	182	0	0	0		1963
95	31	1	0	182	0	0	89	0B	1965
96	31	2	0	700	0	0	90		1963
96	31	2	0	700	0	0	89	0B	1965
50	31	2	0	600	0	0	0	-5	1950
50	31	2	0	600	0	0	0	-6	1955
50	31	2	0	600	0	0	0	3	1960
50	31	2	0	600	0	0	0	-0	1963
50	31	2	0	600	0	0	14	12	1965
97	31	1	0	300A	0	0	88	-34	1960
97	31	2	0	300A	0	0	0	13	1963
97	31	2	0	300A	0	1	5	-28	1965
51	31	1	0	1000A	0	0	0		1950
51	31	2	0	1000	0	0	0		1955
51	31	2	0	1000	0	1	0		1960
51	31	1	0	1000	0	0	90		1963
51	31	1	0	1000	0	0	7		1965
52	31	2	0	167	0	0	0	3	1950
52	31	2	0	167	0	0	0	1	1955
52	31	2	0	167	0	0	0	-7	1960
52	31	2	0	167	0	0	0	-0	1963
52	31	2	0	167	0	0	29	0	1965
53	31	2	0	848	0	0	0	-8	1950
53	31	2	0	848	0	0	0	10	1955
53	31	2	0	848	0	0	0	2	1960
53	31	2	0	848	0	0	0	-212A	1963
53	31	2	0	848	0	0	18		1965
54	31	1	0	848	0	0	0		1950
54	31	1	0	848	0	0	81	26	1955
54	31	1	1	848	1	0	68	19	1960
54	31	0	0	848	0	0	89	-48	1963
54	31	1	0	848	0	0	89		1965
98	31	2	0	535	0	0	0		1963
98	31	1	0	535	1G	0	1	0B	1965
99	31	2	0	140	0	0	0	14	1963
99	31	1	0	140	0	0	8	5	1965
55	31	2	0	999	0	0	0	0	1950
55	31	2	0	999	0	0	0	-4	1955
55	31	2	0	999	0	0	0	-12	1960
55	31	2	0	999	0	0	0	-1	1963
55	31	2	0	999	0	0	4	-74	1965
56	31	1	0	770A	0	0	0		1950
56	31	2	0	770	0	0	0		1955
56	31	2	0	770	0	0	0		1960
56	31	2	0	770	0	0	90		1963
56	31	2	0	770	0	0	0		1965
57	31	1	0	546	0	0	0	2	1950
57	31	2	0	546	0	2	53	2	1955
57	31	1	1	546	0	0	60	-14	1960
57	31	1	0	546	0	0	37D	-3	1963
57	31	1	0	546	0	0	14	-90	1965
58	31	1	1	538	0	0	0	0B	1950
58	31	2	0	538	1	0	0	13B	1955
58	31	2	0	538E	0	0	82	80B	1960
58	31	2	0	538	0	0	86	60B	1963
58	31	2	0	538	0	0	86	1B	1965
59	31	1	0	964	0	0	122	-60	1950
59	31	0	0	964	0	0	0		1955
59	31	1	0	964	0	0	183	17	1960

		71	72	73	74	75	76	77	
59	31	2	0	964	0	0	90	-18	1963
59	31	2	0	964	0	0	89		1965
60	31	1	1	500	0	0	0	-2	1950
60	31	0	1	500	0	0	97	-2	1955
60	31	1	0	500	0	0	0	-6	1960
60	31	1	0	500	0	1	17	-6	1963
60	31	1	0	500	0	2	0	-4	1965
61	31	1	0	802	2	0	0	90	1950
61	31	2	0	802	0	0	0	10	1955
61	31	2	0	802	0	0	36	9	1960
61	31	2	0	802	0	0	0	-5	1963
61	31	2	0	802C	1G	0	14	-19	1965
62	31	1	0	980	0	0	0		1950
62	31	1	0	980	0	0	23		1955
62	31	2	0	980	0	0	44		1960
62	31	2	0	980	0	0	59		1963
62	31	2	0	980	0	0	18		1965
63	31	2	0	997	1	0	0	-1	1950
63	31	2	0	997	0	0	0	1	1955
63	31	2	0	997	0	0	0	17	1960
63	31	2	0	997	0	0	5	-2	1963
63	31	2	0	997	0	0	25	0	1965
64	31	1	0	858	0	0	0		1950
64	31	1	0	858	0	0	0		1955
64	31	2	0	858	0	0	20		1960
64	31	2	0	858	0	0	11		1963
64	31	2	0	858	0	0	38		1965
114	31	1	0	850	0	0	89		1965
65	31	1	0	900	0	0	0		1950
65	31	1	0	900	0	0	0		1955
65	31	2	0	900	0	1	88		1960
65	31	2	0	900	0	0	0	-17	1963
65	31	2	0	900	0	0	23	-18	1965
100	31	2	0	230	0	1	89		1963
100	31	2	0	230	0	0	89	0B	1965
204	31	2	0	200A	0	0	0	-29A	1963
204	31	1	0	200A	0	0	89	0B	1965
101	31	2	0	800	0	0	90	45A	1963
101	31	2	0	800	0	0	37		1965
66	31	1	1	800A	0	0	0		1950
66	31	0	1	800A	0	0	0	3	1955
66	31	1	1	800A	0	0	0	-17	1960
66	31	1	1	800A	0	0	0	-4	1963
66	31	0	1	800A	0	0	12	1	1965
102	31	0	1	400	0	0	0	-116	1960
102	31	1	1	400	0	0	0	307	1963
102	31	1	0	400	0	1	89	0B	1965
67	31	2	0	999	0	0	0	-9	1950
67	31	2	0	999	0	0	0	-0	1955
67	31	2	0	999	0	0	0	-4	1960
67	31	2	0	999	0	0	0	-5	1963
67	31	2	0	999	0	0	4	10	1965
68	31	2	0	748	0	0	0	1	1950
68	31	2	0	748	0	0	0	-0	1955
68	31	2	0	748	0	0	0	-1	1960
68	31	2	0	748	0	0	0	-1	1963
68	31	2	0	748	0	0	0	1	1965

	71	72	73	74	75	76	77	
69 31	0	1F	600	0	1	0	13	1950
69 31	0	0	600	2	0	0	-0	1955
69 31	1	0	600	0	0	0	200	1960
69 31	0	1	600	0	1	89	-3	1963
69 31	1	1	600	0	1	89	-2	1965
109 31	2	0	950	0	0	0		1963
109 31	1	0	950	0	0	7		1965
70 31	0	1	815	0	0	0	-6	1950
70 31	1	0	815	0	0	0	-8	1955
70 31	1	0	815	0	0	0	-4	1960
70 31	2	0	815	0	0	0	-6	1963
70 31	1	0	815	0	0	13	3	1965
103 31	2	0	210	1G	0	90		1963
103 31	1	0	210	0	0	1	0B	1965
216 31	2	0	600	0	0	17	3B	1965
104 31	1	1	300A	0	0	0	-17	1960
104 31	2	0	300A	0	0	0	51	1963
104 31	2	0	300A	0	0	16	3	1965
71 31	2	0	920	0	0	0	4	1950
71 31	2	0	920	0	1	0	3	1955
71 31	1	1	920	0	2	0	-2	1960
71 31	1	0	920	0	0	0	1	1963
71 31	1	0	920	0	1	14	-3	1965
72 31	2	0	611	0	0	0	3	1950
72 31	2	0	611	0	0	0	-2	1955
72 31	2	0	611E	1	0	0	-2	1960
72 31	2	0	611	0	0	0	-2	1963
72 31	2	0	611	0	0	0	1	1965
73 31	2	0	550	0	0	0		1950
73 31	2	0	550	0	0	0		1955
73 31	2	0	550	0	1	45		1960
73 31	2	0	550	0	0	459		1963
73 31	2	0	550	0	0	39		1965
74 31	2	0	854A	0	0	0	1	1950
74 31	2	0	854	0	0	0	0	1955
74 31	2	0	854	0	0	0	1	1960
74 31	2	0	854	0	1	0	3	1963
74 31	2	0	854	0	0	20	1	1965
75 31	2	0	813	1	0	0	1	1950
75 31	2	0	813	0	0	0	0	1955
75 31	2	0	813	0	0	0	1	1960
75 31	2	0	813	1G	0	0	1	1963
75 31	2	0	813	0	0	27	0	1965
219 31	1	0	150	0	0	89		1965
105 31	2	0	600	0	0	72		1963
105 31	2	0	600	0	0	89	0B	1965
76 31	2	0	973	0	1	45	-1	1950
76 31	2	0	973	0	0	93	2	1955
76 31	2	0	973	0	0	81	1	1960
76 31	2	0	973	0	0	85	3	1963
76 31	2	0	973	0	1	84	-7	1965
77 31	0	1	568	1	0	0	1	1950
77 31	1	0	568	0	0	0	-3	1955
77 31	1	0	650	1G	1	87	4	1960
77 31	2	0	568A	1	1	0	-2	1963
77 31	2	0	650	0	0	21	-1	1965

		71	72	73	74	75	76	77	
81	31			851			0		1955
81	31	1	0	851	0	0	0		1960
81	31	2	0	851	0	0	0		1963
81	31	2	0	851	0	0	0		1965
82	31			800			0		1955
82	31	1	0	800	0	0	0	-79	1960
82	31	0	1	800	1G	0	0	127	1963
82	31	0	1	800	0	2	0		1965
78	31	2	0	1000A	0	0	0		1950
78	31	2	0	1000	0	0	1		1955
78	31	1	0	1000	0	0	88		1960
78	31	0	1	1000	0	0	90		1963
78	31	0	1	1000	1	2	89		1965
79	31	1	0	402	0	0	0		1950
79	31	1	0	402	0	0	0	25	1955
79	31	1	0	402	0	0	0	98	1960
79	31	2	0	402	0	0	0	44	1963
79	31	2	0	402			23	-57	1965

		78	79	80	81	82	83	84	
1	32		0	1A	1A	1	0	0	1950
1	32		0	1	0	1	0	0	1955
1	32		0	1		1	0	0	1960
1	32		0	1	0A	1	0	0	1963
1	32		0	1	0	1	0	0	1965
2	32		2	0	0	0	0	0	1950
2	32		2	0	0	0	0	0	1955
2	32		2	0	0	0	0	0	1960
2	32		2	0	0	0	0	0	1963
2	32		2	0	0	0	0	0	1965
106	32		2	1	0	1	1A	0	1965
3	32	-14	2A	1A	2	1	0A	1A	1950
3	32	-45	2B	1	1	1	2	1	1955
3	32	-57	0		2	1	2	0A	1960
3	32	-68	0	1A	2	1	2		1963
3	32	-53	0	2B	2	1	2	1A	1965
4	32	-110	0	2	2	1	2	2	1950
4	32	-523	0	2	2	1	2	2	1955
4	32	-265	0	2	2	1	2	2	1960
4	32	-295	0	2	2	1	2	2	1963
4	32	-295	0	2	2	1	2	2	1965
5	32	4	0	2	2	1	2	2	1955
5	32	-8	0	2	2	1	2	2	1960
5	32	-16	0	2	2	1	2	2	1963
5	32	-21	0	2	2	1	2	2	1965
6	32	-9	0	2	2	1	2	2	1950
6	32	134	0	2	2	1	2	2	1955
6	32	46	0	2	2	1	2	2	1960
6	32	-20	0	2	2	1	2	2	1963
6	32	12	0	2	2	1	2	2	1965
7	32	-3A	0A	1A	2	1		0A	1950
7	32	-8	1B	2	1	1	2	1	1955
7	32	1	1	2	2	1	2	1	1960
7	32	-3	1	2	2	1	2	1	1963
7	32	-4	1	2	2	1	2	1	1965
8	32	-12	0	2	2	1	1	2	1950
8	32	-392	1B	2	2	1	1	2	1955
8	32	-194	0	2	2	1	1	2	1960
8	32	-144	0	2	2	1	1	2	1963
8	32	-259	0	2	2	1	1	2	1965

		78	79	80	81	82	83	84	
9	32		2	0	0	0	0	0	1950
9	32		2	0	0	0	0	0	1955
9	32		2	0	0	0	0	0	1960
9	32		2	0	0	0	0	0	1963
9	32		2	0	0	0	0	0	1965
10	32	-1A	1A	1	0A	1		0A	1950
10	32	-1	2	1	1	1	1	0	1955
10	32	-3	2	1		1			1960
10	32	0	2	1	0A	1	0A	0A	1963
10	32		2	1	0	1	0A	0A	1965
113	32		0	1C	1	1	2	1A	1965
11	32		1	1	0	1	0	0	1955
11	32	-3	1	1	0	1	1	0	1960
11	32	-1	1	1	0	1	0A	0	1963
11	32	-1	1	1	0	1	0A	0	1965
83	32		0	1A	1A	1	2	1	1963
83	32		0	2	2AC	1	2	1	1965
12	32	-311	0	2	2	1	2	2	1950
12	32	-1029	0	2	2	1	2	2	1955
12	32	-538	0	2	2	1	2	2	1960
12	32	-667	0	2	2	1	2	2	1963
12	32	-789	0	2	2	1	2	2	1965
84	32		0	1	0	1	2	0	1963
84	32		0	1	0	1	2	2	1965
13	32	-10	0	2	2	1	1	1	1950
13	32	-33	0	2	2	1	1	1	1955
13	32	-9	0	2	2	1	1	1	1960
13	32	-11	0	2	2	1	1	1	1963
13	32	-3	0	2	2	1	1	2A	1965
85	32		0	1A	1	1	2	0	1963
85	32		0	2	1	1	2	1A	1965
14	32	-59A	0	2	2	1	1	2	1950
14	32	-228	1B	2	2	1	1	2	1955
14	32	-65	0	2	2	1	1	2	1960
14	32	-90	0	2	2	1	1	2	1963
14	32	-121	0	2	2	1	1	2	1965
15	32		2	0	0	0	0	0	1950
15	32		2	0	0	0	0	0	1955
15	32		2	0	0	0	0	0	1960
15	32		2	0	0	0	0	0	1963
15	32		2	0	0	0	0	0	1965
16	32	0	2	1	1	1	0A	0	1955
16	32	0	2A	1A	0A	1	0A	1A	1960
16	32	-4	1A	1A	1A	1	0A	1A	1963
16	32	-3	1	2	1	1	0A	1A	1965
17	32	-30A	0	1	0	1	0A	0A	1950
17	32	-53	0	1	0	1	1	0	1955
17	32	-40	0	2	0A	1	1	1	1960
17	32	-81	0	2	1A	1	1	1	1963
17	32	-79	0	2	1	1	1	1	1965
87	32		0	1A	1	1	2	0	1963
87	32		0	2	1	1	2	0	1965
86	32		0	1A	1A	1	2	0A	1963
86	32	-3	0	2	0	1	2	0A	1965
18	32	-14	2A	2	2	1	2	2	1950
18	32	-21	0	2	2	1	2	2	1955
18	32	-4	0	2	2	1	2	2	1960

	78	79	80	81	82	83	84	
18 32	-7	0	2	2	1	2	2	1963
18 32	-14	0	2	2	1	2	2	1965
19 32	-33	1	2	2A	1	1A	2A	1950
19 32	-123	1B	0	0	1	1	0	1955
19 32		2	0	0A	1A	0A	0	1960
19 32		2	0	0A	0A	0A	0	1963
19 32		2	0	0A	0A	1	0	1965
20 32		2	0	0	0	0	0	1950
20 32		2	0	0	0	0	0	1955
20 32		2	0	0	0	0	0	1960
20 32		2	0	0	0	0	0	1963
20 32		2	0	0	0	0	0	1965
88 32		0	1A	0	1	2	0	1963
88 32		0	2C	1	1	2	0	1965
21 32	-11	0	2	2	1	2	2	1950
21 32	-29	0	2	2	1	2	2	1955
21 32	4	0	2	2	1	2	2	1960
21 32	-8	0	2	2	1	2	2	1963
21 32	-13	0	2	2	1	2	2	1965
22 32	-17A	0	0A	0A	1	0A	0A	1950
22 32	-22	0B	1	0	1	2	0	1955
22 32	-10	0	2	2	1	2	2	1960
22 32	-20	0	2	2	1	2	2	1963
22 32	-12	0	2	2	1	2	2	1965
23 32	-9	0	2	2	1	1A	1A	1950
23 32	-56	0B	2	2	1	1	1	1955
23 32	-23	0	2	2	1	0	1	1960
23 32	-17	0	2	2	1	0	1	1963
23 32	-25	0	2	2	1	0	1	1965
24 32	-31	0	1	0	1	0	0	1950
24 32	-81	1	1	0	1	1	0	1955
24 32	6	2	1	0A	1	0A	0	1960
24 32	-11	2	1	0A	1	0A	0	1963
24 32	-17	2	1	1	1	1A	0	1965
25 32	-1	0	2	2	1	0A	1	1950
25 32	-9	0B	1	0	1	1	0	1955
25 32	-4	0	1	0	1	0	1	1960
25 32	-6	0	1	0	1	0	1	1963
25 32	-8	0	1	1	1	0	1	1965
26 32	0	0	1	0A	1	0	0	1950
26 32	-2	0	1	0	1	0	0	1955
26 32	-5	0	1	0A	1	0	0	1960
26 32	-6	0	1	0A	1	0	0	1963
26 32	-4	0	1	0	1	0	0	1965
27 32	-8	0	2	2	1	2	2	1950
27 32	-31	0	2	2	1	2	2	1955
27 32	-6	0	2	2	1	2	2	1960
27 32	-22	0	2	2	1	2	2	1963
27 32	-41	0	2	2	1	2	2	1965
28 32	-11	0	2	2	1	2	1	1950
28 32	43	0	2	2	1	2	2	1955
28 32	42	0	2	2	1	2	1	1960
28 32	55	0	2	2	1	2	1	1963
28 32	479D	0	2	2	1	2	2A	1965
89 32		0	1A	0	1	2	0	1963
89 32		0	2	0	1	2	1A	1965
29 32		2	0	0	0	0	0	1955
29 32		2	0	0	0	0	0	1960
29 32		2	0	0	0	0	0	1963
29 32		2	0	0	0	0	0	1965

		78	79	80	81	82	83	84	
30	32	-368	0	2	2	1	2	2	1955
30	32	-189	0	2	2	1	2	2	1960
30	32	-310	0	2	2	1	2	2	1963
30	32	-453	0	2	2	1	2	2	1965
90	32	-15	2	1	0	1	1	0	1960
90	32	-25	2	1	0	1	1	0	1963
90	32	-27	2	1	0	1	1	0	1965
31	32	-3	0	2	2	1	2	2	1950
31	32	-1	0	2	2	1	2	1	1955
31	32	4	0	2	2	1	2	2	1960
31	32	-3	0	2	2	1	2	2	1963
31	32	-10	0	2	2	1	2	2	1965
32	32	-3	0	2	2	1	0	1	1950
32	32	-13	0B	1	1	1	1	1	1955
32	32	-5	0	1A		1	0	1	1960
32	32	-5	0	1A	0A	1	0	1	1963
32	32	-11	0	0	0AB	1	0	1	1965
91	32		2	1	0	1	1	0	1963
91	32		2	1	0	1	1	1A	1965
33	32	-5A	0	0A	0	1	0A	0	1950
33	32	-6	0B	1	0	1	0	0	1955
33	32	-4	0	1A	0	1	0A	0	1960
33	32	-6	0	2A	0	1		0	1963
33	32	-4	0	0	0	1	0A	0	1965
34	32	-19	0	2	2	1	0A	1	1950
34	32	-4	0B	2	2	1	1	1	1955
34	32	9	0	2	2	1	0	1	1960
34	32	-6	0	2	2	1	0	1	1963
34	32	-13	0	2	2	1	0	1	1965
35	32		2	0	0	0	0	0	1950
35	32		2	0	0	0C	0	0	1955
35	32		2	0	0	0	0	0	1960
35	32		2	0	0	0	0	0	1963
35	32		2	0	0	0	0	0	1965
36	32	-46	0	2	2	1	2	2	1950
36	32	6	0	2	2	1	2	2	1955
36	32	-89	0	2	2	1	2	2	1960
36	32	-189	0	2	2	1	2	2	1963
36	32	-260	0	2	2	1	2	2	1965
37	32	-33	0	1	0	1	0	0	1950
37	32	-266	2	1	1	1	0	1	1955
37	32	-67	1	1	1A	1	0	0	1960
37	32	-97	1	1	0A	1	0	0	1963
37	32	-94	1	1	0	1	1	0	1965
38	32	-4	0	1	1	1	1A	0	1950
38	32	-128	0	1	1	1	0	0	1955
38	32	-296	0	1	0A	1	0A	0	1960
38	32	-401	0	1	1A	1	1A	0	1963
38	32	-397	0	1	1	1	1A	0	1965
39	32	-41	0	1A	1	1			1950
39	32	-568	0	1	1	1	0	0	1955
39	32	-262	0	1A	0A	1	0A	0A	1960
39	32	-303	0	1A	0A	1	0A	0	1963
39	32	-363	0	2	1	1	1	0A	1965
40	32	26	0	2	2	1	2	2	195
40	32	88	0	2	2	1	2	2	195
40	32	35	0	2	2	1	2	2	196
40	32	38	0	2	2	1	2	2	196
40	32	55	0	2	2	1	2	2	196

		78	79	80	81	82	83	84	
41	32	-1A	2A	2	2	1	2	2	1950
41	32	-59	2	2	2	1	2	2	1955
41	32	-43	1	2	2	1	2	2	1960
41	32	-59	1	2	2	1	2	2	1963
41	32	-57	1	2	2	1	2	2	1965
42	32	-11	0	2	2	1	2	2	1950
42	32	-57	0	2	2	1	2	2	1955
42	32	-29	0	2	2	1	2	2	1960
42	32	-114	0	2	2	1	2	2	1963
42	32	-89	0	2	2	1	2	2	1965
92	32	-20	1	2A	0	1	2	0	1963
92	32	-27	1	2	1	1	2	1A	1965
163	32	-43	0	2	2	1	2	2	1965
43	32	-119	0	2	2	1	2	2	1955
43	32	-33	0	2	2	1	2	2	1960
43	32	-119	0	2	2	1	2	2	1963
43	32	-189	0	2	2	1	2	2	1965
44	32		0	1	1A	1	0	2	1950
44	32	0	0	1	1	1	0	1	1955
44	32		0	1	0A	1	0	0	1960
44	32	2	0	1	1A	1	0	0	1963
44	32	6	0	1	1	1	0	0	1965
45	32		2	0	0	0	0	0	1950
45	32		2	0	0	0	0	0	1955
45	32		2	0	0	0	0	0	1960
45	32		2	0	0	0	0	0	1963
45	32		2	0	0	0	0	0	1965
46	32		2	0A	0	1	0A	0A	1950
46	32	5	1	1	1	1	1	0	1955
46	32	4	1A	1	1A	1	2A	2A	1960
46	32	3	1A	1	2A	1	1A	1A	1963
46	32	1	1A	1	1	1	1A	1A	1965
80	32		0	1	0	1	0	0	1955
80	32		0	1		1	0	0	1960
80	32		0	1	1A	1	0	0	1963
80	32		0	1	0	1	0	0	1965
47	32		0	2	2	1	0A	1	1950
47	32	10A	0	2	1	1	1	1	1955
47	32		0	2		1		1	1960
47	32	22	0	2	1A	1	1A	1	1963
47	32	25	0	2	2	1	1A	1	1965
48	32		0	1	0	1	0	0	1950
48	32	-65	0	2	2	1	1	2	1955
48	32		0	1	0	1	0	0	1960
48	32		0	1	0	1	0	0	1963
48	32		0	2	1	1	0	1A	1965
49	32		0	1	1	1	1	1	1955
49	32	171	0	2	0A	1	1	1	1960
49	32	-2	0	2	1A	1	1	1	1963
49	32	-188	0	1	0	1	1	1	1965
93	32		0	2	2	1	1	1	1963
93	32		0	2	2	1	1	1	1965
94	32		0	2	2	1	2	2	1960
94	32	-59	0	2	2	1	2	2	1963
94	32	-95	0	2	2	1	2	2	1965
95	32		0	1A	0	1	2	1	1963
95	32	-1	0	2	0	1	2	1	1965

		78	79	80	81	82	83	84	
96	32		1	2	0	1	1	1	1963
96	32		1	2	0	1	1	1	1965
50	32	-7A	0	2	2	1	1	1	1950
50	32	-314	0B	2	1B	1B	1B	1B	1955
50	32	-191	0	2	0A	1	1	1	1960
50	32	-266	0	2	2A	1	1	1	1963
50	32	-339	0	2	2	1	1	1	1965
97	32	-20	1	2	0A	1	2	1	1960
97	32	-21	1	2	2A	1	2	1	1963
97	32	-29	1	1	1	1	2	1	1965
51	32		0	1	0	1	0	0	1950
51	32		0	1	0	1	0	0	1955
51	32		0A	1A	0	1	0	0	1960
51	32		1A	1	0A	1	0	0	1963
51	32		0	1	1	1	0	0	1965
52	32	47	0	2	2	1	2	2	1950
52	32	226	0	2	2	1	2	2	1955
52	32	106	0	2	2	1	2	2	1960
52	32	178	0	2	2	1	2	2	1963
52	32	204	0	2	2	1	2	2	1965
53	32	-17	0	2	2	1	2	2	1950
53	32	-66	0	2	2	1	2	2	1955
53	32	-26	0	2	2	1	2	2	1960
53	32	-43	0	2	2	1	2	2	1963
53	32	-47	0	2	2	1	2	2	1965
54	32	-6	0	0A	0	1	0	0A	1950
54	32	-18	0	1	2B	1	1B	0	1955
54	32	-3	0	1	1	1	0	1	1960
54	32	-3	0	1	1	1	0	1	1963
54	32	-13	0	2	1	1	0	1	1965
98	32		0	1A	1A	1	2	0	1963
98	32		0	2	1	1	2	1A	1965
99	32	-48	0	2	1A	1	1A	1	1963
99	32	-147	0	2	2	1	2A	1A	1965
55	32	-8	0	2	2	1	2	2	1950
55	32	-58	0	2	2	1	2	2	1955
55	32	-38	0	2	2	1	2	2	1960
55	32	-58	0	2	2	1	2	2	1963
55	32	-70	0	2	2	1	2	2	1965
56	32		2	0	0	0	0	0	1950
56	32		2	0	0	0	0	0	1955
56	32		2	0	0	0	0	0	1960
56	32		2	0	0	0	0	0	1963
56	32		2	0	0	0	0	0	1965
57	32	-3	0	1	0	1	0	0	1950
57	32	-17	0	1	2	1	1	1	1955
57	32	-7	0A	1	0A	1	0A	0	1960
57	32	-40	1A	1	1A	1	0A	0	1963
57	32	-44	1A	1	1A	1	1A	0	1965
58	32		0	1	0	1	1	0	1950
58	32	-48	0	2	2	1B	1	1	1955
58	32	-10	0	2	2		1	1	1960
58	32	-9	0	2	2	1	1	1	1963
58	32	-20	0	2	2	1	1	1	1965
59	32	-4	0	1	1	1	0	0	1950
59	32	-3	0	1	0	1B	1B	0B	1955
59	32	-2	0	1	1	1	0	0	1960
59	32	-2	0	1	1	1	0	0	1963
59	32	-3	0	1	1	1	0	0	1965

		78	79	80	81	82	83	84	
60	32	-14	0	1	0	1	0	0	1950
60	32	-77	0	1	0	1B	1B	0B	1955
60	32	-66	0	1		1	1		1960
60	32	-72	0	1A	1A	1	1	0A	1963
60	32	-91	0	2	1	1	1	1A	1965
61	32	-29	0	2	2	1	1	2	1950
61	32	-189	0	2	2	1	1	2	1955
61	32	-75	0	2	2	1	1	2	1960
61	32	-17	0	2	2	1	1	2	1963
61	32	-31	0	2	2	1	1	2	1965
62	32		2	0	0	0	0	0	1950
62	32		2	0	0	0	0	0	1955
62	32		2	0	0	0	0	0	1960
62	32		2	0	0	0	0	0	1963
62	32		2	0	0	0	0	0	1965
63	32	5	0	0	0	1	0	0	1950
63	32	9	0	1	0	1	0	0	1955
63	32	3	0	0	0	1	0	0	1960
63	32	-6	0	0	0	1	0	0	1963
63	32	-13	0	0	0	1	0	0	1965
64	32		2	0	0	0	0	0	1950
64	32		2	0	0	0	0	0	1955
64	32		2	0	0	0	0	0	1960
64	32		2	0	0	0	0	0	1963
64	32		2	0	0	0	0	0	1965
114	32		0	2	1	1	2A	1A	1965
65	32		0	1	0	1	0	0	1950
65	32		0	1	0	1	0	0	1955
65	32	-337	0	1	0A	1	0	0	1960
65	32	-450	0	1	0A	1	0	0	1963
65	32	-417	0	1	0	1	0	0	1965
100	32		1	1A	1	1	2	0	1963
100	32		1	2	1	1	2	1A	1965
204	32	-8	0	2	2	1	1	1	1963
204	32	-12	0	2	2	1	1	1	1965
101	32	0	0	1A	1	1	1	1	1963
101	32		0	2	1	1	1	1	1965
66	32		0A	0	0	1	0	0	1950
66	32	-5A	0	1	0	1	0	0	1955
66	32	-14		0	0	1	0	0	1960
66	32	-15	1A	0	0	1	0	0	1963
66	32	-31	0A	0	0	1	0	0	1965
102	32	1	1	1		1		0	1960
102	32	-3	1	1	0A	1	0A	0	1963
102	32	-7	1	1	1	1	1A	1A	1965
67	32	5	0	2	2	1	2	2	1950
67	32	60	0	2	2	1	2	2	1955
67	32	29	0	2	2	1	2	2	1960
67	32	36	0	2	2	1	2	2	1963
67	32	45	0	2	2	1	2	2	1965
68	32	-228	0	2	2	1	2	2	1950
68	32	369	0	2	2	1	2	2	1955
68	32	157	0	2	2	1	2	2	1960
68	32	197	0	2	2	1	2	2	1963
68	32	259	0	2	2	1	2	2	1965
69	32		0	1A	0	1	0A	0A	1950
69	32	-1	0	1	1	1	0	1	1955
69	32		0	1A	0A	1	0A	0A	1960

		78	79	80	81	82	83	84	
69	32	-4	0	0A	0A	1	0A	0A	1963
69	32	-4	0	2	0C	1	2A	1	1965
109	32	-15	1	1A	1	1	2	0	1963
109	32	-14	1	2	1	1	2	0	1965
70	32	-4	0	1	2	1	0	0	1950
70	32	-15	0	1	1	1	0	0	1955
70	32	-5	0	1		1	0	0	1960
70	32	-2	0	1	0A	1	0	0	1963
70	32		0	1	1	1	0	0	1965
103	32		0	1A	1A	1	2	0	1963
103	32	-5	0	1	2	1	1	0	1965
216	32	-60	0	2	2	1	2	2	1965
104	32	2	1	2	0	1	2	0	1960
104	32	-1	1	2	0	1	2	0	1963
104	32	-8	1	2	1	1	2	1A	1965
71	32	-9	1A	2	2	1	2	2	1950
71	32	-30	0	2	2	1	2	2	1955
71	32	-30	0	2	2	1	2	2	1960
71	32	-40	0	2	2	1	2	2	1963
71	32	-55	0	2	2	1	2	2	1965
72	32	-101	0	2	2	1	0	2	1950
72	32	-316A	0	2	1	1	0	2	1955
72	32	-210	0			1	0	2	1960
72	32	-217	0	0A	0A	1	0	2	1963
72	32		0	2	1	1	0	1A	1965
73	32		2	0	0	0	0	0	1950
73	32		2	0	0	0	0	0	1955
73	32		2	0	0	0	0	0	1960
73	32		2	0	0	0	0	0	1963
73	32		2	0	0	0	0	0	1965
74	32	331	0	2	2	1	1	2	1950
74	32	664	0	2	2	1	1	2	1955
74	32	678	0	2	2	1	1	2	1960
74	32	1109	0	2	2	1	1	2	1963
74	32	1316	0	2	2	1	1	2	1965
75	32	1693	0	2	2	1	1	2	1950
75	32	7966	0	2	2	1	1	2	1955
75	32	3443	0	2	2	1	1	2	1960
75	32	4654	0	2	2	1	1	2	1963
75	32	5348	0	2	2	1	1	2	1965
219	32		0	2	1	1	1A	1A	1965
105	32		0	1A	1	1	2	0	1963
105	32		0	2	1	1	2	0	1965
76	32	-44	1A	2	2	1	2	2	1950
76	32	-15	0	2B	1B	1B	1B	1B	1955
76	32	-7	0	2	2	1	2	2	1960
76	32	-10	0	2	2	1	2	2	1963
76	32	-15	0	2	2	1	2	2	1965
77	32	-363	0A	0A	0A	1	0A	0A	1950
77	32	-1825	1B	1B	1B	1B	1B	1B	1955
77	32	-522	1	2	2	1	2	1	1960
77	32	-607	1	2	2	1	2	1	1963
77	32	-706	1	2	2	1	2	1	1965
81	32		2	0	0	0	0	0	1955
81	32		2	0	0	0	0	0	1960
81	32		2	0	0	0	0	0	1963
81	32		2	0	0	0	0	0	1965

		78	79	80	81	82	83	84	
82	32		2	1	0	1	0	0	1955
82	32	-5	2	1A	0	1	1	0	1960
82	32	-4	2	0A	0	1	1	0	1963
82	32	-11	2	1A	0	1	1	0	1965
78	32		0A	1	0	1	0A	0A	1950
78	32		0	1	1	1	0	0	1955
78	32		0A	1A	0A	1A	0	0A	1960
78	32		0A	0A	0A	1	0A	0A	1963
78	32		1A	1A	0A	1	0A	0A	1965
79	32	-1	2	0	0	0	0	0	1950
79	32	-25	2	0	0	0	0	0	1955
79	32	-11	2	0	0	0	0	0	1960
79	32	-34	2	0	0	0	0	0	1963
79	32	-60	2	0	0	0	0	0	1965

		85	86	87	
1	33	1	0		1950
1	33	1A	0	0	1955
1	33	1	0	0	1960
1	33	1	0	0	1963
1	33	1	0	0	1965
2	33	1	1	0	1950
2	33	1A	1	0	1955
2	33	1	1	0	1960
2	33	1	1	0	1963
2	33	1	1	0	1965
106	33	2	0	1	1965
3	33	2	1	0	1950
3	33	2	1	2	1955
3	33	2	1	2	1960
3	33	2	1	1	1963
3	33	1	1	2	1965
4	33	0	2	2	1950
4	33	0	2	2	1955
4	33	0	2	2	1960
4	33	0	2	2	1963
4	33	0	2	2	1965
5	33	0	2	2	1955
5	33	0	2	2	1960
5	33	0	2	2	1963
5	33	0	2	2	1965
6	33	0	2	2	1950
6	33	0	2	2	1955
6	33	0	2	2	1960
6	33	0	2	2	1963
6	33	0	2	2	1965
7	33	2	1	0	1950
7	33	0	1	1	1955
7	33	0	1	0	1960
7	33	0	1	1	1963
7	33	2	1	1	1965
8	33	1	1	2	1950
8	33	2	1	2	1955
8	33	2	1	2	1960
8	33	2	1	1	1963
8	33	2	1	2	1965
9	33	1	1	0	1950
9	33	1	1	0	1955
9	33	1	1	0	1960
9	33	1	1	0	1963
9	33	1	2A	0	1965

		85	86	87	
10	33	1	0	0	1950
10	33	1	0	0	1955
10	33	2	0	1	1960
10	33	2	0	0	1963
10	33	2	0	0	1965
113	33	2	0	1A	1965
11	33	1	0	0	1955
11	33	1	0	1A	1960
11	33	1	0	0	1963
11	33	1	0	0	1965
83	33	0	0	1	1963
83	33	1	0	1	1965
12	33	0	2	2	1950
12	33	0	2	2	1955
12	33	0	2	2	1960
12	33	0	2	2	1963
12	33	0	2	2	1965
84	33	0	0		1963
84	33	2	0	1A	1965
13	33	0	0	2	1950
13	33	0	1	1	1955
13	33	0	1	2	1960
13	33	0	1	1	1963
13	33	0	1	1	1965
85	33	0	0	1	1963
85	33	0	0	1	1965
14	33	0	1	2	1950
14	33	0	1	2	1955
14	33	0	1	2	1960
14	33	0	1	2	1963
14	33	0	2	2	1965
15	33	1	1	0	1950
15	33	1	1	0	1955
15	33	1	1	0A	1960
15	33	1	1	0	1963
15	33	1	1	0	1965
16	33	2	1	1	1955
16	33	2A	1A	1	1960
16	33	1A		1	1963
16	33	1	1A	1	1965
17	33	0	1	0	1950
17	33	2C	1	2	1955
17	33	0	1	2	1960
17	33	0	1	2	1963
17	33	0	1	2	1965
87	33	0	0	1	1963
87	33	0	0	1	1965
86	33		0	1	1963
86	33	2	0	1	1965
18	33	0	0	2	1950
18	33	0	1	2	1955
18	33	0	1	2	1960
18	33	0	1	2	1963
18	33	0	1	2	1965
19	33	1	1	2	1950
19	33	1	1	0	1955
19	33		1	1	1960

		85	86	87	
19	33		1	0	1963
19	33	0	1	0	1965
20	33	1	2	0	1950
20	33	1	1	0	1955
20	33	1	1	0	1960
20	33	1	1	0	1963
20	33	1	2A	0	1965
88	33	0	0		1963
88	33	2	0	1A	1965
21	33	0	2	2	1950
21	33	0	2	2	1955
21	33	0	2	2	1960
21	33	0	2	2	1963
21	33	0	2	2	1965
22	33	1	1	1	1950
22	33	2C	1	1	1955
22	33	0	1	0	1960
22	33	0	1	1	1963
22	33	2	1	1	1965
23	33	1	0	2	1950
23	33	1	1	2	1955
23	33	1	1	2	1960
23	33	1	1	1	1963
23	33	2	1	2	1965
24	33	2B	1	1	1950
24	33	2	1	0	1955
24	33	2	1	0	1960
24	33	2	1	0	1963
24	33	2	1	0	1965
25	33	2B	0	1	1950
25	33	2	1	1	1955
25	33	2	1	2	1960
25	33	2	1	1	1963
25	33	2	1	1	1965
26	33	1	0	1	1950
26	33	1	0	2	1955
26	33	1	0	0	1960
26	33	1	0	0	1963
26	33	1	0	0	1965
27	33	0	2	2	1950
27	33	0	2	2	1955
27	33	0	2	2	1960
27	33	0	2	2	1963
27	33	0	2	2	1965
28	33	0	2	2	1950
28	33	0	2	2	1955
28	33		2	2	1960
28	33		2	2	1963
28	33	0	2	2	1965
89	33	0	0		1963
89	33	1	0	1A	1965
29	33	1	1	0	1955
29	33	1	1	0	1960
29	33	1	1	0	1963
29	33	1	2A	0	1965
30	33	0	2	2	1955
30	33	0	2	2	1960
30	33	0	2	2	1963
30	33	0	2	2	1965

		85	86	87	
90	33	1	1	1	1960
90	33	1	1	0	1963
90	33	1	1	0	1965
31	33	0	1	2	1950
31	33	0	1	2	1955
31	33	0	1	2	1960
31	33	0	1	1	1963
31	33	1	1	2	1965
32	33	1	1	1	1950
32	33	2	1	1	1955
32	33	2	1	1A	1960
32	33	2	1	1	1963
32	33	2	1	1	1965
91	33	1	1	0	1963
91	33	1	1	0	1965
33	33	2	1	1	1950
33	33	2	0	1	1955
33	33	2	1	0	1960
33	33	2	1	0	1963
33	33	1	1	0	1965
34	33	2	1	1	1950
34	33	1	1	1	1955
34	33	2	1	2	1960
34	33	2	1	1	1963
34	33	2	1	1	1965
35	33	1	1	0	1950
35	33	1	1	0	1955
35	33	1	1	0A	1960
35	33	1	1	0	1963
35	33	1	2A	0	1965
36	33	0	0	2	1950
36	33	0	1	2	1955
36	33	0	1	2	1960
36	33	0	1	1	1963
36	33	0	1	2	1965
37	33	1	0	2	1950
37	33	1	0	1	1955
37	33	1		1	1960
37	33	1		0	1963
37	33	2	1A	0	1965
38	33	1	0	1	1950
38	33	1	0	1	1955
38	33	1	0	1	1960
38	33	1	0	1	1963
38	33	1	0	1	1965
39	33	1	0	1	1950
39	33	1	0	1	1955
39	33	2		0	1960
39	33	2		0	1963
39	33	2	0A	0	1965
40	33	0	2	2	1950
40	33	0	2	2	1955
40	33	0	2	2	1960
40	33	0	2	2	1963
40	33	0	2	2	1965
41	33	0	2	0	1950
41	33	0	2	0	1955
41	33	0	2	2	1960
41	33	0	2	2	1963
41	33	0	2	2	1965

		85	86	87	
42	33	0	2	2	1950
42	33	0	2	2	1955
42	33	0	2	2	1960
42	33	0	2	2	1963
42	33	0	2	2	1965
92	33	0	0	1	1963
92	33	0	0	1	1965
163	33	0	1	1A	1965
43	33	0	1	2	1955
43	33	0	1	2	1960
43	33	0	1	2	1963
43	33	0	2A	2	1965
44	33	1	0	0	1950
44	33	1	1	0	1955
44	33	1	0	0	1960
44	33	1	0	1	1963
44	33	1	0	1	1965
45	33	0	1	0	1950
45	33	1A	1A	0	1955
45	33	1	1	0	1960
45	33	1	1	0	1963
45	33	0	1	0	1965
46	33	0B	0	1	1950
46	33	1A	1A	1	1955
46	33	2	1	1	1960
46	33	2	1	1	1963
46	33	2	1	1	1965
80	33	2	0	1	1955
80	33		0	1	1960
80	33		0	1	1963
80	33	2	0	1	1965
47	33	1	1	1	1950
47	33	1	1	1	1955
47	33	1	1	2	1960
47	33	1	1	1	1963
47	33	1	1	2	1965
48	33	1	1		1950
48	33	1	1	1	1955
48	33	1	1	1	1960
48	33	1	1	1	1963
48	33	1	1	1	1965
49	33	0	1	1	1955
49	33	0	1	0	1960
49	33	0	1	1	1963
49	33	0	1	1	1965
93	33	0	0	1	1963
93	33	0	0	1	1965
94	33	0	1	2	1960
94	33	0	1	1	1963
94	33	0	1	2	1965
95	33	0	0	0	1963
95	33	0	0	0	1965
96	33	0	0		1963
96	33	0	0	1A	1965
50	33	1	1	1	1950
50	33	0	1	2	1955
50	33	0	1	2	1960

	85	86	87	
50 33	0	1	1	1963
50 33	0	1	2	1965
97 33	0	1	1	1960
97 33	0	1	1	1963
97 33	0	1	1	1965
51 33	1	0		1950
51 33	0	0	1	1955
51 33		0	1	1960
51 33		0	1	1963
51 33	0	0	1	1965
52 33	0	2	2	1950
52 33	0	2	2	1955
52 33	0	2	2	1960
52 33	0	2	2	1963
52 33	0	2	2	1965
53 33	0	2	2	1950
53 33	0	2	2	1955
53 33	0	2	2	1960
53 33	0	2	2	1963
53 33	0	2	2	1965
54 33	1	1	1	1950
54 33	2	1	1	1955
54 33	2	1	0	1960
54 33	2	1	1	1963
54 33	1	1	1	1965
98 33	0	0		1963
98 33	0	0	1A	1965
99 33	0	0	1	1963
99 33	1	0	1	1965
55 33	0	2	2	1950
55 33	0	2	2	1955
55 33	0	2	2	1960
55 33	0	2	2	1963
55 33	0	2	2	1965
56 33	1	1	0A	1950
56 33	1	1	0	1955
56 33	1	1	0	1960
56 33	1	1	0	1963
56 33	1	1	0	1965
57 33	1	0	2	1950
57 33	1	1	1	1955
57 33	2		1	1960
57 33	2		1	1963
57 33	2	1A	1	1965
58 33	1B	0	1	1950
58 33	1C	1	1	1955
58 33	2	1	2	1960
58 33	2	1	2	1963
58 33	1	1	2	1965
59 33	2	1	2	1950
59 33	2C	1	2	1955
59 33	2	1	0	1960
59 33	2	1	0	1963
59 33	2	1	0	1965
60 33	2	1	1	1950
60 33	2	1	1	1955
60 33	2	1	2	1960
60 33	2	1	1	1963
60 33	1	1	2	1965

		85	86	87	
61	33	1B	0	1	1950
61	33	1	1	1	1955
61	33	0	1	2	1960
61	33	0	1	2	1963
61	33	0	1	2	1965
62	33	1	1	0	1950
62	33	1	1	0	1955
62	33	1	1	0	1960
62	33	1	1	0	1963
62	33	1	2A	0	1965
63	33	1	1	1	1950
63	33	2	1	1	1955
63	33	1	1	0	1960
63	33	1	1	0	1963
63	33	1	1	0	1965
64	33	1	1	0	1950
64	33	1	1	0	1955
64	33	1	1	0	1960
64	33	1	1	0	1963
64	33	1	2A	0	1965
114	33	1	0	1A	1965
65	33	1	0	0	1950
65	33	1	0	0	1955
65	33	1	0	0	1960
65	33	1	0	0	1963
65	33	1	0	0	1965
100	33	1	0	1	1963
100	33	1	0	1	1965
204	33	0	0	1	1963
204	33	0	0	1	1965
101	33		0	1	1963
101	33	1	0	1	1965
66	33	2	1	0	1950
66	33	1	1	0	1955
66	33	1	1	0	1960
66	33	1	1	0	1963
66	33	1	1	0	1965
102	33	2	0	1	1960
102	33	2	0	1	1963
102	33	1	0	1	1965
67	33	0	2	2	1950
67	33	0	2	2	1955
67	33	0	2	2	1960
67	33	0	2	2	1963
67	33	0	2	2	1965
68	33	0	2	2	1950
68	33	0	2	2	1955
68	33	0	2	2	1960
68	33	0	2	2	1963
68	33	0	2	2	1965
69	33	2B	0	1	1950
69	33	2	1	0	1955
69	33	2	1	0	1960
69	33	2	1	0	1963
69	33	2	1	0	1965
109	33	0	0	1	1963
109	33	0	0	1	1965

		85	86	87	
70	33	2	0	2	1950
70	33	1	1	1	1955
70	33	2	0	1	1960
70	33	2	0	1	1963
70	33	2	0	1	1965
103	33	2	0	1	1963
103	33	2	0	1	1965
216	33	0	1	1A	1965
104	33	0	1	1	1960
104	33	0	1	1	1963
104	33	0	1	1	1965
71	33	1	1	1	1950
71	33	1	1	1	1955
71	33	2	1	1	1960
71	33	2	1	1	1963
71	33	2	1	1	1965
72	33	1	2	1	1950
72	33	1	2	1	1955
72	33	1	2	2	1960
72	33	1	2	1	1963
72	33	1	2	1	1965
73	33	1	1	0	1950
73	33	1	1	0	1955
73	33	1	1	0	1960
73	33	1	1	0	1963
73	33	1	2A	0	1965
74	33	0	2	2	1950
74	33	0	2	2	1955
74	33	0	2	2	1960
74	33	0	2	2	1963
74	33	0	2	2	1965
75	33	0	2	2	1950
75	33	0	2	2	1955
75	33	0	2	2	1960
75	33	0	2	2	1963
75	33	0	2	2	1965
219	33	1	0	1	1965
105	33	0	0	0	1963
105	33	1	0	0	1965
76	33	0	1	2	1950
76	33	0	1	2	1955
76	33	0	1	2	1960
76	33	0	1	2	1963
76	33	0	2	2	1965
77	33	2	1	1	1950
77	33	2	1	1	1955
77	33		1	2	1960
77	33		1	1	1963
77	33	1	1	2	1965
81	33	2	1A	0	1955
81	33	1	1	1	1960
81	33	1	1	0	1963
81	33	1	1	0	1965
82	33	2	1A	1	1955
82	33	1		1	1960
82	33	1		1	1963
82	33	2	0A	1	1965

		85	86	87	
78	33	1	0	0A	1950
78	33	1	0	0	1955
78	33	2		0	1960
78	33	2		0	1963
78	33	2	0A	0	1965
79	33	1	0	0	1950
79	33	1	1	0	1955
79	33	1	1	0	1960
79	33	1	1	1	1963
79	33	1	2A	1	1965

		88	89	90	
1	34	1178	3067	2216	1950
1	34	1178	3067	2216	1955
1	34	1178	3067	2216	1960
1	34	1178	3067	2216	1963
1	34	1178	3067	2216	1965
2	34	2828	974	2600	1950
2	34	2828	974	2600	1955
2	34	2828	974	2600	1960
2	34	2828	974	2600	1963
2	34	2828	974	2600	1965
106	34	3185A	172A	2352A	1965
3	34	1742	-2786	-2216	1950
3	34	1742	-2786	-2216	1955
3	34	1742	-2786	-2216	1960
3	34	1742	-2786	-2216	1963
3	34	1742	-2786	-2216	1965
4	34	-2782	1673	-2273	1950
4	34	-2782	1673	-2273	1955
4	34	-2782	1673	-2273	1960
4	34	-2782	1673	-2273	1963
4	34	-2782	1673	-2273	1965
5	34	2550	731	2945	1955
5	34	2550	731	2945	1960
5	34	2550	731	2945	1963
5	34	2550	731	2945	1965
6	34	2488	174	3079	1950
6	34	2488	174	3079	1955
6	34	2488	174	3079	1960
6	34	2488	174	3079	1963
6	34	2488	174	3079	1965
7	34	1428	-3532	-1092	1950
7	34	1428	-3532	-1092	1955
7	34	1428	-3532	-1092	1960
7	34	1428	-3532	-1092	1963
7	34	1428	-3532	-1092	1965
8	34	2668	-2488	-1548	1950
8	34	2668	-2488	-1548	1955
8	34	2741	-2646	-1092	1960
8	34	2741	-2646	-1092	1963
8	34	2741	-2646	-1092	1965
9	34	2711	1151	2651	1950
9	34	2711	1151	2651	1955
9	34	2711	1151	2651	1960
9	34	2711	1151	2651	1963
9	34	2711	1151	2651	1965
10	34	-397	3789	1092	1950
10	34	-397	3789	1092	1955
10	34	-397	3789	1092	1960

		88	89	9C	
10	34	-397	3789	1092	1963
10	34	-397	3789	1092	1965
113	34	3454A	1930A	-221A	1965
11	34	-1006	3758	756	1955
11	34	-1006	3758	756	1960
11	34	-1006	3758	756	1963
11	34	-1006	3758	756	1965
83	34	3881	754	276	1963
83	34	3881	754	276	1965
12	34	726	-2707	2802	1950
12	34	726	-2707	2802	1955
12	34	726	-2707	2802	1960
12	34	726	-2707	2802	1963
12	34	726	-2707	2802	1965
84	34	3760	1221	276	1963
84	34	3760	1221	276	1965
13	34	684	3874	483	1950
13	34	684	3874	483	1955
13	34	684	3874	483	1960
13	34	684	3874	483	1963
13	34	684	3874	483	1965
85	34	3744	1003	824	1963
85	34	3744	1003	824	1965
14	34	1138	-3123	-2158	1950
14	34	1138	-3123	-2158	1955
14	34	1138	-3123	-2158	1960
14	34	1138	-3123	-2158	1963
14	34	1138	-3123	-2158	1965
15	34	-1330	2729	2547	1950
15	34	-1330	2729	2547	1955
15	34	-1330	2729	2547	1960
15	34	-1330	2729	2547	1963
15	34	-1330	2729	2547	1965
16	34	-1849	3080	1675	1955
16	34	-1849	3080	1675	1960
16	34	-1849	3080	1675	1963
16	34	-1849	3080	1675	1965
17	34	1091	-3800	276	1950
17	34	1091	-3800	276	1955
17	34	1091	-3800	276	1960
17	34	1091	-3800	276	1963
17	34	1091	-3800	276	1965
87	34	3819	1023	-276	1963
87	34	3819	1023	-276	1965
86	34	3819	1023	-276	1963
86	34	3819	1023	-276	1965
18	34	409	-3881	688	1950
18	34	409	-3881	688	1955
18	34	409	-3881	688	1960
18	34	409	-3881	688	1963
18	34	409	-3881	688	1965
19	34	509	-3612	1548	1950
19	34	509	-3612	1548	1955
19	34	509	-3612	1548	1960
19	34	509	-3612	1548	1963
19	34	509	-3612	1548	1965

		88	89	90	
20	34	2472	616	3035	1950
20	34	2472	616	3035	1955
20	34	2472	616	3035	1960
20	34	2472	616	3035	1963
20	34	2472	616	3035	1965
88	34	3939	138	414	1963
88	34	3939	138	414	1965
21	34	2224	473	3246	1950
21	34	2224	473	3246	1955
21	34	2224	473	3246	1960
21	34	2224	473	3246	1963
21	34	2224	473	3246	1965
22	34	1290	-3542	1224	1950
22	34	1290	-3542	1224	1955
22	34	1290	-3542	1224	1960
22	34	1290	-3542	1224	1963
22	34	1290	-3542	1224	1965
23	34	825	-3876	-0	1950
23	34	825	-3876	0	1955
23	34	825	-3876	0	1960
23	34	825	-3876	0	1963
23	34	825	-3876	0	1965
24	34	2942	1767	1981	1950
24	34	2942	1767	1981	1955
24	34	2942	1767	1981	1960
24	34	2942	1767	1981	1963
24	34	2942	1767	1981	1965
25	34	69	-3861	891	1950
25	34	69	-3861	891	1955
25	34	69	-3861	891	1960
25	34	69	-3861	891	1963
25	34	69	-3861	891	1965
26	34	3085	2409	620	1950
26	34	3085	2409	620	1955
26	34	3085	2409	620	1960
26	34	3085	2409	620	1963
26	34	3085	2409	620	1965
27	34	1797	838	3432	1950
27	34	1797	838	3432	1955
27	34	1797	838	3432	1960
27	34	1797	838	3432	1963
27	34	1797	838	3432	1965
28	34	2599	91	2990	1950
28	34	2599	91	2990	1955
28	34	2599	91	2990	1960
28	34	2599	91	2990	1963
28	34	2599	91	2990	1965
89	34	3914	620	0	1963
89	34	3914	620	0	1965
29	34	2378	549	3122	1955
29	34	2378	549	3122	1960
29	34	2378	549	3122	1963
29	34	2378	549	3122	1965
30	34	2529	310	3035	1955
30	34	2529	310	3035	1960
30	34	2529	310	3035	1963
30	34	2529	310	3035	1965
90	34	3948	0	345	1960
90	34	3948	-0	345	1963
90	34	3948	-0	345	1965

		88	89	90	
31	34	2875	1220	2439	1950
31	34	2875	1220	2439	1955
31	34	2875	1220	2439	1960
31	34	2875	1220	2439	1963
31	34	2875	1220	2439	1965
32	34	1	-3845	959	1950
32	34	1	-3845	959	1955
32	34	1	-3845	959	1960
32	34	1	-3845	959	1963
32	34	1	-3845	959	1965
91	34	3814	-880	620	1963
91	34	3814	-880	620	1965
33	34	1166	-3584	1224	1950
33	34	1166	-3584	1224	1955
33	34	1166	-3584	1224	1960
33	34	1166	-3584	1224	1963
33	34	1166	-3584	1224	1965
34	34	202	-3840	959	1950
34	34	202	-3840	959	1955
34	34	202	-3840	959	1960
34	34	202	-3840	959	1963
34	34	202	-3840	959	1965
35	34	2556	880	2898	1950
35	34	2556	880	2898	1955
35	34	2556	880	2898	1960
35	34	2556	880	2898	1963
35	34	2556	880	2898	1965
36	34	788	3409	1860	1950
36	34	788	3409	1860	1955
36	34	788	3409	1860	1960
36	34	788	3409	1860	1963
36	34	788	3409	1860	1965
37	34	-1085	3789	-414	1950
37	34	-1085	3789	-414	1955
37	34	-1085	3789	-414	1960
37	34	-1085	3789	-414	1963
37	34	-1085	3789	-414	1965
38	34	2044	2523	2273	1950
38	34	2044	2523	2273	1955
38	34	2044	2523	2273	1960
38	34	2044	2523	2273	1963
38	34	2044	2523	2273	1965
39	34	2391	2309	2158	1950
39	34	2391	2309	2158	1955
39	34	2391	2309	2158	1960
39	34	2391	2309	2158	1963
39	34	2391	2309	2158	1965
40	34	2372	-249	3165	1950
40	34	2372	-249	3165	1955
40	34	2372	-249	3165	1960
40	34	2372	-249	3165	1963
40	34	2372	-249	3165	1965
41	34	2783	1948	2041	1950
41	34	2783	1948	2041	1955
41	34	2783	1948	2041	1960
41	34	2783	1948	2041	1963
41	34	2783	1948	2041	1965
42	34	2881	612	2651	1950
42	34	2881	612	2651	1955
42	34	2881	612	2651	1960

		88	89	90	
42	34	2881	612	2651	1963
42	34	2881	612	2651	1965
92	34	3938	-275	345	1963
92	34	3938	-275	345	1965
163	34	880A	-3665A	1225A	1965
43	34	-2449	2131	2273	1955
43	34	-2449	2131	2273	1960
43	34	-2449	2131	2273	1963
43	34	-2449	2131	2273	1965
44	34	2719	1975	2100	1950
44	34	2719	1975	2100	1955
44	34	2719	1975	2100	1960
44	34	2719	1975	2100	1963
44	34	2719	1975	2100	1965
45	34	-1766	2524	2494	1950
45	34	-1766	2524	2494	1955
45	34	-1766	2524	2494	1960
45	34	-1766	2524	2494	1963
45	34	-1766	2524	2494	1965
46	34	-1904	2529	2385	1950
46	34	-1904	2529	2385	1955
46	34	-1904	2529	2385	1960
46	34	-1904	2529	2385	1963
46	34	-1904	2529	2385	1965
80	34	-782	3687	1224	1955
80	34	-782	3687	1224	1960
80	34	-782	3687	1224	1963
80	34	-782	3687	1224	1965
47	34	2692	1884	2216	1950
47	34	2692	1884	2216	1955
47	34	2692	1884	2216	1960
47	34	2692	1884	2216	1963
47	34	2692	1884	2216	1965
48	34	3881	-684	414	1950
48	34	3881	-684	414	1955
48	34	3881	-684	414	1960
48	34	3881	-684	414	1963
48	34	3881	-684	414	1965
49	34	3239	748	2158	1955
49	34	3239	748	2158	1960
49	34	3239	748	2158	1963
49	34	3239	748	2158	1965
93	34	2556	2740	-1290	1963
93	34	2556	2740	-1290	1965
94	34	-754	3885	207	1960
94	34	-754	3885	207	1963
94	34	-754	3885	207	1965
95	34	3839	-539	824	1963
95	34	3839	-539	824	1965
96	34	3623	-1039	1224	1963
96	34	3623	-1039	1224	1965
50	34	-585	-3701	1290	1950
50	34	-585	-3701	1290	1955
50	34	-585	-3701	1290	1960
50	34	-585	-3701	1290	1963
50	34	-585	-3701	1290	1965

		88	89	90	
97	34	3261	-400	2216	1960
97	34	3261	-400	2216	1963
97	34	3261	-400	2216	1965
51	34	309	3518	1799	1950
51	34	309	3518	1799	1955
51	34	309	3518	1799	1960
51	34	309	3518	1799	1963
51	34	309	3518	1799	1965
52	34	2434B	170B	3122B	1950
52	34	2434B	170B	3122B	1955
52	34	2434B	170B	3122B	1960
52	34	2434B	170B	3122B	1963
52	34	2434B	170B	3122B	1965
53	34	-2975	314	-2600	1950
53	34	-2975	314	-2600	1955
53	34	-2975	314	-2600	1960
53	34	-2975	314	-2600	1963
53	34	-2975	314	-2600	1965
54	34	272	-3867	824	1950
54	34	272	-3867	824	1955
54	34	272	-3867	824	1960
54	34	272	-3867	824	1963
54	34	272	-3867	824	1965
98	34	3859	135	891	1963
98	34	3859	135	891	1965
99	34	3936	206	414	1963
99	34	3936	206	414	1965
55	34	1952	344	3432	1950
55	34	1952	344	3432	1955
55	34	1952	344	3432	1960
55	34	1952	344	3432	1963
55	34	1952	344	3432	1965
56	34	-775	2537	2945	1950
56	34	-775	2537	2945	1955
56	34	-775	2537	2945	1960
56	34	-775	2537	2945	1963
56	34	-775	2537	2945	1965
57	34	973	3178	2158	1950
57	34	973	3178	2158	1955
57	34	973	3178	2158	1960
57	34	973	3178	2158	1963
57	34	973	3178	2158	1965
58	34	748	-3842	620	1950
58	34	748	-3842	620	1955
58	34	748	-3842	620	1960
58	34	748	-3842	620	1963
58	34	748	-3842	620	1965
59	34	1957	-3012	-1675	1950
59	34	1957	-3012	-1675	1955
59	34	1957	-3012	-1675	1960
59	34	1957	-3012	-1675	1963
59	34	1957	-3012	-1675	1965
60	34	873	-3777	-824	1950
60	34	873	-3777	-824	1955
60	34	873	-3777	-824	1960
60	34	873	-3777	-824	1963
60	34	873	-3777	-824	1965
61	34	-1979	3297	959	1950
61	34	-1979	3297	959	1955

		88	89	90	
61	34	-1979	3297	959	1960
61	34	-1979	3297	959	1963
61	34	-1979	3297	959	1965
62	34	2278	874	3122	1950
62	34	2278	874	3122	1955
62	34	2278	874	3122	1960
62	34	2278	874	3122	1963
62	34	2278	874	3122	1965
63	34	3085	-488	2439	1950
63	34	3085	-488	2439	1955
63	34	3085	-488	2439	1960
63	34	3085	-488	2439	1963
63	34	3085	-488	2439	1965
64	34	2563	1250	2753	1950
64	34	2563	1250	2753	1955
64	34	2563	1250	2753	1960
64	34	2563	1250	2753	1963
64	34	2563	1250	2753	1965
114	34	3431A	1981A	-111A	1965
65	34	2515	2604	1612	1950
65	34	2515	2604	1612	1955
65	34	2515	2604	1612	1960
65	34	2515	2604	1612	1963
65	34	2515	2604	1612	1965
100	34	3677	-1124	959	1963
100	34	3677	-1124	959	1965
204	34	3824B	-883B	551B	1963
204	34	3824B	-883B	551B	1965
101	34	2801	2800	138	1963
101	34	2801	2800	138	1965
66	34	3032	-159	2547	1950
66	34	3032	-159	2547	1955
66	34	3032	-159	2547	1960
66	34	3032	-159	2547	1963
66	34	3032	-159	2547	1965
102	34	3247	2028	1026	1960
102	34	3247	2028	1026	1963
102	34	3247	2028	1026	1965
67	34	1931	665	3397	1950
67	34	1931	665	3397	1955
67	34	1931	665	3397	1960
67	34	1931	665	3397	1963
67	34	1931	665	3397	1965
68	34	2683	329	2898	1950
68	34	2683	329	2898	1955
68	34	2683	329	2898	1960
68	34	2683	329	2898	1963
68	34	2683	329	2898	1965
69	34	2689	1953	2158	1950
69	34	2689	1953	2158	1955
69	34	2689	1953	2158	1960
69	34	2689	1953	2158	1963
69	34	2689	1953	2158	1965
109	34	3057	2475	-483	1963
109	34	3057	2475	-483	1965
70	34	-669	3803	891	1950
70	34	-669	3803	891	1955

		88	89	90	
70	34	-669	3803	891	1960
70	34	-669	3803	891	1963
70	34	-669	3803	891	1965
103	34	3941	69	414	1963
103	34	3941	69	414	1965
216	34	1880	-3416	701	1965
104	34	3117	550	2385	1960
104	34	3117	550	2385	1963
104	34	3117	550	2385	1965
71	34	2547	1653	2547	1950
71	34	2547	1653	2547	1955
71	34	2547	1653	2547	1960
71	34	2547	1653	2547	1963
71	34	2547	1653	2547	1965
72	34	3172B	1686B	-1674B	1950
72	34	3172B	1686B	-1675B	1955
72	34	3172B	1686B	-1675B	1960
72	34	3172B	1686B	-1675B	1963
72	34	3172B	1686B	-1675B	1965
73	34	1816	1368	3246	1950
73	34	1816	1368	3246	1955
73	34	1816	1368	3246	1960
73	34	1816	1368	3246	1963
73	34	1816	1368	3246	1965
74	34	2495	0	3079	1950
74	34	2495	-0	3079	1955
74	34	2495	-0	3079	1960
74	34	2495	-0	3079	1963
74	34	2495	-0	3079	1965
75	34	694	-3001	2494	1950
75	34	694	-3001	2494	1955
75	34	694	-3001	2494	1960
75	34	694	-3001	2494	1963
75	34	694	-3001	2494	1965
219	34	3341	2128	0	1965
105	34	3876	-68	824	1963
105	34	3876	-68	824	1965
76	34	1816	-2691	-2273	1950
76	34	1816	-2691	-2273	1955
76	34	1816	-2691	-2273	1960
76	34	1816	-2691	-2273	1963
76	34	1816	-2691	-2273	1965
77	34	1526	-3592	688	1950
77	34	1526	-3592	688	1955
77	34	1526	-3592	688	1960
77	34	1526	-3592	688	1963
77	34	1526	-3592	688	1965
81	34	-1019	3557	1420	1955
81	34	-1019	3557	1420	1960
81	34	-1019	3557	1420	1963
81	34	-1019	3557	1420	1965
82	34	-1074	3752	688	1955
82	34	-1074	3752	689	1960
82	34	-1074	3752	688	1963
82	34	-1074	3752	688	1965
78	34	2754	2659	1026	1950
78	34	2754	2659	1026	1955

		88	89	90	
78	34	2754	2659	1026	1960
78	34	2754	2659	1026	1963
78	34	2754	2659	1026	1965
79	34	2634	958	2802	1950
79	34	2634	958	2802	1955
79	34	2634	958	2802	1960
79	34	2634	958	2802	1963
79	34	2634	958	2802	1965

Set 20

1. A. Estimates
   B. *UN Statistical Yearbook* (1961)
   C. *The World's Telephones–1964,* American Telephone & Telegraph Co.

2. A. Estimates
   B. *Moody's Municipal and Government Manual*
   C. *Oxford Economic Atlas of the World*
   D. *Worldmark Encyclopedia of The Nations*
   E. *International Politics,* Karl W. Deutsch, p. 34
   F. *UN Economic Survey of Latin America* (1956), p. 167
   G. *Yearbook of Labor Statistics* (1967)
   H. *World Almanac* (1964)
   I. *Information Please Almanac* (1964)
   J. *Agricultural Development of African Nations,* vol. 1, S. C. Vora
   K. *Readers' Digest World Almanac* (1966)
   L. *North Korea Today* (1963)
   M. *An Atlas of European Affairs* (1964)
   N. *Atlas of Economic Development*

3. A. Estimates
   B. US Department of State *Research Memorandum REU-6,* September 15, 1961, "Indicators of Economic Strength of Western Europe, Canada, U.S. & the Soviet Block, 1960"

4. A. Estimates
   B. *Demographic Yearbook* (1960)
   C. *Worldmark Encyclopedia of The Nations*
   D. *Basic Facts and Figures* (1959)
   E. *World Survey of Education: Handbook of Educational Organization & Statistics* (1955)
   F. *Atlas of Economic Development,* Norton Ginsburg (ed.)
   G. *UN Statistical Yearbook* (1965)
   H. L. J. Walinsky, *The Planning & Execution of Economic Development,* pp. 190-199
   I. *World Handbook of Political and Social Indicators*
   J. William Peterson, *Population,* pp. 328-332
   K. *Progress in The Asian Region: A Statistical Review,* pp. 71-72
   L. *World Illiteracy at Mid-Century,* pp. 38-44
   M. *New Nations of Africa* (1963)

5. A. Estimates
   B. *UN Statistical Yearbook* (1965)

C. *Statistical Abstract of The US* (1961)
D. US Department of State *Research Memorandum REU-6,* September 15, 1961, "Indicators of Economic Strength of Western Europe, Canada, U.S. & the Soviet Block, 1960"
E. *World Military Expenditures 1966-1967*
F. A. Eckstein, *Communist China's Economic Growth and Foreign Trade,* p. 121
G. *World Handbook of Political and Social Indicators*

6. A. Estimates
B. US Department of State *Research Memorandum REU-6,* September 15, 1961, "Indicators of Economic Strength of Western Europe, Canada, U.S. and the Soviet Block, 1960"

7. A. Estimates
B. *UN Statistical Yearbook* (1959)
C. *Yearbook of National Accounts Statistics* (1966)
D. "Indicators of Market Size for 88 Countries," *Business International* (1965)
E. *The American Annual* (1967)

Set 21

A. Estimates
B. USSR assessment taken as sum of USSR, Byelorussian SSR and Ukrainian SSR
C. *UN Statistical Yearbook*
D. *Moody's Governments and Municipalities*
E. *Statesman's Yearbook*
F. Warsaw Pact contributions
G. *Worldmark Encyclopedia of The Nations*
H. NATO contributions
I. *The Index Translationum* (1965)
J. English is the local language.
K. James Richard Carter, *The Net Cost of Soviet Foreign Aid,* p. 109
L. *Soviet Foreign Aid,* Marshall I. Goldman, p. 28
M. H. J. P. Arnold, *Aid For Development,* p. 164 (figures are for 1964)
N. Due to lack of data for Russian aid, ratios for these nations cannot legitimately be calculated.
P. Fred R. Von der Mihden, *Politics of The Developing Nations,* Chapter 4
Q. *The World Almanac* (1966)
R. "World Defense Expenditures," *Journal of Peace Research* (1966)

S. "Worldwide Defense Expenditures," *Bulletin of The Atomic Scientists* (September 1966)

Z. *Political Handbook and Atlas of The World* (1964)

Set 22

A. Estimates

B. *Yearbook of National Accounts Statistics* (1965)

C. GNP data is not available.

D. *Keesing's Contemporary Archives*

G. Kahin and Lewis, *The United States in Vietnam* (1969), pp. 185, 188

H. *Annual Register of World Events* (1965)

J. Data and estimates referring to the Korean War were based upon three sources:

1. David Reese, *The Limited War* (1964)
2. Mathew Ridgeway, *The Korean War* (1967)
3. *Korean Army History* (vol. 1 - vol. 12)

For China and North Korea the best estimate of number killed in foreign violence was greater than the coding format; therefore, the maximum quantity was entered. Likewise, the number of people killed in domestic violence in Indonesia in 1965. The actual estimates are:

CHN–over 200,000
KON–112,550
INS–250,000.

Set 23

A. Estimates

B. In Afghanistan all inhabitants are subject to the law of Islam.

C*. Measured from Alaska

D*. Measured from Hawaii

*Became states in 1959, thus changing the measured distance for some nations.

Set 24

A. Estimates

B. No legal provision for divorces, therefore the numerator is zero.

C. *Worldmark Encyclopedia of The Nations*

D. *Demographic Yearbook,* year other than primary source.

E. *UN Statistical Yearbook*
L. *Production Yearbook*

Set 25

A. Estimates
B. *Worldmark Encyclopedia of The Nations*
C. Rand McNally's *Cosmopolitan World Atlas*
D. *Statesman's Yearbook*
F. *The Middle East, 1962,* p. 281
G. *Demographic Yearbook*
H. *Information Please Almanac* (1962)

Set 26

A. Estimates
B. *Worldmark Encyclopedia of The Nations*
D. *Yearbook of National Accounts Statistics, 1965,* (New York: UN, 1966)
E. *Yearbook of Labour Statistics,* (Geneva: International Labour Office, 1962)
F. *Moody's Municipal and Government Manual*
G. *Encyclopaedia Britannica World Atlas*
H. *The Middle East, 1962*
I. *Overseas Economic Survey*
J. "Indicators of Market Size for 88 Countries," *Business International* (New York, 1965)
K. *Gross National Product Aid,* Office of Programs Coordination, Statistics and Reports Division

Set 27

A. Estimates
B. *Worldmark Encyclopedia of The Nations*
C. *Moody's Government and Municipalities*
D. *Statesman's Yearbook*
E. *US Economic Assistance Programs Administrated by Aid & Predecessor Agencies 1948-1968*
F. *U.S. Foreign Assistance & Assistance from International Organizations: July 1, 1945 - June 3, 1960*

G. *U.S. Overseas Loans & Grants & Assistance from International Organizations: July 1, 1945 - June 30, 1966*
H. Data only given as "less than $50,000"; recorded as $40,000.
I. *UN Statistical Yearbook*
J. *Laos: World Survey of Cultures* (HARF Press, 1960), p. 247
K. *Professional Manpower & Education in Communist China,* p. 14
L. *U.N. Economic Survey of Latin America,* 1955
M. *U.N. Economic Survey of Asia & The Far East,* 1960
N. *Overseas Economic Surveys* (HMSO, 1954)
P. I. M. D. Little, *International Aid,* Chapter 4
Q. *Development Assistance Efforts & Policies 1965,* OECD
R. *Flow of Financial Resources to Less Developed Countries 1961-65*
S. Data only given as "less than $100,000"; recorded as $90,000.

Set 28

A. Estimates
B. *Yearbook of Labor Statistics* (1954)

Set 29

A. Estimates
B. Russian is native language.
C. *Statesman's Yearbook* (1951)
D. *Brassey's Armed Forces Annual* (1952)
E. *Encyclopaedia Britannica Book of the Year*
F. *Yearbook of The Commonwealth of Australia* No. 38 (1951)
G. *Whitaker's Almanac* (1950)
H. $1 million U.S. has been assumed for those countries with no gold stock to avoid an indeterminate ratio.
I. Imports include foreign aid.
J. Naval data missing.
K. Air Force data missing.
L. Army data missing.
M. *The Military Balance,* Institute for Strategic Studies, London
N. Army data only.
P. Air Force data only.
Q. *Statistical Yearbook* (1968)
R. *Index Translationum,* UNESCO, vol. 18 (1965)

Set 30

A. Estimates
B. *Statesman's Yearbook*
C. *Worldmark Encyclopedia of The Nations*
D. *Monthly Bulletin of Statistics,* Jan-June 1965
E. *Yearbook of National Account Statistics,* 1966
F. *Europa Yearbook,* 1967
G. *Political Handbook & Atlas of The World,* 1964
H. Mehden, *Politics of The Developing Nations*
I. Burnett and Johnson, *Political Forces In Latin America*
J. Since the communist party of the United States was outlawed in 1954, no reliable data sources have been located. FBI information is classified.
K. Furnivall, *Governance of Modern Burma* (1958)
L. Wignon, *Party Politics in India* (1957)
M. Bindn, *Politics in Lebanon*
N. Fgin, *Israel* (1967)
P. Ngorawardana, *Ceylon General Election 1956* (1960)
Q. Marlowe, *Iran* (1963)
R. Majid Khaddrri, *Independent Iraq* (1955)
S. Seale, *The Struggle for Syria* (1965)
T. Little, *Modern Egypt*
U. Robinson, *The First Turkish Republic* (1965)
V. Ingrams, *The Yemen* (1963)
W. R. F. Smith, *Background to Revolution* (1966)
X. Tinker, *India and Pakistan* (1962)
Y. Muron, *A History of Venezuela* (1964)
Z. Kogan, *The Government of Italy* (1962)

Set 31

A. Estimates
B. Nation's total holdings are in US dollars.
C. 37% of Filipinos speak English and 37% speak Tagalog.
D. The UN continues to hold $140,000 in a suspense account for India and Pakistan, relating to a payment made in 1947 toward a Working Capital Fund.
E. *The Gallatin Annual of International Business*
F. R. C. Kingsbury and V. J. G. Pounds, *An Atlas of Middle Eastern Affairs*
G. Murray Clark Havens, Carl Laden, and Karl M. Schmitt, *The Politics of Assassination* (Englewood Cliffs, N.J.: Prentice-Hall, 1970), Appendix A

Set 32

A. Estimates
B. Barnett and Johnson, *Political Forces in Latin America* (1968)
C. *World Almanac* (1971)
D. Data available for 1967 only.

Set 33

A. Estimates
B. *Encyclopaedia Britannica*
C. Robert Putnam, "Toward Expanding Military Intervention in Latin American Politics," *World Politics* 20, no. 1 (October 1967)

Set 34

A. *The International Atlas,* Rand McNally
B. Name of Administrative Seat of Government taken from *Worldmark Encyclopedia* (1963)

Set 20 (Variables 1-7)

		1 TEL-PC	2 %A-POP	3 ENC-PC	4 ILLITE	5 GNP-PC	6 EPXPOP	7 NI
UNIT		x 10^{-4}	%	kg/capita	%	$US	x 10^{-1}	$US x 10^{8}
1950:	MEAN	345.79	49.74	975.87	41.11	386.71	3994.75	85.25
	S.D.	631.32	24.13	1533.01	31.77	376.24	324.26	336.75
1955:	MEAN	428.25	49.19	1068.28	41.33	413.92	4003.96	111.03
	S.D.	746.86	24.34	1491.74	32.20	432.32	332.45	408.85
1960:	MEAN	519.12	47.74	1179.89	36.87	512.49	4012.37	136.77
	S.D.	876.19	23.70	1565.43	31.60	550.37	378.82	498.75
1963:	MEAN	490.28	56.06	1086.58	43.98	486.34	4004.15	157.94
	S.D.	913.95	26.05	1638.06	35.53	593.71	358.20	551.24
1965:	MEAN	523.49	54.14	1191.59	46.31	568.18	4004.28	154.66
	S.D.	978.02	26.34	1767.63	35.53	693.85	359.82	604.04
S-P:	MEAN	470.25	51.95	1110.01	42.29	488.83	4004.46	135.22
	S.D.	856.09	25.25	1612.65	33.67	568.90	351.14	508.81
S-P($\hat{Y}$):	MEAN	468.34	52.76	1092.57	42.29	470.08	4004.50	121.88
	S.D.	854.72	25.04	1595.53	33.63	550.03	350.44	471.60

Set 21 (Variables 8-14)

UNIT		8 POPULA x 10^4	9 %CT-UN % x 10^{-2}	10 DEFEXP $US x 10^6	11 E/TRSL % x 10^{-1}	12 BLOC *rating scale*	13 US/AID x 10^{-4}	14 TOTA *rat sc*
1950:	**MEAN**	2829.39	130.43	774.75	570.40	1.38	7399.49	1
	S.D.	7255.94	493.29	3153.79	854.41	0.72	2304.78	0
1955:	**MEAN**	3075.10	156.05	1384.83	379.56	1.44	6865.34	1
	S.D.	312.55	480.47	6007.11	203.77	0.74	2860.77	0
1960:	**MEAN**	3198.70	116.06	1440.02	456.25	1.33	6895.93	1
	S.D.	8694.86	395.57	6876.82	222.54	0.71	3043.00	0
1963:	**MEAN**	2875.30	91.15	1030.41	355.39	1.27	4972.58	1
	S.D.	8336.70	352.21	5474.87	250.87	0.65	3133.90	0
1965:	**MEAN**	2853.22	95.18	1280.39	401.93	1.36	6889.61	1
	S.D.	8427.17	351.62	6523.32	279.22	0.71	2982.52	0
S-P:	**MEAN**	2959.29	112.93	1172.23	418.63	1.35	6676.80	1
	S.D.	8231.28	405.41	5790.56	379.59	0.70	2969.79	0
S-P($\hat{Y}$):	**MEAN**	2959.29	109.52	1019.22	426.14	1.35	6762.95	1
	S.D.	8231.28	395.24	5344.08	269.69	0.70	2779.32	[illegible]

Set 22 (Variables 15-21)

UNIT		15 IFC/GNP x 10^7	16 THREAT *frequency count*	17 ACCUSA *frequency count*	18 F-KILL *frequency count*	19 MILACT *dichotomous scale*	20 PROTST *frequency count*	21 D-KILL *frequency count*
1950:	MEAN	654.08	0.03	5.87	4164.66	0.36	1.49	17.69
	S.D.	1405.60	0.24	16.38	17921.02	0.48	3.01	61.41
1955:	MEAN	627.59	0.17	7.93	14.98	0.42	0.82	115.97
	S.D.	1235.84	0.64	20.46	64.75	0.50	2.13	673.00
1960:	MEAN	1114.87	0.10	4.56	95.80	0.25	0.77	11.17
	S.D.	3585.45	0.48	13.08	596.22	0.44	1.93	31.03
1963:	MEAN	563.42	0.17	2.05	69.12	0.29	0.93	480.13
	S.D.	997.15	0.65	5.48	561.85	0.46	3.31	3517.16
1965:	MEAN	1415.81	0.21	3.93	389.16	0.29	1.26	1003.53
	S.D.	2834.17	0.73	10.10	1725.73	0.46	4.18	9439.69
S-P:	MEAN	807.30	0.15	4.61	774.15	0.32	1.05	387.73
	S.D.	2177.81	0.60	13.48	7197.20	0.47	3.13	5016.05
S-P($\hat{Y}$):	MEAN	913.85	0.15	4.58	767.28	0.32	1.03	388.03
	S.D.	1873.00	0.60	13.41	7150.36	0.46	3.10	4978.70

Set 23 (Variables 22-28)

UNIT		22 STRIKE	23 RIOTS	24 PURGES	25 DEMONS	26 %CATH	27 US-DIS	28 MED/N
		frequency count	*frequency count*	*frequency count*	*frequency count*	$\% \times 10^{-1}$	in. $\times 10^{-3}$	% x10
1950:	MEAN	0.28	0.33	0.13	0.08	414.87	10968.75	1004.
	S.D.	0.88	0.98	0.37	0.33	427.94	6303.09	395.
1955:	MEAN	0.09	0.39	0.23	0.51	393.44	11522.86	1092.
	S.D.	0.68	2.00	0.53	1.34	426.57	6316.31	539.
1960:	MEAN	0.20	0.67	0.11	0.41	367.41	9594.82	847.
	S.D.	0.61	1.85	0.42	1.68	407.59	4774.34	421.
1963:	MEAN	0.07	0.83	0.16	1.10	319.79	10554.91	855.
	S.D.	0.36	2.74	0.46	6.58	387.69	5001.82	529.
1965:	MEAN	0.09	0.66	0.27	0.70	314.90	10672.56	929.
	S.D.	0.32	1.97	0.56	2.31	369.53	5191.60	512
S-P:	MEAN	0.14	0.60	0.19	0.61	355.38	10639.37	937
	S.D.	0.57	2.05	0.48	3.51	400.90	5487.28	495
S-P($\hat{Y}$):	MEAN	0.14	0.60	0.19	0.61	354.77	10639.37	937
	S.D.	0.57	2.05	0.48	3.51	400.47	5487.27	495

Set 24 (Variables 29-35)

		29 ER-AMB	30 DIV-MR	31 DENSITY	32 %ARABL	33 AREA	34 RDS-KM	35 RRS-KM
UNIT		*frequency count*	ratio $1/10^4$	people/ sq. km	% x 10^{-1}	sq. km x 10^3	km/ sq. km x 10^3	km/ sq. km x 10^4
1950:	MEAN	0.70	756.82	52.88	178.51	1420.71	224.96	30.85
	S.D.	1.74	624.70	63.26	154.87	3385.98	329.32	38.50
1955:	MEAN	0.07	627.56	63.55	194.21	1288.33	204.70	31.18
	S.D.	0.25	512.31	73.09	153.91	3194.69	291.97	39.14
1960:	MEAN	0.43	852.68	66.23	194.71	1256.67	198.36	31.68
	S.D.	1.07	637.81	74.58	151.80	3110.51	277.67	41.65
1963:	MEAN	0.30	902.69	59.78	206.95	1154.19	195.45	27.08
	S.D.	0.68	656.29	75.40	159.21	2821.73	292.87	38.96
1965:	MEAN	0.32	885.62	64.25	204.26	1108.17	229.18	27.20
	S.D.	0.85	679.58	78.18	154.57	2756.93	341.49	38.97
-P:	MEAN	0.35	818.30	61.67	196.64	1225.64	210.27	29.37
	S.D.	1.00	635.05	73.59	154.48	3012.08	306.80	39.34
-P($\hat{Y}$):	MEAN	0.35	888.41	61.47	189.51	1225.64	196.60	28.81
	S.D.	0.99	528.98	73.43	149.90	3012.08	284.96	38.41

Set 25 (Variables 36-42)

UNIT		36 RELGRP *frequency count*	37 IM/I+E % x 10^{-2}	38 RAIN mm	39 RGRP/P %	40 %D-WTR % x 10^{-1}	41 FST/ST % x 10^{-1}	42 NEUT *dichotomous sc*
1950:	MEAN	2.22	577.45	1067.83	82.36	418.96	38.29	0.
	S.D.	1.04	334.89	695.42	20.50	289.33	56.99	0.
1955:	MEAN	2.27	529.91	1100.16	82.31	459.06	52.13	0
	S.D.	1.05	229.74	686.71	20.08	285.43	79.97	0
1960:	MEAN	2.28	461.09	1097.70	82.18	362.91	60.47	0
	S.D.	1.02	259.86	698.33	19.35	319.96	88.42	0
1963:	MEAN	2.38	347.19	1115.90	80.07	367.24	69.10	0
	S.D.	1.07	343.02	690.74	20.60	323.44	117.45	0
1965:	MEAN	2.38	453.59	1115.90	75.80	522.98	88.83	0
	S.D.	1.07	263.87	690.74	21.80	316.73	138.07	0
S-P:	MEAN	2.32	452.74	1101.98	80.17	419.77	67.55	0
	S.D.	1.05	300.88	689.31	20.66	315.82	110.05	0
S-P($\hat{Y}$):	MEAN	2.33	439.80	1102.43	79.98	373.63	69.20	0
	S.D.	1.05	211.39	685.29	19.89	270.37	93.17	0

Set 26 (Variables 43-48)

UNIT		43 NATAGE *rating scale*	44 REL/TI % x 10^{-2}	45 EMG/POP % x 10^{-3}	46 SG/GNP *ratio* x 10^{-5}	47 LAW/NG % x 10^{-2}	48 %UNEMP % x 10^{-2}
1950:	MEAN	2.04	653.00	438.19	364.05	508.10	213.55
	S.D.	1.40	427.59	878.43	410.22	306.02	340.07
1955:	MEAN	1.95	594.59	557.39	345.82	399.88	368.18
	S.D.	1.45	547.69	1050.30	620.81	223.48	518.88
1960:	MEAN	2.09	666.78	246.67	418.37	510.29	219.42
	S.D.	1.54	518.10	241.74	636.06	416.75	224.77
1963:	MEAN	2.64	667.81	141.54	529.22	401.86	186.02
	S.D.	1.80	637.26	237.56	892.25	215.79	237.21
1965:	MEAN	2.76	698.92	252.19	720.94	440.75	397.60
	S.D.	1.83	805.84	335.36	1254.29	301.82	314.22
S-P:	MEAN	2.35	658.67	319.69	502.96	448.10	272.06
	S.D.	1.67	624.46	661.47	885.90	301.41	355.64
S-P($\hat{Y}$):	MEAN	2.35	679.55	307.85	481.94	448.10	265.38
	S.D.	1.67	522.50	469.79	781.91	301.41	233.23

Set 27 (Variables 49-55)

UNIT		49 EX/EPT	50 LANGRP	51 LGRP/P	52 ETHGRP	53 AIDRVD	54 TECRVD	55 %E-
		% x 10^{-2}	*frequency count*	% x 10^{-1}	*frequency count*	\$US x 10^{5}	\$US x 10^{3}	% x 1
1950:	MEAN	3978.73	2.85	785.74	2.97	889.97	448.33	993
	S.D.	2510.54	2.71	226.83	2.14	1902.81	618.00	494
1955:	MEAN	4458.33	2.75	763.60	2.90	787.51	199.51	1220
	S.D.	2284.28	2.61	242.84	2.06	1778.25	258.92	531
1960:	MEAN	3536.68	3.01	757.68	3.54	308.64	304.47	1272
	S.D.	2043.52	2.63	242.86	3.53	704.30	339.96	521
1963:	MEAN	3751.45	3.41	752.67	4.59	826.14	356.52	1393
	S.D.	2189.36	2.73	244.86	4.55	1494.96	289.04	574
1965:	MEAN	3479.42	3.28	769.72	4.43	806.27	3794.54	1537
	S.D.	2302.33	2.57	230.11	4.28	1640.39	9380.57	544
S-P:	MEAN	3799.20	3.12	765.28	3.81	718.58	1261.82	1312
	S.D.	2272.00	2.65	236.77	3.70	1550.64	5164.15	565
S-P($\hat{Y}$):	MEAN	3794.91	3.13	754.13	3.98	720.88	1224.33	1314
	S.D.	2142.89	2.58	216.31	3.60	1350.70	4545.63	496

Set 28 (Variables 56, 57 and 58)

		56 FM/WKS	57 EXP/GNP	58 FMST/FM
UNIT		% x 10^{-2}	% x 10^{-2}	%
1950:	MEAN	2755.76	1526.20	43.29
	S.D.	1150.85	1236.03	9.68
1955:	MEAN	2800.62	1716.52	44.09
	S.D.	1116.30	1107.35	12.32
1960:	MEAN	2699.71	1695.61	42.05
	S.D.	1064.09	981.12	12.11
1963:	MEAN	2928.84	1899.40	43.29
	S.D.	1203.99	1406.91	9.52
1965:	MEAN	2469.68	1893.15	45.00
	S.D.	1428.68	1417.63	12.61
S-P:	MEAN	2713.46	1776.12	43.63
	S.D.	1228.98	1273.96	11.35
S-P($\hat{Y}$):	MEAN	2733.19	1753.49	42.82
	S.D.	1092.97	1162.98	8.55

Set 29 (Variables 59-64)

		59 IP/TRD	60 CAL-PC	61 PR/CAL	62 R/TRSL	63 MIL/POP	64 BOI/GO
UNIT		% x 10^{-2}	% x 10^{-2}	% x 10^{-2}	% x 10^{-2}	% x 10^{-2}	*ratio*
1950:	MEAN	5172.59	803.52	315.71	1353.55	90.16	-173.84
	S.D.	1361.86	1327.99	51.65	2566.73	102.08	643.08
1955:	MEAN	5453.86	672.88	284.47	1267.14	90.92	-530.36
	S.D.	1311.90	1396.86	30.58	2080.60	99.41	1503.08
1960:	MEAN	5657.93	701.16	277.00	889.00	87.95	-167.32
	S.D.	1241.72	1461.59	28.44	1180.32	87.23	1144.89
1963:	MEAN	5600.04	800.67	279.05	699.81	102.44	-220.73
	S.D.	1250.79	1395.37	28.57	1097.62	142.17	921.84
1965:	MEAN	5454.01	842.49	272.85	542.78	80.10	-721.95
	S.D.	1174.27	1365.38	34.29	933.60	123.19	1612.89
S-P:	MEAN	5484.74	767.82	282.31	868.42	89.77	-385.87
	S.D.	1261.80	1386.36	36.54	1560.30	113.55	1276.78
S-P($\hat{Y}$):	MEAN	5496.28	573.90	278.46	841.76	87.97	-365.27
	S.D.	1207.54	1196.99	28.56	1373.64	105.61	1030.46

Set 30 (Variables 65-70)

UNIT		65 PARTYS *frequency count*	66 ART/NGO $\% \times 10^{-2}$	67 COM/POP $\% \times 10^{-3}$	68 GVT/GNP $\% \times 10^{-2}$	69 MONARC *dichotomous scale*	70 PUT-PT *ratio* $\times 10^{-2}$
1950:	MEAN	3.00	271.49	1144.56	1515.02	0.32	3420.92
	S.D.	2.46	193.21	2577.00	714.62	0.47	1106.06
1955:	MEAN	3.84	315.72	1071.46	1711.83	0.24	3434.18
	S.D.	2.47	226.37	2428.58	768.73	0.43	1038.46
1960:	MEAN	3.09	492.08	982.67	1772.06	0.23	3383.33
	S.D.	2.76	277.67	2259.43	679.73	0.42	860.75
1963:	MEAN	2.69	422.02	883.74	2116.86	0.18	3720.94
	S.D.	2.46	229.16	2278.86	1295.97	0.38	1414.64
1965:	MEAN	2.89	443.63	837.02	2092.82	0.19	3583.96
	S.D.	2.45	230.32	2347.91	1033.83	0.40	1212.16
S-P:	MEAN	3.06	398.12	965.02	1884.29	0.23	3527.28
	S.D.	2.54	245.45	2359.73	987.21	0.42	1163.69
S-P($\hat{Y}$):	MEAN	3.06	398.12	949.36	1939.85	0.23	3539.93
	S.D.	2.52	245.45	2339.17	871.88	0.42	1138.20

Set 31 (Variables 71-77)

UNIT		71 LAWTRA	72 LEGIT	73 EGRP/P	74 ASSASS	75 GVTCRS	76 UNDE/A	77 BOP/
		dichoto-mous scale	*dichoto-mous scale*	% x 10^{-1}	*frequency count*	*frequency count*	%	*rat* x 10
1950:	MEAN	1.51	0.10	715.19	0.13	0.14	2.32	-7.
	S.D.	0.58	0.30	251.56	0.37	0.35	15.25	46.
1955:	MEAN	1.42	0.10	730.74	0.14	0.14	12.78	-3.
	S.D.	0.67	0.31	244.90	0.50	0.42	29.31	75.
1960:	MEAN	1.53	0.17	708.63	0.24	0.26	35.62	-6
	S.D.	0.55	0.38	257.88	1.22	0.56	56.52	257
1963:	MEAN	1.67	0.16	645.40	0.08	0.15	32.98	8
	S.D.	0.66	0.37	286.79	0.31	0.58	56.29	60
1965:	MEAN	1.47	0.18	649.54	0.29	0.33	49.59	-19
	S.D.	0.72	0.38	285.87	0.91	0.56	53.29	186
S-P:	MEAN	1.53	0.15	684.43	0.18	0.21	27.68	-5
	S.D.	0.65	0.35	270.01	0.76	0.52	45.48	156
S-P($\hat{Y}$):	MEAN	1.52	0.15	684.43	0.18	0.21	29.17	-7
	S.D.	0.65	0.35	270.01	0.76	0.52	49.81	130

Set 32 (Variables 78-84)

UNIT		78 INVBAL $US x 10^6	79 STYLE *rating scale*	80 CONSTI *rating scale*	81 ELECTO *rating scale*	82 COMMUN *dichoto-mous scale*	83 LEADER *rating scale*	84 POWDIS *rating scale*
1950:	MEAN	8.02	0.47	1.21	1.07	0.85	0.71	0.86
	S.D.	256.71	0.82	0.82	0.97	0.36	0.88	0.93
1955:	MEAN	35.84	0.56	1.27	1.04	0.84	0.90	0.87
	S.D.	1069.41	0.85	0.74	0.88	0.37	0.83	0.89
1960:	MEAN	13.78	0.55	1.29	0.97	0.85	0.88	0.89
	S.D.	458.75	0.84	0.77	0.98	0.36	0.91	0.90
1963:	MEAN	14.65	0.51	1.25	0.97	0.87	1.02	0.77
	S.D.	581.23	0.78	0.75	0.90	0.34	0.89	0.85
1965:	MEAN	18.83	0.50	1.44	1.07	0.88	1.12	0.92
	S.D.	667.40	0.78	0.76	0.85	0.33	0.85	0.81
S-P:	MEAN	18.42	0.52	1.30	1.02	0.86	0.95	0.86
	S.D.	665.02	0.81	0.77	0.91	0.35	0.88	0.87
S-P($\hat{Y}$):	MEAN	16.03	0.52	1.31	1.02	0.86	0.95	0.86
	S.D.	622.50	0.81	0.77	0.90	0.35	0.87	0.87

Set 33 (Variables 85, 86 and 87)

UNIT		85 MILPAR *rating scale*	86 BUREAU *rating scale*	87 CENSOR *rating scale*
1950:	MEAN	0.82	0.94	1.12
	S.D.	0.70	0.75	0.83
1955:	MEAN	0.87	1.09	1.07
	S.D.	0.75	0.61	0.81
1960:	MEAN	0.85	1.10	1.13
	S.D.	0.80	0.60	0.87
1963:	MEAN	0.73	0.89	0.94
	S.D.	0.79	0.69	0.74
1965:	MEAN	0.83	0.94	1.04
	S.D.	0.78	0.77	0.77
S-P:	MEAN	0.82	0.98	1.05
	S.D.	0.77	0.70	0.80
S-P($\hat{Y}$):	MEAN	0.82	0.96	1.04
	S.D.	0.76	0.69	0.80

Set 34 (Variables 88, 89 and 90)

UNIT		88 GEOG-X *index*	89 GEOG-Y *index*	90 GEOG-Z *index*
1950:	MEAN	1385.49	67.32	1468.58
	S.D.	1546.76	2590.75	1638.21
1955:	MEAN	1247.22	331.10	1524.79
	S.D.	1658.48	2576.85	1571.36
1960:	MEAN	1323.72	376.94	1513.44
	S.D.	1689.05	2539.83	1532.56
1963:	MEAN	1764.31	396.77	1292.87
	S.D.	1787.45	2342.88	1476.87
1965:	MEAN	1813.73	368.00	1259.14
	S.D.	1766.06	2354.13	1459.21
S-P:	MEAN	1542.13	323.41	1394.92
	S.D.	1714.80	2457.24	1524.00
S-P($\hat{Y}$):	MEAN	1542.13	323.41	1394.92
	S.D.	1714.80	2457.24	1524.00

NOTES

1. Thus, for example, event data on conflict behavior were collected from the *New York Times,* even though it was known that the frequency of conflict events recorded in the *Times* considerably underreported the actual ones. These data were collected because tests had indicated that, while the *Times* underreported conflict events, the correlation between such *Times* data–the patterns of conflict–reflected actual correlations. See on this Rummel (1972, Chapter 6).

2. This possibility was guarded against by screening all data and checking all extremes greater than an absolute standard score of 2.00. Questionable extremes were then checked back against the source, or other sources, if necessary.

3. Of course, the accuracy of the data vary by variable. Some data, such as population, area, and energy production, are reasonably accurate while data on, say, threats, accusations, and negative sanctions may be less accurate.

4. Note in this case also how data accuracy are assessed relative to the analysis to be done on them.

Appendix III

BEHAVIOR VARIABLES: DEFINITIONS, UNITS, AND PRINCIPAL SOURCES

The following pages provide the necessary information for understanding the dyadic behavior variable data presented in Appendix IV.

The *Set Numbers* (1-11) were used to facilitate the administrative organization of the DON project's data collection. Initially there were seven variables per data set, but due to unavailability or unreliability of data, some variables were omitted prior to analysis. All variables are footnoted by set number. The footnotes are included at the end of each data set listing in Appendix IV, along with a table of means and standard deviations.

The *Variable Numbers* (1-53) are consistent throughout all of the analyses presented in this book. In Appendix IV, the variable numbers appear at the top of each column of data, and are also included in the mean and standard deviation tables.

Further information contained in this appendix includes: the names of the behavior variables; the abbreviation codes used to identify the variables in subsequent analyses; the definitions of the behaviors; the units for which the raw data are given in the tables of Appendix IV; and the primary source(s) for each variable.

SET 1 (VARIABLES 1-6)

1 Economic aid A→B (AID)

The total amount of economic aid that nation A has committed to nation B. Data for this variable includes the amount committed in grants or long-term loans, in cash or in kind, including with the latter category the provision of services as well as of commodities. The data are given in units of ten thousand dollars, US. Sources include the following: *A.I.D. Economic Data Book: Near East and South Asia;* Background Material, *Foreign Assistance Programs,* Committee on Foreign Affairs, "Economic and Military Assistance Programs: Comparative History of Authorizations and Appropriations for Budgeted Programs;" J. R. Carter, *The Net Cost of Soviet Foreign Aid,* Appendices A and B; Alexander Eckstein, *Communist China's Economic Growth and Foreign Trade, Implications for U.S. Policy,* Appendix E, pp. 306-307; *Fe-Ch'ing Nien-Pao;* Official Records of the United Nations, Economic and Social Council, 32nd Session Annexes Agenda, Item No. 5, Document E/3556, Table I, *International Economic Assistance to Underdeveloped Areas, 1958-1960;* OECD, *The Flow of Financial Resources to Less-Developed Countries, 1961-1965,* p. 46; Staff Memorandum on the Communist Economic Offensive, House Committee on Foreign Affairs, March 4, 1958; US Overseas Loans and Grants and Assistance from International Organizations, July 1, 1945-June 30, 1963; US Overseas Loans and Grants and Assistance from International Organizations, June 1, 1945-June 30, 1968; M. I. Goldman, *Soviet Foreign Aid;* Janos Horvath, "Economic Aid Flow from USSR," *Slavic Review* (1970), Table 2; *British Aid,* London: Ministry of Overseas Development, 1967; Harry Price, *The Marshall Plan and Its Meaning.*

2 Relative Economic Aid A→B (R-AID)

The total amount of economic aid nation A has committed to nation B, divided by A's total economic aid commitments. The definition of "economic aid" and sources are the same as variable 1. A datum times 10^{-2} constitutes a percentage. (See note 1 to Appendix I.)

3 Treaties A⟷B (TREATY)

The total number of bilateral and multilateral treaties and agreements signed between nation A and nation B, and filed with the Secretary-General of the United Nations. Accessions, supplementary agreements, and exchanges of notes constituting an agreement are counted along with formal treaties and agreements. *Statement of Treaties and International Agreements,* UN; *Treaties and Alliances of the World: An International Survey Covering Treaties in Force and Communities of States.*

4 Relative Treaties A⟷B (R-TRTY)

The total number of bilateral and multilateral treaties and agreements signed between nation A and nation B, divided by the total number of treaties and agreements nation A has with all other nations. A datum times 10^{-2} constitutes a percentage. Same sources as variable 3.

5 Official Visits A→B (VISITS)

The total number of publicly reported political visits of officials from nation A to nation B. Data include state visits, official visits, or personal visits (e.g., for reasons of health) by the chief of state, cabinet members, or personal representatives of the chief of state. Visits for the purpose of participation in an international conference of three or more countries in nation B are excluded. *New York Times Index.*

6 Co-participation in International Conferences A⟷B (CONFER)

The total number of international conferences of three or more nations attended by officials such as the chief of state, cabinet members, or personal representatives of the chief of state from both nation A and nation B. Regular or emergency meetings of the UN General Assembly or Security Council are excluded. Same source as variable 5.

SET 2 (VARIABLES 7-10)

7 Export of Books and Magazines A→B (BOOKS)

The total value of all printed matter exported from nation A to nation B. "Printed matter" is defined according to the UN's Standard International Trade Classification (SITC) no. 892. Data are given in units of thousands of dollars, US. *Commodity Trade Statistics,* UN; *Trade by Commodities: Statistics Bulletin for Foreign Trade; World Trade Annual,* UN.

8 Relative Export of Books and Magazines A→B (R-BOOK)

The total value of all printed matter exported from nation A to nation B, divided by nation A's total exports of printed matter to all other nations. The definition of "printed matter" and sources are the same as variable 7. A datum times 10^{-2} constitutes a percentage.

9 Book Translations, A of B (TRANSL)

The number of books translated by nation A from the major spoken language of nation B. When the language from which a work was translated differed from the original language of the work, the original language was used in all data counts. *Index Translationum,* UNESCO; *Statistical Yearbook,* UN.

10 Relative Book Translations, A of B (R-TRAN)

The number of books translated by nation A from the major spoken language of nation B, divided by the total number of all foreign books translated by nation A. A datum times 10^{-2} constitutes a percentage. Same sources as variable 9.

SET 3 (VARIABLES 11-15) [1]

11 Warning or Defensive Acts A→B (WARNDF)

A frequency count of acts that are distinctively military in nature, but are nonviolent. The acts are related to a developing conflict situation, thus excluding military acts purely contingent on changes in domestic policy or regime. This category would include any such acts as alerts, mobilizations, maneuvers, military movements, a show of strength, or a strengthening of forces.

12 Violent Actions A→B (VIOLAC)

This is a dichotomous variable with 0 meaning that the dyad experienced no form of violent conflict in the year of collection, and 1 indicating that the dyad experienced either a war, a continuous military action, a discrete military action, or a clash. A war is any continuous military hostility in which the number of soldiers of a nation involved equals or exceeds .02 percent of the population. Continuous military action refers to any military engagement involving violence that continues for more than 24 hours, but where the number of soldiers involved is less than the percentage that defines war. A discrete military action refers to any action completed within 24 hours, such as a firing upon another country's plane or ship, which is not part of a war, continuous military aciton, or clash; it is conflict that is essentially contained in a discrete, one-sided act of violence against another nation. A clash refers to any violent action between opposing forces involving ships, planes, or troops, which is not part of a war or continuous military action and is completed in less than 24 hours. From these definitions, war, continuous military actions, and clashes are symmetric; discrete military actions are asymmetric.

13 Military Actions A→B (MILACT)

This variable gives the total number of continuous military actions, discrete military actions, and clashes nation A directs toward nation B. Again the important discriminating criteria is that continuous military actions and clashes are symmetric, and discrete military actions are asymmetric. Therefore, it is possible to have a numerical coding on both variables 12 and 13 for dyad A→B, but no codings for B→A if only discrete military actions by nation A were recorded.

14 Duration of Violence A→B (DAYSVL)

Recorded in total days, this variables is a measure of the duration of a war, continuous military action, discrete military action or clash. Actions that were coded as lasting less than a day were counted as one day, and estimated figures were collected at the midpoint quantity.

15 Negative Behavior A→B (NEGBEH)

The frequency of any acts or actions reflecting strained, tense, unfriendly, or hostile feelings or relationship and directed by the actor nation toward the object nation.

SET 4 (VARIABLES 16-22)

16 Expulsion or Recall of Diplomats A→B (EXPREC)

The total number of expulsions of ambassador or other diplomatic officials from the object nation by the actor nation, or any recalling of officials of the actor nation for other than administrative reasons. This does not include any expulsion or recall involved in the severance of diplomatic relations.

17 Boycott or Embargo A→B (BCTEMB)

A boycott is any act that constitutes a refusal to deal (e.g., communicate, purchase, negotiate, etc.) with another country. Embargo is either a general or a particular restriction on commerce by nation A directed toward nation B.

18 Aid to Groups Subverting or Rebelling Against the Government of Object Nation A→B (AIDREB)

The total number of reports of nation A aiding groups that are considered by nation B as its enemy. Aid refers to the training of rebels or subversive nationals of another country, giving them economic or military assistance, furnishing them with a base, or direct military assistance to the violent enemies of the object nation.

19 Negative Communications A→B (NEGCOM)

The total number of publicly reported written or oral communications by officials of the actor nation directed at the object nation. These communications include such categories as accusation, representative protest, warning, threat, ultimatum, or denunciation.

20 Accusations A→B (ACCUSN)

The total number of publicly reported negative charges or allegations directed by the government of the actor nation at the object nation. An accusation is a negative communication that may originate without specific provocation.

21 Protests A→B (PROTST)

The total number of publicly reported official diplomatic communications or governmental statements by the executive leaders of the actor nation which have as their purpose the protest of actions of the object nation. A protest is viewed as a response by one nation to the actions, actual or implied, of another.

22 Unofficial Acts A→B (UNOFAC)

The total number of publicly reported acts of unofficial violence, be they planned or unplanned. This type of violence refers to any action or engagement in which the intent is to destroy or damage the property of the object nation, or to injure, wound, or kill any of its members. These actions are assumed to be the result of behavior by persons of the actor nation acting exclusive of official direction.

SET 5 (VARIABLES 23-26)

23 Attack on Embassy A→B (ATKEMB)

Any publicly reported public demonstration (or action) by the citizens of the actor nation directed at the object nation's foreign mission.

24 Nonviolent Behavior A→B (NVIOLB)

Any publicly reported negative acts that reflect strained, unfriendly, or hostile feelings by some of the citizens of the actor nation against the object nation or its policies, such as a protest rally, an antiforeign demonstration, or an unofficial boycott.

25 Weighted UN voting distance A→B (WD-UN)

The factor score distance between nation A and nation B on major rotated dimensions extracted from roll call voting statistics in the UN General Assembly Plenary Sessions. The distances on the issue dimensions are weighted by their percentage contribution to the total variance. The formula for computing the distance is:

$$d_{A \to B} = \left[\sum_{j=1}^{p} (S_{jA} - S_{jB})^2 W_j \right]^{1/2}$$

where W_j is the percentage of the total variance accounted for by the jth dimension, S_j is the jth issue dimension of the p issue dimensions extracted. A datum times 10^{-2} gives the actual factor score distance. Official Records, Plenary Sessions, United Nations General Assembly.

26 Unweighted UN Voting Distance A→B (UWD-UN)

Basically the same calculation as variable 25, except that issue dimensions are not weighted by their percentage of total variance accounted for. Distance are computed by the formula:

$$d_{A \to B} = \left[\sum_{j=1}^{p} (S_{jA} - S_{jB})^2 \right]^{1/2}$$

where $d_{A \to B}$ is the voting distance between nation A and nation B, S_j is the jth issue dimension of the p issue dimensions extracted. Same unit and source as variable 25.

SET 6 (VARIABLES 27-31)

27 Tourists A→B (TOURIS)

The total number of tourists from nation A traveling in nation B. Tourist is defined as any person traveling for a period of 24 hours or more in a country other than that in which he usually resides. Data are in units times one hundred. *International Travel Statistics,* International Union of Official Travel Organization; *Statistical Yearbook,* UN; *Statistical Abstract of Israel* (1967).

28 Relative Tourists A→B (R-TOUR)

The total number of tourists from nation A traveling in nation B (see variable 27), divided by the total number of tourists in nation B from all countries. A datum times 10^{-2} constitutes a percentage. Same sources as variable 27.

29 Tourists A→B as a Percentage of A's Population (T/POPU)

The total number of tourists from nation A traveling in nation B (see variable 27), divided by nation A's total population. A datum times 10^{-3} constitutes a percentage. Same sources as variable 27.

30 Emigrants A→B (EMIGRA)

The total number of people emigrating from nation A to nation B. Emigrants are defined as nationals leaving their country with the intention of staying abroad for a period exceeding one year. A datum times 10^{-1} gives the actual number of emigrants. *Anuario Estatistico Do Brasil–1971,* Instituto Brasileiro de Estatistica, Rio de Janeiro, vol. 32; *Concise Statistical Yearbook of Poland 1970,* Central Statistical Office of the Polish People's Republic, vol. 12; *Cuba 1968: Supplement to the Statistical Abstract of Latin America,* Latin American Center, p. 82; *Demographic Yearbook* 1952, 1957, 1959, 1970, UN; Department of Justice, Immigration and Naturalization Service, *Annual Report,* and releases, Table 6A; *Statistical Abstract of Israel,* Central Bureau of Statistics, 1967, no. 18; *Statistical Yearbook of the Netherlands,* 1971, the Hague, Staatsutgeverij, Netherlands Central Bureau of Statistics; D. R. Taft, and R. Robbins, *International Migrations: The Immigrant in the Modern World,* 1955; US Bureau of the Census, *Statistical Abstract of the United States 1965,* 86th ed.; *Concise Statistical Yearbook of Poland,* vol. 12 (1970).

31 Relative Emigrants A→B (R-EMIG)

The total number of people emigrating from nation A to nation B (see variable 30), divided by the total number of people emigrating from nation A to all other countries. A datum times 10^{-2} constitutes a percentage. Same sources as variable 30.

SET 7 (VARIABLES 32-37)

32 Emigrants A→B as a Percentage of A's Population (E/POPU)

The total number of people emigrating from nation A to nation B (see variable 30), divided by nation A's total population. A datum times 10^{-3} constitutes a percentage. Same sources as variable 30.

33 Students A→B (STUDNT)

The total number of students from nation A studying in nation B. Student is defined as any person who is receiving all or part of their academic training. *Basic Facts and Figures,* UNESCO; *Statistical Yearbook,* UN; *Study Abroad,* UNESCO.

34 Relative Students A→B (R-STUD)

The total number of students from nation A studying in nation B (see variable 33), divided by the total number of students in nation B from all countries. A datum times 10^{-2} constitutes a percentage. Same sources as variable 33.

35 Exports A→B (EXPORT)

The total value of goods (f.o.b.) exported from nation A to nation B. Goods passing through a country only for the purpose of transport are excluded. Data are given in units of ten thousand dollars, US. *Statistical Yearbook,* UN; *Yearbook of International Trade Statistics; Direction of International Trade,* UN; Eckstein's *Communist China's Economic Growth and Foreign Trade; Trade, Aid and Development,* Council on Foreign Relations.

36 Relative Exports A→B (R-EXPT)

The total value of goods (f.o.b.) exported from nation A to nation B (see variable 35), divided by the total value of all goods exported from nation A to all other countries. A datum times 10^{-2} constitutes a percentage. Same sources as variable 35.

37 Exports A→B as a Percentage of A's GNP (E/GNP)

The total value of goods (f.o.b.) exported from nation A to nation B (see variable 35), divided by nation A's GNP. A datum times 10^{-2} constitutes a percentage. Same sources as variable 35.

SET 8 (VARIABLES 38-43)

38 International Governmental Organization Comemberships A←→B (IGO)

The total number of international governmental organizations (IGO's) in which both nation A and nation B have common membership. J. J. Lador-Lederer, *International Non-governmental Organizations; Yearbook of International Organizations;* Moshe Y. Sachs, *Worldmark Encyclopedia of the Nations.*

39 Relative IGO Comemberships A→B (R-IGO)

The total number of IGO's in which both nation A and nation B have common membership (see variable 38), divided by nation A's total IGO membership. A datum times 10^{-2} constitutes a percentage. Same sources as variable 38.

40 International Nongovernmental Organization Comemberships A→B (NGO)

The total number of nongovernmental organizations in which both nation A and nation B have common membership. Same sources as variable 38.

41 Relative NGO Comemberships A→B (R-NGO)

The total number of NGO's in which both nation A and nation B have common membership (see variable 40), divided by nation A's total NGO membership. A datum times 10^{-2} constitutes a percentage. Same sources as variable 38.

42 Membership Ratio of IGO Comemberships A→B (N-IGO)

This variable is a measure of the interaction of dyads in the smaller more specialized IGO's. More concretely, this variable is a composite of the comemberships of the dyad A→B in intergovernmental organizations, divided by the total comemberships of the actor nation in all intergovernmental organizations with all other nations. The variable is calculated by taking the total membership (i.e., the total number of nations) of all the IGO's to which nation A and nation B are both members, and dividing by the total comembership of all the IGO's to which nation A belongs. A datum times 10^{-2} constitutes a ratio. Same sources as variable 38.

43 Membership Ratio of NGO Comemberships A⟷B (N-NGO)

The total membership (i.e., the total number of nations) of all the NGO's to which nation A and nation B are both members, divided by the total comembership of all the NGO's to which nation A belongs. A datum times 10^{-2} constitutes a ratio. Same sources as variable 38.

SET 9 (VARIABLES 44 AND 45)

44 Embassy or Legation A→B (EMBLEG)

This is a dichotomous measure of whether or not nation A has an embassy or legation in nation B. 1 = yes, and 0 = no. Embassy is defined as a diplomatic mission of the first class, headed by an Ambassador Extraordinary. The term refers to the entire mission and staff. Legation is a diplomatic mission headed by an Envoy Extraordinary (second class), or a charge'd'affaires (third class) in the diplomatic relations between small nations. *Diplomatic Yearbook,* UN.

45 Relative Diplomatic Representation A→B (R-EMB)

The total number of embassies or legations that nation A has in nation B, divided by the total number of embassies or legations that nation A has in all other countries. See variable 44 for definitions of embassy and legation. A datum times 10^{-2} constitutes a percentage. Same source as variable 44.

SET 10 (VARIABLES 46, 47 AND 48)

46 Time Since On Opposite Sides In A War A⟷B (WAROPP)

A rating scale measuring the length of time that has passes since the two nations have opposed one another in a war. For the purpose of data collection, hostilities recognized as legal states of war or involving over 50,000 troops were classified as war. In some instances hostilities of lesser magnitude which led to important legal or political results were also included. Coding for the rating scale is as follows:

0 = pre-1900, or never	8 = 1931-1940
1 = 1901-1910	16 = 1941-1950
2 = 1911-1920	32 = 1951-1960
4 = 1921-1930	64 = 1961 on

Quincy Wright, *A Study of War; The World Almanac; Worldmark Encyclopedia of the Nations.*

47 Time Since On Same Sides In A War A⟷B (WARSAM)

A rating scale measuring the length of time that has passed since the two nationa have been on the same side in a war. See variable 46 for qualifications, scale, and sources.

48 Lost Territory A→B (LOSTER)

A dichotomous rating scale of whether or not nation A lost, and not regained, any of its territory to nation B since 1900. Occupation of nation A's territory by nation B during wartime is disregarded. However, if the territorial change becomes permanent after the war has ended, then the loss is counted. Territorial changes for new nations are recorded only after the country has gained independence.

1 = territory was lost to nation B
0 = no territory lost to nation B

Encyclopaedia Britannica; Worldmark Encyclopedia of the Nations.

SET 11 (VARIABLES 49-53)

49 Political Dependency A→B (DEPEND)

A rating scale measuring the length of time that passed since nation A was once a colony, territory, or part of the homeland of nation B. See variable 46 for the scale rating. *Information Please Almanac; Stateman's Yearbook; The World Almanac.*

50 Political Independence of A and B (INDEP)

A dichotomous rating scale of whether or not nation A and nation B were *both* independent countries prior to 1946. A country was classified as independent if it enjoyed some measure of diplomatic recognition as well as effective control over its own foreign affairs and armed forces.

1 = both A and B independent prior to 1946
0 = either A or B, or both not independent

Russett's "National Political Units in the 20th Century," *American Political Science Review* 62, no. 3, pp. 932-951; *Worldmark Encyclopedia of the Nations.*

51 Common Bloc Membership A⟷B (COMBLC)

A rating scale showing whether nation A and nation B are on the same, different, or opposing political blocs. Bloc designations are Eastern, Western and neutral. Eastern and Western bloc membership is determined by military treaties or alliances with the Soviet Union or the United States, respectively. The neutral bloc is a residual category in which nations are catergorized if they have no military treaties or alliances with either of the aforememtioned bloc leaders.

2 = A and B are members of same bloc
1 = A and B are members of different blocs
0 = A and B are members of opposing blocs.

T. N. Dupuy, *The Almanac of World Military Power; Treaties and Alliances of the World.*

52 Bloc Position Index A⟷B (COMPOS)

The bloc position of nation A and nation B, measured as the absolute difference of their respective positions on the following scale:

1	2	4	6	7
USA	not USA, Western bloc member	neutral bloc member	not USSR, Eastern bloc member	USSR

T. N. Dupuy, *The Almanac of World Military Power; Treaties and Alliances of the World; Worldmark Encyclopedia of the Nations.*

53 Military Alliance A←→B (ALLIAN)

A dichotomous rating scale of whether or not nation A and nation B are linked by a military alliance or defense treaty.

1 = a mutual defense treaty exists
0 = no mutual defense treaty.

Same sources as variable 52.

NOTE

1. The data for the dyadic foreign conflict behavior variables (15-24) were originally collected from the *New York Times* and recorded on the DON project's foreign conflict behavior code sheets. Supplemental information was also taken from *Keesing's Contemporary Archives* and *Facts on File.* For a more extensive elaboration of the data collection methods and definitions, see R. J. Rummel's "A Foreign Conflict Behavior Code Sheet," *World Politics* 18 (January 1966).

Appendix IV

DYADIC BEHAVIOR DATA, 1950-1965: MEANS AND STANDARD DEVIATIONS

Following are the dyadic behavioral data, organized in the same format as the attribute data in Appendix II. The qualifications on the reliability of the attribute data given in Appendix II apply equally well to this set of data.

Some of the 1955 data presented here may not correspond to the 1955 data used for these variables in previously published analyses (Rummel, 1972, 1969). Since the completion of those analyses, the 1955 data have been supplemented and improved, and some data errors have been corrected. Consequently, the 1955 data given here constitute a new data set, although one highly correlated with that used in previous analyses.

DATA

This appendix presents the time-series dyadic behavioral data, and is preceded by a list of the selected dyads, a summary variable code, and a number listing for reference.

To illustrate the use of this appendix, the first line of data following the variable code and number listing represents those data on the first six variables for the dyad Brazil→Burma (BRA-BUR) in 1950, and the second line, the data on the same six variables for the same dyad for 1955. To facilitate location of particular items of data, the dyadic codes (1 for BRA-BUR) are printed on the far left column. This dyad code is followed by the set number (1S in this case). Variable numbers are included at the top of each page, and at the end of each data set the *mean* and *standard deviation* for each variable are also printed. Moreover, for each variable is given also the mean over the five years of data (S-P) and the mean over the five years of data with missing data estimated (S-P($\hat{Y}$)).

It is important to remember that different variables have different unit measures. The user of this data book must refer back to Appendix III or the mean and standard deviation tables for information on a particular variable's unit.

All data is footnoted by data set. Footnotes are given after the data. For all data sets the letter A indicates the item of data is an estimate, either as reported in the primary or secondary source, the result of extrapolation of data available from other time point, or as a result of common sense or practical knowledge.

Some data sets contain blank columns. These represent variables that were excluded from the final analysis as a result of insufficient or unreliable data. To carry out the projected analyses of these data, it was necessary to have data on a variable similarly defined for each of the five years.

Selected Dyadic Sample

I.D.	Code	Dyad
1.	BRA→BUR	Brazil→Burma
2.	BRA→CHN	Brazil→China
3.	BRA→CUB	Brazil→Cuba
4.	BRA→EGP	Brazil→Egypt
5.	BRA→IND	Brazil→India
6.	BRA→INS	Brazil→Indonesia
7.	BRA→ISR	Brazil→Israel
8.	BRA→JOR	Brazil→Jordan
9.	BRA→NTH	Brazil→Netherlands
10.	BRA→POL	Brazil→Poland
11.	BRA→USR	Brazil→USSR
12.	BRA→UNK	Brazil→United Kingdom
13.	BRA→USA	Brazil→USA
14.	BUR→BRA	Burma→Brazil
15.	BUR→CHN	Burma→China
16.	BUR→CUB	Burma→Cuba
17.	BUR→EGP	Burma→Egypt
18.	BUR→IND	Burma→India
19.	BUR→INS	Burma→Indonesia
20.	BUR→ISR	Burma→Israel
21.	BUR→JOR	Burma→Jordan
22.	BUR→NTH	Burma→Netherlands
23.	BUR→POL	Burma→Poland
24.	BUR→USR	Burma→USSR
25.	BUR→UK	Burma→United Kingdom
26.	BUR→USA	Burma→USA
27.	CHN→BRA	China→Brazil
28.	CHN→BUR	China→Burma
29.	CHN→CUB	China→Cuba
30.	CHN→EGP	China→Egypt
31.	CHN→IND	China→India
32.	CHN→INS	China→Indonesia
33.	CHN→ISR	China→Israel
34.	CHN→JOR	China→Jordan
35.	CHN→NTH	China→Netherlands
36.	CHN→POL	China→Poland
37.	CHN→USR	China→USSR
38.	CHN→UNK	China→United Kingdom
39.	CHN→USA	China→USA
40.	CUB→BRA	Cuba→Brazil
41.	CUB→BUR	Cuba→Burma
42.	CUB→CHN	Cuba→China
43.	CUB→EGP	Cuba→Egypt
44.	CUB→IND	Cuba→India

I.D.	Code	Dyad
44.	CUB→IND	Cuba→India
45.	CUB→INS	Cuba→Indonesia
46.	CUB→ISR	Cuba→Israel
47.	CUB→JOR	Cuba→Jordan
48.	CUB→NTH	Cuba→Netherlands
49.	CUB→POL	Cuba→Poland
50.	CUB→USR	Cuba→USSR
51.	CUB→UNK	Cuba→United Kingdom
52.	CUB→USA	Cuba→USA
53.	EGP→BRA	Egypt→Brazil
54.	EGP→BUR	Egypt→Burma
55.	EGP→CHN	Egypt→China
56.	EGP→CUB	Egypt→Cuba
57.	EGP→IND	Egypt→India
58.	EGP→INS	Egypt→Indonesia
59.	EGP→ISR	Egypt→Israel
60.	EGP→JOR	Egypt→Jordan
61.	EGP→NTH	Egypt→Netherlands
62.	EGP→POL	Egypt→Poland
63.	EGP→USR	Egypt→USSR
64.	EGP→UNK	Egypt→United Kingdom
65.	EGP→USA	Egypt→USA
66.	IND→BRA	India→Brazil
67.	IND→BUR	India→Burma
68.	IND→CHN	India→China
69.	IND→CUB	India→Cuba
70.	IND→EGP	India→Egypt
71.	IND→INS	India→Indonesia
72.	IND→ISR	India→Israel
73.	IND→JOR	India→Jordan
74.	IND→NTH	India→Netherlands
75.	IND→POL	India→Poland
76.	IND→USR	India→USSR
77.	IND→UNK	India→United Kingdom
78.	IND→USA	India→USA
79.	INS→BRA	Indonesia→Brazil
80.	INS→BUR	Indonesia→Burma
81.	INS→CHN	Indonesia→China
82.	INS→CUB	Indonesia→Cuba
83.	INS→EGP	Indonesia→Egypt
84.	INS→IND	Indonesia→India
85.	INS→ISR	Indonesia→Israel
86.	INS→JOR	Indonesia→Jordan
87.	INS→NTH	Indonesia→Netherlands

Selected Dyadic Sample (continued)

I.D.	Code	Dyad
88.	INS→POL	Indonesia→Poland
89.	INS→USR	Indonesia→USSR
90.	INS→UNK	Indonesia→United Kingdom
91.	INS→USA	Indonesia→USA
92.	ISR→BRA	Israel→Brazil
93.	ISR→BUR	Israel→Burma
94.	ISR→CHN	Israel→China
95.	ISR→CUB	Israel→Cuba
96.	ISR→EGP	Israel→Egypt
97.	ISR→IND	Israel→India
98.	ISR→INS	Israel→Indonesia
99.	ISR→JOR	Israel→Jordan
100.	ISR→NTH	Israel→Netherlands
101.	ISR→POL	Israel→Poland
102.	ISR→USR	Israel→USSR
103.	ISR→UNK	Israel→United Kingdom
104.	ISR→USA	Israel→USA
105.	JOR→BRA	Jordan→Brazil
106.	JOR→BUR	Jordan→Burma
107.	JOR→CHN	Jordan→China
108.	JOR→CUB	Jordan→Cuba
109.	JOR→EGP	Jordan→Egypt
110.	JOR→IND	Jordan→India
111.	JOR→INS	Jordan→Indonesia
112.	JOR→ISR	Jordan→Israel
113.	JOR→NTH	Jordan→Netherlands
114.	JOR→POL	Jordan→Poland
115.	JOR→USR	Jordan→USSR
116.	JOR→UNK	Jordan→United Kingdom
117.	JOR→USA	Jordan→USA
118.	NTH→BRA	Netherlands→Brazil
119.	NTH→BUR	Netherlands→Burma
120.	NTH→CHN	Netherlands→China
121.	NTH→CUB	Netherlands→Cuba
122.	NTH→EGP	Netherlands→Egypt
123.	NTH→IND	Netherlands→India
124.	NTH→INS	Netherlands→Indonesia
125.	NTH→ISR	Netherlands→Israll
126.	NTH→JOR	Netherlands→Jordan
127.	NTH→POL	Netherlands→Poland
128.	NTH→USR	Netherlands→USSR
129.	NTH→UNK	Netherlands→United Kingdom
130.	NTH→USA	Netherlands→USA
131.	POL→BRA	Poland→Brazil
132.	POL→BUR	Poland→Burma
133.	POL→CHN	Poland→China
134.	POL→CUB	Poland→Cuba
135.	POL→EGP	Poland→Egypt
136.	POL→IND	Poland→India
137.	POL→INS	Poland→Indonesia
138.	POL→ISR	Poland→Israel
139.	POL→JOR	Poland→Jordan
140.	POL→NTH	Poland→Netherlands
141.	POL→USR	Poland→USSR
142.	POL→UNK	Poland→United Kingdom
143.	POL→USA	Poland→USA
144.	USR→BRA	USSR→Brazil
145.	USR→BUR	USSR→Burma
146.	USR→CHN	USSR→China
147.	USR→CUB	USSR→Cuba
148.	USR→EGP	USSR→Egypt
149.	USR→IND	USSR→India
150.	USR→INS	USSR→Indonesia
151.	USR→ISR	USSR→Israel
152.	USR→JOR	USSR→Jordan
153.	USR→NTH	USSR→Netherlands
154.	USR→POL	USSR→Poland
155.	USR→UNK	USSR→United Kingdom
156.	USR→USA	USSR→USA
157.	UNK→BRA	United Kingdom→Brazil
158.	UNK→BUR	United Kingdom→Burma
159.	UNK→CHN	United Kingdom→China
160.	UNK→CUB	United Kingdom→Cuba
161.	UNK→EGP	United Kingdom→Egypt
162.	UNK→IND	United Kingdom→India
163.	UNK→INS	United Kingdom→Indones
164.	UNK→ISR	United Kingdom→Israel
165.	UNK→JOR	United Kingdom→Jordan
166.	UNK→NTH	United Kingdom→Netherl
167.	UNK→POL	United Kingdom→Poland
168.	UNK→USR	United Kingdom→USSR
169.	UNK→USA	United Kingdom→USA
170.	USA→BRA	USA→Brazil
171.	USA→BUR	USA→Burma
172.	USA→CHN	USA→China
173.	USA→CUB	USA→Cuba
174.	USA→EGP	USA→Egypt
175.	USA→IND	USA→India
176.	USA→INS	USA→Indonesia
177.	USA→ISR	USA→Israel
178.	USA→JOR	USA→Jordan
179.	USA→NTH	USA→Netherlands
180.	USA→POL	USA→Poland
181.	USA→USR	USA→USSR
182.	USA→UNK	USA→United Kingdom

List of Behavior Variables, 1950

Set	Variables						
1	1 AID	2 R-AID	3 TREATY	4 R-TREATY	5 VISITS	6 CONFER	
2			BOOKS	8 R-BOOK	9 TRANSL	10 R-TRAN	
3	11 WARNDF		12 VIOLAC	13 MILACT	14 DAYSVL	15 NEGBEH	
4	16 EXPREC	17 BCTEMB	18 AIDREB	19 NEGCOM	20 ACCUSN	21 PROTST	22 UNOFAC
5	23 ATKEMB	24 NVIOLB	25 WD-UN	26 UWD-UN			
6			27 TOURIS	28 R-TOUR	29 T/POPU	30 EMIGRA	31 R-EMIG
7	32 E/POPU	33 STUDNT	34 R-STUD	35 EXPORT	36 R-EXPT	37 E/GNP	
8	38 IGO	39 R-IGO	40 NGO	41 R-NGO	42 N-IGO	43 N-NGO	
9		44 EMBLEG	45 R-EMB				
10					46 WAROPP	47 WARSAM	48 LOSTER
11	49 DEPEND	50 INDEP	51 COMBLC	52 COMPOS	53 ALLIAN		

	1	2	3	4	5	6	
1 1S	0A	0A	0	0	0	0	1950
1 1S	0A	0A	0	0	0	0	1955
1 1S	0A	0A	0	0	0	0	1960
1 1S	0	0	1	556	0	0	1963
1 1S	0A	0A	0	0	0	1	1965
2 1S	0A	0A	0	0	0	0	1950
2 1S	0A	0A	0	0	0	0	1955
2 1S	0A	0A	0	0	0	0	1960
2 1S	0	0	0	0	0	0	1963
2 1S	0A	0A	0	0	0	0	1965
3 1S	0A	0A	0	0	0	1	1950
3 1S	0A	0A	0	0	0	0	1955
3 1S	0A	0A	0	0	0	0	1960
3 1S	0	0	0	0	0	1	1963
3 1S	0A	0A	0	0	0	3	1965
4 1S	0A	0A	0	0	0	0	1950
4 1S	0A	0A	0	0	0	0	1955
4 1S	0A	0A	0	0	0	0	1960
4 1S	0	0	3	1667	0	0	1963
4 1S	0A	0A	1	833	0	1	1965
5 1S	0A	0A	0	0	0	0	1950
5 1S	0A	0A	0	0	0	1	1955
5 1S	0A	0A	0	0	0	0	1960
5 1S	0	0	1	556	0	0	1963
5 1S	0A	0A	1	833	0	2	1965
6 1S	0A	0A	0	0	0	0	1950
6 1S	0A	0A	0	0	0	0	1955
6 1S	0A	0A	0	0	0	0	1960
6 1S	0	0	1	556	0	0	1963
6 1S	0A	0A	0	0	0	0	1965
7 1S	0A	0A	0	0	0	0	1950
7 1S	0A	0A	0	0	0	0	1955
7 1S	0A	0A	0	0	0	0	1960
7 1S	0	0	1	556	0	0	1963
7 1S	0A	0A	1	833	0	1	1965
8 1S	0A	0A	0	0	0	0	1950
8 1S	0A	0A	0	0	0	0	1955
8 1S	0A	0A	0	0	0	0	1960
8 1S	0	0	1	556	0	0	1963
8 1S	0A	0A	0	0	0	1	1965
9 1S	0A	0A	2	650	0	0	1950
9 1S	0A	0A	0	0	0	0	1955
9 1S	0A	0A	0	0	0	0	1960
9 1S	0	0	3	1667	0	0	1963
9 1S	0A	0A	1	833	0	1	1965
10 1S	0A	0A	0	0	0	0	1950
10 1S	0A	0A	0	0	0	0	1955
10 1S	0A	0A	0	0	0	0	1960
10 1S	0	0	1	556	0	0	1963
10 1S	0A	0A	1	833	0	2	1965
11 1S	0A	0A	1	320	0	0	1950
11 1S	0A	0A	0	0	0	0	1955
11 1S	0A	0A	0	0	0	0	1960
11 1S	0	0	1	556	0	0	1963
11 1S	0A	0A	1	833	0	3	1965
12 1S	0A	0A	1	320	0	0	1950
12 1S	0A	0A	2	1050	0	1	1955
12 1S	0A	0A	0	0	0	0	1960
12 1S	0	0	2	1111	0	0	1963

		1	2	3	4	5	6	
12	1S	0A	0A	1	833	0	2	1965
13	1S	0A	0A	1	320	0	1	1950
13	1S	0A	0A	14	7370	0	2	1955
13	1S	0A	0A	9	7500	0	0	1960
13	1S	0	0	7	3889	0	1	1963
13	1S	0A	0A	5	4167	0	7	1965
14	1S	0A	0A	0	0	0	0	1950
14	1S	0A	0A	0	0	0	0	1955
14	1S	0A	0A	0	0	0	0	1960
14	1S	0	0	1	1000	0	0	1963
14	1S	0A	0A	0	0	0	1	1965
15	1S	0A	0A	0	0	0	0	1950
15	1S	0A	0A	7A	7000A	0	0	1955
15	1S	0A	0A	8A	4000A	2	0	1960
15	1S	0	0	5A	5000	0	0	1963
15	1S	0A	0A	3A	2500A	1	0	1965
16	1S	0A	0A	0	0	0	0	1950
16	1S	0A	0A	1	1000	0	0	1955
16	1S	0A	0A	1	500A	0	0	1960
16	1S	0	0	0	0	0	0	1963
16	1S	0A	0A	0	0	0	1	1965
17	1S	0A	0A	0	0	0	0	1950
17	1S	0A	0A	2	2000	0	0	1955
17	1S	0A	0A	1	500A	0	0	1960
17	1S	0	0	1	1000	0	0	1963
17	1S	0A	0A	0	0	0	1	1965
18	1S	0A	0A	1	1000	0	0	1950
18	1S	0A	0A	1	1000	1	1	1955
18	1S	0A	0A	1	500A	2	0	1960
18	1S	0A	0A	1	1000	0	0	1963
18	1S	0A	0A	0	0	1	3	1965
19	1S	0A	0A	0	0	0	0	1950
19	1S	0A	0A	0	0	0	1	1955
19	1S	0A	0A	0	0	0	0	1960
19	1S	0	0	1	1000	0	0	1963
19	1S	0A	0A	0	0	0	2	1965
20	1S	0A	0A	0	0	0	0	1950
20	1S	0A	0A	0	0	1	0	1955
20	1S	0A	0A	1	500A	0	0	1960
20	1S	0	0	1	1000	0	0	1963
20	1S	0A	0A	0	0	0	1	1965
21	1S	0A	0A	0	0	0	0	1950
21	1S	0A	0A	0	0	0	0	1955
21	1S	0A	0A	1	500A	0	0	1960
21	1S	0	0	1	1000	0	0	1963
21	1S	0A	0A	0	0	0	1	1965
22	1S	0A	0A	0	0	0	0	1950
22	1S	0A	0A	1	1000	0	0	1955
22	1S	0A	0A	1	500A	0	0	1960
22	1S	0	0	1	1000	0	0	1963
22	1S	0A	0A	0	0	0	1	1965
23	1S	0A	0A	0	0	0	0	1950
23	1S	0A	0A	2	2000	0	0	1955
23	1S	0A	0A	1	500A	0	0	1960
23	1S	0	0	1	1000	0	0	1963
23	1S	0A	0A	0	0	0	1	1965
24	1S	0A	0A	0	0	0	0	1950
24	1S	0A	0A	0	0	1	0	1955
24	1S	0A	0A	1	500A	0	0	1960

		1	2	3	4	5	6	
24	1S	0	0	1	1000	0	0	1963
24	1S	0A	0A	0	0	0	3	1965
25	1S	0A	0A	2	2000	0	0	1950
25	1S	0A	0A	1	1000	1	1	1955
25	1S	0A	0A	1	500A	0	0	1960
25	1S	0	0	3	3000	0	0	1963
25	1S	0A	0A	0	0	0	3	1965
26	1S	0	0	2	2000	0	0	1950
26	1S	0A	0A	1	1000	1	1	1955
26	1S	0A	0A	2	1000	0	0	1960
26	1S	0	0	1	1000	0	0	1963
26	1S	0A	0A	0	0	0	3	1965
27	1S	0	0	0	0	0	0	1950
27	1S	0	0	0	0	0	0	1955
27	1S	0	0	0	0	0	0	1960
27	1S	0	0	0	0	0	0	1963
27	1S	0	0	0	0	0	0	1965
28	1S	0	0	0	0	0	0	1950
28	1S	0	0	7A	588A	0	0	1955
28	1S	0	0	8A	571A	3A	0	1960
28	1S	0	0	5A	352A	2A	0	1963
28	1S	0	0	3A	120A	3	0	1965
29	1S	0	0	0	0	0	0	1950
29	1S	0	0	0	0	0	0	1955
29	1S	600	3109	4A	286A	1A	0	1960
29	1S	0	0	8A	563A	1A	0	1963
29	1S	0	0	10A	400A	1A	0	1965
30	1S	0	0	0	0	0	0	1950
30	1S	0	0	8A	672A	0	0	1955
30	1S	0	0	2A	143A	1A	0	1960
30	1S	0	0	3A	211A	1	2	1963
30	1S	975	3900	6A	240A	2	0	1965
31	1S	0	0	0	0	0	0	1950
31	1S	0	0	7A	588A	1A	0	1955
31	1S	0	0	1A	71A	1	0	1960
31	1S	0	0	0	0	0	2	1963
31	1S	0	0	0	0	0	0	1965
32	1S	0	0	0	0	0	0	1950
32	1S	0	0	5A	420A	1A	0	1955
32	1S	0	0	2A	143A	0	0	1960
32	1S	0	0	3A	211A	2A	2	1963
32	1S	500	2000	20A	800A	3A	1	1965
33	1S	0	0	0	0	0	0	1950
33	1S	0	0	0	0	0	0	1955
33	1S	0	0	0	0	0	0	1960
33	1S	0	0	0	0	0	0	1963
33	1S	0	0	0	0	0	0	1965
34	1S	0	0	0	0	0	0	1950
34	1S	0	0	0	0	0	0	1955
34	1S	0	0	0	0	0	0	1960
34	1S	0	0	0	0	0	0	1963
34	1S	0	0	0	0	0	0	1965
35	1S	0	0	0	0	0	0	1950
35	1S	0	0	0	0	0	0	1955
35	1S	0	0	0	0	0	0	1960
35	1S	0	0	0	0	0	0	1963
35	1S	0	0	0	0	0	0	1965
36	1S	0	0	2A	645A	0	1	1950
36	1S	0	0	5A	420A	2A	0	1955

		1	2	3	4	5	6	
36	1S	0	0	7A	500A	1A	1	1960
36	1S	0	0	4A	282A	0	0	1963
36	1S	0	0	10A	400A	0	0	1965
37	1S	0	0	22A	7094A	2	1	1950
37	1S	0	0	22A	1849A	0	0	1955
37	1S	0	0	12A	852A	2	1	1960
37	1S	0	0	7A	493A	3	2	1963
37	1S	0	0	10A	400A	0	0	1965
38	1S	0	0	0	0	0	0	1950
38	1S	0	0	0	0	0	0	1955
38	1S	0	0	0	0	0	0	1960
38	1S	0	0	0	0	0	0	1963
38	1S	0	0	0	0	0	0	1965
39	1S	0	0	0	0	0	0	1950
39	1S	0	0	1A	84A	0	0	1955
39	1S	0	0	0	0	0	0	1960
39	1S	0	0	0	0	0	1	1963
39	1S	0	0	0	0	0	0	1965
40	1S	0A	0A	0	0	0	1	1950
40	1S	0A	0A	0	0	0	0	1955
40	1S	0A	0A	0	0	0	0	1960
40	1S	0	0	0	0	0	1	1963
40	1S	0A	0A	0	0	0	3	1965
41	1S	0A	0A	0	0	0	0	1950
41	1S	0A	0A	1	1430	0	0	1955
41	1S	0A	0A	1	769	0	0	1960
41	1S	0	0	0	0	0	0	1963
41	1S	0A	0A	0	0	0	1	1965
42	1S	0A	0A	0	0	0	0	1950
42	1S	0A	0A	0	0	0	0	1955
42	1S	0A	0A	4A	3000A	0	0	1960
42	1S	0	0	8	6667	0	0	1963
42	1S	0A	0A	4A	4000A	1	0	1965
43	1S	0A	0A	0	0	0	0	1950
43	1S	0A	0A	0	0	0	0	1955
43	1S	0A	0A	1	769	0	0	1960
43	1S	0	0	0	0	0	0	1963
43	1S	0A	0A	1	1000	1	1	1965
44	1S	0A	0A	1	340	0	0	1950
44	1S	0A	0A	1	1430	0	0	1955
44	1S	0A	0A	1	769	0	0	1960
44	1S	0	0	0	0	0	0	1963
44	1S	0A	0A	1	1000	0	2	1965
45	1S	0A	0A	2	690	0	0	1950
45	1S	0A	0A	0	0	0	0	1955
45	1S	0A	0A	0	0	0	0	1960
45	1S	0	0	0	0	0	0	1963
45	1S	0A	0A	1	1000	0	0	1965
46	1S	0A	0A	0	0	0	0	1950
46	1S	0A	0A	0	0	0	0	1955
46	1S	0A	0A	1	769	0	0	1960
46	1S	0	0	0	0	0	0	1963
46	1S	0A	0A	0	0	0	1	1965
47	1S	0A	0A	0	0	0	0	1950
47	1S	0A	0A	0	0	0	0	1955
47	1S	0A	0A	1	769	0	0	1960
47	1S	0	0	0	0	0	0	1963
47	1S	0A	0A	0	0	0	1	1965
48	1S	0A	0A	1	340	0	0	1950

		1	2	3	4	5	6	
48	1S	0A	0A	1	1430	0	0	1955
48	1S	0A	0A	1	769	0	0	1960
48	1S	0	0	0	0	0	0	1963
48	1S	0A	0A	0	0	0	1	1965
49	1S	0A	0A	0	0	0	0	1950
49	1S	0A	0A	0	0	0	0	1955
49	1S	0A	0A	1	769	0	0	1960
49	1S	0	0	0	0	0	0	1963
49	1S	0A	0A	0	0	0	2	1965
50	1S	0A	0A	0	0	0	0	1950
50	1S	0A	0A	0	0	0	0	1955
50	1S	0A	0A	4	3077	1	0	1960
50	1S	0	0	0	0	1	0	1963
50	1S	0A	0A	0	0	3	2	1965
51	1S	0A	0A	1	340	0	0	1950
51	1S	0A	0A	2	2860	0	0	1955
51	1S	0A	0A	1	769	0	0	1960
51	1S	0	0	0	0	0	0	1963
51	1S	0A	0A	2	2000	0	2	1965
52	1S	0A	0A	3	1030	0	1	1950
52	1S	0A	0A	6	8570	0	0	1955
52	1S	0A	0A	0	0	0	0	1960
52	1S	0	0	0	0	0	1	1963
52	1S	0A	0A	2	2000	0	2	1965
53	1S	0A	0A	0	0	0	0	1950
53	1S	0A	0A	0	0	0	0	1955
53	1S	0A	0A	0	0	0	0	1960
53	1S	0	0	3	1200	0	0	1963
53	1S	0A	0A	1	714	0	1	1965
54	1S	0A	0A	0	0	0	0	1950
54	1S	0A	0A	2	800	0	0	1955
54	1S	0A	0A	1	454	0	0	1960
54	1S	0	0	1	400	0	0	1963
54	1S	0A	0A	0	0	0	1	1965
55	1S	0A	0A	0	0	0	0	1950
55	1S	0A	0A	8A	3200A	0	0	1955
55	1S	0A	0A	2A	908A	1	0	1960
55	1S	0	0	3	1200	1	2	1963
55	1S	0A	0A	2A	1429A	0	0	1965
56	1S	0A	0A	0	0	0	0	1950
56	1S	0A	0A	0	0	0	0	1955
56	1S			1	454	0	0	1960
56	1S	0A	0A	0	0	0	0	1963
56	1S	0A	0A	1	714	0	1	1965
57	1S	0A	0A	1	200	0	0	1950
57	1S	0A	0A	3	1200	0	0	1955
57	1S	0A	0A	3	1364	1	0	1960
57	1S	0	0	1	400	0	2	1963
57	1S	0A	0A	1	714	0	1	1965
58	1S	0A	0A	0	0	0	0	1950
58	1S	0A	0A	1	400	0	0	1955
58	1S	0A	0A	0	0	0	0	1960
58	1S	0	0	1	400	0	2	1963
58	1S			2	1429	0	0	1965
59	1S	0A	0A	3	610	0	0	1950
59	1S	0A	0A	0	0	0	0	1955
59	1S	0A	0A	2	909	0	0	1960
59	1S	0	0	1	400	0	0	1963
59	1S	0A	0A	1	714	0	1	1965

		1	2	3	4	5	6	
60	1S	0A	0A	0	0	0	0	1950
60	1S	0A	0A	0	0	0	0	1955
60	1S	0A	0A	2	909	0	1	1960
60	1S	0	0	2	800	0	1	1963
60	1S	0A	0A	1	714	0	2	1965
61	1S	0A	0A	2	410	0	0	1950
61	1S	0A	0A	3	1200	0	0	1955
61	1S	0A	0A	3	1364	0	0	1960
61	1S	0	0	2	800	0	0	1963
61	1S	0A	0A	1	714	0	1	1965
62	1S	0A	0A	1	200	0	0	1950
62	1S	0A	0A	7	2400	0	0	1955
62	1S	0A	0A	1	454	0	0	1960
62	1S	0	0	1	400	0	0	1963
62	1S	0A	0A	1	714	0	1	1965
63	1S	0A	0A	0	0	0	0	1950
63	1S	0A	0A	0	0	0	0	1955
63	1S	0A	0A	2	909	0	0	1960
63	1S	0	0	1	400	0	2	1963
63	1S	0A	0A	1	714	1	1	1965
64	1S	0A	0A	4	820	0	0	1950
64	1S	0A	0A	5	2000	0	0	1955
64	1S	0A	0A	2	909	0	1	1960
64	1S	0	0	2	800	0	0	1963
64	1S	0A	0A	3	2143	0	1	1965
65	1S	0A	0A	1	200	0	0	1950
65	1S	0A	0A	4	1600	0	1	1955
65	1S	0A	0A	7	3182	0	1	1960
65	1S	0	0	5	2000	3	0	1963
65	1S	0A	0A	3	2143	0	1	1965
66	1S	0A	0A	0	0	0	0	1950
66	1S	0A	0A	0	0	0	1	1955
66	1S	0A	0A	0	0	0	0	1960
66	1S	0	0	1	357	0	0	1963
66	1S	0A	0A	1	454	0	2	1965
67	1S	0A	0A	1	140	0	0	1950
67	1S	0A	0A	1	670	0	1	1955
67	1S	0A	0A	1	454	0	0	1960
67	1S	0A	0A	1	357	0	0	1963
67	1S	0A	0A	0	0	1	3	1965
68	1S	0A	0A	0	0	0	0	1950
68	1S	0A	0A	7A	4670A	0	0	1955
68	1S	0A	0A	1A	454A	0	0	1960
68	1S	0	0	0	0	0	3	1963
68	1S	0A	0A	0	0	0	0	1965
69	1S	0A	0A	1	140	0	0	1950
69	1S	0A	0A	1	670	0	0	1955
69	1S	0A	0A	1	454	0	0	1960
69	1S	0	0	0	0	0	0	1963
69	1S	0A	0A	1	454	0	2	1965
70	1S	0A	0A	1	140	0	0	1950
70	1S	0A	0A	3	2000	4	0	1955
70	1S	0A	0A	3	1364	0	1	1960
70	1S	0	0	1	357	1	2	1963
70	1S	0A	0A	1	454	0	1	1965
71	1S	0A	0A	1	140	0	1	1950
71	1S	0A	0A	1	670	0	3	1955
71	1S	0A	0A	2	909	0	0	1960
71	1S	0	0	1	357	0	2	1963
71	1S	0A	0A	1	454	0	2	1965
72	1S	0A	0A	2	280	0	0	1950
72	1S	0A	0A	0	0	0	0	1955
72	1S	0A	0A	3	1364	0	0	1960
72	1S	0	0	1	357	0	0	1963
72	1S	0A	0A	0	0	0	1	1965

		1	2	3	4	5	6	
73	1S	0A	0A	0	0	0	0	1950
73	1S	0A	0A	0	0	0	0	1955
73	1S	0A	0A	2	909	0	0	1960
73	1S	0	0	1	357	0	0	1963
73	1S	0A	0A	0	0	0	1	1965
74	1S	0A	0A	2	280	0	0	1950
74	1S	0A	0A	4	2670	0	0	1955
74	1S	0A	0A	4	1818	0	0	1960
74	1S	0	0	1	357	0	0	1963
74	1S	0A	0A	2	909	0	1	1965
75	1S	0A	0A	1	140	0	0	1950
75	1S	0A	0A	0	0	1	0	1955
75	1S	0A	0A	1	454	0	0	1960
75	1S	0	0	1	357	0	0	1963
75	1S	0A	0A	1	454	0	2	1965
76	1S	0A	0A	0	0	0	0	1950
76	1S	0A	0A	0	0	1	1	1955
76	1S	0A	0A	2	909	0	1	1960
76	1S	0	0	1	357	0	2	1963
76	1S	0A	0A	1	454	1	4	1965
77	1S	0A	0A	4	580	0	1	1950
77	1S	0A	0A	7	4670	1	3	1955
77	1S	0A	0A	4	1818	0	0	1960
77	1S	0	0	3	1071	1	0	1963
77	1S	0A	0A	3	1364	0	6	1965
78	1S	0A	0A	4	580	0	0	1950
78	1S	0A	0A	2	1330	0	3	1955
78	1S	0A	0A	10	4545	0	0	1960
78	1S	0	0	12A	4286	4	1	1963
78	1S	0A	0A	6	2727	0	4	1965
79	1S	0A	0A	0	0	0	0	1950
79	1S	0A	0A	0	0	0	0	1955
79	1S	0A	0A	0	0	0	0	1960
79	1S	0	0	1	909	0	0	1963
79	1S	0A	0A	0	0	0	0	1965
80	1S	0A	0A	0	0	0	0	1950
80	1S	0A	0A	0	0	0	1	1955
80	1S	0A	0A	0	0	0	0	1960
80	1S	0A	0A	1	909	0	0	1963
80	1S	0A	0A	0	0	0	2	1965
81	1S	0A	0A	0	0	0	0	1950
81	1S	0A	0A	3A	1000A	1	0	1955
81	1S	0A	0A	2A	1333A	0	0	1960
81	1S	0A	0A	3	2727	1	2	1963
81	1S	0A	0A	14A	7000A	2	1	1965
82	1S	0A	0A	2	530	0	0	1950
82	1S	0A	0A	0	0	0	0	1955
82	1S	0A	0A	0	0	1	0	1960
82	1S	0	0	0	0	1	0	1963
82	1S	0A	0A	1	500A	0	0	1965
83	1S	0A	0A	0	0	0	0	1950
83	1S	0A	0A	1	330A	1	0	1955
83	1S	0A	0A	0	0	1	0	1960
83	1S	0	0	1	909	0	2	1963
83	1S	0A	0A	0	0	0	0	1965
84	1S	0A	0A	1	260	0	1	1950
84	1S	0A	0A	1	330A	0	3	1955
84	1S	0A	0A	2	1333	1	0	1960
84	1S	0	0	1	909	0	2	1963
84	1S	0A	0A	1	500A	0	2	1965

		1	2	3	4	5	6	
85	1S	0A	0A	0	0	0	0	1950
85	1S	0A	0A	0	0	0	0	1955
85	1S	0A	0A	1	667	0	0	1960
85	1S	0	0	1A	909	0	0	1963
85	1S	0A	0A	0	0	0	0	1965
86	1S	0A	0A	1	260	0	0	1950
86	1S	0A	0A	0	0	0	0	1955
86	1S	0A	0A	0	0	0	0	1960
86	1S	0	0	1	909	0	0	1963
86	1S	0A	0A	1	500A	0	0	1965
87	1S	0A	0A	2	530	0	0	1950
87	1S	0A	0A	1	330A	0	0	1955
87	1S	0A	0A	2	1333	0	0	1960
87	1S	0	0	1	909	0	0	1963
87	1S	0A	0A	0	0	0	0	1965
88	1S	0A	0A	0	0	0	0	1950
88	1S	0A	0A	0	0	0	0	1955
88	1S	0A	0A	0	0	0	0	1960
88	1S	0	0	1A	909	0	0	1963
88	1S	0A	0A	0	0	1	0	1965
89	1S	0A	0A	0	0	0	0	1950
89	1S	0A	0A	0	0	0	1	1955
89	1S	0A	0A	2	1333	0	0	1960
89	1S	0	0	1A	909	1	2	1963
89	1S	0A	0A	0	0	1	2	1965
90	1S	0A	0A	1	260	0	0	1950
90	1S	0A	0A	1	330A	0	2	1955
90	1S	0A	0A	3	2000	0	0	1960
90	1S	0	0	1A	909	0	0	1963
90	1S	0A	0A	1	500A	0	2	1965
91	1S	0A	0A	5	1320	0	0	1950
91	1S	0A	0A	0	0	0	2	1955
91	1S	0A	0A	8	5333	1	0	1960
91	1S	0	0	3A	2727	1	0	1963
91	1S	0A	0A	1	500A	0	2	1965
92	1S	0A	0A	0	0	0	0	1950
92	1S	0A	0A	0	0	0	0	1955
92	1S	0A	0A	0	0	0	0	1960
92	1S	0	0	1	435	0	0	1963
92	1S	0A	0A	1	476	0	1	1965
93	1S	0A	0A	0	0	0	0	1950
93	1S	0A	0A	0	0	0	0	1955
93	1S	0A	0A	1	588	0	0	1960
93	1S	0A	0A	1	435	0	0	1963
93	1S	0A	0A	0	0	0	1	1965
94	1S	0A	0A	0	0	0	0	1950
94	1S	0A	0A	0	0	0	0	1955
94	1S	0A	0A	0	0	0	0	1960
94	1S	0	0	0	0	0	0	1963
94	1S	0A	0A	0	0	0	0	1965
95	1S	0A	0A	0	0	0	0	1950
95	1S	0A	0A	0	0	0	0	1955
95	1S	0A	0A	1	588	0	0	1960
95	1S	0	0	0	0	0	0	1963
95	1S	0A	0A	0	0	0	1	1965
96	1S	0A	0A	3	560	0	0	1950
96	1S	0A	0A	0	0	0	0	1955
96	1S	0A	0A	2	1176	0	0	1960
96	1S	0	0	1	435	0	0	1963
96	1S	0A	0A	1	476	0	1	1965

		1	2	3	4	5	6	
97	1S	0A	0A	2	370	0	0	1950
97	1S	0A	0A	0	0	0	0	1955
97	1S	0A	0A	3	1765	0	0	1960
97	1S	0A	0A	1	435	0	0	1963
97	1S	0A	0A	0	0	0	1	1965
98	1S	0A	0A	0	0	0	0	1950
98	1S	0A	0A	0	0	0	0	1955
98	1S	0A	0A	1	588	0	0	1960
98	1S	0	0	1A	435	0	0	1963
98	1S	0A	0A	0	0	0	0	1965
99	1S	0A	0A	0	0	0	0	1950
99	1S	0A	0A	0	0	0	0	1955
99	1S	0A	0A	2	1176	0	0	1960
99	1S	0	0	1A	435	0	0	1963
99	1S	0A	0A	0	0	0	1	1965
100	1S	0A	0A	0	0	0	0	1950
100	1S	0A	0A	3	910	0	0	1955
100	1S	0A	0A	3	1765	0	0	1960
100	1S	0	0	3	1304	0	0	1963
100	1S	0A	0A	1	476	0	1	1965
101	1S	0A	0A	0	0	0	0	1950
101	1S	0A	0A	1	300	0	0	1955
101	1S	0A	0A	1	588	0	0	1960
101	1S	0	0	1A	435	0	0	1963
101	1S	0A	0A	1	476	0	1	1965
102	1S	0A	0A	0	0	0	0	1950
102	1S	0A	0A	0	0	0	0	1955
102	1S	0A	0A	1	588	0	0	1960
102	1S	0	0	1A	435	0	0	1963
102	1S	0A	0A	1	476	0	1	1965
103	1S	0A	0A	5	930	0	0	1950
103	1S	0A	0A	0	0	0	0	1955
103	1S	0A	0A	5	2941	0	0	1960
103	1S	0	0	2A	870	0	0	1963
103	1S	0A	0A	2	952	1	1	1965
104	1S	0A	0A	4	740	0	0	1950
104	1S	0A	0A	10	3030	0	0	1955
104	1S	0A	0A	6	3529	1	1	1960
104	1S	0	0	7A	3043	1	0	1963
104	1S	0A	0A	10	4762	0	1	1965
105	1S	0A	0A	1	910	0	0	1950
105	1S	0A	0A	0	0	0	0	1955
105	1S	0A	0A	0	0	0	0	1960
105	1S	0	0	1	1429	0	0	1963
105	1S	0A	0A	0	0	0	1	1965
106	1S	0A	0A	0	0	0	0	1950
106	1S	0A	0A	0	0	0	0	1955
106	1S	0A	0A	1	1429	0	0	1960
106	1S	0	0	1	0	0	0	1963
106	1S	0A	0A	0	0	0	1	1965
107	1S	0A	0A	0	0	0	0	1950
107	1S	0A	0A	0	0	0	0	1955
107	1S	0A	0A	0	0	0	0	1960
107	1S	0	0	0	0	0	0	1963
107	1S	0A	0A	0	0	0	0	1965
108	1S	0A	0A	0	0	0	0	1950
108	1S	0A	0A	0	0	0	0	1955
108	1S	0A	0A	1	1429	0	0	1960
108	1S	0	0	0	2857	0	0	1963
108	1S	0A	0A	0	0	0	1	1965

		1	2	3	4	5	6	
109	1S	0A	0A	0	0	0	0	1950
109	1S	0A	0A	0	0	0	0	1955
109	1S	0A	0A	2	2857	0	1	1960
109	1S	0	0	2	1429	0	1	1963
109	1S	0A	0A	1	3333	1	2	1965
110	1S	0A	0A	0	0	0	0	1950
110	1S	0A	0A	0	0	0	0	1955
110	1S	0A	0A	2	2857	0	0	1960
110	1S	0	0	1	1429	0	0	1963
110	1S	0A	0A	0	0	0	1	1965
111	1S	0A	0A	0	0	0	0	1950
111	1S	0A	0A	0	0	0	0	1955
111	1S	0A	0A	0	0	0	0	1960
111	1S	0	0	1	1429	0	0	1963
111	1S	0A	0A	1	3333	0	0	1965
112	1S	0A	0A	0	0	0	0	1950
112	1S	0A	0A	0	0	0	0	1955
112	1S	0A	0A	2	2857	0	0	1960
112	1S	0	0	1	1429	0	0	1963
112	1S	0A	0A	0	0	0	1	1965
113	1S	0A	0A	0	0	0	0	1950
113	1S	0A	0A	0	0	0	0	1955
113	1S	0A	0A	2	2857	0	0	1960
113	1S	0	0	1	1429	0	0	1963
113	1S	0A	0A	0	0	0	1	1965
114	1S	0A	0A	1	910	0	0	1950
114	1S	0A	0A	0	0	0	0	1955
114	1S	0A	0A	1	1429	0	0	1960
114	1S	0	0	1	1429	0	0	1963
114	1S	0A	0A	0	0	0	1	1965
115	1S	0A	0A	0	0	0	0	1950
115	1S	0A	0A	0	0	0	0	1955
115	1S	0A	0A	1	1429	0	0	1960
115	1S	0	0	1	1429	0	0	1963
115	1S	0A	0A	0	0	0	1	1965
116	1S	0A	0A	0	0	0	0	1950
116	1S	0A	0A	0	0	2	0	1955
116	1S	0A	0A	3	4286	0	0	1960
116	1S	0	0	3	4286	0	0	1963
116	1S	0A	0A	2	6667	0	1	1965
117	1S	0A	0A	0	0	0	0	1950
117	1S	0A	0A	1	2000	0	0	1955
117	1S	0A	0A	1	1429	1	0	1960
117	1S	0	0	2	2857	1	0	1963
117	1S	0A	0A	0	0	0	1	1965
118	1S	0A	0A	2	110	0	0	1950
118	1S	0A	0A	0	0	0	0	1955
118	1S	0A	0A	0	0	0	0	1960
118	1S	0	0	3	938	0	0	1963
118	1S	0A	0A	1	294	0	1	1965
119	1S	0A	0A	0	0	0	0	1950
119	1S	0A	0A	1	150	0	0	1955
119	1S	0A	0A	1	286	0	0	1960
119	1S	0	0	1	313	0	0	1963
119	1S	0A	0A	0	0	0	1	1965
120	1S	0A	0A	0	0	0	0	1950
120	1S	0A	0A	0	0	0	0	1955
120	1S	0A	0A	0	0	0	0	1960
120	1S	0	0	0	0	0	0	1963
120	1S	0A	0A	0	0	0	0	1965

		1	2	3	4	5	6	
121	1S	0A	0A	1	50	0	0	1950
121	1S	0A	0A	1	150	0	0	1955
121	1S	0A	0A	1	286	0	0	1960
121	1S	0	0	0	0	0	0	1963
121	1S	0A	0A	0	0	0	1	1965
122	1S	0A	0A	2	110	0	0	1950
122	1S	0A	0A	3	460	0	0	1955
122	1S	0A	0A	3	857	0	0	1960
122	1S	0	0	2	625	0	0	1963
122	1S	0A	0A	1	294	0	1	1965
123	1S	0A	0A	2	110	0	0	1950
123	1S	0A	0A	4	620	0	0	1955
123	1S	0A	0A	4	1143	0	0	1960
123	1S	0	0	1	313	0	0	1963
123	1S	0A	0A	2	588	0	1	1965
124	1S	0	0	2	110	0	0	1950
124	1S			1	150	0	0	1955
124	1S	1817	8938	2	571	0	0	1960
124	1S	0	0	1	313	0	0	1963
124	1S			0	0	0	0	1965
125	1S	0A	0A	3	160	0	0	1950
125	1S	0A	0A	3	460	0	0	1955
125	1S	0A	0A	3	857	0	0	1960
125	1S	0	0	3	938	0	0	1963
125	1S	0A	0A	1	294	0	1	1965
126	1S	0A	0A	0	0	0	0	1950
126	1S	0A	0A	0	0	0	0	1955
126	1S	0A	0A	2	571	0	0	1960
126	1S	0	0	1	313	0	0	1963
126	1S	0A	0A	0	0	0	1	1965
127	1S	0A	0A	1	50	0	0	1950
127	1S	0A	0A	1	150	0	0	1955
127	1S	0A	0A	2	571	0	0	1960
127	1S	0	0	2	625	0	0	1963
127	1S	0A	0A	2	588	0	1	1965
128	1S	0A	0A	1	50	0	0	1950
128	1S	0A	0A	0	0	0	1	1955
128	1S	0A	0A	1	286	0	0	1960
128	1S	0	0	1	313	0	0	1963
128	1S	0A	0A	2	588	0	1	1965
129	1S	0A	0A	14	750	0	5	1950
129	1S	0A	0A	14	2150	0	3	1955
129	1S	0A	0A	9	2571	0	0	1960
129	1S	0	0	6	1875	0	1	1963
129	1S	0A	0A	5	1470	0	15	1965
130	1S	0A	0A	8	430	0	2	1950
130	1S	0A	0A	12	1850	0	3	1955
130	1S	0A	0A	6	1714	0	0	1960
130	1S	0	0	6	1875	1	1	1963
130	1S	0A	0A	5	1470	2	15	1965
131	1S	0A	0A	0	0	0	0	1950
131	1S	0A	0A	0	0	0	0	1955
131	1S	0A	0A	0	0	0	0	1960
131	1S	0	0	1	476	0	0	1963
131	1S	0A	0A	1	625	0	2	1965
132	1S	0A	0A	0	0	0	0	1950
132	1S	0A	0A	2	2220	0	0	1955
132	1S	0A	0A	1	476	0	0	1960
132	1S	0	0	1	476	0	0	1963
132	1S	0A	0A	0	0	0	1	1965

		1	2	3	4	5	6	
133	1S	0A	0A	2A	600A	0	1	1950
133	1S	0A	0A	5A	5550A	0	0	1955
133	1S	0A	0A	7A	3332A	0	1	1960
133	1S	0A	0A	4	1905	0	0	1963
133	1S	0A	0A	4A	2500A	0	0	1965
134	1S	0A	0A	0	0	0	0	1950
134	1S	0A	0A	0	0	0	0	1955
134	1S	0	0	1	476	0	0	1960
134	1S	0	0	0	0	0	0	1963
134	1S	0	0	0	0	0	2	1965
135	1S	0A	0A	1	300	0	0	1950
135	1S	20		7	6670	0	0	1955
135	1S	0	0	1	476	0	0	1960
135	1S	0	0	1	476	0	0	1963
135	1S	0	0	1	625	0	1	1965
136	1S	0A	0A	1	300	0	0	1950
136	1S	50		0	0	0	0	1955
136	1S	300		1	476	0	0	1960
136	1S	0	0	1	476	0	0	1963
136	1S	0	0	1	625	0	2	1965
137	1S	0A	0A	0	0	0	0	1950
137	1S	0A	0A	0	0	0	0	1955
137	1S	0A	0A	0	0	0	0	1960
137	1S	0	0	1A	476	0	0	1963
137	1S	0A	0A	0	0	0	0	1965
138	1S	0A	0A	1	300	0	0	1950
138	1S	0A	0A	1	1110	0	0	1955
138	1S	0A	0A	1	476	0	0	1960
138	1S	0	0	1A	476	0	0	1963
138	1S	0A	0A	1	625	0	1	1965
139	1S	0A	0A	1	300	0	0	1950
139	1S	0A	0A	0	0	0	0	1955
139	1S	0A	0A	1	476	0	0	1960
139	1S	0	0	1	476	0	0	1963
139	1S	0A	0A	0	0	0	1	1965
140	1S	0A	0A	0	0	0	0	1950
140	1S	0A	0A	1	1110	0	0	1955
140	1S	0A	0A	2	952	0	0	1960
140	1S	0	0	2	952	0	0	1963
140	1S	0A	0A	2	1250	0	1	1965
141	1S	0A	0A	0	0	0	2	1950
141	1S	0A	0A	1	1110	0	2	1955
141	1S	0A	0A	1	476	0	1	1960
141	1S	0	0	3A	1429	0	1	1963
141	1S	0A	0A	5	3125	0	5	1965
142	1S	0A	0A	1	300	0	0	1950
142	1S	0A	0A	0	0	0	0	1955
142	1S	0A	0A	3	1429	0	0	1960
142	1S	0	0	1A	476	0	0	1963
142	1S	0A	0A	2	1250	0	2	1965
143	1S	0A	0A	1	300	0	0	1950
143	1S	0A	0A	0	0	0	0	1955
143	1S	0A	0A	5	2381	0	0	1960
143	1S	0	0	3A	1429	1	0	1963
143	1S	0A	0A	3	1875	0	2	1965
144	1S	0	0A	1	480	0	0	1950
144	1S	0	0	0	0	0	0	1955
144	1S	0	0	0	0	0	0	1960
144	1S	0	0	1	476	0	0	1963
144	1S	0	0	1	588	0	3	1965

		1	2	3	4	5	6	
145	1S	0	0A	0	0	0	0	1950
145	1S	0	0	0	0	1	0	1955
145	1S	100	71	1	400	1	0	1960
145	1S	0	0	1	476	0	0	1963
145	1S	0	0	0	0	0	3	1965
146	1S	3000	7500	3	1430	0	1	1950
146	1S	1414	2765	10A	4300	0	0	1955
146	1S	3730	2635	6A	2400	0	1	1960
146	1S	140	265	7	3333	0	2	1963
146	1S	39	64	5A	2941A	2	0	1965
147	1S	0	0A	0	0	0	0	1950
147	1S	0	0	0	0	0	0	1955
147	1S	0	0	4	1600	0	1	1960
147	1S	579	1097	0	0	0	0	1963
147	1S	163	268	0	0	0	2	1965
148	1S	0	0A	0	0	0	0	1950
148	1S	0	0	0	0	0	0	1955
148	1S	2250	1590	2	800	0	0	1960
148	1S	440	834	1	476	0	2	1963
148	1S	0	0	1	588	0	1	1965
149	1S	0	0A	0	0	0	0	1950
149	1S	1360	2659	0	0	1	1	1955
149	1S	0	0	2	800	2	0	1960
149	1S	0	0	1	476	0	1	1963
149	1S	2110	3460	1	588	1	4	1965
150	1S	0	0A	0	0	0	0	1950
150	1S	0	0	0	0	0	1	1955
150	1S	2500	1766	2	800	1	0	1960
150	1S	0	0	1A	476	0	2	1963
150	1S	30	49	0	0	0	2	1965
151	1S	0	0A	0	0	0	0	1950
151	1S	0	0	1	430	0	0	1955
151	1S	0	0	1	400	0	0	1960
151	1S	0	0	1A	476	0	0	1963
151	1S	0	0	1	588	0	1	1965
152	1S	0	0A	0	0	0	0	1950
152	1S	0	0	0	0	0	0	1955
152	1S	0	0	1	400	0	0	1960
152	1S	0	0	1	476	0	0	1963
152	1S	0	0	0	0	0	1	1965
153	1S	0	0A	1	480	0	0	1950
153	1S	0	0	0	0	0	1	1955
153	1S	0	0	1	400	0	0	1960
153	1S	0	0	1	476	0	0	1963
153	1S	0	0	2	1176	0	1	1965
154	1S	1000	2500	0	0	0	2	1950
154	1S	888	1736	1	430	0	2	1955
154	1S	125	88	1	400	0	1	1960
154	1S	301	568	3A	1429	1	1	1963
154	1S	191	312	5	2941	2	5	1965
155	1S	0	0A	1	480	0	0	1950
155	1S	0	0	1	430	0	9	1955
155	1S	0	0	3	1200	0	3	1960
155	1S	0	0	2A	952	0	4	1963
155	1S	0	0	4	2353	1	5	1965
156	1S	0	0A	1	480	0	0	1950
156	1S	0	0	4	1740	0	8	1955
156	1S	0	0	0	0	0	3	1960
156	1S	0	0	3A	1429	2	4	1963
156	1S	0	0	2	1176	0	6	1965

		1	2	3	4	5	6	
157	1S	0A	0A	3	140	0	0	1950
157	1S	0A	0A	2	160	0	1	1955
157	1S	0B	0A	0	0	0	0	1960
157	1S	0	0	2	256	0	0	1963
157	1S	40	63	1	179	0	2	1965
158	1S	0	0	2	90	0	0	1950
158	1S			1	80	0	1	1955
158	1S	0B		1	104	0	0	1960
158	1S	4	8	3	385	0	0	1963
158	1S	4	6	0	0	0	3	1965
159	1S	0A	0A	0	0	0	0	1950
159	1S	0A	0A	0	0	0	0	1955
159	1S	0A	0A	0	0	0	0	1960
159	1S	0	0	0	0	0	0	1963
159	1S	0A	0A	0	0	0	0	1965
160	1S	0A	0A	1	50	0	0	1950
160	1S	0A	0A	2	160	0	0	1955
160	1S	0A	0A	1	104	0	0	1960
160	1S	0	0	0	0	0	0	1963
160	1S	0A	0A	2	357	0	2	1965
161	1S	0	0	4	190	0	0	1950
161	1S			5	400	0	0	1955
161	1S	0B	0A	2	208	0	0	1960
161	1S	86	162	2	256	0	0	1963
161	1S	18	28	3	536	0	1	1965
162	1S			4	190	0	1	1950
162	1S			7	560	0	3	1955
162	1S	909	2658	4	417	0	0	1960
162	1S	835	1570	3	385	0	0	1963
162	1S	901	1413	3	536	0	6	1965
163	1S	0A	0A	1	50	0	0	1950
163	1S	0A	0A	1	80	0	2	1955
163	1S	0B	0A	3	313	0	0	1960
163	1S	0	0	1	128	0	0	1963
163	1S	0A	0A	1	179	0	2	1965
164	1S	0A	0A	5	240	0	0	1950
164	1S			1	80	0	0	1955
164	1S	0B	0A	5	521	0	0	1960
164	1S	0	0	2	256	0	0	1963
164	1S	0A	0A	2	357	0	1	1965
165	1S	0A	0A	0	0	0	0	1950
165	1S			0	0	0	0	1955
165	1S	89	260	3	313	0	0	1960
165	1S	86	162	3	385	0	0	1963
165	1S	94	147	2	357	0	1	1965
166	1S	0A	0A	14	660	0	5	1950
166	1S	0A	0A	14	1130	0	3	1955
166	1S	0A	0A	9	938	0	0	1960
166	1S	0	0	6	769	1	2	1963
166	1S	0A	0A	5	893	0	15	1965
167	1S	0A	0A	1	50	0	1	1950
167	1S	0A	0A	0	0	0	0	1955
167	1S	0A	0A	3	313	0	1	1960
167	1S	0	0	1	128	0	0	1963
167	1S	0A	0A	2	357	1	2	1965
168	1S	0A	0A	1	50	0	0	1950
168	1S	0A	0A	1	80	0	9	1955
168	1S	0A	0A	3	313	0	2	1960
168	1S	0	0	2	256	0	4	1963
168	1S	0A	0A	4	714	1	6	1965

		1	2	3	4	5	6	
169	1S	0A	0A	10	470	0	3	1950
169	1S	0A	0A	25	1940	0	18	1955
169	1S	0A	0A	15	1563	1	7	1960
169	1S	0	0	9	1154	2	7	1963
169	1S	0A	0A	10	1786	1	23	1965
170	1S	280	57	9	420	0	0	1950
170	1S	1701	615	14	370	0	2	1955
170	1S	205	62	9	361	1	0	1960
170	1S	1423	292	7	317	1	1	1963
170	1S	2730	596	5	273	2	7	1965
171	1S	0	0	2	90	0	0	1950
171	1S	144	52	1	30	0	1	1955
171	1S	-26	-7	2	80	0	0	1960
171	1S	209	43	1	45	0	0	1963
171	1S	39	9	0	0	1	3	1965
172	1S	0A	0A	0	0	0	0	1950
172	1S	0A	0A	1A	30A	0	0	1955
172	1S	0A	0A	0	0	0	0	1960
172	1S	0	0	0	0	0	1	1963
172	1S	0A	0A	0	0	0	0	1965
173	1S	30	6	3	140	0	1	1950
173	1S	23	8	6	200	0	0	1955
173	1S	8	2	0	0	0	0	1960
173	1S	0	0	0	0	0	1	1963
173	1S	0	0	2	109	0	2	1965
174	1S	4	0	1	50	0	0	1950
174	1S	233	84	4	110	0	1	1955
174	1S	929	285	7	281	0	0	1960
174	1S	1784	367	5	226	0	0	1963
174	1S	1257	272	3	164	1	1	1965
175	1S	622	127	4	190	0	0	1950
175	1S	1401	506	2	50	0	3	1955
175	1S	7584	2313	10	402	0	0	1960
175	1S	6849	1409	12	543	2	1	1963
175	1S	6971	1523	6	328	2	4	1965
176	1S	665	136	5	240	0	0	1950
176	1S	223	80	1	30	0	2	1955
176	1S	702	214	8	321	0	0	1960
176	1S	408	83	3	136	1	0	1963
176	1S	-31	-6	1	55	1	2	1965
177	1S	553	113	4	190	0	0	1950
177	1S	585	211	10	260	0	0	1955
177	1S	568	173	6	241	0	1	1960
177	1S	744	153	7	317	0	0	1963
177	1S	528	115	10	546	0	1	1965
178	1S	14	2	0	0	0	0	1950
178	1S	109	39	1	30	0	0	1955
178	1S	510	155	1	40	0	0	1960
178	1S	553	113	2	90	0	0	1963
178	1S	418	91	0	0	0	1	1965
179	1S	3020	618	8	380	0	2	1950
179	1S	13	4	12	320	0	3	1955
179	1S	0	0	6	241	0	1	1960
179	1S	0	0	6	271	1	1	1963
179	1S	0	0	5	273	0	15	1965
180	1S	0A	0A	1	50	0	0	1950
180	1S	60	21	0	0	0	0	1955
180	1S	35	10	5	201	0	0	1960
180	1S	80	16	3	136	0	0	1963
180	1S	41	9	3	164	0	2	1965

		1	2	3	4	5	6	
181	1S	0A	0A	1	50	0	0	1950
181	1S	0A	0A	4	110	0	8	1955
181	1S	0	0	0	0	0	2	1960
181	1S	0	0	3	136	0	4	1963
181	1S	0	0	2	109	2	6	1965
182	1S	9210	1885	10	470	1	3	1950
182	1S	1290	466	25	630	0	17	1955
182	1S	0	0	15	602	0	7	1960
182	1S	0	0	9	407	3	9	1963
182	1S	0	0	10	546	0	23	1965

		7	8	9	10	
1	2S	0A	0A	0	0	1950
1	2S	0A	0A	0	0	1955
1	2S	0A	0A	0	0	1960
1	2S	0A	0A	0	0	1963
1	2S	0A	0A	0	0	1965
2	2S	0A	0A	0	0	1950
2	2S	0A	0A	3	146	1955
2	2S	0A	0A	0	0	1960
2	2S	0A	0A	3	41	1963
2	2S	0A	0A	0	0	1965
3	2S			22	495	1950
3	2S					1955
3	2S			19	407	1960
3	2S			13B	178B	1963
3	2S			20	404	1965
4	2S	0A	0A	2	45	1950
4	2S	0A	0A	0	0	1955
4	2S	0A	0A	0	0	1960
4	2S	0A	0A	8	110	1963
4	2S	0A	0A	2	40	1965
5	2S	0A	0A	3	67	1950
5	2S	0A	0A	0	0	1955
5	2S	0A	0A	0	0	1960
5	2S	0F	0F	0	0	1963
5	2S	0A	0A	0	0	1965
6	2S	0A	0A	0	0	1950
6	2S	0A	0A	0	0	1955
6	2S	0A	0A	0	0	1960
6	2S	0A	0A	0	0	1963
6	2S	0A	0A	0	0	1965
7	2S	0A	0A	2	45	1950
7	2S	0A	0A	0	0	1955
7	2S	0A	0A	0	0	1960
7	2S	0A	0A	5	68	1963
7	2S	0A	0A	1	20	1965
8	2S	0A	0A	2	45	1950
8	2S	0A	0A	0	0	1955
8	2S	0A	0A	0	0	1960
8	2S	0A	0A	8	110	1963
8	2S	0A	0A	2	40	1965
9	2S	0A	0A	0	0	1950
9	2S	0A	0A	1	48	1955
9	2S	0A	0A	0	0	1960
9	2S	0G	0G	0	0	1963
9	2S	0A	0A	1	20	1965
10	2S	0A	0A	2	45	1950
10	2S	0A	0A	0	0	1955
10	2S	0A	0A	0	0	1960

	7	8	9	10	
10 2S	0A	0A	2	27	1963
10 2S	0A	0A	0	0	1965
11 2S			3	67	1950
11 2S			3	144	1955
11 2S			19B	407B	1960
11 2S			26B	356B	1963
11 2S			11	222	1965
12 2S			203	4572	1950
12 2S			200A	4500A	1955
12 2S			210B	4497B	1960
12 2S	6G		358B	4904B	1963
12 2S	10AG		284	5737	1965
13 2S			203	4572	1950
13 2S			200A	4500A	1955
13 2S			210B	4497B	1960
13 2S	11G		358B	4904B	1963
13 2S	15AG		284	5737	1965
14 2S	0A	0A	0	0	1950
14 2S	0A	0A	0	0	1955
14 2S	0A	0A	0	0	1960
14 2S	0A	0A	0	0	1963
14 2S	0A	0A	0	0	1965
15 2S	0A	0A	0	0	1950
15 2S	0A	0A	0	0	1955
15 2S	0A	0A	0	0	1960
15 2S	0A	0A	0	0	1963
15 2S	0A	0A	2	32	1965
16 2S	0A	0A	0	0	1950
16 2S	0A	0A	0	0	1955
16 2S	0A	0A	0B	0B	1960
16 2S	0A	0A	0B	0B	1963
16 2S	0A	0A	0	0	1965
17 2S	0A	0A	0	0	1950
17 2S	0A	0A	0	0	1955
17 2S	0A	0A	0	0	1960
17 2S	0A	0A	0	0	1963
17 2S	0A	0A	1	16	1965
18 2S	0A	0A	0	0	1950
18 2S	0A	0A	0	0	1955
18 2S	0A	0A	0	0	1960
18 2S	0F	0F	0	0	1963
18 2S	0A	0A	3	49	1965
19 2S	0A	0A	0	0	1950
19 2S	0A	0A	0	0	1955
19 2S	0A	0A	0	0	1960
19 2S	0A	0A	0	0	1963
19 2S	0A	0A	0	0	1965
20 2S	0A	0A	0	0	1950
20 2S	0A	0A	0	0	1955
20 2S	0A	0A	0	0	1960
20 2S	0A	0A	0	0	1963
20 2S	0A	0A	1	16	1965
21 2S	0A	0A	0	0	1950
21 2S	0A	0A	0	0	1955
21 2S	0A	0A	0	0	1960
21 2S	0A	0A	0	0	1963
21 2S	0A	0A	1	16	1965
22 2S	0A	0A	0	0	1950
22 2S	0A	0A	0	0	1955

	7	8	9	10	
22 2S	0A	0A	0	0	1960
22 2S	0G	0G	0	0	1963
22 2S	0A	0A	0	0	1965
23 2S	0A	0A	0	0	1950
23 2S	0A	0A	0	0	1955
23 2S	0A	0A	0	0	1960
23 2S	0A	0A	0	0	1963
23 2S	0A	0A	0	0	1965
24 2S	0A	0A	0	0	1950
24 2S	0A	0A	0	0	1955
24 2S	0A	0A	0B	0	1960
24 2S	0A	0A	0B	0B	1963
24 2S	0A	0A	1	16	1965
25 2S	0A	0A	2	714	1950
25 2S	0A	0A	2A	714A	1955
25 2S	0A	0A	27B	7714B	1960
25 2S	0G	0A	25B	7143B	1963
25 2S	0A	0A	103	1669	1965
26 2S	0A	0A	2	714	1950
26 2S	0A	0A	2A	714A	1955
26 2S	0A	0A	27B	7714B	1960
26 2S	0G	0A	25B	7143B	1963
26 2S	0A	0A	103	1669	1965
27 2S	0A	0A	0A	0A	1950
27 2S	0A	0A	3	94	1955
27 2S	0A	0A	0	0	1960
27 2S	0A	0A	0A	0A	1963
27 2S	0A	0A	0	0	1965
28 2S	0A	0A	0A	0A	1950
28 2S	0A	0A	0A	0A	1955
28 2S	0A	0A	0	0	1960
28 2S	0A	0A	0A	0A	1963
28 2S	0A	0A	0	0	1965
29 2S	0A	0A	0A	0A	1950
29 2S	0A	0A	2	63	1955
29 2S	0A	0A	0B	0B	1960
29 2S	0A	0A	0A	0A	1963
29 2S	0A	0A	0	0	1965
30 2S	0A	0A	0A	0A	1950
30 2S	0A	0A	0A	0A	1955
30 2S	0A	0A	0	0	1960
30 2S	0A	0A	0A	0A	1963
30 2S	0A	0A	0	0	1965
31 2S	0A	0A	0A	0A	1950
31 2S	0A	0A	4	125	1955
31 2S	0A	0A	0	0	1960
31 2S	0F	0F	0A	0A	1963
31 2S	0A	0A	0	0	1965
32 2S	0A	0A	0A	0A	1950
32 2S	0A	0A	0	0	1955
32 2S	0A	0A	0	0	1960
32 2S	0A	0A	0A	0A	1963
32 2S	0A	0A	0	0	1965
33 2S	0A	0A	0A	0A	1950
33 2S	0A	0A	0	0	1955
33 2S	0A	0A	0	0	1960
33 2S	0A	0A	0A	0A	1963
33 2S	0A	0A	0	0	1965
34 2S	0A	0A	0A	0A	1950

	7	8	9	10	
34 2S	0A	0A	0	0	1955
34 2S	0A	0A	0	0	1960
34 2S	0A	0A	0A	0A	1963
34 2S	0A	0A	0	0	1965
35 2S	0A	0A	0A	0A	1950
35 2S	0A	0A	2	63	1955
35 2S	0A	0A	0	0	1960
35 2S	0AG	0AG	0A	0A	1963
35 2S	15		0	0	1965
36 2S	0A	0A	0A	0A	1950
36 2S	0A	0A	4	125	1955
36 2S	0A	0A	0	0	1960
36 2S	0A	0A	0A	0A	1963
36 2S	0A	0A	0	0	1965
37 2S	0A	0A			1950
37 2S	0A	0A	67	2094	1955
37 2S	0A	0A			1960
37 2S	0A	0A			1963
37 2S	0A	0A	1	88	1965
38 2S	0A	0A			1950
38 2S	0A	0A	16	500	1955
38 2S	0A	0A			1960
38 2S	0AG	0AG			1963
38 2S	4		100	8772	1965
39 2S	0A	0A			1950
39 2S	0A	0A	16	500	1955
39 2S	0A	0A			1960
39 2S	0AG	0AG			1963
39 2S	0A	0A	100	8772	1965
40 2S	0A	0A			1950
40 2S	0A	0A			1955
40 2S	0A	0A	0	0	1960
40 2S	0A	0A	0A	0A	1963
40 2S	0A	0A	0A	0A	1965
41 2S	0A	0A	0A	0A	1950
41 2S	0A	0A	0	0	1955
41 2S	0A	0A	0	0	1960
41 2S	0A	0A	0A	0A	1963
41 2S	0A	0A	0A	0A	1965
42 2S	0A	0A	0A	0A	1950
42 2S	0A	0A	0	0	1955
42 2S	0A	0A	0	0	1960
42 2S	0A	0A	0A	0A	1963
42 2S	0A	0A	0A	0A	1965
43 2S	0A	0A	0A	0A	1950
43 2S	0A	0A	0	0	1955
43 2S	0A	0A	0	0	1960
43 2S	0A	0A	0A	0A	1963
43 2S	0A	0A	0A	0A	1965
44 2S	0A	0A	0A	0A	1950
44 2S	0A	0A	1	11	1955
44 2S	0A	0A	0	0	1960
44 2S	0A	0A	0A	0A	1963
44 2S	0A	0A	0A	0A	1965
45 2S	0A	0A	0A	0A	1950
45 2S	0A	0A	0	0	1955
45 2S	0A	0A	0	0	1960
45 2S	0A	0A	0A	0A	1963
45 2S	0A	0A	0A	0A	1965

		7	8	9	10	
46	2S	0A	0A	0A	0A	1950
46	2S	0A	0A	7	78	1955
46	2S	0A	0A	0	0	1960
46	2S	0A	0A	0A	0A	1963
46	2S	0A	0A	0A	0A	1965
47	2S	0A	0A	0A	0A	1950
47	2S	0A	0A	0	0	1955
47	2S	0A	0A	0	0	1960
47	2S	0A	0A	0A	0A	1963
47	2S	0A	0A	0A	0A	1965
48	2S	0A	0A	0A	0A	1950
48	2S	0A	0A	3	34	1955
48	2S	0A	0A	0	0	1960
48	2S	0AG	0AG	0A	0A	1963
48	2S	0A	0A	0A	0A	1965
49	2S	0A	0A	0A	0A	1950
49	2S	0A	0A	5	56	1955
49	2S	0A	0A	0	0	1960
49	2S	0A	0A	0A	0A	1963
49	2S	0A	0A	0A	0A	1965
50	2S	0A	0A			1950
50	2S	0A	0A	11	123	1955
50	2S	0A	0A			1960
50	2S	0A	0A			1963
50	2S	0A	0A			1965
51	2S	0A	0A			1950
51	2S	0A	0A	30	336	1955
51	2S	0A	0A	0	0	1960
51	2S	0AG	0AG	1A	0H	1963
51	2S	0A	0A			1965
52	2S	0A	0A			1950
52	2S	0A	0A	30	336	1955
52	2S	0A	0A	0	0	1960
52	2S	0A	0A	1A	0H	1963
52	2S	0A	0A			1965
53	2S	0A	0A	0A	0A	1950
53	2S	0A	0A	0	0	1955
53	2S	0A	0A	0	0	1960
53	2S	0A	0A	0	0	1963
53	2S	0A	0A	0	0	1965
54	2S	0A	0A	0A	0A	1950
54	2S	0A	0A	0	0	1955
54	2S	0A	0A	0	0	1960
54	2S	0A	0A	0	0	1963
54	2S	0A	0A	0	0	1965
55	2S	0A	0A	0A	0A	1950
55	2S	0A	0A	0	0	1955
55	2S	0A	0A	0	0	1960
55	2S	0A	0A	1	40	1963
55	2S	0A	0A	0	0	1965
56	2S	0A	0A	0A	0A	1950
56	2S	0A	0A	0	0	1955
56	2S	0A	0A	5	163	1960
56	2S	0A	0A	1B	40B	1963
56	2S	0A	0A	4	161	1965
57	2S	0A	0A	0A	0A	1950
57	2S	0A	0A	0	0	1955
57	2S	0A	0A	5	163	1960
57	2S	1F	0A	0	0	1963
57	2S	0A	0A	0	0	1965

	7	8	9	10	
58 2S	0A	0A	0A	0A	1950
58 2S	0A	0A	0	0	1955
58 2S	0A	0A	0	0	1960
58 2S	0A	0A	0	0	1963
58 2S	0A	0A	0	0	1965
59 2S	0A	0A	0A	0A	1950
59 2S	0A	0A	0	0	1955
59 2S	0A	0A	0	0	1960
59 2S	0A	0A	0	0	1963
59 2S	0A	0A	0	0	1965
60 2S			0A	0A	1950
60 2S			0	0	1955
60 2S			0A	0A	1960
60 2S			0	0	1963
60 2S			0	0	1965
61 2S	0A	0A	0A	0A	1950
61 2S	0A	0A	1	122	1955
61 2S	0A	0A	0	0	1960
61 2S	0AG	0AG	0	0	1963
61 2S	0A	0A	1	40	1965
62 2S	0A	0A	0A	0A	1950
62 2S	0A	0A	0	0	1955
62 2S	0A	0A	0	0	1960
62 2S	0A	0A	0	0	1963
62 2S	0A	0A	1	40	1965
63 2S	0A	0A	0A	0A	1950
63 2S	0A	0A	0	0	1955
63 2S	0A	0A	11B	359B	1960
63 2S	0A	0A	4B	161B	1963
63 2S	0A	0A	2	81	1965
64 2S	0A	0A			1950
64 2S	0A	0A	40A	4880A	1955
64 2S	0A	0A	234B	7647B	1960
64 2S	0AG	0AG	205B	8266B	1963
64 2S	14		196	7903	1965
65 2S	0A	0A			1950
65 2S	0A	0A	40A	4880A	1955
65 2S	0A	0A	234B	7647B	1960
65 2S	0AG	0AG	205B	8266B	1963
65 2S	56		196	7903	1965
66 2S	0A	0A	0	0	1950
66 2S	0A	0A	0	0	1955
66 2S	0A	0A	0	0	1960
66 2S	0F	0F	0	0	1963
66 2S	0A	0A	0	0	1965
67 2S			0	0	1950
67 2S			0	0	1955
67 2S			0	0	1960
67 2S	569F	2432F	0	0	1963
67 2S			0	0	1965
68 2S	0A	0A	0	0	1950
68 2S	0A	0A	8	226	1955
68 2S	0A	0A	0A	0A	1960
68 2S	0F	0F	4	42	1963
68 2S	0A	0A	2	25	1965
69 2S	0A	0A	0	0	1950
69 2S	0A	0A	0	0	1955
69 2S	0A	0A	0B	0B	1960
69 2S	0F	0F	0B	0B	1963
69 2S	0A	0A	1	13	1965

	7	8	9	10	
70 2S	0A	0A	0	0	1950
70 2S	0A	0A	0	0	1955
70 2S	0A	0A	0	0	1960
70 2S	3F	13F	6	63	1963
70 2S			2	25	1965
71 2S			0	0	1950
71 2S			0	0	1955
71 2S			0	0	1960
71 2S	10F	43F	0	0	1963
71 2S			0	0	1965
72 2S	0A	0A	0	0	1950
72 2S	0A	0A	0	0	1955
72 2S	0A	0A	0	0	1960
72 2S	0F	0F	0	0	1963
72 2S	0A	0A	2	25	1965
73 2S	0A	0A	0	0	1950
73 2S	0A	0A	0	0	1955
73 2S	0A	0A	0	0	1960
73 2S	0F	0F	6	63	1963
73 2S	0A	0A	2	25	1965
74 2S	0A	0A	0	0	1950
74 2S	0A	0A	0	0	1955
74 2S	0A	0A	0	0	1960
74 2S	5G	21G	1	10	1963
74 2S	12		0	0	1965
75 2S	0A	0A	0	0	1950
75 2S	0A	0A	0	0	1955
75 2S	0A	0A	0	0	1960
75 2S	0F	0F	0	0	1963
75 2S	0A	0A	0	0	1965
76 2S	0A	0A	4	388	1950
76 2S	0A	0A	42	1186	1955
76 2S	0A	0A	47B	762B	1960
76 2S	11F	47F	36B	377B	1963
76 2S			21	267	1965
77 2S			21	2039	1950
77 2S	38		92	2599	1955
77 2S			262B	4246B	1960
77 2S	205G	876G	372B	3899B	1963
77 2S	277		475	5814	1965
78 2S			21	2039	1950
78 2S	35		26	734	1955
78 2S			262B	4246B	1960
78 2S	149G	637G	372B	3899B	1963
78 2S	140		475	5814	1965
79 2S	0A	0A	0	0	1950
79 2S	0A	0A	0	0	1955
79 2S	0A	0A	0	0	1960
79 2S	0A	0A	0	0	1963
79 2S	0A	0A	0H	0H	1965
80 2S	0A	0A	0	0	1950
80 2S	0A	0A	0	0	1955
80 2S	0A	0A	0	0	1960
80 2S	0A	0A	0	0	1963
80 2S	0A	0A	0H	0H	1965
81 2S	0A	0A	0	0	1950
81 2S	0A	0A	1	80	1955
81 2S	0A	0A	0	0	1960
81 2S	0A	0A	7	1000	1963
81 2S	0A	0A	9H	769H	1965

	7	8	9	10	
82 2S	0A	0A	0	0	1950
82 2S	0A	0A	0	0	1955
82 2S	0A	0A	4B		1960
82 2S	0A	0A	0B	0B	1963
82 2S	0A	0A	1H	85H	1965
83 2S	0A	0A	0	0	1950
83 2S	0A	0A	0	0	1955
83 2S	0A	0A	3	600	1960
83 2S	0A	0A	4	571	1963
83 2S	0A	0A	4H	342H	1965
84 2S	0A	0A	0	0	1950
84 2S	0A	0A	0	0	1955
84 2S	0A	0A	0	0	1960
84 2S	0F	0F	0	0	1963
84 2S	0A	0A	0H	0H	1965
85 2S	0A	0A	0	0	1950
85 2S	0A	0A	0	0	1955
85 2S	0A	0A	6	1200	1960
85 2S	0A	0A	0	0	1963
85 2S	0A	0A	0H	0H	1965
86 2S	0A	0A	0	0	1950
86 2S	0A	0A	0	0	1955
86 2S	0A	0A	3	600	1960
86 2S	0A	0A	4	571	1963
86 2S	0A	0A	4H	342H	1965
87 2S			0	0	1950
87 2S			73	5840	1955
87 2S			12	2400	1960
87 2S	0AG	0AG	17	2429	1963
87 2S	0A	0A	22H	1880H	1965
88 2S	0A	0A	0	0	1950
88 2S	0A	0A	0	0	1955
88 2S	0A	0A	0	0	1960
88 2S	0A	0A	0	0	1963
88 2S	0A	0A	0H	0H	1965
89 2S	0A	0A	4	470	1950
89 2S	0A	0A	4	320	1955
89 2S	0A	0A	2B	400B	1960
89 2S	0A	0A	3B	429B	1963
89 2S	0A	0A	4H	342H	1965
90 2S	0A	0A	17	2000	1950
90 2S	0A	0A	17A	2240	1955
90 2S	0A	0A	18B	3600B	1960
90 2S	0AG	0AG	33B	4714B	1963
90 2S	0A	0A	55H	4701H	1965
91 2S	0A	0A	17	2000	1950
91 2S	0A	0A	17A	2000A	1955
91 2S	0A	0A	18B	3600B	1960
91 2S	0AG	0AG	33B	4714B	1963
91 2S	0A	0A	55H	4701H	1965
92 2S	0A	0A	0A	0A	1950
92 2S	0A	0A	0	0	1955
92 2S	0A	0A	0	0	1960
92 2S	0A	0A	0	0	1963
92 2S	0A	0A	0	0	1965
93 2S	0A	0A	0A	0A	1950
93 2S	0A	0A	0	0	1955
93 2S	0A	0A	0	0	1960
93 2S	0A	0A	0	0	1963
93 2S	0A	0A	0	0	1965

	7	8	9	10	
94 2S	0A	0A	0A	0A	1950
94 2S	0A	0A	0	0	1955
94 2S	0A	0A	0A	0A	1960
94 2S	0A	0A	0	0	1963
94 2S	0A	0A	0	0	1965
95 2S	0A	0A	0A	0A	1950
95 2S	0A	0A	2	57	1955
95 2S	0A	0A	4B	75B	1960
95 2S	0A	0A	3B	81B	1963
95 2S	0A	0A	0	0	1965
96 2S	0A	0A	0A	0A	1950
96 2S	0A	0A	0	0	1955
96 2S	0A	0A	2	38	1960
96 2S	0A	0A	4	108	1963
96 2S	0A	0A	8	176	1965
97 2S	0A	0A	0A	0A	1950
97 2S	0A	0A	0	0	1955
97 2S	0A	0A	0	0	1960
97 2S	0F	0F	0	0	1963
97 2S	0A	0A	0	0	1965
98 2S	0A	0A	0A	0A	1950
98 2S	0A	0A	0	0	1955
98 2S	0A	0A	0	0	1960
98 2S	0A	0A	0	0	1963
98 2S	0A	0A	0	0	1965
99 2S	0A	0A	0A	0A	1950
99 2S	0A	0A	0	0	1955
99 2S	0A	0A	2	38	1960
99 2S	0A	0A	4	108	1963
99 2S	0A	0A	8	176	1965
100 2S					1950
100 2S			12	344	1955
100 2S			0	0	1960
100 2S	1G	4G	1	27	1963
100 2S	20		0	0	1965
101 2S	0A	0A			1950
101 2S	0A	0A	0	0	1955
101 2S	0A	0A	2	38	1960
101 2S	0A	0A	1	27	1963
101 2S	0A	0A	11	242	1965
102 2S	0A	0A			1950
102 2S	0A	0A	20A	400A	1955
102 2S	0A	0A	21B	395B	1960
102 2S	0A	0A	83B	2231B	1963
102 2S	0A	0A	54	1187	1965
103 2S					1950
103 2S	12		15	430	1955
103 2S	137	467	237B	4455B	1960
103 2S	207G	912G	148B	3978B	1963
103 2S	223		288	6330	1965
104 2S					1950
104 2S	580		15	430	1955
104 2S	1758	5995	237B	4455B	1960
104 2S	1358G	5982G	148B	3978B	1963
104 2S	482		288	6330	1965
105 2S	0A	0A	0A	0A	1950
105 2S	0A	0A	2		1955
105 2S	0A	0A	0	0	1960
105 2S	0A	0A	0	0	1963
105 2S	0A	0A	0H	0H	1965

	7	8	9	10	
106 2S	0A	0A	0A	0A	1950
106 2S	0A	0A	0	0	1955
106 2S	0A	0A	0	0	1960
106 2S	0A	0A	0	0	1963
106 2S	0A	0A	0H	0H	1965
107 2S	0A	0A	0A	0A	1950
107 2S	0A	0A	0	0	1955
107 2S	0A	0A	0	0	1960
107 2S	0A	0A	0	0	1963
107 2S	0A	0A	0H	0H	1965
108 2S	0A	0A	0A	0A	1950
108 2S	0A	0A	3		1955
108 2S	0A	0A	0	0	1960
108 2S	0A	0A	0	0	1963
108 2S	0A	0A	0H	0H	1965
109 2S	0A	0A	0A	0A	1950
109 2S	0A	0A	0	0	1955
109 2S	0A	0A	0	0	1960
109 2S	0A	0A	0	0	1963
109 2S	0A	0A	0H	0H	1965
110 2S	0A	0A	0A	0A	1950
110 2S	0A	0A	2		1955
110 2S	0A	0A	0	0	1960
110 2S	0F	0F	0	0	1963
110 2S	0A	0A	0H	0H	1965
111 2S	0A	0A	0A	0A	1950
111 2S	0A	0A	0	0	1955
111 2S	0A	0A	0	0	1960
111 2S	0A	0A	0	0	1963
111 2S	0A	0A	0H	0H	1965
112 2S	0A	0A	0A	0A	1950
112 2S	0A	0A	0	0	1955
112 2S	0A	0A	0	0	1960
112 2S	0A	0A	0	0	1963
112 2S	0A	0A	0H	0H	1965
113 2S	0A	0A	0A	0A	1950
113 2S	0A	0A	7		1955
113 2S	0A	0A	0	0	1960
113 2S	0G	0G	0	0	1963
113 2S	0A	0A	0H	0H	1965
114 2S	0A	0A	0A	0A	1950
114 2S	0A	0A	0	0	1955
114 2S	0A	0A	0	0	1960
114 2S	0A	0A	0	0	1963
114 2S	0A	0A	0H	0H	1965
115 2S	0A	0A			1950
115 2S	0A	0A	5		1955
115 2S	0A	0A	0	0	1960
115 2S	0A	0A	0	0	1963
115 2S	0A	0A	0H	0H	1965
116 2S	0A	0A			1950
116 2S	0A	0A	6		1955
116 2S	0A	0A	0	0	1960
116 2S	11G		0	0	1963
116 2S	0A	0A	5H	10000H	1965
117 2S	0A	0A			1950
117 2S	0A	0A	6		1955
117 2S	0A	0A	0	0	1960
117 2S	1G		0	0	1963
117 2S	0A	0A	5H	10000H	1965

	7	8	9	10	
118 2S	65	45	1	13	1950
118 2S	89	59	2	18	1955
118 2S	107	46	0	0	1960
118 2S	34	10	2	9	1963
118 2S	55	27	4	19	1965
119 2S	0B	0	0	0	1950
119 2S	22	15	0	0	1955
119 2S			0	0	1960
119 2S	7	2	0	0	1963
119 2S	3	1	0	0	1965
120 2S	0B	0	3	39	1950
120 2S	12	8	0	0	1955
120 2S			0	0	1960
120 2S	3	1	5	23	1963
120 2S	45	22	2	10	1965
121 2S	20	14	6	78	1950
121 2S			2	18	1955
121 2S			9B	70B	1960
121 2S	3	1	13B	59B	1963
121 2S	2	1	10	48	1965
122 2S	0B	0	3	39	1950
122 2S	22	15	1	9	1955
122 2S			0	0	1960
122 2S	21	6	1	5	1963
122 2S	34	17	4	19	1965
123 2S	17	12	2	26	1950
123 2S	34	23	1	9	1955
123 2S			0	0	1960
123 2S	94	28	1	5	1963
123 2S	103	50	0	0	1965
124 2S	6388	4408	0	0	1950
124 2S	2124	1417	1	9	1955
124 2S	494	211	0	0	1960
124 2S	68	20	0	0	1963
124 2S	257	126	1	5	1965
125 2S	0B	0B	2	26	1950
125 2S	0A	0A	4	36	1955
125 2S	127	54	3	23	1960
125 2S	48	14	13	59	1963
125 2S	256	125	12	57	1965
126 2S	0B	0B	3	39	1950
126 2S	0A	0A	0	0	1955
126 2S	0A	0A	0	0	1960
126 2S	20	6	1	5	1963
126 2S	5	2	4	19	1965
127 2S	0B	0B	1	13	1950
127 2S			0	0	1955
127 2S			4	31	1960
127 2S	33	10	5	23	1963
127 2S	47	23	8	38	1965
128 2S	16	11	19	248	1950
128 2S			25	226	1955
128 2S			29B	225B	1960
128 2S	11	3	36B	164B	1963
128 2S	9	4	52	249	1965
129 2S	1797	1240	400	5229	1950
129 2S	1781	1189	482	4366	1955
129 2S	3694	1574	750B	5828B	1960
129 2S	6679	1971	1214B	5533B	1963
129 2S	9883	4842	1055	5045	1965

	7	8	9	10	
130 2S	417	288	400	5229	1950
130 2S	723	482	400A	5000A	1955
130 2S	1711	729	750B	5828B	1960
130 2S	2754	813	1214B	5533B	1963
130 2S	4720	2312	1055	5045	1965
131 2S	0A	0A	0A	0A	1950
131 2S	0A	0A	1	9	1955
131 2S	0A	0A	0	0	1960
131 2S	0A	0A	2	28	1963
131 2S	0A	0A	0	0	1965
132 2S	0A	0A	0A	0A	1950
132 2S	0A	0A	0	0	1955
132 2S	0A	0A	0	0	1960
132 2S	0A	0A	0	0	1963
132 2S	0A	0A	0	0	1965
133 2S	0A	0A	0A	0A	1950
133 2S	0A	0A	4	37	1955
133 2S	0A	0A	5	62	1960
133 2S	0A	0A	1	14	1963
133 2S	0A	0A	2	34	1965
134 2S	0A	0A	0A	0A	1950
134 2S	0A	0A	6	56	1955
134 2S	0A	0A	4B	50B	1960
134 2S	0A	0A	9B	126B	1963
134 2S	0A	0A	4	68	1965
135 2S	0A	0A	0A	0A	1950
135 2S	0A	0A	0	0	1955
135 2S	0A	0A	0	0	1960
135 2S	0A	0A	0	0	1963
135 2S	0A	0A	0	0	1965
136 2S	0A	0A	0A	0A	1950
136 2S	0A	0A	0	0	1955
136 2S	0A	0A	0	0	1960
136 2S	1F		0	0	1963
136 2S	0A	0A	0	0	1965
137 2S	0A	0A	0A	0A	1950
137 2S	0A	0A	0	0	1955
137 2S	0A	0A	0	0	1960
137 2S	0A	0A	0	0	1963
137 2S	0A	0A	0	0	1965
138 2S	0A	0A			1950
138 2S	0A	0A	11	103	1955
138 2S	0A	0A	2	25	1960
138 2S	0A	0A	4	56	1963
138 2S	0A	0A	0	0	1965
139 2S	0A	0A	0A	0A	1950
139 2S	0A	0A	0	0	1955
139 2S	0A	0A	0	0	1960
139 2S	0A	0A	0	0	1963
139 2S	0A	0A	0	0	1965
140 2S	0A	0A	0A	0A	1950
140 2S	0A	0A	0A	0A	1955
140 2S	0A	0A	2	25	1960
140 2S	25G		0	0	1963
140 2S	18		0	0	1965
141 2S					1950
141 2S			620	5789	1955
141 2S			172B	2142B	1960
141 2S			166B	2328B	1963
141 2S			156	2667	1965

	7	8	9	10	
142 2S					1950
142 2S			59	551	1955
142 2S			186B	2316B	1960
142 2S	370G		178B	2496B	1963
142 2S	378		177	3026	1965
143 2S					1950
143 2S	24		22	205	1955
143 2S			186B	2316B	1960
143 2S	118G		178B	2496B	1963
143 2S	94		177	3026	1965
144 2S	0A	0A	0	0	1950
144 2S	0A	0A	3	7	1955
144 2S	0A	0A	6	11	1960
144 2S	0A	0A	15	34	1963
144 2S	0A	0A	15	256	1965
145 2S	0A	0A	0	0	1950
145 2S	0A	0A	0	0	1955
145 2S	0A	0A	0	0	1960
145 2S	0A	0A	3	7	1963
145 2S	0A	0A	0	0	1965
146 2S			5	170	1950
146 2S			59	138	1955
146 2S			40A	100A	1960
146 2S			28	64	1963
146 2S			4	20	1965
147 2S	0A	0A	3	102	1950
147 2S	0A	0A	9	21	1955
147 2S			42B	76B	1960
147 2S			52B	119B	1963
147 2S			28	137	1965
148 2S	0A	0A	0	0	1950
148 2S	0A	0A	0	0	1955
148 2S			9	16	1960
148 2S			12	28	1963
148 2S			11	54	1965
149 2S	0A	0A	0	0	1950
149 2S	0A	0A	1	2	1955
149 2S			12	22	1960
149 2S	9F		6	14	1963
149 2S			5	25	1965
150 2S			0	0	1950
150 2S			1	2	1955
150 2S			4	7	1960
150 2S			8	18	1963
150 2S			3	15	1965
151 2S	0A	0A	0	0	1950
151 2S	0A	0A	0	0	1955
151 2S	0A	0A	0	0	1960
151 2S	0A	0A	0	0	1963
151 2S	0A	0A	0	0	1965
152 2S	0A	0A	0	0	1950
152 2S	0A	0A	0	0	1955
152 2S	0A	0A	9	16	1960
152 2S	0A	0A	12	28	1963
152 2S	0A	0A	11	54	1965
153 2S	0A	0A	0	0	1950
153 2S	0A	0A	27	63	1955
153 2S	0A	0A	5	9	1960
153 2S	0G	0G	5	11	1963
153 2S	2		0	0	1965

	7	8	9	10	
154 2S			8	272	1950
154 2S			34	79	1955
154 2S			63	114	1960
154 2S			66	151	1963
154 2S			64	314	1965
155 2S			68	2313	1950
155 2S			135	315	1955
155 2S			663B	1204B	1960
155 2S	8G		566B	1299B	1963
155 2S	7		478	2345	1965
156 2S			68	2313	1950
156 2S	89		104	243	1955
156 2S	275		663B	1204B	1960
156 2S	206G		566B	1299B	1963
156 2S	111		478	2345	1965
157 2S	341	89	1	21	1950
157 2S	1126	210	1A	20A	1955
157 2S	1273	140	1	24	1960
157 2S	1457	122	1	20	1963
157 2S	2082	525	2	32	1965
158 2S	497	130	0	0	1950
158 2S	342	64	0	0	1955
158 2S	325	35	0	0	1960
158 2S	391	33	0	0	1963
158 2S	795	201	0	0	1965
159 2S	125	33	4	84	1950
159 2S			5	76	1955
159 2S					1960
159 2S	34	3			1963
159 2S	1948	491	3	48	1965
160 2S	41	11	9	188	1950
160 2S	27	5	7A	180A	1955
160 2S			7B	170B	1960
160 2S	23	2	9B	101B	1963
160 2S	288	73	11	175	1965
161 2S	690	180	9	188	1950
161 2S	606	113	2	30	1955
161 2S	213	23	1	24	1960
161 2S	859	72	2	40	1963
161 2S	849	214	2	32	1965
162 2S	941	245	3	63	1950
162 2S	981	183			1955
162 2S	2315	254	0	0	1960
162 2S	3178	266	0	0	1963
162 2S	3226	814	0	0	1965
163 2S	124	32	0	0	1950
163 2S	395	73	2	30	1955
163 2S	3631	399	0	0	1960
163 2S	2294	192	0	0	1963
163 2S	21	5	0	0	1965
164 2S	53	14	6	126	1950
164 2S	428	80	5	76	1955
164 2S	111	12	12	292	1960
164 2S	246	21	5	100	1963
164 2S	334	84	2	32	1965
165 2S	0B	0B	9	188	1950
165 2S			0	0	1955
165 2S	124	13	1	24	1960
165 2S	134	11	2	40	1963
165 2S	319	80	2	32	1965

	7	8	9	10	
166 2S	587	153	7	146	1950
166 2S	905	169	16	243	1955
166 2S	1557	171	6	146	1960
166 2S	2460	206	12	241	1963
166 2S	3229	815	16	254	1965
167 2S	41	11	2	42	1950
167 2S	22	4	4	61	1955
167 2S	123	13	3	73	1960
167 2S	141	12	4	80	1963
167 2S	255	64	6	95	1965
168 2S	0B	0B	30	628	1950
168 2S			27	410	1955
168 2S	364	40	15B	365B	1960
168 2S	102	9	41B	823B	1963
168 2S	387	98	100	1587	1965
169 2S	4353	1134	0D	0D	1950
169 2S	5851	1090	0D	0D	1955
169 2S	11787	1296	0D	0D	1960
169 2S	17472	1464	0D	0D	1963
169 2S	23076	5822	0D	0D	1965
170 2S	1816	271	5	107	1950
170 2S	3000	320	1	12	1955
170 2S	1363	97	4	31	1960
170 2S	3501	198	12	88	1963
170 2S	5504	999	13	60	1965
171 2S	29	43	0	0	1950
171 2S	38	4	0	0	1955
171 2S			0	0	1960
171 2S	31	2	0	0	1963
171 2S	66	12	0	0	1965
172 2S	0B	0B	5	107	1950
172 2S			8	98	1955
172 2S			10A	120A	1960
172 2S	0	0	19	139	1963
172 2S	624	113	24	110	1965
173 2S	1690	253	14	299	1950
173 2S	1455	155	10A	250A	1955
173 2S	888	63	33B	255B	1960
173 2S	0	0	70B	514B	1963
173 2S	0	0	73	335	1965
174 2S	92	138	5	107	1950
174 2S	93	10	2	24	1955
174 2S	136	9	3	23	1960
174 2S	106	6	7	51	1963
174 2S	188	34	11	50	1965
175 2S	769	115	1	21	1950
175 2S	665	71	0A	0A	1955
175 2S	1698	121	0	0	1960
175 2S	2218	125	0	0	1963
175 2S	1942	352	2	9	1965
176 2S	818	122	0	0	1950
176 2S	96	10	2	24	1955
176 2S	934	66	0	0	1960
176 2S	937	53	1	7	1963
176 2S	427	77	0	0	1965
177 2S	308	46	6	128	1950
177 2S	1171	18	14	171	1955
177 2S	290	20	14	108	1960
177 2S	442	25	22	162	1963
177 2S	528	96	36	165	1965

			7	8	9	10	
178	2S		0B	0B	5	107	1950
178	2S				0	0	1955
178	2S				3	23	1960
178	2S		18	1	7	51	1963
178	2S		29	5	11	50	1965
179	2S		338	51	5	107	1950
179	2S		445	47	13	159	1955
179	2S		1270	90	34	263	1960
179	2S		1917	108	22	162	1963
179	2S		3484	632	51	234	1965
180	2S		0B	0B	2	43	1950
180	2S				7	86	1955
180	2S				7	54	1960
180	2S		173	10	7	51	1963
180	2S		259	47	22	101	1965
181	2S		0B	0B	26	554	1950
181	2S				44	538	1955
181	2S				168B	1300B	1960
181	2S		39	2	140B	1028B	1963
181	2S		49	9	333	1528	1965
182	2S		3580	535	0D	0D	1950
182	2S		5531	590	0D	0D	1955
182	2S		12981	925	0D	0D	1960
182	2S		19150	1083	0D	0D	1963
182	2S		26219	4759	0D	0D	1965
1	3S	0	0	0	0	0	1950
1	3S	0	0	0	0	0	1955
1	3S	0	0	0	0	0	1960
1	3S	0	0	0	0	0	1963
1	3S	0	0	0	0	0	1965
2	3S	0	0	0	0	0	1950
2	3S	0	0	0	0	0	1955
2	3S	0	0	0	0	0	1960
2	3S	0	0	0	0	0	1963
2	3S	0	0	0	0	1	1965
3	3S	0	0	0	0	0	1950
3	3S	0	0	0	0	0	1955
3	3S	0	0	0	0	1	1960
3	3S	0	0	0	0	0	1963
3	3S	0	0	0	0	0	1965
4	3S	0	0	0	0	0	1950
4	3S	0	0	0	0	0	1955
4	3S	0	0	0	0	0	1960
4	3S	0	0	0	0	0	1963
4	3S	0	0	0	0	0	1965
5	3S	0	0	0	0	0	1950
5	3S	0	0	0	0	0	1955
5	3S	0	0	0	0	0	1960
5	3S	0	0	0	0	0	1963
5	3S	0	0	0	0	0	1965
6	3S	0	0	0	0	0	1950
6	3S	0	0	0	0	0	1955
6	3S	0	0	0	0	0	1960
6	3S	0	0	0	0	0	1963
6	3S	0	0	0	0	0	1965
7	3S	0	0	0	0	0	1950
7	3S	0	0	0	0	0	1955
7	3S	0	0	0	0	0	1960
7	3S	0	0	0	0	0	1963
7	3S	0	0	0	0	0	1965

	11	12	13	14	15	
8 3S	0	0	0	0	0	1950
8 3S	0	0	0	0	0	1955
8 3S	0	0	0	0	0	1960
8 3S	0	0	0	0	0	1963
8 3S	0	0	0	0	0	1965
9 3S	0	0	0	0	0	1950
9 3S	0	0	0	0	0	1955
9 3S	0	0	0	0	0	1960
9 3S	0	0	0	0	0	1963
9 3S	0	0	0	0	0	1965
10 3S	0	0	0	0	0	1950
10 3S	0	0	0	0	0	1955
10 3S	0	0	0	0	0	1960
10 3S	0	0	0	0	0	1963
10 3S	0	0	0	0	0	1965
11 3S	0	0	0	0	0	1950
11 3S	0	0	0	0	0	1955
11 3S	0	0	0	0	0	1960
11 3S	0	0	0	0	0	1963
11 3S	0	0	0	0	0	1965
12 3S	0	0	0	0	0	1950
12 3S	0	0	0	0	0	1955
12 3S	0	0	0	0	0	1960
12 3S	0	0	0	0	0	1963
12 3S	0	0	0	0	0	1965
13 3S	0	0	0	0	0	1950
13 3S	0	0	0	0	0	1955
13 3S	0	0	0	0	0	1960
13 3S	0	0	0	0	1	1963
13 3S	0	0	0	0	0	1965
14 3S	0	0	0	0	0	1950
14 3S	0	0	0	0	0	1955
14 3S	0	0	0	0	0	1960
14 3S	0	0	0	0	0	1963
14 3S	0	0	0	0	0	1965
15 3S	0	0	0	0	0	1950
15 3S	0	0	0	0	0	1955
15 3S	0	0	0	0	0	1960
15 3S	0	0	0	0	0	1963
15 3S	0	0	0	0	0	1965
16 3S	0	0	0	0	0	1950
16 3S	0	0	0	0	0	1955
16 3S	0	0	0	0	0	1960
16 3S	0	0	0	0	0	1963
16 3S	0	0	0	0	0	1965
17 3S	0	0	0	0	0	1950
17 3S	0	0	0	0	0	1955
17 3S	0	0	0	0	0	1960
17 3S	0	0	0	0	0	1963
17 3S	0	0	0	0	0	1965
18 3S	0	0	0	0	0	1950
18 3S	0	0	0	0	0	1955
18 3S	0	0	0	0	0	1960
18 3S	0	0	0	0	0	1963
18 3S	0	0	0	0	0	1965
19 3S	0	0	0	0	0	1950
19 3S	0	0	0	0	0	1955
19 3S	0	0	0	0	0	1960
19 3S	0	0	0	0	0	1963
19 3S	0	0	0	0	0	1965

	11	12	13	14	15	
20 3S	0	0	0	0	0	1950
20 3S	0	0	0	0	0	1955
20 3S	0	0	0	0	0	1960
20 3S	0	0	0	0	0	1963
20 3S	0	0	0	0	0	1965
21 3S	0	0	0	0	0	1950
21 3S	0	0	0	0	0	1955
21 3S	0	0	0	0	0	1960
21 3S	0	0	0	0	0	1963
21 3S	0	0	0	0	0	1965
22 3S	0	0	0	0	0	1950
22 3S	0	0	0	0	0	1955
22 3S	0	0	0	0	0	1960
22 3S	0	0	0	0	0	1963
22 3S	0	0	0	0	0	1965
23 3S	0	0	0	0	0	1950
23 3S	0	0	0	0	0	1955
23 3S	0	0	0	0	0	1960
23 3S	0	0	0	0	0	1963
23 3S	0	0	0	0	0	1965
24 3S	0	0	0	0	0	1950
24 3S	0	0	0	0	0	1955
24 3S	0	0	0	0	0	1960
24 3S	0	0	0	0	0	1963
24 3S	0	0	0	0	0	1965
25 3S	0	0	0	0	0	1950
25 3S	0	0	0	0	0	1955
25 3S	0	0	0	0	0	1960
25 3S	0	0	0	0	0	1963
25 3S	0	0	0	0	0	1965
26 3S	0	0	0	0	2	1950
26 3S	0	0	0	0	0	1955
26 3S	0	0	0	0	0	1960
26 3S	0	0	0	0	0	1963
26 3S	0	0	0	0	0	1965
27 3S	0	0	0	0	0	1950
27 3S	0	0	0	0	0	1955
27 3S	0	0	0	0	0	1960
27 3S	0	0	0	0	0	1963
27 3S	0	0	0	0	0	1965
28 3S	0	0	0	0	0	1950
28 3S	0	0	0	0	0	1955
28 3S	0	0	0	0	1	1960
28 3S	0	0	0	0	0	1963
28 3S	0	0	0	0	0	1965
29 3S	0	0	0	0	0	1950
29 3S	0	0	0	0	0	1955
29 3S	0	0	0	0	0	1960
29 3S	0	0	0	0	0	1963
29 3S	0	0	0	0	0	1965
30 3S	0	0	0	0	0	1950
30 3S	0	0	0	0	0	1955
30 3S	0	0	0	0	0	1960
30 3S	0	0	0	0	0	1963
30 3S	0	0	0	0	0	1965
31 3S	0	0	0	0	2	1950
31 3S	0	0	0	0	0	1955
31 3S	0	1	1	1	1	1960
31 3S	0	0	0	0	0	1963
31 3S	5	1	15B	15B	3	1965

		11	12	13	14	15	
32	3S	0	0	0	0	0	1950
32	3S	0	0	0	0	0	1955
32	3S	0	0	0	0	0	1960
32	3S	0	0	0	0	0	1963
32	3S	0	0	0	0	2	1965
33	3S	0	0	0	0	0	1950
33	3S	0	0	0	0	0	1955
33	3S	0	0	0	0	0	1960
33	3S	0	0	0	0	0	1963
33	3S	0	0	0	0	0	1965
34	3S	0	0	0	0	0	1950
34	3S	0	0	0	0	0	1955
34	3S	0	0	0	0	0	1960
34	3S	0	0	0	0	0	1963
34	3S	0	0	0	0	0	1965
35	3S	0	1	0	61C	1	1950
35	3S	0	0	0	0	0	1955
35	3S	0	0	0	0	0	1960
35	3S	0	0	0	0	0	1963
35	3S	0	0	0	0	0	1965
36	3S	0	0	0	0	0	1950
36	3S	0	0	0	0	0	1955
36	3S	0	0	0	0	0	1960
36	3S	0	0	0	0	0	1963
36	3S	0	0	0	0	0	1965
37	3S	0	1	1	1	0	1950
37	3S	0	0	0	0	0	1955
37	3S	0	0	0	0	2	1960
37	3S	0	0	0	0	1	1963
37	3S	0	0	0	0	6	1965
38	3S	0	1	0	61C	4	1950
38	3S	0	0	0	0	2	1955
38	3S	0	0	0	0	0	1960
38	3S	0	0	0	0	0	1963
38	3S	0	0	0	0	1	1965
39	3S	0	1	0	61C	11	1950
39	3S	0	1	2	2	4	1955
39	3S	0	0	0	0	0	1960
39	3S	0	0	0	0	0	1963
39	3S	2	1	5	5	1	1965
40	3S	0	0	0	0	0	1950
40	3S	0	0	0	0	0	1955
40	3S	0	0	0	0	1	1960
40	3S	0	0	0	0	0	1963
40	3S	0	0	0	0	0	1965
41	3S	0	0	0	0	0	1950
41	3S	0	0	0	0	0	1955
41	3S	0	0	0	0	0	1960
41	3S	0	0	0	0	0	1963
41	3S	0	0	0	0	0	1965
42	3S	0	0	0	0	1	1950
42	3S	0	0	0	0	0	1955
42	3S	0	0	0	0	0	1960
42	3S	0	0	0	0	0	1963
42	3S	0	0	0	0	0	1965
43	3S	0	0	0	0	0	1950
43	3S	0	0	0	0	0	1955
43	3S	0	0	0	0	0	1960
43	3S	0	0	0	0	0	1963
43	3S	0	0	0	0	0	1965

		11	12	13	14	15	
44	3S	0	0	0	0	0	1950
44	3S	0	0	0	0	0	1955
44	3S	0	0	0	0	0	1960
44	3S	0	0	0	0	0	1963
44	3S	0	0	0	0	0	1965
45	3S	0	0	0	0	0	1950
45	3S	0	0	0	0	0	1955
45	3S	0	0	0	0	0	1960
45	3S	0	0	0	0	0	1963
45	3S	0	0	0	0	1	1965
46	3S	0	0	0	0	0	1950
46	3S	0	0	0	0	0	1955
46	3S	0	0	0	0	0	1960
46	3S	0	0	0	0	0	1963
46	3S	0	0	0	0	0	1965
47	3S	0	0	0	0	0	1950
47	3S	0	0	0	0	0	1955
47	3S	0	0	0	0	0	1960
47	3S	0	0	0	0	0	1963
47	3S	0	0	0	0	0	1965
48	3S	0	0	0	0	0	1950
48	3S	0	0	0	0	0	1955
48	3S	0	0	0	0	1	1960
48	3S	0	0	0	0	0	1963
48	3S	0	0	0	0	0	1965
49	3S	0	0	0	0	0	1950
49	3S	0	0	0	0	0	1955
49	3S	0	0	0	0	0	1960
49	3S	0	0	0	0	0	1963
49	3S	0	0	0	0	0	1965
50	3S	0	0	0	0	0	1950
50	3S	0	0	0	0	0	1955
50	3S	0	0	0	0	0	1960
50	3S	0	0	0	0	0	1963
50	3S	0	0	0	0	0	1965
51	3S	0	0	0	0	0	1950
51	3S	0	0	0	0	0	1955
51	3S	0	0	0	0	0	1960
51	3S	0	0	0	0	0	1963
51	3S	0	0	0	0	1	1965
52	3S	0	0	0	0	0	1950
52	3S	0	0	0	0	0	1955
52	3S	1	1	2	2	30	1960
52	3S	1	2	2	2	1	1963
52	3S	0	0	0	0	6	1965
53	3S	0	0	0	0	0	1950
53	3S	0	0	0	0	0	1955
53	3S	0	0	0	0	0	1960
53	3S	0	0	0	0	0	1963
53	3S	0	0	0	0	0	1965
54	3S	0	0	0	0	0	1950
54	3S	0	0	0	0	0	1955
54	3S	0	0	0	0	0	1960
54	3S	0	0	0	0	0	1963
54	3S	0	0	0	0	0	1965
55	3S	0	0	0	0	0	1950
55	3S	0	0	0	0	0	1955
55	3S	0	0	0	0	0	1960
55	3S	0	0	0	0	0	1963
55	3S	0	0	0	0	0	1965

	11	12	13	14	15	
56 3S	0	0	0	0	0	1950
56 3S	0	0	0	0	0	1955
56 3S	0	0	0	0	1	1960
56 3S	0	0	0	0	0	1963
56 3S	0	0	0	0	0	1965
57 3S	0	0	0	0	0	1950
57 3S	0	0	0	0	0	1955
57 3S	0	0	0	0	0	1960
57 3S	0	0	0	0	0	1963
57 3S	0	0	0	0	0	1965
58 3S	0	0	0	0	0	1950
58 3S	0	0	0	0	0	1955
58 3S	0	0	0	0	0	1960
58 3S	0	0	0	0	0	1963
58 3S	0	0	0	0	0	1965
59 3S	0	0	0	0	2	1950
59 3S	4	1	98B	355B	4	1955
59 3S	3	1	5C	4C	1	1960
59 3S	1	1	1	1	0	1963
59 3S	0	0	0	0	1	1965
60 3S	0	0	0	0	0	1950
60 3S	0	0	0	0	0	1955
60 3S	0	0	0	0	0	1960
60 3S	0	0	0	0	0	1963
60 3S	0	0	0	0	0	1965
61 3S	0	0	0	0	0	1950
61 3S	0	0	0	0	0	1955
61 3S	0	0	0	0	0	1960
61 3S	0	0	0	0	0	1963
61 3S	0	0	0	0	0	1965
62 3S	0	0	0	0	0	1950
62 3S	0	0	0	0	0	1955
62 3S	0	0	0	0	0	1960
62 3S	0	0	0	0	0	1963
62 3S	0	0	0	0	0	1965
63 3S	0	0	0	0	0	1950
63 3S	0	0	0	0	0	1955
63 3S	0	0	0	0	0	1960
63 3S	0	0	0	0	0	1963
63 3S	0	0	0	0	0	1965
64 3S	0	0	0	0	0	1950
64 3S	0	1	1	1	1	1955
64 3S	0	0	0	0	0	1960
64 3S	0	0	0	0	0	1963
64 3S	0	0	0	0	3	1965
65 3S	0	0	0	0	0	1950
65 3S	0	0	0	0	2	1955
65 3S	0	0	0	0	1	1960
65 3S	0	0	0	0	0	1963
65 3S	0	0	0	0	1	1965
66 3S	0	0	0	0	0	1950
66 3S	0	0	0	0	0	1955
66 3S	0	0	0	0	0	1960
66 3S	0	0	0	0	0	1963
66 3S	0	0	0	0	0	1965
67 3S	0	0	0	0	0	1950
67 3S	0	0	0	0	0	1955
67 3S	0	0	0	0	0	1960
67 3S	0	0	0	0	0	1963
67 3S	0	0	0	0	0	1965

	11	12	13	14	15	
68 3S	1	0	0	0	0	1950
68 3S	0	0	0	0	0	1955
68 3S	1	0	0	0	4	1960
68 3S	0	0	0	0	1	1963
68 3S	0	1	16B	18B	1	1965
69 3S	0	0	0	0	0	1950
69 3S	0	0	0	0	0	1955
69 3S	0	0	0	0	0	1960
69 3S	0	0	0	0	0	1963
69 3S	0	0	0	0	0	1965
70 3S	0	0	0	0	0	1950
70 3S	0	0	0	0	0	1955
70 3S	0	0	0	0	0	1960
70 3S	0	0	0	0	0	1963
70 3S	0	0	0	0	0	1965
71 3S	0	0	0	0	0	1950
71 3S	0	0	0	0	0	1955
71 3S	0	0	0	0	0	1960
71 3S	0	0	0	0	0	1963
71 3S	0	0	0	0	0	1965
72 3S	0	0	0	0	0	1950
72 3S	0	0	0	0	0	1955
72 3S	0	0	0	0	0	1960
72 3S	0	0	0	0	0	1963
72 3S	0	0	0	0	0	1965
73 3S	0	0	0	0	0	1950
73 3S	0	0	0	0	0	1955
73 3S	0	0	0	0	0	1960
73 3S	0	0	0	0	0	1963
73 3S	0	0	0	0	0	1965
74 3S	0	0	0	0	0	1950
74 3S	0	0	0	0	0	1955
74 3S	0	0	0	0	0	1960
74 3S	0	0	0	0	0	1963
74 3S	0	0	0	0	0	1965
75 3S	0	0	0	0	0	1950
75 3S	0	0	0	0	0	1955
75 3S	0	0	0	0	0	1960
75 3S	0	0	0	0	0	1963
75 3S	0	0	0	0	0	1965
76 3S	0	0	0	0	0	1950
76 3S	0	0	0	0	0	1955
76 3S	0	0	0	0	0	1960
76 3S	0	0	0	0	0	1963
76 3S	0	0	0	0	0	1965
77 3S	0	0	0	0	0	1950
77 3S	0	0	0	0	1	1955
77 3S	0	0	0	0	0	1960
77 3S	0	0	0	0	0	1963
77 3S	0	0	0	0	0	1965
78 3S	0	0	0	0	0	1950
78 3S	0	0	0	0	1	1955
78 3S	0	0	0	0	1	1960
78 3S	0	0	0	0	0	1963
78 3S	0	0	0	0	1	1965
79 3S	0	0	0	0	0	1950
79 3S	0	0	0	0	0	1955
79 3S	0	0	0	0	0	1960
79 3S	0	0	0	0	0	1963
79 3S	0	0	0	0	0	1965

	11	12	13	14	15	
80 3S	0	0	0	0	0	1950
80 3S	0	0	0	0	0	1955
80 3S	0	0	0	0	0	1960
80 3S	0	0	0	0	0	1963
80 3S	0	0	0	0	0	1965
81 3S	0	0	0	0	0	1950
81 3S	0	0	0	0	0	1955
81 3S	0	0	0	0	0	1960
81 3S	0	0	0	0	0	1963
81 3S	0	1	1	1	2	1965
82 3S	0	0	0	0	0	1950
82 3S	0	0	0	0	0	1955
82 3S	0	0	0	0	0	1960
82 3S	0	0	0	0	0	1963
82 3S	0	0	0	0	4	1965
83 3S	0	0	0	0	0	1950
83 3S	0	0	0	0	0	1955
83 3S	0	0	0	0	0	1960
83 3S	0	0	0	0	0	1963
83 3S	0	0	0	0	0	1965
84 3S	0	0	0	0	0	1950
84 3S	0	0	0	0	0	1955
84 3S	0	0	0	0	0	1960
84 3S	0	0	0	0	0	1963
84 3S	0	0	0	0	0	1965
85 3S	0	0	0	0	0	1950
85 3S	0	0	0	0	0	1955
85 3S	0	0	0	0	0	1960
85 3S	0	0	0	0	0	1963
85 3S	0	0	0	0	0	1965
86 3S	0	0	0	0	0	1950
86 3S	0	0	0	0	0	1955
86 3S	0	0	0	0	0	1960
86 3S	0	0	0	0	0	1963
86 3S	0	0	0	0	0	1965
87 3S	0	0	0	0	1	1950
87 3S	0	0	0	0	1	1955
87 3S	1	0	0	0	3	1960
87 3S	0	0	0	0	0	1963
87 3S	0	0	0	0	1	1965
88 3S	0	0	0	0	0	1950
88 3S	0	0	0	0	0	1955
88 3S	0	0	0	0	0	1960
88 3S	0	0	0	0	0	1963
88 3S	0	0	0	0	0	1965
89 3S	0	0	0	0	0	1950
89 3S	0	0	0	0	0	1955
89 3S	0	0	0	0	0	1960
89 3S	0	0	0	0	0	1963
89 3S	0	0	0	0	1	1965
90 3S	0	0	0	0	0	1950
90 3S	0	0	0	0	0	1955
90 3S	0	0	0	0	0	1960
90 3S	0	1	3	71C	1	1963
90 3S	0	1	11C	11C	0	1965
91 3S	0	0	0	0	0	1950
91 3S	0	0	0	0	0	1955
91 3S	0	0	0	0	1	1960
91 3S	0	0	0	0	0	1963
91 3S	0	0	0	0	12	1965

		11	12	13	14	15	
92	3S	0	0	0	0	0	1950
92	3S	0	0	0	0	0	1955
92	3S	0	0	0	0	0	1960
92	3S	0	0	0	0	0	1963
92	3S	0	0	0	0	0	1965
93	3S	0	0	0	0	0	1950
93	3S	0	0	0	0	0	1955
93	3S	0	0	0	0	0	1960
93	3S	0	0	0	0	0	1963
93	3S	0	0	0	0	0	1965
94	3S	0	0	0	0	0	1950
94	3S	0	0	0	0	0	1955
94	3S	0	0	0	0	0	1960
94	3S	0	0	0	0	0	1963
94	3S	0	0	0	0	0	1965
95	3S	0	0	0	0	0	1950
95	3S	0	0	0	0	0	1955
95	3S	0	0	0	0	0	1960
95	3S	0	0	0	0	0	1963
95	3S	0	0	0	0	0	1965
96	3S	1	1	1	1	2	1950
96	3S	2	1	79B	355B	5	1955
96	3S	2	1	4C	5C	0	1960
96	3S	0	1	1	1	0	1963
96	3S	0	0	0	0	0	1965
97	3S	0	0	0	0	0	1950
97	3S	0	0	0	0	0	1955
97	3S	0	0	0	0	0	1960
97	3S	0	0	0	0	0	1963
97	3S	0	0	0	0	0	1965
98	3S	0	0	0	0	0	1950
98	3S	0	0	0	0	0	1955
98	3S	0	0	0	0	0	1960
98	3S	0	0	0	0	0	1963
98	3S	0	0	0	0	0	1965
99	3S	0	1	5	5	0	1950
99	3S	0	1	17B	26B	2	1955
99	3S	0	1	3	5	1	1960
99	3S	0	1	3	3	0	1963
99	3S	0	1	11C	12C	0	1965
100	3S	0	0	0	0	0	1950
100	3S	0	0	0	0	0	1955
100	3S	0	0	0	0	0	1960
100	3S	0	0	0	0	0	1963
100	3S	0	0	0	0	0	1965
101	3S	0	0	0	0	0	1950
101	3S	0	0	0	0	0	1955
101	3S	0	0	0	0	0	1960
101	3S	0	0	0	0	0	1963
101	3S	0	0	0	0	0	1965
102	3S	0	0	0	0	1	1950
102	3S	0	0	0	0	0	1955
102	3S	0	0	0	0	0	1960
102	3S	0	0	0	0	0	1963
102	3S	0	0	0	0	0	1965
103	3S	0	0	0	0	0	1950
103	3S	0	0	0	0	0	1955
103	3S	0	0	0	0	0	1960
103	3S	0	0	0	0	0	1963
103	3S	0	0	0	0	0	1965

		11	12	13	14	15	
104	3S	0	0	0	0	0	1950
104	3S	0	0	0	0	0	1955
104	3S	0	0	0	0	0	1960
104	3S	0	0	0	0	0	1963
104	3S	0	0	0	0	0	1965
105	3S	0	0	0	0	0	1950
105	3S	0	0	0	0	0	1955
105	3S	0	0	0	0	0	1960
105	3S	0	0	0	0	0	1963
105	3S	0	0	0	0	0	1965
106	3S	0	0	0	0	0	1950
106	3S	0	0	0	0	0	1955
106	3S	0	0	0	0	0	1960
106	3S	0	0	0	0	0	1963
106	3S	0	0	0	0	0	1965
107	3S	0	0	0	0	0	1950
107	3S	0	0	0	0	0	1955
107	3S	0	0	0	0	0	1960
107	3S	0	0	0	0	0	1963
107	3S	0	0	0	0	0	1965
108	3S	0	0	0	0	0	1950
108	3S	0	0	0	0	0	1955
108	3S	0	0	0	0	0	1960
108	3S	0	0	0	0	0	1963
108	3S	0	0	0	0	0	1965
109	3S	0	0	0	0	0	1950
109	3S	0	0	0	0	1	1955
109	3S	0	0	0	0	0	1960
109	3S	0	0	0	0	0	1963
109	3S	0	0	0	0	0	1965
110	3S	0	0	0	0	0	1950
110	3S	0	0	0	0	0	1955
110	3S	0	0	0	0	0	1960
110	3S	0	0	0	0	0	1963
110	3S	0	0	0	0	0	1965
111	3S	0	0	0	0	0	1950
111	3S	0	0	0	0	0	1955
111	3S	0	0	0	0	0	1960
111	3S	0	0	0	0	0	1963
111	3S	0	0	0	0	0	1965
112	3S	0	0	0	0	4	1950
112	3S	0	1	23	25	0	1955
112	3S	1	1	3	5	0	1960
112	3S	0	1	3	3	1	1963
112	3S	1	1	11C	12C	2	1965
113	3S	0	0	0	0	0	1950
113	3S	0	0	0	0	0	1955
113	3S	0	0	0	0	0	1960
113	3S	0	0	0	0	0	1963
113	3S	0	0	0	0	0	1965
114	3S	0	0	0	0	0	1950
114	3S	0	0	0	0	0	1955
114	3S	0	0	0	0	0	1960
114	3S	0	0	0	0	0	1963
114	3S	0	0	0	0	0	1965
115	3S	0	0	0	0	0	1950
115	3S	0	0	0	0	0	1955
115	3S	0	0	0	0	0	1960
115	3S	0	0	0	0	0	1963
115	3S	0	0	0	0	0	1965

	11	12	13	14	15	
116 3S	0	0	0	0	0	1950
116 3S	0	0	0	0	0	1955
116 3S	0	0	0	0	0	1960
116 3S	0	0	0	0	0	1963
116 3S	0	0	0	0	0	1965
117 3S	0	0	0	0	0	1950
117 3S	0	0	0	0	0	1955
117 3S	0	0	0	0	1	1960
117 3S	0	0	0	0	0	1963
117 3S	0	0	0	0	0	1965
118 3S	0	0	0	0	0	1950
118 3S	0	0	0	0	0	1955
118 3S	0	0	0	0	0	1960
118 3S	0	0	0	0	0	1963
118 3S	0	0	0	0	0	1965
119 3S	0	0	0	0	0	1950
119 3S	0	0	0	0	0	1955
119 3S	0	0	0	0	0	1960
119 3S	0	0	0	0	0	1963
119 3S	0	0	0	0	0	1965
120 3S	0	1	0	61C	0	1950
120 3S	0	0	0	0	0	1955
120 3S	0	0	0	0	0	1960
120 3S	0	0	0	0	0	1963
120 3S	0	0	0	0	0	1965
121 3S	0	0	0	0	0	1950
121 3S	0	0	0	0	0	1955
121 3S	0	0	0	0	0	1960
121 3S	0	0	0	0	0	1963
121 3S	0	0	0	0	0	1965
122 3S	0	0	0	0	0	1950
122 3S	0	0	0	0	0	1955
122 3S	0	0	0	0	0	1960
122 3S	0	0	0	0	0	1963
122 3S	0	0	0	0	0	1965
123 3S	0	0	0	0	0	1950
123 3S	0	0	0	0	0	1955
123 3S	0	0	0	0	0	1960
123 3S	0	0	0	0	0	1963
123 3S	0	0	0	0	0	1965
124 3S	0	1	1	1	1	1950
124 3S	0	0	0	0	0	1955
124 3S	1	0	0	0	0	1960
124 3S	0	0	0	0	0	1963
124 3S	0	0	0	0	0	1965
125 3S	0	0	0	0	0	1950
125 3S	0	0	0	0	0	1955
125 3S	0	0	0	0	0	1960
125 3S	0	0	0	0	0	1963
125 3S	0	0	0	0	0	1965
126 3S	0	0	0	0	0	1950
126 3S	0	0	0	0	0	1955
126 3S	0	0	0	0	0	1960
126 3S	0	0	0	0	0	1963
126 3S	0	0	0	0	0	1965
127 3S	0	0	0	0	0	1950
127 3S	0	0	0	0	0	1955
127 3S	0	0	0	0	0	1960
127 3S	0	0	0	0	0	1963
127 3S	0	0	0	0	0	1965

		11	12	13	14	15	
128	3S	0	0	0	0	0	1950
128	3S	0	0	0	0	0	1955
128	3S	0	0	0	0	0	1960
128	3S	0	0	0	0	0	1963
128	3S	0	0	0	0	0	1965
129	3S	0	0	0	0	0	1950
129	3S	0	0	0	0	0	1955
129	3S	0	0	0	0	0	1960
129	3S	0	0	0	0	0	1963
129	3S	0	0	0	0	0	1965
130	3S	0	0	0	0	0	1950
130	3S	0	0	0	0	0	1955
130	3S	0	0	0	0	0	1960
130	3S	0	0	0	0	0	1963
130	3S	0	0	0	0	0	1965
131	3S	0	0	0	0	0	1950
131	3S	0	0	0	0	0	1955
131	3S	0	0	0	0	0	1960
131	3S	0	0	0	0	0	1963
131	3S	0	0	0	0	0	1965
132	3S	0	0	0	0	0	1950
132	3S	0	0	0	0	0	1955
132	3S	0	0	0	0	0	1960
132	3S	0	0	0	0	0	1963
132	3S	0	0	0	0	0	1965
133	3S	0	0	0	0	0	1950
133	3S	0	0	0	0	0	1955
133	3S	0	0	0	0	0	1960
133	3S	0	0	0	0	0	1963
133	3S	0	0	0	0	0	1965
134	3S	0	0	0	0	0	1950
134	3S	0	0	0	0	0	1955
134	3S	0	0	0	0	0	1960
134	3S	0	0	0	0	0	1963
134	3S	0	0	0	0	0	1965
135	3S	0	0	0	0	0	1950
135	3S	0	0	0	0	0	1955
135	3S	0	0	0	0	0	1960
135	3S	0	0	0	0	0	1963
135	3S	0	0	0	0	0	1965
136	3S	0	0	0	0	0	1950
136	3S	0	0	0	0	0	1955
136	3S	0	0	0	0	0	1960
136	3S	0	0	0	0	0	1963
136	3S	0	0	0	0	0	1965
137	3S	0	0	0	0	0	1950
137	3S	0	0	0	0	0	1955
137	3S	0	0	0	0	0	1960
137	3S	0	0	0	0	0	1963
137	3S	0	0	0	0	0	1965
138	3S	0	0	0	0	0	1950
138	3S	0	0	0	0	0	1955
138	3S	0	0	0	0	1	1960
138	3S	0	0	0	0	0	1963
138	3S	0	0	0	0	0	1965
139	3S	0	0	0	0	0	1950
139	3S	0	0	0	0	0	1955
139	3S	0	0	0	0	0	1960
139	3S	0	0	0	0	0	1963
139	3S	0	0	0	0	0	1965

		11	12	13	14	15	
140	3S	0	0	0	0	0	1950
140	3S	0	0	0	0	0	1955
140	3S	0	0	0	0	0	1960
140	3S	0	0	0	0	0	1963
140	3S	0	0	0	0	0	1965
141	3S	0	0	0	0	0	1950
141	3S	0	0	0	0	0	1955
141	3S	0	0	0	0	0	1960
141	3S	0	0	0	0	0	1963
141	3S	0	0	0	0	0	1965
142	3S	0	0	0	0	3	1950
142	3S	0	0	0	0	0	1955
142	3S	0	0	0	0	0	1960
142	3S	0	0	0	0	0	1963
142	3S	0	0	0	0	0	1965
143	3S	0	0	0	0	3	1950
143	3S	0	0	0	0	3	1955
143	3S	0	0	0	0	1	1960
143	3S	0	0	0	0	1	1963
143	3S	0	0	0	0	2	1965
144	3S	0	0	0	0	1	1950
144	3S	0	0	0	0	0	1955
144	3S	0	0	0	0	0	1960
144	3S	0	0	0	0	0	1963
144	3S	0	0	0	0	0	1965
145	3S	0	0	0	0	0	1950
145	3S	0	0	0	0	0	1955
145	3S	0	0	0	0	0	1960
145	3S	0	0	0	0	0	1963
145	3S	0	0	0	0	0	1965
146	3S	0	1	1	1	1	1950
146	3S	0	0	0	0	0	1955
146	3S	0	0	0	0	1	1960
146	3S	0	0	0	0	2	1963
146	3S	0	0	0	0	1	1965
147	3S	0	0	0	0	0	1950
147	3S	0	0	0	0	0	1955
147	3S	0	0	0	0	0	1960
147	3S	0	0	0	0	0	1963
147	3S	0	0	0	0	0	1965
148	3S	0	0	0	0	0	1950
148	3S	0	0	0	0	0	1955
148	3S	0	0	0	0	0	1960
148	3S	0	0	0	0	0	1963
148	3S	0	0	0	0	0	1965
149	3S	0	0	0	0	0	1950
149	3S	0	0	0	0	0	1955
149	3S	0	0	0	0	0	1960
149	3S	0	0	0	0	0	1963
149	3S	0	0	0	0	0	1965
150	3S	0	0	0	0	0	1950
150	3S	0	0	0	0	0	1955
150	3S	0	0	0	0	0	1960
150	3S	0	0	0	0	0	1963
150	3S	0	0	0	0	0	1965
151	3S	0	0	0	0	0	1950
151	3S	0	0	0	0	0	1955
151	3S	0	0	0	0	1	1960
151	3S	0	0	0	0	0	1963
151	3S	0	0	0	0	0	1965

	11	12	13	14	15	
152 3S	0	0	0	0	0	1950
152 3S	0	0	0	0	0	1955
152 3S	0	0	0	0	0	1960
152 3S	0	0	0	0	0	1963
152 3S	0	0	0	0	0	1965
153 3S	0	0	0	0	0	1950
153 3S	0	0	0	0	0	1955
153 3S	0	0	0	0	0	1960
153 3S	0	0	0	0	0	1963
153 3S	0	0	0	0	0	1965
154 3S	0	0	0	0	1	1950
154 3S	0	0	0	0	0	1955
154 3S	0	0	0	0	0	1960
154 3S	0	0	0	0	0	1963
154 3S	0	0	0	0	0	1965
155 3S	0	0	0	0	5	1950
155 3S	0	0	0	0	5	1955
155 3S	0	0	0	0	3	1960
155 3S	0	0	0	0	0	1963
155 3S	0	0	0	0	6	1965
156 3S	1	1	3B	2	23	1950
156 3S	0	1	2	2	10	1955
156 3S	0	1	1	1	13	1960
156 3S	0	0	0	0	1	1963
156 3S	0	0	0	0	14	1965
157 3S	0	0	0	0	0	1950
157 3S	0	0	0	0	0	1955
157 3S	0	0	0	0	0	1960
157 3S	0	0	0	0	0	1963
157 3S	0	0	0	0	0	1965
158 3S	0	0	0	0	0	1950
158 3S	0	0	0	0	0	1955
158 3S	0	0	0	0	0	1960
158 3S	0	0	0	0	0	1963
158 3S	0	0	0	0	0	1965
159 3S	0	1	0	61C	2	1950
159 3S	0	0	0	0	0	1955
159 3S	0	0	0	0	0	1960
159 3S	0	0	0	0	0	1963
159 3S	0	0	0	0	0	1965
160 3S	0	0	0	0	0	1950
160 3S	0	0	0	0	0	1955
160 3S	0	0	0	0	0	1960
160 3S	0	0	0	0	0	1963
160 3S	0	0	0	0	0	1965
161 3S	0	0	0	0	0	1950
161 3S	0	0	0	0	1	1955
161 3S	0	0	0	0	0	1960
161 3S	0	0	0	0	0	1963
161 3S	0	0	0	0	0	1965
162 3S	0	0	0	0	0	1950
162 3S	0	0	0	0	0	1955
162 3S	0	0	0	0	0	1960
162 3S	0	0	0	0	0	1963
162 3S	0	0	0	0	1	1965
163 3S	0	0	0	0	0	1950
163 3S	0	0	0	0	0	1955
163 3S	0	0	0	0	0	1960
163 3S	1	1	2	6	3	1963
163 3S	3	1	11C	11C	1	1965

	11	12	13	14	15	
164 3S	0	0	0	0	0	1950
164 3S	0	0	0	0	1	1955
164 3S	0	0	0	0	0	1960
164 3S	0	0	0	0	0	1963
164 3S	0	0	0	0	0	1965
165 3S	0	0	0	0	0	1950
165 3S	0	0	0	0	0	1955
165 3S	0	0	0	0	0	1960
165 3S	0	0	0	0	0	1963
165 3S	0	0	0	0	0	1965
166 3S	0	0	0	0	0	1950
166 3S	0	0	0	0	0	1955
166 3S	0	0	0	0	0	1960
166 3S	0	0	0	0	0	1963
166 3S	0	0	0	0	0	1965
167 3S	0	0	0	0	0	1950
167 3S	0	0	0	0	0	1955
167 3S	0	0	0	0	0	1960
167 3S	0	0	0	0	0	1963
167 3S	0	0	0	0	0	1965
168 3S	3	0	0	0	5	1950
168 3S	0	0	0	0	3	1955
168 3S	0	0	0	0	3	1960
168 3S	0	0	0	0	0	1963
168 3S	0	0	0	0	1	1965
169 3S	0	0	0	0	3	1950
169 3S	0	0	0	0	1	1955
169 3S	0	0	0	0	0	1960
169 3S	0	0	0	0	0	1963
169 3S	0	0	0	0	0	1965
170 3S	0	0	0	0	0	1950
170 3S	0	0	0	0	0	1955
170 3S	0	0	0	0	0	1960
170 3S	0	0	0	0	0	1963
170 3S	0	0	0	0	0	1965
171 3S	0	0	0	0	0	1950
171 3S	0	0	0	0	2	1955
171 3S	0	0	0	0	0	1960
171 3S	0	0	0	0	0	1963
171 3S	0	0	0	0	0	1965
172 3S	0	1	0	61C	10	1950
172 3S	2	1	2	2	11	1955
172 3S	2	0	0	0	2	1960
172 3S	0	0	0	0	1	1963
172 3S	0	1	3	3	2	1965
173 3S	0	0	0	0	1	1950
173 3S	0	0	0	0	0	1955
173 3S	2	1	1	1	16	1960
173 3S	0	0	0	0	2	1963
173 3S	0	0	0	0	1	1965
174 3S	0	0	0	0	0	1950
174 3S	0	0	0	0	1	1955
174 3S	0	0	0	0	0	1960
174 3S	0	0	0	0	0	1963
174 3S	0	0	0	0	1	1965
175 3S	0	0	0	0	0	1950
175 3S	0	0	0	0	0	1955
175 3S	0	0	0	0	0	1960
175 3S	0	0	0	0	0	1963
175 3S	0	0	0	0	1	1965

	11	12	13	14	15	
176 3S	0	0	0	0	0	1950
176 3S	0	0	0	0	0	1955
176 3S	0	0	0	0	0	1960
176 3S	0	0	0	0	2	1963
176 3S	0	0	0	0	1	1965
177 3S	0	0	0	0	0	1950
177 3S	0	0	0	0	2	1955
177 3S	0	0	0	0	0	1960
177 3S	0	0	0	0	0	1963
177 3S	0	0	0	0	0	1965
178 3S	0	0	0	0	0	1950
178 3S	0	0	0	0	0	1955
178 3S	0	0	0	0	0	1960
178 3S	0	0	0	0	0	1963
178 3S	0	0	0	0	0	1965
179 3S	0	0	0	0	0	1950
179 3S	0	0	0	0	0	1955
179 3S	0	0	0	0	0	1960
179 3S	0	0	0	0	0	1963
179 3S	0	0	0	0	0	1965
180 3S	0	0	0	0	3	1950
180 3S	0	0	0	0	1	1955
180 3S	0	0	0	0	0	1960
180 3S	0	0	0	0	1	1963
180 3S	0	0	0	0	1	1965
181 3S	6	1	2	2	19	1950
181 3S	0	1	1	1	9	1955
181 3S	2	0	0	0	10	1960
181 3S	0	0	0	0	4	1963
181 3S	0	0	0	0	7	1965
182 3S	0	0	0	0	1	1950
182 3S	0	0	0	0	0	1955
182 3S	0	0	0	0	0	1960
182 3S	0	0	0	0	0	1963
182 3S	0	0	0	0	0	1965

	16	17	18	19	20	21	22	
1 4S	0	0	0	0	0	0	0	1950
1 4S	0	0	0	0	0	0	0	1955
1 4S	0	0	0	0	0	0	0	1960
1 4S	0	0	0	0	0	0	0	1963
1 4S	0	0	0	0	0	0	0	1965
2 4S	0	0	0	0	0	0	0	1950
2 4S	0	0	0	0	0	0	0	1955
2 4S	0	0	0	0	0	0	0	1960
2 4S	0	0	0	0	0	0	0	1963
2 4S	0	0	0	0	0	0	0	1965
3 4S	0	0	0	0	0	0	0	1950
3 4S	0	0	0	0	0	0	0	1955
3 4S	0	0	0	0	0	0	0	1960
3 4S	0	0	0	0	0	0	1	1963
3 4S	0	0	0	0	0	0	0	1965
4 4S	0	0	0	0	0	0	0	1950
4 4S	0	0	0	0	0	0	0	1955
4 4S	0	0	0	0	0	0	0	1960
4 4S	0	0	0	0	0	0	0	1963
4 4S	0	0	0	0	0	0	0	1965
5 4S	0	0	0	0	0	0	0	1950
5 4S	0	0	0	0	0	0	0	1955
5 4S	0	0	0	0	0	0	0	1960

	16	17	18	19	20	21	22	
5 4S	0	0	0	0	0	0	0	1963
5 4S	0	0	0	0	0	0	0	1965
6 4S	0	0	0	0	0	0	0	1950
6 4S	0	0	0	0	0	0	0	1955
6 4S	0	0	0	0	0	0	0	1960
6 4S	0	0	0	0	0	0	0	1963
6 4S	0	0	0	0	0	0	0	1965
7 4S	0	0	0	0	0	0	0	1950
7 4S	0	0	0	0	0	0	0	1955
7 4S	0	0	0	0	0	0	0	1960
7 4S	0	0	0	0	0	0	0	1963
7 4S	0	0	0	0	0	0	0	1965
8 4S	0	0	0	0	0	0	0	1950
8 4S	0	0	0	0	0	0	0	1955
8 4S	0	0	0	0	0	0	0	1960
8 4S	0	0	0	0	0	0	0	1963
8 4S	0	0	0	0	0	0	0	1965
9 4S	0	0	0	0	0	0	0	1950
9 4S	0	0	0	0	0	0	0	1955
9 4S	0	0	0	0	0	0	0	1960
9 4S	0	0	0	0	0	0	0	1963
9 4S	0	0	0	0	0	0	0	1965
10 4S	0	0	0	0	0	0	0	1950
10 4S	0	0	0	0	0	0	0	1955
10 4S	0	0	0	0	0	0	0	1960
10 4S	0	0	0	0	0	0	0	1963
10 4S	0	0	0	0	0	0	0	1965
11 4S	0	0	0	0	0	0	0	1950
11 4S	0	0	0	0	0	0	0	1955
11 4S	0	0	0	0	0	0	0	1960
11 4S	0	0	0	0	0	0	1	1963
11 4S	0	0	0	0	0	0	0	1965
12 4S	0	0	0	0	0	0	0	1950
12 4S	0	0	0	0	0	0	0	1955
12 4S	0	0	0	0	0	0	0	1960
12 4S	0	0	0	0	0	0	0	1963
12 4S	0	0	0	0	0	0	0	1965
13 4S	0	0	0	1	0	1	0	1950
13 4S	0	0	0	0	0	0	0	1955
13 4S	0	0	0	0	0	0	0	1960
13 4S	0	0	0	1	0	0	1	1963
13 4S	0	0	0	0	0	0	0	1965
14 4S	0	0	0	0	0	0	0	1950
14 4S	0	0	0	0	0	0	0	1955
14 4S	0	0	0	0	0	0	0	1960
14 4S	0	0	0	0	0	0	0	1963
14 4S	0	0	0	0	0	0	0	1965
15 4S	0	0	0	1	0	0	0	1950
15 4S	0	0	0	0	0	0	0	1955
15 4S	0	0	0	0	0	0	0	1960
15 4S	0	0	0	0	0	0	0	1963
15 4S	0	0	0	0	0	0	0	1965
16 4S	0	0	0	0	0	0	0	1950
16 4S	0	0	0	0	0	0	0	1955
16 4S	0	0	0	0	0	0	0	1960
16 4S	0	0	0	0	0	0	0	1963
16 4S	0	0	0	0	0	0	0	1965
17 4S	0	0	0	0	0	0	0	1950
17 4S	0	0	0	0	0	0	0	1955
17 4S	0	0	0	0	0	0	0	1960

	16	17	18	19	20	21	22	
17 4S	0	0	0	0	0	0	0	1963
17 4S	0	0	0	0	0	0	0	1965
18 4S	0	0	0	0	0	0	0	1950
18 4S	0	0	0	0	0	0	0	1955
18 4S	0	0	0	0	0	0	0	1960
18 4S	0	0	0	0	0	0	0	1963
18 4S	0	0	0	0	0	0	0	1965
19 4S	0	0	0	0	0	0	0	1950
19 4S	0	0	0	0	0	0	0	1955
19 4S	0	0	0	0	0	0	0	1960
19 4S	0	0	0	0	0	0	0	1963
19 4S	0	0	0	0	0	0	0	1965
20 4S	0	0	0	0	0	0	0	1950
20 4S	0	0	0	0	0	0	0	1955
20 4S	0	0	0	0	0	0	0	1960
20 4S	0	0	0	0	0	0	0	1963
20 4S	0	0	0	0	0	0	0	1965
21 4S	0	0	0	0	0	0	0	1950
21 4S	0	0	0	0	0	0	0	1955
21 4S	0	0	0	0	0	0	0	1960
21 4S	0	0	0	0	0	0	0	1963
21 4S	0	0	0	0	0	0	0	1965
22 4S	0	0	0	0	0	0	0	1950
22 4S	0	0	0	0	0	0	0	1955
22 4S	0	0	0	0	0	0	0	1960
22 4S	0	0	0	0	0	0	0	1963
22 4S	0	0	0	0	0	0	0	1965
23 4S	0	0	0	0	0	0	0	1950
23 4S	0	0	0	0	0	0	0	1955
23 4S	0	0	0	0	0	0	0	1960
23 4S	0	0	0	0	0	0	0	1963
23 4S	0	0	0	0	0	0	0	1965
24 4S	0	0	0	0	0	0	0	1950
24 4S	0	0	0	0	0	0	0	1955
24 4S	0	0	0	0	0	0	0	1960
24 4S	0	0	0	0	0	0	0	1963
24 4S	0	0	0	0	0	0	0	1965
25 4S	0	0	0	1	1	0	0	1950
25 4S	0	0	0	0	0	0	0	1955
25 4S	0	0	0	0	0	0	0	1960
25 4S	0	0	0	0	0	0	0	1963
25 4S	0	0	0	0	0	0	0	1965
26 4S	0	0	0	0	0	0	0	1950
26 4S	0	0	0	0	0	0	0	1955
26 4S	0	0	0	0	0	0	0	1960
26 4S	0	0	0	0	0	0	0	1963
26 4S	0	0	0	0	0	0	0	1965
27 4S	0	0	0	0	0	0	0	1950
27 4S	0	0	0	0	0	0	0	1955
27 4S	0	0	0	0	0	0	0	1960
27 4S	0	0	0	0	0	0	0	1963
27 4S	0	0	0	0	0	0	0	1965
28 4S	0	0	0	1	0	0	0	1950
28 4S	0	0	0	0	0	0	0	1955
28 4S	0	0	0	0	0	0	0	1960
28 4S	0	0	0	0	0	0	0	1963
28 4S	0	0	0	0	0	0	0	1965
29 4S	0	0	0	0	0	0	0	1950
29 4S	0	0	0	0	0	0	0	1955
29 4S	0	0	0	0	0	0	0	1960

	16	17	18	19	20	21	22	
29 4S	0	0	0	0	0	0	0	1963
29 4S	0	0	0	0	0	0	0	1965
30 4S	0	0	0	0	0	0	1	1950
30 4S	0	0	0	0	0	0	0	1955
30 4S	0	0	0	0	0	0	0	1960
30 4S	0	0	0	0	0	0	0	1963
30 4S	0	0	0	0	0	0	0	1965
31 4S	0	0	0	1	0	1	0	1950
31 4S	0	0	0	0	0	0	0	1955
31 4S	0	0	0	3	0	1	0	1960
31 4S	0	0	0	5	2	2	0	1963
31 4S	0	0	0	12	2	7	0	1965
32 4S	0	0	0	1	0	0	0	1950
32 4S	0	0	0	0	0	0	0	1955
32 4S	0	0	0	2	1	1	0	1960
32 4S	0	0	0	1	0	1	0	1963
32 4S	0	0	0	8	3	5	0	1965
33 4S	0	0	0	0	0	0	0	1950
33 4S	0	0	0	1	0	0	0	1955
33 4S	0	0	0	0	0	0	0	1960
33 4S	0	0	0	0	0	0	0	1963
33 4S	0	0	0	0	0	0	0	1965
34 4S	0	0	0	0	0	0	0	1950
34 4S	0	0	0	0	0	0	0	1955
34 4S	0	0	0	0	0	0	0	1960
34 4S	0	0	0	0	0	0	0	1963
34 4S	0	0	0	0	0	0	0	1965
35 4S	0	0	0	0	0	0	0	1950
35 4S	0	0	0	0	0	0	0	1955
35 4S	0	0	0	0	0	0	0	1960
35 4S	0	0	0	0	0	0	0	1963
35 4S	0	0	0	0	0	0	0	1965
36 4S	0	0	0	0	0	0	0	1950
36 4S	0	0	0	0	0	0	0	1955
36 4S	0	0	0	0	0	0	0	1960
36 4S	0	0	0	0	0	0	0	1963
36 4S	0	0	0	0	0	0	0	1965
37 4S	0	0	0	0	0	0	0	1950
37 4S	0	0	0	0	0	0	0	1955
37 4S	0	0	0	0	0	0	0	1960
37 4S	0	0	0	19	17	2	0	1963
37 4S	0	1	0	21	16	2	0	1965
38 4S	1	0	0	17	11	3	0	1950
38 4S	0	0	0	8	6	1	0	1955
38 4S	0	0	0	0	0	0	0	1960
38 4S	0	0	0	1	0	1	0	1963
38 4S	0	0	0	7	1	2	0	1965
39 4S	0	0	0	45	29	4	0	1950
39 4S	0	0	0	65	56	2	0	1955
39 4S	0	0	0	57	38	0	0	1960
39 4S	0	0	0	22	20	0	0	1963
39 4S	0	0	1	74	39	0	0	1965
40 4S	0	0	0	0	0	0	0	1950
40 4S	0	0	0	0	0	0	0	1955
40 4S	0	0	0	0	0	0	0	1960
40 4S	0	0	0	0	0	0	0	1963
40 4S	0	0	0	0	0	0	0	1965
41 4S	0	0	0	0	0	0	0	1950
41 4S	0	0	0	0	0	0	0	1955

		16	17	18	19	20	21	22	
41	4S	0	0	0	0	0	0	0	1960
41	4S	0	0	0	0	0	0	0	1963
41	4S	0	0	0	0	0	0	0	1965
42	4S	0	0	0	0	0	0	0	1950
42	4S	0	0	0	0	0	0	0	1955
42	4S	0	0	0	0	0	0	0	1960
42	4S	0	0	0	0	0	0	0	1963
42	4S	0	0	0	1	0	0	0	1965
43	4S	0	0	0	0	0	0	0	1950
43	4S	0	0	0	0	0	0	0	1955
43	4S	0	0	0	0	0	0	0	1960
43	4S	0	0	0	0	0	0	0	1963
43	4S	0	0	0	0	0	0	0	1965
44	4S	0	0	0	0	0	0	0	1950
44	4S	0	0	0	0	0	0	0	1955
44	4S	0	0	0	0	0	0	0	1960
44	4S	0	0	0	0	0	0	0	1963
44	4S	0	0	0	0	0	0	0	1965
45	4S	0	0	0	0	0	0	0	1950
45	4S	0	0	0	0	0	0	0	1955
45	4S	0	0	0	0	0	0	0	1960
45	4S	0	0	0	0	0	0	0	1963
45	4S	0	0	0	0	0	0	0	1965
46	4S	0	0	0	0	0	0	0	1950
46	4S	0	0	0	0	0	0	0	1955
46	4S	0	0	0	0	0	0	0	1960
46	4S	0	0	0	0	0	0	0	1963
46	4S	0	0	0	0	0	0	0	1965
47	4S	0	0	0	0	0	0	0	1950
47	4S	0	0	0	0	0	0	0	1955
47	4S	0	0	0	0	0	0	0	1960
47	4S	0	0	0	0	0	0	0	1963
47	4S	0	0	0	0	0	0	0	1965
48	4S	0	0	0	0	0	0	0	1950
48	4S	0	0	0	0	0	0	0	1955
48	4S	0	0	0	0	0	0	0	1960
48	4S	0	0	0	0	0	0	0	1963
48	4S	0	0	0	0	0	0	0	1965
49	4S	0	0	0	0	0	0	0	1950
49	4S	0	0	0	0	0	0	0	1955
49	4S	0	0	0	0	0	0	0	1960
49	4S	0	0	0	0	0	0	0	1963
49	4S	0	0	0	0	0	0	0	1965
50	4S	0	0	0	0	0	0	0	1950
50	4S	0	0	0	0	0	0	0	1955
50	4S	0	0	0	0	0	0	0	1960
50	4S	0	0	0	0	0	0	0	1963
50	4S	0	0	0	0	0	0	0	1965
51	4S	0	0	0	0	0	0	0	1950
51	4S	0	0	0	0	0	0	0	1955
51	4S	0	0	0	0	0	0	0	1960
51	4S	0	0	0	0	0	0	0	1963
51	4S	0	1	0	0	0	0	0	1965
52	4S	0	0	0	1	0	1	0	1950
52	4S	0	0	0	0	0	0	0	1955
52	4S	1	0	0	55	38	4	2	1960
52	4S	0	0	0	26	20	2	0	1963
52	4S	0	0	0	21	16	0	0	1965
53	4S	0	0	0	0	0	0	0	1950

	16	17	18	19	20	21	22	
53 4S	0	0	0	0	0	0	0	1955
53 4S	0	0	0	0	0	0	0	1960
53 4S	0	0	0	0	0	0	0	1963
53 4S	0	0	0	0	0	0	0	1965
54 4S	0	0	0	0	0	0	0	1950
54 4S	0	0	0	0	0	0	0	1955
54 4S	0	0	0	0	0	0	0	1960
54 4S	0	0	0	0	0	0	0	1963
54 4S	0	0	0	0	0	0	0	1965
55 4S	0	0	0	0	0	0	0	1950
55 4S	0	0	0	0	0	0	0	1955
55 4S	0	0	0	0	0	0	0	1960
55 4S	0	0	0	0	0	0	0	1963
55 4S	0	0	0	0	0	0	0	1965
56 4S	0	0	0	0	0	0	0	1950
56 4S	0	0	0	0	0	0	0	1955
56 4S	0	0	0	0	0	0	0	1960
56 4S	0	0	0	0	0	0	0	1963
56 4S	0	0	0	0	0	0	0	1965
57 4S	0	0	0	0	0	0	0	1950
57 4S	0	0	0	0	0	0	0	1955
57 4S	0	0	0	0	0	0	0	1960
57 4S	0	0	0	0	0	0	0	1963
57 4S	0	0	0	0	0	0	0	1965
58 4S	0	0	0	0	0	0	0	1950
58 4S	0	0	0	0	0	0	0	1955
58 4S	0	0	0	0	0	0	0	1960
58 4S	0	0	0	0	0	0	0	1963
58 4S	0	0	0	0	0	0	0	1965
59 4S	0	1	0	4	4	0	0	1950
59 4S	0	0	0	33	22	5	0	1955
59 4S	0	0	0	10	5	1	0	1960
59 4S	0	0	0	3	2	0	0	1963
59 4S	0	0	0	2	0	0	0	1965
60 4S	0	0	0	0	0	0	0	1950
60 4S	0	0	0	1	0	0	0	1955
60 4S	0	0	0	2	1	0	0	1960
60 4S	0	0	0	0	0	0	0	1963
60 4S	0	0	0	0	0	0	0	1965
61 4S	0	0	0	0	0	0	0	1950
61 4S	0	0	0	0	0	0	0	1955
61 4S	0	0	0	0	0	0	0	1960
61 4S	0	0	0	0	0	0	0	1963
61 4S	0	0	0	0	0	0	0	1965
62 4S	0	0	0	0	0	0	0	1950
62 4S	0	0	0	0	0	0	0	1955
62 4S	0	0	0	0	0	0	0	1960
62 4S	0	0	0	0	0	0	0	1963
62 4S	0	0	0	0	0	0	0	1965
63 4S	0	0	0	0	0	0	0	1950
63 4S	0	0	0	0	0	0	0	1955
63 4S	0	0	0	0	0	0	0	1960
63 4S	0	0	0	0	0	0	0	1963
63 4S	0	0	0	1	0	0	0	1965
64 4S	0	0	0	2	0	0	0	1950
64 4S	0	0	0	3	2	1	0	1955
64 4S	0	0	0	4	1	0	0	1960
64 4S	0	0	0	0	0	0	0	1963
64 4S	1	0	0	1	0	0	0	1965

		16	17	18	19	20	21	22	
65	4S	0	0	0	2	0	1	0	1950
65	4S	1	0	0	10	5	1	0	1955
65	4S	0	1	0	1	0	0	0	1960
65	4S	0	0	0	0	0	0	0	1963
65	4S	0	0	0	4	4	0	0	1965
66	4S	0	0	0	0	0	0	0	1950
66	4S	0	0	0	0	0	0	0	1955
66	4S	0	0	0	0	0	0	0	1960
66	4S	0	0	0	0	0	0	0	1963
66	4S	0	0	0	0	0	0	0	1965
67	4S	0	0	0	0	0	0	0	1950
67	4S	0	0	0	0	0	0	0	1955
67	4S	0	0	0	0	0	0	0	1960
67	4S	0	0	0	0	0	0	0	1963
67	4S	0	0	0	0	0	0	0	1965
68	4S	0	0	0	5	0	0	0	1950
68	4S	0	0	0	0	0	0	0	1955
68	4S	1	0	0	10	7	3	0	1960
68	4S	0	0	0	17	8	7	0	1963
68	4S	0	0	0	11	6	4	0	1965
69	4S	0	0	0	0	0	0	0	1950
69	4S	0	0	0	0	0	0	0	1955
69	4S	0	0	0	0	0	0	0	1960
69	4S	0	0	0	0	0	0	0	1963
69	4S	0	0	0	0	0	0	0	1965
70	4S	0	0	0	0	0	0	0	1950
70	4S	0	0	0	0	0	0	0	1955
70	4S	0	0	0	0	0	0	0	1960
70	4S	0	0	0	0	0	0	0	1963
70	4S	0	0	0	0	0	0	0	1965
71	4S	0	0	0	0	0	0	0	1950
71	4S	0	0	0	0	0	0	0	1955
71	4S	0	0	0	0	0	0	0	1960
71	4S	0	0	0	0	0	0	0	1963
71	4S	0	0	0	0	0	0	2	1965
72	4S	0	0	0	0	0	0	0	1950
72	4S	0	0	0	0	0	0	0	1955
72	4S	0	0	0	0	0	0	0	1960
72	4S	0	0	0	0	0	0	0	1963
72	4S	0	0	0	1	0	1	0	1965
73	4S	0	0	0	0	0	0	0	1950
73	4S	0	0	0	0	0	0	0	1955
73	4S	0	0	0	0	0	0	0	1960
73	4S	0	0	0	0	0	0	0	1963
73	4S	0	0	0	0	0	0	0	1965
74	4S	0	0	0	0	0	0	0	1950
74	4S	0	0	0	0	0	0	0	1955
74	4S	0	0	0	0	0	0	0	1960
74	4S	0	0	0	0	0	0	0	1963
74	4S	0	0	0	0	0	0	0	1965
75	4S	0	0	0	0	0	0	0	1950
75	4S	0	0	0	0	0	0	0	1955
75	4S	0	0	0	0	0	0	0	1960
75	4S	0	0	0	0	0	0	0	1963
75	4S	0	0	0	0	0	0	0	1965
76	4S	0	0	0	1	1	0	0	1950
76	4S	0	0	0	3	1	1	0	1955
76	4S	0	0	0	0	0	0	0	1960
76	4S	0	0	0	0	0	0	0	1963
76	4S	0	0	0	0	0	0	0	1965

	16	17	18	19	20	21	22	
77 4S	0	0	0	0	0	0	0	1950
77 4S	0	0	0	2	1	1	1	1955
77 4S	0	0	0	0	0	0	0	1960
77 4S	0	0	0	0	0	0	0	1963
77 4S	0	0	0	1	1	0	0	1965
78 4S	0	0	0	0	0	0	0	1950
78 4S	0	0	0	3	1	1	0	1955
78 4S	0	0	0	1	0	0	0	1960
78 4S	0	0	0	0	0	0	0	1963
78 4S	0	0	0	2	0	1	0	1965
79 4S	0	0	0	0	0	0	0	1950
79 4S	0	0	0	0	0	0	0	1955
79 4S	0	0	0	0	0	0	0	1960
79 4S	0	0	0	0	0	0	0	1963
79 4S	0	0	0	0	0	0	0	1965
80 4S	0	0	0	0	0	0	0	1950
80 4S	0	0	0	0	0	0	0	1955
80 4S	0	0	0	0	0	0	0	1960
80 4S	0	0	0	0	0	0	0	1963
80 4S	0	0	0	0	0	0	0	1965
81 4S	0	0	0	0	0	0	0	1950
81 4S	0	0	0	0	0	0	0	1955
81 4S	0	0	0	4	2	0	0	1960
81 4S	0	0	0	0	0	0	0	1963
81 4S	0	0	0	3	2	0	4	1965
82 4S	0	0	0	0	0	0	0	1950
82 4S	0	0	0	0	0	0	0	1955
82 4S	0	0	0	0	0	0	0	1960
82 4S	0	0	0	0	0	0	0	1963
82 4S	1	0	0	1	0	0	0	1965
83 4S	0	0	0	0	0	0	0	1950
83 4S	0	0	0	0	0	0	0	1955
83 4S	0	0	0	0	0	0	0	1960
83 4S	0	0	0	0	0	0	0	1963
83 4S	0	0	0	0	0	0	0	1965
84 4S	0	0	0	0	0	0	0	1950
84 4S	0	0	0	0	0	0	0	1955
84 4S	0	0	0	0	0	0	0	1960
84 4S	0	0	0	0	0	0	0	1963
84 4S	0	0	0	1	0	0	1	1965
85 4S	0	0	0	0	0	0	0	1950
85 4S	0	0	0	0	0	0	0	1955
85 4S	0	0	0	0	0	0	0	1960
85 4S	0	0	0	0	0	0	0	1963
85 4S	0	0	0	0	0	0	0	1965
86 4S	0	0	0	0	0	0	0	1950
86 4S	0	0	0	0	0	0	0	1955
86 4S	0	0	0	0	0	0	0	1960
86 4S	0	0	0	0	0	0	0	1963
86 4S	0	0	0	0	0	0	0	1965
87 4S	0	0	0	4	1	1	0	1950
87 4S	0	0	0	3	3	0	0	1955
87 4S	0	0	0	4	3	0	1	1960
87 4S	0	0	0	0	0	0	0	1963
87 4S	0	0	0	0	0	0	0	1965
88 4S	0	0	0	0	0	0	0	1950
88 4S	0	0	0	0	0	0	0	1955
88 4S	0	0	0	0	0	0	0	1960
88 4S	0	0	0	0	0	0	0	1963
88 4S	0	0	0	0	0	0	0	1965

	16	17	18	19	20	21	22	
89 4S	0	0	0	0	0	0	0	1950
89 4S	0	0	0	0	0	0	0	1955
89 4S	0	0	0	0	0	0	0	1960
89 4S	0	0	0	0	0	0	0	1963
89 4S	0	0	0	0	0	0	0	1965
90 4S	0	0	0	0	0	0	0	1950
90 4S	0	0	0	0	0	0	0	1955
90 4S	0	0	0	0	0	0	0	1960
90 4S	0	0	0	0	0	0	2	1963
90 4S	0	0	0	7	4	0	0	1965
91 4S	0	0	0	0	0	0	0	1950
91 4S	0	0	0	0	0	0	0	1955
91 4S	0	0	0	0	0	0	0	1960
91 4S	0	0	0	1	1	0	0	1963
91 4S	0	5	0	10	5	0	6	1965
92 4S	0	0	0	0	0	0	0	1950
92 4S	0	0	0	0	0	0	0	1955
92 4S	0	0	0	0	0	0	0	1960
92 4S	0	0	0	0	0	0	0	1963
92 4S	0	0	0	0	0	0	0	1965
93 4S	0	0	0	0	0	0	0	1950
93 4S	0	0	0	0	0	0	0	1955
93 4S	0	0	0	0	0	0	0	1960
93 4S	0	0	0	0	0	0	0	1963
93 4S	0	0	0	0	0	0	0	1965
94 4S	0	0	0	0	0	0	0	1950
94 4S	0	0	0	0	0	0	0	1955
94 4S	0	0	0	0	0	0	0	1960
94 4S	0	0	0	0	0	0	0	1963
94 4S	0	0	0	0	0	0	0	1965
95 4S	0	0	0	0	0	0	0	1950
95 4S	0	0	0	0	0	0	0	1955
95 4S	0	0	0	0	0	0	0	1960
95 4S	0	0	0	0	0	0	0	1963
95 4S	0	0	0	0	0	0	0	1965
96 4S	0	0	0	2	2	0	0	1950
96 4S	0	1	0	54	42	4	0	1955
96 4S	0	0	0	7	5	0	0	1960
96 4S	0	0	0	0	0	0	0	1963
96 4S	0	0	0	1	0	0	0	1965
97 4S	0	0	0	0	0	0	0	1950
97 4S	0	0	0	0	0	0	0	1955
97 4S	0	0	0	0	0	0	0	1960
97 4S	0	0	0	0	0	0	0	1963
97 4S	0	0	0	0	0	0	0	1965
98 4S	0	0	0	0	0	0	0	1950
98 4S	0	0	0	0	0	0	0	1955
98 4S	0	0	0	0	0	0	0	1960
98 4S	0	0	0	0	0	0	0	1963
98 4S	0	0	0	0	0	0	0	1965
99 4S	0	0	0	7	6	0	0	1950
99 4S	0	0	0	6	5	0	0	1955
99 4S	0	0	0	3	1	0	0	1960
99 4S	0	0	0	1	1	0	0	1963
99 4S	0	0	0	2	1	1	0	1965

DYADIC BEHAVIOR DATA, 1950-1965

	16	17	18	19	20	21	22	
100 4S	0	0	0	0	0	0	0	1950
100 4S	0	0	0	0	0	0	0	1955
100 4S	0	0	0	0	0	0	0	1960
100 4S	0	0	0	0	0	0	0	1963
100 4S	0	0	0	0	0	0	0	1965
101 4S	0	0	0	0	0	0	0	1950
101 4S	0	0	0	0	0	0	0	1955
101 4S	0	0	0	0	0	0	0	1960
101 4S	0	0	0	0	0	0	0	1963
101 4S	0	0	0	0	0	0	0	1965
102 4S	0	0	0	0	0	0	0	1950
102 4S	0	0	0	3	1	1	0	1955
102 4S	0	0	0	2	2	0	0	1960
102 4S	0	0	0	0	0	0	0	1963
102 4S	0	0	0	0	0	0	0	1965
103 4S	0	0	0	4	4	0	0	1950
103 4S	0	0	0	2	2	0	0	1955
103 4S	0	0	0	0	0	0	0	1960
103 4S	0	0	0	0	0	0	0	1963
103 4S	0	0	0	0	0	0	0	1965
104 4S	0	0	0	0	0	0	1	1950
104 4S	0	0	0	1	1	0	0	1955
104 4S	0	0	0	0	0	0	0	1960
104 4S	0	0	0	0	0	0	0	1963
104 4S	0	0	0	0	0	0	0	1965
105 4S	0	0	0	0	0	0	0	1950
105 4S	0	0	0	0	0	0	0	1955
105 4S	0	0	0	0	0	0	0	1960
105 4S	0	0	0	0	0	0	0	1963
105 4S	0	0	0	0	0	0	0	1965
106 4S	0	0	0	0	0	0	0	1950
106 4S	0	0	0	0	0	0	0	1955
106 4S	0	0	0	0	0	0	0	1960
106 4S	0	0	0	0	0	0	0	1963
106 4S	0	0	0	0	0	0	0	1965
107 4S	0	0	0	0	0	0	0	1950
107 4S	0	0	0	0	0	0	0	1955
107 4S	0	0	0	0	0	0	0	1960
107 4S	0	0	0	0	0	0	0	1963
107 4S	0	0	0	0	0	0	0	1965
108 4S	0	0	0	0	0	0	0	1950
108 4S	0	0	0	0	0	0	0	1955
108 4S	0	0	0	0	0	0	0	1960
108 4S	0	0	0	0	0	0	0	1963
108 4S	0	0	0	0	0	0	0	1965
109 4S	0	0	0	0	0	0	0	1950
109 4S	0	0	0	0	0	0	0	1955
109 4S	0	0	0	6	4	0	0	1960
109 4S	0	0	0	1	0	0	0	1963
109 4S	0	0	0	0	0	0	0	1965
110 4S	0	0	0	0	0	0	0	1950
110 4S	0	0	0	0	0	0	0	1955
110 4S	0	0	0	0	0	0	0	1960
110 4S	0	0	0	0	0	0	0	1963
110 4S	0	0	0	0	0	0	0	1965
111 4S	0	0	0	0	0	0	0	1950
111 4S	0	0	0	0	0	0	0	1955
111 4S	0	0	0	0	0	0	0	1960
111 4S	0	0	0	0	0	0	0	1963
111 4S	0	0	0	0	0	0	0	1965

	16	17	18	19	20	21	22	
112 4S	0	0	0	9	7	1	0	1950
112 4S	0	0	0	5	2	0	1	1955
112 4S	0	0	0	5	4	0	0	1960
112 4S	0	0	1	1	1	0	0	1963
112 4S	0	0	0	6	3	1	0	1965
113 4S	0	0	0	0	0	0	0	1950
113 4S	0	0	0	0	0	0	0	1955
113 4S	0	0	0	0	0	0	0	1960
113 4S	0	0	0	0	0	0	0	1963
113 4S	0	0	0	0	0	0	0	1965
114 4S	0	0	0	0	0	0	0	1950
114 4S	0	0	0	0	0	0	0	1955
114 4S	0	0	0	0	0	0	0	1960
114 4S	0	0	0	0	0	0	0	1963
114 4S	0	0	0	0	0	0	0	1965
115 4S	0	0	0	0	0	0	0	1950
115 4S	0	0	0	0	0	0	0	1955
115 4S	0	0	0	0	0	0	0	1960
115 4S	0	0	0	0	0	0	0	1963
115 4S	0	0	0	0	0	0	0	1965
116 4S	0	0	0	0	0	0	0	1950
116 4S	0	0	0	0	0	0	1	1955
116 4S	0	0	0	0	0	0	0	1960
116 4S	0	0	0	0	0	0	0	1963
116 4S	0	0	0	0	0	0	0	1965
117 4S	0	0	0	0	0	0	0	1950
117 4S	0	0	0	2	1	1	2	1955
117 4S	0	1	0	0	0	0	0	1960
117 4S	0	0	0	1	1	0	0	1963
117 4S	0	0	0	0	0	0	0	1965
118 4S	0	0	0	0	0	0	0	1950
118 4S	0	0	0	0	0	0	0	1955
118 4S	0	0	0	0	0	0	0	1960
118 4S	0	0	0	0	0	0	0	1963
118 4S	0	0	0	0	0	0	0	1965
119 4S	0	0	0	0	0	0	0	1950
119 4S	0	0	0	0	0	0	0	1955
119 4S	0	0	0	0	0	0	0	1960
119 4S	0	0	0	0	0	0	0	1963
119 4S	0	0	0	0	0	0	0	1965
120 4S	0	0	0	0	0	0	0	1950
120 4S	0	0	0	0	0	0	0	1955
120 4S	0	0	0	0	0	0	0	1960
120 4S	0	0	0	0	0	0	0	1963
120 4S	0	0	0	0	0	0	0	1965
121 4S	0	0	0	0	0	0	0	1950
121 4S	0	0	0	0	0	0	0	1955
121 4S	0	0	0	0	0	0	0	1960
121 4S	0	0	0	0	0	0	0	1963
121 4S	0	0	0	0	0	0	0	1965
122 4S	0	0	0	0	0	0	0	1950
122 4S	0	0	0	0	0	0	0	1955
122 4S	0	0	0	0	0	0	0	1960
122 4S	0	0	0	0	0	0	0	1963
122 4S	0	0	0	0	0	0	0	1965
123 4S	0	0	0	0	0	0	0	1950
123 4S	0	0	0	0	0	0	0	1955
123 4S	0	0	0	0	0	0	0	1960
123 4S	0	0	0	0	0	0	0	1963
123 4S	0	0	0	0	0	0	0	1965

	16	17	18	19	20	21	22	
124 4S	0	0	0	0	0	0	0	1950
124 4S	0	0	0	3	1	0	0	1955
124 4S	0	0	0	0	0	0	0	1960
124 4S	0	0	0	0	0	0	0	1963
124 4S	0	0	0	0	0	0	0	1965
125 4S	0	0	0	0	0	0	0	1950
125 4S	0	0	0	0	0	0	0	1955
125 4S	0	0	0	0	0	0	0	1960
125 4S	0	0	0	0	0	0	0	1963
125 4S	0	0	0	0	0	0	0	1965
126 4S	0	0	0	0	0	0	0	1950
126 4S	0	0	0	0	0	0	0	1955
126 4S	0	0	0	0	0	0	0	1960
126 4S	0	0	0	0	0	0	0	1963
126 4S	0	0	0	0	0	0	0	1965
127 4S	0	0	0	0	0	0	0	1950
127 4S	0	0	0	0	0	0	0	1955
127 4S	0	0	0	0	0	0	0	1960
127 4S	0	0	0	0	0	0	0	1963
127 4S	0	0	0	0	0	0	0	1965
128 4S	0	0	0	0	0	0	0	1950
128 4S	0	0	0	0	0	0	0	1955
128 4S	0	0	0	0	0	0	0	1960
128 4S	0	0	0	0	0	0	0	1963
128 4S	0	0	0	0	0	0	0	1965
129 4S	0	0	0	0	0	0	0	1950
129 4S	0	0	0	0	0	0	0	1955
129 4S	0	0	0	0	0	0	0	1960
129 4S	0	0	0	0	0	0	0	1963
129 4S	0	0	0	0	0	0	0	1965
130 4S	0	0	0	0	0	0	0	1950
130 4S	0	0	0	1	0	1	0	1955
130 4S	0	0	0	0	0	0	0	1960
130 4S	0	0	0	0	0	0	0	1963
130 4S	0	0	0	0	0	0	0	1965
131 4S	0	0	0	0	0	0	0	1950
131 4S	0	0	0	0	0	0	0	1955
131 4S	0	0	0	0	0	0	0	1960
131 4S	0	0	0	0	0	0	0	1963
131 4S	0	0	0	0	0	0	0	1965
132 4S	0	0	0	0	0	0	0	1950
132 4S	0	0	0	0	0	0	0	1955
132 4S	0	0	0	0	0	0	0	1960
132 4S	0	0	0	0	0	0	0	1963
132 4S	0	0	0	0	0	0	0	1965
133 4S	0	0	0	0	0	0	0	1950
133 4S	0	0	0	0	0	0	0	1955
133 4S	0	0	0	0	0	0	0	1960
133 4S	0	0	0	1	1	0	0	1963
133 4S	0	0	0	1	1	0	0	1965
134 4S	0	0	0	0	0	0	0	1950
134 4S	0	0	0	0	0	0	0	1955
134 4S	0	0	0	0	0	0	0	1960
134 4S	0	0	0	0	0	0	0	1963
134 4S	0	0	0	0	0	0	0	1965
135 4S	0	0	0	0	0	0	0	1950
135 4S	0	0	0	0	0	0	0	1955
135 4S	0	0	0	0	0	0	0	1960
135 4S	0	0	0	0	0	0	0	1963
135 4S	0	0	0	0	0	0	0	1965

	16	17	18	19	20	21	22	
136 4S	0	0	0	0	0	0	0	1950
136 4S	0	0	0	0	0	0	0	1955
136 4S	0	0	0	0	0	0	0	1960
136 4S	0	0	0	0	0	0	0	1963
136 4S	0	0	0	0	0	0	0	1965
137 4S	0	0	0	0	0	0	0	1950
137 4S	0	0	0	0	0	0	0	1955
137 4S	0	0	0	0	0	0	0	1960
137 4S	0	0	0	0	0	0	0	1963
137 4S	0	0	0	0	0	0	0	1965
138 4S	0	0	0	0	0	0	0	1950
138 4S	0	0	0	0	0	0	0	1955
138 4S	1	0	0	0	0	0	0	1960
138 4S	0	0	0	0	0	0	0	1963
138 4S	0	0	0	0	0	0	0	1965
139 4S	0	0	0	0	0	0	0	1950
139 4S	0	0	0	0	0	0	0	1955
139 4S	0	0	0	0	0	0	0	1960
139 4S	0	0	0	0	0	0	0	1963
139 4S	0	0	0	0	0	0	0	1965
140 4S	0	0	0	0	0	0	0	1950
140 4S	0	0	0	0	0	0	0	1955
140 4S	0	0	0	0	0	0	0	1960
140 4S	0	0	0	0	0	0	0	1963
140 4S	0	0	0	0	0	0	0	1965
141 4S	0	0	0	1	1	0	0	1950
141 4S	0	0	0	0	0	0	0	1955
141 4S	0	0	0	1	1	0	0	1960
141 4S	0	0	0	0	0	0	0	1963
141 4S	0	0	0	0	0	0	0	1965
142 4S	1	0	0	3	0	1	0	1950
142 4S	0	0	0	0	0	0	0	1955
142 4S	0	0	0	0	0	0	0	1960
142 4S	0	0	0	0	0	0	0	1963
142 4S	0	0	0	0	0	0	0	1965
143 4S	1	0	1	5	3	1	0	1950
143 4S	0	0	0	3	3	0	0	1955
143 4S	0	0	0	1	1	0	0	1960
143 4S	1	0	0	0	0	0	0	1963
143 4S	1	0	0	8	6	1	0	1965
144 4S	0	0	0	0	0	0	0	1950
144 4S	0	0	0	1	1	0	0	1955
144 4S	0	0	0	0	0	0	0	1960
144 4S	0	0	0	0	0	0	0	1963
144 4S	0	0	0	0	0	0	0	1965
145 4S	0	0	0	0	0	0	0	1950
145 4S	0	0	0	0	0	0	0	1955
145 4S	0	0	0	0	0	0	0	1960
145 4S	0	0	0	0	0	0	0	1963
145 4S	0	0	0	0	0	0	0	1965
146 4S	0	0	0	0	0	0	0	1950
146 4S	0	0	0	1	0	0	0	1955
146 4S	0	0	0	1	0	0	0	1960
146 4S	1	0	1	13	9	2	0	1963
146 4S	0	0	0	9	6	0	0	1965
147 4S	0	0	0	0	0	0	0	1950
147 4S	0	0	0	0	0	0	0	1955
147 4S	0	0	0	0	0	0	0	1960
147 4S	0	0	0	0	0	0	0	1963
147 4S	0	0	0	0	0	0	0	1965

	16	17	18	19	20	21	22	
148 4S	0	0	0	0	0	0	0	1950
148 4S	0	0	0	0	0	0	0	1955
148 4S	0	0	0	0	0	0	0	1960
148 4S	0	0	0	0	0	0	0	1963
148 4S	0	0	0	0	0	0	0	1965
149 4S	0	0	0	0	0	0	0	1950
149 4S	0	0	0	1	1	0	0	1955
149 4S	0	0	0	0	0	0	0	1960
149 4S	0	0	0	0	0	0	0	1963
149 4S	0	0	0	0	0	0	0	1965
150 4S	0	0	0	0	0	0	0	1950
150 4S	0	0	0	0	0	0	0	1955
150 4S	0	0	0	0	0	0	0	1960
150 4S	0	0	0	0	0	0	0	1963
150 4S	0	0	0	1	0	0	0	1965
151 4S	0	0	0	0	0	0	0	1950
151 4S	0	0	0	4	2	0	0	1955
151 4S	0	0	0	1	1	0	0	1960
151 4S	0	0	0	0	0	0	0	1963
151 4S	0	0	0	1	1	0	0	1965
152 4S	0	0	0	0	0	0	0	1950
152 4S	0	0	0	0	0	0	0	1955
152 4S	0	0	0	0	0	0	0	1960
152 4S	0	0	0	0	0	0	0	1963
152 4S	0	0	0	0	0	0	0	1965
153 4S	0	0	0	0	0	0	0	1950
153 4S	0	0	0	3	1	1	0	1955
153 4S	0	0	0	0	0	0	0	1960
153 4S	0	0	0	0	0	0	0	1963
153 4S	0	0	0	0	0	0	0	1965
154 4S	1	0	0	0	0	0	0	1950
154 4S	0	0	0	0	0	0	0	1955
154 4S	0	0	0	0	0	0	0	1960
154 4S	0	0	0	0	0	0	0	1963
154 4S	0	0	0	0	0	0	0	1965
155 4S	0	0	0	21	16	1	0	1950
155 4S	0	0	0	30	23	3	0	1955
155 4S	0	0	0	11	6	2	0	1960
155 4S	0	0	0	1	0	2	0	1963
155 4S	0	1	0	0	0	0	0	1965
156 4S	0	0	0	102	71	8	1	1950
156 4S	0	0	0	90	74	5	0	1955
156 4S	2	0	0	82	50	3	0	1960
156 4S	0	0	0	25	14	6	0	1963
156 4S	3	2	2	84	42	4	2	1965
157 4S	0	0	0	0	0	0	0	1950
157 4S	0	0	0	0	0	0	0	1955
157 4S	0	0	0	0	0	0	0	1960
157 4S	0	0	0	0	0	0	0	1963
157 4S	0	0	0	0	0	0	0	1965
158 4S	0	0	0	0	0	0	0	1950
158 4S	0	0	0	0	0	0	0	1955
158 4S	0	0	0	0	0	0	0	1960
158 4S	0	0	0	0	0	0	0	1963
158 4S	0	0	0	0	0	0	0	1965
159 4S	0	1	0	2	0	0	0	1950
159 4S	0	0	0	3	1	0	0	1955
159 4S	0	0	0	0	0	0	0	1960
159 4S	0	0	0	0	0	0	0	1963
159 4S	0	0	0	0	0	0	0	1965

	16	17	18	19	20	21	22	
160 4S	0	0	0	0	0	0	0	1950
160 4S	0	0	0	0	0	0	0	1955
160 4S	0	0	0	1	0	1	0	1960
160 4S	0	0	0	1	0	1	0	1963
160 4S	0	0	0	1	0	1	0	1965
161 4S	0	0	0	3	0	1	0	1950
161 4S	0	0	0	6	2	4	0	1955
161 4S	0	0	0	0	0	0	0	1960
161 4S	0	0	0	1	1	0	0	1963
161 4S	0	0	0	1	0	1	0	1965
162 4S	0	0	0	0	0	0	0	1950
162 4S	0	0	0	0	0	0	0	1955
162 4S	0	0	0	0	0	0	0	1960
162 4S	0	0	0	0	0	0	0	1963
162 4S	0	0	0	0	0	0	0	1965
163 4S	0	0	0	0	0	0	0	1950
163 4S	0	0	0	0	0	0	0	1955
163 4S	0	0	0	0	0	0	0	1960
163 4S	0	0	0	2	0	1	0	1963
163 4S	0	0	0	1	0	0	0	1965
164 4S	0	0	0	0	0	0	0	1950
164 4S	0	0	0	3	1	2	0	1955
164 4S	0	0	0	0	0	0	0	1960
164 4S	0	0	0	1	0	0	0	1963
164 4S	0	0	0	0	0	0	0	1965
165 4S	0	0	0	0	0	0	0	1950
165 4S	0	0	0	0	0	0	0	1955
165 4S	0	0	0	0	0	0	0	1960
165 4S	0	0	0	0	0	0	0	1963
165 4S	0	0	0	0	0	0	0	1965
166 4S	0	0	0	0	0	0	0	1950
166 4S	0	0	0	0	0	0	0	1955
166 4S	0	0	0	0	0	0	0	1960
166 4S	0	0	0	0	0	0	0	1963
166 4S	0	0	0	0	0	0	0	1965
167 4S	0	0	0	0	0	0	0	1950
167 4S	0	0	0	0	0	0	0	1955
167 4S	0	0	0	0	0	0	0	1960
167 4S	0	0	0	0	0	0	0	1963
167 4S	0	0	0	1	0	1	0	1965
168 4S	0	0	0	17	7	0	2	1950
168 4S	0	0	0	19	9	2	0	1955
168 4S	0	0	0	7	1	1	0	1960
168 4S	0	0	0	6	1	5	0	1963
168 4S	1	0	0	8	1	7	0	1965
169 4S	0	2	0	3	2	0	0	1950
169 4S	0	0	0	7	3	3	0	1955
169 4S	0	0	0	0	0	0	0	1960
169 4S	0	0	0	3	1	1	0	1963
169 4S	0	0	0	1	0	1	0	1965
170 4S	0	0	0	0	0	0	0	1950
170 4S	0	0	0	0	0	0	0	1955
170 4S	0	0	0	0	0	0	0	1960
170 4S	0	0	0	0	0	0	0	1963
170 4S	0	0	0	2	0	0	0	1965
171 4S	0	0	0	0	0	0	0	1950
171 4S	0	0	0	0	0	0	0	1955
171 4S	0	0	0	0	0	0	0	1960
171 4S	0	0	0	0	0	0	0	1963
171 4S	0	0	0	0	0	0	0	1965

	16	17	18	19	20	21	22	
172 4S	0	2	1	10	4	0	0	1950
172 4S	0	0	1	26	18	1	0	1955
172 4S	0	0	1	7	6	0	0	1960
172 4S	0	0	1	0	0	0	0	1963
172 4S	0	0	0	11	7	0	0	1965
173 4S	0	0	0	1	1	0	0	1950
173 4S	0	0	0	0	0	0	0	1955
173 4S	3	2	1	38	21	7	1	1960
173 4S	0	2	0	3	1	2	0	1963
173 4S	0	0	0	2	1	0	0	1965
174 4S	0	0	0	1	0	0	0	1950
174 4S	0	0	0	4	2	1	1	1955
174 4S	0	0	0	0	0	0	0	1960
174 4S	0	0	0	1	0	0	0	1963
174 4S	0	1	0	1	0	0	0	1965
175 4S	0	0	0	2	0	0	0	1950
175 4S	0	0	0	0	0	0	0	1955
175 4S	0	0	0	0	0	0	0	1960
175 4S	0	0	0	0	0	0	0	1963
175 4S	0	0	0	1	0	0	0	1965
176 4S	0	0	0	0	0	0	0	1950
176 4S	0	0	0	1	0	0	0	1955
176 4S	0	0	0	0	0	0	0	1960
176 4S	0	0	0	1	0	0	0	1963
176 4S	0	1	0	8	0	8	0	1965
177 4S	0	0	0	1	0	1	0	1950
177 4S	0	0	0	4	0	0	0	1955
177 4S	0	0	0	0	0	0	0	1960
177 4S	0	0	0	1	0	0	0	1963
177 4S	0	0	0	0	0	0	0	1965
178 4S	0	0	0	0	0	0	0	1950
178 4S	0	0	0	0	0	0	0	1955
178 4S	0	0	0	0	0	0	0	1960
178 4S	0	0	0	0	0	0	0	1963
178 4S	0	0	0	0	0	0	0	1965
179 4S	0	0	0	0	0	0	0	1950
179 4S	0	0	0	0	0	0	0	1955
179 4S	0	0	0	0	0	0	0	1960
179 4S	0	0	0	0	0	0	0	1963
179 4S	0	0	0	0	0	0	0	1965
180 4S	0	1	0	3	1	0	0	1950
180 4S	0	0	0	0	0	0	0	1955
180 4S	0	0	0	0	0	0	0	1960
180 4S	0	0	0	0	0	0	0	1963
180 4S	0	0	0	1	0	1	0	1965
181 4S	0	2	0	76	44	2	0	1950
181 4S	0	0	0	48	34	5	0	1955
181 4S	3	0	0	57	32	1	0	1960
181 4S	1	1	0	13	1	10	0	1963
181 4S	0	1	0	21	6	13	0	1965
182 4S	0	0	0	6	2	2	0	1950
182 4S	0	0	0	1	1	0	0	1955
182 4S	0	0	0	1	1	0	0	1960
182 4S	0	0	0	1	0	1	0	1963
182 4S	0	0	0	0	0	0	0	1965

	23	24	25	26	
1 5S	0	0	-0100	-C494	1950
1 5S	0	0	0719	C627	1955
1 5S	0	0	0615	C396	1960
1 5S	0	0	-0007	C064	1963

		23	24	25	26	
1	5S	0	0	0130	-C020	1965
2	5S	0	0			1950
2	5S	0	0			1955
2	5S	0	0			1960
2	5S	0	0			1963
2	5S	0	0			1965
3	5S	0	0	-1111	-C757	1950
3	5S	0	0	1311	1830	1955
3	5S	0	0	C514	1208	1960
3	5S	1	0	0963	0706	1963
3	5S	0	0	0168	-C046	1965
4	5S	0	0	-0032	-C406	1950
4	5S	0	0	0501	C105	1955
4	5S	0	0	0745	C646	1960
4	5S	0	0	0061	-C247	1963
4	5S	0	0	0030	-C269	1965
5	5S	0	0	0217	C029	1950
5	5S	0	0	1123	C579	1955
5	5S	0	0	0945	C513	1960
5	5S	0	0	0426	C253	1963
5	5S	0	0	-0209	-C338	1965
6	5S	0	0	0101	-C267	1950
6	5S	0	0	0148	-C227	1955
6	5S	0	0	0590	C392	1960
6	5S	0	0	0711	C663	1963
6	5S	0	0			1965
7	5S	0	0	C333	-C351	1950
7	5S	0	0	-0456	-C331	1955
7	5S	0	0	-0151	1071	1960
7	5S	0	0	-0254	C831	1963
7	5S	0	0	0314	0896	1965
8	5S	0	0			1950
8	5S	0	0			1955
8	5S	0	0	1178	1051	1960
8	5S	0	0	-0786	-1104	1963
8	5S	0	0	-0820	-0808	1965
9	5S	0	0	-0240	-C613	1950
9	5S	0	0	-0001	-C302	1955
9	5S	0	0	0100	1326	1960
9	5S	0	0	-0414	C030	1963
9	5S	0	0	0558	-C084	1965
10	5S	0	0	1526	C719	1950
10	5S	0	0	1440	1302	1955
10	5S	0	0	0544	1172	1960
10	5S	0	0	1040	C802	1963
10	5S	0	0	0382	C292	1965
11	5S	0	0	1526	C719	1950
11	5S	0	0	1440	1302	1955
11	5S	0	0	0370	C586	1960
11	5S	0	0	1040	C802	1963
11	5S	0	0	0382	C292	1965
12	5S	0	0	0094	-C002	1950
12	5S	0	0	-0707	-C152	1955
12	5S	0	0	C746	2210	1960
12	5S	0	0	1714	1673	1963
12	5S	0	0	1836	2478	1965
13	5S	0	0	-1476	-1432	1950
13	5S	0	0	-0691	-C428	1955
13	5S	0	1	-0638	0831	1960

	23	24	25	26	
13 5S	0	0	0832	1165	1963
13 5S	0	1	0230	-C184	1965
14 5S	0	0	-0100	-C494	1950
14 5S	0	0	0719	C627	1955
14 5S	0	0	0615	C396	1960
14 5S	0	0	-0007	C064	1963
14 5S	0	0	0130	-C020	1965
15 5S	0	0			1950
15 5S	0	0			1955
15 5S	0	0			1960
15 5S	0	0			1963
15 5S	0	0			1965
16 5S	0	0	-0002	C032	1950
16 5S	0	0	1552	2158	1955
16 5S	0	0	0025	-C055	1960
16 5S	0	0	0702	C458	1963
16 5S	0	0	-0279	C116	1965
17 5S	0	0	-1192	-C913	1950
17 5S	0	0	-0506	C183	1955
17 5S	0	0	-1488	-1341	1960
17 5S	0	0	-0760	-C318	1963
17 5S	0	0	-1033	-C624	1965
18 5S	0	0	-1087	-1017	1950
18 5S	0	0	-1174	-1340	1955
18 5S	0	0	-2055	-2264	1960
18 5S	0	0	-0724	-0843	1963
18 5S	0	0	-0987	-C651	1965
19 5S	0	0	-1690	-1488	1950
19 5S	0	0	-1332	-C921	1955
19 5S	0	0	-1642	-1635	1960
19 5S	0	0	-0546	-C647	1963
19 5S	0	0			1965
20 5S	0	0	-0920	-C567	1950
20 5S	0	0	-0997	-1195	1955
20 5S	0	0	-0042	-C356	1960
20 5S	0	0	-0084	C066	1963
20 5S	0	0	-0034	C227	1965
21 5S	0	0			1950
21 5S	0	0			1955
21 5S	0	0	0331	C277	1960
21 5S	0	0	-0568	-0220	1963
21 5S	0	0	-0489	-C539	1965
22 5S	0	0	0137	-C369	1950
22 5S	0	0	0814	C670	1955
22 5S	0	0	0297	C354	1960
22 5S	0	0	0002	C371	1963
22 5S	0	0	0827	C244	1965
23 5S	0	0	1888	C970	1950
23 5S	0	0	-0367	C017	1955
23 5S	0	0	0235	-C004	1960
23 5S	0	0	0780	C520	1963
23 5S	0	0	0026	C324	1965
24 5S	0	0	1888	C970	1950
24 5S	0	0	-0367	C017	1955
24 5S	0	0	0232	-C204	1960
24 5S	0	0	0780	C520	1963
24 5S	0	0	0026	C324	1965
25 5S	0	0	-0138	-C421	1950
25 5S	0	0	0837	C583	1955
25 5S	0	0	0523	C981	1960

	23	24	25	26	
25 5S	0	0	1360	1034	1963
25 5S	0	0	1982	2765	1965
26 5S	0	0	0271	-C218	1950
26 5S	0	0	1009	1232	1955
26 5S	0	0	0334	C346	1960
26 5S	0	0	0814	C760	1963
26 5S	0	0	1025	C501	1965
27 5S	0	0			1950
27 5S	0	0			1955
27 5S	0	0			1960
27 5S	0	0			1963
27 5S	0	0			1965
28 5S	0	0			1950
28 5S	0	0			1955
28 5S	0	0			1960
28 5S	0	0			1963
28 5S	0	0			1965
29 5S	0	0			1950
29 5S	0	0			1955
29 5S	0	0			1960
29 5S	0	0			1963
29 5S	0	0			1965
30 5S	0	0			1950
30 5S	0	0			1955
30 5S	0	0			1960
30 5S	0	0			1963
30 5S	0	0			1965
31 5S	0	0			1950
31 5S	0	0			1955
31 5S	0	0			1960
31 5S	0	0			1963
31 5S	0	0			1965
32 5S	0	0			1950
32 5S	0	0			1955
32 5S	0	0			1960
32 5S	0	0			1963
32 5S	0	0			1965
33 5S	0	0			1950
33 5S	0	0			1955
33 5S	0	0			1960
33 5S	0	0			1963
33 5S	0	0			1965
34 5S	0	0			1950
34 5S	0	0			1955
34 5S	0	0			1960
34 5S	0	0			1963
34 5S	0	0			1965
35 5S	0	0			1950
35 5S	0	0			1955
35 5S	0	0			1960
35 5S	0	0			1963
35 5S	0	0			1965
36 5S	0	0			1950
36 5S	0	0			1955
36 5S	0	0			1960
36 5S	0	0			1963
36 5S	0	0			1965
37 5S	0	0			1950
37 5S	0	0			1955
37 5S	0	0			1960

	23	24	25	26	
37 5S	0	0			1963
37 5S	0	1			1965
38 5S	0	0			1950
38 5S	0	0			1955
38 5S	0	0			1960
38 5S	0	0			1963
38 5S	0	0			1965
39 5S	0	1			1950
39 5S	1	1			1955
39 5S	0	3			1960
39 5S	0	0			1963
39 5S	0	6			1965
40 5S	0	0	-1111	-C757	1950
40 5S	0	0	1311	1830	1955
40 5S	0	0	0514	1208	1960
40 5S	0	0	0963	C706	1963
40 5S	0	0		-C046	1965
41 5S	0	0	-0002	C032	1950
41 5S	0	0	1552	2158	1955
41 5S	0	0	0025	-C055	1960
41 5S	0	0	0702	C458	1963
41 5S	0	0	-0279	C116	1965
42 5S	0	0			1950
42 5S	0	0			1955
42 5S	0	0			1960
42 5S	0	0			1963
42 5S	0	0			1965
43 5S	0	0	0127	C329	1950
43 5S	0	0	1233	1489	1955
43 5S	0	0	-0838	-C947	1960
43 5S	0	0	1001	C765	1963
43 5S	0	0	-C873	-C498	1965
44 5S	0	0	0455	C647	1950
44 5S	0	0	1749	1964	1955
44 5S	0	0	-0123	-C094	1960
44 5S	0	0	1419	1075	1963
44 5S	0	0	-0492	-C191	1965
45 5S	0	0	-0006	-C168	1950
45 5S	0	0	1103	1482	1955
45 5S	0	0	-0765	-C521	1960
45 5S	0	0	1537	1231	1963
45 5S	0	0			1965
46 5S	0	0	0269	C232	1950
46 5S	0	0	0415	1002	1955
46 5S	0	0	0704	C174	1960
46 5S	0	0	1059	1412	1963
46 5S	0	0	1091	1506	1965
47 5S	0	0			1950
47 5S	0	0			1955
47 5S	0	0	0204	-C294	1960
47 5S	0	0	0551	C378	1963
47 5S	0	0	-0323	-C219	1965
48 5S	0	0	0462	C447	1950
48 5S	0	0	0742	C752	1955
48 5S	0	0	0782	C451	1960
48 5S	0	0	1201	1089	1963
48 5S	0	0	1173	C494	1965
49 5S	0	0	1846	1033	1950
49 5S	0	0	1713	2019	1955
49 5S	0	0	-2194	-2032	1960

		23	24	25	26	
49	5S	0	0	-1525	-1871	1963
49	5S	0	0	-0487	-C151	1965
50	5S	0	0	1846	1033	1950
50	5S	0	0	1713	2019	1955
50	5S	0	1	-1948	-1419	1960
50	5S	0	0	-1525	-1871	1963
50	5S	0	0	-0487	-C151	1965
51	5S	0	0	0630	C743	1950
51	5S	0	0	1472	2126	1955
51	5S	0	0	1099	1257	1960
51	5S	0	0	2137	1791	1963
51	5S	0	0	1938	2432	1965
52	5S	0	0	-0395	C076	1950
52	5S	0	0	-0437	-C285	1955
52	5S	0	2	0549	C446	1960
52	5S	0	0	1269	1167	1963
52	5S	0	1	1172	C441	1965
53	5S	0	0	-0032	-C406	1950
53	5S	0	0	0501	C105	1955
53	5S	0	0	0745	C646	1960
53	5S	0	0	0061	-C247	1963
53	5S	0	0	0030	-C269	1965
54	5S	0	0	-1192	-C913	1950
54	5S	0	0	-0506	C183	1955
54	5S	0	0	-1488	-1341	1960
54	5S	0	0	-0760	-C318	1963
54	5S	0	0	-1033	-C624	1965
55	5S	0	0			1950
55	5S	0	0			1955
55	5S	0	0			1960
55	5S	0	0			1963
55	5S	0	0			1965
56	5S	0	0	0127	C329	1950
56	5S	0	0	1233	1489	1955
56	5S	0	0	-0838	-C947	1960
56	5S	0	0	1001	C765	1963
56	5S	0	0	-0873	-C498	1965
57	5S	0	0	-0415	-C155	1950
57	5S	0	0	-1064	-C694	1955
57	5S	0	0	-1836	-1557	1960
57	5S	0	0	-0936	-C853	1963
57	5S	C	0	-1216	-C935	1965
58	5S	0	0	-1002	-C671	1950
58	5S	0	0	-1600	-1528	1955
58	5S	0	0	-2207	-2075	1960
58	5S	0	0	-0677	-C435	1963
58	5S	0	0			1965
59	5S	0	0	0060	C575	1950
59	5S	C	0	-0217	C058	1955
59	5S	0	0	0411	-C511	1960
59	5S	0	0	0551	1500	1963
59	5S	0	0	0655	1073	1965
60	5S	0	0			1950
60	5S	0	0			1955
60	5S	0	0	-0290	-C585	1960
60	5S	0	0	-0627	-C922	1963
60	5S	0	0	-0598	-C617	1965
61	5S	0	0	0460	C058	1950
61	5S	0	0	0279	C092	1955
61	5S	0	0	0485	C220	1960

	23	24	25	26	
61 5S	0	0	0113	C348	1963
61 5S	0	0	1007	C254	1965
62 5S	0	0	1644	1008	1950
62 5S	0	0	0312	-C576	1955
62 5S	0	0	-0507	-C517	1960
62 5S	0	0	1090	0872	1963
62 5S	0	0	-0165	C122	1965
63 5S	0	0	1644	1008	1950
63 5S	0	0	0312	-C576	1955
63 5S	0	0	-C461	-C480	1960
63 5S	0	0	1090	C872	1963
63 5S	0	0	-0165	C122	1965
64 5S	0	1	0511	C537	1950
64 5S	0	0	0881	C727	1955
64 5S	0	0	0705	1015	1960
64 5S	0	0	1612	1634	1963
64 5S	0	0	1729	2236	1965
65 5S	0	0	0480	C064	1950
65 5S	0	0	0436	C096	1955
65 5S	0	0	0479	-C026	1960
65 5S	0	0	1196	1517	1963
65 5S	0	0	1127	C356	1965
66 5S	0	0	0217	C029	1950
66 5S	0	0	1123	C579	1955
66 5S	0	0	0945	C513	1960
66 5S	0	0	0426	C253	1963
66 5S	0	0	-0209	-C338	1965
67 5S	0	0	-1087	-1017	1950
67 5S	0	0	-1174	-1340	1955
67 5S	0	0	-2055	-2264	1960
67 5S	0	0	-0724	-C843	1963
67 5S	0	0	-0987	-C651	1965
68 5S	0	0			1950
68 5S	0	0			1955
68 5S	0	0			1960
68 5S	0	0			1963
68 5S	0	1			1965
69 5S	0	0	0455	C647	1950
69 5S	0	0	1749	1964	1955
69 5S	0	0	-0123	-C094	1960
69 5S	0	0	1419	1075	1963
69 5S	0	0	-0492	-C191	1965
70 5S	0	0	-0415	-C155	1950
70 5S	0	0	-1064	-C694	1955
70 5S	0	0	-1836	-1557	1960
70 5S	0	0	-0936	-C853	1963
70 5S	0	0	-1216	-C935	1965
71 5S	0	0	-1263	-1200	1950
71 5S	0	0	-1070	-1288	1955
71 5S	0	0	-1955	-2109	1960
71 5S	0	0	-1291	-1495	1963
71 5S	1	1			1965
72 5S	0	0	-0863	-C758	1950
72 5S	0	0	-0160	-C653	1955
72 5S	0	0	0459	-C333	1960
72 5S	0	0	0607	1057	1963
72 5S	0	0	0453	C907	1965
73 5S	0	0			1950
73 5S	0	0			1955
73 5S	0	0	0117	C352	1960

		23	24	25	26	
73	5S	0	0	-0113	-C138	1963
73	5S	0	0	-0683	-C584	1965
74	5S	0	0	0648	C104	1950
74	5S	0	0	0388	C078	1955
74	5S	0	0	0576	C324	1960
74	5S	0	0	0249	C214	1963
74	5S	0	0	0857	C172	1965
75	5S	0	0	1868	1029	1950
75	5S	0	0	-1096	-C643	1955
75	5S	C	0	0090	-C129	1960
75	5S	0	0	1500	1154	1963
75	5S	0	0	0322	C586	1965
76	5S	0	0	1868	1029	1950
76	5S	0	0	-1096	-C643	1955
76	5S	0	0	0086	-C336	1960
76	5S	0	0	1500	1154	1963
76	5S	0	0	0322	C586	1965
77	5S	0	0	0328	C020	1950
77	5S	0	0	1263	C759	1955
77	5S	0	0	0727	C972	1960
77	5S	0	0	1585	1224	1963
77	5S	0	0	1790	2421	1965
78	5S	0	0	0251	-C102	1950
78	5S	0	1	1183	C931	1955
78	5S	0	0	0663	C217	1960
78	5S	0	0	1286	1158	1963
78	5S	0	7	1067	C492	1965
79	5S	0	0	0101	-C267	1950
79	5S	0	0	-0148	-C227	1955
79	5S	0	0	0590	C392	1960
79	5S	0	0	0711	C663	1963
79	5S	0	0			1965
80	5S	0	0	-1690	-1488	1950
80	5S	0	0	-1332	-C921	1955
80	5S	0	0	-1642	-1635	1960
80	5S	0	0	-0546	-C647	1963
80	5S	0	0			1965
81	5S	C	0			1950
81	5S	0	0			1955
81	5S	0	0			1960
81	5S	0	0			1963
81	5S	0	3			1965
82	5S	0	0	-0006	-C168	1950
82	5S	0	0	1103	1482	1955
82	5S	0	0	-0765	-C521	1960
82	5S	0	0	1537	1231	1963
82	5S	0	1			1965
83	5S	0	0	-1002	-C671	1950
83	5S	0	0	-1600	-1528	1955
83	5S	0	0	-2207	-2075	1960
83	5S	0	0	-0677	-C435	1963
83	5S	0	0			1965
84	5S	0	0	-1263	-C758	1950
84	5S	0	0	-1070	-1288	1955
84	5S	0	0	-1955	-2109	1960
84	5S	0	0	-1291	-1495	1963
84	5S	C	3			1965
85	5S	0	0	-1076	-1011	1950
85	5S	0	0	-1003	-C937	1955
85	5S	0	0	0252	-C395	1960

		23	24	25	26	
85	5S	0	0	0814	1213	1963
85	5S	0	0			1965
86	5S	0	0			1950
86	5S	0	0			1955
86	5S	0	0	0088	C140	1960
86	5S	0	0	0172	C309	1963
86	5S	0	0			1965
87	5S	0	0	0514	C022	1950
87	5S	1	0	0427	C068	1955
87	5S	1	0	0547	C491	1960
87	5S	0	0	0407	C271	1963
87	5S	0	0			1965
88	5S	0	0	1988	C971	1950
88	5S	0	0	-0696	-C631	1955
88	5S	0	0	-0532	-C403	1960
88	5S	0	0	1615	1299	1963
88	5S	0	0			1965
89	5S	0	0	1988	C971	1950
89	5S	0	0	-0696	-C631	1955
89	5S	0	0	-0547	-C631	1960
89	5S	0	0	1615	1299	1963
89	5S	0	0			1965
90	5S	0	0	0263	C074	1950
90	5S	0	0	0496	C212	1955
90	5S	0	0	0675	0860	1960
90	5S	2	1	1553	1100	1963
90	5S	0	0			1965
91	5S	0	0	0482	C111	1950
91	5S	0	0	0315	C146	1955
91	5S	0	0	0372	-C084	1960
91	5S	0	2	1336	1085	1963
91	5S	0	16			1965
92	5S	0	0	C333	-C351	1950
92	5S	0	0	-0456	-C331	1955
92	5S	0	0	-0151	1071	1960
92	5S	0	0	-0254	C831	1963
92	5S	0	0	0314	C896	1965
93	5S	0	0	-0920	-C567	1950
93	5S	0	0	-0997	-1195	1955
93	5S	0	0	-0042	-C356	1960
93	5S	0	0	-0084	C066	1963
93	5S	0	0	-0034	C227	1965
94	5S	0	0			1950
94	5S	0	0			1955
94	5S	0	0			1960
94	5S	0	0			1963
94	5S	0	0			1965
95	5S	0	0	0269	C232	1950
95	5S	0	0	0415	1002	1955
95	5S	0	0	0704	C174	1960
95	5S	0	0	1059	1412	1963
95	5S	0	0	1091	1506	1965
96	5S	0	0	0060	C575	1950
96	5S	0	0	-0217	CC58	1955
96	5S	0	0	0411	-C511	1960
96	5S	0	0	0551	1500	1963
96	5S	0	0	0655	1073	1965
97	5S	0	0	-0863	-C758	1950
97	5S	0	0	-0160	-C653	1955
97	5S	0	0	0459	-C333	1960
97	5S	0	0	0607	1057	1963

		23	24	25	26	
97	5S	0	0	0453	C907	1965
98	5S	0	0	-1076	-1011	1950
98	5S	0	0	-1003	-C937	1955
98	5S	0	0	0252	-C395	1960
98	5S	0	0	0814	1213	1963
98	5S	0	0			1965
99	5S	0	0			1950
99	5S	0	0			1955
99	5S	0	0	1692	0827	1960
99	5S	0	0	-0026	1068	1963
99	5S	0	0	0085	C536	1965
100	5S	0	0	0193	C117	1950
100	5S	0	0	0016	-C282	1955
100	5S	0	0	0024	C280	1960
100	5S	0	0	0134	1390	1963
100	5S	0	0	1051	1032	1965
101	5S	0	0	2455	1452	1950
101	5S	0	0	0297	C348	1955
101	5S	0	0	0783	C210	1960
101	5S	0	0	1115	1429	1963
101	5S	0	0	0858	1229	1965
102	5S	0	0	2455	1452	1950
102	5S	0	0	0297	C348	1955
102	5S	0	0	0800	C196	1960
102	5S	0	0	1115	1429	1963
102	5S	0	0	0858	1229	1965
103	5S	0	0	-0318	-C258	1950
103	5S	0	0	-0201	-C100	1955
103	5S	0	0	0762	1662	1960
103	5S	0	0	1631	1681	1963
103	5S	0	0	2927	4082	1965
104	5S	0	0	0529	C499	1950
104	5S	0	0	-0410	-C082	1955
104	5S	0	0	-0863	-C076	1960
104	5S	0	0	0746	1140	1963
104	5S	0	0	1010	1254	1965
105	5S	0	0			1950
105	5S	0	0			1955
105	5S	0	0	1178	1051	1960
105	5S	0	0	-0786	-1104	1963
105	5S	0	0	-0820	-C808	1965
106	5S	0	0			1950
106	5S	0	0			1955
106	5S	0	0	0331	C277	1960
106	5S	0	0	-0568	-C220	1963
106	5S	0	0	-0489	-C539	1965
107	5S	0	0			1950
107	5S	C	0			1955
107	5S	0	0			1960
107	5S	0	0			1963
107	5S	0	0			1965
108	5S	0	0			1950
108	5S	C	0			1955
108	5S	0	0	0204	-C294	1960
108	5S	0	0	0551	C378	1963
108	5S	0	0	-0323	-C219	1965

		23	24	25	26	
109	5S	0	0			1950
109	5S	0	0			1955
109	5S	0	0	-0290	-C585	1960
109	5S	0	0	-0627	-C922	1963
109	5S	0	0	-0598	-C617	1965
110	5S	0	0			1950
110	5S	0	0			1955
110	5S	0	0	0117	C352	1960
110	5S	0	0	-0113	-C138	1963
110	5S	C	0	-0683	-C584	1965
111	5S	0	0			1950
111	5S	0	0			1955
111	5S	C	0	0088	C140	1960
111	5S	0	0	0172	C309	1963
111	5S	0	0			1965
112	5S	0	0			1950
112	5S	0	1			1955
112	5S	0	0	1692	C827	1960
112	5S	0	0	-0026	1068	1963
112	5S	0	0	0085	C536	1965
113	5S	0	0			1950
113	5S	C	0			1955
113	5S	0	0	0968	C587	1960
113	5S	C	0	-0189	C341	1963
113	5S	0	0	1143	C257	1965
114	5S	0	0			1950
114	5S	C	0			1955
114	5S	0	0	0619	C418	1960
114	5S	C	0	0639	C490	1963
114	5S	C	0	-0065	C023	1965
115	5S	0	0			1950
115	5S	0	0			1955
115	5S	C	0	0616	C576	1960
115	5S	0	0	0639	C490	1963
115	5S	0	0	-0065	C023	1965
116	5S	0	0			1950
116	5S	0	0			1955
116	5S	0	0	1227	1491	1960
116	5S	0	0	1661	1756	1963
116	5S	0	0	2185	2674	1965
117	5S	0	0			1950
117	5S	0	0			1955
117	5S	0	0	1133	C682	1960
117	5S	0	0	0927	1407	1963
117	5S	0	0	0942	C199	1965
118	5S	0	0	-0240	-C613	1950
118	5S	0	0	-0001	-C302	1955
118	5S	0	0	0100	1326	1960
118	5S	0	0	-0414	C030	1963
118	5S	C	0	0558	-C084	1965
119	5S	0	0	0137	-C369	1950
119	5S	0	0	0814	C670	1955
119	5S	0	0	0297	C354	1960
119	5S	0	0	0002	C371	1963
119	5S	0	0	0827	C244	1965
120	5S	0	0			1950
120	5S	0	0			1955
120	5S	C	0			1960
120	5S	0	0			1963
120	5S	0	0			1965

		23	24	25	26	
121	5S	0	0	0462	C447	1950
121	5S	0	0	0742	C752	1955
121	5S	0	0	0782	C451	1960
121	5S	0	0	1201	1089	1963
121	5S	0	0	1173	C494	1965
122	5S	0	0	0460	C058	1950
122	5S	0	0	0279	C092	1955
122	5S	0	0	0485	C220	1960
122	5S	0	0	C113	C348	1963
122	5S	0	0	1007	C254	1965
123	5S	0	0	0648	C104	1950
123	5S	0	0	0388	C078	1955
123	5S	0	0	0576	C324	1960
123	5S	0	0	0249	C214	1963
123	5S	0	0	0857	C172	1965
124	5S	0	0	0514	C022	1950
124	5S	0	0	0427	C068	1955
124	5S	0	0	0547	C491	1960
124	5S	0	0	C407	C271	1963
124	5S	0	0			1965
125	5S	0	0	0193	C117	1950
125	5S	0	0	0016	-C282	1955
125	5S	0	0	0024	C280	1960
125	5S	0	0	0134	1390	1963
125	5S	C	0	1051	1032	1965
126	5S	0	0			1950
126	5S	0	0			1955
126	5S	0	0	0968	C587	1960
126	5S	0	0	-0189	C341	1963
126	5S	0	0	1143	C257	1965
127	5S	0	0	1911	1022	1950
127	5S	0	0	0628	C715	1955
127	5S	0	0	0846	C333	1960
127	5S	0	0	1274	1147	1963
127	5S	0	0	1224	C703	1965
128	5S	0	0	1911	1022	1950
128	5S	0	0	0628	C715	1955
128	5S	0	0	0907	C527	1960
128	5S	0	0	1274	1147	1963
128	5S	0	0	1224	C703	1965
129	5S	0	0	-1381	-1190	1950
129	5S	0	0	0150	C297	1955
129	5S	0	0	-0522	1475	1960
129	5S	0	0	0857	C525	1963
129	5S	0	0	1404	2614	1965
130	5S	0	0	-0088	-C598	1950
130	5S	0	0	-0547	-0832	1955
130	5S	0	0	-0427	C603	1960
130	5S	0	0	0061	-C041	1963
130	5S	0	0	-0633	-C343	1965
131	5S	0	0	1526	C719	1950
131	5S	0	0	1440	1302	1955
131	5S	0	0	0544	1172	1960
131	5S	0	0	1040	C802	1963
131	5S	0	0	0382	C292	1965
132	5S	0	0	1888	C970	1950
132	5S	0	0	-0367	C017	1955
132	5S	0	0	0235	-C004	1960
132	5S	0	0	0780	C520	1963
132	5S	0	0	0026	C324	1965

	23	24	25	26	
133 5S	0	0			1950
133 5S	0	0			1955
133 5S	0	0			1960
133 5S	0	0			1963
133 5S	0	0			1965
134 5S	0	0	1846	1033	1950
134 5S	0	0	1713	2019	1955
134 5S	0	0	-2194	-2032	1960
134 5S	0	0	-1525	-1871	1963
134 5S	0	0	-0487	-C151	1965
135 5S	0	0	1644	1008	1950
135 5S	0	0	0312	-C576	1955
135 5S	0	0	-0507	-C517	1960
135 5S	0	0	1090	C872	1963
135 5S	0	0	-0165	C122	1965
136 5S	0	0	1868	1029	1950
136 5S	0	0	-1096	-C643	1955
136 5S	0	0	C090	C324	1960
136 5S	0	0	1500	1154	1963
136 5S	0	0	0322	C586	1965
137 5S	0	0	1988	C971	1950
137 5S	0	0	-0696	-C631	1955
137 5S	0	0	-0532	-C403	1960
137 5S	0	0	1615	1299	1963
137 5S	0	0			1965
138 5S	0	0	2455	1452	1950
138 5S	0	0	0297	C348	1955
138 5S	0	0	0783	C210	1960
138 5S	0	0	1115	1429	1963
138 5S	0	0	0858	1229	1965
139 5S	0	0			1950
139 5S	0	0			1955
139 5S	0	0	0619	C418	1960
139 5S	0	0	0639	C490	1963
139 5S	0	0	-0065	CC23	1965
140 5S	0	0	1911	1022	1950
140 5S	0	0	0628	C715	1955
140 5S	0	0	0846	C333	1960
140 5S	0	0	1274	1147	1963
140 5S	0	0	1224	C703	1965
141 5S	0	0	-2361	-2446	1950
141 5S	0	0	-2630	-2738	1955
141 5S	0	0	-2267	-2006	1960
141 5S	0	0	-1619	-1993	1963
141 5S	0	0	-1884	-1557	1965
142 5S	0	0	2166	1338	1950
142 5S	0	0	1008	C368	1955
142 5S	0	0	1202	1353	1960
142 5S	0	0	2186	1815	1963
142 5S	0	0	2136	2734	1965
143 5S	0	0	1653	C911	1950
143 5S	0	0	1203	1103	1955
143 5S	0	0	0661	C582	1960
143 5S	0	0	1314	1175	1963
143 5S	0	0	0933	C286	1965
144 5S	0	0	1526	C719	1950
144 5S	0	0	1440	1302	1955
144 5S	0	0	0370	C586	1960
144 5S	0	0	1040	C802	1963
144 5S	0	0	0382	C292	1965

		23	24	25	26	
145	5S	0	0	1888	C970	1950
145	5S	0	0	-0367	C017	1955
145	5S	0	0	0232	-C204	1960
145	5S	0	0	0780	C520	1963
145	5S	0	0	0026	C324	1965
146	5S	0	0			1950
146	5S	0	0			1955
146	5S	0	0			1960
146	5S	0	0			1963
146	5S	0	0			1965
147	5S	0	0	1846	1033	1950
147	5S	0	0	1713	2019	1955
147	5S	0	0	-1948	-1419	1960
147	5S	0	0	-1525	-1871	1963
147	5S	0	0	-0487	-C151	1965
148	5S	0	0	1644	1008	1950
148	5S	0	0	0312	-C576	1955
148	5S	0	0	-0461	-C480	1960
148	5S	0	0	1090	C872	1963
148	5S	0	0	-C165	C122	1965
149	5S	0	0	1868	1029	1950
149	5S	0	0	-1096	-C643	1955
149	5S	0	0	0086	-C336	1960
149	5S	0	0	1500	1154	1963
149	5S	0	0	0322	C586	1965
150	5S	0	0	1988	C971	1950
150	5S	0	0	-0696	-C631	1955
150	5S	C	0	-0547	-C631	1960
150	5S	0	0	1615	1299	1963
150	5S	0	0			1965
151	5S	C	0	2455	1452	1950
151	5S	C	0	0297	C348	1955
151	5S	0	0	0800	C196	1960
151	5S	0	0	1115	1429	1963
151	5S	0	0	0858	1229	1965
152	5S	0	0			1950
152	5S	C	0			1955
152	5S	0	0	0616	C576	1960
152	5S	0	0	0639	C490	1963
152	5S	0	0	-C065	C023	1965
153	5S	0	0	1911	1022	1950
153	5S	0	0	0628	C715	1955
153	5S	0	0	0907	C527	1960
153	5S	0	0	1274	1147	1963
153	5S	0	0	1224	C703	1965
154	5S	0	0	-2361	-2446	1950
154	5S	0	0	-2630	-2738	1955
154	5S	0	0	-2267	-2006	1960
154	5S	0	0	-1619	-1993	1963
154	5S	0	0	-1884	-1557	1965
155	5S	0	0	2166	1338	1950
155	5S	0	0	1008	C368	1955
155	5S	0	0	1167	1100	1960
155	5S	0	0	2186	1815	1963
155	5S	0	1	2136	2734	1965
156	5S	0	1	1653	C911	1950
156	5S	0	0	1203	1103	1955
156	5S	0	0	0569	C197	1960
156	5S	0	0	1314	1175	1963
156	5S	0	1	933	C286	1965

	23	24	25	26	
157 5S	0	0	0094	-C002	1950
157 5S	0	0	-0707	-C152	1955
157 5S	0	0	0746	2210	1960
157 5S	0	0	1714	1673	1963
157 5S	0	0	1836	2478	1965
158 5S	0	0	-0138	-C421	1950
158 5S	0	0	0837	C583	1955
158 5S	0	0	0523	C981	1960
158 5S	0	0	1360	1034	1963
158 5S	0	0	1982	2765	1965
159 5S	0	0			1950
159 5S	0	0			1955
159 5S	0	0			1960
159 5S	0	0			1963
159 5S	0	0			1965
160 5S	0	0	0630	C743	1950
160 5S	0	0	1472	2126	1955
160 5S	0	0	1099	1257	1960
160 5S	0	0	2137	1791	1963
160 5S	0	0	1938	2432	1965
161 5S	0	0	0511	C537	1950
161 5S	0	0	0881	C727	1955
161 5S	0	0	0705	1C15	1960
161 5S	0	0	1612	1634	1963
161 5S	0	0	1729	2236	1965
162 5S	0	0	0328	C020	1950
162 5S	0	0	1263	C759	1955
162 5S	0	0	0727	C972	1960
162 5S	0	0	1585	1224	1963
162 5S	0	0	1790	2421	1965
163 5S	0	0	0263	C074	1950
163 5S	0	0	C496	C212	1955
163 5S	0	0	0675	C860	1960
163 5S	0	0	1553	1100	1963
163 5S	0	0			1965
164 5S	0	0	-0318	-C258	1950
164 5S	0	0	-0201	-C100	1955
164 5S	0	0	0762	1662	1960
164 5S	0	0	1631	1681	1963
164 5S	0	0	2927	4082	1965
165 5S	0	0			1950
165 5S	0	0			1955
165 5S	0	0	1227	1491	1960
165 5S	0	0	1661	1756	1963
165 5S	0	0	2185	2674	1965
166 5S	0	0	-1381	-1190	1950
166 5S	0	0	0150	C297	1955
166 5S	0	0	-0522	1475	1960
166 5S	0	0	0857	C525	1963
166 5S	0	0	1404	2614	1965
167 5S	0	0	2166	1338	1950
167 5S	0	0	1008	C368	1955
167 5S	0	0	1202	1353	1960
167 5S	0	0	2186	1815	1963
167 5S	0	0	2136	2734	1965
168 5S	2	1	2166	1338	1950
168 5S	0	0	1008	C368	1955
168 5S	0	0	1167	1100	1960
168 5S	0	0	2186	1815	1963
168 5S	0	0	2136	2734	1965

		23	24	25	26	
169	5S	0	1	0151	-C158	1950
169	5S	0	0	-0241	C362	1955
169	5S	0	2	0115	1130	1960
169	5S	0	1	-0352	-C770	1963
169	5S	0	3	1119	2C02	1965
170	5S	0	0	-1476	-1432	1950
170	5S	0	0	-0691	-C428	1955
170	5S	0	0	0370	C831	1960
170	5S	0	0	0832	1165	1963
170	5S	0	0	0230	-C184	1965
171	5S	0	0	0271	-C218	1950
171	5S	0	0	1009	1232	1955
171	5S	0	0	0334	C346	1960
171	5S	0	0	0814	C760	1963
171	5S	0	0	1025	C501	1965
172	5S	0	0			1950
172	5S	0	0			1955
172	5S	0	0			1960
172	5S	0	0			1963
172	5S	0	0			1965
173	5S	0	0	-0395	C076	1950
173	5S	0	0	-0437	-C285	1955
173	5S	0	1	0549	C446	1960
173	5S	0	1	1269	1167	1963
173	5S	0	1	1172	C441	1965
174	5S	0	0	C480	C064	1950
174	5S	0	0	0436	C096	1955
174	5S	0	2	0479	-CC26	1960
174	5S	0	0	1196	1517	1963
174	5S	0	0	1127	C356	1965
175	5S	0	0	0251	-C102	1950
175	5S	0	0	1183	C931	1955
175	5S	0	0	0663	C217	1960
175	5S	0	0	1286	1158	1963
175	5S	0	0	1067	C492	1965
176	5S	0	0	0482	C111	1950
176	5S	0	0	0315	C146	1955
176	5S	0	0	0372	-C084	1960
176	5S	0	0	1336	1085	1963
176	5S	0	0			1965
177	5S	0	0	0529	C499	1950
177	5S	0	0	-041C	-C082	1955
177	5S	0	0	-0863	-C076	1960
177	5S	0	1	C746	1140	1963
177	5S	0	0	1010	1254	1965
178	5S	0	0			1950
178	5S	0	0			1955
178	5S	0	0	1133	C682	1960
178	5S	0	0	0927	14C7	1963
178	5S	0	0	0942	C199	1965
179	5S	0	0	-0088	-C598	1950
179	5S	0	0	-0547	-C832	1955
179	5S	0	0	-0427	C603	1960
179	5S	0	0	0061	-C041	1963
179	5S	0	0	-0633	-C343	1965
180	5S	0	0	1653	C911	1950
180	5S	0	2	1203	11C3	1955
180	5S	0	0	0661	C582	1960
180	5S	0	0	1314	1175	1963
180	5S	0	0	0933	C286	1965

		23	24	25	26				
181	5S	0	1	1653	C911				1950
181	5S	0	5	1203	1103				1955
181	5S	0	3	0569	C197				1960
181	5S	0	0	1314	1175				1963
181	5S	0	2	0933	C286				1965
182	5S	0	0	0151	-C158				1950
182	5S	0	0	-0241	C362				1955
182	5S	0	0	0115	1130				1960
182	5S	0	0	-0352	-C770				1963
182	5S	0	0	1119	2002				1965
1	6S			0A	0A	0A	0A	0A	1950
1	6S			0A	0A	0A	0A	0A	1955
1	6S			0A	0A	0A	0A	0A	1960
1	6S			0A	0A	0A	0A	0A	1963
1	6S			0A	0A	0A	0A	0A	1965
2	6S			0A	0A	0A	0A	0A	1950
2	6S			0A	0A	0A	0A	0A	1955
2	6S			0A	0A	0A	0A	0A	1960
2	6S			0A	0A	0A	0A	0A	1963
2	6S			0A	0A	0A	0A	0A	1965
3	6S								1950
3	6S								1955
3	6S								1960
3	6S			0A	0A	0A	0A	0A	1963
3	6S			0A	0A	0A	0A	0A	1965
4	6S						0A	0A	1950
4	6S				0A	0A	0A	0A	1955
4	6S						0A	0A	1960
4	6S			0A	0A	0A	0A	0A	1963
4	6S			0A	0A	0A	0A	0A	1965
5	6S			4	20	1	0A	0A	1950
5	6S			1	0	0	0A	0A	1955
5	6S			1	10	0	0A	0A	1960
5	6S			2	14	0	0A	0A	1963
5	6S						0A	0A	1965
6	6S			0A	0A	0A	0A	0A	1950
6	6S			0A	0A	0A	0A	0A	1955
6	6S			0A	0A	0A	0A	0A	1960
6	6S			0A	0A	0A	0A	0A	1963
6	6S			0A	0A	0A	0A	0A	1965
7	6S			35	113	7	9		1950
7	6S			4	80	1	13		1955
7	6S			12	105	2	10		1960
7	6S			30	151	4			1963
7	6S			26	88	3			1965
8	6S			0A	0A	0A	0A	0A	1950
8	6S			0A	0A	0A	0A	0A	1955
8	6S			0A	0A	0A	0A	0A	1960
8	6S			0A	0A	0A	0A	0A	1963
8	6S			0A	0A	0A	0A	0A	1965
9	6S						7		1950
9	6S						25		1955
9	6S								1960
9	6S			0A	0A	0A			1963
9	6S			0A	0A	0A			1965
				27	28	29	30	31	
10	6S			0A	0A	0A	0A	0A	1950
10	6S			0A	0A	0A	0A	0A	1955
10	6S			0A	0A	0A	0A	0A	1960

	27	28	29	30	31	
10 6S	0A	0A	0A	0A	0A	1963
10 6S	0A	0A	0A	0A	0A	1965
11 6S	0A	0A	0A	0A	0A	1950
11 6S	0A	0A	0A	0A	0A	1955
11 6S	0A	0A	0A	0A	0A	1960
11 6S	0A	0A	0A	0A	0A	1963
11 6S	0A	0A	0A	0A	0A	1965
12 6S				43		1950
12 6S	18	20	1	36		1955
12 6S	50	30	7	19		1960
12 6S	62	29	8			1963
12 6S						1965
13 6S	987	46	187	45B		1950
13 6S	101	20	2	133		1955
13 6S	122	133	20	268		1960
13 6S	159	126	21	294B		1963
13 6S	213	29	26	368		1965
14 6S	0A	0A	0A	0A	0A	1950
14 6S	0A	0A	0A	0A	0A	1955
14 6S	0A	0A	0A	0A	0A	1960
14 6S	0A	0A	0A	0A	0A	1963
14 6S	0A	0A	0A	0A	0A	1965
15 6S	0A	0A	0A	0A	0A	1950
15 6S	0A	0A	0A	0A	0A	1955
15 6S	0A	0A	0A	0A	0A	1960
15 6S	0A	0A	0A	0A	0A	1963
15 6S	0A	0A	0A	0A	0A	1965
16 6S	0A	0A	0A	0A	0A	1950
16 6S	0A	0A	0A	0A	0A	1955
16 6S	0A	0A	0A	0A	0A	1960
16 6S	0A	0A	0A	0A	0A	1963
16 6S	0A	0A	0A	0A	0A	1965
17 6S	0A	0A	0A	0A	0A	1950
17 6S	0A	0A	0A	0A	0A	1955
17 6S	0A	0A	0A	0A	0A	1960
17 6S	0A	0A	0A	0A	0A	1963
17 6S	0A	0A	0A	0A	0A	1965
18 6S						1950
18 6S	11	240	1			1955
18 6S	14	114	6			1960
18 6S	5	36	2			1963
18 6S						1965
19 6S	0A	0A	0A			1950
19 6S						1955
19 6S						1960
19 6S						1963
19 6S						1965
20 6S	0A	0A	0A	0A	0A	1950
20 6S	0A	0A	0A	0A	0A	1955
20 6S	0A	0A	0A	0A	0A	1960
20 6S	0A	0A	0A	0A	0A	1963
20 6S	0A	0A	0A	0A	0A	1965
21 6S	0A	0A	0A	0A	0A	1950
21 6S	0A	0A	0A	0A	0A	1955
21 6S	0A	0A	0A	0A	0A	1960
21 6S	0A	0A	0A	0A	0A	1963
21 6S	0A	0A	0A	0A	0A	1965
22 6S	0A	0A	0A	0A	0A	1950
22 6S	0A	0A	0A	0A	0A	1955
22 6S	0A	0A	0A	0A	0A	1960

	27	28	29	30	31	
22 6S	0A	0A	0A	0A	0A	1963
22 6S	0A	0A	0A	0A	0A	1965
23 6S	0A	0A	0A	0A	0A	1950
23 6S	0A	0A	0A	0A	0A	1955
23 6S	0A	0A	0A	0A	0A	1960
23 6S	0A	0A	0A	0A	0A	1963
23 6S	0A	0A	0A	0A	0A	1965
24 6S	0A	0A	0A	0A	0A	1950
24 6S	0A	0A	0A	0A	0A	1955
24 6S	0A	0A	0A	0A	0A	1960
24 6S	0A	0A	0A	0A	0A	1963
24 6S	0A	0A	0A	0A	0A	1965
25 6S				0A	0A	1950
25 6S	5	0	1	0A	0A	1955
25 6S	5	3	2	0A	0A	1960
25 6S	4	2	2	0A	0A	1963
25 6S				0A	0A	1965
26 6S						1950
26 6S	0A	0A	0A	0A	0A	1955
26 6S	0A	0A	0A	0A	0A	1960
26 6S	0A	0A	0A	0B	0	1963
26 6S	0A	0A	0A	0A	0A	1965
27 6S	0A	0A	0A	0A	0A	1950
27 6S	0A	0A	0A	0A	0A	1955
27 6S	0A	0A	0A	0A	0A	1960
27 6S	0A	0A	0A	0A	0A	1963
27 6S	0A	0A	0A	0A	0A	1965
28 6S	0A	0A	0A	0A	0A	1950
28 6S	1A	100A	0A	0A	0A	1955
28 6S	1A	100A	0A	0A	0A	1960
28 6S	1A	100A	0A	0A	0A	1963
28 6S	1A	100A	0A	0A	0A	1965
29 6S	0A	0A	0A	0A	0A	1950
29 6S	0A	0A	0A	0A	0A	1955
29 6S	1A	50A	0A	0A	0A	1960
29 6S	1A	50A	0A	0A	0A	1963
29 6S	1A	50A	0A	0A	0A	1965
30 6S	0A	0A	0A	0A	0A	1950
30 6S	1A	0A	0A	0A	0A	1955
30 6S	1A	0A	0A	0A	0A	1960
30 6S	1A	0A	0A	0A	0A	1963
30 6S	1A	0A	0A	0A	0A	1965
31 6S	0	0A	0A	0A	0A	1950
31 6S	1A	0A	0A	0A	0A	1955
31 6S	1A	0A	0A	0A	0A	1960
31 6S	0A	0A	0A	0A	0A	1963
31 6S	0A	0A	0A	0A	0A	1965
32 6S	0A	0A	0A	0A	0A	1950
32 6S	1A	0A	0A	0A	0A	1955
32 6S	1A	50A	0A	0A	0A	1960
32 6S	2A	50A	0	0A	0A	1963
32 6S	3A	50A	0A	0A	0A	1965
33 6S	0A	0A	0A	34A	0A	1950
33 6S	0A	0A	0A	2	0A	1955
33 6S	0A	0A	0A	0A	0A	1960
33 6S	0A	0A	0A	0A	0A	1963
33 6S	0A	0A	0A	0A	0A	1965
34 6S	0A	0A	0A	0A	0A	1950
34 6S	0A	0A	0A	0A	0A	1955
34 6S	0A	0A	0A	0A	0A	1960

	27	28	29	30	31	
34 6S	0A	0A	0A	0A	0A	1963
34 6S	0A	0A	0A	0A	0A	1965
35 6S	0A	0A	0A	0A	0A	1950
35 6S	0A	0A	0A	0A	0A	1955
35 6S	0A	0A	0A	0A	0A	1960
35 6S	0A	0A	0A	0A	0A	1963
35 6S	0A	0A	0A	0A	0A	1965
36 6S	0A	0A	0A	0A	0A	1950
36 6S	1A	10A	0A	0A	0A	1955
36 6S	2A	10A	0A	0A	0A	1960
36 6S	2A	10A	0A	0A	0A	1963
36 6S	1A	10A	0A	0A	0A	1965
37 6S	400A	500A	5A	0A	0A	1950
37 6S	400A	500A	5A	0A	0A	1955
37 6S	361	507	6	0A	0A	1960
37 6S	231	248	3	0A	0A	1963
37 6S	277	219	4	0A	0A	1965
38 6S	0A	0A	0A	44A	0A	1950
38 6S	0A	0A	0A	7	0A	1955
38 6S	0A	0A	0A	0A	0A	1960
38 6S	0A	0A	0A	0A	0A	1963
38 6S	0A	0A	0A	0A	0A	1965
39 6S	0A	0A	0A	128A		1950
39 6S	0A	0A	0A	57		1955
39 6S	0A	0A	0A	138		1960
39 6S	0A	0A	0A	161A		1963
39 6S	0A	0A	0A	161		1965
40 6S						1950
40 6S						1955
40 6S						1960
40 6S						1963
40 6S	1	10	1			1965
41 6S	0A	0A	0A	0A	0A	1950
41 6S	0A	0A	0A	0A	0A	1955
41 6S	0A	0A	0A	0A	0A	1960
41 6S	0A	0A	0A	0A	0A	1963
41 6S	0A	0A	0A	0A	0A	1965
42 6S	0A	0A	0A	0A	0A	1950
42 6S	0A	0A	0A	0A	0A	1955
42 6S	0A	0A	0A	0A	0A	1960
42 6S	0A	0A	0A	0A	0A	1963
42 6S	0A	0A	0A	0A	0A	1965
43 6S	0A	0A	0A	0A	0A	1950
43 6S	0A	0A	0A	0A	0A	1955
43 6S	0A	0A	0A	0A	0A	1960
43 6S	0A	0A	0A	0A	0A	1963
43 6S	0A	0A	0A	0A	0A	1965
44 6S	1	5	187	0A	0A	1950
44 6S	0A	0A	0A	0A	0A	1955
44 6S	0A	0A	0A	0A	0A	1960
44 6S	0A	0A	0A	0A	0A	1963
44 6S	0A	0A	0A	0A	0A	1965
45 6S	0A	0A	0A	0A	0A	1950
45 6S	0A	0A	0A	0A	0A	1955
45 6S	0A	0A	0A	0A	0A	1960
45 6S	0A	0A	0A	0A	0A	1963
45 6S	0A	0A	0A	0A	0A	1965
46 6S						1950
46 6S	0A	0A	0A	0A	0A	1955
46 6S	0A	0A	0A	0A	0A	1960

	27	28	29	30	31	
46 6S	0A	0A	0A	0A	0A	1963
46 6S	0A	0A	0A	0A	0A	1965
47 6S	0A	0A	0A	0A	0A	1950
47 6S	0A	0A	0A	0A	0A	1955
47 6S	0A	0A	0A	0A	0A	1960
47 6S	0A	0A	0A	0A	0A	1963
47 6S	0A	0A	0A	0A	0A	1965
48 6S				0A	0A	1950
48 6S				0A	0A	1955
48 6S	0A	0A	0A	0A	0A	1960
48 6S	0A	0A	0A	0A	0A	1963
48 6S	0A	0A	0A	0A	0A	1965
49 6S	0A	0A	0A	0A	0A	1950
49 6S	0A	0A	0A	0A	0A	1955
49 6S				0A	0A	1960
49 6S				0A	0A	1963
49 6S				0A	0A	1965
50 6S	0A	0A	0A	0A	0A	1950
50 6S	0A	0A	0A	0A	0A	1955
50 6S						1960
50 6S	37	40	51			1963
50 6S	58	46	76			1965
51 6S						1950
51 6S						1955
51 6S				0A	0A	1960
51 6S	4	2	6	0A	0A	1963
51 6S				0A	0A	1965
52 6S	7847	362	14640			1950
52 6S	1019	180	166			1955
52 6S	427	460	625	813		1960
52 6S	8	6	11	507		1963
52 6S				1316	5839	1965
53 6S	0A	0A	0A	0A	0A	1950
53 6S	0A	0A	0A	0A	0A	1955
53 6S	0A	0A	0A	8	2	1960
53 6S	0A	0A	0A	0A	0A	1963
53 6S	0A	0A	0A	19		1965
54 6S	0A	0A	0A	0A	0A	1950
54 6S	CA	0A	0A	0A	0A	1955
54 6S	0A	0A	0A	0A	0A	1960
54 6S	0A	0A	0A	0A	0A	1963
54 6S	0A	0A	0A	0A	0A	1965
55 6S	0A	0A	0A	0A	0A	1950
55 6S	0A	0A	0A	0A	0A	1955
55 6S	0A	0A	0A	0A	0A	1960
55 6S	0A	0A	0A	0A	0A	1963
55 6S	0A	0A	0A	0A	0A	1965
56 6S				0A	0A	1950
56 6S	0A	0A	0A	0A	0A	1955
56 6S	0A	0A	0A	0A	0A	1960
56 6S	CA	0A	0A	0A	0A	1963
56 6S	0A	0A	0A	0A	0A	1965
57 6S	0	0	0	0A	0A	1950
57 6S	1	30	1	0A	0A	1955
57 6S				0A	0A	1960
57 6S	0A	0A	0A	0A	0A	1963
57 6S	0A	0A	0A	0A	0A	1965
58 6S	0A	0A	0A	0A	0A	1950
58 6S	0A	0A	0A	0A	0A	1955
58 6S	0A	0A	0A	0A	0A	1960

	27	28	29	30	31	
58 6S	0A	0A	0A	0A	0A	1963
58 6S	0A	0A	0A	0A	0A	1965
59 6S	0A	0A	0A	665		1950
59 6S	0A	0A	0A	68	0	1955
59 6S	0A	0A	0A	1300	339	1960
59 6S	0A	0A	0A			1963
59 6S	0A	0A	0A			1965
60 6S						1950
60 6S						1955
60 6S						1960
60 6S	20	57	7			1963
60 6S	44	88	15			1965
61 6S	0A	0A	0A	0A	0A	1950
61 6S	0A	0A	0A	0A	0A	1955
61 6S	0A	0A	0A	0A	0A	1960
61 6S	0A	0A	0A	0A	0A	1963
61 6S	0A	0A	0A	0A	0A	1965
62 6S	0A	0A	0A	0A	0A	1950
62 6S	0A	0A	0A	0A	0A	1955
62 6S	0A	0A	0A	0A	0A	1960
62 6S	0A	0A	0A	0A	0A	1963
62 6S	0A	0A	0A	0A	0A	1965
63 6S	0A	0A	0A	0A	0A	1950
63 6S	0A	0A	0A	0A	0A	1955
63 6S	0A	0A	0A	0A	0A	1960
63 6S	0A	0A	0A	0A	0A	1963
63 6S	0A	0A	0A	0A	0A	1965
64 6S	376	61	184	372		1950
64 6S	47	50	2	222		1955
64 6S	44	26	20	11	3	1960
64 6S	43	20	15			1963
64 6S						1965
65 6S				168		1950
65 6S	5	0	1	13		1955
65 6S	19	20	7	34	9	1960
65 6S	14	11	5	338		1963
65 6S				30		1965
66 6S	0A	0A	0A	0A	0A	1950
66 6S	0A	0A	0A	0A	0A	1955
66 6S	0A	0A	0A	1	34	1960
66 6S	0A	0A	0A			1963
66 6S	0A	0A	0A			1965
67 6S						1950
67 6S				306	18	1955
67 6S				1		1960
67 6S						1963
67 6S						1965
68 6S	0A	0A	0A	0A	0A	1950
68 6S	0A	0A	0A	0A	0A	1955
68 6S	0A	0A	0A	0A	0A	1960
68 6S	0A	0A	0A	0A	0A	1963
68 6S	0A	0A	0A	0A	0A	1965
69 6S	0A	0A	0A	0A	0A	1950
69 6S	0A	0A	0A	0A	0A	1955
69 6S	0A	0A	0A	0A	0A	1960
69 6S	0A	0A	0A	0A	0A	1963
69 6S	0A	0A	0A	0A	0A	1965
70 6S	0A	0A	0A	0A	0A	1950
70 6S	0A	0A	0A	0A	0A	1955
70 6S	0A	0A	0A	0A	0A	1960

	27	28	29	30	31	
70 6S	0A	0A	0A	0A	0A	1963
70 6S	0A	0A	0A	0A	0A	1965
71 6S	0A	0A	0A	0A	0A	1950
71 6S						1955
71 6S						1960
71 6S	3		0	0A	0A	1963
71 6S				0A	0A	1965
72 6S				95		1950
72 6S				51	51	1955
72 6S				96C	3700	1960
72 6S	0	0	0	0A	0A	1963
72 6S	0A	0A	0A	0A	0A	1965
73 6S	0A	0A	0A	0A	0A	1950
73 6S	CA	0A	0A	0A	0A	1955
73 6S	0A	0A	0A	0A	0A	1960
73 6S	0	0	0	0A	0A	1963
73 6S	0A	0A	0A	0A	0A	1965
74 6S	0A	0A	0A	0A	0A	1950
74 6S						1955
74 6S						1960
74 6S	0	0	0	0A	0A	1963
74 6S	0A	0A	0A	0A	0A	1965
75 6S	0A	0A	0A	0A	0A	1950
75 6S	3	40	1	0A	0A	1955
75 6S				0A	0A	1960
75 6S	0	0	0	0A	0A	1963
75 6S	0A	0A	0A	0A	0A	1965
76 6S				0A	0A	1950
76 6S				0A	0A	1955
76 6S	48	67	1	0A	0A	1960
76 6S	53	57	1	0A	0A	1963
76 6S	90	71	2	0A	0A	1965
77 6S				1195		1950
77 6S	125	120	1	700	429	1955
77 6S				1	54	1960
77 6S	0	0	0			1963
77 6S						1965
78 6S				12B		1950
78 6S				19	12	1955
78 6S	52	57	1	24		1960
78 6S	62	49	1	97B		1963
78 6S				47		1965
79 6S	0A	0A	0A	0A	0A	1950
79 6S	0A	0A	0A	0A	0A	1955
79 6S	0A	0A	0A	1		1960
79 6S	0A	0A	0A	0A	0A	1963
79 6S	0A	0A	0A	0A	0A	1965
80 6S	0A	0A	0A	0A	0A	1950
80 6S						1955
80 6S	CA	0A	0A			1960
80 6S						1963
80 6S	0A	0A	0A			1965
81 6S	0A	0A	0A	0A	0A	1950
81 6S	0A	0A	0A	0A	0A	1955
81 6S	0A	0A	0A	0A	0A	1960
81 6S	0A	0A	0A	0A	0A	1963
81 6S	0A	0A	0A	0A	0A	1965

	27	28	29	30	31	
82 6S	0A	0A	0A	0A	0A	1950
82 6S	0A	0A	0A	0A	0A	1955
82 6S	0A	0A	0A	0A	0A	1960
82 6S	0A	0A	0A	0A	0A	1963
82 6S	0A	0A	0A	0A	0A	1965
83 6S	0A	0A	0A	0A	0A	1950
83 6S	0A	0A	0A	0A	0A	1955
83 6S	0A	0A	0A	0A	0A	1960
83 6S	0A	0A	0A	0A	0A	1963
83 6S	0A	0A	0A	0A	0A	1965
84 6S	0A	0A	0A	0A	0A	1950
84 6S	1	20	1	0A	0A	1955
84 6S	5	41	1	0A	0A	1960
84 6S	6	43	1	0A	0A	1963
84 6S	3	20	0	0A	0A	1965
85 6S	0A	0A	0A	0A	0A	1950
85 6S	0A	0A	0A	0A	0A	1955
85 6S	0A	0A	0A	0A	0A	1960
85 6S	0	0	0	0A	0A	1963
85 6S	0A	0A	0A	0A	0A	1965
86 6S	0A	0A	0A	0A	0A	1950
86 6S	0A	0A	0A	0A	0A	1955
86 6S	0A	0A	0A	0A	0A	1960
86 6S	0	0	0	0A	0A	1963
86 6S	0A	0A	0A	0A	0A	1965
87 6S				5612		1950
87 6S	45	40	1	2405		1955
87 6S				200		1960
87 6S	0	0	0	122		1963
87 6S	0A	0A	0A			1965
88 6S	0A	0A	0A	0A	0A	1950
88 6S	0A	0A	0A	0A	0A	1955
88 6S	0A	0A	0A	0A	0A	1960
88 6S	0	0	0	0A	0A	1963
88 6S	0A	0A	0A	0A	0A	1965
89 6S				0A	0A	1950
89 6S				0A	0A	1955
89 6S				0A	0A	1960
89 6S	0	0	0	0A	0A	1963
89 6S	0A	0A	0A	0A	0A	1965
90 6S				11		1950
90 6S	6	0	1A	7		1955
90 6S	8	5	1	5		1960
90 6S	8	4	1			1963
90 6S						1965
91 6S				58		1950
91 6S				7		1955
91 6S	12	13	1	30		1960
91 6S	11	9	1	0B	0	1963
91 6S				11		1965
92 6S				11	110	1950
92 6S				33	516	1955
92 6S				37	319	1960
92 6S				31	121	1963
92 6S	4	39	16	6	32	1965
93 6S	0A	0A	0A	0A	0A	1950
93 6S	0A	0A	0A	0A	0A	1955
93 6S	0A	0A	0A	0A	0A	1960
93 6S	0A	0A	0A	0A	0A	1963
93 6S	0A	0A	0A	0A	0A	1965

	27	28	29	30	31	
94 6S	0A	0A	0A	0A	0A	1950
94 6S	0A	0A	0A	0A	0A	1955
94 6S	0A	0A	0A	0A	0A	1960
94 6S	0A	0A	0A	0A	0A	1963
94 6S	0A	0A	0A	0A	0A	1965
95 6S						1950
95 6S						1955
95 6S	0A	0A	0A	0A	0A	1960
95 6S	0A	0A	0A	0A	0A	1963
95 6S	0A	0A	0A	0A	0A	1965
96 6S	0A	0A	0A	2	20	1950
96 6S	0A	0A	0A	0	0	1955
96 6S	0A	0A	0A			1960
96 6S	0A	0A	0A	0A	0A	1963
96 6S	0A	0A	0A	0A	0A	1965
97 6S	15	75	119	4	40	1950
97 6S	1	10	1	2	31	1955
97 6S	2	16	10	2	14	1960
97 6S	0	0	0	0	0	1963
97 6S	0A	0A	0A	0A	0A	1965
98 6S	0A	0A	0A	0A	0A	1950
98 6S	0A	0A	0A	0	0	1955
98 6S	0A	0A	0A	0A	0A	1960
98 6S	0A	0A	0A	0A	0A	1963
98 6S	0A	0A	0A	0A	0A	1965
99 6S	0A	0A	0A			1950
99 6S	0A	0A	0A	0A	0A	1955
99 6S	0A	0A	0A	0A	0A	1960
99 6S	0	0	0	0A	0A	1963
99 6S	0A	0A	0A	0A	0A	1965
100 6S				1	10	1950
100 6S				15	234	1955
100 6S				3	23	1960
100 6S	0	0	0	40	157	1963
100 6S	0A	0A	0A			1965
101 6S	0A	0A	0A	2	20	1950
101 6S	0A	0A	0A	1	5	1955
101 6S	0A	0A	0A	8	66	1960
101 6S	0	0	0	2	8	1963
101 6S	0A	0A	0A	0A	0A	1965
102 6S	0A	0A	0A	0A	0A	1950
102 6S	0A	0A	0A	2	31	1955
102 6S	0A	0A	0A	4	34	1960
102 6S	0	0	0	0	0	1963
102 6S	0A	0A	0A	0A	0A	1965
103 6S	464	75	3683	26	261	1950
103 6S	62	60	35	9	141	1955
103 6S	125	75	590	10	87	1960
103 6S	161	75	676	96	381	1963
103 6S	204	57	797			1965
104 6S				79	792	1950
104 6S	28	0	16	153	2391	1955
104 6S	68	74	320	448	5091	1960
104 6S	110	87	462	821	3243	1963
104 6S	148	20	578	200	1065	1965
105 6S	0A	0A	0A	0A	0A	1950
105 6S	0A	0A	0A	0A	0A	1955
105 6S	0A	0A	0A	0A	0A	1960
105 6S	0A	0A	0A	0A	0A	1963
105 6S	0A	0A	0A	0A	0A	1965

	27	28	29	30	31	
106 6S	0A	0A	0A	0A	0A	1950
106 6S	0A	0A	0A	0A	0A	1955
106 6S	0A	0A	0A	0A	0A	1960
106 6S	0A	0A	0A	0A	0A	1963
106 6S	0A	0A	0A	0A	0A	1965
107 6S	0A	0A	0A	0A	0A	1950
107 6S	0A	0A	0A	0A	0A	1955
107 6S	0A	0A	0A	0A	0A	1960
107 6S	0A	0A	0A	0A	0A	1963
107 6S	0A	0A	0A	0A	0A	1965
108 6S	0A	0A	0A	0A	0A	1950
108 6S	0A	0A	0A	0A	0A	1955
108 6S	0A	0A	0A	0A	0A	1960
108 6S	0A	0A	0A	0A	0A	1963
108 6S	0A	0A	0A	0A	0A	1965
109 6S						1950
109 6S						1955
109 6S	69A	242	406			1960
109 6S	88	218	481			1963
109 6S	207	382	1084			1965
110 6S	0A	0A	0A	0A	0A	1950
110 6S	0A	0A	0A	0A	0A	1955
110 6S	0A	0A	0A	0A	0A	1960
110 6S	0	0	0	0A	0A	1963
110 6S	0A	0A	0A	0A	0A	1965
111 6S	0A	0A	0A	0A	0A	1950
111 6S	0A	0A	0A	0A	0A	1955
111 6S	0A	0A	0A	0A	0A	1960
111 6S	0A	0A	0A	0A	0A	1963
111 6S	0A	0A	0A	0	0	1965
112 6S	0A	0A	0A	0A	0A	1950
112 6S	0A	0A	0A	0A	0A	1955
112 6S	0A	0A	0A	0A	0A	1960
112 6S	0	0	0	0A	0A	1963
112 6S	0A	0A	0A	0A	0A	1965
113 6S		0A	0A	0A	0A	1950
113 6S		0A	0A	0A	0A	1955
113 6S		0A	0A	0A	0A	1960
113 6S	0	0	0	0A	0A	1963
113 6S		0A	0A	0A	0A	1965
114 6S	0A	0A	0A	0A	0A	1950
114 6S	0A	0A	0A	0A	0A	1955
114 6S	0A	0A	0A	0A	0A	1960
114 6S	0	0	0	0A	0A	1963
114 6S	0A	0A	0A	0A	0A	1965
115 6S		0A	0A	0A	0A	1950
115 6S		0A	0A	0A	0A	1955
115 6S		0A	0A	0A	0A	1960
115 6S	0	0	0	0A	0A	1963
115 6S		0A	0A	0A	0A	1965
116 6S						1950
116 6S						1955
116 6S						1960
116 6S	0	0	0	0	0	1963
116 6S				0	0	1965
117 6S						1950
117 6S						1955
117 6S	4	4	24	44		1960
117 6S	6	5	33	60B		1963
117 6S				50		1965

	27	28	29	30	31	
118 6S				59	1	1950
118 6S				58	101	1955
118 6S				33	74	1960
118 6S				19F	275	1963
118 6S	8	78	7			1965
119 6S	0A	0A	0A	0A	0A	1950
119 6S	0A	0A	0A	0A	0A	1955
119 6S	0A	0A	0A	0A	0A	1960
119 6S	0A	0A	0A	0F	0	1963
119 6S	0A	0A	0A	0A	0A	1965
120 6S	0A	0A	0A	0A	0A	1950
120 6S	0A	0A	0A	0A	0A	1955
120 6S	0A	0A	0A	0A	0A	1960
120 6S	0A	0A	0A	0F	0	1963
120 6S	0A	0A	0A	0A	0A	1965
121 6S				0A	0A	1950
121 6S				0A	0A	1955
121 6S				0A	0A	1960
121 6S	0A	0A	0A	0A	0A	1963
121 6S	0A	0A	0A	0A	0	1965
122 6S				0A	0A	1950
122 6S	19	120	2	0A	0A	1955
122 6S	28	98	24	0A	0A	1960
122 6S	30	74	25	0A	0A	1963
122 6S	68	125	55	0A	0	1965
123 6S	30	150	30	0A	0A	1950
123 6S	4	80	1	0A	0A	1955
123 6S	10	81	9	0A	0A	1960
123 6S	13	92	11	0A	0A	1963
123 6S	13	88	11	0A	0	1965
124 6S				963	190	1950
124 6S				452	789	1955
124 6S				296	605	1960
124 6S	0A	0A	0A	17	5	1963
124 6S	0A	0A	0A			1965
125 6S	71	229	70	22	4	1950
125 6S	8	160	1	18	31	1955
125 6S	24	211	20	4	9	1960
125 6S	49	247	41			1963
125 6S	79	266	64			1965
126 6S	0A	0A	0A	0A	0A	1950
126 6S	0A	0A	0A	0A	0A	1955
126 6S	11	84	10	0A	0A	1960
126 6S	25	71	21	0A	0A	1963
126 6S	28	56	23	0A	0A	1965
127 6S	0A	0A	0A	6	1	1950
127 6S	9	120	1	1	2	1955
127 6S	15	82	13	0A	0A	1960
127 6S	16	56	13	0A	0A	1963
127 6S	31	27	25	0A	0A	1965
128 6S				0A	0A	1950
128 6S				0A	0A	1955
128 6S	47	66	40	0A	0A	1960
128 6S	64	69	53	0A	0A	1963
128 6S	68	54	55	0A	0A	1965
129 6S	5999	971	5934	214	42	1950
129 6S	674	650	63	189	330	1955
129 6S	1011	606	880			1960
129 6S	1231	570	103	0E	0	1963
129 6S	1687	469	1373	0A	0A	1965

	27	28	29	30	31	
130 6S	2118	98	2095	332	65	1950
130 6S	250	40	23	25	44	1955
130 6S	139	150	120	865	1769	1960
130 6S	199	158	166	409F	127	1963
130 6S	260	35	212	235	54	1965
131 6S	0A	0A	0A	0A	0A	1950
131 6S	0A	0A	0A	0A	0A	1955
131 6S	0A	0A	0A	20	14	1960
131 6S	0A	0A	0A			1963
131 6S	1	10	0	29	9	1965
132 6S	0A	0A	0A	0A	0A	1950
132 6S	0A	0A	0A	0A	0A	1955
132 6S	0A	0A	0A	0A	0A	1960
132 6S	0A	0A	0A	0A	0A	1963
132 6S	0A	0A	0A	0A	0A	1965
133 6S	0A	0A	0A	0A	0A	1950
133 6S	0A	0A	0A	0A	0A	1955
133 6S	0A	0A	0A	0A	0A	1960
133 6S	0A	0A	0A	0A	0A	1963
133 6S	0A	0A	0A	0A	0A	1965
134 6S	0A	0A	0A	0A	0A	1950
134 6S	0A	0A	0A	0A	0A	1955
134 6S	0A	0A	0A	0A	0A	1960
134 6S	0A	0A	0A	0A	0A	1963
134 6S	0A	0A	0A	0A	0A	1965
135 6S	0A	0A	0A	0A	0A	1950
135 6S	CA	0A	0A	0A	0A	1955
135 6S	0A	0A	0A	0A	0A	1960
135 6S	0A	0A	0A	0A	0A	1963
135 6S	0A	0A	0A	0A	0A	1965
136 6S	3	15	1	0A	0A	1950
136 6S	2	30	1	0A	0A	1955
136 6S	0A	0A	0A	0A	0A	1960
136 6S	0	0	0	0A	0A	1963
136 6S	0A	0A	0A	0A	0A	1965
137 6S	0A	0A	0A	0A	0A	1950
137 6S	0A	0A	0A	0A	0A	1955
137 6S	0A	0A	0A	0A	0A	1960
137 6S	0A	0A	0A	0A	0A	1963
137 6S	0A	0A	0A	0A	0A	1965
138 6S	4	13	2	2649		1950
138 6S	1	10	1	21	886	1955
138 6S	0A	0A	0A	422	1755	1960
138 6S	0	0	0			1963
138 6S	0A	0A	0A			1965
139 6S	0A	0A	0A	0A	0A	1950
139 6S	0A	0A	0A	0A	0A	1955
139 6S	0A	0A	0A	0A	0A	1960
139 6S	0	0	0	0A	0A	1963
139 6S	0A	0A	0A	0A	0A	1965
140 6S	0A	0A	0A	6	252	1950
140 6S	0A	0A	0A			1955
140 6S	0A	0A	0A			1960
140 6S	0	0	0			1963
140 6S	0A	0A	0A			1965
141 6S						1950
141 6S						1955
141 6S	944	1326	320			1960
141 6S	1323	1418	431			1963
141 6S	1934	1530	614			1965

	27	28	29	30	31	
142 6S						1950
142 6S						1955
142 6S	62	37	20			1960
142 6S	77	36	25		0A	1963
142 6S						1965
143 6S				228	948	1950
143 6S				25	1062	1955
143 6S	16	20	5	201		1960
143 6S	25	20	8	6798	3029	1963
143 6S				709	221	1965
144 6S	0A	0A	0A	0A	0A	1950
144 6S	0A	0A	0A	0A	0A	1955
144 6S	0A	0A	0A	0	0A	1960
144 6S	0A	0A	0A	0A	0A	1963
144 6S	0A	0A	0A	11	0A	1965
145 6S	0A	0A	0A	0A	0A	1950
145 6S	0A	0A	0A	0A	0A	1955
145 6S	0A	0A	0A	0A	0A	1960
145 6S	0A	0A	0A	0A	0A	1963
145 6S	0A	0A	0A	0A	0A	1965
146 6S				0A	0A	1950
146 6S				0A	0A	1955
146 6S				0A	0A	1960
146 6S				0A	0A	1963
146 6S				0A	0A	1965
147 6S	0A	0A	0A	0A	0A	1950
147 6S	0A	0A	0A	0A	0A	1955
147 6S				0A	0A	1960
147 6S				0A	0A	1963
147 6S				0A	0A	1965
148 6S				0A	0A	1950
148 6S	0A	100	1	0A	0A	1955
148 6S				0A	0A	1960
148 6S	0A	0A	0A	0A	0A	1963
148 6S				0A	0A	1965
149 6S	7	35	0	0A	0A	1950
149 6S	4	0A	0A	0A	0A	1955
149 6S	30	244	1	0A	0A	1960
149 6S	32	227	1	0A	0A	1963
149 6S	24	162	1	0A	0A	1965
150 6S				0A	0A	1950
150 6S	0A	0A	0A	0A	0A	1955
150 6S				0A	0A	1960
150 6S	1		4	0A	0A	1963
150 6S				0A	0A	1965
151 6S	7	23	0	229		1950
151 6S	0A	0A	0A	12	0	1955
151 6S	0A	0A	0A	149		1960
151 6S	0	0	0			1963
151 6S	0A	0A	0A			1965
152 6S	0A	0A	0A	0A	0A	1950
152 6S	0A	0A	0A	0A	0A	1955
152 6S	0A	0A	0A	0A	0A	1960
152 6S	0	0	0	0A	0A	1963
152 6S	0A	0A	0A	0A	0A	1965
153 6S						1950
153 6S	0A	0A	0A	0A	0A	1955
153 6S	0A	0A	0A	0A	0A	1960
153 6S	0	0	0	0A	0A	1963
153 6S	0A	0A	0A	0A	0A	1965

	27	28	29	30	31	
154 6S						1950
154 6S	58	760	1			1955
154 6S	2977	16180	140			1960
154 6S	318	1115	14			1963
154 6S	1482	1274	64			1965
155 6S						1950
155 6S	8	10	1	0	0	1955
155 6S	26	16	1			1960
155 6S	17	8	1	0A	0A	1963
155 6S				0A	0A	1965
156 6S				1B		1950
156 6S				16	0	1955
156 6S	22	24	1	22		1960
156 6S	18	14	1	12B	6263	1963
156 6S	20	3	1	19		1965
157 6S				49	4	1950
157 6S				32	27	1955
157 6S				40	35	1960
157 6S				0F	0	1963
157 6S	31	301	6	0A	0A	1965
158 6S				0A	0A	1950
158 6S	0A	0A	0A	0A	0A	1955
158 6S	0A	0A	0A	0A	0A	1960
158 6S	0A	0A	0A	0F	0	1963
158 6S	0A	0A	0A	0A	0A	1965
159 6S	0A	0A	0A	0A	0A	1950
159 6S	0A	0A	0A	8	7	1955
159 6S	0A	0A	0A	0A	0A	1960
159 6S	0A	0A	0A	0E	0	1963
159 6S	0A	0A	0A	0A	0A	1965
160 6S				33	3	1950
160 6S						1955
160 6S	0A	0A	0A	0A	0A	1960
160 6S	0A	0A	0A	0F	0	1963
160 6S	0A	0A	0A	0A	0A	1965
161 6S				375	29	1950
161 6S	162	1080	3	112	96	1955
161 6S	162	568	30	9	8	1960
161 6S	284	703	53	0E	0	1963
161 6S	417	769	87	0A	0A	1965
162 6S	598	2990	118	475	36	1950
162 6S	87	1990	2	249	214	1955
162 6S	187	1520	40	242	215	1960
162 6S	232	1648	43	290E	153	1963
162 6S	224	1514	41			1965
163 6S		0A	0A	12	1	1950
163 6S	0A	0A	0A	10	9	1955
163 6S	0A	0A	0A	7	7	1960
163 6S	15	0A	3	0E	0	1963
163 6S		0A	0A	0A	0A	1965
164 6S	399	1287	79	35	3	1950
164 6S	49	1020	1	14	12	1955
164 6S	109	960	20	3	3	1960
164 6S	255	1286	47		0	1963
164 6S	330	1111	61			1965
165 6S						1950
165 6S	0A	0A	0A	0A	0A	1955
165 6S	70	534	13	0A	0A	1960
165 6S	151	431	21	0E	0	1963
165 6S	193	385	35	0A	0A	1965

	27	28	29	30	31	
166 6S	5890	1601	1164	124	10	1950
166 6S	1198	1150	23	142	122	1955
166 6S	1954	1320	370			1960
166 6S	2190	1334	407	0E	0	1963
166 6S	2556	1404	470	0A	0A	1965
167 6S				0A	0A	1950
167 6S	16	210	1	0A	0A	1955
167 6S	73	400	14	0A	0A	1960
167 6S	100	351	19	0E	0	1963
167 6S	163	140	30	0A	0A	1965
168 6S				0A	0A	1950
168 6S				0A	0A	1955
168 6S	193	270	40	0A	0A	1960
168 6S	241	257	45	0E	0	1963
168 6S	268	212	49	0A	0A	1965
169 6S	8677	400	1714	1276	98	1950
169 6S	934	160	18	2188	1880	1955
169 6S	906	986	170	2087	2240	1960
169 6S	1317	1046		2366E	221	1963
169 6S	1832	250	337	2428E	85	1965
170 6S				69B	25	1950
170 6S				37	150	1955
170 6S				25	1	1960
170 6S						1963
170 6S	245	2379	13			1965
171 6S	0A	0A	0A	0A	0A	1950
171 6S	0A	0A	0A	0A	0A	1955
171 6S	0A	0A	0A	0A	0A	1960
171 6S	0A	0A	0A	0A	0A	1963
171 6S	0A	0A	0A	0A	0A	1965
172 6S	0A	0A	0A	0A	0A	1950
172 6S	0A	0A	0A	8	32	1955
172 6S	0A	0A	0A	0A	0A	1960
172 6S	0A	0A	0A	0A	0A	1963
172 6S	0A	0A	0A	0A	0A	1965
173 6S						1950
173 6S						1955
173 6S	0A	0A	0A	0A	0A	1960
173 6S	0A	0A	0A	0A	0A	1963
173 6S	0A	0A	0A	0A	0A	1965
174 6S				14B	5	1950
174 6S	255	1700	2	18	73	1955
174 6S	340	1190	20	8	0	1960
174 6S	525	1299	28	0A	0A	1963
174 6S	531	980	27	0A	0A	1965
175 6S	350	1750	23	36B	13	1950
175 6S	110	2530	1	52	211	1955
175 6S	272	2210	15	22	1	1960
175 6S	389	2763	21	0A	0A	1963
175 6S	393	2655	20	0A	0A	1965
176 6S				2B	1	1950
176 6S				6	24	1955
176 6S				4	0	1960
176 6S	41		2	0A	0A	1963
176 6S				0A	0A	1965
177 6S	952	3071	63	41	15	1950
177 6S	183	3800	1	42	171	1955
177 6S	497	4360	28	20	1	1960
177 6S	683	3444	36			1963
177 6S	832	2801	43			1965

	27	28	29	30	31	
178 6S				0A	0A	1950
178 6S	0A	0A	0A	0A	0A	1955
178 6S	234	1786	10	0A	0A	1960
178 6S	371	1059	20	0A	0A	1963
178 6S	444	886	23	0A	0A	1965
179 6S	4701	1277	311	79	28	1950
179 6S	1268	1210	8	160	650	1955
179 6S	2081	1410	120	32	1	1960
179 6S	2292	1397	121	151	5	1963
179 6S	2810	1544	144			1965
180 6S				88	3	1950
180 6S	7	90	1	6	24	1955
180 6S	108	590	6	3	0	1960
180 6S	99	347	5	0A	0A	1963
180 6S	130	112	7	0A	0A	1965
181 6S				178	1	1950
181 6S			14	16	65	1955
181 6S	174	240	10	16	1	1960
181 6S	196	210	10	0A	0A	1963
181 6S	230	182	12	0A	0A	1965
182 6S	12758	2064	844	632	227	1950
182 6S	2391	2310		1445	5869	1955
182 6S	4265	2560	240	98	4	1960
182 6S	5091	2358	269			1963
182 6S	6743	1875	347	830	27	1965

	32	33	34	35	36	37	
1 7S	0A	0	0	0A	0A	0A	1950
1 7S	0	0	0	0	0	0	1955
1 7S	0	0	0	0A	0	0	1960
1 7S	0	0A	0A	0F	0	0	1963
1 7S	0	0A	0A	0A	0A	0A	1965
2 7S	0A	0	0	25	19	2	1950
2 7S	0	0	0	46	32	9	1955
2 7S	0	0	0	5	4	0	1960
2 7S	0	0	0	2	1	0	1963
2 7S	0	0A	0A	4	2	0	1965
3 7S	0A	0	0	1	1	0	1950
3 7S	0	0A	0A	1	1	1	1955
3 7S	0	0	0	3A	2	0	1960
3 7S	0A	0	0	28	20	2	1963
3 7S	0A	0A	0A	0A	0A	0A	1965
4 7S	0A	0	0	33	25	2	1950
4 7S	0	0	0	5	4	1	1955
4 7S	0	0A	0A	1	0	0	1960
4 7S	0	0A	0A	14	10	1	1963
4 7S	0	0A	0A				1965
5 7S	0A	0	0	0A	0A	0A	1950
5 7S	0	0	0	19	13	4	1955
5 7S	0	0	0	1	1	0	1960
5 7S	0	0A	0A	2	1	0	1963
5 7S	0	0A	0A	2	1	0	1965
6 7S	0A	0	0	0A	0A	0A	1950
6 7S	0	0	0	0	0	0	1955
6 7S	0	0	0	13	10	1	1960
6 7S	0	0A	0A	0	0	0	1963
6 7S	0	0A	0A	0	0	0	1965
7 7S	2	0	0	18	13	1	1950
7 7S	2			1	1	1	1955
7 7S	0	0	0	3	3	0	1960

	32	33	34	35	36	37	
7 7S	0	0	0	7	5	0	1963
7 7S	0						1965
8 7S	0A	0	0	0A	0A	0A	1950
8 7S	0	0	0	0	0	0	1955
8 7S	0	0	0	4	3	0	1960
8 7S	0	0A	0A	4	3	0	1963
8 7S	0	0A	0A				1965
9 7S	1	0	0	188	140	14	1950
9 7S	4	0	0	424	298	39	1955
9 7S	0	0	0	517	407	40	1960
9 7S	0	2	17	1088	773	72	1963
9 7S	0			814	510	42	1965
10 7S	0A	0	0	16	12	1	1950
10 7S	0	0	0	129	91	24	1955
10 7S	0	0	0	249	196	19	1960
10 7S	0	0A	0A	128	91	8	1963
10 7S	0	0A	0A	111	69	6	1965
11 7S		0	0	0A			1950
11 7S	0	0	0	7	5	1	1955
11 7S	0	0	0	134	105	10	1960
11 7S	0	20	0	401	285	26	1963
11 7S	0	0A	0A	293	184	15	1965
12 7S	8	0	0	1139	846	84	1950
12 7S	6	17	16	604	424	55	1955
12 7S	0	14	10	646	509	50	1960
12 7S	0	29	21	554	394	37	1963
12 7S	0	39	46	617	387	32	1965
13 7S	9	471	155	7145	5308	525	1950
13 7S	23			6016	4227	547	1955
13 7S	38	521	90	5637	4442	441	1960
13 7S	38	673	90	5309	3773	350	1963
13 7S	46	885	518	5202	3259	270	1965
14 7S	0A	0	0	0A	0A	0A	1950
14 7S	0	0	0	0	0	0	1955
14 7S	0	0	0	0A	0	0	1960
14 7S	0	0A	0A	0G	0	0	1963
14 7S	0	0A	0A	0A	0A	0A	1965
15 7S	0A	0A	0A	49	353	61	1950
15 7S	0	0A	0A	175	772	175	1955
15 7S	0	0	0	79	349	53	1960
15 7S	0A	5	0	123	454	72	1963
15 7S	0A			187	832	106	1965
16 7S	0A	0	0	0A	0A	0A	1950
16 7S	0	0	0	0	0	0	1955
16 7S	0	0	0	0A	0	0	1960
16 7S	0	0A	0A	0A	0	0	1963
16 7S	0	0A	0A	0A	0A	0A	1965
17 7S	0A	0	0	0A	0A	0A	1950
17 7S	0	0	0	0	0	0	1955
17 7S	0	0A	0A	0A	0	0	1960
17 7S	0	0A	0A	0	0	0	1963
17 7S	0	9	25	0	1	0	1965
18 7S				264	1899	330	1950
18 7S	0	90	247	416	1834	416	1955
18 7S	0	0	0	343	1516	230	1960
18 7S	0	0	0	212	782	123	1963
18 7S	0	60	50	231	1024	131	1965
19 7S				185	1331	231	1950
19 7S	0			120	529	120	1955
19 7S	0	0	0	431	1905	289	1960

	32	33	34	35	36	37	
19 7S		0	0	314	1159	183	1963
19 7S		0A	CA	80	356	46	1965
20 7S		0	C	0A	0A	0A	1950
20 7S	0	0	0	2	9	2	1955
20 7S	0	0	C	7	33	5	1960
20 7S	0	0A	0A	7	26	4	1963
20 7S	0	0A	CA	0	0	0	1965
21 7S	0A	0	0	0A	0A	0A	1950
21 7S	0	0	0	0	0	0	1955
21 7S	0	0	0	0A	0	0	1960
21 7S	0	0A	0A	0A	0	0	1963
21 7S	0	0A	CA	0A	0A	0A	1965
22 7S	0A	0	0	7	50	9	1950
22 7S	0	0	0	22	97	22	1955
22 7S	0	0	C	22	97	15	1960
22 7S	0	0	0	36	133	21	1963
22 7S	0			46	206	26	1965
23 7S	0A	0	0	0A	0A	0A	1950
23 7S	0	0	0	24	106	24	1955
23 7S	0	0	0	1	4	1	1960
23 7S	0	0A	0A	26	96	15	1963
23 7S	0	0A	0A	6	27	3	1965
24 7S		0	0	0A			1950
24 7S	0	3	3	152	670	152	1955
24 7S	0	0	0	50	219	33	1960
24 7S	0	50	0	91	336	53	1963
24 7S	0			135	600	77	1965
25 7S				71	511	89	1950
25 7S	0	78	72	194	855	194	1955
25 7S	0	72	54	214	949	144	1960
25 7S	0	50	35	264	974	154	1963
25 7S	0	56	66	128	571	73	1965
26 7S		90	30	7	50	9	1950
26 7S	0	0	C	12	53	12	1955
26 7S	0	220	38	8	35	5	1960
26 7S	0	158	21	4	15	2	1963
26 7S	0	92	54	8	36	5	1965
27 7S	0A	0	0	0A	0A	0A	1950
27 7S	0	0	0	0	0	0	1955
27 7S	0	0	0	0	0	0	1960
27 7S	0	0A	0A	9F	5	0	1963
27 7S	0	0A	0A	0	0	0	1965
28 7S				34			1950
28 7S	0	0	C	23	18	1	1955
28 7S	0	0	0	247	121	5	1960
28 7S	0	0	0	264F	157	2	1963
28 7S	0	0A	0A	250	129	3	1965
29 7S	0A	0	0	1	0A	0A	1950
29 7S	0	0	0	0	0	0	1955
29 7S	0	0	0	112A	55	2	1960
29 7S	0	0	C	907F	540	8	1963
29 7S	0	0A	0A	1289	668	17	1965
30 7S	0A	0	0	9	0A	0A	1950
30 7S	0	0	0	9	7	0	1955
30 7S	0	0A	CA	195	96	4	1960
30 7S	0	0A	0A	180F	107	2	1963
30 7S	0	1	3	241	124	3	1965
31 7S	0A	0A	0A	10			1950
31 7S	0	20	55	54	42	2	1955
31 7S	0	0	0	54	26	1	1960

	32	33	34	35	36	37	
31 7S	0	0	0	2F	1	0	1963
31 7S	0	8	7	0	0	0	1965
32 7S	0A	0A	0A	25			1950
32 7S	0	0A	0A	101	79	3	1955
32 7S	0	0	0	570	279	12	1960
32 7S	0	0	0	399AF	237	3	1963
32 7S	0	0A	0A	0	0	0	1965
33 7S	1	0	0	1	0A	0A	1950
33 7S	1B	0	0	0	0	0	1955
33 7S	0	0	0	0E	0	0	1960
33 7S	0	0A	0A	0A	0	0	1963
33 7S	0	0A	0A	0	0	0	1965
34 7S	0A	0	0	0A	0A	0A	1950
34 7S	0	0	0	0	0	0	1955
34 7S	0	0	0	11	5	0	1960
34 7S	0	0A	0A	18F	11	0	1963
34 7S	0	0A	0A	33	15	1	1965
35 7S	0A			125	0A	2	1950
35 7S	0	1	7	81	63	2	1955
35 7S	0	0	0	214	105	4	1960
35 7S	0	0	0	142F	85	1	1963
35 7S	0			229	119	3	1965
36 7S	0A			0A	0A	0A	1950
36 7S	0	16	172	352	274	10	1955
36 7S	0	0	0	464	227	10	1960
36 7S	0	0	0	248F	148	2	1963
36 7S	0			0	0	0	1965
37 7S		500		1913			1950
37 7S	0	4964	4393	6435	5009	184	1955
37 7S	0	7500		8481	4149	175	1960
37 7S	0	0	0	4130F	2458	36	1963
37 7S	0	65		2256	1170	30	1965
38 7S	1B			302			1950
38 7S	1B	8	7	344	268	10	1955
38 7S	0	7	0	697	341	14	1960
38 7S	2B	0	0	468F	279	4	1963
38 7S	0	18	21	749	388	10	1965
39 7S	3B	0	0	0A	0A	0A	1950
39 7S	1B	0	0	2	2	1	1955
39 7S	2	0A	0	3	1	0	1960
39 7S	0	0A	0A	3F	2	0	1963
39 7S	2B	0A	0A	0	0	0	1965
40 7S				0A			1950
40 7S	0			1	2	1	1955
40 7S	0	0	0	29	46	10	1960
40 7S		0	0	0AF	0	0	1963
40 7S				0	0	0	1965
41 7S	0A	0	0	0A	0A	0A	1950
41 7S	0	0	0	0	0	0	1955
41 7S	0	0	0	0A	0	0	1960
41 7S	0	0A	0A	0A	0	0	1963
41 7S	0	0A	0A				1965
42 7S	0A	0	0	55	86	28	1950
42 7S	0	0	0	4	7	2	1955
42 7S	0	0	0	321	519	117	1960
42 7S	0	0	0	727	1339	192	1963
42 7S	0			999	1456	312	1965
43 7S	0A	0	0	18	28	9	1950
43 7S	0	0	0	0	0	0	1955
43 7S	0	0A	0A	89	144	33	1960

		32	33	34	35	36	37	
43	7S	0	0A	0A	153	282	40	1963
43	7S	0	1	3	73	107	23	1965
44	7S	0A	0	0	32	50	16	1950
44	7S	0	0	0	9	15	4	1955
44	7S	0	0	0	5	8	2	1960
44	7S	0	0A	0A	0	0	0	1963
44	7S	0	0A	CA	0	0	0	1965
45	7S	0A	0	0	0A	0A	0A	1950
45	7S	0	0	0	0	0	0	1955
45	7S	0	0	0	0A	0	0	1960
45	7S	0	0A	0A	0A	0	0	1963
45	7S	0						1965
46	7S		0	0	0A	0A	0A	1950
46	7S	0	0	0	37	62	17	1955
46	7S	0	0	0	0	0	0	1960
46	7S	0	0A	0A	0	0	0	1963
46	7S	0	0A	0A	5	8	2	1965
47	7S	0A	0	0	0A	0A	0A	1950
47	7S	0	0	0	0	0	0	1955
47	7S	0	0	0	0A	0	0	1960
47	7S	0	0A	0A	0F	0	0	1963
47	7S	0	0A	0A	0A	0A	0A	1965
48	7S				265	413	133	1950
48	7S	0	1	7	109	183	50	1955
48	7S	0	0	0	113	182	41	1960
48	7S	0	1	9	84	155	22	1963
48	7S	0			45	66	14	1965
49	7S	0A	0	0	0A	0A	0A	1950
49	7S	0	0	0	0	0	0	1955
49	7S	0	0	0	97	156	35	1960
49	7S	0	0	0	182	335	48	1963
49	7S	0			41	60	13	1965
50	7S	0A	0	0	1	2	1	1950
50	7S	0	0	0	364	613	165	1955
50	7S	0	0	0	1035	1675	377	1960
50	7S	0A	0	0	1639	3018	432	1963
50	7S	0A			3224	4699	1007	1965
51	7S				1072	1670	536	1950
51	7S	0	2	19	70	118	32	1955
51	7S	0	3	2	85	137	31	1960
51	7S	0	2	1	227	418	60	1963
51	7S	0	0A	0A	121	176	38	1965
52	7S		675	222	4055	6316	2028	1950
52	7S		0	0	4013	6754	1824	1955
52	7S	1190	1094	188	3289	5322	1197	1960
52	7S	700	0A	0A	0	0	0	1963
52	7S	1725A			0	0	0	1965
53	7S	0A	0	0	0A			1950
53	7S	0	0	0	0	0	0	1955
53	7S	33	0	0	1	2	0	1960
53	7S	0	0A	0A	1	2	0	1963
53	7S	6	0A	CA	0	0	0	1965
54	7S	0A	0	C	0A			1950
54	7S	0	0	0	3	7	1	1955
54	7S	0	0	0	0	0	0	1960
54	7S	0	0A	0A	7F	13	2	1963
54	7S	0	0A	CA				1965
55	7S	0A	0	0	35	69	13	1950
55	7S	0	0	0	245	584	79	1955
55	7S	0	0	0	445	784	125	1960

	32	33	34	35	36	37	
55 7S	0	0	0	164	314	42	1963
55 7S	0	0A	CA	451	747	96	1965
56 7S		0	0	0A			1950
56 7S	0	0	0	0	0	0	1955
56 7S	0	0	0	93	163	26	1960
56 7S	0	0A	0A	104	199	27	1963
56 7S	0	0A	0A	92	153	20	1965
57 7S		0	0	628	1246	242	1950
57 7S	0	2	5	371	885	120	1955
57 7S	0	0	0	386	680	108	1960
57 7S	0	0	0	297	569	76	1963
57 7S	0	9	8	259	429	55	1965
58 7S		0	C	7	14	3	1950
58 7S	0	0	0	19	45	6	1955
58 7S	0	0	0	2	4	1	1960
58 7S	0	0A	0A	17	33	4	1963
58 7S	0	0A	0A	1	2	0	1965
59 7S	326	0	C	0A	0A	0A	1950
59 7S	29			0	0	0	1955
59 7S	5034	0	0	0A	0	0	1960
59 7S		0	0	0A	0	0	1963
59 7S		0A	0A	0A	0A	0A	1965
60 7S		0	0	0A			1950
60 7S	0			0	0	0	1955
60 7S				23	40	6	1960
60 7S		0	0	1C3	197	26	1963
60 7S				35	57	7	1965
61 7S	0	0		179	355	69	1950
61 7S	0	7	51	95	227	31	1955
61 7S		0	C	52	92	15	1960
61 7S	0	10	86	57	109	15	1963
61 7S	0			73	120	15	1965
62 7S	0A			27	54	10	1950
62 7S	0	0	0	83	198	27	1955
62 7S		0	0	221	390	62	1960
62 7S	0	0	0	109	209	28	1963
62 7S	0			161	267	34	1965
63 7S	0A			252	500	97	1950
63 7S	0	14	12	202	482	65	1955
63 7S		0	0	887	1561	248	1960
63 7S	0	225	0	1017	1948	261	1963
63 7S	0			1304	2158	277	1965
64 7S	182			1094	2171	421	1950
64 7S	96	279	256	231	551	75	1955
64 7S	42	344	257	132	232	37	1960
64 7S	0	452	320	181	347	46	1963
64 7S	0	328	7024	170	281	36	1965
65 7S	8	344	113	443	879	170	1950
65 7S	6	0	0	260	620	84	1955
65 7S	132	923	159	285	502	80	1960
65 7S	12	1217	163	226	433	58	1963
65 7S	10	993	1176	191	316	41	1965
66 7S	0A	0	0	13	11	1	1950
66 7S		0	0	2	2	1	1955
66 7S	0	0	0	5	4	0	1960
66 7S	0	0A	0A	7F	4	0	1963
66 7S	0	0A	CA				1965
67 7S	0A	0A	0A	488	416	24	1950
67 7S	0A	0A	0A	285	223	10	1955
67 7S	0	0	0	137	103	4	1960

		32	33	34	35	36	37	
67	7S	0	0	0	98	60	2	1963
67	7S	0	0A	0A	76	45	2	1965
68	7S	0A	0A	0A	51	44	3	1950
68	7S	0	0A	0A	143	112	5	1955
68	7S	0A	0	0	111	83	3	1960
68	7S	0	0	0	0	0	0	1963
68	7S	0	0A	0A	0A	0A	0A	1965
69	7S	0A	0	0	140	119	7	1950
69	7S	0	0	0	96	75	4	1955
69	7S	0A	0	0	154	115	4	1960
69	7S	0	0	0	88	54	2	1963
69	7S	0	0A	0A	6	4	0	1965
70	7S	0A	0	0	140	119	7	1950
70	7S		0	0	204	160	7	1955
70	7S		18A	19A	282	212	8	1960
70	7S	0	18	19	250	152	6	1963
70	7S	0	18	51	568	337	12	1965
71	7S		0A	0A	46	39	2	1950
71	7S		0A	0A	237	186	9	1955
71	7S		0	0	65	49	2	1960
71	7S	0	0	0	51	31	1	1963
71	7S	0	0A	0A	17	10	0	1965
72	7S	3	0	0	3	3	0	1950
72	7S	1	0A	0A	0	0	0	1955
72	7S	22	0	0	7	5	0	1960
72	7S	0	0	0	1	1	0	1963
72	7S	0	0A	0A	0A	0A	0A	1965
73	7S	0A	0	0	0A	0A	0A	1950
73	7S	0	0	0	0	0	0	1955
73	7S	0A	0	0	3	2	0	1960
73	7S	0	0A	0A	10	6	0	1963
73	7S	0	0A	0A				1965
74	7S	0A			189	161	9	1950
74	7S	0	7	51	374	293	14	1955
74	7S	0A	0	0	178	133	5	1960
74	7S	0	14	120	227	138	6	1963
74	7S	0			166	98	3	1965
75	7S	0A	0A	0A	4	3	0	1950
75	7S	0	0	0	9	7	1	1955
75	7S	0A	0	0	81	61	2	1960
75	7S	0	0A	0A	196	119	5	1963
75	7S	0	0A	0A	192	113	4	1965
76	7S	0A			28	24	1	1950
76	7S	0	8	7	52	41	2	1955
76	7S	0A	0	0	605	455	17	1960
76	7S	0A	210	0	1030	627	26	1963
76	7S	0A			1951	1156	40	1965
77	7S	33			2489	2124	124	1950
77	7S	18	1532	1407	3531	2766	129	1955
77	7S	0	1660	1240	3587	2695	103	1960
77	7S		1543	1093	3633	2211	91	1963
77	7S		1711	2027	3040	1801	53	1965
78	7S	1	1099	361	2144	1829	107	1950
78	7S	1	2144	496	1949	1527	71	1955
78	7S	1	5621	968	2107	1583	61	1960
78	7S	2	6387	854	2728	1660	68	1963
78	7S	1	7518	4402	3090	1831	64	1965
79	7S	0A	0	0	0A	0A	0A	1950
79	7S	0	0	0	218	231	21	1955

	32	33	34	35	36	37	
79 7S	0	0	C	0	0	0	1960
79 7S	0	0A	0A	0A	0	0	1963
79 7S	0	0A	CA	7	9	1	1965
80 7S	0A	0	0	0A			1950
80 7S	0A	0A	0A	25	26	2	1955
80 7S	0A	0	0	17	20	3	1960
80 7S	0A	0	0	2F	3	0	1963
80 7S	0A	0A	0A	27	37	3	1965
81 7S	0A	0A	0A	0A	0A	0A	1950
81 7S	0	0A	CA	65	69	6	1955
81 7S	0A	0	0	354	422	55	1960
81 7S	0	5	0	344	494	43	1963
81 7S	0	300		400	564	47	1965
82 7S	0A	0	0	0A	0A	0A	1950
82 7S	0	0	0	0	0	0	1955
82 7S	0A	0	0	0A	0	0	1960
82 7S	0	0A	0	CA	0	0	1963
82 7S	0	0A	0A	CA	0A	0A	1965
83 7S	0A	0	0	28	39	2	1950
83 7S	0	41	311	8	8	1	1955
83 7S	0A	54A	58A	0	0	0	1960
83 7S	0	54	58	0	0	0	1963
83 7S	0	108	305	10	14	1	1965
84 7S	0A			62	86	4	1950
84 7S	0	20	55	28	30	3	1955
84 7S	0A	0	0	56	67	9	1960
84 7S	0	0	0	1F	1	0	1963
84 7S	0	11	9	16	23	2	1965
85 7S	0A	0	0	0A	0A	0A	1950
85 7S	0A	0	0	0	0	0	1955
85 7S	0A	0	0	0	0	0	1960
85 7S	0	0A	0	0A	0	0	1963
85 7S	0	0A	0A	0A	0A	0A	1965
86 7S	0A	0	0	0A	0A	0A	1950
86 7S	0	0A	0A	0	0	0	1955
86 7S	0A	0	0	0A	0	0	1960
86 7S	0	0	0	0A	0	0	1963
86 7S	0	0A	0A	0A	0A	0A	1965
87 7S	743			1341	1870	87	1950
87 7S	294	629	4611	1508	1595	144	1955
87 7S	3636			24	29	4	1960
87 7S	12	238	2038	138F	198	17	1963
87 7S	0			919	1298	108	1965
88 7S	0A	0A	0A	3	4	0	1950
88 7S	0	0	0	128	135	12	1955
88 7S	0A	0	0	4	5	1	1960
88 7S	0	0A	0	52	75	6	1963
88 7S	0	0A	CA	39	54	5	1965
89 7S	0A			0A	0A	0A	1950
89 7S	0	8	7	0	0	0	1955
89 7S	0A	0	0	281	335	43	1960
89 7S	0	370	0	383	550	47	1963
89 7S	0			263	372	31	1965
90 7S	1			357	498	23	1950
90 7S	1	40	37	919	972	88	1955
90 7S	5	47	35	914	1088	142	1960
90 7S	0	29	21	233F	335	29	1963
90 7S	0	18	21	60	85	7	1965
91 7S	1	130	43	1573	2194	101	1950
91 7S	1	0	0	1671	1767	159	1955

		32	33	34	35	36	37	
91	7S	3	653	112	1937	2306	300	1960
91	7S	1	727	97	1133F	1628	140	1963
91	7S	1	412	241	1584	2237	186	1965
92	7S	87A	0	C	0A	0A	0A	1950
92	7S	189	0A	0A	0	0	0	1955
92	7S	1768	0	0	12	52	4	1960
92	7S	130	0	C	8	24	3	1963
92	7S	23A	0A	0A	7	16	2	1965
93	7S	0A	0	0	0A	0A	0A	1950
93	7S	0	0	C	1	11	1	1955
93	7S	0A	0	0	2	8	1	1960
93	7S	0	0A	0	5	15	2	1963
93	7S	0	0A	0A	3	7	1	1965
94	7S	0A	0	C	0A	0A	0A	1950
94	7S	0	0	0	0	0	0	1955
94	7S	0A	0	0	0A	0	0	1960
94	7S	0	0	0	0A	0	0	1963
94	7S	0	0A	CA	0A	0A	0A	1965
95	7S	0A	0	C	0A	0A	0A	1950
95	7S	0	0A	0A	0	0	0	1955
95	7S	0A	0	0	0	1	0	1960
95	7S	0	0	C	0	0	0	1963
95	7S	0	0A	0A	0	0	0	1965
96	7S	16A	0	0	0A	0A	0A	1950
96	7S	0	0	0	0	0	0	1955
96	7S	0A	0A	0A	0A	0	0	1960
96	7S	0	0A	0	0A	0	0	1963
96	7S	0	0A	0A	0A	0A	0A	1965
97	7S	32A	0	0	0A	0A	0A	1950
97	7S	11	4	11	0	0	0	1955
97	7S	76	0	0	0	2	0	1960
97	7S	0	0	0	3	9	1	1963
97	7S	0	0A	0A	0A	0A	0A	1965
98	7S	0A	0	0	0A	0A	0A	1950
98	7S	0	0	0	0	0	0	1955
98	7S	0A	0	0	0	0	0	1960
98	7S	0	0A	0	0G	0	0	1963
98	7S	0	0A	0A	0A	0A	0A	1965
99	7S	0A	0	C	0A	0A	0A	1950
99	7S	0	0	0	0	0	0	1955
99	7S	0A	0	0	0A	0	0	1960
99	7S	0	0A	0	0A	0	0	1963
99	7S	0	0A	CA	0A	0A	0A	1965
100	7S	8			15	429	11	1950
100	7S	86	19	139	31	353	34	1955
100	7S	128	0	0	122	552	47	1960
100	7S	168	52	445	238	706	90	1963
100	7S	0A			366	901	108	1965
101	7S	16A	0	0	13	371	9	1950
101	7S	0	0A	0A	5	57	6	1955
101	7S	370	0	0	6	26	1	1960
101	7S	8	0	C	25	74	9	1963
101	7S	0A	0A	0A	53	131	16	1965
102	7S	CA	0	0	0A			1950
102	7S	11	0	0	18	205	20	1955
102	7S	190	0	0	3	14	1	1960
102	7S	0	0	0	6	18	2	1963
102	7S	0	0A	0A	6	15	2	1965
103	7S	206A	0	C	145	4143	104	1950
103	7S	51	92	84	182	2073	202	1955

		32	33	34	35	36	37	
103	7S	483	121	90	360	1637	44	1960
103	7S	403	111	79	480	1424	182	1963
103	7S		128	152	501	1234	148	1965
104	7S	627	779	256	79	2257	56	1950
104	7S	874	716	166	163	1856	86	1955
104	7S	2123	1013	174	293	1333	117	1960
104	7S	3450	1382	185	465	1380	176	1963
104	7S	781	1878	1100	624	1537	184	1965
105	7S	0A	0	0	0A	0A	0A	1950
105	7S	0A	0	C	0	0	0	1955
105	7S	0A	0	0	0	0	0	1960
105	7S	0	0A	0	0	0	0	1963
105	7S	0	0A	0A	0	0	0	1965
106	7S	0A	0	C	0A	0A	0A	1950
106	7S	0	0	0	0	0	0	1955
106	7S	0A	0	0	0A	0	0	1960
106	7S	0	0A	0	0A	0	0	1963
106	7S	0	0A	0A	0A	0A	0A	1965
107	7S	0A	0	0	0A	0A	0A	1950
107	7S	C	0	0	0	0	0	1955
107	7S	0A	0	C	0	0	0	1960
107	7S	0	0	0	0	0	0	1963
107	7S	0	0A	CA	0A	0A	0A	1965
108	7S	0A	0	0	0A	0A	0A	1950
108	7S	0	0	0	0	0	0	1955
108	7S	0A	0	C	0A	0	0	1960
108	7S	0	0A	0	0	0	0	1963
108	7S	0	0A	0A	0	0	0	1965
109	7S				0A	0A	0A	1950
109	7S		377	830	0	0	0	1955
109	7S		1798A	1932A	0	0	0	1960
109	7S		1798	1932	0	0	0	1963
109	7S		4828	13638	0	4	0	1965
110	7S	0A	0A	0A	0A	0A	0A	1950
110	7S	0A	0	0	2	274	20	1955
110	7S	0A	0	0	8	736	28	1960
110	7S	0	0A	0	10	556	28	1963
110	7S	0	23	19	17	611	37	1965
111	7S	0A	0A	0A	0A	0A	0A	1950
111	7S	0A	0	0	0	0	0	1955
111	7S	0A	0	0	0A	0	0	1960
111	7S	0	0	0	0G	0	0	1963
111	7S	0	0A	0A	0	0	0	1965
112	7S		0A	0A	0A	0A	0A	1950
112	7S		0	C	0	0	0	1955
112	7S		0	0	0A	0	0	1960
112	7S		0A	0	0A	0	0	1963
112	7S		0A	CA	0A	0A	0A	1965
113	7S	0A			0A	0A	0A	1950
113	7S	0A	1	7	0	0	0	1955
113	7S	0A	0	C	0	0	0	1960
113	7S	0	4	34	3	167	8	1963
113	7S	0			0	0	0	1965
114	7S	0A	0A	0A	0A	0A	0A	1950
114	7S	C	0	0	0	0	0	1955
114	7S	0A	0	C	5	427	16	1960
114	7S	0	0A	0	2	111	6	1963
114	7S	0	0A	0A	0	0	0	1965
115	7S	0A	0A	0A	0A	0A	0A	1950
115	7S	0	0	0	0	0	0	1955
115	7S	0A	0	0	0A	0	0	1960

		32	33	34	35	36	37	
115	7S	0	10	C	0	0	0	1963
115	7S	0			0	0	0	1965
116	7S				0A	0A	0A	1950
116	7S		57	52	0	0	0	1955
116	7S		59	44	0	9	0	1960
116	7S	0	56	40	0	0	0	1963
116	7S	0	96	114	0	4	0	1965
117	7S		179	59	0A	0A	0A	1950
117	7S		0	0	1	137	10	1955
117	7S	259	655	113	1	45	2	1960
117	7S	328	686	92	0	0	0	1963
117	7S	262	717	420	1	29	2	1965
118	7S	58	0	0	151	107	30	1950
118	7S	54	0	0	243	90	32	1955
118	7S	286	0	0	252	63	22	1960
118	7S	16	0	C	182	37	13	1963
118	7S		0A	0A	162	25	9	1965
119	7S	0A	0	0	18	13	4	1950
119	7S	C	0	0	91	34	12	1955
119	7S	0A	0	0	77	19	7	1960
119	7S	0	0A	0	82	17	6	1963
119	7S	0	0A	CA	63	10	3	1965
120	7S	0A	0	C	3	2	1	1950
120	7S	0	0	0	29	11	4	1955
120	7S	CA	0	C	69	17	6	1960
120	7S	0	0A	0	129	26	9	1963
120	7S	0	0A	CA	190	30	10	1965
121	7S	0A	0	0	19	13	4	1950
121	7S	0	0	0	66	25	9	1955
121	7S	0A	0	C	74	18	7	1960
121	7S	0	0	0	1C9	22	8	1963
121	7S	0A	0A	0A	36	6	2	1965
122	7S	0	0	0	126	89	25	1950
122	7S	C	0	0	165	61	22	1955
122	7S	0A	1A	1A	172	43	15	1960
122	7S	0	1	1	135	27	10	1963
122	7S	0A	0A	0A	152	24	8	1965
123	7S	0A	0	0	84	59	17	1950
123	7S	0	0	0	227	84	30	1955
123	7S	0A	0	C	209	52	18	1960
123	7S	0	0A	0A	185	37	13	1963
123	7S	CA	0A	0A	394	62	21	1965
124	7S	953	0A	CA	789	558	158	1950
124	7S	420	0A	0A	680	253	89	1955
124	7S	258	0	C	263	65	23	1960
124	7S	14	0	0	87	18	6	1963
124	7S		0A	0A	327	51	17	1965
125	7S	22	0A	0A	57	40	11	1950
125	7S	17	0A	0A	98	36	13	1955
125	7S	36	0	0	224	56	20	1960
125	7S	0	0	0	171	34	12	1963
125	7S		0A	CA	218	34	11	1965
126	7S	0A	0	0	0A	0A	0A	1950
126	7S	0	0	C	0	0	0	1955
126	7S	0A	0	0	37	9	3	1960
126	7S	0	0A	0A	33	7	2	1963
126	7S	0A	0A	0A	46	7	2	1965
127	7S	6	0	0	90	64	18	1950
127	7S	1	0A	0A	75	28	10	1955
127	7S	0A	0	0	142	35	13	1960

		32	33	34	35	36	37	
127	7S	0	0	0	91	18	7	1963
127	7S	0A	0A	0A	130	20	7	1965
128	7S				5	4	1	1950
128	7S	0	0	C	156	58	21	1955
128	7S		0	0	119	29	10	1960
128	7S	0	0A	0A	237	48	17	1963
128	7S	0A			293	46	15	1965
129	7S	212			2058	1455	412	1950
129	7S	176	57	52	3324	1237	437	1955
129	7S		54	43	4411	1095	389	1960
129	7S	0	61	43	4770	961	343	1963
129	7S		98	116	5557	869	292	1965
130	7S	328	385	126	608	430	122	1950
130	7S	23	0	0	1585	590	209	1955
130	7S	753	372	64	1982	492	175	1960
130	7S	342	434	58	2033	410	146	1963
130	7S	191	719	421	2437	381	128	1965
131	7S	0A	0	C	0A	0A	0A	1950
131	7S	C	0	0	0	0	0	1955
131	7S	66	0	C	199	150	9	1960
131	7S	0	0A	0A	133	75	1	1963
131	7S	9A	0A	0A	46	20	2	1965
132	7S	0A	0	0	0A	0A	0A	1950
132	7S	0	0	0	0	0	0	1955
132	7S	0A	0	0	142	107	7	1960
132	7S	0	0A	0A	35F	20	0	1963
132	7S	0	0A	0A				1965
133	7S	0A	0	0	0A	0A	0A	1950
133	7S	0	0A	0A	349	382	24	1955
133	7S	0A	0	0	500	377	24	1960
133	7S	0	0	C	112	63	6	1963
133	7S	C	0A	0A	192	86	7	1965
134	7S	0A	0	0	1	0A	0A	1950
134	7S	0	0	0	0	0	0	1955
134	7S		U	0	41	31	2	1960
134	7S	0	0	C	243	137	2	1963
134	7S	0	0A	0A	53	24	2	1965
135	7S	0A	0	0	13	0A	0A	1950
135	7S	0	0	0	C	0	0	1955
135	7S	0A	0A	0A	90	68	4	1960
135	7S	0	0A	0A	137	77	7	1963
135	7S	0	0A	0A	152	68	5	1965
136	7S	0A	0	C	5	0A	0A	1950
136	7S	0	0	0	0	0	0	1955
136	7S	0A	0	0	62	47	3	1960
136	7S	0	0A	0A	206	116	10	1963
136	7S	0	1	1	321	144	11	1965
137	7S	0A	0	0	0A	0A	0A	1950
137	7S	0	0	0	0	0	0	1955
137	7S	0A	0	0	19	14	1	1960
137	7S	0	0A	0A	122	69	1	1963
137	7S	0	0A	CA	154	69	5	1965
138	7S	30A	0	0	73			1950
138	7S		0A	CA	0	0	0	1955
138	7S	30A	0	0	9	7	0	1960
138	7S	0	0	C	53F	30	0	1963
138	7S	C	0A	0A	45	20	2	1965
139	7S	0A	0	0	0A	0A	0A	1950
139	7S	0	0	C	0	0	0	1955
139	7S	0A	0	0	8	6	0	1960

		32	33	34	35	36	37	
139	7S	0	0A	CA	11F	6	0	1963
139	7S	0	0A	0A				1965
140	7S	2			67			1950
140	7S	0	5	37	0	0	0	1955
140	7S		0	0	93	70	4	1960
140	7S		6	51	134	76	1	1963
140	7S				189	85	7	1965
141	7S							1950
141	7S		1184	1048	2805	3071	193	1955
141	7S		0	0	3902	2943	183	1960
141	7S		0	0	6175	3489	312	1963
141	7S				7814	3507	272	1965
142	7S				536		17	1950
142	7S		2	2	779	853	54	1955
142	7S		27	20	989	746	46	1960
142	7S		32	23	1128	637	57	1963
142	7S		37	44	1275	572	44	1965
143	7S	9	0	0	111			1950
143	7S		0	0	0	0	0	1955
143	7S	142	70	12	315	238	15	1960
143	7S	221	127	170	418	236	21	1963
143	7S	225	273	160	695	312	24	1965
144	7S	0A	0	0	0A	0A	0A	1950
144	7S	0	0A	0A	0	0	0	1955
144	7S	C	0	C	158	28	1	1960
144	7S	0	0	0	294	40	2	1963
144	7S	1A	0A	0A	277	34	1	1965
145	7S	0A	0A	0A	0A	0A	0A	1950
145	7S	0	0	0	2	1	0	1955
145	7S	0A	0	0	17	3	0	1960
145	7S	C	0A	CA	67	9	0	1963
145	7S	0	0A	0A	53	7	0	1965
146	7S	0A			3882		73	1950
146	7S	0			7484	2158	50	1955
146	7S	CA	0	0	8171	1469	35	1960
146	7S	0	0	C	1872	257	10	1963
146	7S	0	15		1917	234	6	1965
147	7S	0A	0	0	0A	0A	0A	1950
147	7S	0	0	0	0	0	0	1955
147	7S	0A	0	0	708	127	3	1960
147	7S	0A	0	C	3998	550	21	1963
147	7S	0A	0A	0A	3754	459	12	1965
148	7S	0A	0	0	168		3	1950
148	7S	0	0	0	110	32	1	1955
148	7S	0A	1A	1A	696	125	3	1960
148	7S	0	1	1	1352	186	7	1963
148	7S	C	3	8	2087	255	7	1965
149	7S	0A	0A	0A	35		1	1950
149	7S	0	0	C	73	21	0	1955
149	7S	0A	0	0	470	85	2	1960
149	7S	0	0A	0A	2219	305	12	1963
149	7S	0	30	25	2150	263	7	1965
150	7S	0A	0	0	0A	0A	0A	1950
150	7S	0	0	C	1	0	1	1955
150	7S	0A	0	0	162	29	1	1960
150	7S	0	0A	0A	499	69	3	1963
150	7S	0	0A	0A	544	67	2	1965
151	7S	12	0	0	1		0	1950
151	7S		0	C	68	20	1	1955
151	7S	69	0	0	1	0	0	1960

		32	33	34	35	36	37	
151	7S	0	0	0	1F	0	0	1963
151	7S	0	0A	0A	0A	0A	0A	1965
152	7S	0A	0	0	0A	0A	0A	1950
152	7S	0	0	0	0	0	0	1955
152	7S	0A	0	0	0A	0	0	1960
152	7S	0	0A	0A	15F	2	0	1963
152	7S	0	0A	0A				1965
153	7S	0A	0A	0A	23		0	1950
153	7S	0	0	0	329	95	2	1955
153	7S	0A	0	0	489	88	2	1960
153	7S	0	1	9	422	58	2	1963
153	7S	0			643	79	2	1965
154	7S							1950
154	7S				4318	1245	29	1955
154	7S		0	0	4908	882	21	1960
154	7S		0	0	6626	911	35	1963
154	7S				7267	889	23	1965
155	7S				958		18	1950
155	7S	0	2	2	1692	488	11	1955
155	7S	0A	12	9	1924	346	8	1960
155	7S	0	16	11	2150	296	11	1963
155	7S	0	14	17	2911	356	9	1965
156	7S	1			382		7	1950
156	7S	1	0	0	238	69	2	1955
156	7S	1	37	6	244	44	1	1960
156	7S	1	50	7	248	34	1	1963
156	7S	1	56	33	344	42	1	1965
157	7S	10	0	0	1213	192	33	1950
157	7S	2	0A	0A	188	22	4	1955
157	7S	75	0	0	529	53	7	1960
157	7S	0	0	0	529	46	6	1963
157	7S	0	0A	0A	298	23	3	1965
158	7S	0A	0	0	252	44	7	1950
158	7S	0	0	0	615	73	12	1955
158	7S	0A	0	0	323	33	4	1960
158	7S	0	0A	0A	290	25	3	1963
158	7S	0	0A	0A	222	17	2	1965
159	7S	0A	0	0	101	16	3	1950
159	7S	2	0	0	223	26	4	1955
159	7S	0A	0	0	880	88	12	1960
159	7S	0	0A	0A	374	33	5	1963
159	7S	0	0A	0A	696	53	7	1965
160	7S	7	0	0	96	15	3	1950
160	7S	0	0	0	138	16	3	1955
160	7S	0A	0	0	205	21	3	1960
160	7S	0	0	0	58	5	1	1963
160	7S	0	0A	0A	414	31	4	1965
161	7S	74			1202	190	32	1950
161	7S	22	0	0	816	96	16	1955
161	7S	18	11A	12A	543	55	8	1960
161	7S	0	11	12	937	82	11	1963
161	7S	0	6	17	548	41	6	1965
162	7S	94			2723	431	73	1950
162	7S	49	8	23	3668	433	72	1955
162	7S	462	0	0	4205	422	58	1960
162	7S	54	0	0	3862	338	47	1963
162	7S		20	17	3195	241	32	1965
163	7S	2	0	0	240	38	6	1950
163	7S	2	0	0	320	38	6	1955
163	7S	14	0	0	542	54	8	1960

	32	33	34	35	36	37	
163 7S	0	0A	0A	387	34	5	1963
163 7S	0	0A	CA	252	19	3	1965
164 7S	7			281	45	8	1950
164 7S	3			276	33	5	1955
164 7S	6	0	C	426	43	6	1960
164 7S		0	0	665	58	8	1963
164 7S				1478	112	15	1965
165 7S		0	C	0A	0A	0A	1950
165 7S		0	0	0	0	0	1955
165 7S		0	C	167	17	2	1960
165 7S	0	0A	0A	253	22	3	1963
165 7S	0	0A	CA	251	19	3	1965
166 7S	24			2134	338	57	1950
166 7S	28	22	161	3188	376	62	1955
166 7S				3231	325	45	1960
166 7S	C	32	274	4911	430	59	1963
166 7S	0			5408	409	55	1965
167 7S	0A	0A	0A	223	35	6	1950
167 7S	0	0A	0A	195	23	4	1955
167 7S	0A	0	C	407	41	6	1960
167 7S	C	0	0	786	69	9	1963
167 7S	0	0A	0A	683	52	7	1965
168 7S	0A	0A	CA	397	63	11	1950
168 7S	0	0	0	894	106	17	1955
168 7S	0A	0	0	1038	104	14	1960
168 7S	0	0	0	1788	157	22	1963
168 7S	0	0A	0A	1313	99	13	1965
169 7S	252	1054	346	3571	566	96	1950
169 7S	427	862	200	5589	660	109	1955
169 7S	397	1109	191	9114	915	126	1960
169 7S	440	1777	238	1C167	891	123	1963
169 7S	446	3118	1826	13958	1054	141	1965
170 7S	5	0	0	3435	334	12	1950
170 7S	2	0A	0A	2536	163	7	1955
170 7S	14	0	0	4224	208	8	1960
170 7S		0	0	3818	166	7	1963
170 7S		0A	0A	3480	128	5	1965
171 7S	0A	0	0	9	1	0	1950
171 7S	0	0	0	46	3	0	1955
171 7S	0A	0	0	83	4	0	1960
171 7S	0	0A	0A	118	5	0	1963
171 7S	0	0A	0A	236	9	0	1965
172 7S	0A	0A	0A	0A	68	2	1950
172 7S	1	0	0	0	0	0	1955
172 7S	0A	0	0	0E	0	0	1960
172 7S	0	0A	0A	0	0	0	1963
172 7S	0	0A	0A	0	0	0	1965
173 7S	0A			4561	444	16	1950
173 7S				4585	295	12	1955
173 7S		0	0	2216	109	4	1960
173 7S	0	0	C	365	16	1	1963
173 7S	0	0A	0A	0	0	0	1965
174 7S	1			321	31	1	1950
174 7S	1	0	0	797	51	2	1955
174 7S	5	17A	18A	1505	74	3	1960
174 7S	0	17	18	2098	91	4	1963
174 7S	0	10	28	1580	58	2	1965
175 7S	2			2124	207	7	1950
175 7S	3	17	47	1914	123	5	1955
175 7S	12	0	0	6390	314	12	1960

		32	33	34	35	36	37	
175	7S	0	0	0	8168	356	14	1963
175	7S	0	22	18	9280	341	14	1965
176	7S	1			784	76	3	1950
176	7S	1			775	50	2	1955
176	7S	2	0	C	856	42	2	1960
176	7S	0	0	0	1092	47	2	1963
176	7S	0	0A	0A	420	15	1	1965
177	7S	3			923	90	3	1950
177	7S	3			900	58	2	1955
177	7S	11	0	C	1183	58	2	1960
177	7S		0	0	1669	73	3	1963
177	7S				2240	82	3	1965
178	7S	0A	0	C	0A	0A	0A	1950
178	7S	0	0	0	65	4	1	1955
178	7S	0A	0	C	169	8	0	1960
178	7S	C	0A	0A	372	16	1	1963
178	7S	0	0A	CA	276	10	0	1965
179	7S	5			2239	218	8	1950
179	7S	10	168	1232	48C1	309	12	1955
179	7S	17			7062	347	14	1960
179	7S	8	136	1164	7818	340	14	1963
179	7S				1C880	400	16	1965
180	7S	1			89	9	0	1950
180	7S	1	0	C	31	2	1	1955
180	7S	2	0	0	1431	70	3	1960
180	7S	C	0	C	1089	47	2	1963
180	7S	0	0A	0A	350	13	1	1965
181	7S	1	0A	0A	7	1	0	1950
181	7S	1	0	0	3	0	1	1955
181	7S	9	0	0	392	19	1	1960
181	7S	0	0	0	226	10	0	1963
181	7S	0			450	17	1	1965
182	7S	42			5113	498	18	1950
182	7S	87	910	836	9304	598	24	1955
182	7S	54	1146	856	11386	682	27	1960
182	7S		1295	917	11729	511	20	1963
182	7S	43	1991	2358	16150	594	24	1965

		38	39	40	41	42	43	
1	8S	8	1905	29	1174	64	46	1950
1	8S	15	34C9	55	1511	88	53	1955
1	8S	16	3810	74	1859	89	59	1960
1	8S	15	3191	84	1768	68	0052	1963
1	8S	18	3333	92	1829	65	51	1965
2	8S	0A	0A	78	3158	0A	125	1950
2	8S	0	0	4	110	0	4	1955
2	8S	0A	0A	19	477	0A	15	1960
2	8S	0	0	21	C442	0	0013	1963
2	8S	8	1481	97	1928	29	54	1965
3	8S	30	7143	114	4615	240	182	1950
3	8S	35	7955	176	4835	206	168	1955
3	8S	32	7619	201	5050	178	160	1960
3	8S	31	6596	215	4526	142	0133	1963
3	8S	31	5740	206	4095	112	114	1965
4	8S	18	4286	124	5020	144	198	1950
4	8S	21	4773	179	4918	124	171	1955
4	8S	21	5000	171	4296	117	136	1960
4	8S	24	5106	213	4484	109	0132	1963
4	8S	29	5370	229	4553	105	127	1965
5	8S	20	4762	133	5385	160	212	1950

		38	39	40	41	42	43	
5	8S	22	5000	206	5659	129	197	1955
5	8S	24	5714	240	6030	133	190	1960
5	8S	27	5745	292	6147	123	0180	1963
5	8S	32	5925	304	6044	116	168	1965
6	8S	14	3333	41	1660	112	65	1950
6	8S	19	4318	83	2280	112	79	1955
6	8S	22	5238	118	2965	122	94	1960
6	8S	23	4894	135	2842	105	0083	1963
6	8S	25	4629	142	2823	90	79	1965
7	8S	12	2857	95	3846	96	152	1950
7	8S	21	4773	176	4835	124	168	1955
7	8S	21	5000	229	5754	117	182	1960
7	8S	26	5532	281	5916	119	0174	1963
7	8S	32	5925	322	6402	116	178	1965
8	8S	5	1190	8	324	40	13	1950
8	8S	12	2727	20	549	71	19	1955
8	8S	14	3333	34	854	78	27	1960
8	8S	15	3191	43	C905	68	0027	1963
8	8S	17	3148	52	1034	61	29	1965
9	8S	21	5000	206	8340	168	329	1950
9	8S	26	5909	309	8489	153	295	1955
9	8S	28	6667	338	8492	156	268	1960
9	8S	29	6170	399	8400	132	0247	1963
9	8S	37	6851	410	8151	134	227	1965
10	8S	16	3809	113	4575	128	180	1950
10	8S	21	4773	143	3929	124	137	1955
10	8S	19	4524	184	4623	106	146	1960
10	8S	20	4255	238	5011	91	0147	1963
10	8S	25	4629	254	5050	90	140	1965
11	8S	8	1905	36	1457	64	57	1950
11	8S	15	3409	59	1621	88	56	1955
11	8S	14	3333	107	2688	78	85	1960
11	8S	19	4043	163	3432	87	0101	1963
11	8S	22	4074	179	3559	80	99	1965
12	8S	24	5714	201	8138	192	321	1950
12	8S	30	6818	299	8214	177	286	1955
12	8S	28	6667	320	8040	156	254	1960
12	8S	33	7021	395	8316	151	0244	1963
12	8S	38	7037	404	8032	138	223	1965
13	8S	35	8333	214	8664	279	342	1950
13	8S	40	9091	328	9011	235	314	1955
13	8S	38	9047	348	8744	211	276	1960
13	8S	40	8511	413	8695	183	0255	1963
13	8S	48	8888	437	8688	174	242	1965
14	8S	8	6154	29	6591	158	193	1950
14	8S	15	7500	55	7432	145	198	1955
14	8S	16	6957	74	7957	134	190	1960
14	8S	15	6521	84	7636	108	0162	1963
14	8S	18	7500	92	8364	107	157	1965
15	8S	0A	0A	31	7045	0A	206	1950
15	8S	0	0	4	541	0	14	1955
15	8S	1	435	13	1398	8	33	1960
15	8S	0	0	8	C727	0	0015	1963
15	8S	2	0833	44	4000	11	75	1965
16	8S	8	6154	20	4545	158	133	1950
16	8S	16	8000	39	5270	154	141	1955
16	8S	16	6957	52	5591	134	133	1960
16	8S	13	5652	63	5727	93	0122	1963
16	8S	13	5416	60	5455	77	102	1965
17	8S	8	6154	28	6364	158	186	1950

		38	39	40	41	42	43	
17	8S	16	8000	47	6351	154	169	1955
17	8S	17	7391	64	6882	142	164	1960
17	8S	17	7391	75	6818	122	0145	1963
17	8S	19	7916	77	7000	113	131	1965
18	8S	10	7692	42	9545	198	279	1950
18	8S	19	9500	72	9730	183	260	1955
18	8S	22	9565	88	9462	184	226	1960
18	8S	23	10000	105	9545	166	0203	1963
18	8S	24	10000	104	9455	143	177	1965
19	8S	11	8461	22	5000	217	146	1950
19	8S	19	9500	39	5270	183	141	1955
19	8S	21	9130	56	6021	175	144	1960
19	8S	21	9130	72	6545	151	0139	1963
19	8S	21	8750	73	6636	125	124	1965
20	8S	7	5385	27	6136	138	179	1950
20	8S	15	7500	46	6216	145	166	1955
20	8S	15	6522	60	6452	125	154	1960
20	8S	15	6521	75	6818	108	0145	1963
20	8S	16	6666	83	7545	95	141	1965
21	8S	4	3077	9	2045	79	60	1950
21	8S	11	5500	14	1892	106	50	1955
21	8S	13	5652	23	2473	109	59	1960
21	8S	13	5652	26	2364	94	0050	1963
21	8S	14	5833	36	3273	83	61	1965
22	8S	11	8461	38	8636	217	252	1950
22	8S	15	7500	64	8649	145	231	1955
22	8S	20	8696	83	8925	167	213	1960
22	8S	20	8695	96	8727	144	0186	1963
22	8S	21	8750	99	9000	125	169	1965
23	8S	6	4615	20	4545	119	133	1950
23	8S	11	5500	30	4054	106	108	1955
23	8S	13	5652	39	4193	109	100	1960
23	8S	9	3913	50	4545	64	0097	1963
23	8S	13	5416	54	4909	77	92	1965
24	8S	3	2308	15	3409	59	100	1950
24	8S	10	5000	20	2703	96	72	1955
24	8S	9	3913	26	2796	75	67	1960
24	8S	10	4347	35	3182	72	0068	1963
24	8S	9	3750	43	3909	53	73	1965
25	8S	13	9999	41	9318	257	272	1950
25	8S	20	10000	65	8784	193	234	1955
25	8S	21	9130	84	9032	175	216	1960
25	8S	21	9130	97	8818	151	0188	1963
25	8S	22	9166	98	8909	131	167	1965
26	8S	13	9999	40	9091	257	266	1950
26	8S	19	9500	68	9189	183	245	1955
26	8S	20	8696	84	9032	167	216	1960
26	8S	20	8695	95	8636	144	0184	1963
26	8S	21	8750	99	9000	125	169	1965
27	8S	0A	0A	78	6783	0A	222	1950
27	8S	0	0	4	4000	0	137	1955
27	8S	0A	0A	19	6333	0A	151	1960
27	8S	0	0	21	6563	0	0161	1963
27	8S	8	6153	97	7638	169	172	1965
28	8S	0A	0A	31	2696	0A	88	1950
28	8S	0	0	4	4000	0	137	1955
28	8S	0A	0A	13	4333	0A	103	1960
28	8S	0	0	8	2500	0	0061	1963
28	8S	2	1538	44	3465	42	78	1965
29	8S	0A	0A	57	4957	0A	162	1950
29	8S	0	0	4	4000	0	137	1955

		38	39	40	41	42	43	
29	8S	0A	0A	14	4667	0A	111	1960
29	8S	0	0	17	5313	0	0130	1963
29	8S	7	5384	59	4646	147	105	1965
30	8S	0A	0A	71	6174	0A	202	1950
30	8S	0	0	3	3000	0	103	1955
30	8S	0A	0A	21	7000	0A	167	1960
30	8S	1	2500	18	5625	192	0138	1963
30	8S	6	4615	75	5906	127	133	1965
31	8S	0A	0A	95	8261	0A	271	1950
31	8S	0	0	8	8000	0	275	1955
31	8S	0A	0A	25	8333	0A	199	1960
31	8S	1	2500	26	8125	192	0200	1963
31	8S	8	6153	110	8661	169	195	1965
32	8S	0A	0A	35	3043	0A	100	1950
32	8S	0	0	5	5000	0	172	1955
32	8S	0A	0A	13	4333	0A	103	1960
32	8S	0	0	16	5000	0	0123	1963
32	8S	5	3846	55	4331	105	98	1965
33	8S	0A	0A	53	4609	0A	151	1950
33	8S	0	0	3	3000	0	103	1955
33	8S	0A	0A	17	5667	0A	135	1960
33	8S	1	2500	18	5625	192	0138	1963
33	8S	5	3846	81	6378	105	144	1965
34	8S	0A	0A	10	870	0A	29	1950
34	8S	0	0	2	2000	0	69	1955
34	8S	0A	0A	8	2667	0A	63	1960
34	8S	0	0	5	1563	0	0038	1963
34	8S	2	1538	26	2047	42	46	1965
35	8S	0A	0A	98	8522	0A	279	1950
35	8S	0	0	6	6000	0	206	1955
35	8S	0A	0A	24	8000	0A	191	1960
35	8S	0	0	24	7500	0	0184	1963
35	8S	8	6153	108	8504	169	192	1965
36	8S	0A	0A	63	5478	0A	179	1950
36	8S	0	0	8	8000	0	275	1955
36	8S	1A	10000A	25	8333		199	1960
36	8S	3	7500	27	8438	576	0207	1963
36	8S	10	7692	86	6772	211	153	1965
37	8S	0A	0A	33	2870	0A	94	1950
37	8S	0	0	8	8000	0	275	1955
37	8S	1A	10000A	22	7333		175	1960
37	8S	2	5000	24	7500	384	0184	1963
37	8S	7	5384	71	5591	147	126	1965
38	8S	0A	0A	104	9043	0A	296	1950
38	8S	0	0	5	5000	0	172	1955
38	8S	0A	0A	24	8000	0A	191	1960
38	8S	0	0	24	7500	0	0184	1963
38	8S	7	5384	105	8268	147	187	1965
39	8S	0A	0A	107	9304	0A	305	1950
39	8S	0	0	6	6000	0	206	1955
39	8S	0A	0A	23	7667	0A	183	1960
39	8S	0	0	25	7813	0	0192	1963
39	8S	7	5384	110	8661	147	195	1965
40	8S	30	8571	114	8028	266	276	1950
40	8S	35	8537	176	8800	217	269	1955
40	8S	32	9143	201	8778	198	244	1960
40	8S	31	8857	215	9034	176	0225	1963
40	8S	31	8857	206	8957	159	208	1965
41	8S	8	2286	20	1408	71	48	1950
41	8S	16	3902	39	1950	99	60	1955

		38	39	40	41	42	43	
41	8S	16	4571	52	2271	99	63	1960
41	8S	13	3714	63	2647	74	0066	1963
41	8S	13	3714	60	2609	66	61	1965
42	8S	0A	0A	57	4014	0A	138	1950
42	8S	0	0	4	200	0	6	1955
42	8S	0A	0A	14	611	0A	17	1960
42	8S	0	0	17	C714	0	0018	1963
42	8S	7	2000	59	2565	35	60	1965
43	8S	19	5429	71	5000	168	172	1950
43	8S	22	5366	99	4950	136	151	1955
43	8S	21	6000	100	4367	130	121	1960
43	8S	20	5714	125	5252	113	0131	1963
43	8S	23	6571	125	5435	118	126	1965
44	8S	17	4857	87	6127	151	211	1950
44	8S	22	5366	120	6000	136	183	1955
44	8S	22	6286	152	6638	136	184	1960
44	8S	21	6000	166	6975	119	0174	1963
44	8S	23	6571	152	6609	118	154	1965
45	8S	13	3714	30	2113	115	73	1950
45	8S	22	5366	54	2700	136	82	1955
45	8S	21	6000	84	3668	130	102	1960
45	8S	18	5142	90	3782	102	0094	1963
45	8S	20	5714	94	4087	102	95	1965
46	8S	10	2857	63	4437	89	153	1950
46	8S	17	4146	105	5250	105	160	1955
46	8S	18	5143	141	6157	111	171	1960
46	8S	19	5428	154	6471	108	0161	1963
46	8S	21	6000	156	6783	107	158	1965
47	8S	4	1143	5	352	35	12	1950
47	8S	13	3171	13	650	81	20	1955
47	8S	14	4000	28	1222	86	34	1960
47	8S	12	3428	30	1261	68	0031	1963
47	8S	11	3142	36	1565	56	36	1965
48	8S	20	5714	112	7887	177	271	1950
48	8S	23	5610	156	7800	143	238	1955
48	8S	25	7143	189	8253	154	229	1960
48	8S	23	6571	197	8277	131	0206	1963
48	8S	26	7428	190	8261	133	192	1965
49	8S	17	4857	66	4648	151	160	1950
49	8S	20	4878	82	4100	124	125	1955
49	8S	17	4857	101	4410	105	122	1960
49	8S	14	4000	130	5462	79	0136	1963
49	8S	19	5428	141	6130	97	142	1965
50	8S	5	1429	28	1972	44	68	1950
50	8S	13	3171	39	1950	81	60	1955
50	8S	12	3429	61	2664	74	74	1960
50	8S	14	4000	96	4034	79	0100	1963
50	8S	15	4285	103	4478	77	104	1965
51	8S	21	6000	113	7958	186	274	1950
51	8S	27	6585	155	7750	167	237	1955
51	8S	23	6571	184	8035	142	223	1960
51	8S	22	6285	192	8067	125	0201	1963
51	8S	24	6857	182	7913	123	184	1965
52	8S	32	9143	129	9085	284	313	1950
52	8S	38	9268	185	9250	236	282	1955
52	8S	32	9143	204	8908	198	247	1960
52	8S	31	8857	209	8782	176	0219	1963
52	8S	31	8857	200	8696	159	202	1965
53	8S	18	6207	124	6631	177	239	1950
53	8S	21	7241	179	7521	155	239	1955

		38	39	40	41	42	43	
53	8S	21	7000	171	7634	144	205	1960
53	8S	24	6315	213	7717	128	0192	1963
53	8S	29	6304	229	7951	116	186	1965
54	8S	8	2759	28	1497	79	54	1950
54	8S	16	5517	47	1975	118	63	1955
54	8S	17	5667	64	2857	117	77	1960
54	8S	17	4473	75	2717	90	0068	1963
54	8S	19	4130	77	2674	76	63	1965
55	8S	0A	0A	71	3797	0A	137	1950
55	8S	0	0	3	126	0	4	1955
55	8S	0A	0A	21	938	0A	25	1960
55	8S	1	263	18	0652	5	0016	1963
55	8S	6	1304	75	2604	24	61	1965
56	8S	19	6552	71	3797	187	137	1950
56	8S	22	7586	99	4160	163	132	1955
56	8S	21	7000	100	4464	144	120	1960
56	8S	20	5263	125	4529	106	0113	1963
56	8S	23	5000	125	4340	92	102	1965
57	8S	21	7241	123	6577	207	237	1950
57	8S	21	7241	162	6807	155	216	1955
57	8S	22	7333	171	7634	151	205	1960
57	8S	23	6052	210	7609	122	0189	1963
57	8S	32	6956	218	7569	129	177	1965
58	8S	15	5172	39	2086	148	75	1950
58	8S	19	6552	73	3067	141	97	1955
58	8S	21	7000	93	4152	144	112	1960
58	8S	20	5263	114	4130	106	0103	1963
58	8S	25	5434	117	4063	100	95	1965
59	8S	12	4138	98	5241	118	189	1950
59	8S	20	6897	138	5798	148	184	1955
59	8S	22	7333	152	6786	151	182	1960
59	8S	26	6842	200	7246	138	0180	1963
59	8S	32	6956	217	7535	129	177	1965
60	8S	6	2069	13	695	59	25	1950
60	8S	13	4483	24	1008	96	32	1955
60	8S	16	5333	35	1562	110	42	1960
60	8S	19	5000	44	1594	101	0040	1963
60	8S	20	4347	49	1701	80	40	1965
61	8S	20	6897	172	9198	197	331	1950
61	8S	22	7586	220	9244	163	293	1955
61	8S	24	8000	213	9509	164	256	1960
61	8S	28	7368	256	9275	149	0231	1963
61	8S	34	7391	266	9236	137	217	1965
62	8S	19	6552	91	4866	187	175	1950
62	8S	20	6897	107	4496	148	143	1955
62	8S	16	5333	123	5491	110	148	1960
62	8S	16	4210	168	6087	85	0151	1963
62	8S	23	5000	182	6319	92	148	1965
63	8S	6	2069	35	1872	59	67	1950
63	8S	12	4138	51	2143	89	68	1955
63	8S	11	3667	86	3839	75	103	1960
63	8S	15	3947	121	4384	80	0109	1963
63	8S	19	4130	132	4583	76	107	1965
64	8S	24	8276	168	8984	237	324	1950
64	8S	23	7931	213	8950	170	284	1955
64	8S	24	8000	208	9286	164	250	1960
64	8S	28	7368	253	9167	149	0228	1963
64	8S	34	7391	255	8854	137	208	1965
65	8S	23	7931	169	9037	227	325	1950
65	8S	23	7931	216	9076	170	288	1955

		38	39	40	41	42	43	
65	8S	23	7667	205	9152	158	246	1960
65	8S	25	6578	249	9022	133	0224	1963
65	8S	30	6521	261	9063	120	212	1965
66	8S	20	6061	133	5429	193	214	1950
66	8S	22	6667	206	6458	159	227	1955
66	8S	24	5854	240	6266	147	198	1960
66	8S	27	5869	292	6606	131	0190	1963
66	8S	32	6153	304	6552	125	182	1965
67	8S	10	3030	42	1714	96	68	1950
67	8S	19	5758	72	2257	137	79	1955
67	8S	22	5366	88	2298	135	73	1960
67	8S	23	5000	105	2376	112	0068	1963
67	8S	24	4615	104	2241	94	62	1965
68	8S	0A	0A	95	3877	0A	153	1950
68	8S	0	0	8	251	0	9	1955
68	8S	0A	0A	25	653	0A	21	1960
68	8S	1	217	26	C588	4	0017	1963
68	8S	8	1538	110	2371	31	66	1965
69	8S	17	5152	87	3551	164	140	1950
69	8S	22	6667	120	3762	159	132	1955
69	8S	22	5366	152	3969	134	125	1960
69	8S	21	4565	166	3756	102	0108	1963
69	8S	23	4423	152	3276	90	91	1965
70	8S	21	6364	123	5C20	203	198	1950
70	8S	21	6364	162	5078	151	178	1955
70	8S	22	5366	171	4465	134	141	1960
70	8S	23	5000	210	4751	112	0137	1963
70	8S	32	6153	218	4698	125	130	1965
71	8S	15	4545	52	2122	145	84	1950
71	8S	24	7273	93	2915	173	102	1955
71	8S	26	6341	135	3525	159	111	1960
71	8S	29	6304	157	3552	141	0102	1963
71	8S	30	5769	152	3276	117	91	1965
72	8S	12	3636	113	4612	116	182	1950
72	8S	20	6061	162	5078	144	178	1955
72	8S	20	4878	238	6214	122	196	1960
72	8S	25	5434	290	6561	122	0189	1963
72	8S	29	5576	325	7004	113	194	1965
73	8S	4	1212	11	449	39	18	1950
73	8S	13	3939	23	721	94	25	1955
73	8S	14	3415	40	1044	86	33	1960
73	8S	15	3260	42	C950	73	0027	1963
73	8S	17	3269	52	1121	66	31	1965
74	8S	24	7273	219	8939	231	353	1950
74	8S	24	7273	284	8903	173	312	1955
74	8S	29	7073	338	8825	177	279	1960
74	8S	34	7391	388	8778	166	0252	1963
74	8S	37	7115	397	8556	145	237	1965
75	8S	17	5151	93	3796	164	150	1950
75	8S	16	4848	115	3605	115	126	1955
75	8S	21	5122	174	4543	128	143	1960
75	8S	19	4130	228	5158	92	0148	1963
75	8S	27	5192	235	5065	105	141	1965
76	8S	7	2121	39	1592	67	63	1950
76	8S	13	3939	55	1724	94	60	1955
76	8S	14	3415	110	2872	86	91	1960
76	8S	17	3695	151	3416	83	0098	1963
76	8S	21	4038	165	3556	82	99	1965
77	8S	31	9394	220	8980	299	355	1950
77	8S	31	9394	291	9122	223	320	1955
77	8S	35	8537	341	8903	214	281	1960

		38	39	40	41	42	43	
77	8S	40	8695	402	9095	195	0261	1963
77	8S	44	8461	415	8944	172	248	1965
78	8S	25	7576	224	9143	241	361	1950
78	8S	27	8182	288	9028	195	317	1955
78	8S	27	6585	328	8564	165	271	1960
78	8S	33	7173	383	8665	161	0249	1963
78	8S	36	6923	405	8728	141	242	1965
79	8S	14	6667	41	6308	186	197	1950
79	8S	19	6786	83	7545	149	216	1955
79	8S	22	7097	118	7662	150	197	1960
79	8S	23	6764	135	7500	131	0174	1963
79	8S	25	7142	142	7978	120	168	1965
80	8S	11	5238	22	3385	146	106	1950
80	8S	19	6786	39	3545	149	102	1955
80	8S	21	6774	56	3636	143	93	1960
80	8S	21	6176	72	4000	119	0093	1963
80	8S	21	6000	73	4101	100	86	1965
81	8S	0A	0A	35	5385	0A	168	1950
81	8S	0	0	5	455	0	13	1955
81	8S	0A	0A	13	844	0A	22	1960
81	8S	0	0	16	0889	0	0021	1963
81	8S	5	1428	55	3090	24	65	1965
82	8S	13	6190	30	4615	173	144	1950
82	8S	22	7857	54	4909	172	141	1955
82	8S	21	6774	84	5454	143	140	1960
82	8S	18	5294	90	5000	102	0116	1963
82	8S	20	5714	94	5281	96	111	1965
83	8S	15	7143	39	6000	199	187	1950
83	8S	19	6786	73	6636	149	190	1955
83	8S	21	6774	93	6039	143	155	1960
83	8S	20	5882	114	6333	113	0147	1963
83	8S	25	7142	117	6573	120	138	1965
84	8S	15	7143	52	8000	199	249	1950
84	8S	24	8571	93	8455	188	242	1955
84	8S	26	8387	135	8766	177	225	1960
84	8S	29	8529	157	8722	165	0203	1963
84	8S	30	8571	152	8539	144	180	1965
85	8S	10	4762	34	5231	133	163	1950
85	8S	17	6071	69	6273	133	180	1955
85	8S	21	6774	98	6364	143	163	1960
85	8S	22	6470	119	6611	125	0154	1963
85	8S	22	6285	126	7079	105	149	1965
86	8S	5	2381	8	1231	66	38	1950
86	8S	13	4643	15	1364	102	39	1955
86	8S	14	4516	21	1364	95	35	1960
86	8S	14	4117	22	1222	79	0028	1963
86	8S	14	4000	31	1742	67	37	1965
87	8S	15	7143	57	8769	199	274	1950
87	8S	22	7857	102	9273	172	266	1955
87	8S	27	8710	139	9026	184	232	1960
87	8S	26	7647	161	8944	148	0208	1963
87	8S	30	8571	159	8933	144	188	1965
88	8S	10	4762	37	5692	133	177	1950
88	8S	16	5714	56	5091	125	146	1955
88	8S	17	5484	76	4935	116	127	1960
88	8S	16	4705	102	5667	91	0132	1963
88	8S	21	6000	102	5730	100	121	1965
89	8S	4	1905	23	3538	53	110	1950
89	8S	11	3929	27	2455	86	70	1955
89	8S	11	3548	55	3571	75	92	1960

		38	39	40	41	42	43	
89	8S	16	4705	81	4500	91	0105	1963
89	8S	17	4857	79	4438	81	93	1965
90	8S	17	8095	56	8615	226	269	1950
90	8S	25	8929	96	8727	196	250	1955
90	8S	28	9032	134	8701	191	224	1960
90	8S	31	9117	158	8778	176	0204	1963
90	8S	30	8571	156	8764	144	184	1965
91	8S	18	8571	58	8923	239	279	1950
91	8S	25	8929	99	9000	196	258	1955
91	8S	25	8065	138	8961	170	230	1960
91	8S	27	7941	153	8500	153	0198	1963
91	8S	27	7714	156	8764	129	184	1965
92	8S	12	8571	95	5555	190	207	1950
92	8S	21	8077	176	7126	165	235	1955
92	8S	21	7000	229	6189	142	199	1960
92	8S	26	6666	281	6445	131	0191	1963
92	8S	32	7441	322	6479	127	186	1965
93	8S	7	5000	27	1579	111	59	1950
93	8S	15	5769	46	1862	118	61	1955
93	8S	15	5000	60	1622	102	52	1960
93	8S	15	3846	75	1720	75	0051	1963
93	8S	16	3720	83	1670	63	48	1965
94	8S	0A	0A	53	3099	0A	116	1950
94	8S	0	0	3	121	0	4	1955
94	8S	0A	0A	17	459	0A	15	1960
94	8S	1	256	18	C413	5	0012	1963
94	8S	5	1162	81	1630	19	47	1965
95	8S	10	7143	63	3684	159	138	1950
95	8S	17	6538	105	4251	134	140	1955
95	8S	18	6000	141	3811	122	122	1960
95	8S	19	4871	154	3532	96	0104	1963
95	8S	21	4883	156	3139	83	90	1965
96	8S	12	8571	98	5731	190	214	1950
96	8S	20	7692	138	5587	158	184	1955
96	8S	22	7333	152	4108	149	132	1960
96	8S	26	6666	200	4587	131	0136	1963
96	8S	32	7441	217	4366	127	125	1965
97	8S	12	8571	113	6608	190	247	1950
97	8S	20	7692	162	6559	158	216	1955
97	8S	20	6667	238	6432	136	207	1960
97	8S	25	6410	290	6651	126	0197	1963
97	8S	29	6744	325	6539	115	188	1965
98	8S	10	7143	34	1988	159	74	1950
98	8S	17	6538	69	2794	134	92	1955
98	8S	21	7000	98	2649	142	85	1960
98	8S	22	5641	119	2729	111	0081	1963
98	8S	22	5116	126	2535	87	73	1965
99	8S	5	3571	8	468	79	17	1950
99	8S	13	5000	16	648	102	21	1955
99	8S	14	4667	29	784	95	25	1960
99	8S	17	4358	38	0872	86	0026	1963
99	8S	18	4186	51	1026	71	29	1965
100	8S	13	9286	157	9181	206	343	1950
100	8S	20	7692	230	9312	158	307	1955
100	8S	26	8667	347	9378	176	301	1960
100	8S	31	7948	404	9266	156	0274	1963
100	8S	36	8372	453	9115	143	261	1965
101	8S	12	8571	79	4620	190	173	1950
101	8S	17	6538	105	4251	134	140	1955
101	8S	19	6333	185	5000	129	161	1960

		38	39	40	41	42	43	
101	8S	18	4615	234	5367	91	0159	1963
101	8S	25	5813	263	5292	99	152	1965
102	8S	3	2143	33	1930	48	72	1950
102	8S	12	4615	46	1862	95	61	1955
102	8S	14	4667	118	3189	95	102	1960
102	8S	18	4615	160	3670	91	0108	1963
102	8S	22	5116	182	3662	87	105	1965
103	8S	14	9999	152	8889	222	332	1950
103	8S	23	8846	225	9109	181	300	1955
103	8S	27	9000	334	9027	183	290	1960
103	8S	34	8717	394	9037	172	0267	1963
103	8S	37	8604	442	8893	147	255	1965
104	8S	12	8571	153	8947	190	334	1950
104	8S	21	8077	219	8866	165	292	1955
104	8S	21	7000	320	8649	142	278	1960
104	8S	26	6666	378	8670	131	0256	1963
104	8S	31	7209	429	8632	123	248	1965
105	8S	5	7143	8	6154	184	168	1950
105	8S	12	8571	20	7407	143	181	1955
105	8S	14	8750	34	7555	138	173	1960
105	8S	15	7500	43	7963	110	0165	1963
105	8S	17	8500	52	7879	103	148	1965
106	8S	4	5714	9	6923	147	189	1950
106	8S	11	7857	14	5185	131	127	1955
106	8S	13	8125	23	5111	128	117	1960
106	8S	13	6500	26	4815	96	0100	1963
106	8S	14	7000	36	5455	85	102	1965
107	8S	0A	0A	10	7692	0A	211	1950
107	8S	0	0	2	741	0	18	1955
107	8S	0A	0A	8	1778	0A	41	1960
107	8S	0	0	5	0926	0	0019	1963
107	8S	2	1000	26	3939	12	74	1965
108	8S	4	5714	5	3846	147	105	1950
108	8S	13	9286	13	4815	155	118	1955
108	8S	14	8750	28	6222	138	142	1960
108	8S	12	6000	30	5556	88	0115	1963
108	8S	11	5500	36	5455	67	102	1965
109	8S	6	8571	13	9999	221	274	1950
109	8S	13	9286	24	8889	155	217	1955
109	8S	16	10000	35	7778	157	178	1960
109	8S	19	9500	44	8148	140	0169	1963
109	8S	20	10000	49	7424	122	139	1965
110	8S	4	5714	11	8461	147	232	1950
110	8S	13	9286	23	8519	155	208	1955
110	8S	14	8750	40	8889	138	203	1960
110	8S	15	7500	42	7778	110	0161	1963
110	8S	17	8500	52	7879	103	148	1965
111	8S	5	7143	8	6154	184	168	1950
111	8S	13	9286	15	5556	155	136	1955
111	8S	14	8750	21	4667	138	107	1960
111	8S	14	7000	22	4074	103	0084	1963
111	8S	14	7000	31	4697	85	88	1965
112	8S	5	7143	8	6154	184	168	1950
112	8S	13	9286	16	5926	155	145	1955
112	8S	14	8750	29	6444	138	147	1960
112	8S	17	8500	38	7037	125	0146	1963
112	8S	18	9000	51	7727	110	145	1965
113	8S	5	7143	10	7692	184	211	1950
113	8S	9	6429	23	8519	107	208	1955
113	8S	14	8750	40	8889	138	203	1960

		38	39	40	41	42	43	
113	8S	17	8500	48	8889	125	0184	1963
113	8S	17	8500	58	8788	103	165	1965
114	8S	3	4286	7	5385	110	147	1950
114	8S	9	6429	9	3333	107	81	1955
114	8S	11	6875	16	3555	108	81	1960
114	8S	10	5000	25	4630	73	0096	1963
114	8S	14	7000	38	5758	85	108	1965
115	8S	1	1429	3	2308	37	63	1950
115	8S	7	5000	6	2222	83	54	1955
115	8S	8	5000	10	2222	79	51	1960
115	8S	10	5000	18	3333	73	0069	1963
115	8S	11	5500	25	3788	67	71	1965
116	8S	5	7143	10	7692	184	211	1950
116	8S	12	8571	23	8519	143	208	1955
116	8S	14	8750	39	8667	138	199	1960
116	8S	16	8000	45	8333	111	0173	1963
116	8S	17	8500	52	7879	103	148	1965
117	8S	5	7143	10	7692	184	211	1950
117	8S	13	9286	24	8889	155	217	1955
117	8S	14	8750	41	9111	138	208	1960
117	8S	15	7500	46	8519	110	0177	1963
117	8S	16	8000	56	8485	97	159	1965
118	8S	21	3889	206	4000	164	213	1950
118	8S	26	4194	309	4421	159	212	1955
118	8S	28	3733	338	4132	132	182	1960
118	8S	29	3717	399	3455	114	0167	1963
118	8S	37	4404	410	3528	120	159	1965
119	8S	11	2037	38	738	86	39	1950
119	8S	15	2419	64	916	92	44	1955
119	8S	20	2667	83	1015	94	45	1960
119	8S	20	2564	96	C831	79	0040	1963
119	8S	21	2500	99	852	68	38	1965
120	8S	0A	0A	98	1903	0A	101	1950
120	8S	0	0	6	86	0	4	1955
120	8S	0A	0A	24	293	0A	13	1960
120	8S	0	0	24	C208	0	0010	1963
120	8S	8	0952	108	929	26	42	1965
121	8S	20	3704	112	2175	156	116	1950
121	8S	23	3710	156	2232	141	107	1955
121	8S	25	3333	189	2310	118	102	1960
121	8S	23	2948	197	1706	90	0083	1963
121	8S	26	3095	190	1635	84	74	1965
122	8S	20	3704	172	3340	156	178	1950
122	8S	22	3548	220	3147	134	151	1955
122	8S	24	3200	213	2604	113	115	1960
122	8S	28	3589	256	2216	110	0107	1963
122	8S	34	4047	266	2289	110	103	1965
123	8S	24	4444	219	4252	187	226	1950
123	8S	24	3871	284	4063	147	195	1955
123	8S	29	3867	338	4132	137	182	1960
123	8S	34	4358	388	3359	134	0163	1963
123	8S	37	4404	397	3417	120	154	1965
124	8S	15	2778	57	1107	117	59	1950
124	8S	22	3548	102	1459	134	70	1955
124	8S	27	3600	139	1699	127	75	1960
124	8S	26	3333	161	1394	102	0067	1963
124	8S	30	3571	159	1368	97	62	1965
125	8S	13	2407	157	3049	101	162	1950
125	8S	20	3226	230	3290	122	158	1955
125	8S	26	3467	347	4242	123	187	1960

	38	39	40	41	42	43	
125 8S	31	3974	404	3498	122	0169	1963
125 8S	36	4285	453	3898	117	176	1965
126 8S	5	926	10	194	39	10	1950
126 8S	9	1452	23	329	55	16	1955
126 8S	14	1867	40	489	66	21	1960
126 8S	17	2179	48	C416	67	0020	1963
126 8S	17	2023	58	499	55	23	1965
127 8S	22	4074	178	3456	172	184	1950
127 8S	21	3387	193	2761	128	133	1955
127 8S	27	3600	303	3704	127	163	1960
127 8S	27	3461	369	3195	106	0155	1963
127 8S	34	4047	382	3287	110	148	1965
128 8S	9	1667	50	971	70	52	1950
128 8S	11	1774	72	1030	67	49	1955
128 8S	19	2533	158	1931	90	85	1960
128 8S	24	3076	216	1870	94	0091	1963
128 8S	27	3214	226	1945	87	88	1965
129 8S	47	8704	426	8272	367	440	1950
129 8S	48	7742	579	8283	293	398	1955
129 8S	57	7600	654	7995	269	353	1960
129 8S	57	7307	784	6788	225	0329	1963
129 8S	65	7738	811	6979	211	315	1965
130 8S	35	6481	365	7087	273	377	1950
130 8S	38	6129	475	6795	232	326	1955
130 8S	37	4933	527	6442	174	284	1960
130 8S	40	5128	605	5238	158	0254	1963
130 8S	43	5119	628	5404	139	244	1965
131 8S	16	5926	113	5765	170	229	1950
131 8S	21	7500	143	6908	165	228	1955
131 8S	19	5429	184	5593	130	187	1960
131 8S	20	5555	238	6056	132	0184	1963
131 8S	25	5681	254	6150	116	175	1965
132 8S	6	2222	20	1C20	64	41	1950
132 8S	11	3929	30	1449	86	48	1955
132 8S	13	3714	39	1185	89	40	1960
132 8S	9	2500	50	1272	59	0039	1963
132 8S	13	2954	54	1308	60	37	1965
133 8S	0A	0A	63	3214	0A	128	1950
133 8S	0	0	8	386	0	13	1955
133 8S	1A	10000	25	760		25	1960
133 8S	3	833	27	C687	19	0021	1963
133 8S	10	2272	86	2082	46	59	1965
134 8S	17	6296	66	3367	181	134	1950
134 8S	20	7143	82	3961	157	131	1955
134 8S	17	4857	101	3070	116	103	1960
134 8S	14	3888	130	3308	93	0101	1963
134 8S	19	4318	141	3414	88	97	1965
135 8S	19	7037	91	4643	202	185	1950
135 8S	20	7143	107	5169	157	170	1955
135 8S	16	4571	123	3739	110	125	1960
135 8S	16	4444	168	4275	106	0130	1963
135 8S	23	5227	182	4407	107	126	1965
136 8S	17	6296	93	4745	181	189	1950
136 8S	16	5714	115	5556	126	183	1955
136 8S	21	6000	174	5289	144	177	1960
136 8S	19	5277	228	5802	126	0176	1963
136 8S	27	6136	235	5690	125	162	1965
137 8S	10	3704	37	1888	106	75	1950
137 8S	16	5714	56	2705	126	89	1955
137 8S	17	4857	76	2310	116	77	1960
137 8S	16	4444	102	2595	106	0079	1963

		38	39	40	41	42	43	
137	8S	21	4772	102	2470	97	70	1965
138	8S	12	4444	79	4031	128	160	1950
138	8S	17	6071	105	5072	134	167	1955
138	8S	19	5429	185	5623	130	188	1960
138	8S	18	5000	234	5954	119	0181	1963
138	8S	25	5681	263	6368	116	182	1965
139	8S	3	1111	7	357	32	14	1950
139	8S	9	3214	9	435	71	14	1955
139	8S	11	3143	16	486	75	16	1960
139	8S	10	2777	25	C636	66	0019	1963
139	8S	14	3181	38	920	65	26	1965
140	8S	22	8148	178	9082	234	361	1950
140	8S	21	7500	193	9324	165	308	1955
140	8S	27	7714	303	9210	185	308	1960
140	8S	27	7500	369	9389	179	0285	1963
140	8S	34	7727	382	9249	158	264	1965
141	8S	9	3333	49	2500	96	99	1950
141	8S	15	5357	70	3382	118	112	1955
141	8S	25	7143	150	4559	171	152	1960
141	8S	25	6944	209	5318	166	0162	1963
141	8S	30	6818	225	5448	139	155	1965
142	8S	22	8148	166	8469	234	337	1950
142	8S	22	7857	181	8744	173	288	1955
142	8S	27	7714	285	8663	185	290	1960
142	8S	27	7500	349	8880	179	0270	1963
142	8S	35	7954	367	8886	162	253	1965
143	8S	18	6667	153	7806	192	310	1950
143	8S	20	7143	176	8502	157	280	1955
143	8S	22	6286	246	7477	151	250	1960
143	8S	20	5555	307	7812	132	0237	1963
143	8S	26	5909	325	7869	121	224	1965
144	8S	8	5000	36	6316	196	194	1950
144	8S	15	7895	59	7108	167	205	1955
144	8S	14	5000	107	5978	128	180	1960
144	8S	19	5588	163	6820	129	0188	1963
144	8S	22	6111	179	6992	127	183	1965
145	8S	3	1875	15	2632	73	81	1950
145	8S	10	5263	20	2410	111	69	1955
145	8S	9	3214	26	1452	82	44	1960
145	8S	10	2941	35	1464	68	0040	1963
145	8S	9	2500	43	1680	52	44	1965
146	8S	0A	0A	33	5789	0A	178	1950
146	8S	0	0	8	964	0	28	1955
146	8S	1A		22	1229		37	1960
146	8S	2	588	24	1004	13	0028	1963
146	8S	7	1944	71	2773	40	73	1965
147	8S	5	3125	28	4912	123	151	1950
147	8S	13	6842	39	4699	144	135	1955
147	8S	12	4286	61	3408	110	103	1960
147	8S	14	4117	96	4017	95	0111	1963
147	8S	15	4166	103	4023	86	105	1965
148	8S	6	3750	35	6140	147	189	1950
148	8S	12	6316	51	6145	133	177	1955
148	8S	11	3929	86	4804	101	145	1960
148	8S	15	4411	121	5063	102	0139	1963
148	8S	19	5277	132	5156	110	135	1965
149	8S	7	4375	39	6842	172	210	1950
149	8S	13	6842	55	6627	144	191	1955
149	8S	14	5000	110	6145	128	185	1960
149	8S	17	5000	151	6318	115	0174	1963

		38	39	40	41	42	43	
149	8S	21	5833	165	6445	121	169	1965
150	8S	4	2500	23	4035	98	124	1950
150	8S	11	5789	27	3253	122	94	1955
150	8S	11	3929	55	3073	101	92	1960
150	8S	16	4705	81	3389	108	0093	1963
150	8S	17	4722	79	3086	98	81	1965
151	8S	3	1875	33	5789	73	178	1950
151	8S	12	6316	46	5542	133	160	1955
151	8S	14	5000	118	6592	128	199	1960
151	8S	18	5294	160	6695	122	0184	1963
151	8S	22	6111	182	7109	127	186	1965
152	8S	1	625	3	526	25	16	1950
152	8S	7	3684	6	723	78	21	1955
152	8S	8	2857	10	559	73	17	1960
152	8S	10	2941	18	0753	68	0021	1963
152	8S	11	3055	25	977	63	26	1965
153	8S	9	5625	50	8772	221	269	1950
153	8S	11	5789	72	8675	122	250	1955
153	8S	19	6786	158	8827	174	266	1960
153	8S	24	7058	216	9038	163	0249	1963
153	8S	27	7500	226	8828	156	231	1965
154	8S	9	5625	49	8596	221	264	1950
154	8S	15	7895	70	8434	167	243	1955
154	8S	25	8929	150	8380	229	252	1960
154	8S	25	7352	209	8745	170	0241	1963
154	8S	30	8333	225	8789	173	230	1965
155	8S	14	8750	46	8070	343	248	1950
155	8S	17	8947	70	8434	189	243	1955
155	8S	21	7500	156	8715	192	262	1960
155	8S	26	7647	216	9038	176	0249	1963
155	8S	29	8055	234	9141	168	239	1965
156	8S	12	7500	48	8421	294	259	1950
156	8S	16	8421	73	8795	178	254	1955
156	8S	18	6429	152	8492	165	256	1960
156	8S	22	6470	207	8661	149	0239	1963
156	8S	24	6666	220	8594	139	225	1965
157	8S	24	3582	201	4136	168	216	1950
157	8S	30	4412	299	4593	162	214	1955
157	8S	28	3733	320	4420	132	183	1960
157	8S	33	4177	395	4473	126	0178	1963
157	8S	38	4578	404	4382	123	167	1965
158	8S	13	1940	41	844	91	44	1950
158	8S	20	2941	65	998	108	46	1955
158	8S	21	2800	84	1160	99	48	1960
158	8S	21	2658	97	1099	80	0044	1963
158	8S	22	2650	98	1063	71	41	1965
159	8S	0A	0A	104	2140	0A	112	1950
159	8S	0	0	5	77	0	4	1955
159	8S	0A	0A	24	331	0A	14	1960
159	8S	0	0	24	C272	0	0011	1963
159	8S	7	0843	105	1139	22	44	1965
160	8S	21	3134	113	2325	147	121	1950
160	8S	27	3971	155	2381	146	111	1955
160	8S	23	3067	184	2541	109	105	1960
160	8S	22	2784	192	2174	84	0087	1963
160	8S	24	2891	182	1974	77	75	1965
161	8S	24	3582	168	3457	168	180	1950
161	8S	23	3382	213	3272	125	152	1955
161	8S	24	3200	208	2973	113	119	1960
161	8S	28	3544	253	2865	107	0114	1963

		38	39	40	41	42	43	
161	8S	34	4096	255	2766	110	106	1965
162	8S	31	4627	220	4527	217	236	1950
162	8S	31	4559	291	4470	168	208	1955
162	8S	35	4667	341	4710	165	195	1960
162	8S	40	5063	402	4553	153	0181	1963
162	8S	44	5301	415	4501	142	172	1965
163	8S	17	2537	56	1152	119	60	1950
163	8S	25	3676	96	1475	135	69	1955
163	8S	28	3733	134	1851	132	77	1960
163	8S	31	3924	158	1789	118	0071	1963
163	8S	30	3614	156	1692	97	65	1965
164	8S	14	2090	152	3128	98	163	1950
164	8S	23	3382	225	3456	125	161	1955
164	8S	27	3600	334	4613	127	191	1960
164	8S	34	4303	394	4462	130	0178	1963
164	8S	37	4457	442	4794	120	183	1965
165	8S	5	746	10	206	35	11	1950
165	8S	12	1765	23	353	65	16	1955
165	8S	14	1867	39	539	66	22	1960
165	8S	16	2025	45	C510	61	0020	1963
165	8S	17	2048	52	564	55	22	1965
166	8S	47	7015	426	8765	329	457	1950
166	8S	48	7059	579	8894	260	414	1955
166	8S	57	7600	654	9033	269	374	1960
166	8S	57	7215	784	8879	218	0354	1963
166	8S	65	7831	811	8796	210	336	1965
167	8S	22	3284	166	3416	154	178	1950
167	8S	22	3235	181	2780	119	129	1955
167	8S	27	3600	285	3936	127	163	1960
167	8S	27	3417	349	3952	103	0157	1963
167	8S	35	4216	367	3980	113	152	1965
168	8S	14	2089	46	947	98	49	1950
168	8S	17	2500	70	1075	92	50	1955
168	8S	21	2800	156	2155	99	89	1960
168	8S	26	3291	216	2446	99	0097	1963
168	8S	29	3493	234	2538	94	97	1965
169	8S	48	7164	376	7737	336	404	1950
169	8S	42	6176	494	7588	227	353	1955
169	8S	44	5867	522	7210	208	298	1960
169	8S	47	5949	623	7055	180	0281	1963
169	8S	49	5903	651	7061	158	270	1965
170	8S	35	5469	214	4853	242	236	1950
170	8S	40	6452	328	5795	216	245	1955
170	8S	38	6230	348	5677	189	213	1960
170	8S	40	6349	413	5866	169	0205	1963
170	8S	48	7272	437	5850	170	196	1965
171	8S	13	2031	40	907	90	44	1950
171	8S	19	3065	68	1201	102	51	1955
171	8S	20	3279	84	1370	99	51	1960
171	8S	20	3174	95	1349	84	0047	1963
171	8S	21	3181	99	1325	74	44	1965
172	8S	0A	0A	107	2426	0A	118	1950
172	8S	0	0	6	106	0	4	1955
172	8S	0A	0A	23	375	0A	14	1960
172	8S	0	0	25	C355	0	0012	1963
172	8S	7	1060	110	1473	24	49	1965
173	8S	32	5000	129	2925	221	143	1950
173	8S	38	6129	185	3269	205	138	1955
173	8S	32	5246	204	3328	159	125	1960
173	8S	31	4920	209	2969	131	0104	1963
173	8S	31	4696	200	2677	110	90	1965

		38	39	40	41	42	43	
174	8S	23	3594	169	3832	159	187	1950
174	8S	23	3710	216	3816	124	161	1955
174	8S	23	3770	205	3344	114	126	1960
174	8S	25	3968	249	3537	106	0124	1963
174	8S	30	4545	261	3494	106	117	1965
175	8S	25	3906	224	5079	173	247	1950
175	8S	27	4355	288	5088	146	215	1955
175	8S	27	4426	328	5351	134	201	1960
175	8S	33	5238	383	5440	139	0190	1963
175	8S	36	5454	405	5422	128	182	1965
176	8S	18	2813	58	1315	124	64	1950
176	8S	25	4032	99	1749	135	74	1955
176	8S	25	4098	138	2251	124	84	1960
176	8S	27	4285	153	2173	114	0076	1963
176	8S	27	4090	156	2088	96	70	1965
177	8S	12	1875	153	3469	83	169	1950
177	8S	21	3387	219	3869	113	164	1955
177	8S	21	3443	320	5220	104	196	1960
177	8S	26	4126	378	5369	110	0188	1963
177	8S	31	4696	429	5743	110	192	1965
178	8S	5	781	10	227	35	11	1950
178	8S	13	2097	24	424	70	18	1955
178	8S	14	2295	41	669	70	25	1960
178	8S	15	2380	46	C653	63	0023	1963
178	8S	16	2424	56	750	56	25	1965
179	8S	35	5469	365	8277	242	403	1950
179	8S	38	6129	475	8392	205	355	1955
179	8S	37	6066	527	8597	184	323	1960
179	8S	40	6349	605	8594	169	0300	1963
179	8S	43	6515	628	8407	152	282	1965
180	8S	18	2813	153	3469	124	169	1950
180	8S	20	3226	176	3110	108	131	1955
180	8S	22	3607	246	4013	109	151	1960
180	8S	20	3174	307	4361	84	0152	1963
180	8S	26	3939	325	4351	92	146	1965
181	8S	12	1875	48	1088	83	53	1950
181	8S	16	2581	73	1290	86	55	1955
181	8S	18	2951	152	2480	90	93	1960
181	8S	22	3492	207	2940	93	0103	1963
181	8S	24	3636	220	2945	85	99	1965
182	8S	48	7500	376	8526	331	416	1950
182	8S	42	6774	494	8728	226	369	1955
182	8S	44	7213	522	8515	219	320	1960
182	8S	47	7460	623	8849	199	0309	1963
182	8S	49	7424	651	8715	174	292	1965

		44	45	
1	9S	0	0	1950
1	9S	0	0	1955
1	9S	0	0	1960
1	9S	0	0	1963
1	9S	0	0	1965
2	9S	0A	CA	1950
2	9S	0	0	1955
2	9S	0	0	1960
2	9S	0	0	1963
2	9S	0	0	1965
3	9S	1	238	1950
3	9S	1	170	1955
3	9S	1	188	1960
3	9S	1	175	1963

	44	45	
3 9S	0	0	1965
4 9S	1	238	1950
4 9S	1	170	1955
4 9S	1	188	1960
4 9S	1	175	1963
4 9S	1	172	1965
5 9S	0	C	1950
5 9S	1	170	1955
5 9S	1	188	1960
5 9S	1	175	1963
5 9S	1	172	1965
6 9S	1A	238A	1950
6 9S	1	170	1955
6 9S	1	188	1960
6 9S	1	175	1963
6 9S	1	172	1965
7 9S	0	C	1950
7 9S	0	0	1955
7 9S	0	0	1960
7 9S	0	0	1963
7 9S	0	0	1965
8 9S	0	C	1950
8 9S	0	0	1955
8 9S	0	C	1960
8 9S	0	0	1963
8 9S	0	0	1965
9 9S	1	238	1950
9 9S	1	170	1955
9 9S	1	188	1960
9 9S	1	175	1963
9 9S	1	172	1965
10 9S	1	238	1950
10 9S	1	170	1955
10 9S	1	188	1960
10 9S	1	175	1963
10 9S	1	172	1965
11 9S	0	0	1950
11 9S	1	170	1955
11 9S	0	0	1960
11 9S	1	175	1963
11 9S	1	172	1965
12 9S	1	238	1950
12 9S	1	170	1955
12 9S	1	188	1960
12 9S	1	175	1963
12 9S	1	172	1965
13 9S	1	238	1950
13 9S	1	170	1955
13 9S	1	188	1960
13 9S	1	175	1963
13 9S	1	172	1965
14 9S	0	0	1950
14 9S	0	0	1955
14 9S	0	0	1960
14 9S	0	C	1963
14 9S	0	0	1965
15 9S	1A		1950
15 9S	1	380	1955
15 9S	1	400	1960
15 9S	1	40C	1963

	44	45	
15 9S	1	384	1965
16 9S	0	0	1950
16 9S	0	C	1955
16 9S	0	0	1960
16 9S	0	C	1963
16 9S	0	0	1965
17 9S	0	0	1950
17 9S	1	380	1955
17 9S	1	400	1960
17 9S	1	400	1963
17 9S	1	384	1965
18 9S	1	1667	1950
18 9S	1	380	1955
18 9S	1	400	1960
18 9S	1	400	1963
18 9S	1	384	1965
19 9S			1950
19 9S	1	38C	1955
19 9S	1	400	1960
19 9S	1	400	1963
19 9S	1	384	1965
20 9S	0	0	1950
20 9S	1	380	1955
20 9S	1	400	1960
20 9S	1	400	1963
20 9S	1	384	1965
21 9S	0	0	1950
21 9S	0	0	1955
21 9S	0	0	1960
21 9S	0	0	1963
21 9S	0	0	1965
22 9S	0	0	1950
22 9S	1	380	1955
22 9S	1	400	1960
22 9S	1	400	1963
22 9S	0	0	1965
23 9S	0	0	1950
23 9S	0	0	1955
23 9S	0	0	1960
23 9S	0	C	1963
23 9S	1	384	1965
24 9S	0	0	1950
24 9S	1	380	1955
24 9S	1	400	1960
24 9S	1	400	1963
24 9S	1	384	1965
25 9S	1	1667	1950
25 9S	1	38C	1955
25 9S	1	400	1960
25 9S	1	400	1963
25 9S	1	384	1965
26 9S	1	1667	1950
26 9S	1	380	1955
26 9S	1	400	1960
26 9S	1	400	1963
26 9S	1	384	1965
27 9S	0	C	1950
27 9S	0	0	1955
27 9S	0A	CA	1960
27 9S	0	0	1963
27 9S	0	C	1965

	44	45	
28 9S	1	500A	1950
28 9S	1	400A	1955
28 9S	1A	250A	1960
28 9S	1	243	1963
28 9S	1	200	1965
29 9S	0	0	1950
29 9S	0A	0A	1955
29 9S	1A	250A	1960
29 9S	1	243	1963
29 9S	1	200	1965
30 9S	0	0	1950
30 9S	0A	0A	1955
30 9S	1A	250A	1960
30 9S	1	243	1963
30 9S	1	200A	1965
31 9S	1	500A	1950
31 9S	1	400A	1955
31 9S	1A	25CA	1960
31 9S	1	243	1963
31 9S	1	20C	1965
32 9S	0	C	1950
32 9S	1	400A	1955
32 9S	1A	250A	1960
32 9S	1	243	1963
32 9S	1	200	1965
33 9S	0	0	1950
33 9S	0A	0A	1955
33 9S	0A	CA	1960
33 9S	0A	0A	1963
33 9S	0A	0A	1965
34 9S	0	0	1950
34 9S	0	0	1955
34 9S	0A	0A	1960
34 9S	0	0	1963
34 9S	0	0	1965
35 9S	0	0	1950
35 9S	1	400A	1955
35 9S	1A	250A	1960
35 9S	1	243	1963
35 9S	1	200	1965
36 9S	1	500A	1950
36 9S	1	400A	1955
36 9S	1A	250A	1960
36 9S	1	243	1963
36 9S	1	200	1965
37 9S	1A	500A	1950
37 9S	1	40CA	1955
37 9S	1A	250A	1960
37 9S	1	243	1963
37 9S	1	200	1965
38 9S	0	0	1950
38 9S	1	400A	1955
38 9S	1A	250A	1960
38 9S	1	243	1963
38 9S	1	200	1965
39 9S	0	0	1950
39 9S	0	C	1955
39 9S	0A	0A	1960
39 9S	0	0	1963
39 9S	0	0	1965

	44	45	
40 9S	1	323	1950
40 9S	1	230	1955
40 9S	1	188	1960
40 9S	1	192	1963
40 9S	0	0	1965
41 9S	0	0	1950
41 9S	0	0	1955
41 9S	0	0	1960
41 9S	0	0	1963
41 9S	0	0	1965
42 9S	0A	CA	1950
42 9S	0A	0A	1955
42 9S	1	188	1960
42 9S	1	192	1963
42 9S	1	188	1965
43 9S	0	0	1950
43 9S	1	230	1955
43 9S	1	188	1960
43 9S	1	192	1963
43 9S	1	188	1965
44 9S	0	C	1950
44 9S	1	230	1955
44 9S	1	188	1960
44 9S	1	192	1963
44 9S	1	188	1965
45 9S			1950
45 9S	1	230	1955
45 9S	1	188	1960
45 9S	1	192	1963
45 9S	1	188	1965
46 9S	0	0	1950
46 9S	1	230	1955
46 9S	1	188	1960
46 9S	1	192	1963
46 9S	1	188	1965
47 9S	0	0	1950
47 9S	0	0	1955
47 9S	0	0	1960
47 9S	0	C	1963
47 9S	0	0	1965
48 9S	1	323	1950
48 9S	1	230	1955
48 9S	1	188	1960
48 9S	1	192	1963
48 9S	1	188	1965
49 9S	0	0	1950
49 9S	1	230	1955
49 9S	1	188	1960
49 9S	1	192	1963
49 9S	1	188	1965
50 9S	0	0	1950
50 9S	1	230	1955
50 9S	1	188	1960
50 9S	1	192	1963
50 9S	1	188	1965
51 9S	1	323	1950
51 9S	1	230	1955
51 9S	1	188	1960
51 9S	1	192	1963
51 9S	1	188	1965

	44	45	
52 9S	1	323	1950
52 9S	1	190	1955
52 9S	0	0	1960
52 9S	0	0	1963
52 9S	0	0	1965
53 9S	1	303	1950
53 9S	1	190A	1955
53 9S	1	188	1960
53 9S	1	181	1963
53 9S	1	135	1965
54 9S	0	0	1950
54 9S	1	190A	1955
54 9S	1	188	1960
54 9S	1	181	1963
54 9S	1	135	1965
55 9S	0A	0A	1950
55 9S	0A	0A	1955
55 9S	1	188	1960
55 9S	1	181	1963
55 9S	1	135	1965
56 9S	0	0	1950
56 9S	1	190A	1955
56 9S	1	188	1960
56 9S	1	181	1963
56 9S	1	135	1965
57 9S	0	0	1950
57 9S	1	190A	1955
57 9S	1	188	1960
57 9S	1	181	1963
57 9S	1	135	1965
58 9S			1950
58 9S	1	190A	1955
58 9S	1	188	1960
58 9S	1	181	1963
58 9S	1	135	1965
59 9S	0	0	1950
59 9S	0	0	1955
59 9S	0	0	1960
59 9S	0	0	1963
59 9S	0	0	1965
60 9S	1	303	1950
60 9S	1	190A	1955
60 9S	1	188	1960
60 9S	1	181	1963
60 9S	0	0	1965
61 9S	1	303	1950
61 9S	1	190A	1955
61 9S	1	188	1960
61 9S	1	181	1963
61 9S	1	135	1965
62 9S	1	303	1950
62 9S	1	190A	1955
62 9S	1	188	1960
62 9S	1	181	1963
62 9S	1	135	1965
63 9S	1	303	1950
63 9S	1	190A	1955
63 9S	1	188	1960
63 9S	1	181	1963
63 9S	1	135	1965

		44	45	
64	9S	1	303	1950
64	9S	1	190A	1955
64	9S	1	188	1960
64	9S	1	181	1963
64	9S	1	135	1965
65	9S	1	303	1950
65	9S	1	190A	1955
65	9S	1	188	1960
65	9S	1	181	1963
65	9S	1	135	1965
66	9S	1	333	1950
66	9S	1	130	1955
66	9S	1	147	1960
66	9S	1	133	1963
66	9S	1	126	1965
67	9S	1	333	1950
67	9S	1	130	1955
67	9S	1	147	1960
67	9S	1	133	1963
67	9S	0	0	1965
68	9S	1	333	1950
68	9S	1	130	1955
68	9S	1	147	1960
68	9S	1	133	1963
68	9S	1	126	1965
69	9S	0	0	1950
69	9S	1	130	1955
69	9S	1	147	1960
69	9S	1	133	1963
69	9S	1	126	1965
70	9S	1	333	1950
70	9S	1	130	1955
70	9S	1	147	1960
70	9S	1	133	1963
70	9S	1	126	1965
71	9S	0	0	1950
71	9S	1	130	1955
71	9S	1	147	1960
71	9S	1	133	1963
71	9S	0	0	1965
72	9S	0	0	1950
72	9S	0	0	1955
72	9S	0	0	1960
72	9S	0	0	1963
72	9S	0	0	1965
73	9S	1	333	1950
73	9S	1	130	1955
73	9S	1	147	1960
73	9S	1	133	1963
73	9S	1	126	1965
74	9S	1	333	1950
74	9S	1	130	1955
74	9S	1	147	1960
74	9S	1	133	1963
74	9S	1	126	1965
75	9S	0	0	1950
75	9S	1	130	1955
75	9S	1	147	1960
75	9S	1	133	1963
75	9S	0	0	1965

	44	45	
76 9S	1	333	1950
76 9S	1	130	1955
76 9S	1	147	1960
76 9S	1	133	1963
76 9S	1	126	1965
77 9S	1	333	1950
77 9S	1	130	1955
77 9S	1	147	1960
77 9S	1	133	1963
77 9S	1	126	1965
78 9S	1	333	1950
78 9S	1	130	1955
78 9S	1	147	1960
78 9S	1	133	1963
78 9S	1	126	1965
79 9S	0	0	1950
79 9S	1	190	1955
79 9S	1	217	1960
79 9S	1	196	1963
79 9S	1	175	1965
80 9S	1		1950
80 9S	1	190	1955
80 9S	1	217	1960
80 9S	1	196	1963
80 9S	1	175	1965
81 9S	0	0	1950
81 9S	1	190	1955
81 9S	1	217	1960
81 9S	1	196	1963
81 9S	1	175	1965
82 9S	0	0	1950
82 9S	0	0	1955
82 9S	0	0	1960
82 9S	0	0	1963
02 9S	1	175	1965
83 9S	0	0	1950
83 9S	1	190	1955
83 9S	1	217	1960
83 9S	1	196	1963
83 9S	1	175	1965
84 9S	0	0	1950
84 9S	1	190	1955
84 9S	1	217	1960
84 9S	1	196	1963
84 9S	1	175	1965
85 9S	0	0	1950
85 9S	0	0	1955
85 9S	0	0	1960
85 9S	0	0	1963
85 9S	0	0	1965
86 9S	0	0	1950
86 9S	1	190	1955
86 9S	1	217	1960
86 9S	1	196	1963
86 9S	1	175	1965
87 9S	1		1950
87 9S	0	0	1955
87 9S	0	0	1960
87 9S	1	196	1963
87 9S	1	175	1965

		44	45	
88	9S	0		1950
88	9S	1	190	1955
88	9S	0	0	1960
88	9S	1	196	1963
88	9S	1	175	1965
89	9S	0		1950
89	9S	1	190	1955
89	9S	1	217	1960
89	9S	1	196	1963
89	9S	1	175	1965
90	9S	1		1950
90	9S	1	190	1955
90	9S	1	217	1960
90	9S	1	196	1963
90	9S	1	175	1965
91	9S	1		1950
91	9S	1	190	1955
91	9S	1	217	1960
91	9S	1	196	1963
91	9S	1	175	1965
92	9S	0	0	1950
92	9S	1	180	1955
92	9S	1	181	1960
92	9S	1	192	1963
92	9S	1	120	1965
93	9S	0	0	1950
93	9S	1	180	1955
93	9S	1	181	1960
93	9S	1	192	1963
93	9S	1	120	1965
94	9S	0	0	1950
94	9S	0	C	1955
94	9S	0	0	1960
94	9S	0	C	1963
94	9S	0	0	1965
95	9S	0	0	1950
95	9S	1	18C	1955
95	9S	1	181	1960
95	9S	1	192	1963
95	9S	1	120	1965
96	9S	0	0	1950
96	9S	0	C	1955
96	9S	0	0	1960
96	9S	0	C	1963
96	9S	0	0	1965
97	9S	0	0	1950
97	9S	0	0	1955
97	9S	0	0	1960
97	9S	0	0	1963
97	9S	0	0	1965
98	9S	0	0	1950
98	9S	0	0	1955
98	9S	0	0	1960
98	9S	0	0	1963
98	9S	0	0	1965
99	9S	0	0	1950
99	9S	0	0	1955
99	9S	0	0	1960
99	9S	0	0	1963
99	9S	0	0	1965

	44	45	
100 9S	1	833	1950
100 9S	1	180	1955
100 9S	1	181	1960
100 9S	1	192	1963
100 9S	1	120	1965
101 9S	1	833	1950
101 9S	1	180	1955
101 9S	1	181	1960
101 9S	1	192	1963
101 9S	1	120	1965
102 9S	1	833	1950
102 9S	1	180	1955
102 9S	1	181	1960
102 9S	1	192	1963
102 9S	1	120	1965
103 9S	1	833	1950
103 9S	1	180	1955
103 9S	1	181	1960
103 9S	1	192	1963
103 9S	1	120	1965
104 9S	1	833	1950
104 9S	1	180	1955
104 9S	1	181	1960
104 9S	1	192	1963
104 9S	1	120	1965
105 9S	0	0	1950
105 9S	0	0	1955
105 9S	0	0	1960
105 9S	0	0	1963
105 9S	0	C	1965
106 9S	0	C	1950
106 9S	0	0	1955
106 9S	0	0	1960
106 9S	0	0	1963
106 9S	0	0	1965
107 9S	0	0	1950
107 9S	0	0	1955
107 9S	0	0	1960
107 9S	0	0	1963
107 9S	0	0	1965
108 9S	0	0	1950
108 9S	0	0	1955
108 9S	0	0	1960
108 9S	0	0	1963
108 9S	0	0	1965
109 9S	1	833	1950
109 9S	1A	560A	1955
109 9S	1	625	1960
109 9S	1A	555A	1963
109 9S	1	416	1965
110 9S	0	0	1950
110 9S	1	560	1955
110 9S	0	0	1960
110 9S	1	555	1963
110 9S	1	416	1965
111 9S	0A	0A	1950
111 9S	0	0	1955
111 9S	0	0	1960
111 9S	0	0	1963
111 9S	0	0	1965

	44	45	
112 9S	0	0	1950
112 9S	0	0	1955
112 9S	0	C	1960
112 9S	0	0	1963
112 9S	0	0	1965
113 9S	0	0	1950
113 9S	0	0	1955
113 9S	0	0	1960
113 9S	0	0	1963
113 9S	0	0	1965
114 9S	0	0	1950
114 9S	0	0	1955
114 9S	0	0	1960
114 9S	0	0	1963
114 9S	0	0	1965
115 9S	0	0	1950
115 9S	0	0	1955
115 9S	0	0	1960
115 9S	0	0	1963
115 9S	1	416	1965
116 9S	1	833	1950
116 9S	1	560	1955
116 9S	1	625	1960
116 9S	1	555	1963
116 9S	1	416	1965
117 9S	1	833	1950
117 9S	1	560	1955
117 9S	1	625	1960
117 9S	1	555	1963
117 9S	1	416	1965
118 9S	1	185	1950
118 9S	1	120	1955
118 9S	1	123	1960
118 9S	1	107	1963
118 9S	1	93	1965
119 9S	1	185	1950
119 9S	1	120	1955
119 9S	1	123	1960
119 9S	1	107	1963
119 9S	1	93	1965
120 9S	0	0	1950
120 9S	1	120	1955
120 9S	1	123	1960
120 9S	1	107	1963
120 9S	1	93	1965
121 9S	1	185	1950
121 9S	1	120	1955
121 9S	1	123	1960
121 9S	1	107	1963
121 9S	1	93	1965
122 9S	1	185	1950
122 9S	1	120	1955
122 9S	1	123	1960
122 9S	1	107	1963
122 9S	1	93	1965
123 9S	1	185	1950
123 9S	1	120	1955
123 9S	1	123	1960
123 9S	1	107	1963
123 9S	1	93	1965

	44	45	
124 9S	1	85	1950
124 9S	0	0	1955
124 9S	0	C	1960
124 9S	1	107	1963
124 9S	1	93	1965
125 9S	1	185	1950
125 9S	1	120	1955
125 9S	1	123	1960
125 9S	1	107	1963
125 9S	1	93	1965
126 9S	0	0	1950
126 9S	1	120	1955
126 9S	1	123	1960
126 9S	1	107	1963
126 9S	1	93	1965
127 9S	1	185	1950
127 9S	1	120	1955
127 9S	1	123	1960
127 9S	1	107	1963
127 9S	1	93	1965
128 9S	1	185	1950
128 9S	1	120	1955
128 9S	1	123	1960
128 9S	1	107	1963
128 9S	1	93	1965
129 9S	1	185	1950
129 9S	1	120	1955
129 9S	1	123	1960
129 9S	1	107	1963
129 9S	1	93	1965
130 9S	1	185	1950
130 9S	1	120	1955
130 9S	1	123	1960
130 9S	1	107	1963
130 9S	1	93	1965
131 9S	1	294	1950
131 9S	1	210	1955
131 9S	1	217	1960
131 9S	1	277	1963
131 9S	1	163	1965
132 9S	0	0	1950
132 9S	0	C	1955
132 9S	0	0	1960
132 9S	0	0	1963
132 9S	1	163	1965
133 9S	1	294	1950
133 9S	1	210	1955
133 9S	1	217	1960
133 9S	1	277	1963
133 9S	1	163	1965
134 9S	1	294	1950
134 9S	1	210	1955
134 9S	1	217	1960
134 9S	1	277	1963
134 9S	1	163	1965
135 9S	1	294	1950
135 9S	1	210	1955
135 9S	1	217	1960
135 9S	1	277	1963
135 9S	1	163	1965

		44	45	
136	9S	0	0	1950
136	9S	0	0	1955
136	9S	0	0	1960
136	9S	0	0	1963
136	9S	1	163	1965
137	9S	0	0	1950
137	9S	1	210	1955
137	9S	1	217	1960
137	9S	1	277	1963
137	9S	1	163	1965
138	9S	0	0	1950
138	9S	1	210	1955
138	9S	1	217	1960
138	9S	1	277	1963
138	9S	1	163	1965
139	9S	0	0	1950
139	9S	0	0	1955
139	9S	0	0	1960
139	9S	0	0	1963
139	9S	1	163	1965
140	9S	1	294	1950
140	9S	1	210	1955
140	9S	1	217	1960
140	9S	1	277	1963
140	9S	1	163	1965
141	9S	1	294	1950
141	9S	1	210	1955
141	9S	1	217	1960
141	9S	1	277	1963
141	9S	1	163	1965
142	9S	1	294	1950
142	9S	1	210	1955
142	9S	1	217	1960
142	9S	1	277	1963
142	9S	1	163	1965
143	9S	1	294	1950
143	9S	1	210	1955
143	9S	1	217	1960
143	9S	1	277	1963
143	9S	1	163	1965
144	9S	0	0	1950
144	9S	0	0	1955
144	9S	0	0	1960
144	9S	0	0	1963
144	9S	0	0	1965
145	9S	0	0	1950
145	9S	1	190	1955
145	9S	1	192	1960
145	9S	1	200	1963
145	9S	1	161	1965
146	9S	1	270	1950
146	9S	1	190	1955
146	9S	1	192	1960
146	9S	1	200	1963
146	9S	1	161	1965
147	9S	1	270	1950
147	9S	1	190	1955
147	9S	1	192	1960
147	9S	1	200	1963
147	9S	1	161	1965

		44	45	
148	9S	1	270	1950
148	9S	1	190	1955
148	9S	1	192	1960
148	9S	1	200	1963
148	9S	1	161	1965
149	9S	1	270	1950
149	9S	1	190	1955
149	9S	1	192	1960
149	9S	1	200	1963
149	9S	1	161	1965
150	9S	1	270	1950
150	9S	1	190	1955
150	9S	1	192	1960
150	9S	1	200	1963
150	9S	1	161	1965
151	9S	1	270	1950
151	9S	1	190	1955
151	9S	1	192	1960
151	9S	1	200	1963
151	9S	1	161	1965
152	9S	0	0	1950
152	9S	0	0	1955
152	9S	0	0	1960
152	9S	0	0	1963
152	9S	0	0	1965
153	9S	1	270	1950
153	9S	1	190	1955
153	9S	1	192	1960
153	9S	1	200	1963
153	9S	1	161	1965
154	9S	1	270	1950
154	9S	1	190	1955
154	9S	1	192	1960
154	9S	1	200	1963
154	9S	1	161	1965
155	9S	1	270	1950
155	9S	1	190	1955
155	9S	1	192	1960
155	9S	1	200	1963
155	9S	1	161	1965
156	9S	1	270	1950
156	9S	1	190	1955
156	9S	1	192	1960
156	9S	1	200	1963
156	9S	1	161	1965
157	9S	1	156	1950
157	9S	1	130	1955
157	9S	1G	130A	1960
157	9S	1H	128	1963
157	9S	1G	130A	1965
158	9S	1	156	1950
158	9S	1	130	1955
158	9S	1G	130A	1960
158	9S	1H	128	1963
158	9S	1G	130A	1965
159	9S	0	0	1950
159	9S	1	130	1955
159	9S	1A	130A	1960
159	9S	1H	128	1963
159	9S	1G	130A	1965

		44	45	
160	9S	1	156	1950
160	9S	1	130	1955
160	9S	0G	0A	1960
160	9S	1H	128	1963
160	9S	1G	130A	1965
161	9S	1	156	1950
161	9S	1	130	1955
161	9S	1G	130A	1960
161	9S	1H	128	1963
161	9S	1G	130A	1965
162	9S	1	156	1950
162	9S	1	130A	1955
162	9S	1A	130A	1960
162	9S	1H	128	1963
162	9S	1G	130A	1965
163	9S	1A	156A	1950
163	9S	1	130	1955
163	9S	1A	130A	1960
163	9S	1H	128	1963
163	9S	1G	130A	1965
164	9S	1	156	1950
164	9S	1	130	1955
164	9S	1G	130A	1960
164	9S	1H	128	1963
164	9S	1G	130A	1965
165	9S	1	156	1950
165	9S	1	130	1955
165	9S	1G	130A	1960
165	9S	1H	128	1963
165	9S	1G	130A	1965
166	9S	1	156	1950
166	9S	1	130	1955
166	9S	1G	130A	1960
166	9S	1H	128	1963
166	9S	1G	130A	1965
167	9S	1	156	1950
167	9S	1	130	1955
167	9S	1G	130A	1960
167	9S	1H	128	1963
167	9S	1G	130A	1965
168	9S	1	156	1950
168	9S	1	130	1955
168	9S	1A	130	1960
168	9S	1H	128	1963
168	9S	1G	130A	1965
169	9S	1	156	1950
169	9S	1	130	1955
169	9S	1A	130A	1960
169	9S	1	128	1963
169	9S	1G	130A	1965
170	9S	1	159	1950
170	9S	1	110	1955
170	9S	1G	110A	1960
170	9S	1G	107	1963
170	9S	1G	100A	1965
171	9S	1	159	1950
171	9S	1	110	1955
171	9S	1G	110A	1960
171	9S	1G	107	1963
171	9S	1G	100A	1965

	44	45	
181 9S	1	159	1950
181 9S	1	110	1955
181 9S	1G	110A	1960
181 9S	1G	107	1963
181 9S	1G	100A	1965
182 9S	1	159	1950
182 9S	1	110	1955
182 9S	1G	110A	1960
182 9S	1G	107	1963
182 9S	1G	100A	1965
172 9S	0	0	1950
172 9S	0	0	1955
172 9S	0	0	1960
172 9S	0G	0	1963
172 9S	0G	0	1965
173 9S	1	159	1950
173 9S	1	110	1955
173 9S	1G	110A	1960
173 9S	0G	0	1963
173 9S	0G	0	1965
174 9S	1	159	1950
174 9S	1	110	1955
174 9S	1G	110A	1960
174 9S	1G	107	1963
174 9S	1G	100A	1965
175 9S	1	159	1950
175 9S	1	110	1955
175 9S	1G	110A	1960
175 9S	1G	107	1963
175 9S	1G	100A	1965
176 9S	1A	159A	1950
176 9S	1	110	1955
176 9S	1G	110A	1960
176 9S	1G	107	1963
176 9S	1G	100A	1965
177 9S	1	159	1950
177 9S	1	110	1955
177 9S	1G	110A	1960
177 9S	1G	107	1963
177 9S	1G	100A	1965
178 9S	1	159	1950
178 9S	1	110	1955
178 9S	1G	110A	1960
178 9S	1G	107	1963
178 9S	1G	100A	1965
179 9S	1	159	1950
179 9S	1	110	1955
179 9S	1G	110A	1960
179 9S	1G	107	1963
179 9S	1G	100A	1965
180 9S	1	159	1950
180 9S	1	110	1955
180 9S	1G	110A	1960
180 9S	1G	107	1963
180 9S	1G	100A	1965

	46	47	48	
110S	0	0	0	1950
110S	0	0	0	1955
110S	0	0	0	1960
110S	0	0	0	1963

	46	47	48	
110S	0	0	0	1965
210S	0	16	0	1950
210S	0	16	0	1955
210S	0	16A	0	1960
210S	0	16	0	1963
210S	0	16	0	1965
310S	0	16	0	1950
310S	0	16	0	1955
310S	0	16A	0	1960
310S	0	16	0	1963
310S	0	16	0	1965
410S	0	16	0	1950
410S	0	16	0	1955
410S	0	16A	0	1960
410S	0	16	0	1963
410S	0	16	0	1965
510S	0	16	0	1950
510S	0	16	0	1955
510S	0	16A	0	1960
510S	0	16	0	1963
510S	0	16	0	1965
610S	0	0	0	1950
610S	0	0	0	1955
610S	0	0	0	1960
610S	0	0	0	1963
610S	0	0	0	1965
710S	0	0A	0	1950
710S	0	0	0	1955
710S	0	0A	0	1960
710S	0	0A	0	1963
710S	0	0A	0	1965
810S	0	0A	0	1950
810S	0	0	0	1955
810S	0	0A	0	1960
810S	0	0A	0	1963
810S	0	0A	0	1965
910S	0	16	0	1950
910S	0	16	0	1955
910S	0	16A	0	1960
910S	0	16	0	1963
910S	0	16	0	1965
1010S	0	16	0	1950
1010S	0	16	0	1955
1010S	0	16A	0	1960
1010S	0	16	0	1963
1010S	0	16	0	1965
1110S	0	16	0	1950
1110S	0	16	0	1955
1110S	0	16A	0	1960
1110S	0	16	0	1963
1110S	0	16	0	1965
1210S	0	16	0	1950
1210S	0	16	0	1955
1210S	0	16A	0	1960
1210S	0	16	0	1963
1210S	0	16	0	1965
1310S	0	16	0	1950
1310S	0	16	0	1955
1310S	0	16A	0	1960
1310S	0	16	0	1963

	46	47	48	
1310S	0	16	0	1965
1410S	0	0	0	1950
1410S	0A	0	0	1955
1410S	0	0	0	1960
1410S	0	0	0	1963
1410S	0	0	0	1965
1510S	0	0	0	1950
1510S	0A	0	0	1955
1510S	0	0	0	1960
1510S	0	0	0	1963
1510S	0	0	0	1965
1610S	0	0	0	1950
1610S	0A	0	0	1955
1610S	0	0	0	1960
1610S	0	0	0	1963
1610S	0	0	0	1965
1710S	0	0	0	1950
1710S	0A	0	0	1955
1710S	0	0	0	1960
1710S	0	0	0	1963
1710S	0	0	0	1965
1810S	0	0	0	1950
1810S	0A	0	0	1955
1810S	0	0	0	1960
1810S	0	0	0	1963
1810S	0	0	0	1965
1910S	0	0	0	1950
1910S	0A	0	0	1955
1910S	0	0	0	1960
1910S	0	0	0	1963
1910S	0	0	0	1965
2010S	0	0	0	1950
2010S	0A	0	0	1955
2010S	0	0	0	1960
2010S	0	0	0	1963
2010S	0	0	0	1965
2110S	0	0	0	1950
2110S	0A	0	0	1955
2110S	0	0	0	1960
2110S	0	0	0	1963
2110S	0	0	0	1965
2210S	0	0	0	1950
2210S	0A	0	0	1955
2210S	0	0	0	1960
2210S	0	0	0	1963
2210S	0	0	0	1965
2310S	0	0	0	1950
2310S	0A	0	0	1955
2310S	0	0	0	1960
2310S	0	0	0	1963
2310S	0	0	0	1965
2410S	0	0	0	1950
2410S	0A	0	0	1955
2410S	0	0	0	1960
2410S	0	0	0	1963
2410S	0	0	0	1965
2510S	16	0	0	1950
2510S	16	0	0	1955
2510S	16A	0	0	1960
2510S	16B	0	0	1963

	46	47	48	
2510S	16	0	0	1965
2610S	16	0	0	1950
2610S	16	0	0	1955
2610S	16A	0	0	1960
2610S	16B	0	0	1963
2610S	16	0	0	1965
2710S	0	16	0	1950
2710S	0	16	0	1955
2710S	0	16A	0	1960
2710S	0	16	0	1963
2710S	0	16	0	1965
2810S	0	0	0	1950
2810S	0A	0	0	1955
2810S	0	0	0	1960
2810S	0	0	0	1963
2810S	0	0	0	1965
2910S	0	16	0	1950
2910S	0	16	0	1955
2910S	0	16A	0	1960
2910S	0	16	0	1963
2910S	0	16	0	1965
3010S	0	16	0	1950
3010S	0	16	0	1955
3010S	0	16A	0	1960
3010S	0	16	0	1963
3010S	0	16	0	1965
3110S	0	16	0	1950
3110S	0	16	0	1955
3110S	0A	16A	0	1960
3110S	64	16	0	1963
3110S	64	16	0	1965
3210S	0	0	0	1950
3210S	0	0	0	1955
3210S	0	0	0	1960
3210S	0	0	0	1963
3210S	0	0	0	1965
3310S	0	0A	0	1950
3310S	0	0	0	1955
3310S	0	0A	0	1960
3310S	0	0A	0	1963
3310S	0	0A	0	1965
3410S	0	0A	0	1950
3410S	0	0	0	1955
3410S	0	0A	0	1960
3410S	0	0A	0	1963
3410S	0	0A	0	1965
3510S	0	16	0	1950
3510S	0	16	0	1955
3510S	0	16A	0	1960
3510S	0	16	0	1963
3510S	0	16	0	1965
3610S	0	16	0	1950
3610S	0	16	0	1955
3610S	0	16A	0	1960
3610S	0	16	0	1963
3610S	0	16	0	1965
3710S	0	16	0	1950
3710S	0	16	0	1955
3710S	0	16A	0	1960
3710S	0	16	0	1963

	46	47	48	
3710S	0	16	0	1965
3810S	0	16	0	1950
3810S	32	16	0	1955
3810S	32	16A	0	1960
3810S	32	16	0	1963
3810S	32	16	0	1965
3910S	32	16	0	1950
3910S	32	16	0	1955
3910S	32A	16A	0	1960
3910S	32	16	0	1963
3910S	32	16	0	1965
4010S	0	16	0	1950
4010S	0	16	0	1955
4010S	0	16A	0	1960
4010S	0	16	0	1963
4010S	0	16	0	1965
4110S	0	0	0	1950
4110S	0	0	0	1955
4110S	0	0	0	1960
4110S	0	0	0	1963
4110S	0	0	0	1965
4210S	0	16	0	1950
4210S	0	16	0	1955
4210S	0	16A	0	1960
4210S	0	16	0	1963
4210S	0	16	0	1965
4310S	0	16	0	1950
4310S	0	16	0	1955
4310S	0	16A	0	1960
4310S	0	16	0	1963
4310S	0	16	0	1965
4410S	0	16	0	1950
4410S	0	16	0	1955
4410S	0	16A	0	1960
4410S	0	16	0	1963
4410S	0	16	0	1965
4510S	0	0	0	1950
4510S	0	0	0	1955
4510S	0	0	0	1960
4510S	0	0	0	1963
4510S	0	0	0	1965
4610S	0	0A	0	1950
4610S	0	0	0	1955
4610S	0	0A	0	1960
4610S	0	0A	0	1963
4610S	0	0A	0	1965
4710S	0	0A	0	1950
4710S	0	0	0	1955
4710S	0	0A	0	1960
4710S	0	0A	0	1963
4710S	0	0A	0	1965
4810S	0	16	0	1950
4810S	0	16	0	1955
4810S	0	16A	0	1960
4810S	0	16	0	1963
4810S	0	16	0	1965
4910S	0	16	0	1950
4910S	0	16	0	1955
4910S	0	16A	0	1960
4910S	0	16	0	1963

	46	47	48	
4910S	0	16	0	1965
5010S	0	16	0	1950
5010S	0	16	0	1955
5010S	0	16A	0	1960
5010S	0	16	0	1963
5010S	0	16	0	1965
5110S	0	16	0	1950
5110S	0	16	0	1955
5110S	0	16A	0	1960
5110S	0	16	0	1963
5110S	0	16	0	1965
5210S	0	16	0	1950
5210S	0	16	0	1955
5210S	0A	16A	0	1960
5210S	64	16	0	1963
5210S	64	16	0	1965
5310S	0	16	0	1950
5310S	0	16	0	1955
5310S	0	16A	0	1960
5310S	0	16	0	1963
5310S	0	16	0	1965
5410S	0	0	0	1950
5410S	0	0	0	1955
5410S	0	0	0	1960
5410S	0	0	0	1963
5410S	0	0	0	1965
5510S	0	16	0	1950
5510S	0	16	0	1955
5510S	0	16A	0	1960
5510S	0	16	0	1963
5510S	0	16	0	1965
5610S	0	16	0	1950
5610S	0	16	0	1955
5610S	0	16A	0	1960
5610S	0	16	0	1963
5610S	0	16	0	1965
5710S	0	16	0	1950
5710S	0	16	0	1955
5710S	0	16A	0	1960
5710S	0	16	0	1963
5710S	0	16	0	1965
5810S	0	0	0	1950
5810S	0	0	0	1955
5810S	0	0	0	1960
5810S	0	0	0	1963
5810S	0	0	0	1965
5910S	16	0A	0	1950
5910S	16	0	0	1955
5910S	32A	0A	0	1960
5910S	32	0A	0	1963
5910S	32	0	0	1965
6010S	0	16	0	1950
6010S	0	16	0	1955
6010S	0	16A	0	1960
6010S	0	16B	0	1963
6010S	0	16	0	1965
6110S	0	16	0	1950
6110S	0	16	0	1955
6110S	0	16A	0	1960
6110S	0	16	0	1963

	46	47	48	
6110S	0	16	0	1965
6210S	0	16	0	1950
6210S	0	16	0	1955
6210S	0	16A	0	1960
6210S	0	16	0	1963
6210S	0	16	0	1965
6310S	0	16	0	1950
6310S	0	16	0	1955
6310S	0	16A	0	1960
6310S	0	16	0	1963
6310S	0	16	0	1965
6410S	0	16	0	1950
6410S	0	16	0	1955
6410S	32A	16A	0	1960
6410S	32	16	0	1963
6410S	32	16	0	1965
6510S	0	16	0	1950
6510S	0	16	0	1955
6510S	0	16A	0	1960
6510S	0	16	0	1963
6510S	0	16	0	1965
6610S	0	16	0	1950
6610S	0	16	0	1955
6610S	0	16A	0	1960
6610S	0	16	0	1963
6610S	0	16	0	1965
6710S	0	0	0	1950
6710S	0A	0	0	1955
6710S	0	0	0	1960
6710S	0	0	0	1963
6710S	0	0	0	1965
6810S	0	16	0	1950
6810S	0	16	0	1955
6810S	0A	16A	0	1960
6810S	64	16	0	1963
6810S	64	16	0	1965
6910S	0	16	0	1950
6910S	0	16	0	1955
6910S	0	16A	0	1960
6910S	0	16	0	1963
6910S	0	16	0	1965
7010S	0	16	0	1950
7010S	0	16	0	1955
7010S	0	16A	0	1960
7010S	0	16	0	1963
7010S	0	16	0	1965
7110S	0	0	0	1950
7110S	0	0	0	1955
7110S	0	0	0	1960
7110S	0	0	0	1963
7110S	0	0	0	1965
7210S	0	0A	0	1950
7210S	0	0	0	1955
7210S	0	0A	0	1960
7210S	0	0A	0	1963
7210S	0	0A	0	1965
7310S	0	0A	0	1950
7310S	0	0	0	1955
7310S	0	0A	0	1960
7310S	0	0A	0	1963

	46	47	48	
7310S	0	0A	0	1965
7410S	0	16	0	1950
7410S	0	16	0	1955
7410S	0	16A	0	1960
7410S	0	16	0	1963
7410S	0	16	0	1965
7510S	0	16	0	1950
7510S	0	16	0	1955
7510S	0	16A	0	1960
7510S	0	16	0	1963
7510S	0	16	0	1965
7610S	0	16	0	1950
7610S	0	16	0	1955
7610S	0	16A	0	1960
7610S	0	16	0	1963
7610S	0	16	0	1965
7710S	0	16	0	1950
7710S	0	16	0	1955
7710S	0	16A	0	1960
7710S	0	16	0	1963
7710S	0	16	0	1965
7810S	0	16	0	1950
7810S	0	16	0	1955
7810S	0	16A	0	1960
7810S	0	16	0	1963
7810S	0	16	0	1965
7910S	0	0	0	1950
7910S	0	0	0	1955
7910S	0	0	0	1960
7910S	0	0	0	1963
7910S	0	0	0	1965
8010S	0	0	0	1950
8010S	0A	0	0	1955
8010S	0	0	0	1960
8010S	0	0	0	1963
8010S	0	0	0	1965
8110S	0	0	0	1950
8110S	0	0	0	1955
8110S	0	0	0	1960
8110S	0	0	0	1963
8110S	0	0	0	1965
8210S	0	0	0	1950
8210S	0	0	0	1955
8210S	0	0	0	1960
8210S	0	0	0	1963
8210S	0	0	0	1965
8310S	0	0	0	1950
8310S	0	0	0	1955
8310S	0	0	0	1960
8310S	0	0	0	1963
8310S	0	0	0	1965
8410S	0	0	0	1950
8410S	0	0	0	1955
8410S	0	0	0	1960
8410S	0	0	0	1963
8410S	0	0	0	1965
8510S	0	0	0	1950
8510S	0	0	0	1955
8510S	0	0	0	1960
8510S	0	0	0	1963

	46	47	48	
8510S	0	0	0	1965
8610S	0	0	0	1950
8610S	0	0	0	1955
8610S	0	0	0	1960
8610S	0	0	0	1963
8610S	0	0	0	1965
8710S	16	0	0	1950
8710S	16	0	0	1955
8710S	16A	0	0	1960
8710S	16	0	0	1963
8710S	16	0	0	1965
8810S	0	0	0	1950
8810S	0	0	0	1955
8810S	0	0	0	1960
8810S	0	0	0	1963
8810S	0	0	0	1965
8910S	0	0	0	1950
8910S	0	0	0	1955
8910S	0	0	0	1960
8910S	0	0	0	1963
8910S	0	0	0	1965
9010S	0	0	0	1950
9010S	0	0	0	1955
9010S	0	0	0	1960
9010S	0	0	0	1963
9010S	0	0	0	1965
9110S	0	0	0	1950
9110S	0	0	0	1955
9110S	0	0	0	1960
9110S	0	0	0	1963
9110S	0	0	0	1965
9210S	0	0A	0	1950
9210S	0	0	0	1955
9210S	0	0A	0	1960
9210S	0	0A	0	1963
9210S	0	0A	0	1965
9310S	0	0	0	1950
9310S	0A	0	0	1955
9310S	0	0	0	1960
9310S	0	0	0	1963
9310S	0	0	0	1965
9410S	0	0A	0	1950
9410S	0	0	0	1955
9410S	0	0A	0	1960
9410S	0	0A	0	1963
9410S	0	0A	0	1965
9510S	0	0A	0	1950
9510S	0	0	0	1955
9510S	0	0A	0	1960
9510S	0	0A	0	1963
9510S	0	0A	0	1965
9610S	16	0A	0	1950
9610S	16	0	0	1955
9610S	32A	0A	0	1960
9610S	32	0A	0	1963
9610S	32	0	0	1965
9710S	0	0A	0	1950
9710S	0	0	0	1955
9710S	0	0A	0	1960
9710S	0	0A	0	1963

	46	47	48	
9710S	0	0A	0	1965
9810S	0	0	0	1950
9810S	0	0	0	1955
9810S	0	0	0	1960
9810S	0	0	0	1963
9810S	0	0	0	1965
9910S	16	0A	1	1950
9910S	16	0	1	1955
9910S	16A	0A	1	1960
9910S	16	0A	1	1963
9910S	16	0A	1	1965
10010S	0	0A	0	1950
10010S	0	0	0	1955
10010S	0	0A	0	1960
10010S	0	0A	0	1963
10010S	0	0A	0	1965
10110S	0	0A	0	1950
10110S	0	0	0	1955
10110S	0	0A	0	1960
10110S	0	0A	0	1963
10110S	0	0A	0	1965
10210S	0	0A	0	1950
10210S	0	0	0	1955
10210S	0	0A	0	1960
10210S	0	0A	0	1963
10210S	0	0A	0	1965
10310S	0	0A	0	1950
10310S	0	0	0	1955
10310S	0	0A	0	1960
10310S	0	32B	0	1963
10310S	0	32	0	1965
10410S	0	0A	0	1950
10410S	0	0	0	1955
10410S	0	32A	0	1960
10410S	0	32A	0	1963
10410S	0	32A	0	1965
10510S	0	0A	0	1950
10510S	0	0	0	1955
10510S	0	0A	0	1960
10510S	0	0A	0	1963
10510S	0	0A	0	1965
10610S	0	0	0	1950
10610S	0A	0	0	1955
10610S	0	0A	0	1960
10610S	0	0	0	1963
10610S	0	0	0	1965
10710S	0	0A	0	1950
10710S	0	0	0	1955
10710S	0	0	0	1960
10710S	0	0A	0	1963
10710S	0	0A	0	1965
10810S	0	0A	0	1950
10810S	0	0	0	1955
10810S	0	0A	0	1960
10810S	0	0A	0	1963
10810S	0	0A	0	1965
10910S	0	32A	0	1950
10910S	0	32A	0	1955
10910S	0	32A	0	1960
10910S	0	32A	0	1963
10910S	0	32A	0	1965

	46	47	48	
11010S	0	0A	0	1950
11010S	0	0	0	1955
11010S	0	0A	0	1960
11010S	0	0A	0	1963
11010S	0	0A	0	1965
11110S	0	0	0	1950
11110S	0	0	0	1955
11110S	0	0A	0	1960
11110S	0	0	0	1963
11110S	0	0	0	1965
11210S	16	0A	0	1950
11210S	32	0	0	1955
11210S	32	0	0	1960
11210S	32	0A	0	1963
11210S	32	0A	0	1965
11310S	0	0A	0	1950
11310S	0	0	0	1955
11310S	0	0A	0	1960
11310S	0	0A	0	1963
11310S	0	0A	0	1965
11410S	0	0A	0	1950
11410S	0	0	0	1955
11410S	0	0A	0	1960
11410S	0	0A	0	1963
11410S	0	0A	0	1965
11510S	0	0A	0	1950
11510S	0	0	0	1955
11510S	0	0A	0	1960
11510S	0	0A	0	1963
11510S	0	0A	0	1965
11610S	0	0A	0	1950
11610S	0	0	0	1955
11610S	0	0A	0	1960
11610S	0	0A	0	1963
11610S	0	0A	0	1965
11710S	0	0A	0	1950
11710S	0	0	0	1955
11710S	0	0A	0	1960
11710S	0	0A	0	1963
11710S	0	0A	0	1965
11810S	0	16	0	1950
11810S	0	16	0	1955
11810S	0	16A	0	1960
11810S	0	16	0	1963
11810S	0	16	0	1965
11910S	0	0	0	1950
11910S	0A	0	0	1955
11910S	0	0	0	1960
11910S	0	0	0	1963
11910S	0	0	0	1965
12010S	0	16	0	1950
12010S	0	16	0	1955
12010S	0	16A	0	1960
12010S	0	16	0	1963
12010S	0	16	0	1965
12110S	0	16	0	1950
12110S	0	16	0	1955
12110S	0	16A	0	1960
12110S	0	16	0	1963
12110S	0	16	0	1965

	46	47	48	
12210S	0	16	0	1950
12210S	0	16	0	1955
12210S	0	16A	0	1960
12210S	0	16	0	1963
12210S	0	16	0	1965
12310S	0	16	0	1950
12310S	0	16	0	1955
12310S	0	16A	0	1960
12310S	0	16	0	1963
12310S	0	16	0	1965
12410S	16	0	1	1950
12410S	16	0	1A	1955
12410S	16A	0	1	1960
12410S	16	0	1	1963
12410S	16	0	1A	1965
12510S	0	0A	0	1950
12510S	0	0	0	1955
12510S	0	0A	0	1960
12510S	0	0A	0	1963
12510S	0	0A	0	1965
12610S	0	0A	0	1950
12610S	0	0	0	1955
12610S	0	0A	0	1960
12610S	0	0A	0	1963
12610S	0	0A	0	1965
12710S	0	16	0	1950
12710S	0	16	0	1955
12710S	0	16A	0	1960
12710S	0	16	0	1963
12710S	0	16	0	1965
12810S	0	16	0	1950
12810S	0	16	0	1955
12810S	0	16A	0	1960
12810S	0	16	0	1963
12810S	0	16	0	1965
12910S	0	16	0	1950
12910S	0	16	0	1955
12910S	0	16A	0	1960
12910S	0	16	0	1963
12910S	0	16	0	1965
13010S	0	16	0	1950
13010S	0	16	0A	1955
13010S	0	16A	0A	1960
13010S	0	16	0A	1963
13010S	0	16	0	1965
13110S	0	16	0	1950
13110S	0	16	0	1955
13110S	0	16A	0	1960
13110S	0	16	0	1963
13110S	0	16	0	1965
13210S	0	0	0	1950
13210S	0A	0	0	1955
13210S	0	0	0	1960
13210S	0	0	0	1963
13210S	0	0	0	1965
13310S	0	16	0	1950
13310S	0	16	0	1955
13310S	0	16A	0	1960
13310S	0	16	0	1963
13310S	0	16	0	1965

	46	47	48	
13410S	0	16	0	1950
13410S	0	16	0	1955
13410S	0	16A	0	1960
13410S	0	16	0	1963
13410S	0	16	0	1965
13510S	0	16	0	1950
13510S	0	16	0	1955
13510S	0	16A	0	1960
13510S	0	16	0	1963
13510S	0	16	0	1965
13610S	0	16	0	1950
13610S	0	16	0	1955
13610S	0	16A	0	1960
13610S	0	16	0	1963
13610S	0	16	0	1965
13710S	0	0	0	1950
13710S	0	0	0	1955
13710S	0	0	0	1960
13710S	0	0	0	1963
13710S	0	0	0	1965
13810S	0	0A	0	1950
13810S	0	0	0	1955
13810S	0	0A	0	1960
13810S	0	0A	0	1963
13810S	0	0A	0	1965
13910S	0	0A	0	1950
13910S	0	0	0	1955
13910S	0	0A	0	1960
13910S	0	0A	0	1963
13910S	0	0A	0	1965
14010S	0	16	0	1950
14010S	0	16	0	1955
14010S	0	16A	0	1960
14010S	0	16	0	1963
14010S	0	16	0	1965
14110S	8	16	1	1950
14110S	8A	16	1	1955
14110S	8A	16A	1	1960
14110S	8C	16	1	1963
14110S	8	16	1	1965
14210S	0	16	0	1950
14210S	0	16	0	1955
14210S	0	16A	0	1960
14210S	0	16	0	1963
14210S	0	16	0	1965
14310S	0	16	0	1950
14310S	0	16	0	1955
14310S	0	16A	0	1960
14310S	0	16	0	1963
14310S	0	16	0	1965
14410S	0	16	0	1950
14410S	0	16	0	1955
14410S	0	16A	0	1960
14410S	0	16	0	1963
14410S	0	16	0	1965
14510S	0	0	0	1950
14510S	0A	0	0	1955
14510S	0	0	0	1960
14510S	0	0	0	1963
14510S	0	0	0	1965

	46	47	48	
14610S	0	16	0	1950
14610S	0	16	0	1955
14610S	0	16A	0	1960
14610S	0	16	0	1963
14610S	0	16	0	1965
14710S	0	16	0	1950
14710S	0	16	0	1955
14710S	0	16A	0	1960
14710S	0	16	0	1963
14710S	0	16	0	1965
14810S	0	16	0	1950
14810S	0	16	0	1955
14810S	0	16A	0	1960
14810S	0	16	0	1963
14810S	0	16	0	1965
14910S	0	16	0	1950
14910S	0	16	0	1955
14910S	0	16A	0	1960
14910S	0	16	0	1963
14910S	0	16	0	1965
15010S	0	0	0	1950
15010S	0	0	0	1955
15010S	0	0	0	1960
15010S	0	0	0	1963
15010S	0	0	0	1965
15110S	0	0A	0	1950
15110S	0	0	0	1955
15110S	0	0A	0	1960
15110S	0	0A	0	1963
15110S	0	0A	0	1965
15210S	0	0A	0	1950
15210S	0	0	0	1955
15210S	0	0A	0	1960
15210S	0	0A	0	1963
15210S	0	0A	0	1965
15310S	0	16	0	1950
15310S	0	16	0	1955
15310S	0	16A	0	1960
15310S	0	16	0	1963
15310S	0	16	0	1965
15410S	8	16	0	1950
15410S	8	16	0	1955
15410S	8A	16A	0	1960
15410S	8C	16	0	1963
15410S	8	16	0	1965
15510S	2	16	0	1950
15510S	2	16	0	1955
15510S	2A	16A	0	1960
15510S	2	16	0	1963
15510S	2	16	0	1965
15610S	2	16	0	1950
15610S	2	16	0	1955
15610S	2A	16A	0	1960
15610S	2	16	0	1963
15610S	2	16	0	1965
15710S	0	16	0	1950
15710S	0	16	0	1955
15710S	0	16A	0	1960
15710S	0	16	0	1963
15710S	0	16	0	1965

	46	47	48	
15810S	16	0	0	1950
15810S	16	0	0	1955
15810S	16A	0	0	1960
15810S	16B	0	0	1963
15810S	16	0	0	1965
15910S	16	16	0	1950
15910S	32	16	0	1955
15910S	32	16A	0	1960
15910S	32	16	0	1963
15910S	32	16	0	1965
16010S	0	16	0	1950
16010S	0	16	0	1955
16010S	0	16A	0	1960
16010S	0	16	0	1963
16010S	0	16	0	1965
16110S	0	16	0	1950
16110S	0	16	0	1955
16110S	32	16A	0	1960
16110S	32	16	0	1963
16110S	32	16A	0	1965
16210S	0	16	0	1950
16210S	0	16	0	1955
16210S	0	16A	0	1960
16210S	0	16	0	1963
16210S	0	16A	0	1965
16310S	0	0	0	1950
16310S	0	0	0	1955
16310S	0	0	0	1960
16310S	0	0	0	1963
16310S	0	0	0	1965
16410S	0	16	0	1950
16410S	0	16	0	1955
16410S	0	32A	0	1960
16410S	0	32B	0	1963
16410S	0	32	0	1965
16510S	0	0A	0	1950
16510S	0	0	0	1955
16510S	0	0A	0	1960
16510S	0	0A	0	1963
16510S	0	0	0	1965
16610S	0	16	0	1950
16610S	0	16	0	1955
16610S	0	16A	0	1960
16610S	0	16	0	1963
16610S	0	16A	0	1965
16710S	0	16	0	1950
16710S	0	16	0	1955
16710S	0	16A	0	1960
16710S	0	16	0	1963
16710S	0	16A	0	1965
16810S	2	16	0	1950
16810S	2	16	0	1955
16810S	2A	16A	0	1960
16810S	2	16	0	1963
16810S	2	16	0	1965
16910S	0	16	0	1950
16910S	0	32	0	1955
16910S	0	32A	0	1960
16910S	0	32A	0	1963
16910S	0	32A	0	1965

	46	47	48	
17010S	0	16	0	1950
17010S	0	16	0	1955
17010S	0	16A	0	1960
17010S	0	16	0	1963
17010S	0	16A	0	1965
17110S	0A	0	0	1950
17110S	0	0	0	1955
17110S	0A	0	0	1960
17110S	0A	0	0	1963
17110S	0A	0	0	1965
17210S	16	16	0	1950
17210S	32	16	0	1955
17210S	32A	16A	0	1960
17210S	32	16	0	1963
17210S	32	16A	0	1965
17310S	2	16	0	1950
17310S	2	16	0	1955
17310S	2	16A	0	1960
17310S	64	16	0	1963
17310S	64	16	0	1965
17410S	0	16	0	1950
17410S	0	16	0	1955
17410S	0	16A	0	1960
17410S	0	16	0	1963
17410S	0	16	0	1965
17510S	0	16	0	1950
17510S	0	16	0	1955
17510S	0	16A	0	1960
17510S	0	16	0	1963
17510S	0	16	0	1965
17610S	0	0	0	1950
17610S	0	0	0	1955
17610S	0	0	0	1960
17610S	0	0	0	1963
17610S	0	0	0	1965
17710S	0	0A	0	1950
17710S	0	0	0	1955
17710S	0	0A	0	1960
17710S	0	0A	0	1963
17710S	0	0	0	1965
17810S	0	0A	0	1950
17810S	0	0	0	1955
17810S	0	0A	0	1960
17810S	0	0A	0	1963
17810S	0	0	0	1965
17910S	0	16	0	1950
17910S	0	16	0	1955
17910S	0	16A	0	1960
17910S	0	16	0	1963
17910S	0	16	0	1965
18010S	0	16	0	1950
18010S	0	16	0	1955
18010S	0	16A	0	1960
18010S	0	16	0	1963
18010S	0	16	0	1965

	46	47	48	
18110S	2	16	0	1950
18110S	2	16	0	1955
18110S	2A	16A	0	1960
18110S	2	16	0	1963
18110S	2	16	0	1965
18210S	0	16	0	1950
18210S	0	32	0	1955
18210S	0	32	0	1960
18210S	0	32	0	1963
18210S	0	32	0	1965

	49	50	51	52	53	
111S	0	0	1	2	0	1950
111S	0	0A	1	2	0	1955
111S	0	0	1	2	0	1960
111S	0	0	1	2	0	1963
111S	0	0	1	2	0	1965
211S	0	1	0	4	0	1950
211S	0	1	0	4	0	1955
211S	0	1	0	4	0	1960
211S	0	1	0	4	0	1963
211S	0	1	0	4	0	1965
311S	0	1	2	0	1	1950
311S	0	1	2	0	1	1955
311S	0	1	2	0	1	1960
311S	0	1	0	4	0	1963
311S	0	1	0A	4	0	1965
411S	0	1	1	2	0	1950
411S	0	1	1	2	0	1955
411S	0	1	1	2	0	1960
411S	0	1	1	2	0	1963
411S	0	1	1	2	0	1965
511S	0	0	1	2	0	1950
511S	0	0	1	2	0	1955
511S	0	0	1	2	0	1960
511S	0	0	1	2	0	1963
511S	0	0	1	2	0	1965
611S	0	0	1	2	0	1950
611S	0	0	1	2	0	1955
611S	0	0	1	2	0	1960
611S	0	0	1	2	0	1963
611S	0	0	1	2	0	1965
711S	0	0	1	2	0	1950
711S	0	0	1	2	0	1955
711S	0	0	1	2	0	1960
711S	0	0	1	2	0	1963
711S	0	0	1	2	0	1965
811S	0	0	1	2	0	1950
811S	0	0	1	2	0	1955
811S	0	0	1	2	0	1960
811S	0	0A	1	2	0	1963
811S	0	0A	1	2	0	1965
911S	0	1	2	0	0	1950
911S	0	1	2	0	0	1955
911S	0	1	2	0	0	1960
911S	0	1	2	0	0	1963
911S	0	1	2	0	0	1965
1011S	0	1	0	4	0	1950
1011S	0	1	0	4	0	1955
1011S	0	1	0	4	0	1960
1011S	0	1	0	4	0	1963

	49	50	51	52	53	
1011S	0	1	0	4	0	1965
1111S	0	1	0	5	0	1950
1111S	0	1	0	5	0	1955
1111S	0	1	0	5	0	1960
1111S	0	1	0	5	0	1963
1111S	0	1	0	5	0	1965
1211S	0	1	2	0	0	1950
1211S	0	1	2	0	0	1955
1211S	0	1	2	0	0	1960
1211S	0	1	2	0	0	1963
1211S	0	1	2	0	0	1965
1311S	0	1	2	1	1	1950
1311S	0	1	2	1	1	1955
1311S	0	1	2	1	1	1960
1311S	0	1	2	1	1	1963
1311S	0	1	2	1	1	1965
1411S	0	0	1	2	0	1950
1411S	0	0	1	2	0	1955
1411S	0	0	1	2	0	1960
1411S	0	0	1	2	0	1963
1411S	0	0	1	2	0	1965
1511S	0	0	1	2	0	1950
1511S	0	0	1	2	0	1955
1511S	0	0	1	2	0	1960
1511S	0	0	1	2	0	1963
1511S	0	0	1	2	0	1965
1611S	0	0	1	2	0	1950
1611S	0	0	1	2	0	1955
1611S	0	0	1	2	0	1960
1611S	0	0	1	2	0	1963
1611S	0	0	1	2	0	1965
1711S	0	0	2	0	0	1950
1711S	0	0	2	0	0	1955
1711S	0	0	2	0	0	1960
1711S	0	0	2	0	0	1963
1711S	0	0	2	0	0	1965
1811S	0	0	2	0	0	1950
1811S	0	0	2	0	0	1955
1811S	0	0	2	0	0	1960
1811S	0	0	2	0	0	1963
1811S	0	0	2	0	0	1965
1911S	0	0	2	0	0	1950
1911S	0	0	2	0	0	1955
1911S	0	0	2	0	0	1960
1911S	0	0	2	0	0	1963
1911S	0	0	2	0	0	1965
2011S	0	0	2	0	0	1950
2011S	0	0	2	0	0	1955
2011S	0	0	2	0	0	1960
2011S	0	0	2	0	0	1963
2011S	0	0	2	0	0	1965
2111S	0	0	2	0	0	1950
2111S	0	0	1	0	0	1955
2111S	0	0	2	0	0	1960
2111S	0	0	2	0	0	1963
2111S	0	0	2	0	0	1965
2211S	0	0	1	2	0	1950
2211S	0	0	1	2	0	1955
2211S	0	0	1	2	0	1960
2211S	0	0	1	2	0	1963
2211S	0	0	1	2	0	1965

	49	50	51	52	53	
2311S	0	0	1	2	0	1950
2311S	0	1	1	2	0	1955
2311S	0	0	1	2	0	1960
2311S	0	0	1	2	0	1963
2311S	0	0	1	2	0	1965
2411S	0	0	1	3	0	1950
2411S	0	0	1	3	0	1955
2411S	0	0	1	3	0	1960
2411S	0	0	1	3	0	1963
2411S	0	0	1	3	0	1965
2511S	16	0	1	2	0	1950
2511S	16	0	1	2	0	1955
2511S	16	0	1	2	0	1960
2511S	16	0	1	2	0	1963
2511S	16	0	1	2	0	1965
2611S	0	0	1	3	0	1950
2611S	0	0	1	3	0	1955
2611S	0	0	1	3	0	1960
2611S	0	0	1	3	0	1963
2611S	0	0	1	3	0	1965
2711S	0	1	0	4	0	1950
2711S	0	1	0	4	0	1955
2711S	0	1	0	4	0	1960
2711S	0	1	0	4	0	1963
2711S	0	1	0	4	0	1965
2811S	0	0	1	2	0	1950
2811S	0	0	1	2	0	1955
2811S	0	0	1	2	0	1960
2811S	0	0	1	2	0	1963
2811S	0	0	1	2	0	1965
2911S	0	1	0	4	0	1950
2911S	0	1	0	4	0	1955
2911S	0	1	0	4	0	1960
2911S	0	1	2	0	0	1963
2911S	0	1	2	0	1	1965
3011S	0	1	1	2	0	1950
3011S	0	1	1	2	0	1955
3011S	0	1	1	2	0	1960
3011S	0	1	1	2	0	1963
3011S	0	1	1	2	0	1965
3111S	0	0	1	2	0	1950
3111S	0	0	1	2	0	1955
3111S	0	0	1	2	0	1960
3111S	0	0	1	2	0	1963
3111S	0	0	1	2	0	1965
3211S	0	0	1	2	0	1950
3211S	0	0	1	2	0	1955
3211S	0	0	1	2	0	1960
3211S	0	0	1	2	0	1963
3211S	0	0	1	2	0	1965
3311S	0	0	1	2	0	1950
3311S	0	0	1	2	0	1955
3311S	0	0	1	2	0	1960
3311S	0	0	1	2	0	1963
3311S	0	0	1	2	0	1965
3411S	0	0	1	2	0	1950
3411S	0	0	1	2	0	1955
3411S	0	0	1	2	0	1960
3411S	0	1	1	2	0	1963
3411S	0	1	1	2	0	1965

	49	50	51	52	53	
3511S	0	1	0	4	0	1950
3511S	0	1	0	4	0	1955
3511S	0	1	0	4	0	1960
3511S	0	1	0	4	0	1963
3511S	0	1	0	4	0	1965
3611S	0	1	2	0	0	1950
3611S	0	1	2	0	0	1955
3611S	0	1	2	0	0	1960
3611S	0	1	2	0	0	1963
3611S	0	1	2	0	0	1965
3711S	0	1	2	1	1	1950
3711S	0	1	2	1	1	1955
3711S	0	1	2	1	1	1960
3711S	0	1	2	1	1	1963
3711S	0	1	2	1	0	1965
3811S	0	1	0	4	0	1950
3811S	0	1	0	4	0	1955
3811S	0	1	0	4	0	1960
3811S	0	1	0	4	0	1963
3811S	0	1	0	4	0	1965
3911S	0	1	0	5	0	1950
3911S	0	1	0	5	0	1955
3911S	0	1	0	5	0	1960
3911S	0	1	0	5	0	1963
3911S	0	1	0	5	0	1965
4011S	0	1	2	0	1	1950
4011S	0	1	2	0	1	1955
4011S	0	1	2	0	1	1960
4011S	0	1	0	4	0	1963
4011S	0	1	1	4	0	1965
4111S	0	0	1	2	0	1950
4111S	0	0	1	2	0	1955
4111S	0	0	1	2	0	1960
4111S	0	0	1	2	0	1963
4111S	0	0	1	2	0	1965
4211S	0	1	0	4	0	1950
4211S	0	1	0	4	0	1955
4211S	0	1	0	4	0	1960
4211S	0	1	2	0	0	1963
4211S	0	1	2	0	0	1965
4311S	0	1	1	2	0	1950
4311S	0	1	1	2	0	1955
4311S	0	1	1	2	0	1960
4311S	0	1	1	2	0	1963
4311S	0	1	1	2	0	1965
4411S	0	0	1	2	0	1950
4411S	0	0	1	2	0	1955
4411S	0	0	1	2	0	1960
4411S	0	0	1	2	0	1963
4411S	0	0	1	2	0	1965
4511S	0	0	1	2	0	1950
4511S	0	0	1	2	0	1955
4511S	0	0	1	2	0	1960
4511S	0	0	1	2	0	1963
4511S	0	0	1	2	0	1965
4611S	0	0	1	2	0	1950
4611S	0	0	1	2	0	1955
4611S	0	0	1	2	0	1960
4611S	0	0	1	2	0	1963
4611S	0	0	1	2	0	1965

	49	50	51	52	53	
4711S	0	0	1	2	0	1950
4711S	0	0	1	2	0	1955
4711S	0	0	1	2	0	1960
4711S	0	0A	1	2	0	1963
4711S	0	0A	1	2	0	1965
4811S	0	1	2	0	0	1950
4811S	0	1	2	0	0	1955
4811S	0	1	2	0	0	1960
4811S	0	1	0	4	0	1963
4811S	0	1	0	4	0	1965
4911S	0	1	0	4	0	1950
4911S	0	1	0	4	0	1955
4911S	0	1	0	4	0	1960
4911S	0	1	2	0	0	1963
4911S	0	1	2	0	0	1965
5011S	0	1	0	5	0	1950
5011S	0	1	0	5	0	1955
5011S	0	1	0	5	0	1960
5011S	0	1	2	1	1	1963
5011S	0	1	2	1	1	1965
5111S	0	1	2	0	0	1950
5111S	0	1	2	0	0	1955
5111S	0	1	2	0	0	1960
5111S	0	1	0	4	0	1963
5111S	0	1	0	4	0	1965
5211S	1	1	2	1	1	1950
5211S	1	1	2	1	1	1955
5211S	1	1	2	1	1	1960
5211S	1	1	0	5	0	1963
5211S	1	1	0	5	0	1965
5311S	0	1	1	2	0	1950
5311S	0	1	1	2	0	1955
5311S	0	1	1	2	0	1960
5311S	0	1	1	2	0	1963
5311S	0	1	1	2	0	1965
5411S	0	0	2	0	0	1950
5411S	0	0A	2	0	0	1955
5411S	0	0	2	0	0	1960
5411S	0	0	2	0	0	1963
5411S	0	0	2	0	0	1965
5511S	0	1	1	2	0	1950
5511S	0	1	1	2	0	1955
5511S	0	1	1	2	0	1960
5511S	0	1	1	2	0	1963
5511S	0	1	1	2	0	1965
5611S	0	1	1	2	0	1950
5611S	0	1	1	2	0	1955
5611S	0	1	1	2	0	1960
5611S	0	1	1	2	0	1963
5611S	0	1	1	2	0	1965
5711S	0	0	2	0	0	1950
5711S	0	0	2	0	0	1955
5711S	0	0	2	0	0	1960
5711S	0	0	2	0	0	1963
5711S	0	0	2	0	0	1965
5811S	0	0	2	0	0	1950
5811S	0	0	2	0	0	1955
5811S	0	0	2	0	0	1960
5811S	0	0	2	0	0	1963
5811S	0	0	2	0	0	1965

	49	50	51	52	53	
5911S	0	0	2	0	0	1950
5911S	0	0	2	0	0	1955
5911S	0	0	2	0	0	1960
5911S	0	0	2	0	0	1963
5911S	0	0	2	0	0	1965
6011S	0	0	2	0	1	1950
6011S	0	0	2	0	1	1955
6011S	0	0	2	0	0	1960
6011S	0	1	2	0	1	1963
6011S	0	1	2	0	1	1965
6111S	0	1	1	2	0	1950
6111S	0	1	1	2	0	1955
6111S	0	1	1	2	0	1960
6111S	0	1	1	2	0	1963
6111S	0	1	1	2	0	1965
6211S	0	1	1	2	0	1950
6211S	0	1	1	2	0	1955
6211S	0	1	1	2	0	1960
6211S	0	1	1	2	0	1963
6211S	0	1	1	2	0	1965
6311S	0	1	1	3	0	1950
6311S	0	1	1	3	0	1955
6311S	0	1	1	3	0	1960
6311S	0	1	1	3	0	1963
6311S	0	1	1	3	0	1965
6411S	8	1	1	2	0	1950
6411S	8A	1	1	2	0	1955
6411S	8	1	1	2	0	1960
6411S	8A	1	1	2	0	1963
6411S	8A	1	1	2	0	1965
6511S	0	1	1	3	0	1950
6511S	0	1	1	3	0	1955
6511S	0	1	1	3	0	1960
6511S	0	1	1	3	0	1963
6511S	0	1	1	3	0	1965
6611S	0	0	1	2	0	1950
6611S	0	0	1	2	0	1955
6611S	0	0	1	2	0	1960
6611S	0	0	1	2	0	1963
6611S	0	0	1	2	0	1965
6711S	0	0	2	0	0	1950
6711S	0	0	2	0	0	1955
6711S	0	0	2	0	0	1960
6711S	0	0	2	0	0	1963
6711S	0	0	2	0	0	1965
6811S	0	0	1	2	0	1950
6811S	0	0	1	2	0	1955
6811S	0	0	1	2	0	1960
6811S	0	0	1	2	0	1963
6811S	0	0	1	2	0	1965
6911S	0	0	1	2	0	1950
6911S	0	0	1	2	0	1955
6911S	0	0	1	2	0	1960
6911S	0	0	1	2	0	1963
6911S	0	0	1	2	0	1965
7011S	0	0	2	0	0	1950
7011S	0	0	2	0	0	1955
7011S	0	0	2	0	0	1960
7011S	0	0	2	0	0	1963
7011S	0	0	2	0	0	1965

	49	50	51	52	53	
7111S	0	0	2	0	0	1950
7111S	0	0	2	0	0	1955
7111S	0	0	2	0	0	1960
7111S	0	0	2	0	0	1963
7111S	0	0	2	0	0	1965
7211S	0	0	2	0	0	1950
7211S	0	0	2	0	0	1955
7211S	0	0	2	0	0	1960
7211S	0	0	2	0	0	1963
7211S	0	0	2	0	0	1965
7311S	0	0	2	0	0	1950
7311S	0	0	2	0	0	1955
7311S	0	0	2	0	0	1960
7311S	0	0	2	0	0	1963
7311S	0	0	2	0	0	1965
7411S	0	0	1	2	0	1950
7411S	0	0	1	2	0	1955
7411S	0	0	1	2	0	1960
7411S	0	0	1	2	0	1963
7411S	0	0	1	2	0	1965
7511S	0	0	1	2	0	1950
7511S	0	0	1	2	0	1955
7511S	0	0	1	2	0	1960
7511S	0	0	1	2	0	1963
7511S	0	0	1	2	0	1965
7611S	0	0	1	3	0	1950
7611S	0	0	1	3	0	1955
7611S	0	0	1	3	0	1960
7611S	0	0	1	3	0	1963
7611S	0	0	1	3	0	1965
7711S	16	0	1	2	0	1950
7711S	16	0	1	2	0	1955
7711S	16	0	1	2	0	1960
7711S	16	0	1	2	0	1963
7711S	16	0	1	2	0	1965
7811S	0	0	1	3	0	1950
7811S	0	0	1	3	0	1955
7811S	0	0	1	3	0	1960
7811S	0	0	1	3	0	1963
7811S	0	0	1	3	1	1965
7911S	0	0	1	2	0	1950
7911S	0	0	1	2	0	1955
7911S	0	0	1	2	0	1960
7911S	0	0	1	2	0	1963
7911S	0	0	1	2	0	1965
8011S	0	0	2	0	0	1950
8011S	0	0	2	0	0	1955
8011S	0	0	2	0	0	1960
8011S	0	0	2	0	0	1963
8011S	0	0	2	0	0	1965
8111S	0	0	1	2	0	1950
8111S	0	0	1	2	0	1955
8111S	0	0	1	2	0	1960
8111S	0	0	1	2	0	1963
8111S	0	0	1	2	0	1965
8211S	0	0	1	2	0	1950
8211S	0	0	1	2	0	1955
8211S	0	0	1	2	0	1960
8211S	0	0	1	2	0	1963
8211S	0	0	1	2	0	1965

	49	50	51	52	53	
8311S	0	0	2	0	0	1950
8311S	0	0	2	0	0	1955
8311S	0	0	2	0	0	1960
8311S	0	0	2	0	0	1963
8311S	0	0	2	0	0	1965
8411S	0	0	2	0	0	1950
8411S	0	0	2	0	0	1955
8411S	0	0	2	0	0	1960
8411S	0	0	2	0	0	1963
8411S	0	0	2	0	0	1965
8511S	0	0	2	0	0	1950
8511S	0	0	2	0	0	1955
8511S	0	0	2	0	0	1960
8511S	0	0	2	0	0	1963
8511S	0	0	2	0	0	1965
8611S	0	0	2	0	0	1950
8611S	0	0	2	0	0	1955
8611S	0	0	2	0	0	1960
8611S	0	0	2	0	0	1963
8611S	0	0	2	0	0	1965
8711S	16	0	1	2	0	1950
8711S	16	0	1	2	0	1955
8711S	16	0	1	2	0	1960
8711S	16	0	1	2	0	1963
8711S	16	0	1	2	0	1965
8811S	0	0	1	2	0	1950
8811S	0	0	1	2	0	1955
8811S	0	0	1	2	0	1960
8811S	0	0	1	2	0	1963
8811S	0	0	1	2	0	1965
8911S	0	0	1	3	0	1950
8911S	0	0	1	3	0	1955
8911S	0	0	1	3	0	1960
8911S	0	0	1	3	0	1963
8911S	0	0	1	3	0	1965
9011S	0	0	1	2	0	1950
9011S	0	0	1	2	0	1955
9011S	0	0	1	2	0	1960
9011S	0	0	1	2	0	1963
9011S	0	0	1	2	0	1965
9111S	0	0	1	3	0	1950
9111S	0	0	1	3	0	1955
9111S	0	0	1	3	0	1960
9111S	0	0	1	3	0	1963
9111S	0	0	1	3	1	1965
9211S	0	0	1	2	0	1950
9211S	0	0	1	2	0	1955
9211S	0	0	1	2	0	1960
9211S	0	0	1	2	0	1963
9211S	0	0	1	2	0	1965
9311S	0	0	2	0	0	1950
9311S	0	0	2	0	0	1955
9311S	0	0	2	0	0	1960
9311S	0	0	2	0	0	1963
9311S	0	0	2	0	0	1965
9411S	0	0	1	2	0	1950
9411S	0	0	1	2	0	1955
9411S	0	0	1	2	0	1960
9411S	0	0	1	2	0	1963
9411S	0	0	1	2	0	1965

	49	50	51	52	53	
9511S	0	0	1	2	0	1950
9511S	0	0	1	2	0	1955
9511S	0	0	1	2	0	1960
9511S	0	0	1	2	0	1963
9511S	0	0	1	2	0	1965
9611S	0	0	2	0	0	1950
9611S	0	0	2	0	0	1955
9611S	0	0	2	0	0	1960
9611S	0	0	2	0	0	1963
9611S	0	0	2	0	0	1965
9711S	0	0	2	0	0	1950
9711S	0	0	2	0	0	1955
9711S	0	0	2	0	0	1960
9711S	0	0	2	0	0	1963
9711S	0	0	2	0	0	1965
9811S	0	0	2	0	0	1950
9811S	0	0	2	0	0	1955
9811S	0	0	2	0	0	1960
9811S	0	0	2	0	0	1963
9811S	0	0	2	0	0	1965
9911S	0	0	2	0	0	1950
9911S	0	0	2	0	0	1955
9911S	0	0	2	0	0	1960
9911S	0	0	2	0	0	1963
9911S	0	0	2	0	0	1965
10011S	0	0	1	2	0	1950
10011S	0	0	1	2	0	1955
10011S	0	0	1	2	0	1960
10011S	0	0	1	2	0	1963
10011S	0	0	1	2	0	1965
10111S	0	0	1	2	0	1950
10111S	0	0	1	2	0	1955
10111S	0	0	1	2	0	1960
10111S	0	0	1	2	0	1963
10111S	0	0	1	2	0	1965
10211S	0	0	1	3	0	1950
10211S	0	0	1	3	0	1955
10211S	0	0	1	3	0	1960
10211S	0	0	1	3	0	1963
10211S	0	0	1	3	0	1965
10311S	16	0	1	2	0	1950
10311S	16	0	1	2	0	1955
10311S	16	0	1	2	0	1960
10311S	16	0	1	2	0	1963
10311S	0	0	1	2	0	1965
10411S	0	0	1	3	0	1950
10411S	0	0	1	3	1	1955
10411S	0	0	1	3	0	1960
10411S	0	0	1	3	0	1963
10411S	0	0	1	3	1	1965
10511S	0	0	1	2	0	1950
10511S	0	0	1	2	0	1955
10511S	0	0	1	2	0	1960
10511S	0	0	1	2	0	1963
10511S	0	0	1	2	0	1965
10611S	0	0	2	0	0	1950
10611S	0	0	2	0	0	1955
10611S	0	0	2	0	0	1960
10611S	0	0	2	0	0	1963
10611S	0	0	2	0	0	1965

	49	50	51	52	53	
10711S	0	0	1	2	0	1950
10711S	0	0	1	2	0	1955
10711S	0	0	1	2	0	1960
10711S	0	0	1	2	0	1963
10711S	0	0	1	2	0	1965
10811S	0	0	1	2	0	1950
10811S	0	0	1	2	0	1955
10811S	0	0	1	2	0	1960
10811S	0	0	1	2	0	1963
10811S	0	0	1	2	0	1965
10911S	0	0	2	0	1	1950
10911S	0	0	2	0	1	1955
10911S	0	0	2	0	1	1960
10911S	0	0	2	0	1	1963
10911S	0	0	2	0	1	1965
11011S	0	0	2	0	0	1950
11011S	0	0	2	0	0	1955
11011S	0	0	2	0	0	1960
11011S	0	0	2	0	0	1963
11011S	0	0	2	0	0	1965
11111S	0	0	2	0	0	1950
11111S	0	0	2	0	0	1955
11111S	0	0	2	0	0	1960
11111S	0	0	2	0	0	1963
11111S	0	0	2	0	0	1965
11211S	0	0	2	0	0	1950
11211S	0	0	2	0	0	1955
11211S	0	0	2	0	0	1960
11211S	0	0	2	0	0	1963
11211S	0	0	2	0	0	1965
11311S	0	0	1	2	0	1950
11311S	0	0	1	2	0	1955
11311S	0	0	1	2	0	1960
11311S	0	0	1	2	0	1963
11311S	0	0	1	2	0	1965
11411S	0	0	1	2	0	1950
11411S	0	0	1	2	0	1955
11411S	0	0	1	2	0	1960
11411S	0	0	1	2	0	1963
11411S	0	0	1	2	0	1965
11511S	0	0	1	3	0	1950
11511S	0	0	1	3	0	1955
11511S	0	0	1	3	0	1960
11511S	0	0	1	3	0	1963
11511S	0	0	1	3	0	1965
11611S	16	0	1	2	0	1950
11611S	16	0	1	2	1	1955
11611S	16	0	1	2	0	1960
11611S	16	0	1	2	0	1963
11611S	16	0	1	2	0	1965
11711S	0	0	1	3	0	1950
11711S	0	0	1	3	0	1955
11711S	0	0	1	3	0	1960
11711S	0	0	1	3	0	1963
11711S	0	0	1	3	0	1965
11811S	0	1	2	0	0	1950
11811S	0	1	2	0	0	1955
11811S	0	1	2	0	0	1960
11811S	0	1	2	0	0	1963
11811S	0	1	2	0	0	1965

	49	50	51	52	53	
11911S	0	0	1	2	0	1950
11911S	0	0	1	2	0	1955
11911S	0	0	1	2	0	1960
11911S	0	0	1	2	0	1963
11911S	0	0	1	2	0	1965
12011S	0	1	0	4	0	1950
12011S	0	1	0	4	0	1955
12011S	0	1	0	4	0	1960
12011S	0	1	0	4	0	1963
12011S	0	1	0	4	0	1965
12111S	0	1	2	0	0	1950
12111S	0	1	2	0	0	1955
12111S	0	1	2	0	0	1960
12111S	0	1	0	4	0	1963
12111S	0	1	0	4	0	1965
12211S	0	1	1	2	0	1950
12211S	0	1	1	2	0	1955
12211S	0	1	1	2	0	1960
12211S	0	1	1	2	0	1963
12211S	0	1	1	2	0	1965
12311S	0	0	1	2	0	1950
12311S	0	0	1	2	0	1955
12311S	0	0	1	2	0	1960
12311S	0	0	1	2	0	1963
12311S	0	0	1	2	0	1965
12411S	0	0	1	2	0	1950
12411S	0	0	1	2	0	1955
12411S	0	0	1	2	0	1960
12411S	0	0	1	2	0	1963
12411S	0	0	1	2	0	1965
12511S	0	0	1	2	0	1950
12511S	0	0	1	2	0	1955
12511S	0	0	1	2	0	1960
12511S	0	0	1	2	0	1963
12511S	0	0	1	2	0	1965
12611S	0	0	1	2	0	1950
12611S	0	0	1	2	0	1955
12611S	0	0	1	2	0	1960
12611S	0	1	1	2	0	1963
12611S	0	1	1	2	0	1965
12711S	0	1	0	4	0	1950
12711S	0	1	0	4	0	1955
12711S	0	1	0	4	0	1960
12711S	0	1	0	4	0	1963
12711S	0	1	0	4	0	1965
12811S	0	1	0	5	0	1950
12811S	0	1	0	5	0	1955
12811S	0	1	0	5	0	1960
12811S	0	1	0	5	0	1963
12811S	0	1	0	5	0	1965
12911S	0	1	2	0	1	1950
12911S	0	1	2	0	1	1955
12911S	0	1	2	0	1	1960
12911S	0	1	2	0	1	1963
12911S	0	1	2	0	1	1965
13011S	0	1	2	1	1	1950
13011S	0	1	2	1	1	1955
13011S	0	1	2	1	1	1960
13011S	0	1	2	1	1	1963
13011S	0	1	2	1	1	1965

	49	50	51	52	53	
13111S	0	1	0	4	0	1950
13111S	0	1	0	4	0	1955
13111S	0	1	0	4	0	1960
13111S	0	1	0	4	0	1963
13111S	0	1	0	4	0	1965
13211S	0	0	1	2	0	1950
13211S	0	0	1	2	0	1955
13211S	0	0	1	2	0	1960
13211S	0	0	1	2	0	1963
13211S	0	0	1	2	0	1965
13311S	0	1	2	0	0	1950
13311S	0	1	2	0	0	1955
13311S	0	1	2	0	0	1960
13311S	0	1	2	0	0	1963
13311S	0	1	2	0	0	1965
13411S	0	1	0	4	0	1950
13411S	0	1	0	4	0	1955
13411S	0	1	0	4	0	1960
13411S	0	1	2	0	0	1963
13411S	0	1	2	0	0	1965
13511S	0	1	1	2	0	1950
13511S	0	1	1	2	0	1955
13511S	0	1	1	2	0	1960
13511S	0	1	1	2	0	1963
13511S	0	1	1	2	0	1965
13611S	0	0	1	2	0	1950
13611S	0	0	1	2	0	1955
13611S	0	0	1	2	0	1960
13611S	0	0	1	2	0	1963
13611S	0	0	1	2	0	1965
13711S	0	0	1	2	0	1950
13711S	0	0	1	2	0	1955
13711S	0	0	1	2	0	1960
13711S	0	0	1	2	0	1963
13711S	0	0	1	2	0	1965
13811S	0	0	1	2	0	1950
13811S	0	0	1	2	0	1955
13811S	0	0	1	2	0	1960
13811S	0	0	1	2	0	1963
13811S	0	0	1	2	0	1965
13911S	0	0	1	2	0	1950
13911S	0	0	1	2	0	1955
13911S	0	0	1	2	0	1960
13911S	0	0	1	2	0	1963
13911S	0	0	1	2	0	1965
14011S	0	1	0	4	0	1950
14011S	0	1	0	4	0	1955
14011S	0	1	0	4	0	1960
14011S	0	1	0	4	0	1963
14011S	0	1	0	4	0	1965
14111S	2C	1	2	1	1	1950
14111S	2B	1	2	1	1	1955
14111S	2	1	2	1	1	1960
14111S	2B	1	2	1	1	1963
14111S	2	1	2	1	1	1965
14211S	0	1	0	4	0	1950
14211S	0	1	0	4	0	1955
14211S	C	1	0	4	0	1960
14211S	0	1	0	4	0	1963
14211S	0	1	0	4	0	1965

	49	50	51	52	53	
14311S	0	1	0	5	0	1950
14311S	0	1	0	5	0	1955
14311S	0	1	0	5	0	1960
14311S	0	1	0	5	0	1963
14311S	0	1	0	5	0	1965
14411S	0	1	0	5	0	1950
14411S	0	1	0	5	0	1955
14411S	0	1	0	5	0	1960
14411S	0	1	0	5	0	1963
14411S	0	1	0	5	0	1965
14511S	0	0	1	3	0	1950
14511S	0	0	1	3	0	1955
14511S	0	0	1	3	0	1960
14511S	0	0	1	3	0	1963
14511S	0	0	1	3	0	1965
14611S	0	1	2	1	1	1950
14611S	0	1	2	1	1	1955
14611S	0	1	2	1	1	1960
14611S	0	1	2	1	1	1963
14611S	0	1	2	1	0	1965
14711S	0	1	0	5	0	1950
14711S	0	1	0	5	0	1955
14711S	0	1	0	5	0	1960
14711S	0	1	2	1	1	1963
14711S	0	1	2	1	1	1965
14811S	0	1	1	3	0	1950
14811S	0	1	1	3	0	1955
14811S	0	1	1	3	0	1960
14811S	0	1	1	3	0	1963
14811S	0	1	1	3	0	1965
14911S	0	0	1	3	0	1950
14911S	0	0	1	3	0	1955
14911S	0	0	1	3	0	1960
14911S	0	0	1	3	0	1963
14911S	0	0	1	3	0	1965
15011S	0	0	1	3	0	1950
15011S	0	0	1	3	0	1955
15011S	0	0	1	3	0	1960
15011S	0	0	1	3	0	1963
15011S	0	0	1	3	0	1965
15111S	0	0	1	3	0	1950
15111S	0	0	1	3	0	1955
15111S	0	0	1	3	0	1960
15111S	0	0	1	3	0	1963
15111S	0	0	1	3	0	1965
15211S	0	0	1	3	0	1950
15211S	0	0	1	3	0	1955
15211S	0	0	1	3	0	1960
15211S	0	1	1	3	0	1963
15211S	0	1	1	3	0	1965
15311S	0	1	0	5	0	1950
15311S	0	1	0	5	0	1955
15311S	0	1	0	5	0	1960
15311S	0	1	0	5	0	1963
15311S	0	1	0	5	0	1965
15411S	0	1	2	1	1	1950
15411S	0	1	2	1	1	1955
15411S	0	1	2	1	1	1960
15411S	0	1	2	1	1	1963
15411S	0	1	2	1	1	1965

	49	50	51	52	53	
15511S	0	1	0	5	0	1950
15511S	0	1	0	5	0	1955
15511S	0	1	0	5	0	1960
15511S	0	1	0	5	0	1963
15511S	0	1	0	5	0	1965
15611S	0	1	0	6	0	1950
15611S	0	1	0	6	0	1955
15611S	0	1	0	6	0	1960
15611S	0	1	0	6	0	1963
15611S	0	1	0	6	0	1965
15711S	0	1	2	0	0	1950
15711S	0	1	2	0	0	1955
15711S	0	1	2	0	0	1960
15711S	0	1	2	0	0	1963
15711S	0	1	2	0	0	1965
15811S	0	0	1	2	0	1950
15811S	0	0	1	2	0	1955
15811S	0	0	1	2	0	1960
15811S	0	0	1	2	0	1963
15811S	0	0	1	2	0	1965
15911S	0	1	0	4	0	1950
15911S	0	1	0	4	0	1955
15911S	0	1	0	4	0	1960
15911S	0	1	0	4	0	1963
15911S	0	1	0	4	0	1965
16011S	0	1	2	0	0	1950
16011S	0	1	2	0	0	1955
16011S	0	1	2	0	0	1960
16011S	0	1	0	4	0	1963
16011S	0	1	0	4	0	1965
16111S	0	1	1	2	0	1950
16111S	0	1	1	2	0	1955
16111S	0	1	1	2	0	1960
16111S	0	1	1	2	0	1963
16111S	0	1	1	2	0	1965
16211S	0	0	1	2	0	1950
16211S	0	0	1	2	0	1955
16211S	0	0	1	2	0	1960
16211S	0	0	1	2	0	1963
16211S	0	0	1	2	0	1965
16311S	0	0	1	2	0	1950
16311S	0	0	1	2	0	1955
16311S	0	0	1	2	0	1960
16311S	0	0	1	2	0	1963
16311S	0	0	1	2	0	1965
16411S	0	0	1	2	0	1950
16411S	0	0	1	2	0	1955
16411S	0	0	1	2	0	1960
16411S	0	0	1	2	0	1963
16411S	0	0	1	2	0	1965
16511S	0	0	1	2	0	1950
16511S	0	0	1	2	1	1955
16511S	0	0	1	2	0	1960
16511S	0	1	1	2	0	1963
16511S	0	1	1	2	0	1965
16611S	0	1	2	0	1	1950
16611S	0	1	2	0	1	1955
16611S	0	1	2	0	1	1960
16611S	0	1	2	0	1	1963
16611S	0	1	2	0	1	1965

	49	50	51	52	53	
16711S	0	1	0	4	0	1950
16711S	0	1	0	4	0	1955
16711S	0	1	0	4	0	1960
16711S	0	1	0	4	0	1963
16711S	0	1	0	4	0	1965
16811S	0	1	0	5	0	1950
16811S	0	1	0	5	0	1955
16811S	0	1	0	5	0	1960
16811S	0	1	0	5	0	1963
16811S	0	1	0	5	0	1965
16911S	0	1	2	1	1	1950
16911S	0	1	2	1	1	1955
16911S	0	1	2	1	1	1960
16911S	0	1	2	1	1	1963
16911S	0	1	2	1	1	1965
17011S	0	1	2	1	1	1950
17011S	0	1	2	1	1	1955
17011S	0	1	2	1	1	1960
17011S	0	1	2	1	1	1963
17011S	0	1	2	1	1	1965
17111S	0	0	1	3	0	1950
17111S	0	0	1	3	0	1955
17111S	0	0	1	3	0	1960
17111S	0	0	1	3	0	1963
17111S	0	0	1	3	0	1965
17211S	0	1	0	5	0	1950
17211S	0	1	0	5	0	1955
17211S	0	1	0	5	0	1960
17211S	0	1	0	5	0	1963
17211S	0	1	0	5	0	1965
17311S	0	1	2	1	1	1950
17311S	0	1	2	1	1	1955
17311S	0	1	2	1	1	1960
17311S	0	1	0	5	0	1963
17311S	0	1	0	5	0	1965
17411S	0	1	1	3	0	1950
17411S	0	1	1	3	0	1955
17411S	0	1	1	3	0	1960
17411S	0	1	1	3	0	1963
17411S	0	1	1	3	0	1965
17511S	0	0	1	3	0	1950
17511S	0	0	1	3	0	1955
17511S	0	0	1	3	0	1960
17511S	0	0	1	3	0	1963
17511S	0	0	1	3	1	1965
17611S	0	0	1	3	0	1950
17611S	0	0	1	3	0	1955
17611S	0	0	1	3	0	1960
17611S	0	0	1	3	0	1963
17611S	0	0	1	3	1	1965
17711S	0	0	1	3	0	1950
17711S	0	0	1	3	1	1955
17711S	0	0	1	3	0	1960
17711S	0	0	1	3	1	1963
17711S	0	0	1	3	1	1965
17811S	0	0	1	3	0	1950
17811S	0	0	1	3	0	1955
17811S	0	0	1	3	0	1960
17811S	0	1	1	3	0	1963
17811S	0	1	1	3	0	1965

	49	50	51	52	53	
17911S	0	1	2	1	1	1950
17911S	0	1	2	1	1	1955
17911S	0	1	2	1	1	1960
17911S	0	1	2	1	1	1963
17911S	0	1	2	1	1	1965
18011S	0	1	0	5	0	1950
18011S	0	1	0	5	0	1955
18011S	0	1	0	5	0	1960
18011S	0	1	0	5	0	1963
18011S	0	1	0	5	0	1965
18111S	0	1	0	6	0	1950
18111S	0	1	0	6	0	1955
18111S	0	1	0	6	0	1960
18111S	0	1	C	6	0	1963
18111S	0	1	0	6	0	1965
18211S	C	1	2	1	1	1950
18211S	0	1	2	1	1	1955
18211S	0	1	2	1	1	1960
18211S	0	1	2	1	1	1963
18211S	0	1	2	1	1	1965

Set 1

A. Estimates

B. Taken from UN Economic and Social Council Documents (E/3556). Figure is between 0 – $50,000. Exact amount unknown.

Set 2

A. Estimates

B. *UN Statistical Yearbook*

D. Nations A and B have same language.

F. *Monthly Statistics of the Foreign Trade of India,* vol. I (1964)

G. *Trade by Commodities* (Paris: OECD, 1963)

H. *Index Translationum*

Set 3

B. Supplemental information taken from *Keesing's Contemporary Archives*

C. Supplemental information taken from *Facts on File*

Set 6

A. Estimates

B. *Statistical Abstract of the US* (1952-1965)

C. Data for Federation of Malaysia are included in data for Indonesia.

E. *Great Britain Central Office Annual Abstract of Statistics,* 1965

F. *The International Migration Digest* 1 (Fall 1964)

G. *International Migration, 1945-1957* (Geneva, 1959)

Set 7

A. Estimates

B. No indication in primary source whether emigration data refers to CHT or CHN.

F. Derived from trade returns of the importing country.

G. *Economic Bulletin for Asia and the Far East* 18 (September 1966)

H. *Monthly Statistics of the Foreign Trade of India* 1 (March 1964)

Set 8

A. Estimates

Set 9

A. Estimates
G. *Europa Yearbook,* vols. 1 and 2
H. *The Foreign Office List and Diplomatic and Consular Yearbook for 1964*

Set 10

A. Estimates
B. John L. Snell, *Illustion and Necessity* (Boston, 1963), p. 96

Set 11

A. Estimates
B. *Information Please Almanac* (1964)
C. Military occupation during World War II ignored.

Set 1 (Variables 1-6)

UNIT		1 AID	2 R-AID	3 TREATY	4 R-TRTY	5 VISITS	6 CONFER
		\$US x 10^4	% x 10^{-2}	*frequency count*	% x 10^{-2}	*frequency count*	*frequency count*
1950:	MEAN	101.65	71.51	1.34	228.90	0.02	0.21
	S.D.	757.51	603.51	2.74	609.91	0.17	0.71
1955:	MEAN	54.06	53.14	2.16	667.86	0.12	0.74
	S.D.	252.19	323.92	4.21	1390.27	0.44	2.29
1960:	MEAN	126.71	135.88	2.21	819.57	0.15	0.23
	S.D.	692.94	791.53	2.79	1093.35	0.46	0.85
1963:	MEAN	79.78	39.24	1.86	754.64	0.23	0.50
	S.D.	543.09	193.53	2.21	967.64	0.63	1.18
1965:	MEAN	94.02	79.11	1.67	644.00	0.25	2.00
	S.D.	591.73	441.07	2.79	1089.68	0.61	3.30
S-P:	MEAN	91.44	75.78	1.85	622.99	0.15	0.73
	S.D.	594.21	515.40	3.03	1078.24	0.50	2.04
S-P($\hat{Y}$):	MEAN	91.32	76.00	1.85	622.99	0.15	0.73
	S.D.	591.28	511.77	3.03	1078,24	0.50	2.04

Set 2 (Variables 7-10)

		7 BOOKS	8 R-BOOK	9 TRANSL	10 R-TRAN
UNIT		$US x 10^3	% x 10^{-2}	*frequency count*	% x 10^{-2}
1950:	MEAN	161.20	59.78	10.41	246.71
	S.D.	713.86	374.04	49.94	853.56
1955:	MEAN	183.20	42.54	18.17	359.72
	S.D.	738.77	186.02	69.87	1091.30
1960:	MEAN	338.00	88.10	34.37	553.28
	S.D.	1529.86	531.33	116.46	1552.71
1963:	MEAN	406.84	110.36	41.27	569.99
	S.D.	2080.57	556.39	152.45	1569.74
1965:	MEAN	556.10	159.82	43.36	776.22
	S.D.	2860.66	755.53	139.85	2029.87
S-P:	MEAN	332.77	91.90	29.87	507.28
	S.D.	1809.96	515.92	114.20	1497.65
S-P($\hat{Y}$):	MEAN	398.39	94.48	29.20	530.11
	S.D.	1808.02	481.69	112.02	1486.87

Set 3 (Variables 11-15)

UNIT		11 WARNDF *frequency count*	12 VIOLAC *dichoto- mous scale*	13 MILACT *frequency count*	14 DAYSVL *days*	15 NEGBEH *frequency count*
1950:	MEAN	0.07	0.07	0.08	2.08	0.62
	S.D.	0.51	0.26	0.48	10.92	2.56
1955:	MEAN	0.04	0.05	1.24	4.23	0.41
	S.D.	0.36	0.22	9.52	37.17	1.49
1960:	MEAN	0.09	0.04	0.11	0.13	0.56
	S.D.	0.40	0.21	0.59	0.72	2.82
1963:	MEAN	0.02	0.04	0.08	0.48	0.13
	S.D.	0.13	0.23	0.45	5.29	0.49
1965:	MEAN	0.06	0.05	0.46	0.48	0.50
	S.D.	0.46	0.22	2.30	2.43	1.70
S-P:	MEAN	0.06	0.05	0.39	1.48	0.44
	S.D.	0.39	0.23	4.41	17.55	2.00
S-P($\hat{Y}$):	MEAN	0.06	0.05	0.39	1.48	0.44
	S.D.	0.39	0.23	4.41	17.55	2.00

Set 4 (Variables 16-22)

UNIT		16 EXPREC *frequency count*	17 BCTEMB *frequency count*	18 AIDREB *frequency count*	19 NEGCOM *frequency count*	20 ACCUSN *frequency count*	21 PROTST *frequency count*	22 UNOFAC *frequency count*
1950:	MEAN	0.02	0.05	0.01	2.01	1.20	0.17	0.03
	S.D.	0.15	0.28	0.10	10.22	6.71	0.76	0.20
1955:	MEAN	0.01	0.01	0.01	2.55	1.80	0.26	0.03
	S.D.	0.07	0.07	0.07	10.47	8.31	0.87	0.21
1960:	MEAN	0.06	0.02	0.01	2.11	1.28	0.14	0.02
	S.D.	0.37	0.18	0.10	9.83	6.12	0.70	0.18
1963:	MEAN	0.02	0.02	0.02	0.96	0.56	0.25	0.03
	S.D.	0.13	0.17	0.13	3.87	2.77	1.12	0.20
1965:	MEAN	0.04	0.07	0.02	1.99	0.96	0.34	0.08
	S.D.	0.27	0.43	0.17	8.84	4.65	1.46	0.58
S-P:	MEAN	0.03	0.03	0.01	1.92	1.16	0.23	0.04
	S.D.	0.22	0.26	0.12	8.99	6.02	1.02	0.31
S-P($\hat{Y}$):	MEAN	0.03	0.03	0.01	1.92	1.16	0.23	0.04
	S.D.	0.22	0.26	0.12	8.99	6.02	1.02	0.31

Set 5 (Variables 23-26)

UNIT		23 ATKEMB *frequency count*	24 NVIOLB *frequency count*	25 WD–UN *factor score distance x 10^{-2}*	26 UWD–UN *factor score distance x 10^{-2}*
1950:	MEAN	0.01	0.03	434.85	118.38
	S.D.	0.15	0.18	1147.31	813.04
1955:	MEAN	0.01	0.05	209.91	217.23
	S.D.	0.10	0.42	940.98	965.79
1960:	MEAN	0.01	0.08	111.42	145.10
	S.D.	0.07	0.42	908.92	936.48
1963:	MEAN	0.02	0.03	606.92	596.90
	S.D.	0.17	0.21	908.64	903.86
1965:	MEAN	0.01	0.27	499.48	582.58
	S.D.	0.07	1.43	957.30	1097.47
S–P:	MEAN	0.01	0.10	371.43	334.67
	S.D.	0.12	0.71	987.79	967.31
S–P($\hat{Y}$):	MEAN	0.01	0.o0	388.76	347.60
	S.D.	0.12	0.71	910.53	875.00

Set 6 (Variables 27-31)

		27 TOURIS	28 R-TOUR	29 T/POPU	30 EMIGRA	31 R-EMIG
UNIT		x 10^2	% x 10^{-2}	% x 10^{-3}	x 10^{-1}	% x 10^{-2}
1950:	MEAN	439.11	140.09	255.78	101.24	22.78
	S.D.	1779.44	501.89	1472.98	516.94	109.59
1955:	MEAN	67.98	144.79	2.84	57.85	110.13
	S.D.	278.80	505.46	15.32	285.11	549.78
1960:	MEAN	125.35	280.38	32.00	50.58	113.14
	S.D.	497.94	1407.25	116.22	220.70	584.99
1963:	MEAN	111.37	152.42	22.71	40.31	93.88
	S.D.	488.19	477.81	88.21	216.45	625.76
1965:	MEAN	165.73	159.97	43.97	43.42	52.00
	S.D.	679.04	476.98	173.57	243.87	499.34
S-P:	MEAN	170.47	176.53	63.70	58.95	79.01
	S.D.	863.10	770.38	612.00	318.49	510.81
S-P($\hat{Y}$):	MEAN	174.30	180.45	65.18	63.40	89.93
	S.D.	793.68	705.91	560.10	306.61	487.54

Set 7 (Variables 32-37)

		32 E/POPU	33 STUDNT	34 R-STUD	35 EXPORT	36 R-EXPT	37 E/GNP
UNIT		% x 10^{-3}	*frequency count*	% x 10^{-2}	\$US x 10^{4}	% x 10^{-2}	% x 10^{-2}
1950:	MEAN	29.27	41.65	12.67	396.57	309.54	43.83
	S.D.	119.00	170.19	54.78	1010.34	857.97	178.14
1955:	MEAN	18.34	84.91	101.37	552.72	312.24	40.12
	S.D.	87.26	451.98	518.55	1415.61	828.66	151.65
1960:	MEAN	112.11	141.88	38.51	711.99	316.35	36.25
	S.D.	539.82	741.58	198.44	1744.05	744.44	111.29
1963:	MEAN	38.02	113.10	59.71	730.84	271.37	27.69
	S.D.	278.02	548.91	256.96	1759.41	578.43	65.03
1965:	MEAN	23.44	180.70	252.34	883.69	288.60	31.01
	S.D.	155.25	818.40	1348.72	2246.88	635.85	93.86
S-P:	MEAN	44.35	113.77	90.50	652.94	299.45	35.67
	S.D.	290.51	597.34	640.97	1683.35	732.60	125.47
S-P($\hat{Y}$):	MEAN	45.84	121.94	108.20	657.23	297.35	35.99
	S.D.	277.82	573.88	642.52	1678.51	718.91	123.67

Set 8 (Variables 38-43)

UNIT		38 IGO *frequency*	39 R-IGO % x 10^{-2}	40 NGO *frequency*	41 R-NGO % x 10^{-2}	42 N-IGO % x 10^{-2}	43 N-NGO % x 10^{-2}
1950:	MEAN	12.50	4325.21	85.56	4864.47	135.38	176.62
	S.D.	10.22	2868.47	81.98	2758.28	86.37	99.54
1955:	MEAN	16.93	5167.41	108.78	4712.77	122.40	154.83
	S.D.	10.04	2840.63	114.17	2926.30	62.72	95.49
1960:	MEAN	18.23	5183.03	140.64	4972.28	118.37	147.69
	S.D.	10.43	2718.64	127.10	2799.13	56.83	82.33
1963:	MEAN	19.53	4856.72	169.55	5016.20	109.93	138.95
	S.D.	11.11	2440.82	150.92	2807.38	64.31	76.47
1965:	MEAN	23.07	5413.82	187.18	5208.77	105.20	134.76
	S.D.	11.33	2117.64	151.31	2640.95	38.98	67.50
S-P:	MEAN	18.05	4989.02	138.34	4954.90	118.25	150.57
	S.D.	11.16	2633.71	132.85	2786.47	64.44	86.18
S-P($\hat{Y}$):	MEAN	18.05	4986.33	138.34	4954.90	118.51	150.57
	S.D.	11.16	2633.51	132.85	2786.47	64.57	86.18

Set 9 (Variables 44 and 45)

		44 EMBLEG	45 R-EMB
UNIT		0 or 1	% x 10^{-2}
1950:	MEAN	0.56	189.58
	S.D.	0.50	281.52
1955:	MEAN	0.76	153.19
	S.D.	0.43	123.74
1960:	MEAN	0.75	149.28
	S.D.	0.43	118.24
1963:	MEAN	0.78	154.75
	S.D.	0.42	117.70
1965:	MEAN	0.78	131.71
	S.D.	0.42	101.06
S-P:	MEAN	0.73	155.32
	S.D.	0.45	161.75
S-P($\hat{Y}$):	MEAN	0.73	155.20
	S.D.	0.45	161.09

Set 10 (Variables 46, 47 and 48)

UNIT		46 WAROPP *rating scale*	47 WARSAM *rating scale*	48 LOSTER 0 or 1
1950:	MEAN	1.29	8.26	0.02
	S.D.	4.51	8.19	0.13
1955:	MEAN	1.73	8.44	0.02
	S.D.	6.12	8.52	0.13
1960:	MEAN	2.25	8.70	0.02
	S.D.	7.42	8.83	0.13
1963:	MEAN	3.65	8.88	0.02
	S.D.	11.72	8.98	0.13
1965:	MEAN	3.65	8.88	0.02
	S.D.	11.72	8.98	0.13
S-P:	MEAN	2.51	8.63	0.02
	S.D.	8.84	8.69	0.13
S-P($\hat{Y}$):	MEAN	2.51	8.63	0.02
	S.D.	8.84	8.69	0.13

Set 11 (Variables 49-53)

UNIT		49 DEPEND *rating scale*	50 INDEP 0 or 1	51 COMBLC *rating scale*	52 COMPOS *rating scale*	53 ALLIAN 0 or 1
1950:	MEAN	0.50	0.40	1.14	2.00	0.10
	S.D.	2.68	0.49	0.67	1.52	0.30
1955:	MEAN	0.50	0.40	1.14	2.00	0.12
	S.D.	2.68	0.49	0.67	1.52	0.33
1960:	MEAN	0.50	0.40	1.14	2.00	0.09
	S.D.	2.68	0.49	0.67	1.52	0.29
1963:	MEAN	0.50	0.43	1.12	2.04	0.09
	S.D.	2.68	0.50	0.68	1.52	0.29
1965:	MEAN	0.41	0.43	1.13	2.04	0.12
	S.D.	2.42	0.50	0.67	1.52	0.32
S-P:	MEAN	0.48	0.41	1.13	2.02	0.10
	S.D.	2.63	0.49	0.67	1.51	0.31
S-P($\hat{Y}$):	MEAN	0.48	0.41	1.13	2.02	0.10
	S.D.	2.63	0.49	0.67	1.51	0.31